ALL GLORY TO ŚRĪ GURU AND GAURĀṄGA

ŚRĪMAD BHĀGAVATAM

of

KṚṢṆA-DVAIPĀYANA VYĀSA

अहमेवासमेवाग्रे नान्यद् यत् सदसत् परम् ।
पश्चादहं यदेतच्च योऽवशिष्येत सोऽस्म्यहम् ॥३३॥

aham evāsam evāgre
nānyad yat sad-asat param
paścād ahaṁ yad etac ca
yo 'vaśiṣyeta so 'smy aham

(p. 538)

BOOKS by
His Divine Grace
A. C. Bhaktivedanta Swami Prabhupāda

Bhagavad-gītā As It Is
Śrīmad-Bhāgavatam, cantos 1–10 (12 vols.)
Śrī Caitanya-caritāmṛta (17 vols.)
Teachings of Lord Caitanya
The Nectar of Devotion
The Nectar of Instruction
Śrī Īśopaniṣad
Easy Journey to Other Planets
Kṛṣṇa Consciousness: The Topmost Yoga System
Kṛṣṇa, The Supreme Personality of Godhead (3 vols.)
Perfect Questions, Perfect Answers
Teachings of Lord Kapila, the Son of Devahūti
Transcendental Teachings of Prahlāda Mahārāja
Dialectic Spiritualism—A Vedic View of Western Philosophy
Teachings of Queen Kuntī
Kṛṣṇa, the Reservoir of Pleasure
The Science of Self-Realization
The Path of Perfection
Search for Liberation
Life Comes from Life
The Perfection of Yoga
Beyond Birth and Death
On the Way to Kṛṣṇa
Geetār-gan (Bengali)
Vairāgya-vidyā (Bengali)
Buddhi-yoga (Bengali)
Bhakti-ratna-bolī (Bengali)
Rāja-vidyā: The King of Knowledge
Elevation to Kṛṣṇa Consciousness
Kṛṣṇa Consciousness: The Matchless Gift
Back to Godhead magazine (founder)

A complete catalog is available upon request.

Bhaktivedanta Book Trust
3764 Watseka Avenue
Los Angeles, California 90034

Bhaktivedanta Book Trust
P.O. Box 262
Botany
N. S. W. 2019, Australia

ŚRĪMAD BHĀGAVATAM

Second Canto
"The Cosmic Manifestation"

With the Original Sanskrit Text,
Its Roman Transliteration, Synonyms,
Translation and Elaborate Purports

by

His Divine Grace
A.C. Bhaktivedanta Swami Prabhupāda
Founder-*Ācārya* of the International Society for Krishna Consciousness

THE BHAKTIVEDANTA BOOK TRUST
Los Angeles · London · Stockholm · Bombay · Sydney

Readers interested in the subject matter of this book are invited by the International Society for Krishna Consciousness to correspond with its Secretary at either of the following addresses:

International Society for Krishna Consciousness
P. O. Box 262
Botany
N. S. W. 2019
Australia

International Society for Krishna Consciousness
3764 Watseka Avenue
Los Angeles, California 90034

First Printing, 1987: 5,000 copies

Printed in Singapore

Library of Congress Cataloging in Publication Data (Revised)

Purāṇas. Bhāgavatapurāṇa. English and Sanskrit.
Śrīmad-Bhāgavatam: with the original Sanskrit text, its roman transliteration, synonyms, translation and elaborate purports.

In English and Sanskrit.
Translation of: Bhāgavatapurāṇa
Includes index.
Contents: 1st canto. Creation—2nd canto. The cosmic manifestation—3rd canto. The status quo (2 v)—4th canto. The creation of the fourth order (2 v)—5th canto. The creative impetus—6th canto. Prescribed duties for mankind—7th canto. The science of God—8th canto. Withdrawal of the cosmic creations—9th canto. Liberation—10th canto. The summum bonum (4 v)—11th canto. General history (2 v)—12th canto. The age of deterioration.
Cantos 10 (v 2-4), 11 and 12 by Hridayananda dāsa Goswami, completing the great work of His Divine Grace A. C. Bhaktivedanta Swami Prabhupāda; Sanskrit editing by Gopīparāṇadhana dāsa Adhikārī.
1. Purāṇas. Bhāgavatapurāṇa—Criticism, interpretation, etc. I. Bhaktivedanta Swami, A. C., 1896-1977. II. Title.
BL1140.4.B432E5 1987 294.5'925 87-25585
ISBN 0-89213-251-5 (v. 2)

Table of Contents

CHAPTER TWO

The Lord in the Heart 65

Appendixes

Preface

We must know the present need of human society. And what is that need? Human society is no longer bounded by geographical limits to particular countries or communities. Human society is broader than in the Middle Ages, and the world tendency is toward one state or one human society. The ideals of spiritual communism, according to *Śrīmad-Bhāgavatam,* are based more or less on the oneness of the entire human society, nay, of the entire energy of living beings. The need is felt by great thinkers to make this a successful ideology. *Śrīmad-Bhāgavatam* will fill this need in human society. It begins, therefore, with an aphorism of Vedānta philosophy, *janmādy asya yataḥ,* to establish the ideal of a common cause.

Human society, at the present moment, is not in the darkness of oblivion. It has made rapid progress in the fields of material comforts, education and economic development throughout the entire world. But there is a pinprick somewhere in the social body at large, and therefore there are large-scale quarrels, even over less important issues. There is need of a clue as to how humanity can become one in peace, friendship and prosperity with a common cause. *Śrīmad-Bhāgavatam* will fill this need, for it is a cultural presentation for the respiritualization of the entire human society.

Śrīmad-Bhāgavatam should be introduced also in the schools and colleges, for it is recommended by the great student-devotee Prahlāda Mahārāja in order to change the demoniac face of society.

kaumāra ācaret prājño
dharmān bhāgavatān iha
durlabhaṁ mānuṣaṁ janma
tad apy adhruvam artha-dam
(*Bhāg.* 7.6.1)

Disparity in human society is due to lack of principles in a godless civilization. There is God, or the Almighty One, from whom everything emanates, by whom everything is maintained and in whom everything is merged to rest. Material science has tried to find the ultimate source of creation very insufficiently, but it is a fact that there is one ultimate source of everything that be. This ultimate source is explained rationally and authoritatively in the beautiful *Bhāgavatam*, or *Śrīmad-Bhāgavatam*.

Śrīmad-Bhāgavatam is the transcendental science not only for knowing the ultimate source of everything but also for knowing our relation with Him and our duty toward perfection of the human society on the basis of this perfect knowledge. It is powerful reading matter in the Sanskrit language, and it is now rendered into English elaborately so that simply by a careful reading one will know God perfectly well, so much so that the reader will be sufficiently educated to defend himself from the onslaught of atheists. Over and above this, the reader will be able to convert others to accepting God as a concrete principle.

Śrīmad-Bhāgavatam begins with the definition of the ultimate source. It is a bona fide commentary on the *Vedānta-sūtra* by the same author, Śrīla Vyāsadeva, and gradually it develops into nine cantos up to the highest state of God realization. The only qualification one needs to study this great book of transcendental knowledge is to proceed step by step cautiously and not jump forward haphazardly as with an ordinary book. It should be gone through chapter by chapter, one after another. The reading matter is so arranged with the original Sanskrit text, its English transliteration, synonyms, translation and purports so that one is sure to become a God-realized soul at the end of finishing the first nine cantos.

The Tenth Canto is distinct from the first nine cantos because it deals directly with the transcendental activities of the Personality of Godhead, Śrī Kṛṣṇa. One will be unable to capture the effects of the Tenth Canto without going through the first nine cantos. The book is complete in twelve cantos, each independent, but it is good for all to read them in small installments one after another.

I must admit my frailties in presenting *Śrīmad-Bhāgavatam*, but still I am hopeful of its good reception by the thinkers and leaders of society on the strength of the following statement of *Śrīmad-Bhāgavatam* (1.5.11):

tad-vāg-visargo janatāgha-viplavo
yasmin prati-ślokam abaddhavaty api

nāmāny anantasya yaśo 'ṅkitāni yac
chṛṇvanti gāyanti gṛṇanti sādhavaḥ

"On the other hand, that literature which is full of descriptions of the transcendental glories of the name, fame, form and pastimes of the unlimited Supreme Lord is a transcendental creation meant for bringing about a revolution in the impious life of a misdirected civilization. Such transcendental literature, even though irregularly composed, is heard, sung and accepted by purified men who are thoroughly honest."

Oṁ tat sat

A. C. Bhaktivedanta Swami

Introduction

"This *Bhāgavata Purāṇa* is as brilliant as the sun, and it has arisen just after the departure of Lord Kṛṣṇa to His own abode, accompanied by religion, knowledge, etc. Persons who have lost their vision due to the dense darkness of ignorance in the age of Kali shall get light from this *Purāṇa.*" (*Śrīmad-Bhāgavatam* 1.3.43)

The timeless wisdom of India is expressed in the *Vedas,* ancient Sanskrit texts that touch upon all fields of human knowledge. Originally preserved through oral tradition, the *Vedas* were first put into writing five thousand years ago by Śrīla Vyāsadeva, the "literary incarnation of God." After compiling the *Vedas,* Vyāsadeva set forth their essence in the aphorisms known as *Vedānta-sūtras. Śrīmad-Bhāgavatam* (*Bhāgavata Purāṇa*) is Vyāsadeva's commentary on his own *Vedānta-sūtras.* It was written in the maturity of his spiritual life under the direction of Nārada Muni, his spiritual master. Referred to as "the ripened fruit of the tree of Vedic literature," *Śrīmad-Bhāgavatam* is the most complete and authoritative exposition of Vedic knowledge.

After compiling the *Bhāgavatam,* Vyāsa imparted the synopsis of it to his son, the sage Śukadeva Gosvāmī. Śukadeva Gosvāmī subsequently recited the entire *Bhāgavatam* to Mahārāja Parīkṣit in an assembly of learned saints on the bank of the Ganges at Hastināpura (now Delhi). Mahārāja Parīkṣit was the emperor of the world and was a great *rājarṣi* (saintly king). Having received a warning that he would die within a week, he renounced his entire kingdom and retired to the bank of the Ganges to fast until death and receive spiritual enlightenment. The *Bhāgavatam* begins with Emperor Parīkṣit's sober inquiry to Śukadeva Gosvāmī: "You are the spiritual master of great saints and devotees. I am therefore begging you to show the way of perfection for all persons, and especially for one who is about to die. Please let me know what a man should hear, chant, remember and worship, and also what he should not do. Please explain all this to me."

Śukadeva Gosvāmī's answer to this question, and numerous other questions posed by Mahārāja Parīkṣit, concerning everything from the nature of the self to the origin of the universe, held the assembled sages in rapt attention continuously for the seven days leading up to the king's death. The sage Sūta Gosvāmī, who was present in that assembly when Śukadeva Gosvāmī first recited *Śrīmad-Bhāgavatam*, later repeated the *Bhāgavatam* before a gathering of sages in the forest of Naimiṣāraṇya. Those sages, concerned about the spiritual welfare of the people in general, had gathered to perform a long, continuous chain of sacrifices to counteract the degrading influence of the incipient age of Kali. In response to the sages' request that he speak the essence of Vedic wisdom, Sūta Gosvāmī repeated from memory the entire eighteen thousand verses of *Śrīmad-Bhāgavatam*, as spoken by Śukadeva Gosvāmī to Mahārāja Parīkṣit.

The reader of *Śrīmad-Bhāgavatam* hears Sūta Gosvāmī relate the questions of Mahārāja Parīkṣit and the answers of Śukadeva Gosvāmī. Also, Sūta Gosvāmī sometimes responds directly to questions put by Śaunaka Ṛṣi, the spokesman for the sages gathered at Naimiṣāraṇya. One therefore simultaneously hears two dialogues: one between Mahārāja Parīkṣit and Śukadeva Gosvāmī on the bank of the Ganges, and another at Naimiṣāraṇya between Sūta Gosvāmī and the sages at Naimiṣāraṇya forest, headed by Śaunaka Ṛṣi. Furthermore, while instructing King Parīkṣit, Śukadeva Gosvāmī often relates historical episodes and gives accounts of lengthy philosophical discussions between such great souls as Nārada Muni and Vasudeva. With this understanding of the history of the *Bhāgavatam*, the reader will easily be able to follow its intermingling of dialogues and events from various sources. Since philosophical wisdom, not chronological order, is most important in the text, one need only be attentive to the subject matter of *Śrīmad-Bhāgavatam* to appreciate fully its profound message.

The translators of this edition compare the *Bhāgavatam* to sugar candy—wherever you taste it, you will find it equally sweet and relishable. Therefore, to taste the sweetness of the *Bhāgavatam*, one may begin by reading any of its volumes. After such an introductory taste, however, the serious reader is best advised to go back to the First Canto and then proceed through the *Bhāgavatam*, canto after canto, in its natural order.

This edition of the *Bhāgavatam* is the first complete English translation of this important text with an elaborate commentary, and it is the first widely available to the English-speaking public. The first twelve volumes (Canto One through Canto Ten, Part One) are the product of the scholarly and devotional effort of His Divine Grace A. C. Bhaktivedanta Swami Prabhupāda, the founder-*ācārya* of the International

Society for Krishna Consciousness and the world's most distinguished teacher of Indian religious and philosophical thought. His consummate Sanskrit scholarship and intimate familiarity with Vedic culture and thought as well as the modern way of life combine to reveal to the West a magnificent exposition of this important classic. After the departure of Śrīla Prabhupāda from this world in 1977, his monumental work of translating and annotating *Śrīmad-Bhāgavatam* has been continued by his disciples Hridayananda dāsa Goswami and Gopīparāṇadhana dāsa.

Readers will find this work of value for many reasons. For those interested in the classical roots of Indian civilization, it serves as a vast reservoir of detailed information on virtually every one of its aspects. For students of comparative philosophy and religion, the *Bhāgavatam* offers a penetrating view into the meaning of India's profound spiritual heritage. To sociologists and anthropologists, the *Bhāgavatam* reveals the practical workings of a peaceful and scientifically organized Vedic culture, whose institutions were integrated on the basis of a highly developed spiritual world view. Students of literature will discover the *Bhāgavatam* to be a masterpiece of majestic poetry. For students of psychology, the text provides important perspectives on the nature of consciousness, human behavior and the philosophical study of identity. Finally, to those seeking spiritual insight, the *Bhāgavatam* offers simple and practical guidance for attainment of the highest self-knowledge and realization of the Absolute Truth. The entire multivolume text, presented by the Bhaktivedanta Book Trust, promises to occupy a significant place in the intellectual, cultural and spiritual life of modern man for a long time to come.

—The Publishers

CHAPTER ONE

The First Step in God Realization

INVOCATION

ॐ नमो भगवते वासुदेवाय ॥

oṁ namo bhagavate vāsudevāya

oṁ—O my Lord; *namaḥ*—my respectful obeisances unto You; *bhagavate*—unto the Personality of Godhead; *vāsudevāya*—unto Lord Kṛṣṇa, the son of Vasudeva.

TRANSLATION

O my Lord, the all-pervading Personality of Godhead, I offer my respectful obeisances unto You.

PURPORT

Vāsudevāya means "to Kṛṣṇa, the son of Vasudeva." Since by chanting the name of Kṛṣṇa, Vāsudeva, one can achieve all the good results of charity, austerity and penances, it is to be understood that by the chanting of this *mantra, oṁ namo bhagavate vāsudevāya,* the author or the speaker or any one of the readers of *Śrīmad-Bhāgavatam* is offering respectful obeisances unto the Supreme Lord, Kṛṣṇa, the reservoir of all pleasure. In the First Canto of *Śrīmad-Bhāgavatam,* the principles of creation are described, and thus the First Canto may be called "Creation."

Similarly, in the Second Canto, the postcreation cosmic manifestation is described. The different planetary systems are described in the Second Canto as different parts of the universal body of the Lord. For this reason, the Second Canto may be called "The Cosmic Manifestation." There are ten chapters in the Second Canto, and in these ten chapters the purpose of *Śrīmad-Bhāgavatam* and the different symptoms of this purpose are narrated. The first chapter describes the glories of chanting, and it hints at the process by which the neophyte devotees may perform meditation on the universal form of the Lord. In the first verse, Śukadeva Gosvāmī replies to the questions of Mahārāja Parīkṣit, who asked him about one's duties at the point of death. Mahārāja Parīkṣit was glad to receive Śukadeva Gosvāmī, and he was proud of being a descendant of Arjuna, the intimate friend of Kṛṣṇa. Personally, he was very humble and meek, but he expressed his gladness that Lord Kṛṣṇa was very kind to his grandfathers, the sons of Pāṇḍu, especially his own grandfather, Arjuna. And because Lord Kṛṣṇa was always pleased with Mahārāja Parīkṣit's family, at the verge of Mahārāja Parīkṣit's death Śukadeva Gosvāmī was sent to help him in the process of self-realization. Mahārāja Parīkṣit was a devotee of Lord Kṛṣṇa from his childhood, so he had natural affection for Kṛṣṇa. Śukadeva Gosvāmī could understand his devotion. Therefore, he welcomed the questions about the King's duty. Because the King hinted that worship of Lord Kṛṣṇa is the ultimate function of every living entity, Śukadeva Gosvāmī welcomed the suggestion and said, "Because you have raised questions about Kṛṣṇa, your question is most glorious." The translation of the first verse is as follows.

TEXT 1

श्रीशुक उवाच
वरीयानेष ते प्रश्नः कृतो लोकहितं नृप ।
आत्मवित्सम्मतः पुंसां श्रोतव्यादिषु यः परः ॥ १ ॥

śrī-śuka uvāca
varīyān eṣa te praśnaḥ
kṛto loka-hitaṁ nṛpa
ātmavit-sammataḥ puṁsāṁ
śrotavyādiṣu yaḥ paraḥ

śrī-śukaḥ uvāca—Śrī Śukadeva Gosvāmī said; *varīyān*—glorious; *eṣaḥ*—this; *te*—your; *praśnaḥ*—question; *kṛtaḥ*—made by you; *loka-hitam*—beneficial for all men; *nṛpa*—O King; *ātmavit*—transcendentalist; *sammataḥ*—approved; *puṁsām*—of all men; *śrotavya-ādiṣu*—in all kinds of hearing; *yaḥ*—what is; *paraḥ*—the supreme.

TRANSLATION

Śrī Śukadeva Gosvāmī said: My dear King, your question is glorious because it is very beneficial to all kinds of people. The answer to this question is the prime subject matter for hearing, and it is approved by all transcendentalists.

PURPORT

Even the very question is so nice that it is the best subject matter for hearing. Simply by such questioning and hearing, one can achieve the highest perfectional stage of life. Because Lord Kṛṣṇa is the original Supreme Person, any question about Him is original and perfect. Lord Śrī Caitanya Mahāprabhu said that the highest perfection of life is to achieve the transcendental loving service of Kṛṣṇa. Because questions and answers about Kṛṣṇa elevate one to that transcendental position, the questions of Mahārāja Parīkṣit about Kṛṣṇa philosophy are greatly glorified. Mahārāja Parīkṣit wanted to absorb his mind completely in Kṛṣṇa, and such absorption can be effected simply by hearing about the uncommon activities of Kṛṣṇa. For instance, in the *Bhagavad-gītā* it is stated that simply by understanding the transcendental nature of Lord Kṛṣṇa's appearance, disappearance, and activities, one can immediately return home, back to Godhead, and never come back to this miserable condition of material existence. It is very auspicious, therefore, to hear always about Kṛṣṇa. So Mahārāja Parīkṣit requested Śukadeva Gosvāmī to narrate the activities of Kṛṣṇa so that he could engage his mind in Kṛṣṇa. The activities of Kṛṣṇa are nondifferent from Kṛṣṇa Himself. As long as one is engaged in hearing such transcendental activities of Kṛṣṇa, he remains aloof from the conditional life of material existence. The topics of Lord Kṛṣṇa are so auspicious that they purify the speaker, the hearer and the inquirer. They are compared to the Ganges waters, which flow from the toe of Lord Kṛṣṇa. Wherever the Ganges waters go, they purify the land and the person who bathes in them. Similarly, *kṛṣṇa-kathā*, or the topics of Kṛṣṇa, are so pure that wherever they are spoken, the place, the hearer, the inquirer, the speaker and all concerned become purified.

TEXT 2

श्रोतव्यादीनि राजेन्द्र नृणां सन्ति सहस्रशः ।
अपश्यतामात्मतत्त्वं गृहेषु गृहमेधिनाम् ॥ २ ॥

śrotavyādīni rājendra
nṛṇāṁ santi sahasraśaḥ
apaśyatām ātma-tattvaṁ
gṛheṣu gṛha-medhinām

śrotavya-ādīni—subject matters for hearing; *rājendra*—O Emperor; *nṛṇām*—of human society; *santi*—there are; *sahasraśaḥ*—hundreds and thousands; *apaśyatām*—of the blind; *ātma-tattvam*—knowledge of self, the ultimate truth; *gṛheṣu*—at home; *gṛha-medhinām*—of persons too materially engrossed.

TRANSLATION

Those persons who are materially engrossed, being blind to the knowledge of ultimate truth, have many subject matters for hearing in human society, O Emperor.

PURPORT

In the revealed scriptures there are two nomenclatures for the householder's life. One is *gṛhastha*, and the other is *gṛhamedhī*. The *gṛhasthas* are those who live together with wife and children but live transcendentally for realizing the ultimate truth. The *gṛhamedhīs*, however, are those who live only for the benefit of the family members, extended or centralized, and thus are envious of others. The word *medhī* indicates jealousy of others. The *gṛhamedhīs*, being interested in family affairs only, are certainly envious of others. Therefore, one *gṛhamedhī* is not on good terms with another *gṛhamedhī*, and in the extended form, one community, society or nation is not on good terms with another counterpart of selfish interest. In the age of Kali, all the householders are jealous of one another because they are blind to the knowledge of ultimate truth. They have many subject matters for hearing—political, scientific, social, economic and so on—but due to a poor fund of knowledge, they set aside the question of the ultimate miseries of life, namely miseries of birth, death, old age and disease. Factually, the human life is meant for making an ultimate solution to birth, death, old age and disease, but the *gṛhamedhīs*, being illusioned by the material nature, forget everything about self-realization. The ultimate solution to the problems of life is to go back home, back to Godhead, and thus, as stated in the *Bhagavad-gītā* (8.16), the miseries of material existence—birth, death, old age and disease—are removed.

The process of going back home, back to Godhead, is to hear about the Supreme Lord and His name, form, attributes, pastimes, paraphernalia and variegatedness. Foolish people do not know this. They want to hear something about the name, form, etc., of everything temporary, and they do not know how to utilize this propensity of hearing for the ultimate good. Misguided as they are, they also create some false literatures about the name, form, attributes, etc., of the ultimate truth. One should not, therefore, become a *gṛhamedhī* simply to exist for envying others; one should become a real householder in terms of the scriptural injunctions.

TEXT 3

निद्रया ह्रियते नक्तं व्यवायेन च वा वयः ।
दिवा चार्थेहया राजन् कुटुम्बभरणेन वा ॥ ३ ॥

nidrayā hriyate naktaṁ
vyavāyena ca vā vayaḥ
divā cārthehayā rājan
kuṭumba-bharaṇena vā

nidrayā—by sleeping; *hriyate*—wastes; *naktam*—night; *vyavāyena*—sex indulgence; *ca*—also; *vā*—either; *vayaḥ*—duration of life; *divā*—days; *ca*—and; *artha*—economic; *īhayā*—development; *rājan*—O King; *kuṭumba*—family members; *bharaṇena*—maintaining; *vā*—either.

TRANSLATION

The lifetime of such an envious householder is passed at night either in sleeping or in sex indulgence, and in the daytime either in making money or maintaining family members.

PURPORT

The present human civilization is primarily based on the principles of sleeping and sex indulgence at night and earning money in the day and spending the same for family maintenance. Such a form of human civilization is condemned by the *Bhāgavata* school.

Because human life is a combination of matter and spirit soul, the whole process of Vedic knowledge is directed at liberating the spirit soul from the contamination of matter. The knowledge concerning this is called *ātma-tattva*. Those men who are too materialistic are unaware of this knowledge and are more inclined to economic development for material enjoyment. Such materialistic men are called *karmīs*, or fruitive laborers, and they are allowed regulated economic development or association of woman for sex indulgence. Those who are above the *karmīs*, that is, the *jñānīs*, *yogīs* and devotees, are strictly prohibited from sex indulgence. The *karmīs* are more or less devoid of *ātma-tattva* knowledge, and as such, their life is spent without spiritual profit. The human life is not meant for hard labor for economic development, nor is it meant for sex indulgence like that of the dogs and hogs. It is specially meant for making a solution to the problems of material life and the miseries thereof. So the *karmīs* waste their valuable human life by sleeping and sex indulgence at night, and by laboring hard in the daytime to accumulate wealth, and after doing so, they try to improve the standard of materialistic life. The materialistic way of life is described herein in a nutshell, and how foolishly men waste the boon of human life is described as follows.

TEXT 4

देहापत्यकलत्रादिष्वात्मसैन्येष्वसत्स्वपि ।
तेषां प्रमत्तो निधनं पश्यन्नपि न पश्यति ॥ ४ ॥

dehāpatya-kalatrādiṣv
ātma-sainyeṣv asatsv api
teṣāṁ pramatto nidhanaṁ
paśyann api na paśyati

deha—body; *apatya*—children; *kalatra*—wife; *ādiṣu*—and in everything in relation to them; *ātma*—own; *sainyeṣu*—fighting soldiers;

asatsu—fallible; *api*—in spite of; *teṣām*—of all of them; *pramattaḥ*—too attached; *nidhanam*—destruction; *paśyan*—having been experienced; *api*—although; *na*—does not; *paśyati*—see it.

TRANSLATION

Persons devoid of ātma-tattva do not inquire into the problems of life, being too attached to the fallible soldiers like the body, children and wife. Although sufficiently experienced, they still do not see their inevitable destruction.

PURPORT

This material world is called the world of death. Every living being, beginning from Brahmā, whose duration of life is some thousands of millions of years, down to the germs who live for a few seconds only, is struggling for existence. Therefore, this life is a sort of fight with material nature, which imposes death upon all. In the human form of life, a living being is competent enough to come to an understanding of this great struggle for existence, but being too attached to family members, society, country, etc., he wants to win over the invincible material nature by the aid of bodily strength, children, wife, relatives, etc. Although he is sufficiently experienced in the matter by dint of past experience and previous examples of his deceased predecessors, he does not see that the so-called fighting soldiers like the children, relatives, society members and countrymen are all fallible in the great struggle. One should examine the fact that his father or his father's father has already died, and that he himself is therefore also sure to die, and similarly, his children, who are the would-be fathers of their children, will also die in due course. No one will survive in this struggle with material nature. The history of human society definitely proves it, yet the foolish people still suggest that in the future they will be able to live perpetually, with the help of material science. This poor fund of knowledge exhibited by human society is certainly misleading, and it is all due to ignoring the constitution of the living soul. This material world exists only as a dream, due to our attachment to it. Otherwise, the living soul is always different from the material nature. The great ocean of material nature is tossing with the waves of time, and the so-called living conditions are something like foaming bubbles, which appear before us as bodily self, wife, children, society, countrymen, etc. Due to a lack of knowledge of self, we become victimized by the force of ignorance and thus spoil the valuable energy of human life in a vain search after permanent living conditions, which are impossible in this material world.

Our friends, relatives and so-called wives and children are not only fallible, but also bewildered by the outward glamor of material existence. As such, they cannot save us. Still we think that we are safe within the orbit of family, society or country.

The whole materialistic advancement of human civilization is like the decoration of a dead body. Everyone is a dead body flapping only for a few days, and yet all the energy of human life is being wasted in the decoration of this dead body. Śukadeva Gosvāmī is pointing out the duty of the human being after showing the actual position of bewildered human activities. Persons who are devoid of the knowledge of *ātma-tattva* are misguided, but those who are devotees of the Lord and have perfect realization of transcendental knowledge are not bewildered.

TEXT 5

तस्माद्भारत सर्वात्मा भगवानीश्वरो हरिः ।
श्रोतव्यः कीर्तितव्यश्च स्मर्तव्यश्चेच्छताभयम् ॥ ५ ॥

tasmād bhārata sarvātmā
bhagavān īśvaro hariḥ
śrotavyaḥ kīrtitavyaś ca
smartavyaś cecchatābhayam

tasmāt—for this reason; *bhārata*—O descendant of Bharata; *sarvātmā*—the Supersoul; *bhagavān*—the Personality of Godhead; *īśvaraḥ*—the controller; *hariḥ*—the Lord, who vanquishes all miseries; *śrotavyaḥ*—is to be heard; *kīrtitavyaḥ*—to be glorified; *ca*—also; *smartavyaḥ*—to be remembered; *ca*—and; *icchatā*—of one who desires; *abhayam*—freedom.

TRANSLATION

O descendant of King Bharata, one who desires to be free from all miseries must hear about, glorify and also remember the Per-

sonality of Godhead, who is the Supersoul, the controller and the savior from all miseries.

PURPORT

In the previous verse, Śrī Śukadeva Gosvāmī has described how the foolish materially attached men are wasting their valuable time in the improvement of the material conditions of life by sleeping, indulging in sex life, developing economic conditions and maintaining a band of relatives who are to be vanquished in the air of oblivion. Being engaged in all these materialistic activities, the living soul entangles himself in the cycle of the law of fruitive actions. This entails the chain of birth and death in the 8,400,000 species of life: the aquatics, the vegetables, the reptiles, the birds, the beasts, the uncivilized man, and then again the human form, which is the chance for getting out of the cycle of fruitive action. Therefore, if one desires freedom from this vicious circle, then one must cease to act as a *karmī* or enjoyer of the results of one's own work, good or bad. One should not do anything, either good or bad, on his own account, but must execute everything on behalf of the Supreme Lord, the ultimate proprietor of everything that be. This process of doing work is recommended in the *Bhagavad-gītā* (9.27) also, where instruction is given for working on the Lord's account. Therefore, one should first of all hear about the Lord. When one has perfectly and scrutinizingly heard, one must glorify His acts and deeds, and thus it will become possible to remember constantly the transcendental nature of the Lord. Hearing about and glorifying the Lord are identical with the transcendental nature of the Lord, and by so doing, one will be always in the association of the Lord. This brings freedom from all sorts of fear. The Lord is the Supersoul (Paramātmā) present in the hearts of all living beings, and thus by the above hearing and glorifying process, the Lord invites the association of all in His creation. This process of hearing about and glorifying the Lord is applicable for everyone, whoever he may be, and it will lead one to the ultimate success in everything in which one may be engaged by providence. There are many classes of human beings: the fruitive workers, the empiric philosophers, the mystic *yogīs*, and ultimately, the unalloyed devotees. For all of them, one and the same process is applicable for achieving the desired success. Everyone wants to be free from all kinds of fear, and everyone wants the fullest extent of happiness in life. The perfect process for achieving this, here and now, is recommended in the *Śrīmad-Bhāgavatam*, which is uttered by such a great authority as Śrīla Śukadeva Gosvāmī. By hearing about and glorifying the Lord, all a person's activities become molded into spiritual activities, and thus all conceptions of material miseries become completely vanquished.

TEXT 6

एतावान् सांख्ययोगाभ्यां स्वधर्मपरिनिष्ठया ।
जन्मलाभः परः पुंसामन्ते नारायणस्मृतिः ॥ ६ ॥

etāvān sāṅkhya-yogābhyāṁ
sva-dharma-pariniṣṭhayā
janma-lābhaḥ paraḥ puṁsām
ante nārāyaṇa-smṛtiḥ

etāvān—all these; *sāṅkhya*—complete knowledge of matter and spirit; *yogābhyām*—knowledge of mystic power; *sva-dharma*—particular occupational duty; *pariniṣṭhayā*—by full perception; *janma*—birth; *lābhaḥ*—gain; *paraḥ*—the supreme; *puṁsām*—of a person; *ante*—at the end; *nārāyaṇa*—the Personality of Godhead; *smṛtiḥ*—remembrance.

TRANSLATION

The highest perfection of human life, achieved either by complete knowledge of matter and spirit, by practice of mystic powers, or by perfect discharge of occupational duty, is to remember the Personality of Godhead at the end of life.

PURPORT

Nārāyaṇa is the transcendental Personality of Godhead beyond the material creation. Everything that is created, sustained, and at the end annihilated is within the compass of the *mahat-tattva* (material principle) and is known as the material world. The existence of Nārāyaṇa, or the Personality of Godhead, is not within the jurisdiction of this *mahat-*

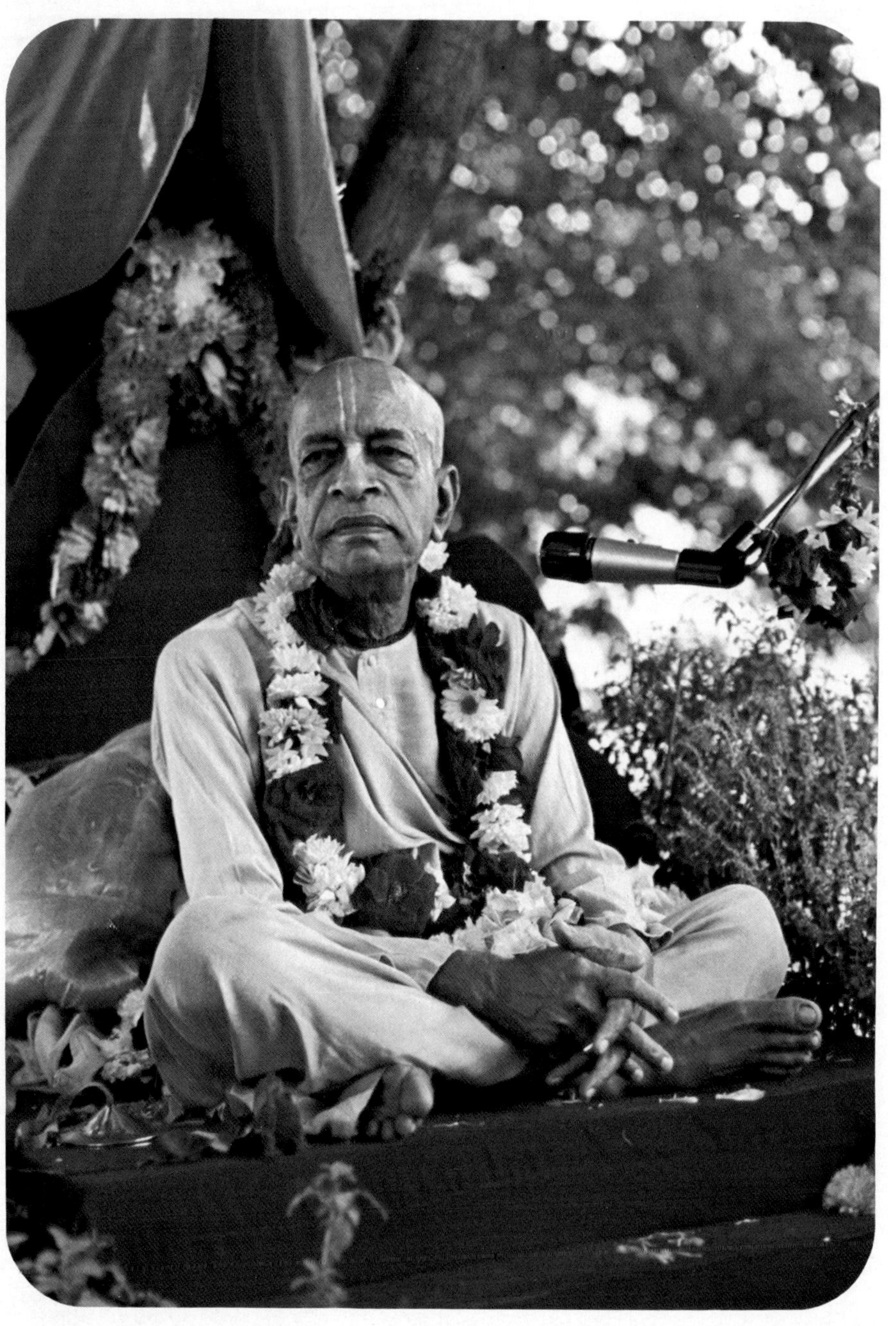

His Divine Grace A.C. Bhaktivedanta Swami Prabhupāda
Founder-Ācārya of the International Society for Krishna Consciousness

PLATE ONE: A plenary portion of the Supreme Personality of Godhead known as the Supersoul resides within the body in the region of the heart. The Lord's magnanimous pastimes and the glowing glancing of His smiling face indicate His extensive benedictions. (*pp. 80-85*)

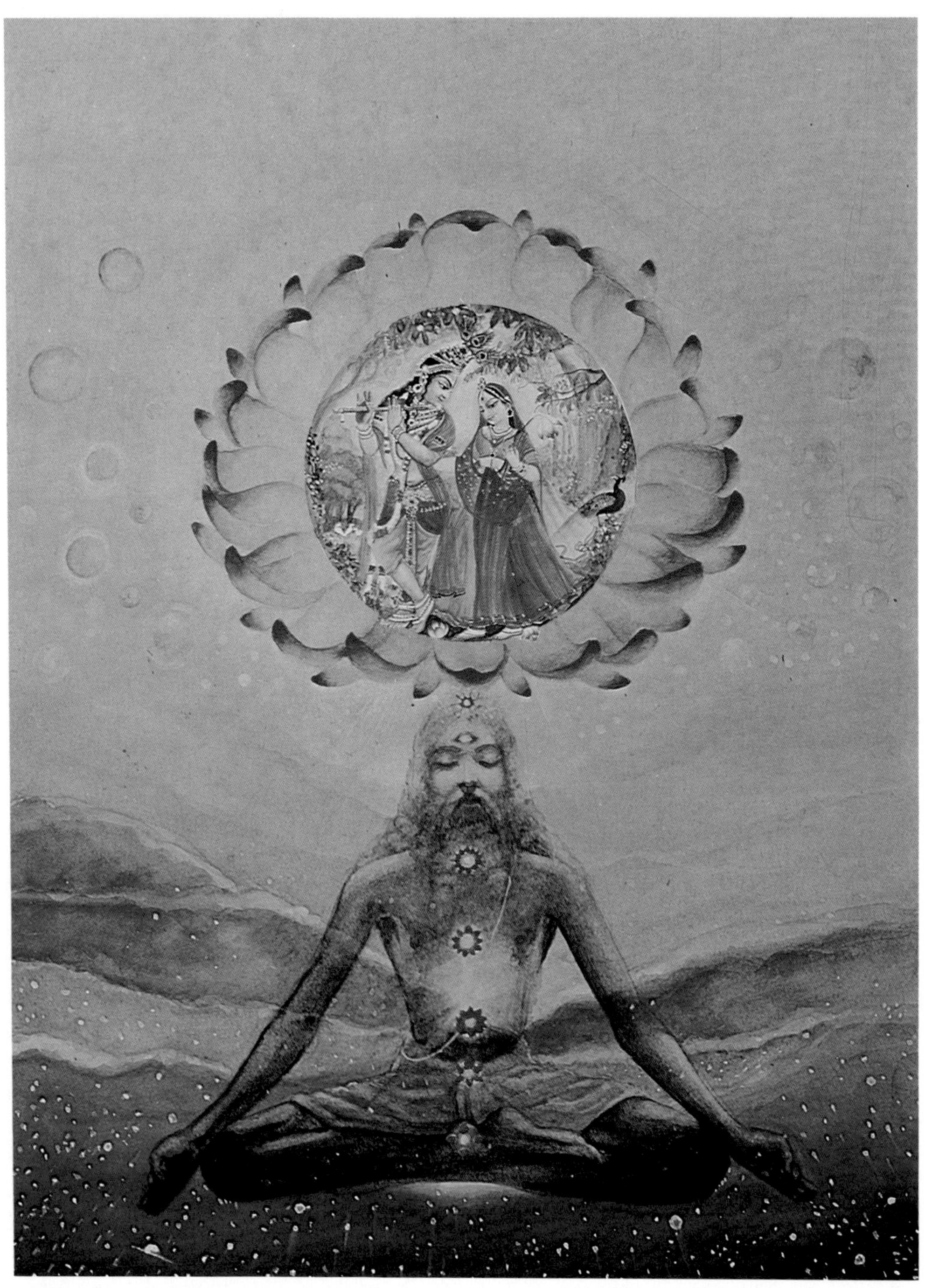

PLATE TWO: Following the process of mystic yoga, the meditative devotee pushes up his life air from the navel to the heart, then to the root of the palate, then to the space between the eyebrows, and finally out of the cerebral hole. Thus he gives up his material connection and goes back to Godhead. (*pp. 99-102*)

PLATE THREE: While Brahmā sat in meditation, the sound of Kṛṣṇa's flute entered his ear as the Vedic *mantra oṁ*. Thus Brahmā attained complete Vedic knowledge and became the original spiritual master of all living entities. (*p. 123*)

PLATE FOUR: Lord Kṛṣṇa's ten most prominent pastime incarnations are, from the upper lefthand corner, (1) Lord Matsya, the fish incarnation; (2) Lord Kūrma, the tortoise incarnation; (3) Lord Varāha, the boar incarnation; (4) Lord Nṛsiṁhadeva, the half-man, half-lion incarnation; (5) Lord Vāmanadeva, the dwarf-*brāhmaṇa* incarnation; (6) Lord Paraśurāma; (7) Lord Rāmacandra; (8) Lord Kṛṣṇa Himself; (9) Lord Buddha; and (10) Lord Kalki. (*p. 197*)

PLATE FIVE: When Nārada Muni approached his father, Lord Brahmā, and asked who the original creator of the universe is, Brahmā replied that it is Lord Kṛṣṇa, the Supreme Personality of Godhead. *(pp. 238–49)*

PLATE SIX: Lord Kṛṣṇa exists eternally on His effulgent spiritual planet, Goloka Vṛndāvana, where He enjoys Himself with His ever-liberated associates. To create the material universes, He expands Himself as four-armed Mahā-viṣṇu, who, lying within the Causal Ocean, produces numberless universes from the pores of His skin. (*p. 278*)

PLATE SEVEN: As Lord Varāha, the boar incarnation, lifted the earth up from the depths of the Garbhodaka Ocean, the ferocious demon Hiraṇyākṣa attacked Him. A great battle ensued. (*pp. 360–65*)

PLATE EIGHT: Lord Nṛsiṁhadeva took the powerful demon Hiraṇyakaśipu upon His lap, tore out his heart and then disemboweled him. (*pp. 383-84*)

PLATE NINE: The elephant Gajendra prayerfully lifted a lotus aloft as an offering to Lord Viṣṇu, who came to deliver him from the crocodile, and also from material life. (*pp. 384–88*)

PLATE TEN: Having been coronated after His long exile and His battle with the demon Rāvaṇa, Lord Rāmacandra ruled Ayodhyā in the company of His brother Lakṣmaṇa; His consort, Sītā; and His faithful servant Hanumān. (*pp. 399-404*)

PLATE ELEVEN: When the world was overburdened by many atheistic kings, Lord Kṛṣṇa descended with His plenary portion Balarāma just to relieve the world's distress. (*p. 404*)

PLATE TWELVE: As the demoness Pūtanā, who had tried to poison Kṛṣṇa, perished and fell down, she assumed her original, gigantic form, said to be as long as six miles. (*p. 407*)

PLATE THIRTEEN: The demon Śakaṭāsura took the form of a cart, but baby Kṛṣṇa, lying beneath it on a bed, kicked His legs in anger and destroyed the cart demon. (*p. 408*)

PLATE FOURTEEN: Lord Kṛṣṇa chased after Śaṅkhacūḍa, swiftly approached him, and with a blow of His fist removed the demon's head. (*p. 416*)

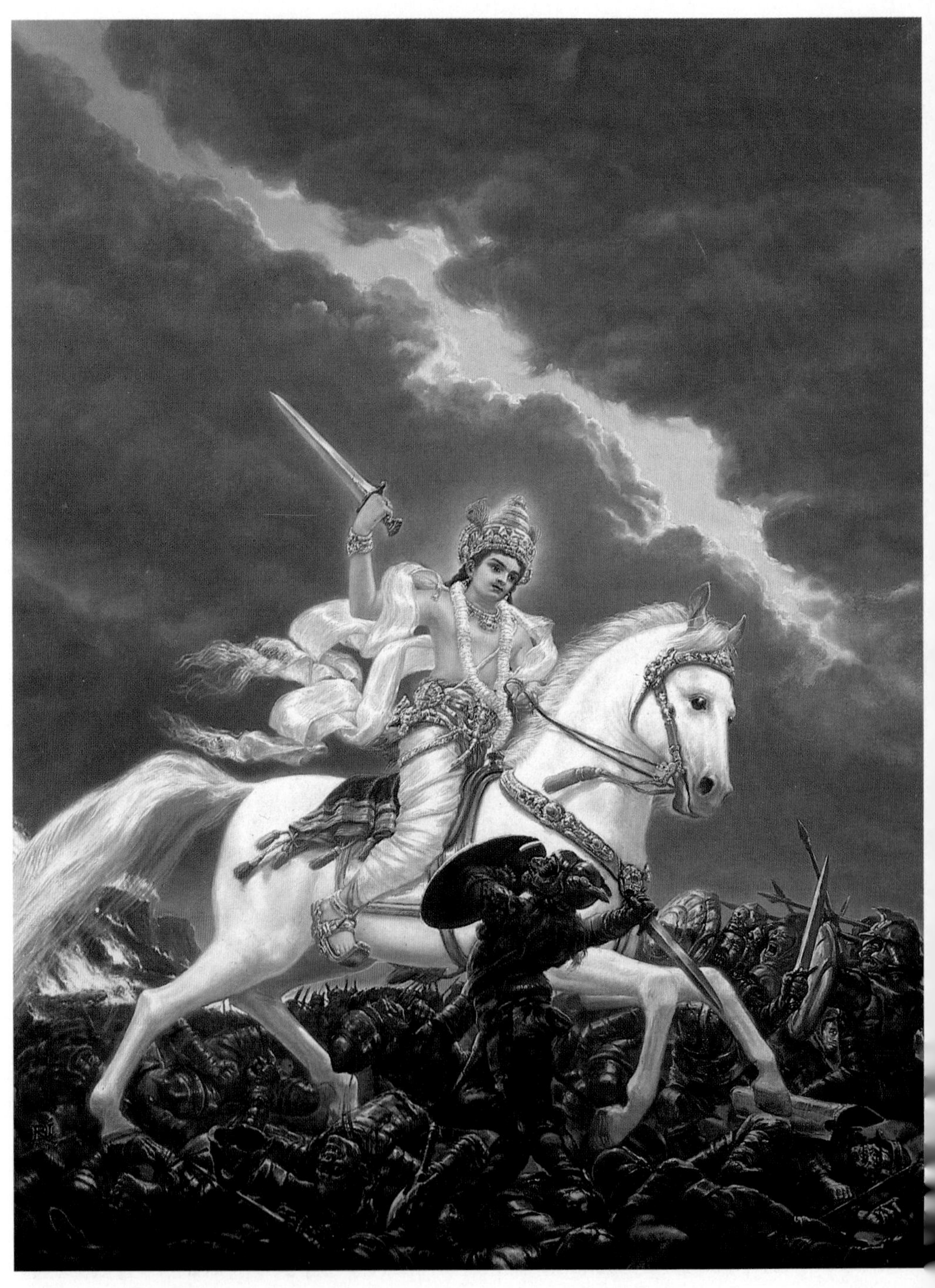

PLATE FIFTEEN: When human society becomes totally degraded, the Lord will incarnate as Kalki, the supreme chastiser, and kill all the demons. (*pp. 422-24*)

tattva, and as such, the name, form, attributes, etc. of Nārāyaṇa are beyond the jurisdiction of the material world. By the speculation of empiric philosophy, which discerns matter from spirit, or by cultivation of mystic powers, which ultimately helps the performer to reach any planet of the universe or beyond the universe, or by discharge of religious duties, one can achieve the highest perfection, provided one is able to reach the stage of *nārāyaṇa-smṛti*, or constant remembrance of the Personality of Godhead. This is possible only by the association of a pure devotee, who can give a finishing touch to the transcendental activities of all *jñānīs*, *yogīs*, or *karmīs*, in terms of prescribed duties defined in the scriptures. There are many historical instances of the achievement of spiritual perfection, such as that of the Sanakādi Ṛṣis or the nine celebrated Yogendras, who attained perfection only after being situated in the devotional service of the Lord. None of the devotees of the Lord ever deviated from the path of devotional service by taking to other methods as adopted by the *jñānīs* or *yogīs*. Everyone is anxious to achieve the highest perfection of his particular activity, and it is indicated herein that such perfection is *nārāyaṇa-smṛti*, for which everyone must endeavor his best. In other words, life should be molded in such a manner that one is able to progressively remember the Personality of Godhead in every step of life.

TEXT 7

प्रायेण मुनयो राजन्निवृत्ता विधिषेधतः ।
नैर्गुण्यस्था रमन्ते स्म गुणानुकथने हरेः ॥ ७ ॥

prāyeṇa munayo rājan
nivṛttā vidhi-ṣedhataḥ
nairguṇya-sthā ramante sma
guṇānukathane hareḥ

prāyeṇa—mainly; *munayaḥ*—all sages; *rājan*—O King; *nivṛttāḥ*—above; *vidhi*—regulative principles; *sedhataḥ*—from restrictions; *nairguṇya-sthāḥ*—transcendentally situated; *ramante*—take pleasure in; *sma*—distinctly; *guṇa-anukathane*—describing the glories; *hareḥ*—of the Lord.

TRANSLATION

O King Parīkṣit, mainly the topmost transcendentalists, who are above the regulative principles and restrictions, take pleasure in describing the glories of the Lord.

PURPORT

The topmost transcendentalist is a liberated soul and is therefore not within the purview of the regulative principles. A neophyte, who is intended to be promoted to the spiritual plane, is guided by the spiritual master under regulative principles. He may be compared to a patient who is treated by various restrictions under medical jurisdiction. Generally, liberated souls also take pleasure in describing the transcendental activities. As mentioned above, since Nārāyaṇa, Hari, the Personality of Godhead, is beyond the material creation, His form and attributes are not material. The topmost transcendentalists or the liberated souls realize Him by advanced experience of transcendental knowledge, and therefore they take pleasure in the discussion of the transcendental qualities of the Lord's pastimes. In the *Bhagavad-gītā* (4.9), the Personality of Godhead declares that His appearance and activities are all *divyam,* or transcendental. The common man, who is under the spell of material energy, takes it for granted that the Lord is like one of us, and therefore he refuses to accept the transcendental nature of the Lord's form, name, etc. The topmost transcendentalist is not interested in anything material, and his taking interest in the matter of the Lord's activities is definite proof that the Lord is not like one of us in the material world. In the Vedic literatures also, it is confirmed that the Supreme Lord is one, but that He is engaged in His transcendental pastimes in the company of His unalloyed devotees and that simultaneously He is present as the Supersoul, an expansion of Baladeva, in the heart of all living entities. Therefore, the highest perfection of transcendental realization is to take pleasure in hearing and describing the transcendental qualities of the Lord and not in merging into His impersonal Brahman existence, for which the impersonalist monist aspires. Real transcendental pleasure is realized in the glorification of the transcendental Lord, and not in the feeling of being situated in His impersonal feature. But there are also others who are not the topmost transcendentalists but are in a lower status, and who do not take pleasure in describing the transcendental activities of the Lord. Rather, they discuss such activities of the Lord formally with the aim of merging into His existence.

TEXT 8

इदं भागवतं नाम पुराणं ब्रह्मसम्मितम् ।
अधीतवान् द्वापरादौ पितुर्द्वैपायनादहम् ॥ ८ ॥

idaṁ bhāgavataṁ nāma
purāṇaṁ brahma-sammitam
adhītavān dvāparādau
pitur dvaipāyanād aham

idam—this; *bhāgavatam*—*Śrīmad-Bhāgavatam;* *nāma*—of the name; *purāṇam*—Vedic supplement; *brahma-sammitam*—approved as the essence of the *Vedas;* *adhītavān*—studied; *dvāpara-ādau*—at the end of the Dvāpara-yuga; *pituḥ*—from my father; *dvaipāyanāt*—Dvaipāyana Vyāsadeva; *aham*—myself.

TRANSLATION

At the end of the Dvāpara-yuga, I studied this great supplement of Vedic literature named Śrīmad-Bhāgavatam, which is equal to all the Vedas, from my father, Śrīla Dvaipāyana Vyāsadeva.

PURPORT

The statement made by Śrīla Śukadeva Gosvāmī that the topmost transcendentalist, who is beyond the jurisdiction of regulations and restrictions, mainly takes to the task of hearing about and glorifying the Personality of Godhead, is verified by his personal example. Śukadeva Gosvāmī, being a recognized liberated soul and the topmost transcendentalist, was accepted by all of the topmost sages present in the meeting during the last seven days of Mahārāja Parīkṣit. He cites from the example of his life that he himself was attracted by the transcendental activities of the Lord, and he studied *Śrīmad-Bhāgavatam* from his great father, Śrī Dvaipāyana Vyāsadeva. *Śrīmad-Bhāgavatam*, or, for that matter, any other scientific literature, cannot be studied at home by one's own intellectual capacity. Medical books of anatomy or physiology are available in the market, but no one can become a qualified medical practitioner simply by reading such books at home. One has to be admitted to the medical college and study the books under the guidance of learned professors. Similarly, *Śrīmad-Bhāgavatam, the postgraduate study of the science of Godhead*, can only be learned by studying it at the feet of a realized soul like Śrīla Vyāsadeva. Although Śukadeva Gosvāmī was a liberated soul from the very day of his birth, he still had to take lessons of *Śrīmad-Bhāgavatam* from his great father, Vyāsadeva, who compiled the *Śrīmad-Bhāgavatam* under the instruction of another great soul, Śrī Nārada Muni. Lord Śrī Caitanya Mahāprabhu instructed a learned *brāhmaṇa* to study *Śrīmad-Bhāgavatam* from a personal *bhāgavata. Śrīmad-Bhāgavatam* is based on the transcendental name, form, attributes, pastimes, entourage and variegatedness of the Supreme Person, and it is spoken by the incarnation of the Personality of Godhead, Śrīla Vyāsadeva. Pastimes of the Lord are executed in cooperation with His pure devotees, and consequently historical incidences are mentioned in this great literature because they are related to Kṛṣṇa. It is called *brahma-sammitam* because it is the sound representative of Lord Kṛṣṇa—like the *Bhagavad-gītā. Bhagavad-gītā* is the sound incarnation of the Lord because it is spoken by the Supreme Lord, and *Śrīmad-Bhāgavatam* is the sound representative of the Lord because it was spoken by the incarnation of the Lord about the activities of the Lord. As stated in the beginning of this book, it is the essence of the Vedic desire tree and the natural commentation on the *Brahma-sūtras*, the topmost philosophical thesis on the subject matter of Brahman. Vyāsadeva appeared at the end of Dvāpara-yuga as the son of Satyavatī, and therefore the word *dvāpara-ādau*, or "the beginning of Dvāpara-yuga," in this context means just prior to the beginning of the Kali-yuga. The logic of this statement, according to Śrīla Jīva Gosvāmī, is comparable to that of calling the upper portion of the tree the beginning. The root of the tree is the beginning of the tree, but in common knowledge the upper portion of the tree is first seen. In that way the end of the tree is accepted as its beginning.

TEXT 9

परिनिष्ठितोऽपि नैर्गुण्य उत्तमश्लोकलीलया ।
गृहीतचेता राजर्षे आख्यानं यदधीतवान् ॥ ९ ॥

parinişṭhito 'pi nairguṇya
uttama-śloka-līlayā
gṛhīta-cetā rājarṣe
ākhyānaṁ yad adhītavān

parinişṭhitaḥ—fully realized; *api*—in spite of; *nairguṇye*—in transcendence; *uttama*—enlightened; *śloka*—verse; *līlayā*—by the pastimes; *gṛhīta*—being attracted; *cetāḥ*—attention; *rājarṣe*—O saintly King; *ākhyānam*—delineation; *yat*—that; *adhītavān*—I have studied.

TRANSLATION

O saintly King, I was certainly situated perfectly in transcendence, yet I was still attracted by the delineation of the pastimes of the Lord, who is described by enlightened verses.

PURPORT

The Absolute Truth is realized as the impersonal Brahman at the first instance by philosophical speculation and later as the Supersoul by further progress of transcendental knowledge. But if, by the grace of the Lord, an impersonalist is enlightened by the superior statements of *Śrīmad-Bhāgavatam,* he is also converted into a transcendental devotee of the Personality of Godhead. With a poor fund of knowledge, we cannot adjust to the idea of the personality of the Absolute Truth, and the personal activities of the Lord are deplored by the less intelligent impersonalists; but reasons and arguments together with the transcendental process of approaching the Absolute Truth help even the staunch impersonalist to become attracted by the personal activities of the Lord. A person like Śukadeva Gosvāmī cannot be attracted by any mundane activity, but when such a devotee is convinced by a superior method, he is certainly attracted by the transcendental activities of the Lord. The Lord is transcendental, as are His activities. He is neither inactive nor impersonal.

TEXT 10

तदहं तेऽभिधास्यामि महापौरुषिको भवान् ।
यस्य श्रद्दधतामाशु स्यान्मुकुन्दे मतिः सती ॥१०॥

tad ahaṁ te 'bhidhāsyāmi
mahā-pauruṣiko bhavān
yasya śraddadhatām āśu
syān mukunde matiḥ satī

tat—that; *aham*—I; *te*—unto you; *abhidhāsyāmi*—shall recite; *mahā-pauruṣikaḥ*—the most sincere devotee of Lord Kṛṣṇa; *bhavān*—your good self; *yasya*—of which; *śraddadhatām*—of one who gives full respect and attention; *āśu*—very soon; *syāt*—it so becomes; *mukunde*—unto the Lord, who awards salvation; *matiḥ*—faith; *satī*—unflinching.

TRANSLATION

That very Śrīmad-Bhāgavatam I shall recite before you because you are the most sincere devotee of Lord Kṛṣṇa. One who gives full attention and respect to hearing Śrīmad-Bhāgavatam achieves unflinching faith in the Supreme Lord, the giver of salvation.

PURPORT

Śrīmad-Bhāgavatam is recognized Vedic wisdom, and the system of receiving Vedic knowledge is called *avaroha-panthā*, or the process of receiving transcendental knowledge through bona fide disciplic succession. For advancement of material knowledge there is a need for personal ability and researching aptitude, but in the case of spiritual knowledge, all progress depends more or less on the mercy of the spiritual master. The spiritual master must be satisfied with the disciple; only then is knowledge automatically manifest before the student of spiritual science. The process should not, however, be misunderstood to be something like magical feats whereby the spiritual master acts like a magician and injects spiritual knowledge into his disciple, as if surcharging him with an electrical current. The bona fide spiritual master reasonably explains everything to the disciple on the authorities of Vedic wisdom. The disciple can receive such teachings not exactly intellectually, but by submissive inquiries and a service attitude. The idea is that both the spiritual master and the disciple must be bona fide. In this case, the spiritual master, Śukadeva Gosvāmī, is ready to recite exactly what he has learned from his great father Śrīla Vyāsadeva, and the disciple, Mahārāja Parīkṣit, is a great devotee of Lord Kṛṣṇa. A devotee of Lord Kṛṣṇa is he who believes sincerely that by becoming a devotee of the Lord one becomes fully equipped with everything spiritual. This teaching is imparted by the Lord Himself in the pages of the *Bhagavad-gītā*, in which it is clearly described that the Lord (Śrī Kṛṣṇa) is everything, and that to surrender unto Him solely and wholly makes one the most perfectly pious man. This unflinching faith in Lord Kṛṣṇa prepares one to become a student of *Śrīmad-Bhāgavatam*, and one who hears *Śrīmad-Bhāgavatam* from a devotee like Śukadeva Gosvāmī is sure to attain salvation at the end, as Mahārāja Parīkṣit did. The professional reciter of *Śrīmad-Bhāgavatam* and the pseudodevotees whose faith is based on one week's hearing are different from Śukadeva Gosvāmī and Mahārāja Parīkṣit. Śrīla Vyāsadeva explained *Śrīmad-Bhāgavatam* unto Śukadeva Gosvāmī from the very beginning of the *janmādy asya* verse, and so Śukadeva Gosvāmī also explained it to the King. Lord Kṛṣṇa is described as the Mahāpuruṣa in the *Śrīmad-Bhāgavatam* (Canto Eleven) in His devotional feature as Lord Śrī Caitanya Mahāprabhu. Śrī Caitanya Mahāprabhu is Lord Kṛṣṇa Himself in His devotional attitude, descended on earth to bestow special favors upon the fallen souls of this age of Kali. There are two verses particularly suitable to offer as prayers to this Mahāpuruṣa feature of Lord Kṛṣṇa.

dhyeyaṁ sadā paribhava-ghnam abhīṣṭa-dohaṁ
tīrthāspadaṁ śiva-viriñci-nutaṁ śaraṇyam
bhṛtyārti-haṁ praṇata-pāla bhavābdhi-potaṁ
vande mahāpuruṣa te caraṇāravindam

tyaktvā sudustyaja-surepsita-rājya-lakṣmīṁ
dharmiṣṭha ārya-vacasā yad agād araṇyam
māyā-mṛgaṁ dayitayepsitam anvadhāvad
vande mahāpuruṣa te caraṇāravindam
(*Bhāg.* 11.5.33–34)

In other words, *puruṣa* means the enjoyer, and *mahāpuruṣa* means the supreme enjoyer, or the Supreme Personality of Godhead Śrī Kṛṣṇa. One who deserves to approach the Supreme Lord Śrī Kṛṣṇa is called the *mahā-pauruṣika.* Anyone who hears *Śrīmad-Bhāgavatam* attentively from its bona fide reciter is sure to become a sincere devotee of the Lord, who is able to award liberation. There was none so attentive as Mahārāja Parīkṣit in the matter of hearing *Śrīmad-Bhāgavatam,* and there was none so qualified as Śukadeva Gosvāmī to recite the text of *Śrīmad-Bhāgavatam.* Therefore, anyone who follows in the footsteps of either the ideal reciter or the ideal hearer, Śukadeva Gosvāmī and Mahārāja Parīkṣit respectively, will undoubtedly attain salvation like them. Mahārāja Parīkṣit attained salvation by hearing only, and Śukadeva Gosvāmī attained salvation only by reciting. Recitation and hearing are two processes out of nine devotional activities, and by strenuously following the principles, either in all or by parts, one can attain the absolute plane. So the complete text of *Śrīmad-Bhāgavatam,* beginning with the *janmādy asya* verse up to the last one in the Twelfth Canto, was spoken by Śukadeva Gosvāmī for the attainment of salvation by Mahārāja Parīkṣit. In the *Padma Purāṇa,* it is mentioned that Gautama Muni advised Mahārāja Ambarīṣa to hear regularly *Śrīmad-Bhāgavatam* as it was recited by Śukadeva Gosvāmī, and herein it is confirmed that Mahārāja Ambarīṣa heard *Śrīmad-Bhāgavatam* from the very beginning to the end, as it was spoken by Śukadeva Gosvāmī. One who is actually interested in the *Bhāgavatam,* therefore, must not play with it by reading or hearing a portion from here and a portion from there; one must follow in the footsteps of great kings like Mahārāja Ambarīṣa or Mahārāja Parīkṣit and hear it from a bona fide representative of Śukadeva Gosvāmī.

TEXT 11

एतन्निर्विद्यमानानामिच्छतामकुतोभयम् ।
योगिनां नृप निर्णीतं हरेर्नामानुकीर्तनम् ॥११॥

etan nirvidyamānānām
icchatām akuto-bhayam
yoginām nṛpa nirṇītaṁ
harer nāmānukīrtanam

etat—it is; *nirvidyamānānām*—of those who are completely free from all material desires; *icchatām*—of those who are desirous of all sorts of material enjoyment; *akutaḥ-bhayam*—free from all doubts and fear; *yoginām*—of all who are self-satisfied; *nṛpa*—O King; *nirṇītam*—decided truth; *hareḥ*—of the Lord, Śrī Kṛṣṇa; *nāma*—holy name; *anu*—after someone, always; *kīrtanam*—chanting.

TRANSLATION

O King, constant chanting of the holy name of the Lord after the ways of the great authorities is the doubtless and fearless way of success for all, including those who are free from all material desires, those who are desirous of all material enjoyment, and also those who are self-satisfied by dint of transcendental knowledge.

PURPORT

In the previous verse, the great necessity for attaining attachment to Mukunda has been accredited. There are different types of persons who desire to attain success in different varieties of pursuits. Generally the persons are materialists who desire to enjoy the fullest extent of material gratification. Next to them are the transcendentalists, who have attained perfect knowledge about the nature of material enjoyment and thus are aloof from such an illusory way of life. More or less, they are satisfied in themselves by self-realization. Above them are the devotees of the Lord, who neither aspire to enjoy the material world nor desire to get out of it. They are after the satisfaction of the Lord, Śrī Kṛṣṇa. In other words, the devotees of the Lord do not want anything on their personal account. If the Lord desires, the devotees can accept all sorts of material facilities, and if the Lord does not desire this, the devotees can leave aside all sorts of facilities, even up to the limit of salvation. Nor are they self-satisfied, because they want the satisfaction of the Lord only. In this verse, Śrī Śukadeva Gosvāmī recommends the transcendental chanting of the holy name of the Lord. By offenseless chanting and hearing of the holy name of the Lord, one becomes acquainted with the transcendental form of the Lord, and then with the attributes of the Lord, and then with the transcendental nature of His pastimes, etc. Here it is mentioned that one should constantly chant the holy name of the Lord after hearing it from authorities. This means that hearing from the authorities is the first essential. Hearing of the holy name gradually promotes one to the stage of hearing about His form, about His attributes, His pastimes and so on, and thus the necessity of the chanting of His glories develops successively. This process is recommended not only for the successful execution of devotional service, but also even for those who are materially attached. According to Śrī Śukadeva Gosvāmī, this way of attaining success is an established fact, concluded not only by him, but also by all other previous *ācāryas.* Therefore, there is no need of further evidence. The process is recommended not only for the progressive students in different departments of ideological success, but also for those who are already successful in their achievement as fruitive workers, as philosophers or as devotees of the Lord.

Śrīla Jīva Gosvāmī instructs that chanting of the holy name of the Lord should be loudly done, and it should be performed offenselessly as well, as recommended in the *Padma Purāṇa.* One can deliver himself from the effects of all sins by surrendering himself unto the Lord. One can deliver himself from all offenses at the feet of the Lord by taking shelter of His holy name. But one cannot protect himself if one commits an offense at the feet of the holy name of the Lord. Such offenses are mentioned in the *Padma Purāṇa* as being ten in number. The first offense is to vilify the great devotees who have preached about the glories of the Lord. The second offense is to see the holy names of the Lord in terms of worldly distinction. The Lord is the proprietor of all the universes, and therefore He may be known in different places by different names, but that does not in any way qualify the fullness of the Lord. Any nomenclature which is meant for the Supreme Lord is as holy as the others because they are all meant for the Lord. Such holy names are as powerful as the Lord, and there is no bar for anyone in any part of the creation to chant and glorify the Lord by the particular name of the Lord as it is locally understood. They are all auspicious, and one should not distinguish such names of the Lord as material commodities. The third offense is to neglect the orders of the authorized *ācāryas* or spiritual masters. The fourth offense is to vilify scriptures or Vedic knowledge. The fifth offense is to define the holy name of the Lord in terms of one's mundane calculation. The holy name of the Lord is identical with the Lord Himself, and one should understand the holy name of the Lord to be nondifferent from Him. The sixth offense is to interpret the holy name. The Lord is not imaginary, nor is His holy name. There are persons with a poor fund of knowledge who think the Lord to be an imagination of the worshiper and therefore think His holy name to be imaginary. Such a chanter of the name of the Lord cannot achieve the desired success in the matter of chanting the holy name. The seventh offense is to commit sins intentionally on the strength of the holy name. In the scriptures it is said that one can be liberated from the effects of all sinful actions simply by chanting the holy name of the Lord. One who takes advantage of this transcendental method and continues to commit sins on the expectation of neutralizing the effects of sins by chanting the holy name of the Lord is the greatest offender at the feet of the holy name. Such an offender cannot purify himself by any recommended method of purification. In other words, one may be a sinful man before chanting the holy name of the Lord, but after taking shelter in the holy name of the Lord and becoming immune, one should strictly restrain oneself from committing sinful acts with a hope that his method of chanting the holy name will give him protection. The eighth offense is to consider the holy name of the Lord and His chanting method to be equal to some material auspicious activity. There are various kinds of good works for material benefits, but the holy name and His chanting are not mere auspicious holy services. Undoubtedly the holy name is holy service, but He should never be utilized for such purposes. Since the holy name and the Lord are of one and the same identity, one should not try to bring the holy name into the service of mankind. The idea is that the Supreme Lord is the supreme enjoyer. He is no one's servant or order supplier. Similarly, since the holy name of the Lord is identical with the Lord, one should not try to utilize the holy name for one's personal service.

The ninth offense is to instruct those who are not interested in chanting the holy name of the Lord about the transcendental nature of the holy name. If such instruction is imparted to an unwilling audience, the act is considered to be an offense at the feet of the holy name. The tenth offense is to become uninterested in the holy name of the Lord even after hearing of the transcendental nature of the holy name. The effect of chanting the holy name of the Lord is perceived by the chanter as liberation from the conception of false egoism. False egoism is exhibited by thinking oneself to be the enjoyer of the world and thinking everything in the world to be meant for the enjoyment of one's self only. The whole materialistic world is moving under such false egoism of "I" and "mine," but the factual effect of chanting the holy name is to become free from such misconceptions.

TEXT 12

किं प्रमत्तस्य बहुभिः परोक्षैर्हायनैरिह ।
वरं मुहूर्तं विदितं घटते श्रेयसे यतः ॥१२॥

kiṁ pramattasya bahubhiḥ
parokṣair hāyanair iha
varaṁ muhūrtaṁ viditaṁ
ghaṭate śreyase yataḥ

kim—what is; *pramattasya*—of the bewildered; *bahubhiḥ*—by many; *parokṣaiḥ*—inexperienced; *hāyanaiḥ*—years; *iha*—in this world; *varam*—better; *muhūrtam*—a moment; *viditam*—conscious; *ghaṭate*—one can try for; *śreyase*—in the matter of the supreme interest; *yataḥ*—by that.

TRANSLATION

What is the value of a prolonged life which is wasted, inexperienced by years in this world? Better a moment of full consciousness, because that gives one a start in searching after his supreme interest.

PURPORT

Śrīla Śukadeva Gosvāmī instructed Mahārāja Parīkṣit about the importance of the chanting of the holy name of the Lord by every progressive gentleman. In order to encourage the King, who had only seven remaining days of life, Śrīla Śukadeva Gosvāmī asserted that there is no use in living hundreds of years without any knowledge of the problems of life—better to live for a moment with full consciousness of the supreme interest to be fulfilled. The supreme interest of life is eternal, with full knowledge and bliss. Those who are bewildered by the external features of the material world and are engaged in the animal propensities of the eat-drink-and-be-merry type of life are simply wasting their lives by the unseen passing away of valuable years. We should know in perfect consciousness that human life is bestowed upon the conditioned soul to achieve spiritual success, and the easiest possible procedure to attain this end is to chant the holy name of the Lord. In the previous verse, we have discussed this point to a certain extent, and we may further be enlightened on the different types of offenses committed unto the feet of the holy name. Śrīla Jīva Gosvāmī Prabhu has quoted many passages from authentic scriptures and has ably supported the statements in the matter of offenses at the feet of the holy name. From *Viṣṇu-yāmala Tantra*, Śrīla Jīva Gosvāmī has proven that one can be liberated from the effects of all sins simply by chanting the holy name of the Lord. Quoting from the *Mārkaṇḍeya Purāṇa*, Śrī Gosvāmījī says that one should neither blaspheme the devotee of the Lord nor indulge in hearing others who are engaged in belittling a devotee of the Lord. A devotee should try to restrict the vilifier by cutting out his tongue, and being unable to do so, one should commit suicide rather than hear the blaspheming of the devotee of the Lord. The conclusion is that one should neither hear nor allow vilification of a devotee of the Lord. As far as distinguishing the Lord's holy name from the names of the demigods, the revealed scriptures disclose (Bg. 10.41) that all extraordinarily powerful beings are but parts and parcels of the supreme energetic, Lord Kṛṣṇa. Except for the Lord Himself, everyone is subordinate; no one is independent of the Lord. Since no one is more powerful than or equal to the energy of the Supreme Lord, no one's name can be as powerful as that of the Lord. By chanting the Lord's holy name, one can derive all the stipulated energy synchronized from all sources. Therefore, one should not equalize the supreme holy name of the Lord with any other name. Brahmā, Śiva or any other powerful god can never be equal to the Supreme Lord Viṣṇu. The powerful holy name of the Lord can certainly deliver one from sinful effects, but one who desires to utilize this transcendental potency of the holy name of the Lord in one's sinister activities is the most degraded person in the world. Such persons are never excused by the Lord or by any agent of the Lord. One should, therefore, utilize one's life in glorifying the Lord by all means, without any offense. Such activity of life, even for a moment, is never to be compared to a prolonged life of ignorance, like the lives of the tree and other living entities who may live for thousands of years without prosecuting spiritual advancement.

TEXT 13

खट्वाङ्गो नाम राजर्षिर्ज्ञात्वेयत्तामिहायुषः ।
मुहूर्तात्सर्वमुत्सृज्य गतवानभयं हरिम् ॥१३॥

khaṭvāṅgo nāma rājarṣir
jñātveyattām ihāyuṣaḥ
muhūrtāt sarvam utsṛjya
gatavān abhayaṁ harim

khaṭvāṅgaḥ—King Khaṭvāṅga; *nāma*—name; *rāja-ṛṣiḥ*—saintly king; *jñātvā*—by knowing; *iyattām*—duration; *iha*—in this world; *āyuṣaḥ*—of one's life; *muhūrtāt*—within only a moment; *sarvam*—everything; *utsṛjya*—leaving aside; *gatavān*—had undergone; *abhayam*—fully safe; *harim*—the Personality of Godhead.

TRANSLATION

The saintly King Khaṭvāṅga, after being informed that the duration of his life would be only a moment more, at once freed himself from all material activities and took shelter of the supreme safety, the Personality of Godhead.

PURPORT

A fully responsible man should always be conscious of the prime duty of the present human form of life. The activities to meet the immediate necessities of material life are not everything. One should always be alert in his duty for attainment of the best situation in the next life. Human life is meant for preparing ourselves for that prime duty. Mahārāja Khaṭvāṅga is mentioned herein as a saintly king because even within the responsibility of the state management, he was not at all forgetful of the prime duty of life. Such was the case with other *rājarṣis* (saintly kings), like Mahārāja Yudhiṣṭhira and Mahārāja Parīkṣit. They were all exemplary personalities on account of their being alert in discharging their prime duty. Mahārāja Khaṭvāṅga was invited by the demigods in the higher planets to fight demons, and as a king he fought the battles to the full satisfaction of the demigods. The demigods, being fully satisfied with him, wanted to give him some benediction for material enjoyment, but Mahārāja Khaṭvāṅga, being very much alert to his prime duty, inquired from the demigods about his remaining duration of life. This means that he was not as anxious to accumulate some material benediction from the demigods as he was to prepare himself for the next life. He was informed by the demigods, however, that his life would last only a moment longer. The king at once left the heavenly kingdom, which is always full of material enjoyment of the highest standard, and coming down to this earth, took ultimate shelter of the all-safe Personality of Godhead. He was successful in his great attempt and achieved liberation. This attempt, even for a moment, by the saintly king, was successful because he was always alert to his prime duty. Mahārāja Parīkṣit was thus encouraged by the great Śukadeva Gosvāmī, even though he had only seven days left in his life to execute the prime duty of hearing the glories of the Lord in the form of *Śrīmad-Bhāgavatam.* By the will of the Lord, Mahārāja Parīkṣit instantly met the great Śukadeva Gosvāmī, and the great treasure of spiritual success left by him is nicely mentioned in the *Śrīmad-Bhāgavatam.*

TEXT 14

तवाप्येतर्हि कौरव्य सप्ताहं जीवितावधिः ।
उपकल्पय तत्सर्वं तावद्यत्साम्परायिकम् ॥१४॥

tavāpy etarhi kauravya
saptāhaṁ jīvitāvadhiḥ
upakalpaya tat sarvaṁ
tāvad yat sāmparāyikam

tava—your; *api*—also; *etarhi*—thercfore; *kauravya*—O one born in the family of Kuru; *saptāham*—seven days; *jīvita*—duration of life; *avadhiḥ*—up to the limit of; *upakalpaya*—get them performed; *tat*—those; *sarvam*—all; *tāvat*—so long; *yat*—which are; *sāmparāyikam*—rituals for the next life.

TRANSLATION

Mahārāja Parīkṣit, now your duration of life is limited to seven more days, so during this time you can perform all those rituals which are needed for the best purpose of your next life.

PURPORT

Śukadeva Gosvāmī, after citing the example of Mahārāja Khaṭvāṅga, who prepared himself for the next life within a very short time, encouraged Mahārāja Parīkṣit by saying that since he still had seven days at his disposal, he could easily take advantage of the time to prepare himself for the next life. Indirectly, the Gosvāmī told Mahārāja Parīkṣit that he should take shelter of the sound representation of the Lord for the seven days still remaining in the duration of his life and thus get himself liberated. In other words, everyone can best prepare himself for the next life simply by hearing *Śrīmad-Bhāgavatam*, as it was recited by Śukadeva Gosvāmī to Mahārāja Parīkṣit. The rituals are not formal, but there are also some favorable conditions, which are required to be carried out, as instructed hereafter.

TEXT 15

अन्तकाले तु पुरुष आगते गतसाध्वसः ।
छिन्द्यादसङ्गशस्त्रेण स्पृहां देहेऽनु ये च तम् ॥१५॥

anta-kāle tu puruṣa
āgate gata-sādhvasaḥ
chindyād asaṅga-śastreṇa
spṛhāṁ dehe 'nu ye ca tam

anta-kāle—at the last stage of life; *tu*—but; *puruṣaḥ*—a person; *āgate*—having arrived; *gata-sādhvasaḥ*—without any fear of death; *chindyāt*—must cut off; *asaṅga*—nonattachment; *śastreṇa*—by the weapon of; *spṛhām*—all desires; *dehe*—in the matter of the material tabernacle; *anu*—pertaining; *ye*—all that; *ca*—also; *tam*—them.

TRANSLATION

At the last stage of one's life, one should be bold enough not to be afraid of death. But one must cut off all attachment to the material body and everything pertaining to it and all desires thereof.

PURPORT

The foolishness of gross materialism is that people think of making a permanent settlement in this world, although it is a settled fact that one has to give up everything here that has been created by valuable human energy. Great statesmen, scientists, philosophers, etc., who are foolish, without any information of the spirit soul, think that this life of a few years only is all in all and that there is nothing more after death. This poor fund of knowledge, even in the so-called learned circles of the world, is killing the vitality of human energy, and the awful result is being keenly felt. And yet the foolish materialistic men do not care about what is going to happen in the next life. The preliminary instruction in the *Bhagavad-gītā* is that one should know that the identity of the individual living entity is not lost even after the end of this present body, which is nothing but an outward dress only. As one changes an old garment, so the individual living being also changes his body, and this change of body is called death. Death is therefore a process of changing the body at the end of the duration of the present life. An intelligent person must be prepared for this and must try to have the best type of body in the next life. The best type of body is a spiritual body, which is obtained by those who go back to the kingdom of God or enter the realm of Brahman. In the second chapter of this canto, this matter will be broadly discussed, but as far as the change of body is concerned, one must prepare now for the next life. Foolish people attach more importance to the present temporary life, and thus the foolish leaders make appeals to the body and the bodily relations. The bodily relations extend not only to this body but also to the family members, wife, children, society, country and so many other things which end at the end of life. After death one forgets everything about the present bodily relations; we have a little experience of this at night when we go to sleep. While sleeping, we forget everything about this body and bodily relations, although this forgetfulness is a temporary situation for only a few hours. Death is nothing but sleeping for a few months in order to develop another term of bodily encagement, which we are awarded by the law of nature according to our aspiration. Therefore, one has only to change the aspiration during the course of this present body, and for this there is need of training in the current duration of human life. This training can be begun at any stage of life, or even a few seconds before death, but the usual procedure is for one to get the training from very early life, from the stage of *brahmacarya,* and gradually progress to the *gṛhastha, vānaprastha* and *sannyāsa* orders of life. The institution which gives such training is called *varṇāśrama-dharma,* or the system of *sanātana-dharma,* the best procedure for making the human life perfect. One is therefore required to give up the attachment to family or social or political life just at the age of fifty years, if not earlier, and the training in the *vānaprastha* and *sannyāsa-āśramas* is given for preparation of the next life. Foolish materialists, in the garb of leaders of the people in general, stick to family affairs without attempting to cut off relations with them, and thus they become victims of nature's law and get gross bodies again, according to their work. Such foolish leaders may have some respect from the people at the end of life, but that does not mean that such leaders will be immune to the natural laws under which everyone is tightly bound by the hands and feet. The best thing is, therefore, that everyone voluntarily give up family relations by transferring the attachment from family, society, country and everything thereof to the devotional service of the Lord. It is stated herein that one should give up all desires of family attachment. One must have a chance for better desires; otherwise there is no chance of giving up such morbid desires. Desire is the concomitant factor of the living entity. The living entity is eternal, and therefore his desires, which are natural for a living being, are also eternal. One cannot, therefore, stop desiring, but the subject matter for desires can be changed. So one must develop the desires for returning home, back to Godhead, and automatically the desires for material gain, material honor and material popularity will diminish in proportion to the development of devotional service. A living being is meant for service activities, and his desires are centered around such a service attitude. Beginning from the top executive head of the state down to the insignificant pauper in the street, all are rendering some sort of service to others. The perfection of such a service attitude is only attained simply by transferring the desire of service from matter to spirit, or from Satan to God.

TEXT 16

गृहात् प्रव्रजितो धीरः पुण्यतीर्थजलाप्लुतः ।
शुचौ विविक्त आसीनो विधिवत्कल्पितासने ॥१६॥

gṛhāt pravrajito dhīraḥ
puṇya-tīrtha-jalāplutaḥ
śucau vivikta āsīno
vidhivat kalpitāsane

gṛhāt—from one's home; *pravrajitaḥ*—having gone out; *dhīraḥ*—self-controlled; *puṇya*—pious; *tīrtha*—sacred place; *jala-āplutaḥ*—fully washed; *śucau*—cleansed; *vivikte*—solitary; *āsīnaḥ*—seated; *vidhivat*—according to regulations; *kalpita*—having done; *āsane*—on a sitting place.

TRANSLATION

One should leave home and practice self-control. In a sacred place he should bathe regularly and sit down in a lonely place duly sanctified.

PURPORT

To prepare oneself for the better next life, one must get out of one's so-called home. The system of *varṇāśrama-dharma*, or *sanātana-dharma*, prescribes retirement from family encumbrances as early as possible after one has passed fifty years of age. Modern civilization is based on family comforts, the highest standard of amenities, and therefore after retirement everyone expects to live a very comfortable life in a well-furnished home decorated with fine ladies and children, without any desire to get out of such a comfortable home. High government officers and ministers stick to their prize posts until death, and they neither dream nor desire to get out of homely comforts. Bound by such hallucinations, materialistic men prepare various plans for a still more comfortable life, but suddenly cruel death comes without mercy and takes away the great planmaker against his desire, forcing him to give up the present body for another body. Such a planmaker is thus forced to accept another body in one of the 8,400,000 species of life according to the fruits of the work he has performed. In the next life, persons who are too much attached to family comforts are generally awarded lower species of life on account of sinful acts performed during a long duration of sinful life, and thus all the energy of the human life is spoiled. In order to be saved from the danger of spoiling the human form of life and being attached to unreal things, one must take warning of death at the age of fifty, if not earlier. The principle is that one should take it for granted that the death warning is already there, even prior to the attainment of fifty years of age, and thus at any stage of life one should prepare himself for a better next life. The system of the *sanātana-dharma* institution is so made that the follower is trained for the better next life without any chance that the human life will be spoiled. The holy places all over the world are meant for the residential purposes of retired persons getting ready for a better next life. Intelligent persons must go there at the end of life, and for that matter, after fifty years of age, to live a life of spiritual regeneration for the sake of being freed from family attachment, which is considered to be the shackle of material life. One is recommended to quit home just to get rid of material attachment because one who sticks to family life until death cannot get rid of material attachment and as long as one is materially attached one cannot understand spiritual freedom. One should not, however, become self-complacent simply by leaving home or by creating another home at the holy place, either lawfully or unlawfully. Many persons leave home and go to such holy places, but due to bad association, again become family men by illicit connection with the opposite sex. The illusory energy of matter is so strong that one is apt to be under such illusion at every stage of life, even after quitting one's happy home. Therefore, it is essential that one practice self-control by celibacy without the least desire for sex indulgence. For a man desiring to improve the condition of his existence, sex indulgence is considered suicidal, or even worse. Therefore, to live apart from family life means to become self-controlled in regard to all sense desires, especially sex desires. The method is that one should have a duly sanctified sitting place made of straw, deerskin and carpet, and thus sitting on it one should chant the holy name of the Lord without offense, as prescribed above. The whole process is to drag the mind from material engagements and fix it on the lotus feet of the Lord. This simple process alone will help one advance to the highest stage of spiritual success.

TEXT 17

अभ्यसेन्मनसा शुद्धं त्रिवृद्ब्रह्माक्षरं परम् ।
मनो यच्छेज्जितश्वासो ब्रह्मबीजमविस्मरन् ॥१७॥

abhyasen manasā śuddhaṁ
trivṛd-brahmākṣaraṁ param
mano yacchej jita-śvāso
brahma-bījam avismaran

abhyaset—one should practice; *manasā*—by the mind; *śuddham*—sacred; *tri-vṛt*—composed of the three; *brahma-akṣaram*—transcendental letters; *param*—the supreme; *manaḥ*—mind; *yacchet*—get under control; *jita-śvāsaḥ*—by regulating the breathing air; *brahma*—absolute; *bījam*—seed; *avismaran*—without being forgotten.

TRANSLATION

After sitting in the above manner, make the mind remember the three transcendental letters [a-u-m], and by regulating the breathing process, control the mind so as not to forget the transcendental seed.

PURPORT

Oṁkāra, or the *praṇava*, is the seed of transcendental realization, and it is composed of the three transcendental letters *a-u-m.* By its chanting by the mind, in conjunction with the breathing process, which is a transcendental but mechanical way of getting into trance, as devised by the experience of great mystics, one is able to bring the mind, which is materially absorbed, under control. This is the way of changing the habit of the mind. The mind is not to be killed. Mind or desire cannot be stopped, but to develop a desire to function for spiritual realization, the quality of engagement by the mind has to be changed. The mind is the pivot of the active sense organs, and as such if the quality of thinking, feeling and willing is changed, naturally the quality of actions by the instrumental senses will also change. *Oṁkāra* is the seed of all transcendental sound and it is only the transcendental sound which can bring about the desired change of the mind and the senses. Even a mentally deranged man can be cured by treatment of transcendental sound. In the *Bhagavad-gītā*, the *praṇava* (*oṁkāra*) has been accepted as the direct, literal representation of the Supreme Absolute Truth. One who is not able to chant directly the holy name of the Lord, as recommended above, can easily chant the *praṇava* (*oṁkāra*). This *oṁkāra* is a note of address, such as "O my Lord," just as *oṁ hari om* means "O my Lord, the Supreme Personality of Godhead." As we have explained before, the Lord's holy name is identical with the Lord Himself. So also is *oṁkāra.* But persons who are unable to realize the transcendental personal form or name of the Lord on account of their imperfect senses (in other words, the neophytes) are trained to the practice of self-realization by this mechanical process of regulating the breathing function and simultaneously repeating the *praṇava* (*oṁkāra*) within the mind. As we have several times expressed, since the transcendental name, form, attributes, pastimes, etc., of the Personality of Godhead are impossible to understand with the present material senses, it is necessary that through the mind, the center of sensual activities, such transcendental realization be set into motion. The devotees directly fix their minds on the Person of the Absolute Truth. But one who is unable to accommodate such personal features of the Absolute is disciplined in impersonality to train the mind to make further progress.

TEXT 18

नियच्छेद्विषयेभ्योऽक्षान्मनसा बुद्धिसारथिः ।
मनः कर्मभिराक्षिप्तं शुभार्थे धारयेद्धिया ॥१८॥

niyacched viṣayebhyo 'kṣān
manasā buddhi-sārathiḥ
manaḥ karmabhir ākṣiptaṁ
śubhārthe dhārayed dhiyā

niyacchet—withdraw; *viṣayebhyaḥ*—from sense engagements; *akṣān*—the senses; *manasā*—by dint of the mind; *buddhi*—intelligence; *sārathiḥ*—driver; *manaḥ*—the mind; *karmabhiḥ*—by the fruitive work; *ākṣiptam*—being absorbed in; *śubha-arthe*—for the sake of the Lord; *dhārayet*—hold up; *dhiyā*—in full consciousness.

TRANSLATION

Gradually, as the mind becomes progressively spiritualized, withdraw it from sense activities, and by intelligence the senses will be controlled. The mind too absorbed in material activities can be engaged in the service of the Personality of Godhead and become fixed in full transcendental consciousness.

PURPORT

The first process of spiritualizing the mind by mechanical chanting of the *praṇava* (*oṁkāra*) and by control of the breathing system is technically called the mystic or yogic process of *prāṇāyāma*, or fully controlling the breathing air. The ultimate state of this *prāṇāyāma* system is to be fixed in trance, technically called *samādhi*. But experience has proven that even the *samādhi* stage also fails to control the materially absorbed mind. For example, the great mystic Viśvāmitra Muni, even in the stage of *samādhi*, became a victim of the senses and cohabited with Menakā. History has already recorded this. The mind, although ceasing to think of sensual activities at present, remembers past sensual activities from the subconscious status and thus disturbs one from cent percent engagement in self-realization. Therefore, Śukadeva Gosvāmī recommends the next step of assured policy, namely to fix one's mind in the service of the Personality of Godhead. Lord Śrī Kṛṣṇa, the Supreme Personality of Godhead, also recommends this direct process in the *Bhagavad-gītā* (6.47). Thus, the mind being spiritually cleansed, one should at once engage himself in the transcendental loving service of the Lord by the different devotional activities of hearing, chanting, etc. If performed under proper guidance, that is the surest path of progress, even for the disturbed mind.

TEXT 19

तत्रैकावयवं ध्यायेदव्युच्छिन्नेन चेतसा ।
मनो निर्विषयं युक्त्वा ततः किञ्चन न स्मरेत् ।
पदं तत्परमं विष्णोर्मनो यत्र प्रसीदति ॥१९॥

tatraikāvayavaṁ dhyāyed
avyucchinnena cetasā
mano nirviṣayaṁ yuktvā
tataḥ kiñcana na smaret
padaṁ tat paramaṁ viṣṇor
mano yatra prasīdati

tatra—thereafter; *eka*—one by one; *avayavam*—limbs of the body; *dhyāyet*—should be concentrated upon; *avyucchinnena*—without being deviated from the complete form; *cetasā*—by the mind; *manaḥ*—mind; *nirviṣayam*—without being contaminated by sense objects; *yuktvā*—being dovetailed; *tataḥ*—after that; *kiñcana*—anything; *na*—do not; *smaret*—think of; *padam*—personality; *tat*—that; *paramam*—Supreme; *viṣṇoḥ*—of Viṣṇu; *manaḥ*—the mind; *yatra*—whereupon; *prasīdati*—becomes reconciled.

TRANSLATION

Thereafter, you should meditate upon the limbs of Viṣṇu, one after another, without being deviated from the conception of the complete body. Thus the mind becomes free from all sense objects. There should be no other thing to be thought upon. Because the Supreme Personality of Godhead, Viṣṇu, is the Ultimate Truth, the mind becomes completely reconciled in Him only.

PURPORT

Foolish persons, bewildered by the external energy of Viṣṇu, do not know that the ultimate goal of the progressive search after happiness is to get in touch directly with Lord Viṣṇu, the Personality of Godhead. *Viṣṇu-tattva* is an unlimited expansion of different transcendental forms of the Personality of Godhead, and the supreme or original form of *viṣṇu-tattva* is Govinda, or Lord Kṛṣṇa, the supreme cause of all causes. Therefore, thinking of Viṣṇu or meditating upon the transcendental form of Viṣṇu, specifically upon Lord Kṛṣṇa, is the last word on the subject of meditation. This meditation may be begun from the lotus feet of the Lord. One should not, however, forget or be misled from the complete form of the Lord; thus one should practice thinking of the different parts of His transcendental body, one after another. Here in this verse, it is definitely assured that the Supreme Lord is not impersonal. He is a person, but His body is different from those of conditioned persons like us. Otherwise, meditation beginning from the *praṇava* (*oṁkāra*) up to the limbs of the personal body of Viṣṇu would not have been recommended by Śukadeva Gosvāmī for the attainment of complete spiritual perfection. The Viṣṇu forms of worship in great temples of India are not, therefore, arrangements of idol worship, as they are wrongly interpreted to be by a class of men with a poor fund of knowledge; rather, they are different spiritual centers of meditation on the transcendental limbs of the body of Viṣṇu. The worshipable Deity in the temple of Viṣṇu is identical with Lord Viṣṇu by the inconceivable potency of the Lord. Therefore, a neophyte's concentration or meditation upon the limbs of Viṣṇu in the temple, as contemplated in the revealed scriptures, is an easy opportunity for meditation for persons who are unable to sit down tightly at one place and then concentrate upon *praṇava oṁkāra* or the limbs of the body of Viṣṇu, as recommended herein by Śukadeva Gosvāmī, the great authority. The common man can benefit more by meditating on the form of Viṣṇu in the temple than on the *oṁkāra*, the spiritual combination of *a-u-m* as explained before. There is no difference between *oṁkāra* and the forms of Viṣṇu, but persons unacquainted with the science of Absolute Truth try to create dissension by differentiating between the forms of Viṣṇu and that of *oṁkāra*. Here it is indicated that the Viṣṇu form is the ultimate goal of meditation, and as such it is better to concentrate upon the forms of Viṣṇu than on impersonal *oṁkāra*. The latter process is also more difficult than the former.

TEXT 20

रजस्तमोभ्यामाक्षिप्तं विमूढं मन आत्मनः ।
यच्छेद्धारणया धीरो हन्ति या तत्कृतं मलम् ॥२०॥

rajas-tamobhyām ākṣiptaṁ
vimūḍhaṁ mana ātmanaḥ
yacched dhāraṇayā dhīro
hanti yā tat-kṛtaṁ malam

rajaḥ—the passionate mode of nature; *tamobhyām*—as well as by the ignorant mode of material nature; *ākṣiptam*—agitated; *vimūḍham*—bewildered; *manaḥ*—the mind; *ātmanaḥ*—of one's own; *yacchet*—get it rectified; *dhāraṇayā*—by conception (of Viṣṇu); *dhīraḥ*—the pacified; *hanti*—destroys; *yā*—all those; *tat-kṛtam*—done by them; *malam*—dirty things.

TRANSLATION

One's mind is always agitated by the passionate mode of material nature and bewildered by the ignorant mode of nature. But one can rectify such conceptions by the relation of Viṣṇu and thus become pacified by cleansing the dirty things created by them.

PURPORT

Persons generally conducted by the modes of passion and ignorance cannot be bona fide candidates for being situated in the transcendental stage of God realization. Only persons conducted by the mode of goodness can have the knowledge of the Supreme Truth. Effects of the modes of passion and ignorance are manifested by too much hankering after wealth and women. And those who are too much after wealth and women can rectify their leanings only by constant remembrance of Viṣṇu in His potential impersonal feature. Generally the impersonalists or monists are influenced by the modes of passion and ignorance. Such impersonalists think of themselves as liberated souls, but they have no knowledge of the transcendental personal feature of the Absolute Truth. Actually they are impure in heart on account of being devoid of knowledge of the personal feature of the Absolute. In the *Bhagavad-gītā*, it is said that after many hundreds of births, the impersonal philosopher surrenders unto the Personality of Godhead. To acquire such a qualification of God realization in the personal feature, the neophyte impersonalist is given a chance to realize the relation of the Lord in everything by the philosophy of pantheism.

Pantheism in its higher status does not permit the student to form an impersonal conception of the Absolute Truth, but it extends the conception of the Absolute Truth into the field of the so-called material energy. Everything created by the material energy can be dovetailed with the

Absolute by an attitude of service, which is the essential part of living energy. The pure devotee of the Lord knows the art of converting everything into its spiritual existence by this service attitude, and only in that devotional way can the theory of pantheism be perfected.

TEXT 21

यस्यां सन्धार्यमाणायां योगिनो भक्तिलक्षणः ।
आशु सम्पद्यते योग आश्रयं भद्रमीक्षतः ॥२१॥

yasyāṁ sandhāryamāṇāyāṁ
yogino bhakti-lakṣaṇaḥ
āśu sampadyate yoga
āśrayaṁ bhadram īkṣataḥ

yasyām—by such systematic remembrance; *sandhāryamāṇāyām*—and thus being fixed in the habit of; *yoginaḥ*—the mystics; *bhakti-lakṣaṇaḥ*—being practiced to the devotional system; *āśu*—very soon; *sampadyate*—attains success; *yogaḥ*—connection by devotional service; *āśrayam*—under the shelter of; *bhadram*—the all-good; *īkṣataḥ*—which seeing that.

TRANSLATION

O King, by this system of remembrance and by being fixed in the habit of seeing the all-good personal conception of the Lord, one can very soon attain devotional service to the Lord, under His direct shelter.

PURPORT

Success of mystic performances is achieved only by the help of the devotional attitude. Pantheism, or the system of feeling the presence of the Almighty everywhere, is a sort of training of the mind to become accustomed to the devotional conception, and it is this devotional attitude of the mystic that makes possible the successful termination of such mystic attempts. One is not, however, elevated to such a successful status without the tinge of mixture in devotional service. The devotional atmosphere created by pantheistic vision develops into devotional service in later days, and that is the only benefit for the impersonalist. It is confirmed in the *Bhagavad-gītā* (12.5) that the impersonal way of self-realization is more troublesome because it reaches the goal in an indirect way, although the impersonalist also becomes obsessed with the personal feature of the Lord after a long time.

TEXT 22

राजोवाच
यथा सन्धार्यते ब्रह्मन् धारणा यत्र सम्मता ।
यादृशी वा हरेदाशु पुरुषस्य मनोमलम् ॥२२॥

rājovāca
yathā sandhāryate brahman
dhāraṇā yatra sammatā
yādṛśī vā hared āśu
puruṣasya mano-malam

rājā uvāca—the fortunate King said; *yathā*—as it is; *sandhāryate*—the conception is made; *brahman*—O *brāhmaṇa; dhāraṇā*—conception; *yatra*—where and how; *sammatā*—in a summary; *yādṛśī*—the way by which; *vā*—or; *haret*—extricated; *āśu*—without delay; *puruṣasya*—of a person; *manaḥ*—of the mind; *malam*—dirty things.

TRANSLATION

The fortunate King Parīkṣit, inquiring further, said: O brāhmaṇa, please describe in full detail how and where the mind has to be applied and how the conception can be fixed so that the dirty things in a person's mind can be removed.

PURPORT

The dirty things in the heart of a conditioned soul are the root cause of all troubles for him. A conditioned soul is surrounded by the manifold miseries of material existence, but on account of his gross ignorance he is unable to remove the troubles due to dirty things in the heart, accumulated during the long prison life in the material world. He is actually meant to serve the will of the Supreme Lord, but on account of the dirty things in the heart, he likes to serve his concocted desires. These desires, instead of giving him any peace of mind, create new problems and thus bind him to the cycle of repeated birth and death. These dirty things of fruitive work and empiric philosophy can be removed only by association with the Supreme Lord. The Lord, being omnipotent, can offer His association by His inconceivable potencies. Thus persons who are unable to pin their faith on the personal feature of the Absolute are given a chance to associate with His *virāṭ-rūpa*, or the cosmic impersonal feature of the Lord. The cosmic impersonal feature of the Lord is a feature of His unlimited potencies. Since the potent and potencies are identical, even the conception of His impersonal cosmic feature helps the conditioned soul to associate with the Lord indirectly and thus gradually rise to the stage of personal contact.

Mahārāja Parīkṣit was already directly connected with the personal feature of the Lord Śrī Kṛṣṇa, and as such he had no need to inquire from Śukadeva Gosvāmī about where and how to apply the mind in the impersonal *virāṭ-rūpa* of the Lord. But he inquired after a detailed description of the matter for the benefit of others, who are unable to conceive of the transcendental personal feature of the Lord as the form of eternity, knowledge and bliss. The nondevotee class of men cannot think of the personal feature of the Lord. Because of their poor fund of knowledge, the personal form of the Lord, like Rāma or Kṛṣṇa, is completely revolting to them. They have a poor estimation of the potency of the Lord. In the *Bhagavad-gītā* (9.11) it is explained by the Lord Himself that people with a poor fund of knowledge deride the supreme personality of the Lord, taking Him to be a common man. Such men are ignorant of the inconceivable potency of the Lord. By the inconceivable potency of the Lord, He can move in human society or any other society of living beings and yet remain the same omnipotent Lord, without deviating in the slightest from His transcendental position. So, for the benefit of men who are unable to accept the Lord in His personal eternal form, Mahārāja Parīkṣit inquired from Śukadeva Gosvāmī how to fix the mind on Him in the beginning, and the Gosvāmī replied in detail as follows.

TEXT 23

श्रीशुक उवाच
जितासनो जितश्वासो जितसङ्गो जितेन्द्रियः ।
स्थूले भगवतो रूपे मनः सन्धारयेद्धिया ॥२३॥

śrī-śuka uvāca
jitāsano jita-śvāso
jita-saṅgo jitendriyaḥ
sthūle bhagavato rūpe
manaḥ sandhārayed dhiyā

śrī-śukaḥ uvāca—Śukadeva Gosvāmī said; *jita-āsanaḥ*—controlled sitting posture; *jita-śvāsaḥ*—controlled breathing process; *jita-saṅgaḥ*—controlled association; *jita-indriyaḥ*—controlled senses; *sthūle*—in the gross matter; *bhagavataḥ*—unto the Personality of Godhead; *rūpe*—in the feature of; *manaḥ*—the mind; *sandhārayet*—must apply; *dhiyā*—by intelligence.

TRANSLATION

Śukadeva Gosvāmī answered: One should control the sitting posture, regulate the breathing process by the yogic prāṇāyāma and thus control the mind and senses and with intelligence apply the mind to the gross potencies of the Lord [called the virāṭ-rūpa].

PURPORT

The materially absorbed mind of the conditioned soul does not allow him to transcend the limit of the bodily conception of self, and thus the *yoga* system for meditation (controlling the sitting posture and breathing process and fixing the mind upon the Supreme) is prescribed in order to mold the character of the gross materialist. Unless such materialists are able to cleanse the materially absorbed mind, it is impossible for them to concentrate upon thoughts of transcendence. And to do so one may fix one's mind on the gross material or external feature of the Lord. The different parts of the gigantic form of the Lord are described in the following verses. The materialistic men are very anxious to have some mystic powers as a result of such a controlling process, but the real purpose of yogic regulations is to eradicate the accumulated dirty things like lust, anger, avarice and all such material contaminations. If the mystic *yogī* is diverted by the accompanying feats of mystic control, then his mission of yogic success is a failure, because the ultimate aim is God realization. He is therefore recommended to fix his gross materialistic mind by a different conception and thus realize the potency of the Lord. As soon as the potencies are understood to be instrumental manifestations of the transcendence, one automatically advances to the next step, and gradually the stage of full realization becomes possible for him.

TEXT 24

विशेषस्तस्य देहोऽयं स्थविष्ठश्च स्थवीयसाम् ।
यत्रेदं व्यज्यते विश्वं भूतं भव्यं भवच्च सत् ॥२४॥

viśeṣas tasya deho 'yaṁ
sthaviṣṭhaś ca sthavīyasām
yatredaṁ vyajyate viśvaṁ
bhūtaṁ bhavyaṁ bhavac ca sat

viśeṣaḥ—personal; *tasya*—His; *dehaḥ*—body; *ayam*—this; *sthaviṣṭhaḥ*—grossly material; *ca*—and; *sthavīyasām*—of all matter; *yatra*—wherein; *idam*—all these phenomena; *vyajyate*—is experienced; *viśvam*—universe; *bhūtam*—past; *bhavyam*—future; *bhavat*—present; *ca*—and; *sat*—resultant.

TRANSLATION

This gigantic manifestation of the phenomenal material world as a whole is the personal body of the Absolute Truth, wherein the universal resultant past, present and future of material time is experienced.

PURPORT

Anything, either material or spiritual, is but an expansion of the energy of the Supreme Personality of Godhead, and as stated in the

Bhagavad-gītā (13.13), the omnipotent Lord has His transcendental eyes, heads and other bodily parts distributed everywhere. He can see, hear, touch or manifest Himself anywhere and everywhere, for He is present everywhere as the Supersoul of all infinitesimal souls, although He has His particular abode in the absolute world. The relative world is also His phenomenal representation because it is nothing but an expansion of His transcendental energy. Although He is in His abode, His energy is distributed everywhere, just as the sun is localized as well as expanded everywhere, since the rays of the sun, being nondifferent from the sun, are accepted as expansions of the sun disc. In the *Viṣṇu Purāṇa* (1.22.52) it is said that as fire expands its rays and heat from one place, similarly the Supreme Spirit, the Personality of Godhead, expands Himself by His manifold energy everywhere and anywhere. The phenomenal manifestation of the gigantic universe is only a part of His *virāṭ* body. Less intelligent men cannot conceive of the transcendental all-spiritual form of the Lord, but they are astounded by His different energies, just as the aborigines are struck with wonder by the manifestation of lightning, a gigantic mountain or a hugely expanded banyan tree. The aborigines praise the strength of the tiger and the elephant because of their superior energy and strength. The *asuras* cannot recognize the existence of the Lord, although there are vivid descriptions of the Lord in the revealed scriptures, although the Lord incarnates and exhibits His uncommon strength and energy, and although He is accepted as the Supreme Personality of Godhead by learned scholars and saints like Vyāsadeva, Nārada, Asita and Devala in the past and by Arjuna in the *Bhāgavad-gītā*, as also by the *ācāryas* like Śaṅkara, Rāmānuja, Madhva and Lord Śrī Caitanya in the modern age. The *asuras* do not accept any evidential proof from the revealed scriptures, nor do they recognize the authority of the great *ācāryas.* They want to see with their own eyes at once. Therefore they can see the gigantic body of the Lord as *virāṭ*, which will answer their challenge, and since they are accustomed to paying homage to superior material strength like that of the tiger, elephant and lightning, they can offer respect to the *virāṭ-rūpa.* Lord Kṛṣṇa, by the request of Arjuna, exhibited His *virāṭ-rūpa* for the *asuras.* A pure devotee of the Lord, being unaccustomed to looking into such a mundane gigantic form of the Lord, requires special vision for the purpose. The Lord, therefore, favored Arjuna with special vision for looking into His *virāṭ-*

rūpa, which is described in the Eleventh Chapter of the *Bhagavad-gītā*. This *virāṭ-rūpa* of the Lord was especially manifested, not for the benefit of Arjuna, but for that unintelligent class of men who accept anyone and everyone as an incarnation of the Lord and so mislead the general mass of people. For them, the indication is that one should ask the cheap incarnation to exhibit his *virāṭ-rūpa* and thus be established as an incarnation. The *virāṭ-rūpa* manifestation of the Lord is simultaneously a challenge to the atheist and a favor for the *asuras*, who can think of the Lord as *virāṭ* and thus gradually cleanse the dirty things from their hearts in order to become qualified to actually see the transcendental form of the Lord in the near future. This is a favor of the all-merciful Lord to the atheists and the gross materialists.

TEXT 25

अण्डकोशे शरीरेऽस्मिन् सप्तावरणसंयुते ।
वैराजः पुरुषो योऽसौ भगवान् धारणाश्रयः ॥२५॥

aṇḍa-kośe śarīre 'smin
saptāvaraṇa-saṁyute
vairājaḥ puruṣo yo 'sau
bhagavān dhāraṇāśrayaḥ

aṇḍa-kośe—within the universal shell; *śarīre*—in the body of; *asmin*—this; *sapta*—sevenfold; *āvaraṇa*—coverings; *saṁyute*—having so done; *vairājaḥ*—the gigantic universal; *puruṣaḥ*—form of the Lord; *yaḥ*—that; *asau*—He; *bhagavān*—the Personality of Godhead; *dhāraṇā*—conception; *āśrayaḥ*—object of.

TRANSLATION

The gigantic universal form of the Personality of Godhead, within the body of the universal shell, which is covered by sevenfold material elements, is the subject for the virāṭ conception.

PURPORT

Simultaneously, the Lord has multifarious other forms, and all of them are identical with the original fountainhead form of the Lord, Śrī

Kṛṣṇa. In the *Bhagavad-gītā,* it has been proven that the original transcendental and eternal form of the Lord is Śrī Kṛṣṇa, the Absolute Personality of Godhead, but by His inconceivable internal potency, *ātma-māyā,* He can expand Himself by multifarious forms and incarnations simultaneously, without being diminished in His full potency. He is complete, and although innumerable complete forms emanate from Him, He is still complete, without any loss. That is His spiritual or internal potency. In the Eleventh Chapter of the *Bhagavad-gītā,* the Personality of Godhead, Lord Kṛṣṇa, manifested His *virāṭ-rūpa* just to convince the less intelligent class of men, who cannot conceive of the Lord as appearing just like a human being, that He factually has the potency of His claim to be the Supreme Absolute Person without any rival or superior. Materialistic men can think, although very imperfectly, of the huge universal space, comprehending an innumerable number of planets as big as the sun. They can see only the circular sky overhead, without any information that this universe, as well as many other hundreds of thousands of universes, are each covered by sevenfold material coverings of water, fire, air, sky, ego, noumenon and material nature, just like a huge football, pumped and covered, floating on the water of the Causal Ocean, wherein the Lord is lying as Mahā-Viṣṇu. All the universes in seed are emanating from the breathing of the Mahā-Viṣṇu, who is but part of a partial expansion of the Lord, and all the universes presided over by the Brahmās vanish when the Mahā-Viṣṇu withdraws His great breath. In this way, the material worlds are being created and vanished by the supreme will of the Lord. The poor foolish materialist can just imagine how ignorantly he puts forward an insignificant creature to become His rival incarnation, simply on the allegations of a dying man. The *virāṭ-rūpa* was particularly exhibited by the Lord just to give lessons to such foolish men, so that one can accept a person as the incarnation of Godhead only if such a person is able to exhibit such a *virāṭ-rūpa* as Lord Kṛṣṇa did. The materialistic person may concentrate his mind upon the *virāṭ* or gigantic form of the Lord in his own interest and as recommended by Śukadeva Gosvāmī, but he must be on his guard not to be misled by pretenders who claim to be the identical person as Lord Kṛṣṇa but are not able to act like Him or exhibit the *virāṭ-rūpa,* comprehending the whole of the universe.

TEXT 26

पातालमेतस्य हि पादमूलं
पठन्ति पार्ष्णिप्रपदे रसातलम् ।
महातलं विश्वसृजोऽथ गुल्फौ
तलातलं वै पुरुषस्य जङ्घे ॥२६॥

pātālam etasya hi pāda-mūlaṁ
paṭhanti pārṣṇi-prapade rasātalam
mahātalaṁ viśva-sṛjo 'tha gulphau
talātalaṁ vai puruṣasya jaṅghe

pātālam—the planets at the bottom of the universe; *etasya*—of His; *hi*—exactly; *pāda-mūlam*—soles of the feet; *paṭhanti*—they study it; *pārṣṇi*—the heels; *prapade*—the toes; *rasātalam*—the planets named Rasātala; *mahātalam*—the planets named Mahātala; *viśva-sṛjaḥ*—of the creator of the universe; *atha*—thus; *gulphau*—the ankles; *talātalam*—the planets named Talātala; *vai*—as they are; *puruṣasya*—of the gigantic person; *jaṅghe*—the shanks.

TRANSLATION

Persons who have realized it have studied that the planets known as Pātāla constitute the bottoms of the feet of the universal Lord, and the heels and the toes are the Rasātala planets. The ankles are the Mahātala planets, and His shanks constitute the Talātala planets.

PURPORT

Outside the bodily existence of the Supreme Personality of Godhead, the manifested cosmic existence has no reality. Everything and anything of the manifested world rests on Him, as confirmed in the *Bhagavad-gītā* (9.4), but that does not imply that everything and anything in the vision of a materialist is the Supreme Personality. The conception of the universal form of the Lord gives a chance to the materialist to think of the Supreme Lord, but the materialist must know for certain that his visualization of the world in a spirit of lording over it is not God realization.

The materialistic view of exploitation of the material resources is occasioned by the illusion of the external energy of the Lord, and as such, if anyone wants to realize the Supreme Truth by conceiving of the universal form of the Lord, he must cultivate the service attitude. Unless the service attitude is revived, the conception of *virāṭ* realization will have very little effect on the seer. The transcendental Lord, in any conception of His form, is never a part of the material creation. He keeps His identity as Supreme Spirit in all circumstances and is never affected by the three material qualities, for everything material is contaminated. The Lord always exists by His internal energy.

The universe is divided into fourteen planetary systems. Seven planetary systems, called Bhūr, Bhuvar, Svar, Mahar, Janas, Tapas and Satya, are upward planetary systems, one above the other. There are also seven planetary systems downward, known as Atala, Vitala, Sutala, Talātala, Mahātala, Rasātala and Pātāla, gradually, one below the other. In this verse, the description begins from the bottom because it is in the line of devotion that the Lord's bodily description should begin from His feet. Śukadeva Gosvāmī is a recognized devotee of the Lord, and he is exactly correct in the description.

TEXT 27

द्वे जानुनी सुतलं विश्वमूर्ते-
रूरुद्वयं वितलं चातलं च ।
महीतलं तज्जघनं महीपते
नभस्तलं नाभिसरो गृणन्ति ॥२७॥

dve jānunī sutalaṁ viśva-mūrter
ūru-dvayaṁ vitalaṁ cātalaṁ ca
mahītalaṁ taj-jaghanaṁ mahīpate
nabhastalaṁ nābhi-saro gṛṇanti

dve—two; *jānunī*—two knees; *sutalam*—the planetary system named Sutala; *viśva-mūrteḥ*—of the universal form; *ūru-dvayam*—the two thighs; *vitalam*—the planetary system named Vitala; *ca*—also; *atalam*—the planets named Atala; *ca*—and; *mahītalam*—the planetary system named Mahītala; *tat*—of that; *jaghanam*—the hips; *mahīpate*—

O King; *nabhastalam*—outer space; *nābhi-saraḥ*—the depression of the navel; *gṛṇanti*—they take it so.

TRANSLATION

The knees of the universal form are the planetary system of the name Sutala, and the two thighs are the Vitala and Atala planetary systems. The hips are Mahītala, and outer space is the depression of His navel.

TEXT 28

उरःस्थलं ज्योतिरनीकमस्य
ग्रीवा महर्वदनं वै जनोऽस्य ।
तपो वराटीं विदुरादिपुंसः
सत्यं तु शीर्षाणि सहस्रशीर्ष्णः ॥२८॥

uraḥ-sthalaṁ jyotir-anīkam asya
grīvā mahar vadanaṁ vai jano 'sya
tapo varāṭīṁ vidur ādi-puṁsaḥ
satyaṁ tu śīrṣāṇi sahasra-śīrṣṇaḥ

uraḥ—high; *sthalam*—place (the chest); *jyotiḥ-anīkam*—the luminary planets; *asya*—of Him; *grīvā*—the neck; *mahaḥ*—the planetary system above the luminaries; *vadanam*—mouth; *vai*—exactly; *janaḥ*—the planetary system above Mahar; *asya*—of Him; *tapaḥ*—the planetary system above the Janas; *varāṭīm*—forehead; *viduḥ*—is known; *ādi*—the original; *puṁsaḥ*—personality; *satyam*—the topmost planetary system; *tu*—but; *śīrṣāṇi*—the head; *sahasra*—one thousand; *śīrṣṇaḥ*—one with heads.

TRANSLATION

The chest of the Original Personality of the gigantic form is the luminary planetary system, His neck is the Mahar planets, His mouth is the Janas planets, and His forehead is the Tapas planetary system. The topmost planetary system, known as Satyaloka, is the head of He who has one thousand heads.

PURPORT

The effulgent luminary planets like the sun and the moon are situated almost in the midplace of the universe, and as such they are to be known as the chest of the original gigantic form of the Lord. And above the luminary planets, called also the heavenly places of the universal directorate demigods, are the Mahar, Janas and Tapas planetary systems, and, above all, the Satyaloka planetary system, where the chief directors of the modes of material nature reside, namely Viṣṇu, Brahmā and Śiva. This Viṣṇu is known as the Kṣīrodakaśāyī Viṣṇu, and He acts as the Supersoul in every living being. There are innumerable universes floating on the Causal Ocean, and in each of them the representation of the *virāṭ* form of the Lord is there along with innumerable suns, moons, heavenly demigods, Brahmās, Viṣṇus and Śivas, all of them situated in one part of the inconceivable potency of Lord Kṛṣṇa, as stated in the *Bhagavad-gītā* (10.42).

TEXT 29

इन्द्रादयो बाहव आहुरुस्राः
कर्णौ दिशः श्रोत्रममुष्य शब्दः ।
नासत्यदस्रौ परमस्य नासे
घ्राणोऽस्य गन्धो मुखमग्निरिद्धः ॥२९॥

indrādayo bāhava āhur usrāḥ
karṇau diśaḥ śrotram amuṣya śabdaḥ
nāsatya-dasrau paramasya nāse
ghrāṇo 'sya gandho mukham agnir iddhaḥ

indra-ādayaḥ—demigods headed by the heavenly king, Indra; *bāhavaḥ*—arms; *āhuḥ*—are called; *usrāḥ*—the demigods; *karṇau*—the ears; *diśaḥ*—the four directions; *śrotram*—the sense of hearing; *amuṣya*—of the Lord; *śabdaḥ*—sound; *nāsatya-dasrau*—the demigods known as the Aśvinī-kumāras; *paramasya*—of the Supreme; *nāse*—nostrils; *ghrāṇaḥ*—the sense of smell; *asya*—of Him; *gandhaḥ*—fragrance; *mukham*—the mouth; *agniḥ*—fire; *iddhaḥ*—blazing.

TRANSLATION

His arms are the demigods headed by Indra, the ten directional sides are His ears, and physical sound is His sense of hearing. His nostrils are the two Aśvinī-kumāras, and material fragrance is His sense of smell. His mouth is the blazing fire.

PURPORT

The description of the gigantic form of the Personality of Godhead made in the Eleventh Chapter of the *Bhagavad-gītā* is further explained here in the *Śrīmad-Bhāgavatam.* The description in the *Bhagavad-gītā* (11.30) runs as follows: "O Viṣṇu, I see You devouring all people in Your blazing mouths and covering all the universe by Your immeasurable rays. Scorching the worlds, You are manifest." In that way, *Śrīmad-Bhāgavatam* is the postgraduate study for the student of the *Bhagavad-gītā.* Both of them are the science of Kṛṣṇa, the Absolute Truth, and so they are interdependent.

The conception of the *virāt-puruṣa,* or the gigantic form of the Supreme Lord, is said to include all the dominating demigods as well as the dominated living beings. Even the minutest part of a living being is controlled by the empowered agency of the Lord. Since the demigods are included in the gigantic form of the Lord, worship of the Lord, whether in His gigantic material conception or in His eternal transcendental form as Lord Śrī Kṛṣṇa, also appeases the demigods and all the other parts and parcels, as much as watering the root of a tree distributes energy to all of the tree's other parts. Consequently, for a materialist also, worship of the universal gigantic form of the Lord leads one to the right path. One need not risk being misled by approaching many demigods for fulfillment of different desires. The real entity is the Lord Himself, and all others are imaginary, for everything is included in Him only.

TEXT 30

द्यौरक्षिणी चक्षुरभूत्पतङ्गः
पक्ष्माणि विष्णोरहनी उभे च ।
तद्भ्रूविजृम्भः परमेष्ठिधिष्ण्य-
मापोऽस्य तालू रस एव जिह्वा ॥३०॥

dyaur akṣiṇī cakṣur abhūt pataṅgaḥ
pakṣmāṇi viṣṇor ahanī ubhe ca
tad-bhrū-vijṛmbhaḥ parameṣṭhi-dhiṣṇyam
āpo 'sya tālū rasa eva jihvā

dyauḥ—the sphere of outer space; *akṣiṇī*—the eyeballs; *cakṣuḥ*—of eyes (senses); *abhūt*—it so became; *pataṅgaḥ*—the sun; *pakṣmāṇi*—eyelids; *viṣṇoḥ*—of the Personality of Godhead, Śrī Viṣṇu; *ahanī*—day and night; *ubhe*—both; *ca*—and; *tat*—His; *bhrū*—eyebrows; *vijṛmbhaḥ*—movements; *parameṣṭhi*—the supreme entity (Brahmā); *dhiṣṇyam*—post; *āpaḥ*—Varuṇa, the director of water; *asya*—His; *tālū*—palate; *rasaḥ*—juice; *eva*—certainly; *jihvā*—the tongue.

TRANSLATION

The sphere of outer space constitutes His eyepits, and the eyeball is the sun as the power of seeing. His eyelids are both the day and night, and in the movements of His eyebrows, the Brahmā and similar supreme personalities reside. His palate is the director of water, Varuṇa, and the juice or essence of everything is His tongue.

PURPORT

To common sense the description in this verse appears to be somewhat contradictory because sometimes the sun has been described as the eyeball and sometimes as the outer space sphere. But there is no room for common sense in the injunctions of the *śāstras.* We must accept the description of the *śāstras* and concentrate more on the form of the *virāṭ-rūpa* than on common sense. Common sense is always imperfect, whereas the description in the *śāstras* is always perfect and complete. If there is any incongruity, it is due to our imperfection and not the *śāstras*'. That is the method of approaching Vedic wisdom.

TEXT 31

छन्दांस्यनन्तस्य शिरो गृणन्ति
दंष्ट्रा यमः स्नेहकला द्विजानि ।
हासो जनोन्मादकरी च माया
दुरन्तसर्गो यदपाङ्गमोक्षः ॥३१॥

chandāṁsy anantasya śiro gṛṇanti
daṁṣṭrā yamaḥ sneha-kalā dvijāni
hāso janonmāda-karī ca māyā
duranta-sargo yad-apāṅga-mokṣaḥ

chandāṁsi—the Vedic hymns; *anantasya*—of the Supreme; *śiraḥ*—the cerebral passage; *gṛṇanti*—they say; *daṁṣṭrāḥ*—the jaws of teeth; *yamaḥ*—Yamarāja, the director of sinners; *sneha-kalāḥ*—the art of affection; *dvijāni*—the set of teeth; *hāsaḥ*—smile; *jana-unmāda-karī*—the most alluring; *ca*—also; *māyā*—illusory energy; *duranta*—insurpassable; *sargaḥ*—the material creation; *yat-apāṅga*—whose glance; *mokṣaḥ*—casting over.

TRANSLATION

They say that the Vedic hymns are the cerebral passage of the Lord, and His jaws of teeth are Yama, god of death, who punishes the sinners. The art of affection is His set of teeth, and the most alluring illusory material energy is His smile. This great ocean of material creation is but the casting of His glance over us.

PURPORT

According to Vedic assertion, this material creation is the result of the Lord's casting a glance over the material energy, which is described herein as the most alluring illusory energy. The conditioned souls who are allured by such materialism should know that the material temporary creation is simply an imitation of the reality and that those who are captivated by such alluring glances of the Lord are put under the direction of the controller of sinners called Yamarāja. The Lord smiles affectionately, displaying His teeth. The intelligent person who can grasp these truths about the Lord becomes a soul fully surrendered unto Him.

TEXT 32

व्रीडोत्तरौष्ठोऽधर एव लोभो
धर्मः स्तनोऽधर्मपथोऽस्य पृष्ठम् ।
कस्तस्य मेढ्रं वृषणौ च मित्रौ
कुक्षिः समुद्रा गिरयोऽस्थिसङ्घाः ॥३२॥

vrīḍottarauṣṭho 'dhara eva lobho
dharmaḥ stano 'dharma-patho 'sya pṛṣṭham
kas tasya meḍhraṁ vṛṣaṇau ca mitrau
kukṣiḥ samudrā girayo 'sthi-saṅghāḥ

vrīḍa—modesty; *uttara*—upper; *oṣṭha*—lip; *adharaḥ*—chin; *eva*—certainly; *lobhaḥ*—hankering; *dharmaḥ*—religion; *stanaḥ*—breast; *adharma*—irreligion; *pathaḥ*—way; *asya*—His; *pṛṣṭham*—back; *kaḥ*—Brahmā; *tasya*—His; *meḍhram*—genitals; *vṛṣaṇau*—testicles; *ca*—also; *mitrau*—the Mitrā-varuṇas; *kukṣiḥ*—waist; *samudrāḥ*—the oceans; *girayaḥ*—the hills; *asthi*—bones; *saṅghāḥ*—stack.

TRANSLATION

Modesty is the upper portion of His lips, hankering is His chin, religion is the breast of the Lord, and irreligion is His back. Brahmājī, who generates all living beings in the material world, is His genitals, and the Mitrā-varuṇas are His two testicles. The ocean is His waist, and the hills and mountains are the stacks of His bones.

PURPORT

The Supreme Lord is not impersonal, as misconceived by less intelligent thinkers. Rather, He is the Supreme Person, as confirmed in all authentic Vedic literatures. But His personality is different from what we can conceive. It is stated here that Brahmājī acts as His genitals and that the Mitrā-varuṇas are His two testicles. This means that as a person He is complete with all bodily organs, but they are of different types with different potencies. When the Lord is described as impersonal, therefore, it should be understood that His personality is not exactly the type of personality found within our imperfect speculation. One can, however, worship the Lord even by seeing the hills and mountains or the ocean and the sky as different parts and parcels of the gigantic body of the Lord, the *virāṭ-puruṣa.* The *virāṭ-rūpa,* as exhibited by Lord Kṛṣṇa to Arjuna, is a challenge to the unbelievers.

TEXT 33

नद्योऽस्य नाड्योऽथ तनूरुहाणि
महीरुहा विश्वतनोर्नृपेन्द्र ।
अनन्तवीर्यः श्वसितं मातरिश्वा
गतिर्वयः कर्म गुणप्रवाहः ॥३३॥

nadyo 'sya nāḍyo 'tha tanū-ruhāṇi
mahī-ruhā viśva-tanor nṛpendra
ananta-vīryaḥ śvasitaṁ mātariśvā
gatir vayaḥ karma guṇa-pravāhaḥ

nadyaḥ—the rivers; *asya*—of Him; *nāḍyaḥ*—veins; *atha*—and thereafter; *tanū-ruhāṇi*—hairs on the body; *mahī-ruhāḥ*—the plants and trees; *viśva-tanoḥ*—of the universal form; *nṛpa-indra*—O King; *ananta-vīryaḥ*—of the omnipotent; *śvasitam*—breathing; *mātariśvā*—air; *gatiḥ*—movement; *vayaḥ*—passing ages; *karma*—activity; *guṇa-pravāhaḥ*—reactions of the modes of nature.

TRANSLATION

O King, the rivers are the veins of the gigantic body, the trees are the hairs of His body, and the omnipotent air is His breath. The passing ages are His movements, and His activities are the reactions of the three modes of material nature.

PURPORT

The Personality of Godhead is not a dead stone, nor is He inactive, as is poorly thought by some schools. He moves with the progress of time, and therefore He knows all about the past and future, along with His present activities. There is nothing unknown to Him. The conditioned souls are driven by the reactions of the modes of material nature, which are the activities of the Lord. As stated in the *Bhagavad-gītā* (7.12), the modes of nature act under His direction only, and as such no natural functions are blind or automatic. The power behind the activities is the supervision of the Lord, and thus the Lord is never inactive as is wrongly conceived. The *Vedas* say that the Supreme Lord has nothing to do personally, as is always the case with superiors, but everything is done by His direction. As it is said, not a blade of grass moves without His sanction. In the *Brahma-saṁhitā* (5.48), it is said that all the universes and the heads of them (the Brahmās) exist only for the duration of His breathing period. The same is confirmed here. The air on which the universes and the planets within the universes exist is nothing but a bit of the breath of the unchallengeable *virāṭ-puruṣa.* So even by studying the rivers, trees, air and passing ages, one can conceive of the Personality of Godhead without being misled by the formless conception of the Lord. In the *Bhagavad-gītā* (12.5) it is stated that those who are much inclined to the formless conception of the Supreme Truth are more troubled than those who can intelligently conceive of the personal form.

TEXT 34

ईशस्य केशान् विदुरम्बुवाहान्
वासस्तु सन्ध्यां कुरुवर्य भूम्नः ।
अव्यक्तमाहुर्हृदयं मनश्च
स चन्द्रमाः सर्वविकारकोशः ॥३४॥

īśasya keśān vidur ambuvāhān
vāsas tu sandhyāṁ kuru-varya bhūmnaḥ
avyaktam āhur hṛdayaṁ manaś ca
sa candramāḥ sarva-vikāra-kośaḥ

īśasya—of the supreme controller; *keśān*—hairs on the head; *viduḥ*—you may know it from me; *ambu-vāhān*—the clouds which carry water; *vāsaḥ tu*—the dress; *sandhyām*—termination of day and night; *kuru-varya*—O best of the Kurus; *bhūmnaḥ*—of the Almighty; *avyaktam*—the prime cause of material creation; *āhuḥ*—it is said; *hṛdayam*—intelligence; *manaḥ ca*—and the mind; *saḥ*—He; *candramāḥ*—the moon; *sarva-vikāra-kośaḥ*—the reservoir of all changes.

TRANSLATION

O best amongst the Kurus, the clouds which carry water are the hairs on His head, the terminations of days or nights are His dress,

and the supreme cause of material creation is His intelligence. His mind is the moon, the reservoir of all changes.

TEXT 35

विज्ञानशक्तिं महिमामनन्ति
सर्वात्मनोऽन्तःकरणं गिरित्रम् ।
अश्वाश्वतर्युष्ट्रगजा नखानि
सर्वे मृगाः पशवः श्रोणिदेशे ॥३५॥

vijñāna-śaktiṁ mahim āmananti
sarvātmano 'ntaḥ-karaṇaṁ giritram
aśvāśvatary-uṣṭra-gajā nakhāni
sarve mṛgāḥ paśavaḥ śroṇi-deśe

vijñāna-śaktim—consciousness; *mahim*—the principle of matter; *āmananti*—they call it so; *sarva-ātmanaḥ*—of the omnipresent; *antaḥ-karaṇam*—ego; *giritram*—Rudra (Śiva); *aśva*—horse; *aśvatari*—mule; *uṣṭra*—camel; *gajāḥ*—elephant; *nakhāni*—nails; *sarve*—all other; *mṛgāḥ*—stags; *paśavaḥ*—quadrupeds; *śroṇi-deśe*—on the region of the belt.

TRANSLATION

The principle of matter [mahat-tattva] is the consciousness of the omnipresent Lord, as asserted by the experts, and Rudradeva is His ego. The horse, mule, camel and elephant are His nails, and wild animals and all quadrupeds are situated in the belt zone of the Lord.

TEXT 36

वयांसि तद्व्याकरणं विचित्रं
मनुर्मनीषा मनुजो निवासः ।
गन्धर्वविद्याधरचारणाप्सरः
स्वरस्मृतीरसुरानीकवीर्यः ॥३६॥

vayāṁsi tad-vyākaraṇaṁ vicitraṁ
manur manīṣā manujo nivāsaḥ

gandharva-vidyādhara-cāraṇāpsaraḥ
svara-smṛtīr asurānīka-vīryaḥ

vayāṁsi—varieties of birds; *tat-vyākaraṇam*—vocables; *vicitram*—artistic; *manuḥ*—the father of mankind; *manīṣā*—thoughts; *manujaḥ*—mankind (the sons of Manu); *nivāsaḥ*—residence; *gandharva*—the human beings named Gandharvas; *vidyādhara*—the Vidyādharas; *cāraṇa*—the Cāraṇas; *apsaraḥ*—the angels; *svara*—musical rhythm; *smṛtīḥ*—remembrance; *asura-anīka*—the demoniac soldiers; *vīryaḥ*—prowess.

TRANSLATION

Varieties of birds are indications of His masterful artistic sense. Manu, the father of mankind, is the emblem of His standard intelligence, and humanity is His residence. The celestial species of human beings, like the Gandharvas, Vidyādharas, Cāraṇas and angels, all represent His musical rhythm, and the demoniac soldiers are representations of His wonderful prowess.

PURPORT

The aesthetic sense of the Lord is manifested in the artistic, colorful creation of varieties of birds like the peacock, parrot and cuckoo. The celestial species of human beings, like the Gandharvas and Vidyādharas, can sing wonderfully and can entice even the minds of the heavenly demigods. Their musical rhythm represents the musical sense of the Lord. How then can He be impersonal? His musical taste, artistic sense and standard intelligence, which is never fallible, are different signs of His supreme personality. The *Manu-saṁhitā* is the standard lawbook for humanity, and every human being is advised to follow this great book of social knowledge. Human society is the residential quarters for the Lord. This means that the human being is meant for God realization and association with God. This life is a chance for the conditioned soul to regain his eternal God consciousness and thus fulfill the mission of life. Mahārāja Prahlāda is the right type of representative of the Lord in the family of *asuras*. None of the living beings is away from the Lord's gigantic body. Each and every one has a particular duty in relation to the supreme body. Disruption in the matter of discharging the specific duty assigned to each and every living being is the cause of disharmony between one living being and another, but when the relation is reestablished in relation with the Supreme Lord, there is complete unity between all living beings, even up to the limit of the wild animals and human society. Lord Caitanya Mahāprabhu displayed this living unity in the jungle of Madhya Pradesh, where even the tigers, elephants and many other ferocious animals perfectly cooperated in glorifying the Supreme Lord. That is the way to peace and amity all over the world.

TEXT 37

ब्रह्माननं क्षत्रभुजो महात्मा
विड्डूरुरङ्घ्रिश्रितकृष्णवर्णः ।
नानाभिधाभीज्यगणोपपन्नो
द्रव्यात्मकः कर्म वितानयोगः ॥३७॥

brahmānanaṁ kṣatra-bhujo mahātmā
viḍ ūrur aṅghri-śrita-kṛṣṇa-varṇaḥ
nānābhidhābhījya-gaṇopapanno
dravyātmakaḥ karma vitāna-yogaḥ

brahma—the *brāhmaṇas; ānanam*—the face; *kṣatra*—the *kṣatriyas; bhujaḥ*—the arms; *mahātmā*—the *virāṭ-puruṣa; viṭ*—the *vaiśyas; ūruḥ*—the thighs; *aṅghri-śrita*—under the protection of His feet; *kṛṣṇa-varṇaḥ*—the *śūdras; nānā*—various; *abhidhā*—by names; *abhījya-gaṇa*—the demigods; *upapannaḥ*—being overtaken; *dravya-ātmakaḥ*—with feasible goods; *karma*—activities; *vitāna-yogaḥ*—performances of sacrifice.

TRANSLATION

The virāṭ-puruṣa's face is the brāhmaṇas, His arms are the kṣatriyas, His thighs are the vaiśyas, and the śūdras are under the protection of His feet. All the worshipable demigods are also overtaken by Him, and it is the duty of everyone to perform sacrifices with feasible goods to appease the Lord.

PURPORT

Monotheism is practically suggested here. Offering sacrifices to many demigods under different names is mentioned in the Vedic literatures, but the suggestion made in this verse is that all those varieties of demigods are included in the form of the Supreme Personality of Godhead; they are only the parts and parcels of the original whole. Similarly, the divisions of the orders of human society, namely the *brāhmaṇas* (the intelligent class), the *kṣatriyas* (the administrators), the *vaiśyas* (the mercantile community) and the *śūdras* (the laborer class), are all included in the body of the Supreme. As such, sacrifice by every one of them in terms of pleasing the Supreme by feasible goods is recommended. Generally, the sacrifice is offered with clarified butter and grains, but with the progress of time, human society has produced varieties of goods by transforming materials supplied by God's material nature. Human society, therefore, *must learn to offer sacrifices not only with clarified butter, but also with other manufactured goods in the propagation of the Lord's glory, and that will bring about perfection in human society.* The intelligent class of men, or *brāhmaṇas*, may give direction for such sacrifices in consultation with the previous *ācāryas;* the administrators may give all facilities to perform such sacrifices; the *vaiśya* class or mercantile community, who produce such goods, may offer them for sacrifice; and the *śūdra* class may offer their manual labor for the successful termination of such sacrifice. Thus by the cooperation of all classes of human beings, the sacrifice recommended in this age, namely the sacrifice of congregational chanting of the holy name of the Lord, may be executed for the common welfare of all the people of the world.

TEXT 38

इयानसावीश्वरविग्रहस्य
यः सन्निवेशः कथितो मया ते ।
सन्धार्यतेऽस्मिन् वपुषि स्थविष्ठे
मनः स्वबुद्ध्या न यतोऽस्ति किञ्चित् ॥३८॥

iyān asāv īśvara-vigrahasya
yaḥ sanniveśaḥ kathito mayā te

sandhāryate 'smin vapuṣi sthaviṣṭhe
manaḥ sva-buddhyā na yato 'sti kiñcit

iyān—all these; *asau*—that; *īśvara*—Supreme Lord; *vigrahasya*—of the form; *yaḥ*—whatsoever; *sanniveśaḥ*—as they are located; *kathitaḥ*—explained; *mayā*—by me; *te*—unto you; *sandhāryate*—one may concentrate; *asmin*—in this; *vapuṣi*—form of *virāṭ; sthaviṣṭhe*—in the gross; *manaḥ*—mind; *sva-buddhyā*—by one's intelligence; *na*—not; *yataḥ*—beyond Him; *asti*—there is; *kiñcit*—anything else.

TRANSLATION

I have thus explained to you the gross material gigantic conception of the Personality of Godhead. One who seriously desires liberation concentrates his mind on this form of the Lord, because there is nothing more than this in the material world.

PURPORT

In the *Bhagavad-gītā* (9.10), the Supreme Personality of Godhead has verily explained that the material nature is only an order-carrying agent of His. She is one of the different potencies of the Lord, and she acts under His direction only. As the supreme transcendental Lord, He simply casts a glance over the material principle, and thus the agitation of matter begins, and the resultant actions are manifested one after another by six kinds of gradual differentiations. All material creation is moving in that way, and thus it appears and disappears in due course.

Less intelligent persons with a poor fund of knowledge cannot accommodate the thought of this inconceivable potency of the Lord Śrī Kṛṣṇa, by which He appears just like a human being (Bg. 9.11). His appearance in the material world as one of us is also His causeless mercy upon the fallen souls. He is transcendental to all material conceptions, but by His unbounded mercy upon His pure devotees, He comes down and manifests Himself as the Personality of Godhead. Materialistic philosophers and scientists are too much engrossed with atomic energy and the gigantic situation of the universal form, and they offer respect more seriously to the external phenomenal feature of material manifestations than to the noumenal principle of spiritual existence. The transcendental form of the Lord is beyond the jurisdiction of such materialistic activities, and it is very difficult to conceive that the Lord can be simultaneously localized and all-pervasive, because the materialistic philosophers and scientists think of everything in terms of their own experience. Because they are unable to accept the personal feature of the Supreme Lord, the Lord is kind enough to demonstrate the *virāṭ* feature of His transcendental form, and herein Śrīla Śukadeva Gosvāmī has vividly described this form of the Lord. He concludes that there is nothing beyond this gigantic feature of the Lord. None of the materialistic thoughtful men can go beyond this conception of the gigantic form. The minds of the materialistic men are flickering and constantly changing from one aspect to another. Therefore, one is advised to think of the Lord by thinking of any part of His gigantic body, and by one's intelligence only one can think of Him in any manifestation of the material world—the forest, the hill, the ocean, the man, the animal, the demigod, the bird, the beast or anything else. Each and every item of the material manifestation entails a part of the body of the gigantic form, and thus the flickering mind can be fixed in the Lord only and nothing else. This process of concentrating on the different bodily parts of the Lord will gradually diminish the demoniac challenge of godlessness and bring about gradual development of devotional service to the Lord. Everything being a part and parcel of the Complete Whole, the neophyte student will gradually realize the hymns of *Īśopaniṣad* which state that the Supreme Lord is everywhere, and thus he will learn the art of not committing any offense to the body of the Lord. This sense of God-mindedness will diminish one's pride in challenging the existence of God. Thus one can learn to show respect to everything, for all things are parts and parcels of the supreme body.

TEXT 39

स सर्वधीवृत्त्यनुभूतसर्व
आत्मा यथा स्वप्नजनेक्षितैकः ।
तं सत्यमानन्दनिधिं भजेत
नान्यत्र सज्जेद् यत आत्मपातः ॥३९॥

sa sarva-dhī-vṛtty-anubhūta-sarva
ātmā yathā svapna-janekṣitaikaḥ
taṁ satyam ānanda-nidhiṁ bhajeta
nānyatra sajjed yata ātma-pātaḥ

saḥ—He (the Supreme Person); *sarva-dhī-vṛtti*—the process of realization by all sorts of intelligence; *anubhūta*—cognizant; *sarve*—everyone; *ātmā*—the Supersoul; *yathā*—as much as; *svapna-jana*—a person dreaming; *īkṣita*—seen by; *ekaḥ*—one and the same; *tam*—unto Him; *satyam*—the Supreme Truth; *ānanda-nidhim*—the ocean of bliss; *bhajeta*—must one worship; *na*—never; *anyatra*—anything else; *sajjet*—be attached; *yataḥ*—whereby; *ātma-pātaḥ*—degradation of oneself.

TRANSLATION

One should concentrate his mind upon the Supreme Personality of Godhead, who alone distributes Himself in so many manifestations just as ordinary persons create thousands of manifestations in dreams. One must concentrate the mind on Him, the only all-blissful Absolute Truth. Otherwise one will be misled and will cause his own degradation.

PURPORT

In this verse, the process of devotional service is indicated by the great Gosvāmī, Śrīla Śukadeva. He tries to impress upon us that instead of diverting our attention to several branches of self-realization, we should concentrate upon the Supreme Personality of Godhead as the supreme object of realization, worship and devotion. Self-realization is, as it were, offering a fight for eternal life against the material struggle for existence, and therefore by the illusory grace of the external energy, the *yogī* or the devotee is faced with many allurements which can entangle a great fighter again in the bondage of material existence. A *yogī* can attain miraculous successes in material achievements, such as *aṇimā* and *laghimā*, by which one can become more minute than the minutest or lighter than the lightest, or in the ordinary sense, one may achieve material benedictions in the shape of wealth and women. But one is warned against such allurements because entanglement again in such illusory pleasure means degradation of the self and further imprisonment in the material world. By this warning, one should follow one's vigilant intelligence only.

The Supreme Lord is one, and His expansions are various. He is therefore the Supersoul of everything. When a man sees anything, he must know that his seeing is secondary and the Lord's seeing is primary. One cannot see anything without the Lord's having first seen it. That is the instruction of the *Vedas* and the *Upaniṣads*. So whatever we see or do, the Supersoul of all acts of seeing or doing is the Lord. This theory of simultaneous oneness and difference between the individual soul and the Supersoul is propounded by Lord Śrī Caitanya Mahāprabhu as the philosophy of *acintya-bhedābheda-tattva*. The *virāṭ-rūpa*, or the gigantic feature of the Supreme Lord, includes everything materially manifested, and therefore the *virāṭ* or gigantic feature of the Lord is the Supersoul of all living and nonliving entities. But the *virāṭ-rūpa* is also the manifestation of Nārāyaṇa or Viṣṇu, and going further on and on one will eventually see that Lord Kṛṣṇa is the ultimate Supersoul of everything that be. The conclusion is that one should unhesitatingly become a worshiper of Lord Kṛṣṇa, or, for that matter, His plenary expansion Nārāyaṇa, and none else. In the Vedic hymns, it is clearly said that first of all Nārāyaṇa cast a glance over matter and thus there was creation. Before creation, there was neither Brahmā nor Śiva, and what to speak of others. Śrīpāda Śaṅkarācārya has definitely accepted this, that Nārāyaṇa is beyond the material creation and that all others are within the material creation. The whole material creation, therefore, is one with and different from Nārāyaṇa, simultaneously, and this supports the *acintya-bhedābheda-tattva* philosophy of Lord Śrī Caitanya Mahāprabhu. Being an emanation from the glancing potency of Nārāyaṇa, the whole material creation is nondifferent from Him. But because it is the effect of His external energy (*bahiraṅgā māyā*) and is aloof from the internal potency (*ātma-māyā*), the whole material creation is different from Him at the same time. The example given in this verse very nicely is that of the dreaming man. The dreaming man creates many things in his dream, and thus he himself becomes the entangled seer of the dream and is also affected by the consequences. This material creation is also exactly a dreamlike creation of the Lord, but He, being the transcendental Supersoul, is neither entangled nor affected by the reactions of such a dreamlike creation. He is always in His transcendental position, but essentially He is everything, and nothing is apart from Him. As a part of Him, one should therefore concentrate on Him only, without deviation; otherwise one is sure to be overcome by the potencies of the material creation, one after another. It is confirmed in the *Bhagavad-gītā* (9.7) as follows:

sarva-bhūtāni kaunteya
prakṛtiṁ yānti māmikām
kalpa-kṣaye punas tāni
kalpādau visṛjāmy aham

"O son of Kuntī, at the end of the millennium every material manifestation enters into My nature, and at the beginning of another millennium, by My potency, I again create."

The human life, however, is an opportunity to get out of this repetition of creation and annihilation. It is a means whereby one may escape the Lord's external potency and enter into His internal potency.

Thus end the Bhaktivedanta purports of the Second Canto, First Chapter, of the Śrīmad-Bhāgavatam, *entitled "The First Step in God Realization."*

CHAPTER TWO

The Lord in the Heart

TEXT 1

श्रीशुक उवाच

एवं पुरा धारणयात्मयोनि-
नैष्टां स्मृतिं प्रत्यवरुध्य तुष्टात् ।
तथा ससर्जेदममोघदृष्टि-
र्यथाप्ययात् प्राग् व्यवसायबुद्धिः ॥ १ ॥

śrī-śuka uvāca
evaṁ purā dhāraṇayātma-yonir
naṣṭāṁ smṛtiṁ pratyavarudhya tuṣṭāt
tathā sasarjedam amogha-dṛṣṭir
yathāpyayāt prāg vyavasāya-buddhiḥ

śrī-śukaḥ uvāca—Śrī Śukadeva Gosvāmī said; *evam*—just in the same way; *purā*—prior to the manifestation of the cosmos; *dhāraṇayā*—by such a conception; *ātma-yoniḥ*—of Brahmājī; *naṣṭām*—lost; *smṛtim*—remembrance; *pratyavarudhya*—by regaining consciousness; *tuṣṭāt*—because of appeasing the Lord; *tathā*—thereafter; *sasarja*—created; *idam*—this material world; *amogha-dṛṣṭiḥ*—one who has attained clear vision; *yathā*—as; *apyayāt*—created; *prāk*—as formerly; *vyavasāya*—ascertained; *buddhiḥ*—intelligence.

TRANSLATION

Śrī Śukadeva Gosvāmī said: Formerly, prior to the manifestation of the cosmos, Lord Brahmā, by meditating on the virāṭ-rūpa, regained his lost consciousness by appeasing the Lord. Thus he was able to rebuild the creation as it was before.

PURPORT

The example cited herein of Śrī Brahmājī is one of forgetfulness. Brahmājī is the incarnation of one of the mundane attributes of the Lord. Being the incarnation of the passion mode of material nature, he is empowered by the Lord to generate the beautiful material manifestation. Yet due to his being one of the numerous living entities, he is apt to forget the art of his creative energy. This forgetfulness of the living being—beginning from Brahmā down to the lowest insignificant ant—is a tendency which can be counteracted by meditation on the *virāṭ-rūpa* of the Lord. This chance is available in the human form of life, and if a human being follows the instruction of *Śrīmad-Bhāgavatam* and begins to meditate upon the *virāṭ-rūpa,* then revival of his pure consciousness and counteraction of the tendency to forget his eternal relationship with the Lord can follow simultaneously. And as soon as this forgetfulness is removed, the *vyavasāya-buddhi,* as mentioned here and in the *Bhagavad-gītā* (2.41), follows at once. This ascertained knowledge of the living being leads to loving service to the Lord, which the living being requires. The kingdom of God is unlimited; therefore the number of the assisting hands of the Lord is also unlimited. The *Bhagavad-gītā* (13.14) asserts that the Lord has His hands, legs, eyes and mouths in every nook and corner of His creation. This means that the expansions of differentiated parts and parcels, called *jīvas* or living entities, are assisting hands of the Lord, and all of them are meant for rendering a particular pattern of service to the Lord. The conditioned soul, even in the position of a Brahmā, forgets this by the influence of illusory, material energy generated out of false egoism. One can counteract such false egoism by invoking God consciousness. Liberation means getting out of the slumber of forgetfulness and becoming situated in the real loving service of the Lord, as exemplified in the case of Brahmā. The service of Brahmā is the sample of service in liberation distinguished from the so-called altruistic services full of mistakes and forgetfulness. Liberation is never inaction, but service without human mistakes.

TEXT 2

शाब्दस्य हि ब्रह्मण एष पन्था
यन्नामभिर्ध्यायति धीरपार्थैः ।

परिभ्रमंस्तत्र न विन्दतेऽर्थान्
मायामये वासनया शयानः ॥ २ ॥

śābdasya hi brahmaṇa eṣa panthā
yan nāmabhir dhyāyati dhīr apārthaiḥ
paribhramaṁs tatra na vindate 'rthān
māyāmaye vāsanayā śayānaḥ

śābdasya—of the Vedic sound; *hi*—certainly; *brahmaṇaḥ*—of the *Vedas; eṣaḥ*—these; *panthāḥ*—the way; *yat*—what is; *nāmabhiḥ*—by different names; *dhyāyati*—ponders; *dhīḥ*—intelligence; *apārthaiḥ*—by meaningless ideas; *paribhraman*—wandering; *tatra*—there; *na*—never; *vindate*—enjoys; *arthān*—realities; *māyā-maye*—in illusory things; *vāsanayā*—by different desires; *śayānaḥ*—as if dreaming in sleep.

TRANSLATION

The way of presentation of the Vedic sounds is so bewildering that it directs the intelligence of the people to meaningless things like the heavenly kingdoms. The conditioned souls hover in dreams of such heavenly illusory pleasures, but actually they do not relish any tangible happiness in such places.

PURPORT

The conditioned soul is always engaged in laying out plans for happiness within the material world, even up to the end of the universal limit. He is not even satisfied with available amenities on this planet earth, where he has exploited the resources of nature to the best of his ability. He wants to go to the moon or the planet Venus to exploit resources there. But the Lord has warned us in the *Bhagavad-gītā* (8.16) about the worthlessness of all the innumerable planets of this universe, as well as those planets within other systems. There are innumerable universes and also innumerable planets in each of them. But none of them is immune to the chief miseries of material existence, namely the pangs of birth, the pangs of death, the pangs of old age and the pangs of disease. The Lord says that even the topmost planet, known as the Brahmaloka or

Satyaloka, (and what to speak of other planets, like the heavenly planets) is not a happy land for residential purposes, due to the presence of material pangs, as above mentioned. Conditioned souls are strictly under the laws of fruitive activities, and as such they sometimes go up to Brahmaloka and again come down to Pātālaloka, as if they were unintelligent children on a merry-go-round. The real happiness is in the kingdom of God, where no one has to undergo the pangs of material existence. Therefore, the Vedic ways of fruitive activities for the living entities are misleading. One thinks of a superior way of life in this country or that, or on this planet or another, but nowhere in the material world can he fulfill his real desire of life, namely eternal life, full intelligence and complete bliss. Indirectly, Śrīla Śukadeva Gosvāmī affirms that Mahārāja Parīkṣit, in the last stage of life, should not desire to transfer himself to the so-called heavenly planets, but should prepare himself for going back home, back to Godhead. None of the material planets, nor the amenities available there for living conditions, is everlasting; therefore one must have a factual reluctance to enjoy such temporary happiness as they afford.

TEXT 3

अतः कविर्नामसु यावदर्थः
स्यादप्रमत्तो व्यवसायबुद्धिः ।
सिद्धेऽन्यथार्थे न यतेत तत्र
परिश्रमं तत्र समीक्षमाणः ॥ ३ ॥

ataḥ kavir nāmasu yāvad arthaḥ
syād apramatto vyavasāya-buddhiḥ
siddhe 'nyathārthe na yateta tatra
pariśramaṁ tatra samīkṣamāṇaḥ

ataḥ—for this reason; *kaviḥ*—the enlightened person; *nāmasu*—in names only; *yāvat*—minimum; *arthaḥ*—necessity; *syāt*—must be; *apramattaḥ*—without being mad after them; *vyavasāya-buddhiḥ*—intelligently fixed; *siddhe*—for success; *anyathā*—otherwise; *arthe*—in the interest of; *na*—should never; *yateta*—endeavor for; *tatra*—there;

pariśramam—laboring hard; *tatra*—there; *samīkṣamāṇaḥ*—one who sees practically.

TRANSLATION

For this reason the enlightened person should endeavor only for the minimum necessities of life while in the world of names. He should be intelligently fixed and never endeavor for unwanted things, being competent to perceive practically that all such endeavors are merely hard labor for nothing.

PURPORT

The *bhāgavata-dharma*, or the cult of *Śrīmad-Bhāgavatam*, is perfectly distinct from the way of fruitive activities, which are considered by the devotees to be merely a waste of time. The whole universe, or for that matter all material existence, is moving on as *jagat*, simply for planning business to make one's position very comfortable or secure, although everyone sees that this existence is neither comfortable nor secure and can never become comfortable or secure at any stage of development. Those who are captivated by the illusory advancement of material civilization (following the way of phantasmagoria) are certainly madmen. The whole material creation is a *jugglery of names* only; in fact, it is nothing but a bewildering creation of matter like earth, water and fire. The buildings, furniture, cars, bungalows, mills, factories, industries, peace, war or even the highest perfection of material science, namely atomic energy and electronics, are all simply bewildering names of material elements with their concomitant reactions of the three modes. Since the devotee of the Lord knows them perfectly well, he is not interested in creating unwanted things for a situation which is not at all reality, but simply names of no more significance than the babble of sea waves. The great kings, leaders and soldiers fight with one another in order to perpetuate their names in history. They are forgotten in due course of time, and they make a place for another era in history. But the devotee realizes how much history and historical persons are useless products of flickering time. The fruitive worker aspires after a big fortune in the matter of wealth, woman and worldly adoration, but those who are fixed in perfect reality are not at all interested in such false things. For them it is all a waste of time. Since every second of human life is important, an enlightened man should be very careful to utilize time very cautiously. One second of human life wasted in the vain research of planning for happiness in the material world can never be replaced, even if one spends millions of coins of gold. Therefore, the transcendentalist desiring freedom from the clutches of *māyā*, or the illusory activities of life, is warned herewith not to be captivated by the external features of fruitive actors. Human life is never meant for sense gratification, but for self-realization. *Śrīmad-Bhāgavatam* instructs us solely on this subject from the very beginning to the end. Human life is simply meant for self-realization. The civilization which aims at this utmost perfection never indulges in creating unwanted things, and such a perfect civilization prepares men only to accept the bare necessities of life or to follow the principle of the best use of a bad bargain. Our material bodies and our lives in that connection are bad bargains because the living entity is actually spirit, and spiritual advancement of the living entity is absolutely necessary. Human life is intended for the realization of this important factor, and one should act accordingly, accepting only the bare necessities of life and depending more on God's gift without diversion of human energy for any other purpose, such as being mad for material enjoyment. The materialistic advancement of civilization is called "the civilization of the demons," which ultimately ends in wars and scarcity. The transcendentalist is specifically warned herewith to be fixed in mind, so that even if there is difficulty in plain living and high thinking he will not budge even an inch from his stark determination. For a transcendentalist, it is a suicidal policy to be intimately in touch with the sense gratifiers of the world, because such a policy will frustrate the ultimate gain of life. Śukadeva Gosvāmī met Mahārāja Parīkṣit when the latter felt a necessity for such a meeting. It is the duty of a transcendentalist to help persons who desire real salvation and to support the cause of salvation. One might note that Śukadeva Gosvāmī never met Mahārāja Parīkṣit while he was ruling as a great king. For a transcendentalist, the mode of activities is explained in the next *śloka*.

TEXT 4

सत्यां क्षितौ किं कशिपोः प्रयासै-
र्बाहौ स्वसिद्धे ह्युपबर्हणैः किम् ।

सत्यञ्जलौ किं पुरुधान्नपात्र्या
दिग्वल्कलादौ सति किं दुकूलैः ॥ ४ ॥

satyāṁ kṣitau kiṁ kaśipoḥ prayāsair
bāhau svasiddhe hy upabarhaṇaiḥ kim
saty añjalau kiṁ purudhānna-pātryā
dig-valkalādau sati kiṁ dukūlaiḥ

satyām—being in possession; *kṣitau*—earthly flats; *kim*—where is the necessity; *kaśipoḥ*—of beds and cots; *prayāsaiḥ*—endeavoring for; *bāhau*—the arms; *sva-siddhe*—being self-sufficient; *hi*—certainly; *upabarhaṇaiḥ*—bed and bedstead; *kim*—what is the use; *sati*—being present; *añjalau*—the palms of the hands; *kim*—what is the use; *purudhā*—varieties of; *anna*—eatables; *pātryā*—by the utensils; *dik*—open space; *valkala-ādau*—skins of trees; *sati*—being existent; *kim*—what is the use of; *dukūlaiḥ*—clothes.

TRANSLATION

When there are ample earthly flats to lie on, what is the necessity of cots and beds? When one can use his own arms, what is the necessity of a pillow? When one can use the palms of his hands, what is the necessity of varieties of utensils? When there is ample covering, or the skins of trees, what is the necessity of clothing?

PURPORT

The necessities of life for the protection and comfort of the body must not be unnecessarily increased. Human energy is spoiled in a vain search after such illusory happiness. If one is able to lie down on the floor, then why should one endeavor to get a good bedstead or soft cushion to lie on? If one can rest without any pillow and make use of the soft arms endowed by nature, there is no necessity of searching after a pillow. If we make a study of the general life of the animals, we can see that they have no intelligence for building big houses, furniture, and other household paraphernalia, and yet they maintain a healthy life by lying down on the open land. They do not know how to cook or prepare foodstuff, yet they still live healthy lives more easily than the human being. This does not mean that human civilization should revert to animal life or that the human being should live naked in the jungles without any culture, education and sense of morality. An intelligent human cannot live the life of an animal; rather, man should try to utilize his intelligence in arts and science, poetry and philosophy. In such a way he can further the progressive march of human civilization. But here the idea given by Śrīla Śukadeva Gosvāmī is that the reserve energy of human life, which is far superior to that of animals, should simply be utilized for self-realization. Advancement of human civilization must be towards the goal of establishing our lost relationship with God, which is not possible in any form of life other than the human. One must realize the nullity of the material phenomenon, considering it a passing phantasmagoria, and must endeavor to make a solution to the miseries of life. Self-complacence with a polished type of animal civilization geared to sense gratification is delusion, and such a "civilization" is not worthy of the name. In pursuit of such false activities, a human being is in the clutches of *māyā*, or illusion. Great sages and saints in the days of yore were not living in palatial buildings furnished with good furniture and so-called amenities of life. They used to live in huts and groves and sit on the flat ground, and yet they have left immense treasures of high knowledge with all perfection. Śrīla Rūpa Gosvāmī and Śrīla Sanātana Gosvāmī were high-ranking ministers of state, but they were able to leave behind them immense writings on transcendental knowledge, while residing only for one night underneath one tree. They did not live even two nights under the same tree, and what to speak of well-furnished rooms with modern amenities. And still they were able to give us most important literatures of self-realization. So-called comforts of life are not actually helpful for progressive civilization; rather, they are detrimental to such progressive life. In the system of *sanātana-dharma*, of four divisions of social life and four orders of progressive realization, there are ample opportunities and sufficient directions for a happy termination of the progressive life, and the sincere followers are advised therein to accept a voluntary life of renunciation in order to achieve the desired goal of life. If one is not accustomed to abiding by the life of renunciation and self-abnegation from the beginning, one should try to get into the habit at a later stage of life as recommended by Śrīla Śukadeva Gosvāmī, and that will help one to achieve the desired success.

TEXT 5

चीराणि किं पथि न सन्ति दिशन्ति भिक्षां
नैवाङ्घ्रिपाः परभृतः सरितोऽप्यशुष्यन् ।
रुद्धा गुहाः किमजितोऽवति नोपसन्नान्
कस्माद् भजन्ति कवयो धनदुर्मदान्धान् ॥ ५ ॥

cīrāṇi kiṁ pathi na santi diśanti bhikṣāṁ
naivāṅghripāḥ para-bhṛtaḥ sarito 'py aśuṣyan
ruddhā guhāḥ kim ajito 'vati nopasannān
kasmād bhajanti kavayo dhana-durmadāndhān

cīrāṇi—torn clothes; *kim*—whether; *pathi*—on the road; *na*—not; *santi*—there is; *diśanti*—give in charity; *bhikṣām*—alms; *na*—not; *eva*—also; *aṅghripāḥ*—the trees; *para-bhṛtaḥ*—one who maintains others; *saritaḥ*—the rivers; *api*—also; *aśuṣyan*—have dried up; *ruddhāḥ*—closed; *guhāḥ*—caves; *kim*—whether; *ajitaḥ*—the Almighty Lord; *avati*—give protection; *na*—not; *upasannān*—the surrendered soul; *kasmāt*—what for, then; *bhajanti*—flatters; *kavayaḥ*—the learned; *dhana*—wealth; *durmada-andhān*—too intoxicated by.

TRANSLATION

Are there no torn clothes lying on the common road? Do the trees, which exist for maintaining others, no longer give alms in charity? Do the rivers, being dried up, no longer supply water to the thirsty? Are the caves of the mountains now closed, or, above all, does the Almighty Lord not protect the fully surrendered souls? Why then do the learned sages go to flatter those who are intoxicated by hard-earned wealth?

PURPORT

The renounced order of life is never meant for begging or living at the cost of others as a parasite. According to the dictionary, a parasite is a sycophant who lives at the cost of society without making any contribution to that society. The renounced order is meant for contributing something substantial to society and not depending on the earnings of the householders. On the contrary, acceptance of alms from the householders by the bona fide mendicant is an opportunity afforded by the saint for the tangible benefit of the donor. In the *sanātana-dharma* institution, almsgiving to the mendicant is part of a householder's duty, and it is advised in the scriptures that the householders should treat the mendicants as their family children and should provide them with food, clothing, etc., without being asked. Pseudomendicants, therefore, should not take advantage of the charitable disposition of the faithful householders. The first duty of a person in the renounced order of life is to contribute some literary work for the benefit of the human being in order to give him realized direction toward self-realization. Amongst the other duties in the renounced order of life of Śrīla Sanātana, Śrīla Rūpa and the other Gosvāmīs of Vṛndāvana, the foremost duty discharged by them was to hold learned discourses amongst themselves at Sevākuñja, Vṛndāvana (the spot where Śrī Rādhā-Dāmodara Temple was established by Śrīla Jīva Gosvāmī and where the actual *samādhi* tombs of Śrīla Rūpa Gosvāmī and Śrīla Jīva Gosvāmī are laid). For the benefit of all in human society, they left behind them immense literatures of transcendental importance. Similarly, all the *ācāryas* who voluntarily accepted the renounced order of life aimed at benefiting human society and not at living a comfortable or irresponsible life at the cost of others. However, those who cannot give any contribution should not go to the householders for food, for such mendicants asking bread from the householders are an insult to the highest order. Śukadeva Gosvāmī gave this warning especially for those mendicants who adopt this line of profession to solve their economic problems. Such mendicants are in abundance in the age of Kali. When a man becomes a mendicant willfully or by circumstances, he must be of firm faith and conviction that the Supreme Lord is the maintainer of all living beings everywhere in the universe. Why, then, would He neglect the maintenance of a surrendered soul who is cent percent engaged in the service of the Lord? A common master looks to the necessities of his servant, so how much more would the all-powerful, all-opulent Supreme Lord look after the necessities of life for a fully surrendered soul. The general rule is that a mendicant devotee will accept a simple small loincloth without asking anyone to give it in charity. He simply salvages it from the rejected torn cloth thrown in the street. When he is hungry he may go to a magnanimous tree which drops fruits, and when he is thirsty he may drink water from the flowing river. He does not require to live in a comfortable house, but should find a cave in the hills and not be afraid of jungle animals, keeping faith in God, who lives in everyone's heart. The Lord may dictate to tigers and other jungle animals not to disturb His devotee. Haridāsa Ṭhākura, a great devotee of Lord Śrī Caitanya, used to live in such a cave, and by chance a great venomous snake was a copartner of the cave. Some admirer of Ṭhākura Haridāsa who had to visit the Ṭhākura every day feared the snake and suggested that the Ṭhākura leave that place. Because his devotees were afraid of the snake and they were regularly visiting the cave, Ṭhākura Haridāsa agreed to the proposal on their account. But as soon as this was settled, the snake actually crawled out of its hole in the cave and left the cave for good before everyone present. By the dictation of the Lord, who lived also within the heart of the snake, the snake gave preference to Haridāsa and decided to leave the place and not disturb him. So this is a tangible example of how the Lord gives protection to a bona fide devotee like Ṭhākura Haridāsa. According to the regulations of the *sanātana-dharma* institution, one is trained from the beginning to depend fully on the protection of the Lord in all circumstances. The path of renunciation is recommended for acceptance by one who is fully accomplished and fully purified in his existence. This stage is described also in the *Bhagavad-gītā* (16.5) as *daivī sampat.* A human being is required to accumulate *daivī sampat,* or spiritual assets; otherwise, the next alternative, *āsurī sampat,* or material assets, will overcome him disproportionately, and thus one will be forced into the entanglement of different miseries of the material world. A *sannyāsī* should always live alone, without company, and he must be fearless. He should never be afraid of living alone, although he is never alone. The Lord is residing in everyone's heart, and unless one is purified by the prescribed process, one will feel that he is alone. But a man in the renounced order of life must be purified by the process; thus he will feel the presence of the Lord everywhere and will have nothing to fear (such as being without any company). Everyone can become a fearless and honest person if his very existence is purified by discharging the prescribed duty for each and every order of life. One can become fixed in one's prescribed duty by faithful aural reception of Vedic instructions and assimilation of the essence of Vedic knowledge by devotional service to the Lord.

TEXT 6

एवं स्वचित्ते स्वत एव सिद्ध
आत्मा प्रियोऽर्थो भगवाननन्तः ।
तं निर्वृतो नियतार्थो भजेत
संसारहेतूपरमश्च यत्र ॥ ६ ॥

evaṁ sva-citte svata eva siddha
ātmā priyo 'rtho bhagavān anantaḥ
taṁ nirvṛto niyatārtho bhajeta
saṁsāra-hetūparamaś ca yatra

evam—thus; *sva-citte*—in one's own heart; *svataḥ*—by His omnipotency; *eva*—certainly; *siddhaḥ*—fully represented; *ātmā*—the Supersoul; *priyaḥ*—very dear; *arthaḥ*—substance; *bhagavān*—the Supreme Personality of Godhead; *anantaḥ*—the eternal unlimited; *tam*—unto Him; *nirvṛtaḥ*—being detached from the world; *niyata*—permanent; *arthaḥ*—the supreme gain; *bhajeta*—one must worship; *saṁsāra-hetu*—the cause of the conditioned state of existence; *uparamaḥ*—cessation; *ca*—certainly; *yatra*—in which.

TRANSLATION

Thus being fixed, one must render service unto the Supersoul situated in one's own heart by His omnipotency. Because He is the Almighty Personality of Godhead, eternal and unlimited, He is the ultimate goal of life, and by worshiping Him one can end the cause of the conditioned state of existence.

PURPORT

As confirmed in *Bhagavad-gītā* (18.61), the Supreme Personality of Godhead Śrī Kṛṣṇa is the all-pervading omnipresent Supersoul. Therefore one who is a *yogī* can worship only Him because He is the substance and not illusion. Every living creature is engaging in the service of something else. A living being's constitutional position is to render service, but in the atmosphere of *māyā*, or illusion, or the conditional state of existence, the conditioned soul seeks the service of illusion. A conditioned soul works in the service of his temporary body, bodily relatives like the wife and children, and the necessary paraphernalia for maintaining the body and bodily relations, such as the house, land, wealth, society and country, but he does not know that all such renderings of service are totally illusory. As we have discussed many times before, this material world is itself an illusion, like a mirage in the desert. In the desert there is an illusion of water, and the foolish animals become entrapped by such an illusion and run after water in the desert, although there is no water at all. But because there is no water in the desert, one does not conclude that there is no water at all. The intelligent person knows well that there is certainly water, water in the seas and oceans, but such vast reservoirs of water are far, far away from the desert. One should therefore search for water in the vicinity of seas and oceans and not in the desert. Every one of us is searching after real happiness in life, namely eternal life, eternal or unlimited knowledge and unending blissful life. But foolish people who have no knowledge of the substance search after the reality of life in the illusion. This material body does not endure eternally, and everything in relation with this temporary body, such as the wife, children, society and country, also changes along with the change of body. This is called *saṁsāra*, or repetition of birth, death, old age and disease. We would like to find a solution for all these problems of life, but we do not know the way. Herein it is suggested that anyone who wants to make an end to these miseries of life, namely repetition of birth, death, disease, and old age, must take to this process of worshiping the Supreme Lord and not others, as it is also ultimately suggested in the *Bhagavad-gītā* (18.65). If we at all want to end the cause of our conditioned life, we must take to the worship of Lord Śrī Kṛṣṇa, who is present in everyone's heart by His natural affection for all living beings, who are actually the parts and parcels of the Lord (Bg. 18.61). The baby in the lap of his mother is naturally attached to the mother, and the mother is attached to the child. But when the child grows up and becomes overwhelmed by circumstances, he gradually becomes detached from the mother, although the mother always expects some sort of service from the grown-up child and is equally affectionate toward her child, even though the child is forgetful. Similarly, because we are all part and parcel of the Lord, the Lord is always affectionate to us, and He always tries to get us back home, back to Godhead. But we, the conditioned souls, do not care for Him and run instead after the illusory bodily connections. We must therefore extricate ourselves from all illusory connections of the world and seek reunion with the Lord, trying to render service unto Him because He is the ultimate truth. Actually we are hankering after Him as the child seeks the mother. And to search out the Supreme Personality of Godhead, we need not go anywhere else, because the Lord is within our hearts. This does not suggest, however, that we should not go to the places of worship, namely the temples, churches and mosques. Such holy places of worship are also occupied by the Lord because the Lord is omnipresent. For the common man these holy places are centers of learning about the science of God. When the temples are devoid of activities, the people in general become uninterested in such places, and consequently the mass of people gradually become godless, and a godless civilization is the result. Such a hellish civilization artificially increases the conditions of life, and existence becomes intolerable for everyone. The foolish leaders of a godless civilization try to devise various plans to bring about peace and prosperity in the godless world under a patent trademark of materialism, and because such attempts are illusory only, the people elect incompetent, blind leaders, one after another, who are incapable of offering solutions. If we want at all to end this anomaly of a godless civilization, we must follow the principles of revealed scriptures like the *Śrīmad-Bhāgavatam* and follow the instruction of a person like Śrī Śukadeva Gosvāmī who has no attraction for material gain.

TEXT 7

कस्तां त्वनादृत्य परानुचिन्ता-
मृते पशूनसतीं नाम कुर्यात् ।
पश्यञ्जनं पतितं वैतरण्यां
स्वकर्मजान् परितापाञ्जुषाणम् ॥ ७ ॥

kas tāṁ tv anādṛtya parānucintām
ṛte paśūn asatīṁ nāma kuryāt
paśyañ janaṁ patitaṁ vaitaraṇyāṁ
sva-karmajān paritāpāñ juṣāṇam

kaḥ—who else; *tām*—that; *tu*—but; *anādṛtya*—by neglecting; *para-anucintām*—transcendental thoughts; *ṛte*—without; *paśūn*—the materialists; *asatīm*—in the nonpermanent; *nāma*—name; *kuryāt*—will adopt; *paśyan*—seeing definitely; *janam*—the general mass of people; *patitam*—fallen; *vaitaraṇyām*—in Vaitaraṇī, the river of suffering; *sva-karma-jān*—produced from one's own work; *paritāpān*—suffering; *juṣāṇam*—being overtaken by.

TRANSLATION

Who else but the gross materialists will neglect such transcendental thought and take to the nonpermanent names only, seeing the mass of people fallen in the river of suffering as the consequence of accruing the result of their own work?

PURPORT

In the *Vedas* it is said that persons who are attached to demigods to the exclusion of the Supreme Personality of Godhead are like the animals who follow the herdsman even though they are taken to the slaughterhouse. The materialists, like animals, also do not know how they are being misdirected by neglecting the transcendental thought of the Supreme Person. No one can remain vacant of thought. It is said that an idle brain is a devil's workshop because a person who cannot think in the right way must think of something which may bring about disaster. The materialists are always worshiping some minor demigods, although this is condemned in the *Bhagavad-gītā* (7.20). As long as a person is illusioned by material gains, he petitions the respective demigods to draw some particular benefit which is, after all, illusory and nonpermanent. The enlightened transcendentalist is not captivated by such illusory things; therefore he is always absorbed in the transcendental thought of the Supreme in different stages of realization, namely Brahman, Paramātmā and Bhagavān. In the previous verse it is suggested that one should think of the Supersoul, which is one step higher than the impersonal thought of Brahman, as it was suggested in the case of contemplating the *virāṭ-rūpa* of the Personality of Godhead.

Intelligent persons who can see properly may look into the general conditions of the living entities who are wandering in the cycle of the

8,400,000 species of life, as well as in different classes of human beings. It is said that there is an everlasting belt of water called the River Vaitaraṇī at the entrance of the Plutonic planet of Yamarāja, who punishes sinners in different manners. After being subjected to such sufferings, a sinner is awarded a particular species of life according to his deeds in the past. Such living entities as are punished by Yamarāja are seen in different varieties of conditioned life. Some of them are in heaven, and some of them are in hell. Some of them are *brāhmaṇas*, and some of them are misers. But no one is happy in this material world, and all of them are either class A, B or C prisoners suffering because of their own deeds. The Lord is impartial to all circumstances of the sufferings of the living entities, but to one who takes shelter at His lotus feet, the Lord gives proper protection, and He takes such a living entity back home, back to Himself.

TEXT 8

केचित् स्वदेहान्तर्हृदयावकाशे
प्रादेशमात्रं पुरुषं वसन्तम् ।
चतुर्भुजं कञ्जरथाङ्गशङ्ख-
गदाधरं धारणया स्मरन्ति ॥ ८ ॥

kecit sva-dehāntar-hṛdayāvakāśe
prādeśa-mātram puruṣaṁ vasantam
catur-bhujaṁ kañja-rathāṅga-śaṅkha-
gadā-dharaṁ dhāraṇayā smaranti

kecit—others; *sva-deha-antaḥ*—within the body; *hṛdaya-avakāśe*—in the region of the heart; *prādeśa-mātram*—measuring only eight inches; *puruṣam*—the Personality of Godhead; *vasantam*—residing; *catuḥ-bhujam*—with four hands; *kañja*—lotus; *ratha-aṅga*—the wheel of a chariot; *śaṅkha*—conchshell; *gadā-dharam*—and with a club in the hand; *dhāraṇayā*—conceiving in that way; *smaranti*—do meditate upon Him.

TRANSLATION

Others conceive of the Personality of Godhead residing within the body in the region of the heart and measuring only eight

inches, with four hands carrying a lotus, a wheel of a chariot, a conchshell and a club respectively.

PURPORT

The all-pervading Personality of Godhead resides as Paramātmā in the heart of each and every living entity. The measurement of the localized Personality of Godhead is estimated to expand from the ring finger to the end of the thumb, more or less eight inches. The form of the Lord described in this verse with distribution of different symbols—beginning from the lower right hand up and down to the lower left hand with lotus, wheel of a chariot, conchshell and club respectively—is called Janārdana, or the plenary portion of the Lord who controls the general mass. There are many other forms of the Lord with varied situations of the symbols of lotus, conchshell, etc., and they are differently known as Puruṣottama, Acyuta, Narasiṁha, Trivikrama, Hṛṣīkeśa, Keśava, Mādhava, Aniruddha, Pradyumna, Saṅkarṣaṇa, Śrīdhara, Vāsudeva, Dāmodara, Janārdana, Nārāyaṇa, Hari, Padmanābha, Vāmana, Madhusūdana, Govinda, Kṛṣṇa, Viṣṇumūrti, Adhokṣaja and Upendra. These twenty-four forms of the localized Personality of Godhead are worshiped in different parts of the planetary system, and in each system there is an incarnation of the Lord having a different Vaikuṇṭha planet in the spiritual sky, which is called the *paravyoma.* There are many other hundreds and scores of different forms of the Lord, and each and every one of them has a particular planet in the spiritual sky, of which this material sky is only a fragmental offshoot. The Lord exists as *puruṣa*, or the male enjoyer, although there is no comparing Him to any male form in the material world. But all such forms are *advaita,* nondifferent from one another, and each of them is eternally young. The young Lord with four hands is nicely decorated, as described below.

TEXT 9

प्रसन्नवक्त्रं नलिनायतेक्षणं
कदम्बकिञ्जल्कपिशङ्गवाससम् ।
लसन्महारत्नहिरण्मयाङ्गदं
स्फुरन्महारत्नकिरीटकुण्डलम् ॥ ९ ॥

prasanna-vaktraṁ nalināyatekṣaṇaṁ
kadamba-kiñjalka-piśaṅga-vāsasam
lasan-mahā-ratna-hiraṇmayāṅgadaṁ
sphuran-mahā-ratna-kirīṭa-kuṇḍalam

prasanna—expresses happiness; *vaktram*—mouth; *nalina-āyata*—spread like the petals of a lotus; *īkṣaṇam*—eyes; *kadamba*—*kadamba* flower; *kiñjalka*—saffron; *piśaṅga*—yellow; *vāsasam*—garments; *lasat*—hanging; *mahā-ratna*—valuable jewels; *hiraṇmaya*—made of gold; *aṅgadam*—ornament; *sphurat*—glowing; *mahā-ratna*—valuable jewels; *kirīṭa*—headdress; *kuṇḍalam*—earrings.

TRANSLATION

His mouth expresses His happiness. His eyes spread like the petals of a lotus, and His garments, yellowish like the saffron of a kadamba flower, are bedecked with valuable jewels. His ornaments are all made of gold, set with jewels, and He wears a glowing headdress and earrings.

TEXT 10

उन्निद्रहृत्पङ्कजकर्णिकालये
योगेश्वरास्थापितपादपल्लवम् ।
श्रीलक्षणं कौस्तुभरत्नकन्धर-
मम्लानलक्ष्म्या वनमालयाचितम् ॥१०॥

unnidra-hṛt-paṅkaja-karṇikālaye
yogeśvarāsthāpita-pāda-pallavam
śrī-lakṣaṇaṁ kaustubha-ratna-kandharam
amlāna-lakṣmyā vana-mālayācitam

unnidra—blooming; *hṛt*—heart; *paṅkaja*—lotus flower; *karṇikā-ālaye*—on the surface of the whorl; *yoga-īśvara*—the great mystics; *āsthāpita*—placed; *pāda-pallavam*—lotus feet; *śrī*—the goddess of fortune, or a beautiful calf; *lakṣaṇam*—marked in that way; *kaustubha*—the Kaustubha jewel; *ratna*—other jewels; *kandharam*—on the shoulder; *amlāna*—quite fresh; *lakṣmyā*—beauty; *vana-mālayā*—by a flower garland; *ācitam*—spread over.

TRANSLATION

His lotus feet are placed over the whorls of the lotuslike hearts of great mystics. On His chest is the Kaustubha jewel, engraved with a beautiful calf, and there are other jewels on His shoulders. His complete torso is garlanded with fresh flowers.

PURPORT

The ornaments, flowers, clothing and all the other decorations on the transcendental body of the Personality of Godhead are identical with the body of the Lord. None of them are made of material ingredients; otherwise there would be no chance of their decorating the body of the Lord. As such, in the *paravyoma*, spiritual varieties are also distinguished from the material variegatedness.

TEXT 11

विभूषितं मेखलयाङ्गुलीयकै-
र्महाधनैर्नूपुरकङ्कणादिभिः ।
स्निग्धामलाकुञ्चितनीलकुन्तलै-
र्विरोचमानाननहासपेशलम् ॥११॥

vibhūṣitaṁ mekhalayāṅgulīyakair
mahā-dhanair nūpura-kaṅkaṇādibhiḥ
snigdhāmalākuñcita-nīla-kuntalair
virocamānānana-hāsa-peśalam

vibhūṣitam—well decorated; *mekhalayā*—with an ornamental wreath about the waist; *aṅgulīyakaiḥ*—by finger rings; *mahā-dhanaiḥ*—all highly valuable; *nūpura*—ringing leglets; *kaṅkaṇa-ādibhiḥ*—also by bangles; *snigdha*—slick; *amala*—spotless; *ākuñcita*—curling; *nīla*—bluish; *kuntalaiḥ*—hair; *virocamāna*—very pleasing; *ānana*—face; *hāsa*—smile; *peśalam*—beautiful.

TRANSLATION

He is well decorated with an ornamental wreath about His waist and rings studded with valuable jewels on His fingers. His leglets, His bangles, His oiled hair, curling with a bluish tint, and His beautiful smiling face are all very pleasing.

PURPORT

The Supreme Personality of Godhead is the most beautiful person amongst all others, and Śrīla Śukadeva Gosvāmī describes every part of His transcendental beauty, one after another, in order to teach the impersonalist that the Personality of Godhead is not an imagination by the devotee for facility of worship, but is the Supreme Person in fact and figure. The impersonal feature of the Absolute Truth is but His radiation, as the sun rays are but radiations from the sun.

TEXT 12

अदीनलीलाहसितेक्षणोल्लसद्-
भ्रूभङ्गसंसूचितभूर्यनुग्रहम् ।
ईक्षेत चिन्तामयमेनमीश्वरं
यावन्मनो धारणयावतिष्ठते ॥१२॥

adīna-līlā-hasitekṣaṇollasad-
bhrū-bhaṅga-saṁsūcita-bhūry-anugraham
īkṣeta cintāmayam enam īśvaraṁ
yāvan mano dhāraṇayāvatiṣṭhate

adīna—very magnanimous; *līlā*—pastimes; *hasita*—smiling; *īkṣaṇa*—by glancing over; *ullasat*—glowing; *bhrū-bhaṅga*—signals of the eyebrow; *saṁsūcita*—indicated; *bhūri*—extensive; *anugraham*—benediction; *īkṣeta*—one must concentrate on; *cintāmayam*—transcendental; *enam*—this particular; *īśvaram*—the Supreme Lord; *yāvat*—as long as; *manaḥ*—the mind; *dhāraṇayā*—by meditation; *avatiṣṭhate*—can be fixed.

TRANSLATION

The Lord's magnanimous pastimes and the glowing glancing of His smiling face are all indications of His extensive benedictions. One must therefore concentrate on this transcendental form of the Lord, as long as the mind can be fixed on Him by meditation.

PURPORT

In *Bhagavad-gītā* (12.5) it is said that the impersonalist undergoes a series of difficult programs on account of his impersonal meditation. But the devotee, due to the Lord's personal service, progresses very easily. Impersonal meditation is therefore a source of suffering for the impersonalist. Here, the devotee has an advantage over the impersonalist philosopher. The impersonalist is doubtful about the personal feature of the Lord, and therefore he always tries to meditate upon something which is not objective. For this reason there is an authentic statement in the *Bhāgavatam* regarding the positive concentration of the mind on the factual form of the Lord.

The process of meditation recommended herein is *bhakti-yoga*, or the process of devotional service after one is liberated from the material conditions. *Jñāna-yoga* is the process of liberation from the material conditions. After one is liberated from the conditions of material existence, i.e., when one is *nivṛtta*, as previously stated herein, or when one is freed from all material necessities, one becomes qualified to discharge the process of *bhakti-yoga*. Therefore *bhakti-yoga* includes *jñāna-yoga*, or, in other words, the process of pure devotional service simultaneously serves the purpose of *jñāna-yoga;* liberation from material conditions is automatically achieved by the gradual development of pure devotional service. These effects of *bhakti-yoga* are called *anartha-nivṛtti*. Things which are artificially acquired gradually disappear along with the progress of *bhakti-yoga*. Meditation on the lotus feet of the Personality of Godhead, the first processional step, must show its effect by *anartha-nivṛtti*. The grossest type of *anartha* which binds the conditioned soul in material existence is sex desire, and this sex desire gradually develops in the union of the male and female. When the male and female are united, the sex desire is further aggravated by the accumulation of buildings, children, friends, relatives and wealth. When all these are acquired, the conditioned soul becomes overwhelmed by such entanglements, and the false sense of egoism, or the sense of "myself" and "mine," becomes prominent, and the sex desire expands to various political, social, altruistic, philanthropic and many other unwanted engagements, resembling the foam of the sea waves, which becomes very prominent at one time and at the next moment vanishes as quickly as a cloud in the sky. The conditioned soul is encircled by such products, as well as products of sex desire, and therefore *bhakti-yoga* leads to gradual evaporation of the sex desire, which is summarized in three headings, namely *profit, adoration* and *distinction.* All conditioned souls are mad after these different forms of sex desire, and one shall see for himself how much he has been freed from such material hankerings based primarily on the sex desire. As a person feels his hunger satisfied after eating each morsel of foodstuff, he must similarly be able to see the degree to which he has been freed from sex desire. The sex desire is diminished along with its various forms by the process of *bhakti-yoga* because *bhakti-yoga* automatically, by the grace of the Lord, effectively results in knowledge and renunciation, even if the devotee is not materially very well educated. Knowledge means knowing things as they are, and if by deliberation it is found that there are things which are at all unnecessary, naturally the person who has acquired knowledge leaves aside such unwanted things. When the conditioned soul finds by culture of knowledge that material necessities are unwanted things, he becomes detached from such unwanted things. This stage of knowledge is called *vairāgya*, or detachment from unwanted things. We have previously discussed that the transcendentalist is required to be self-sufficient and should not beg from the rich blind persons to fulfill the bare necessities of life. Śukadeva Gosvāmī has suggested some alternatives for the bare necessities of life, namely the problem of eating, sleeping and shelter, but he has not suggested any alternative for sex satisfaction. One who has the sex desire still with him should not at all try to accept the renounced order of life. For one who has not attained to this stage, there is no question of a renounced order of life. So by the gradual process of devotional service under the guidance of a proper spiritual master, and following the principles of the *Bhāgavatam*, one must be able at least to control the gross sex desire before one accepts the renounced order of life factually.

So purification means getting free gradually from sex desire, and this is attained by meditation on the person of the Lord as described herein, beginning from the feet. One should not try to go upwards artificially without seeing for himself how much he has been released from the sex desire. The smiling face of the Lord is the Tenth Canto of *Śrīmad-Bhāgavatam*, and there are many upstarts who at once try to begin with the Tenth Canto and especially with the five chapters which delineate the *rāsa-līlā* of the Lord. This is certainly improper. By such improper study or hearing of *Bhāgavatam*, the material opportunists have played havoc by indulgence in sex life in the name of *Bhāgavatam*. This vilification of *Bhāgavatam* is rendered by the acts of the so-called devotees; one should be free from all kinds of sex desire before he tries to make a show of recital of *Bhāgavatam*. Śrī Viśvanātha Cakravartī Ṭhākura clearly defines the import of purification as cessation from sex indulgence. He says, *yathā yathā dhīś ca śudhyati viṣaya-lāmpaṭyaṁ tyajati, tathā tathā dhārayed iti citta-śuddhi-tāratamyenaiva dhyāna-tāratamyam uktam.* And as one gets free from the intoxication of sex indulgence by purification of intelligence, one should step forward for the next meditation, or in other words, the progress of meditation on the different limbs of the transcendental body of the Lord should be enhanced in proportion to the progress of purification of the heart. The conclusion is that those who are still entrapped by sex indulgence should never progress to meditation above the feet of the Lord; therefore recital of *Śrīmad-Bhāgavatam* by them should be restricted to the First and Second Cantos of the great literature. One must complete the purificatory process by assimilating the contents of the first nine cantos. Then one should be admitted into the realm of the Tenth Canto of *Śrīmad-Bhāgavatam*.

TEXT 13

एकैकशोऽङ्गानि धियानुभावयेत्
पादादि यावद्धसितं गदाभृतः ।
जितं जितं स्थानमपोह्य धारयेत्
परं परं शुद्ध्यति धीर्यथा यथा ॥१३॥

ekaikaśo 'ṅgāni dhiyānubhāvayet
pādādi yāvad dhasitaṁ gadābhṛtaḥ

jitaṁ jitaṁ sthānam apohya dhārayet
paraṁ paraṁ śuddhyati dhīr yathā yathā

eka-ekaśaḥ—one to one, or one after another; *aṅgāni*—limbs; *dhiyā*—by attention; *anubhāvayet*—meditate upon; *pāda-ādi*—legs, etc.; *yāvat*—until; *hasitam*—smiling; *gadā-bhṛtaḥ*—the Personality of Godhead; *jitam jitam*—gradually controlling the mind; *sthānam*—place; *apohya*—leaving; *dhārayet*—meditate upon; *param param*—higher and higher; *śuddhyati*—purified; *dhīḥ*—intelligence; *yathā yathā*—as much as.

TRANSLATION

The process of meditation should begin from the lotus feet of the Lord and progress to His smiling face. The meditation should be concentrated upon the lotus feet, then the calves, then the thighs, and in this way higher and higher. The more the mind becomes fixed upon the different parts of the limbs, one after another, the more the intelligence becomes purified.

PURPORT

The process of meditation recommended in the *Śrīmad-Bhāgavatam* is not to fix one's attention on something impersonal or void. The meditation should concentrate on the Person of the Supreme Godhead, either in His *virāṭ-rūpa*, the gigantic universal form, or in His *sac-cid-ānanda-vigraha*, as described in the scriptures. There are authorized descriptions of Viṣṇu forms, and there are authorized representations of Deities in the temples. Thus one can practice meditating upon the Deity, concentrating his mind on the lotus feet of the Lord and gradually rising higher and higher, up to His smiling face.

According to the *Bhāgavata* school, the Lord's *rāsa* dancing is the smiling face of the Lord. Since it is recommended in this verse that one should gradually progress from the lotus feet up to the smiling face, we shall not jump at once to understand the Lord's pastimes in the *rāsa* dance. It is better to practice concentrating our attention by offering flowers and *tulasī* to the lotus feet of the Lord. In this way, we gradually become purified by the *arcanā* process. We dress the Lord, bathe Him, etc., and all these transcendental activities help us purify our existence.

When we reach the higher standard of purification, if we see the smiling face of the Lord or hear the *rāsa* dance pastimes of the Lord, then we can relish His activities. In the *Śrīmad-Bhāgavatam*, therefore, the *rāsa* dance pastimes are delineated in the Tenth Canto (Chapters 29–34).

The more one concentrates on the transcendental form of the Lord, either on the lotus feet, the calves, the thighs or the chest, the more one becomes purified. In this verse it is clearly stated, "the more the intelligence becomes purified," which means the more one becomes detached from sense gratification. Our intelligence in the present conditioned state of life is impure due to being engaged in sense gratification. The result of meditation on the transcendental form of the Lord will be manifested by one's detachment from sense gratification. Therefore, the ultimate purpose of meditation is purification of one's intelligence.

Those who are too engrossed in sense gratification cannot be allowed to participate in *arcanā* or to touch the transcendental form of the Rādhā-Kṛṣṇa or Viṣṇu Deities. For them it is better to meditate upon the gigantic *virāṭ-rūpa* of the Lord, as recommended in the next verse. The impersonalists and the voidists are therefore recommended to meditate upon the universal form of the Lord, whereas the devotees are recommended to meditate on the Deity worship in the temple. Because the impersonalists and the voidists are not sufficiently purified in their spiritual activities, *arcanā* is not meant for them.

TEXT 14

यावन्न जायेत परावरेऽस्मिन्
विश्वेश्वरे द्रष्टरि भक्तियोगः ।
तावत् स्थवीयः पुरुषस्य रूपं
क्रियावसाने प्रयतः स्मरेत ॥१४॥

yāvan na jāyeta parāvare 'smin
viśveśvare draṣṭari bhakti-yogaḥ
tāvat sthavīyaḥ puruṣasya rūpaṁ
kriyāvasāne prayataḥ smareta

yāvat—as long as; *na*—does not; *jāyeta*—develop; *para*—transcendental; *avare*—mundane; *asmin*—in this form of; *viśva-īśvare*—the

Lord of all worlds; *draṣṭari*—unto the seer; *bhakti-yogaḥ*—devotional service; *tāvat*—so long; *sthavīyaḥ*—the gross materialist; *puruṣasya*—of the *virāṭ-puruṣa; rūpam*—universal form; *kriyā-avasāne*—at the end of one's prescribed duties; *prayataḥ*—with proper attention; *smareta*—one should remember.

TRANSLATION

Unless the gross materialist develops a sense of loving service unto the Supreme Lord, the seer of both the transcendental and material worlds, he should remember or meditate upon the universal form of the Lord at the end of his prescribed duties.

PURPORT

The Supreme Lord is the seer of all worlds, both material and transcendental. In other words, the Supreme Lord is the ultimate beneficiary and enjoyer of all worlds, as confirmed in the *Bhagavad-gītā* (5.29). The spiritual world is the manifestation of His internal potency, and the material world is the manifestation of His external potency. The living entities are also His marginal potency, and by their own choice they can live in either the transcendental or material worlds. The material world is not a fit place for living entities because they are spiritually one with the Lord and in the material world the living entities become conditioned by the laws of the material world. The Lord wants all living entities, who are His parts and parcels, to live with Him in the transcendental world, and for enlightening conditioned souls in the material world, all the *Vedas* and the revealed scriptures are there—expressly to recall the conditioned souls back home, back to Godhead. Unfortunately, the conditioned living entities, although suffering continually the threefold miseries of conditioned life, are not very serious about going back to Godhead. It is due to their misguided way of living, complicated by sins and virtues. Some of them who are virtuous by deeds begin to reestablish the lost relation with the Lord, but they are unable to understand the personal feature of the Lord. The real purpose of life is to make contact with the Lord and be engaged in His service. That is the natural position of living entities. But those who are impersonalists and are unable to render any loving service to the Lord have been advised to meditate upon His impersonal feature, the *virāṭ-rūpa*, or universal form. Some way or other, one must try to reestablish one's forgotten relation with the Lord if one at all desires to gain real happiness in life, and to reclaim his natural unfettered condition. For the less intelligent beginners, meditation on the impersonal feature, the *virāṭ-rūpa*, or universal form of the Lord, will gradually qualify one to rise to personal contact. One is advised herewith to meditate upon the *virāṭ-rūpa* specified in the previous chapters in order to understand how the different planets, seas, mountains, rivers, birds, beasts, human beings, demigods and all that we can conceive are but different parts and limbs of the Lord's *virāṭ* form. This sort of thinking is also a type of meditation on the Absolute Truth, and as soon as such meditation begins, one develops one's godly qualities, and the whole world appears to be a happy and peaceful residence for all the people of the world. Without such meditation on God, either personal or impersonal, all good qualities of the human being become covered with misconceptions regarding his constitutional position, and without such advanced knowledge, the whole world becomes a hell for the human being.

TEXT 15

स्थिरं सुखं चासनमास्थितो यति-
र्यदा जिहासुरिममङ्ग लोकम् ।
काले च देशे च मनो न सज्जयेत्
प्राणान् नियच्छेन्मनसा जितासुः ॥१५॥

sthiraṁ sukhaṁ cāsanam āsthito yatir
yadā jihāsur imam aṅga lokam
kāle ca deśe ca mano na sajjayet
prāṇān niyacchen manasā jitāsuḥ

sthiram—without being disturbed; *sukham*—comfortable; *ca*—also; *āsanam*—sitting accommodation; *āsthitaḥ*—being situated; *yatiḥ*—the sage; *yadā*—whenever; *jihāsuḥ*—desires to give up; *imam*—this; *aṅga*—O King; *lokam*—this body; *kāle*—in time; *ca*—and; *deśe*—in a proper place; *ca*—also; *manaḥ*—the mind; *na*—not; *sajjayet*—may not be perplexed; *prāṇān*—the senses; *niyacchet*—must control; *manasā*—by the mind; *jita-asuḥ*—conquering the life air.

TRANSLATION

O King, whenever the yogī desires to leave this planet of human beings, he should not be perplexed about the proper time or place, but should comfortably sit without being disturbed and, regulating the life air, should control the senses by the mind.

PURPORT

In the *Bhagavad-gītā* (8.14) it is clearly stated that a person who is totally engaged in the transcendental loving service of the Lord, and who constantly remembers Him at every step, easily obtains the mercy of the Lord by entering into His personal contact. Such devotees do not need to seek an opportune moment to leave the present body. But those who are mixed devotees, alloyed with fruitive action or empirical philosophical speculation, require an opportune moment for quitting this body. For them the opportune moments are stated in the *Bhagavad-gītā* (8.23–26). But these opportune moments are not as important as one's being a successful *yogī* who is able to quit his body as he likes. Such a *yogī* must be competent to control his senses by the mind. The mind is easily conquered simply by engaging it at the lotus feet of the Lord. Gradually, by such service, all the senses become automatically engaged in the service of the Lord. That is the way of merging into the Supreme Absolute.

TEXT 16

मनः स्वबुद्ध्यामलया नियम्य
क्षेत्रज्ञ एतां निनयेत् तमात्मनि ।
आत्मानमात्मन्यवरुध्य धीरो
लब्धोपशान्तिर्विरमेत कृत्यात् ॥१६॥

manaḥ sva-buddhyāmalayā niyamya
kṣetra-jña etāṁ ninayet tam ātmani
ātmānam ātmany avarudhya dhīro
labdhopaśāntir virameta kṛtyāt

manaḥ—the mind; *sva-buddhyā*—by his own intelligence; *amalayā*—unalloyed; *niyamya*—by regulating; *kṣetra-jñe*—unto the living entity; *etām*—all of them; *ninayet*—merge; *tam*—that; *ātmani*—the self; *ātmānam*—the self; *ātmani*—in the Superself; *avarudhya*—being locked up; *dhīraḥ*—the fully satisfied; *labdha-upaśāntiḥ*—one who has attained full bliss; *virameta*—ceases from; *kṛtyāt*—all other activities.

TRANSLATION

Thereafter, the yogī should merge his mind, by his unalloyed intelligence, into the living entity, and then merge the living entity into the Superself. And by doing this, the fully satisfied living entity becomes situated in the supreme stage of satisfaction, so that he ceases from all other activities.

PURPORT

The functions of the mind are thinking, feeling and willing. When the mind is materialistic, or absorbed in material contact, it acts for material advancement of knowledge, destructively ending in discovery of nuclear weapons. But when the mind acts under spiritual urge, it acts wonderfully for going back home, back to Godhead, for life in complete bliss and eternity. Therefore the mind has to be manipulated by good and unalloyed intelligence. Perfect intelligence is to render service unto the Lord. One should be intelligent enough to understand that the living being is, in all circumstances, a servant of the circumstances. Every living being is serving the dictates of desire, anger, lust, illusion, insanity and enviousness—all materially affected. But even while executing such dictations of different temperaments, he is perpetually unhappy. When one actually feels this and turns his intelligence to inquiring about it from the right sources, he gets information of the transcendental loving service of the Lord. Instead of serving materially for the above-mentioned different humors of the body, the living entity's intelligence then becomes freed from the unhappy illusion of materialistic temperament, and thus, by unalloyed intelligence, the mind is brought into the service of the Lord. The Lord and His service are identical, being on the absolute plane. Therefore the unalloyed intelligence and the mind are merged into the Lord, and thus the living entity does not remain a seer himself but becomes seen by the Lord transcendentally. When the living entity is directly seen by the Lord, the Lord dictates to him to act according to His desire, and when the living entity follows Him perfectly, the living entity ceases to discharge any other duty for his illusory satisfaction. In his pure unalloyed state, the living being attains the stage of full bliss, *labdhopaśānti,* and ceases all material hankerings.

TEXT 17

न यत्र कालोऽनिमिषां परः प्रभुः
कुतो नु देवा जगतां य ईशिरे ।
न यत्र सत्त्वं न रजस्तमश्च
न वै विकारो न महान् प्रधानम् ॥१७॥

na yatra kālo 'nimiṣāṁ paraḥ prabhuḥ
kuto nu devā jagatāṁ ya īśire
na yatra sattvaṁ na rajas tamaś ca
na vai vikāro na mahān pradhānam

na—not; *yatra*—wherein; *kālaḥ*—destructive time; *animiṣām*—of the heavenly demigods; *paraḥ*—superior; *prabhuḥ*—controller; *kutaḥ*—where is there; *nu*—certainly; *devāḥ*—the demigods; *jagatām*—the mundane creatures; *ye*—those; *īśire*—rules; *na*—not; *yatra*—therein; *sattvam*—mundane goodness; *na*—nor; *rajaḥ*—mundane passion; *tamaḥ*—mundane ignorance; *ca*—also; *na*—nor; *vai*—certainly; *vikāraḥ*—transformation; *na*—nor; *mahān*—the material Causal Ocean; *pradhānam*—material nature.

TRANSLATION

In that transcendental state of labdhopaśānti, there is no supremacy of devastating time, which controls even the celestial demigods who are empowered to rule over mundane creatures. (And what to speak of the demigods themselves?) Nor is there the mode of material goodness, nor passion, nor ignorance, nor even the false ego, nor the material Causal Ocean, nor the material nature.

PURPORT

Devastating time, which controls even the celestial demigods by its manifestations of past, present and future, does not act on the transcendental plane. The influence of time is exhibited by the symptoms of birth, death, old age and disease, and these four principles of material conditions are present everywhere in any part of the material cosmos up to the planet Brahmaloka, where the duration of life of the inhabitants appears to us to be fabulous. Insurmountable time even brings about the death of Brahmā, so what to speak of other demigods like Indra, Candra, Sūrya, Vāyu and Varuṇa? The astronomical influence directed by the different demigods over mundane creatures is also conspicuous by its absence. In material existence, the living entities are afraid of Satanic influence, but for a devotee on the transcendental plane there is no such fear at all. The living entities change their material bodies in different shapes and forms under the influence of the different modes of material nature, but in the transcendental state the devotee is *guṇātīta*, or above the material modes of goodness, passion and ignorance. Thus the false ego of "I am the lord of all I survey" does not arise there. In the material world the false ego of the living being trying to lord it over the material nature is something like the moth's falling in a blazing fire. The moth is captivated by the glaring beauty of the fire, and when he comes to enjoy it, the blazing fire consumes him. In the transcendental state the living being is pure in his consciousness, and as such he has no false ego to lord it over the material nature. Rather, his pure consciousness directs him to surrender unto the Supreme Lord, as stated in the *Bhagavad-gītā* (7.19): *vāsudevaḥ sarvam iti sa mahātmā sudurlabhaḥ*. All this indicates that in the transcendental state there is neither material creation nor the Causal Ocean for material nature.

The above-mentioned state of affairs is factual on the transcendental plane, but is factually revealed in a transcendentalist's knowledge of the advanced state of pure consciousness. Such transcendentalists are of two types, namely the impersonalists and the devotees. For the impersonalist the ultimate goal or destination is the *brahmajyoti* of the spiritual sky, but for the devotees the ultimate goal is the Vaikuṇṭha planets. The devotees experience the above-mentioned state of affairs by attainment of spiritual forms for activity in the transcendental loving service of the Lord. But the impersonalist, because of his neglecting the association of the Lord, does not develop a spiritual body for spiritual activity, but remains a spiritual spark only, merged in the effulgent spiritual rays of the Supreme Personality of Godhead. The Lord is the full-fledged form of eternity, bliss and knowledge, but the formless *brahmajyoti* is simply eternity and knowledge. The Vaikuṇṭha planets are also forms of eternity, bliss and knowledge, and therefore the devotees of the Lord, who are admitted into the abode of the Lord, also get bodies of eternity, bliss and knowledge. As such there is no difference between one and another. The Lord's abode, name, fame, entourage, etc., are of the same transcendental quality, and how this transcendental quality differs from the material world is explained herewith in this verse. In the *Bhagavad-gītā*, three principal subjects have been explained by Lord Śrī Kṛṣṇa, namely *karma-yoga*, *jñāna-yoga* and *bhakti-yoga*, but one can reach the Vaikuṇṭha planets by the practice of *bhakti-yoga* only. The other two are incompetent in helping one reach the Vaikuṇṭhalokas, although they can, however, conveniently take one to the effulgent *brahmajyoti*, as described above.

TEXT 18

परं पदं वैष्णवमामनन्ति तद्
यन्नेति नेतीत्यतदुत्सिसृक्षवः ।
विसृज्य दौरात्म्यमनन्यसौहृदा
हृदोपगुह्यार्हपदं पदे पदे ॥१८॥

paraṁ padaṁ vaiṣṇavam āmananti tad
yan neti netīty atad utsisṛkṣavaḥ
visṛjya daurātmyam ananya-sauhṛdā
hṛdopaguhyārha-padaṁ pade pade

param—the supreme; *padam*—situation; *vaiṣṇavam*—in relation with the Personality of Godhead; *āmananti*—do they know; *tat*—that; *yat*—which; *na iti*—not this; *na iti*—not this; *iti*—thus; *atat*—godless; *utsisṛkṣavaḥ*—those who desire to avoid; *visṛjya*—giving it up completely; *daurātmyam*—perplexities; *ananya*—absolutely; *sauhṛdāḥ*—in good will; *hṛdā upaguhya*—taking them into his heart; *arha*—that which is only worshipable; *padam*—lotus feet; *pade pade*—at every moment.

TRANSLATION

The transcendentalists desire to avoid everything godless, for they know that supreme situation in which everything is related

with the Supreme Lord Viṣṇu. Therefore a pure devotee who is in absolute harmony with the Lord does not create perplexities, but worships the lotus feet of the Lord at every moment, taking them into his heart.

PURPORT

In the *Bhagavad-gītā, mad-dhāma* ("My abode") is mentioned several times, and according to the version of the Supreme Personality of Godhead Śrī Kṛṣṇa there exists the unlimited spiritual sky, wherein the planets are called Vaikuṇṭhas, or the abode of the Personality of Godhead. In that sky, which is far, far beyond the material sky and its sevenfold coverings, there is no need of the sun or the moon, nor is there necessity of electricity for illumination, because the planets are self-illuminating and more brilliant than the material suns. Pure devotees of the Lord are absolutely in harmony with the Personality of Godhead, or in other words, they always think of the Lord as their only dependable friend and well-wisher. They do not care for any mundane creature, up to the status of Brahmā, the lord of the universe. Only they can definitely have a clear vision of the Vaikuṇṭha planets. Such pure devotees, being perfectly directed by the Supreme Lord, do not create any artificial perplexity in the matter of transcendental understanding by wasting time in discussing what is Brahman and what is non-Brahman, or *māyā*, nor do they falsely think of themselves as one with the Lord, or argue that there is no existence of the Lord separately, or that there is no God at all, or that living beings are themselves God, or that when God incarnates Himself He assumes a material body. Nor do they concern themselves with many obscure speculative theories, which are in actuality so many stumbling blocks on the path of transcendental understanding. Apart from the class of impersonalists or nondevotees, there are also classes who pose themselves as devotees of the Lord but at heart maintain the idea of salvation by becoming one with the impersonal Brahman. They wrongly manufacture their own way of devotional service by open debauchery and mislead others who are simpletons or debauchees like themselves. All these nondevotees and debauchees are, according to Viśvanātha Cakravartī, *durātmās,* or crooked souls in the dress of *mahātmās,* or great souls. Such nondevotees and debauchees are completely excluded from the list of transcendentalists by the presentation of this particular verse by Śukadeva Gosvāmī.

So the Vaikuṇṭha planets are factually the supreme residential places called the *paraṁ padam.* The impersonal *brahmajyoti* is also called the *paraṁ padam* due to its being the rays of the Vaikuṇṭha planets, as the sun rays are the rays of the sun. In the *Bhagavad-gītā* (14.27) it is clearly said that the impersonal *brahmajyoti* rests on the person of the Lord, and because everything rests on the *brahmajyoti* directly and indirectly, everything is generated from the Lord, everything rests on Him, and after annihilation, everything is merged in Him only. Therefore, nothing is independent of Him. A pure devotee of the Lord no longer wastes valuable time in discriminating the Brahman from non-Brahman because he knows perfectly well that the Lord Parabrahman, by His Brahman energy, is interwoven in everything, and thus everything is looked upon by a devotee as the property of the Lord. The devotee tries to engage everything in His service and does not create perplexities by falsely lording it over the creation of the Lord. He is so faithful that he engages himself, as well as everything else, in the transcendental loving service of the Lord. In everything, the devotee sees the Lord, and he sees everything in the Lord. The specific disturbance created by a *durātmā,* or crooked soul, is due to his maintaining that the transcendental form of the Lord is something material.

TEXT 19

इत्थं मुनिस्तूपरमेद् व्यवस्थितो
विज्ञानदृग्वीर्यसुरन्धिताशयः ।
स्वपार्ष्णिनापीड्य गुदं ततोऽनिलं
स्थानेषु षट्सून्नमयेज्जितक्लमः ॥१९॥

itthaṁ munis tūparamed vyavasthito
vijñāna-dṛg-vīrya-surandhitāśayaḥ
sva-pārṣṇināpīḍya gudaṁ tato 'nilaṁ
sthāneṣu ṣaṭsūnnamayej jita-klamaḥ

ittham—thus, by Brahman realization; *muniḥ*—the philosopher; *tu*—but; *uparamet*—should retire; *vyavasthitaḥ*—well situated; *vijñāna-dṛk*—by scientific knowledge; *vīrya*—strength; *su-randhita*—well regulated; *āśayaḥ*—aim of life; *sva-pārṣṇinā*—with the heel of one's foot; *āpīḍya*—by blocking; *gudam*—the air hole; *tataḥ*—thereafter; *anilam*—life air; *sthāneṣu*—in the places; *ṣaṭsu*—six primary; *unnamayet*—must be lifted; *jita-klamaḥ*—by extinguishing material desires.

TRANSLATION

By the strength of scientific knowledge, one should be well situated in absolute realization and thus be able to extinguish all material desires. One should then give up the material body by blocking the air hole [through which stool is evacuated] with the heel of one's foot and by lifting the life air from one place to another in the six primary places.

PURPORT

There are many *durātmās* who claim to have realized themselves as Brahman and yet are unable to conquer material desires. In the *Bhagavad-gītā* (18.54) it is clearly explained that an absolutely self-realized soul becomes completely aloof from all material desires. Material desires are based on the false ego of the living being and are exhibited by his childish and useless activities to conquer the laws of material nature and by his desire to lord it over the resources of the five elements. With such a mentality, one is led to believe in the strength of material science, with its discovery of atomic energy and space travel by mechanical vehicles, and by such tiny advancements in material science the false egoist tries to challenge even the strength of the Supreme Lord, who can finish all man's tiny endeavors in less than a second. The well-situated self, or Brahman-realized soul, perfectly understands that the Supreme Brahman, or the Personality of Godhead, is the all-powerful Vāsudeva and that he (the self-realized living being) is a part and parcel of the supreme whole. As such, his constitutional position is to cooperate with Him in all respects in the transcendental relation of the served and the servitor. Such a self-realized soul ceases to exhibit his useless activities of attempting to lord it over material nature. Being scientifically well informed, he fully engages himself in faithful devotion to the Lord.

The expert *yogī* who has thoroughly practiced the control of the life air by the prescribed method of the *yoga* system is advised to quit the body as follows. He should plug up the evacuating hole with the heel of the foot and then progressively move the life air on and on to six places: the navel, abdomen, heart, chest, palate, eyebrows and cerebral pit. Controlling the life air by the prescribed yogic process is mechanical, and the practice is more or less a physical endeavor for spiritual perfection. In olden days such practice was very common for the transcendentalist, for the mode of life and character in those days were favorable. But in modern days, when the influence of Kali Age is so disturbing, practically everyone is untrained in this art of bodily exercise. Concentration of the mind is more easily attained in these days by the chanting of the holy name of the Lord. The results are more effective than those derived from the inner exercise of the life air.

TEXT 20

नाभ्यां स्थितं हृद्यधिरोप्य तस्मा-
दुदानगत्योरसि तं नयेन्मुनिः ।
ततोऽनुसन्धाय धिया मनस्वी
स्वतालुमूलं शनकैर्नयेत ॥२०॥

nābhyāṁ sthitaṁ hṛdy adhiropya tasmād
udāna-gatyorasi taṁ nayen muniḥ
tato 'nusandhāya dhiyā manasvī
sva-tālu-mūlaṁ śanakair nayeta

nābhyām—on the navel; *sthitam*—situated; *hṛdi*—in the heart; *adhiropya*—by placing; *tasmāt*—from there; *udāna*—soaring; *gatya*—force; *urasi*—on the chest; *tam*—thereafter; *nayet*—should draw; *muniḥ*—the meditative devotee; *tataḥ*—them; *anusandhāya*—just to search out; *dhiyā*—by intelligence; *manasvī*—the meditative; *sva-tālu-mūlam*—at the root of the palate; *śanakaiḥ*—slowly; *nayeta*—may be brought in.

TRANSLATION

The meditative devotee should slowly push up the life air from the navel to the heart, from there to the chest and from there to

the root of the palate. He should search out the proper places with intelligence.

PURPORT

There are six circles of the movement of the life air, and the intelligent *bhakti-yogī* should search out these places with intelligence and in a meditative mood. Among these, mentioned above is the *svādhiṣṭhāna-cakra,* or the powerhouse of the life air, and above this, just below the abdomen and navel, is the *maṇi-pūraka-cakra.* When upper space is further searched out in the heart, one reaches the *anāhata-cakra,* and further up, when the life air is placed at the root of the palate, one reaches the *viśuddhi-cakra.*

TEXT 21

तस्माद् भ्रुवोरन्तरमुन्नयेत
निरुद्धसप्तायतनोऽनपेक्षः ।
स्थित्वा मुहूर्तार्धमकुण्ठदृष्टि-
र्निर्भिद्य मूर्धन् विसृजेत्परं गतः ॥२१॥

tasmād bhruvor antaram unnayeta
niruddha-saptāyatano 'napekṣaḥ
sthitvā muhūrtārdham akuṇṭha-dṛṣṭir
nirbhidya mūrdhan visṛjet paraṁ gataḥ

tasmāt—from there; *bhruvoḥ*—of the eyebrows; *antaram*—in between; *unnayeta*—should be brought in; *niruddha*—by blocking; *sapta*—seven; *āyatanaḥ*—outlets of the life air; *anapekṣaḥ*—independent of all material enjoyment; *sthitvā*—by keeping; *muhūrta*—of a moment; *ardham*—half; *akuṇṭha*—back home, back to Godhead; *dṛṣṭiḥ*—one whose aim is targeted like that; *nirbhidya*—punching; *mūrdhan*—the cerebral hole; *visṛjet*—should give up his body; *param*—the Supreme; *gataḥ*—having gone to.

TRANSLATION

Thereafter the bhakti-yogī should push the life air up between the eyebrows, and then, blocking the seven outlets of the life air,

he should maintain his aim for going back home, back to Godhead. If he is completely free from all desires for material enjoyment, he should then reach the cerebral hole and give up his material connections, having gone to the Supreme.

PURPORT

The process of giving up all material connections and returning home, back to Godhead, the Supreme, is recommended herein. The condition is that one should be completely freed from desire for material enjoyment. There are different grades of material enjoyments in respect to duration of life and sensual gratification. The highest plane of sensual enjoyment for the longest period of life is mentioned in the *Bhagavad-gītā* (9.20). All are but material enjoyments, and one should be thoroughly convinced that he has no need of such a long duration of life, even in the Brahmaloka planet. He must return home, back to Godhead, and must not be attracted by any amount of material facilities. In the *Bhagavad-gītā* (2.59) it is said that this sort of material detachment is possible to attain when one is acquainted with the supreme association of life. *Paraṁ dṛṣṭvā nivartate.* One cannot be freed from material attraction unless he has complete understanding of the nature of spiritual life. The propaganda by a certain class of impersonalists that spiritual life is void of all varieties is dangerous propaganda to mislead the living beings into becoming more and more attracted by material enjoyments. As such, persons with a poor fund of knowledge cannot have any conception of the *param,* the Supreme; they try to stick to the varieties of material enjoyments, although they may flatter themselves as being Brahman-realized souls. Such less intelligent persons cannot have any conception of the *param,* as mentioned in this verse, and therefore they cannot reach the Supreme. The devotees have full knowledge of the spiritual world, the Personality of Godhead and His transcendental association in unlimited spiritual planets called Vaikuṇṭhalokas. Herein *akuṇṭha-dṛṣṭiḥ* is mentioned. *Akuṇṭha* and *vaikuṇṭha* convey the same import, and only one who has his aim fixed upon that spiritual world and personal association with the Godhead can give up his material connections even while living in the material world. This *param* and the *paraṁ dhāma* mentioned in several places in the *Bhagavad-gītā* are one and the same thing. One who goes to the *paraṁ dhāma* does not return to the material world. This freedom is not possible even by reaching the topmost *loka* of the material world.

The life air passes through seven openings, namely two eyes, two nostrils, two ears and one mouth. Generally it passes through the mouth at the time of an ordinary man's death. But the *yogī*, as above mentioned, who controls the life air in his own way, generally releases the life air by puncturing the cerebral hole in the head. The *yogī* therefore blocks up all the above-mentioned seven openings, so that the life air will naturally burst forth through the cerebral hole. This is the sure sign of a great devotee's leaving the material connection.

TEXT 22

यदि प्रयास्यन् नृप पारमेष्ठ्यं
वैहायसानामुत यद् विहारम् ।
अष्टाधिपत्यं गुणसन्निवाये
सहैव गच्छेन्मनसेन्द्रियैश्च ॥२२॥

yadi prayāsyan nṛpa pārameṣṭhyaṁ
vaihāyasānām uta yad vihāram
aṣṭādhipatyaṁ guṇa-sannivāye
sahaiva gacchen manasendriyaiś ca

yadi—however; *prayāsyan*—maintaining a desire; *nṛpa*—O King; *pārameṣṭhyam*—the governing planet of the material world; *vaihāyasānām*—of the beings known as the Vaihāyasas; *uta*—it is said; *yat*—what is; *vihāram*—place of enjoyment; *aṣṭa-ādhipatyam*—lording it over with eightfold achievements; *guṇa-sannivāye*—in the world of three modes of nature; *saha*—along with; *eva*—certainly; *gacchet*—should go; *manasā*—accompanied by the mind; *indriyaiḥ*—and the senses; *ca*—also.

TRANSLATION

However, O King, if a yogī maintains a desire for improved material enjoyments, like transference to the topmost planet, Brahmaloka, or the achievement of the eightfold perfections, travel in outer space with the Vaihāyasas, or a situation in one of

the millions of planets, then he has to take away with him the materially molded mind and senses.

PURPORT

In the upper status of the planetary systems there are facilities thousands and thousands of times greater for material enjoyments than in the lower planetary systems. The topmost planetary systems consist of planets like Brahmaloka and Dhruvaloka (the polestar), and all of them are situated beyond Maharloka. The inhabitants of those planets are empowered with eightfold achievements of mystic perfection. They do not have to learn and practice the mystic processes of *yoga* perfection and achieve the power of becoming small like a particle (*aṇimā-siddhi*), or lighter than a soft feather (*laghimā-siddhi*). They do not have to get anything and everything from anywhere and everywhere (*prāpti-siddhi*), to become heavier than the heaviest (*mahimā-siddhi*), to act freely even to create something wonderful or to annihilate anything at will (*īśitva-siddhi*), to control all material elements (*vaśitva-siddhi*), to possess such power as will never be frustrated in any desire (*prākāmya-siddhi*), or to assume any shape or form one may even whimsically desire (*kāmāvasāyitā-siddhi*). All these expediencies are as common as natural gifts for the inhabitants of those higher planets. They do not require any mechanical help to travel in outer space, and they can move and travel at will from one planet to any other planet within no time. The inhabitants of the earth cannot move even to the nearest planet except by mechanical vehicles like spacecraft, but the highly talented inhabitants of such higher planets can do everything very easily.

Since a materialist is generally inquisitive to experience what is actually in such planetary systems, he wants to see everything personally. As inquisitive persons tour all over the world to gain direct local experience, the less intelligent transcendentalist similarly desires to have some experience of those planets about which he has heard so many wonderful things. The *yogī* can, however, easily fulfill his desire by going there with the present materialistic mind and senses. The prime inclination of the materialistic mind is to lord it over the material world, and all the *siddhis* mentioned above are features of domination over the world. The devotees of the Lord are not ambitious to dominate a false and temporary phenomenon. On the contrary, a devotee wants to be dominated by the supreme predominator, the Lord. A desire to serve the Lord, the supreme predominator, is spiritual or transcendental, and one has to attain this purification of the mind and the senses to get admission into the spiritual kingdom. With the materialistic mind one can reach the best planet in the universe, but no one can enter into the kingdom of God. Senses are called spiritually purified when they are not involved in sense gratification. Senses require engagements, and when the senses are engaged totally in the transcendental loving service of the Lord, they have no chance to become contaminated by material infections.

TEXT 23

योगेश्वराणां गतिमाहुरन्त-
बहिस्त्रिलोक्याः पवनान्तरात्मनाम् ।
न कर्मभिस्तां गतिमाप्नुवन्ति
विद्यातपोयोगसमाधिभाजाम् ॥२३॥

yogeśvarāṇāṁ gatim āhur antar-
bahis-tri-lokyāḥ pavanāntar-ātmanām
na karmabhis tāṁ gatim āpnuvanti
vidyā-tapo-yoga-samādhi-bhājām

yoga-īśvarāṇām—of the great saints and devotees; *gatim*—destination; *āhuḥ*—it is said; *antaḥ*—within; *bahiḥ*—without; *tri-lokyāḥ*—of the three planetary systems; *pavana-antaḥ*—within the air; *ātmanām*—of the subtle body; *na*—never; *karmabhiḥ*—by fruitive activities; *tām*—that; *gatim*—speed; *āpnuvanti*—achieve; *vidyā*—devotional service; *tapaḥ*—austerities; *yoga*—mystic power; *samādhi*—knowledge; *bhājām*—of those who entertain.

TRANSLATION

The transcendentalists are concerned with the spiritual body. As such, by the strength of their devotional service, austerities, mystic power and transcendental knowledge, their movements are unrestricted, within and beyond the material worlds. The fruitive workers, or the gross materialists, can never move in such an unrestricted manner.

PURPORT

The materialistic scientist's endeavor to reach other planets by mechanical vehicles is only a futile attempt. One can, however, reach heavenly planets by virtuous activities, but one can never expect to go beyond Svarga or Janaloka by such mechanical or materialistic activities, either gross or subtle. The transcendentalists who have nothing to do with the gross material body can move anywhere within or beyond the material worlds. Within the material worlds they move in the planetary systems of the Mahar-, Janas-, Tapas- and Satya-loka, and beyond the material worlds they can move in the Vaikuṇṭhas as unrestricted spacemen. Nārada Muni is one of the examples of such spacemen, and Durvāsā Muni is one of such mystics. By the strength of devotional service, austerities, mystic powers and transcendental knowledge, everyone can move like Nārada Muni or Durvāsā Muni. It is said that Durvāsā Muni traveled throughout the entirety of material space and part of spiritual space within one year only. The speed of the transcendentalists can never be attained by the gross or subtle materialists.

TEXT 24

वैश्वानरं याति विहायसा गतः
सुषुम्णया ब्रह्मपथेन शोचिषा ।
विधूतकल्कोऽथ हरेरुदस्तात्
प्रयाति चक्रं नृप शैशुमारम् ॥२४॥

vaiśvānaraṁ yāti vihāyasā gataḥ
suṣumṇayā brahma-pathena śociṣā
vidhūta-kalko 'tha harer udastāt
prayāti cakraṁ nṛpa śaiśumāram

vaiśvānaram—the controlling deity of fire; *yāti*—goes; *vihāyasā*—by the path in the sky (the Milky Way); *gataḥ*—by passing over; *suṣumṇayā*—by the Suṣumṇā; *brahma*—Brahmaloka; *pathena*—on the way to; *śociṣā*—illuminating; *vidhūta*—being washed off; *kalkaḥ*—dirt; *atha*—thereafter; *hareḥ*—of Lord Hari; *udastāt*—upwards; *prayāti*—does reach; *cakram*—circle; *nṛpa*—O King; *śaiśumāram*—named Śiśumara.

TRANSLATION

O King, when such a mystic passes over the Milky Way by the illuminating Suṣumṇā to reach the highest planet, Brahmaloka, he goes first to Vaiśvānara, the planet of the deity of fire, wherein he becomes completely cleansed of all contaminations, and thereafter he still goes higher, to the circle of Śiśumāra, to relate with Lord Hari, the Personality of Godhead.

PURPORT

The polar star of the universe and the circle thereof is called the Śiśumāra circle, and therein the local residential planet of the Personality of Godhead (Kṣīrodakaśāyī Viṣṇu) is situated. Before reaching there, the mystic passes over the Milky Way to reach Brahmaloka, and while going there he first reaches Vaiśvānara-loka, where the demigod controls fire. On Vaiśvānara-loka the *yogī* becomes completely cleansed of all dirty sins acquired while in contact with the material world. The Milky Way in the sky is indicated herein as the way leading to Brahmaloka, the highest planet of the universe.

TEXT 25

तद् विश्वनाभिं त्वतिवर्त्य विष्णो-
रणीयसा विरजेनात्मनैकः ।
नमस्कृतं ब्रह्मविदामुपैति
कल्पायुषो यद् विबुधा रमन्ते ॥२५॥

tad viśva-nābhiṁ tv ativartya viṣṇor
aṇīyasā virajenātmanaikaḥ
namaskṛtaṁ brahma-vidām upaiti
kalpāyuṣo yad vibudhā ramante

tat—that; *viśva-nābhim*—navel of the universal Personality of Godhead; *tu*—but; *ativartya*—crossing over; *viṣṇoḥ*—of Lord Viṣṇu, the Personality of Godhead; *aṇīyasā*—due to mystic perfection; *virajena*—by the purified; *ātmanā*—by the living entity; *ekaḥ*—alone; *namaskṛtam*—worshipable; *brahma-vidām*—by those who are transcendentally situated; *upaiti*—reaches; *kalpa-āyuṣaḥ*—a period of 4,300,000,000 solar years; *yat*—the place; *vibudhāḥ*—self-realized souls; *ramante*—do enjoy.

TRANSLATION

This Śiśumāra is the pivot for the turning of the complete universe, and it is called the navel of Viṣṇu [Garbhodakaśāyī Viṣṇu]. The yogī alone goes beyond this circle of Śiśumāra and attains the planet [Maharloka] where purified saints like Bhṛgu enjoy a duration of life of 4,300,000,000 solar years. This planet is worshipable even for the saints who are transcendentally situated.

TEXT 26

अथो अनन्तस्य मुखानलेन
दन्दह्यमानं स निरीक्ष्य विश्वम् ।
निर्याति सिद्धेश्वरयुष्टधिष्ण्यं
यद् द्वैपरार्ध्यं तदु पारमेष्ठ्यम् ॥२६॥

atho anantasya mukhānalena
dandahyamānaṁ sa nirīkṣya viśvam
niryāti siddheśvara-yuṣṭa-dhiṣṇyaṁ
yad dvai-parārdhyaṁ tad u pārameṣṭhyam

atho—thereupon; *anantasya*—of Ananta, the resting incarnation of Godhead; *mukha-analena*—by the fire emanating from His mouth; *dandahyamānam*—burning to ashes; *saḥ*—he; *nirīkṣya*—by seeing this; *viśvam*—the universe; *niryāti*—goes out; *siddheśvara-yuṣṭa-dhiṣṇyam*—airplanes used by the great purified souls; *yat*—the place; *dvai-parārdhyam*—15,480,000,000,000 solar years; *tat*—that; *u*—the exalted; *pārameṣṭhyam*—Satyaloka, where Brahmā resides.

TRANSLATION

At the time of the final devastation of the complete universe [the end of the duration of Brahmā's life], a flame of fire emanates

from the mouth of Ananta [from the bottom of the universe]. The yogī sees all the planets of the universe burning to ashes, and thus he leaves for Satyaloka by airplanes used by the great purified souls. The duration of life in Satyaloka is calculated to be 15,480,000,000,000 years.

PURPORT

It is indicated herein that the residents of Maharloka, where the purified living entities or demigods possess a duration of life calculated to be 4,300,000,000 solar years, have airships by which they reach Satyaloka, the topmost planet of the universe. In other words, the *Śrīmad-Bhāgavatam* gives us many clues about other planets far, far away from us which modern planes and spacecraft cannot reach, even by imaginary speeds. The statements of *Śrīmad-Bhāgavatam* are accepted by great *ācāryas* like Śrīdhara Svāmī, Rāmānujācārya and Vallabhācārya. Lord Śrī Caitanya Mahāprabhu specifically accepts *Śrīmad-Bhāgavatam* as the spotless Vedic authority, and as such no sane man can ignore the statements of *Śrīmad-Bhāgavatam* when it is spoken by the self-realized soul Śrīla Śukadeva Gosvāmī, who follows in the footsteps of his great father, Śrīla Vyāsadeva, the compiler of all Vedic literatures. In the creation of the Lord there are many wonderful things we can see with our own eyes every day and night, but we are unable to reach them equipped by modern materialistic science. We should not, therefore, depend on the fragmentary authority of materialistic science for knowing things beyond the range of scientific purview. For a common man, both modern science and Vedic wisdom are simply to be accepted because none of the statements either of modern science or of Vedic literature can be verified by him. The alternative for a common man is to believe either of them or both of them. The Vedic way of understanding, however, is more authentic because it has been accepted by the *ācāryas*, who are not only faithful and learned men, but are also liberated souls without any of the flaws of conditioned souls. The modern scientists, however, are conditioned souls liable to so many errors and mistakes; therefore the safe side is to accept the authentic version of Vedic literatures, like *Śrīmad-Bhāgavatam*, which is accepted unanimously by the great *ācāryas*.

TEXT 27

न यत्र शोको न जरा न मृत्यु-
र्नार्तिर्न चोद्वेग ऋते कुतश्चित् ।
यच्चित्ततोऽदः कृपयानिदंविदां
दुरन्तदुःखप्रभवानुदर्शनात् ॥२७॥

na yatra śoko na jarā na mṛtyur
nārtir na codvega ṛte kutaścit
yac cit tato 'daḥ kṛpayānidaṁ-vidāṁ
duranta-duḥkha-prabhavānudarśanāt

na—never; *yatra*—there are; *śokaḥ*—bereavement; *na*—nor; *jarā*—old age; *na*—nor; *mṛtyuḥ*—death; *na*—nor; *artiḥ*—pains; *na*—nor; *ca*—also; *udvegaḥ*—anxieties; *ṛte*—save and except; *kutaścit*—sometimes; *yat*—because of; *cit*—consciousness; *tataḥ*—therefore; *adaḥ*—compassion; *kṛpayā*—out of heartfelt sympathy; *an-idam-vidām*—of those who are ignorant of the process of devotional service; *duranta*—unsurpassable; *duḥkha*—misery; *prabhava*—repeated birth and death; *anudarśanāt*—by successive experience.

TRANSLATION

In that planet of Satyaloka, there is neither bereavement, nor old age nor death. There is no pain of any kind, and therefore there are no anxieties, save that sometimes, due to consciousness, there is a feeling of compassion for those unaware of the process of devotional service, who are subjected to unsurpassable miseries in the material world.

PURPORT

Foolish men of materialistic temperament do not take advantage of successive authorized knowledge. The Vedic knowledge is authorized and is acquired not by experiment but by authentic statements of the Vedic literatures explained by bona fide authorities. Simply by becoming an academic scholar one cannot understand the Vedic statements; one has to approach the real authority who has received the Vedic knowledge by disciplic succession, as clearly explained in the *Bhagavad-gītā* (4.2). Lord Kṛṣṇa affirmed that the system of knowledge as explained in the *Bhagavad-gītā* was explained to the sun-god, and the knowledge descended by disciplic succession from the sun-god to his son Manu, and from Manu to King Ikṣvāku (the forefather of Lord Rāmacandra), and thus the system of knowledge was explained down the line of great sages, one after another. But in due course of time the authorized succession was broken, and therefore, just to reestablish the true spirit of the knowledge, the Lord again explained the same knowledge to Arjuna, who was a bona fide candidate for understanding due to his being a pure devotee of the Lord. *Bhagavad-gītā,* as it was understood by Arjuna, is also explained (Bg. 10.12–13), but there are many foolish men who do not follow in the footsteps of Arjuna in understanding the spirit of *Bhagavad-gītā.* They create instead their own interpretations, which are as foolish as they themselves, and thereby only help to put a stumbling block on the path of real understanding, misdirecting the innocent followers who are less intelligent, or the *śūdras.* It is said that one should become a *brāhmaṇa* before one can understand the Vedic statements, and this stricture is as important as the stricture that no one shall become a lawyer who has not qualified himself as a graduate. Such a stricture is not an impediment in the path of progress for anyone and everyone, but it is necessary for an unqualified understanding of a particular science. Vedic knowledge is misinterpreted by those who are not qualified *brāhmaṇas.* A qualified *brāhmaṇa* is one who has undergone strict training under the guidance of a bona fide spiritual master.

The Vedic wisdom guides us to understanding our relation with the Supreme Lord Śrī Kṛṣṇa and to acting accordingly in order to achieve the desired result of returning home, back to Godhead. But materialistic men do not understand this. They want to make a plan to become happy in a place where there is no happiness. For false happiness they try to reach other planets, either by Vedic rituals or by spacecraft, but they should know for certain that any amount of materialistic adjustment for becoming happy in a place which is meant for distress cannot benefit the misguided man because, after all, the whole universe with all its paraphernalia will come to an end after a certain period. Then all plans of materialistic happiness will automatically come to an end. The intelligent person therefore makes a plan to return home, back to Godhead. Such an intelligent person surpasses all the pangs of material existence, like birth, death, disease and old age. He is actually happy because he has no anxieties of material existence, but as a compassionate sympathizer he feels unhappiness for the suffering materialistic men, and thus he occasionally comes before the materialistic men to teach them the necessity of going back to Godhead. All the bona fide *ācāryas* preach this truth of returning home, back to Godhead, and warn men not to make a false plan for happiness in a place where happiness is only a myth.

TEXT 28

ततो विशेषं प्रतिपद्य निर्भय-
स्तेनात्मनापोऽनलमूर्तिरत्वरन् ।
ज्योतिर्मयो वायुमुपेत्य काले
वाय्वात्मना खं बृहदात्मलिङ्गम् ॥२८॥

tato viśeṣaṁ pratipadya nirbhayas
tenātmanāpo 'nala-mūrtir atvaran
jyotirmayo vāyum upetya kāle
vāyv-ātmanā khaṁ bṛhad ātma-liṅgam

tataḥ—thereafter; *viśeṣam*—particularly; *pratipadya*—by obtaining; *nirbhayaḥ*—without any doubt; *tena*—by that; *ātmanā*—pure self; *āpaḥ*—water; *anala*—fire; *mūrtiḥ*—forms; *atvaran*—by surpassing; *jyotiḥ-mayaḥ*—effulgent; *vāyum*—atmosphere; *upetya*—having reached there; *kāle*—in due course of time; *vāyu*—air; *ātmanā*—by the self; *kham*—ethereal; *bṛhat*—great; *ātma-liṅgam*—the real form of the self.

TRANSLATION

After reaching Satyaloka, the devotee is specifically able to be incorporated fearlessly by the subtle body in an identity similar to that of the gross body, and one after another he gradually attains stages of existence from earthly to watery, fiery, glowing and airy, until he reaches the ethereal stage.

PURPORT

Anyone who can reach Brahmaloka, or Satyaloka, by dint of spiritual perfection and practice is qualified to attain three different types of perfection. One who has attained a specific planet by dint of pious activities attains places in terms of his comparative pious activities. One who has attained the place by dint of *virāṭ* or Hiraṇyagarbha worship is liberated along with the liberation of Brahmā. But one who attains the place by dint of devotional service is specifically mentioned here, in relation to how he can penetrate into the different coverings of the universe and thus ultimately disclose his spiritual identity in the absolute atmosphere of supreme existence.

According to Śrīla Jīva Gosvāmī, all the universes are clustered together up and down, and each and every one of them is separately sevenfold-covered. The watery portion is beyond the sevenfold coverings, and each covering is ten times more expansive than the previous covering. The Personality of Godhead who creates all such universes by His breathing period lies above the cluster of the universes. The water of the Causal Ocean is differently situated than the covering water of the universe. The water that serves as covering for the universe is material, whereas the water of the Causal Ocean is spiritual. As such, the watery covering mentioned herein is considered to be the false egoistic covering of all living entities, and the gradual process of liberation from the material coverings, one after another, as mentioned herein, is the gradual process of being liberated from false egoistic conceptions of the material gross body, and then being absorbed in the identification of the subtle body till the attainment of the pure spiritual body in the absolute realm of the kingdom of God.

Śrīla Śrīdhara Svāmī confirms that a part of the material nature, after being initiated by the Lord, is known as the *mahat-tattva.* A fractional portion of the *mahat-tattva* is called the false ego. A portion of the ego is the vibration of sound, and a portion of sound is atmospheric air. A portion of the airy atmosphere is turned into forms, and the forms constitute the power of electricity or heat. Heat produces the smell of the aroma of the earth, and the gross earth is produced by such aroma. And all these combined together constitute the cosmic phenomenon. The extent of the cosmic phenomenon is calculated to be diametrically (both ways) four billion miles. Then the coverings of the universe begin. The first stratum of the covering is calculated to extend eighty million miles, and the subsequent coverings of the universe are respectively of fire, effulgence, air and ether, one after another, each extending ten times further than the previous. The fearless devotee of the Lord penetrates each one of them and ultimately reaches the absolute atmosphere where everything is of one and the same spiritual identity. Then the devotee enters one of the Vaikuṇṭha planets, where he assumes exactly the same form as the Lord and engages in the loving transcendental service of the Lord. That is the highest perfection of devotional life. Beyond this there is nothing to be desired or achieved by the perfect *yogī.*

TEXT 29

घ्राणेन गन्धं रसनेन वै रसं
रूपं तु दृष्ट्या श्वसनं त्वचैव ।
श्रोत्रेण चोपेत्य नभोगुणत्वं
प्राणेन चाकूतिमुपैति योगी ॥२९॥

ghrāṇena gandhaṁ rasanena vai rasaṁ
rūpaṁ ca dṛṣṭyā śvasanaṁ tvacaiva
śrotreṇa copetya nabho-guṇatvaṁ
prāṇena cākūtim upaiti yogī

ghrāṇena—by smelling; *gandham*—aroma; *rasanena*—by taste; *vai*—exactly; *rasam*—palate; *rūpam*—forms; *ca*—also; *dṛṣṭyā*—by vision; *śvasanam*—contact; *tvacā*—touch; *eva*—as it were; *śrotreṇa*—by vibration of the ear; *ca*—also; *upetya*—by achieving; *nabhaḥ-guṇatvam*—identification of ether; *prāṇena*—by sense organs; *ca*—also; *ākūtim*—material activities; *upaiti*—attains; *yogī*—the devotee.

TRANSLATION

The devotee thus surpasses the subtle objects of different senses like aroma by smelling, the palate by tasting, vision by seeing forms, touch by contacting, the vibrations of the ear by ethereal identification, and the sense organs by material activities.

PURPORT

Beyond the sky there are subtle coverings, resembling the elementary coverings of the universes. The gross coverings are a development of partial ingredients of the subtle causes. So the *yogī* or devotee, along with liquidation of the gross elements, relinquishes the subtle causes like aroma by smelling. The pure spiritual spark, the living entity, thus becomes completely cleansed of all material contamination to become eligible for entrance into the kingdom of God.

TEXT 30

स भूतसूक्ष्मेन्द्रियसंनिकर्षं
मनोमयं देवमयं विकार्यम् ।
संसाद्य गत्या सह तेन याति
विज्ञानतत्त्वं गुणसंनिरोधम् ॥३०॥

sa bhūta-sūkṣmendriya-sannikarṣaṁ
manomayaṁ devamayaṁ vikāryam
saṁsādya gatyā saha tena yāti
vijñāna-tattvaṁ guṇa-sannirodham

saḥ—he (the devotee); *bhūta*—the gross; *sūkṣma*—and the subtle; *indriya*—senses; *sannikarṣam*—the point of neutralization; *manaḥ-mayam*—the mental plane; *deva-mayam*—in the mode of goodness; *vikāryam*—egoism; *saṁsādya*—surpassing; *gatyā*—by the progress; *saha*—along with; *tena*—them; *yāti*—goes; *vijñāna*—perfect knowledge; *tattvam*—truth; *guṇa*—the material modes; *sannirodham*—completely suspended.

TRANSLATION

The devotee, thus surpassing the gross and the subtle forms of coverings, enters the plane of egoism. And in that status he merges the material modes of nature [ignorance and passion] in this point of neutralization and thus reaches egoism in goodness. After this,

all egoism is merged in the mahat-tattva, and he comes to the point of pure self-realization.

PURPORT

Pure self-realization, as we have several times discussed, is the pure consciousness of admitting oneself to be the eternal servitor of the Lord. Thus one is reinstated in his original position of transcendental loving service to the Lord, as will be clearly explained in the following verse. This stage of rendering transcendental loving service to the Lord without any hopes of emolument from the Lord, or any other way, can be attained when the material senses are purified and the original pure state of the senses is revived. It is suggested herein that the process of purifying the senses is by the yogic way, namely the gross senses are merged in the mode of ignorance, and the subtle senses are merged in the mode of passion. The mind belongs to the mode of goodness and therefore is called *devamaya,* or godly. Perfect purification of the mind is made possible when one is fixed in the conviction of being the eternal servitor of the Lord. Therefore simple attainment of goodness is also a material mode; one has to surpass this stage of material goodness and reach the point of purified goodness, or *vasudeva-sattva.* This *vasudeva-sattva* helps one to enter into the kingdom of God.

We may also remember in this connection that the process of gradual emancipation by the devotees in the manner mentioned above, although authoritative, is not viable in the present age because of people's being primarily unaware of *yoga* practice. The so-called *yoga* practice by the professional protagonists may be physiologically beneficial, but such small successes cannot help one in the attainment of spiritual emancipation as mentioned herein. Five thousand years ago, when the social status of human society was in perfect Vedic order, the *yoga* process mentioned herein was a common affair for everyone because everyone, and especially the *brāhmaṇa* and *kṣatriya,* was trained in the transcendental art under the care of the spiritual master far away from home, in the status of *brahmacarya.* Modern man, however, is incompetent to understand it perfectly.

Lord Śrī Caitanya, therefore, made it easier for the prospective devotee of the present age in the following specific manner. Ultimately there is no difference in the result. The first and foremost point is that one must understand the prime importance of *bhakti-yoga.* The living beings in different species of life are undergoing different terms of encagement according to their fruitive actions and reactions. But in the execution of different activities, one who secures some resources in *bhakti-yoga* can understand the importance of service to the Lord through the causeless mercy of the Lord, as well as that of the spiritual master. A sincere soul is helped by the Lord through meeting a bona fide spiritual master, the representative of the Lord. By the instruction of such a spiritual master, one gets the seed of *bhakti-yoga.* Lord Śrī Caitanya Mahāprabhu recommends that the devotee sow the seed of *bhakti-yoga* in his heart and nurture it by the watering of hearing and chanting the holy name, fame, etc., of the Lord. The simple process of offenselessly chanting and hearing the holy name of the Lord will gradually promote one very soon to the stage of emancipation. There are three stages in chanting the holy name of the Lord. The first stage is the offensive chanting of the holy name, and the second is the reflective stage of chanting the holy name. The third stage is the offenseless chanting of the holy name of the Lord. In the second stage only, the stage of reflection, between the offensive and offenseless stages, one automatically attains the stage of emancipation. And in the offenseless stage, one actually enters into the kingdom of God, although physically he may apparently be within the material world. To attain the offenseless stage, one must be on guard in the following manner.

When we speak of hearing and chanting, it means that not only should one chant and hear of the holy name of the Lord as Rāma, Kṛṣṇa (or systematically the sixteen names Hare Kṛṣṇa, Hare Kṛṣṇa, Kṛṣṇa Kṛṣṇa, Hare Hare/ Hare Rāma, Hare Rāma, Rāma Rāma, Hare Hare), but one should also read and hear the *Bhagavad-gītā* and *Śrīmad-Bhāgavatam* in the association of devotees. The primary practice of *bhakti-yoga* will cause the seed already sowed in heart to sprout, and by a regular watering process, as mentioned above, the *bhakti-yoga* creeper will begin to grow. By systematic nurturing, the creeper will grow to such an extent that it will penetrate the coverings of the universe, as we have heard in the previous verses, reach the effulgent sky, the *brahmajyoti,* and go farther and farther and reach the spiritual sky, where there are innumerable spiritual planets called Vaikuṇṭhalokas. Above all of them is Kṛṣṇaloka, or Goloka Vṛndāvana, wherein the growing creeper enters and takes repose at the lotus feet of Lord Śrī Kṛṣṇa, the original Personality of Godhead. When one reaches the lotus feet of Lord Kṛṣṇa at Goloka Vṛndāvana, the watering process of hearing and reading, as also chanting of the holy name in the pure devotional stage, fructifies, and the fruits grown there in the form of love of God are tangibly tasted by the devotee, even though he is here in this material world. The ripe fruits of love of God are relished only by the devotees constantly engaged in the watering process as described above. But the working devotee must always be mindful so that the creeper which has so grown will not be cut off. Therefore he should be mindful of the following considerations:

1) Offense by one at the feet of a pure devotee may be likened to the mad elephant who devastates a very good garden if it enters.

2) One must be very careful to guard himself against such offenses at the feet of pure devotees, just as one protects a creeper by all-around fencing.

3) It so happens that by the watering process some weeds are also grown, and unless such weeds are uprooted, the nurturing of the main creeper, or the creeper of *bhakti-yoga*, may be hampered.

4) Actually these weeds are material enjoyment, merging of the self in the Absolute without separate individuality, and many other desires in the field of religion, economic development, sense enjoyment and emancipation.

5) There are many other weeds, like disobedience to the tenets of the revered scriptures, unnecessary engagements, killing animals, and hankering after material gain, prestige and adoration.

6) If sufficient care is not taken, then the watering process may only help to breed the weeds, stunting the healthy growth of the main creeper and resulting in no fructification of the ultimate requirement: love of God.

7) The devotee must therefore be very careful to uproot the different weeds in the very beginning. Only then will the healthy growth of the main creeper not be stunted.

8) And by so doing, the devotee is able to relish the fruit of love of God and thus live practically with Lord Kṛṣṇa, even in this life, and be able to see the Lord in every step.

The highest perfection of life is to enjoy life constantly in the association of the Lord, and one who can relish this does not aspire after any temporary enjoyment of the material world via other media.

TEXT 31

तेनात्मनात्मानमुपैति शान्त-
मानन्दमानन्दमयोऽवसाने ।
एतां गतिं भागवतीं गतो यः
स वै पुनर्नेह विषज्जतेऽङ्ग ॥३१॥

tenātmanātmānam upaiti śāntam
ānandam ānandamayo 'vasāne
etāṁ gatiṁ bhāgavatīṁ gato yaḥ
sa vai punar neha viṣajjate 'ṅga

tena—by that purified; *ātmanā*—by the self; *ātmānam*—the Supersoul; *upaiti*—attains; *śāntam*—rest; *ānandam*—satisfaction; *ānandamayaḥ*—naturally so being; *avasāne*—being freed from all material contamination; *etām*—such; *gatim*—destination; *bhāgavatīm*—devotional; *gataḥ*—attained by; *yaḥ*—the person; *saḥ*—he; *vai*—certainly; *punaḥ*—again; *na*—never; *iha*—in this material world; *viṣajjate*—becomes attracted; *aṅga*—O Mahārāja Parīkṣit.

TRANSLATION

Only the purified soul can attain the perfection of associating with the Personality of Godhead in complete bliss and satisfaction in his constitutional state. Whoever is able to renovate such devotional perfection is never again attracted by this material world, and he never returns.

PURPORT

We should specially note in this verse the description of *gatiṁ bhāgavatīm.* To become merged in the rays of the Parabrahman, the Supreme Personality of Godhead, as desired by the *brahmavādī* impersonalist, is not *bhāgavatīm* perfection. The *bhāgavatas* never accept merging in the impersonal rays of the Lord, but always aspire after personal association with the Supreme Lord in one of the Vaikuṇṭha spiritual planets in the spiritual sky. The whole of the spiritual sky, of which the total number of the material skies is only an insignificant part, is full of unlimited numbers of Vaikuṇṭha planets. The destination of the devotee (the *bhāgavata*) is to enter into one of the Vaikuṇṭha planets, in each of which the Personality of Godhead, in His unlimited personal expansions, enjoys Himself in the association of unlimited numbers of pure devotee associates. The conditioned souls in the material world, after gaining emancipation by devotional service, are promoted to these planets. But the number of ever-liberated souls is far, far greater than the number of conditioned souls in the material world, and the ever-liberated souls in the Vaikuṇṭha planets never care to visit this miserable material world.

The impersonalists, who aspire to merge in the impersonal *brahmajyoti* effulgence of the Supreme Lord but have no conception of loving devotional service to Him in His personal form in the spiritual manifestation, may be compared to certain species of fish, who, being born in the rivers and rivulets, migrate to the great ocean. They cannot stay in the ocean indefinitely, for their urge for sense gratification brings them back to the rivers and streams to spawn. Similarly, when the materialist becomes frustrated in his attempts to enjoy himself in the limited material world, he may seek impersonal liberation by merging either with the Causal Ocean or with the impersonal *brahmajyoti* effulgence. However, as neither the Causal Ocean nor the impersonal *brahmajyoti* effulgence affords any superior substitute for association and engagement of the senses, the impersonalist will fall again into the limited material world to become entangled once more in the wheel of births and deaths, drawn on by the inextinguishable desire for sensual engagement. But any devotee who enters the kingdom of God by transcendental engagement of his senses in devotional service, and who associates with the liberated souls and the Personality of Godhead there, will never be attracted to the limited surroundings of the material world.

In the *Bhagavad-gītā* (8.15) also the same is confirmed, as the Lord says, "The great *mahātmās*, or the *bhakti-yogīs*, after attaining My association, never come back to this material world, which is full of miseries and is nonpermanent." The highest perfection of life, therefore, is to attain His association, and nothing else. The *bhakti-yogī*, being completely engaged in the Lord's service, has no attraction for any other process of liberation like *jñāna* or *yoga.* A pure devotee is a one hundred percent devotee of the Lord and nothing more.

We should further note in this verse the two words *śāntam* and *ānandam*, which denote that devotional service of the Lord can really bestow upon the devotee two important benedictions, namely peace and satisfaction. The impersonalist is desirous of becoming one with the Supreme, or in other words, he wants to become the Supreme. This is a myth only. The mystic *yogīs* become encumbered by various mystic powers and so have neither peace nor satisfaction. So neither the impersonalists nor the *yogī* can have real peace and satisfaction, but the devotee can become fully peaceful and satisfied because of his association with the complete whole. Therefore, merging in the Absolute or attaining some mystic powers has no attraction for the devotee.

Attainment of love of Godhead means complete freedom from all other attractions. The conditioned soul has many aspirations such as becoming a religious man, a rich man, or a first-class enjoyer or becoming God himself, or becoming powerful like the mystics and acting wonderfully by getting anything or doing anything, but all these aspirations should be rejected by the prospective devotee who actually wants to revive his dormant love of God. The impure devotee aspires after all of the above-mentioned material things by perfection of devotion. But a pure devotee has none of the tinges of the above contaminations, which are the influence of material desires, impersonal speculations and attainment of mystic powers. One can attain the stage of love of God by pure devotional service, or by "a learned labor of love," for the sake of the devotee's lovable object, the Personality of Godhead.

To be more clear, if one wants to attain the stage of love of Godhead, he must give up all desires for material enjoyment, he should refrain from worshiping any of the demigods, and he should devote himself only to the worship of the Supreme Personality of Godhead. He must give up the foolish idea of becoming one with the Lord and the desire to have some wonderful powers just to get the ephemeral adoration of the world. The pure devotee is only favorably engaged in the service of the Lord, without any hope of emolument. This will bring about love of Godhead, or the stage of *śāntam* and *ānandam*, as stated in this verse.

TEXT 32

एते सृती ते नृप वेदगीते
त्वयाभिपृष्टे च सनातने च ।
ये वै पुरा ब्रह्मण आह तुष्ट
आराधितो भगवान् वासुदेवः ॥३२॥

ete sṛtī te nṛpa veda-gīte
tvayābhipṛṣṭe ca sanātane ca
ye vai purā brahmaṇa āha tuṣṭa
ārādhito bhagavān vāsudevaḥ

ete—all that is described; *sṛtī*—way; *te*—unto you; *nṛpa*—O Mahārāja Parīkṣit; *veda-gīte*—according to the version of the *Vedas; tvayā*—by Your Majesty; *abhipṛṣṭe*—being properly inquired; *ca*—also; *sanātane*—in the matter of eternal truth; *ca*—verily; *ye*—which; *vai*—certainly; *purā*—before; *brahmaṇe*—unto Lord Brahmā; *āha*—said; *tuṣṭaḥ*—being satisfied; *ārādhitaḥ*—being worshiped; *bhagavān*—the Personality of Godhead; *vāsudevaḥ*—Lord Kṛṣṇa.

TRANSLATION

Your Majesty Mahārāja Parīkṣit, know that all that I have described in reply to your proper inquiry is just according to the version of the Vedas, and it is eternal truth. This was described personally by Lord Kṛṣṇa unto Brahmā, with whom the Lord was satisfied upon being properly worshiped.

PURPORT

The two different ways of reaching the spiritual sky and thereby getting emancipation from all material bondage, namely either the direct process of reaching the kingdom of God or the gradual process through the other higher planets of the universe, are set forth exactly according to the version of the *Vedas*. The Vedic versions in this connection are, *yadā sarve pramucyante kāmā ye 'sya hṛdi śritāḥ / atha martyo 'mṛto bhavaty atra brahma samaśnute* (*Bṛhad-āraṇyaka Up.* 4.4.7) and *te 'rcir abhisambhavanti* (*Bṛhad-āraṇyaka Up.* 6.2.15): "Those who are free from all material desires, which are diseases of the heart, are able to conquer death and enter the kingdom of God through the Arci planets." These Vedic versions corroborate the version of the *Śrīmad-Bhāgavatam,* and the latter is further confirmed by Śukadeva Gosvāmī, who affirms that the truth was disclosed by the Supreme Personality of Godhead Lord Śrī Kṛṣṇa, Vāsudeva, to Brahmā, the first authority on the *Vedas.* The disciplic succession holds that the *Vedas* were uttered by Lord Kṛṣṇa to Brahmā, by Brahmā to Nārada, and by Nārada to Vyāsadeva, and then by Vyāsadeva to Śukadeva Gosvāmī and so on. So there is no difference between the versions of all the authorities. The truth is eternal, and as such there cannot be any new opinion about the truth. That is the way of knowing the knowledge contained in the *Vedas.* It is not a thing to be understood by one's erudite scholarship or by the fashionable interpretations of mundane scholars. There is nothing to be added and nothing to be subtracted, because the truth is the truth. One has to accept, after all, *some* authority. The modern scientists are also authorities for the common man for some scientific truths. The common man follows the version of the scientist. This means that the common man follows the authority. The Vedic knowledge is also received in that way. The common man cannot argue about what is beyond the sky or beyond the universe; he must accept the versions of the *Vedas* as they are understood by the authorized disciplic succession. In the *Bhagavad-gītā* also the same process of understanding the *Gītā* is stated in the Fourth Chapter. If one does not follow the authoritative version of the *ācāryas,* he will vainly search after the truth mentioned in the *Vedas.*

TEXT 33

न ह्यतोऽन्यः शिवः पन्था विशतः संसृताविह ।
वासुदेवे भगवति भक्तियोगो यतो भवेत् ॥३३॥

na hy ato 'nyaḥ śivaḥ panthā
viśataḥ saṁsṛtāv iha
vāsudeve bhagavati
bhakti-yogo yato bhavet

na—never; *hi*—certainly; *ataḥ*—beyond this; *anyaḥ*—any other; *śivaḥ*—auspicious; *panthāḥ*—means; *viśataḥ*—wandering; *saṁsṛtau*—

in the material world; *iha*—in this life; *vāsudeve*—unto Lord Vāsudeva, Kṛṣṇa; *bhagavati*—the Personality of Godhead; *bhakti-yogaḥ*—direct devotional service; *yataḥ*—wherein; *bhavet*—may result in.

TRANSLATION

For those who are wandering in the material universe, there is no more auspicious means of deliverance than what is aimed at in the direct devotional service of Lord Kṛṣṇa.

PURPORT

As will be clarified in the next verse, devotional service, or direct *bhakti-yoga*, is the only absolute and auspicious means of deliverance from the grip of material existence. There are many indirect methods for deliverance from the clutches of material existence, but none of them is as easy and auspicious as *bhakti-yoga*. The means of *jñāna* and *yoga* and other allied disciplines are not independent in delivering a performer. Such activities help one to reach the stage of *bhakti-yoga* after many, many years. In the *Bhagavad-gītā* (12.5) it is said that those who are attached to the impersonal feature of the Absolute are liable to many troubles in the pursuit of their desired goal, and the empiricist philosophers, searching after the Absolute Truth, realize the importance of Vāsudeva realization as all in all after many, many births (Bg. 7.19). As far as *yoga* systems are concerned, it is also said in the *Bhagavad-gītā* (6.47) that amongst the mystics who pursue the Absolute Truth, the one who is always engaged in the service of the Lord is the greatest of all. And the last instruction in the *Bhagavad-gītā* (18.66) advises fully surrendering unto the Lord, leaving aside all other engagements or different processes for self-realization and liberation from material bondage. And the purport of all Vedic literatures is to induce one to accept the transcendental loving service of the Lord by all means.

As already explained in the texts of *Śrīmad-Bhāgavatam* (First Canto), either direct *bhakti-yoga* or the means which ultimately culminate in *bhakti-yoga*, without any tinge of fruitive activity, constitutes the highest form of religion. Everything else is simply a waste of time for the performer.

Śrīla Śrīdhara Svāmī and all other *ācāryas*, like Jīva Gosvāmī, agree that *bhakti-yoga* is not only easy, simple, natural and free from trouble, but is the only source of happiness for the human being.

TEXT 34

भगवान् ब्रह्म कार्त्स्न्येन त्रिरन्वीक्ष्य मनीषया ।
तदध्यवस्यत् कूटस्थो रतिरात्मन् यतो भवेत् ॥३४॥

bhagavān brahma kārtsnyena
trir anvīkṣya manīṣayā
tad adhyavasyat kūṭa-stho
ratir ātman yato bhavet

bhagavān—the great personality Brahmā; *brahma*—the *Vedas;* *kārtsnyena*—by summarization; *triḥ*—three times; *anvīkṣya*—scrutinizingly examined; *manīṣayā*—with scholarly attention; *tat*—that; *adhyavasyat*—ascertained it; *kūṭa-sthaḥ*—with concentration of the mind; *ratiḥ*—attraction; *ātman* (*ātmani*)—unto the Supreme Personality of Godhead Śrī Kṛṣṇa; *yataḥ*—by which; *bhavet*—it so happens.

TRANSLATION

The great personality Brahmā, with great attention and concentration of the mind, studied the Vedas three times, and after scrutinizingly examining them, he ascertained that attraction for the Supreme Personality of Godhead Śrī Kṛṣṇa is the highest perfection of religion.

PURPORT

Śrī Śukadeva Gosvāmī is referring to the highest Vedic authority, Lord Brahmā, who is the qualitative incarnation of Godhead. The *Vedas* were taught to Brahmājī in the beginning of the material creation. Although Brahmājī was to hear Vedic instructions directly from the Personality of Godhead, in order to satisfy the inquisitiveness of all prospective students of the *Vedas*, Brahmājī, just like a scholar, studied the *Vedas* three times, as generally done by all scholars. He studied with great attention, concentrating on the purpose of the *Vedas*, and after scrutinizingly examining the whole process, he ascertained that becoming a pure, unalloyed devotee of the Supreme Personality of Godhead Śrī Kṛṣṇa is the topmost perfection of all religious principles. And this is the last instruction of the *Bhagavad-gītā* directly presented by the Personality of Godhead. The Vedic conclusion is thus accepted by all *ācāryas*, and those who are against this conclusion are only *veda-vāda-ratas*, as explained in the *Bhagavad-gītā* (2.42).

TEXT 35

भगवान् सर्वभूतेषु लक्षितः स्वात्मना हरिः ।
दृश्यैर्बुद्ध्यादिभिर्द्रष्टा लक्षणैरनुमापकैः ॥३५॥

bhagavān sarva-bhūteṣu
lakṣitaḥ svātmanā hariḥ
dṛśyair buddhy-ādibhir draṣṭā
lakṣaṇair anumāpakaiḥ

bhagavān—the Personality of Godhead; *sarva*—all; *bhūteṣu*—in the living entities; *lakṣitaḥ*—is visible; *sva-ātmanā*—along with the self; *hariḥ*—the Lord; *dṛśyaiḥ*—by what is seen; *buddhi-ādibhiḥ*—by intelligence; *draṣṭā*—one who sees; *lakṣaṇaiḥ*—by different signs; *anumāpakaiḥ*—by hypothesis.

TRANSLATION

The Personality of Godhead Lord Śrī Kṛṣṇa is in every living being along with the individual soul. And this fact is perceived and hypothesized in our acts of seeing and taking help from the intelligence.

PURPORT

The general argument of the common man is that since the Lord is not visible to our eyes, how can one either surrender unto Him or render transcendental loving service unto Him? To such a common man, here is a practical suggestion given by Śrīla Śukadeva Gosvāmī as to how one can perceive the Supreme Lord by reason and perception. Actually the Lord is not perceivable by our present materialized senses, but when one is convinced of the presence of the Lord by a practical service attitude, there is a revelation by the Lord's mercy, and such a pure devotee of the Lord can perceive the Lord's presence always and everywhere. He can perceive that intelligence is the form-direction of the Paramātmā plenary portion of the Personality of Godhead. The presence of Paramātmā in everyone's company is not very difficult to realize, even for the common man. The procedure is as follows. One can perceive one's self-identification and feel positively that he exists. He may not feel it very abruptly, but by using a little intelligence, he can feel that he is not the body. He can feel that the hand, the leg, the head, the hair and the limbs are all his bodily parts and parcels, but as such the hand, the leg, the head, etc., cannot be identified with his self. Therefore just by using intelligence he can distinguish and separate his self from other things that he sees. So the natural conclusion is that the living being, either man or beast, is the seer, and he sees besides himself all other things. So there is a difference between the seer and the seen. Now, by a little use of intelligence we can also readily agree that the living being who sees the things beyond himself by ordinary vision has no power to see or to move independently. All our ordinary actions and perceptions depend on various forms of energy supplied to us by nature in various combinations. Our senses of perception and of action, that is to say, our five perceptive senses of (1) hearing, (2) touch, (3) sight, (4) taste and (5) smell, as well as our five senses of action, namely (1) hands, (2) legs, (3) speech, (4) evacuation organs and (5) reproductive organs, and also our three subtle senses, namely (1) mind, (2) intelligence and (3) ego (thirteen senses in all), are supplied to us by various arrangements of gross or subtle forms of natural energy. And it is equally evident that our objects of perception are nothing but the products of the inexhaustible permutations and combinations of the forms taken by natural energy. As this conclusively proves that the ordinary living being has no independent power of perception or of motion, and as we undoubtedly feel our existence being conditioned by nature's energy, we conclude that he who sees is spirit, and that the senses as well as the objects of perception are material. The spiritual quality of the seer is manifest in our dissatisfaction with the limited state of materially conditioned existence. That is the difference between spirit and matter. There are some less intelligent arguments that matter develops the power of seeing and moving as a certain organic development, but such an argument cannot be accepted because there is no experimental evidence that matter has anywhere produced a living entity. Trust no future, however pleasant. Idle talks regarding future development of matter into spirit are actually foolish because no matter has ever developed the power of seeing or moving in any part of the world. Therefore it is definite that matter and spirit are two different identities, and this conclusion is arrived at by the use of intelligence. Now we come to the point that the things which are seen by a little use of intelligence cannot be animate unless we accept someone as the user of or director of the intelligence. Intelligence gives one direction like some higher authority, and the living being cannot see or move or eat or do anything without the use of intelligence. When one fails to take advantage of intelligence he becomes a deranged man, and so a living being is dependent on intelligence or the direction of a superior being. Such intelligence is all-pervading. Every living being has his intelligence, and this intelligence, being the direction of some higher authority, is just like a father giving direction to his son. The higher authority, who is present and residing within every individual living being, is the Superself.

At this point in our investigation, we may consider the following question: on the one hand we realize that all our perceptions and activities are conditioned by arrangements of material nature, yet we also ordinarily feel and say, "I am perceiving" or "I am doing." Therefore we can say that our material senses of perception and action are moving because we are identifying the self with the material body, and that the superior principle of Superself is guiding and supplying us according to our desire. By taking advantage of the guidance of Superself in the form of intelligence, we can either continue to study and to put into practice our conclusion that "I am not this body," or we can choose to remain in the false material identification, fancying ourselves to be the possessors and doers. Our freedom consists in orienting our desire either toward the ignorant, material misconception or the true, spiritual conception. We can easily attain to the true, spiritual conception by recognizing the Superself (Paramātmā) to be our friend and guide and by dovetailing our intelligence with the superior intelligence of Paramātmā. The Superself and the individual self are both spirit, and therefore the Superself and the individual self are both qualitatively one and distinct from matter. But the

Superself and the individual self cannot be on an equal level because the Superself gives direction or supplies intelligence and the individual self follows the direction, and thus actions are performed properly. The individual is completely dependent on the direction of the Superself because in every step the individual self follows the direction of the Superself in the matter of seeing, hearing, thinking, feeling, willing, etc.

So far as common sense is concerned, we come to the conclusion that there are three identities, namely matter, spirit and Superspirit. Now if we go to the *Bhagavad-gītā*, or the Vedic intelligence, we can further understand that all three identities, namely matter, individual spirit, and the Superspirit, are all dependent on the Supreme Personality of Godhead. The Superself is a partial representation or plenary portion of the Supreme Personality of Godhead. The *Bhagavad-gītā* affirms that the Supreme Personality of Godhead dominates all over the material world by His partial representation only. God is great, and He cannot be simply an order supplier of the individual selves; therefore the Superself cannot be a full representation of the Supreme Self, Puruṣottama, the Absolute Personality of Godhead. Realization of the Superself by the individual self is the beginning of self-realization, and by the progress of such self-realization one is able to realize the Supreme Personality of Godhead by intelligence, by the help of authorized scriptures, and, principally, by the grace of the Lord. The *Bhagavad-gītā* is the preliminary conception of the Personality of Godhead Śrī Kṛṣṇa, and *Śrīmad-Bhāgavatam* is the further explanation of the science of Godhead. So if we stick to our determination and pray for the mercy of the director of intelligence sitting within the same bodily tree, like a bird sitting with another bird (as explained in the *Upaniṣads*), certainly the purport of the revealed information in the *Vedas* becomes clear to our vision, and there is no difficulty in realizing the Supreme Personality of Godhead, Vāsudeva. The intelligent man therefore, after many births of such use of intelligence, surrenders himself at the lotus feet of Vāsudeva, as confirmed by the *Bhagavad-gītā* (7.19).

TEXT 36

तस्मात् सर्वात्मना राजन् हरिः सर्वत्र सर्वदा ।
श्रोतव्यः कीर्तितव्यश्च स्मर्तव्यो भगवान्नृणाम् ॥३६॥

tasmāt sarvātmanā rājan
hariḥ sarvatra sarvadā
śrotavyaḥ kīrtitavyaś ca
smartavyo bhagavān nṛṇām

tasmāt—therefore; *sarva*—all; *ātmanā*—soul; *rājan*—O King; *hariḥ*—the Lord; *sarvatra*—everywhere; *sarvadā*—always; *śrotavyaḥ*—must be heard; *kīrtitavyaḥ*—glorified; *ca*—also; *smartavyaḥ*—be remembered; *bhagavān*—the Personality of Godhead; *nṛṇām*—by the human being.

TRANSLATION

O King, it is therefore essential that every human being hear about, glorify and remember the Supreme Lord, the Personality of Godhead, always and everywhere.

PURPORT

Śrīla Śukadeva Gosvāmī begins this verse with the word *tasmāt*, or "therefore," because in the previous verse he has already explained that there is no auspicious means for salvation other than the sublime process of *bhakti-yoga*. The *bhakti-yoga* process is practiced by the devotees in different methods like hearing, chanting, remembering, serving the lotus feet of the Lord, worshiping, praying, rendering service in love, becoming friendly, and offering all that one may possess. All nine methods are bona fide methods, and either all of them, some of them or even one of them can bring about the desired result for the sincere devotee. But out of all the nine different methods, the first one, namely hearing, is the most important function in the process of *bhakti-yoga*. Without hearing sufficiently and properly, no one can make any progress by any of the methods of practice. And for hearing only, all the Vedic literatures are there, compiled by authorized persons like Vyāsadeva, who is the powerful incarnation of Godhead. And since it has been ascertained that the Lord is the Supersoul of everything, He should therefore be heard and glorified everywhere and always. That is the special duty of the human being. When the human being gives up the process of hearing about the all-pervading Personality of Godhead, he becomes victim to hearing rubbish transmitted by man-made machines. Machinery is not bad because through the machine one can take advantage of hearing about the Lord, but because machinery is used for ulterior purposes, it is creating rapid degradation in the standard of human civilization. It is said here that it is incumbent upon the human beings to hear because the scriptures like *Bhagavad-gītā* and *Śrīmad-Bhāgavatam* are made for that purpose. Living beings other than human beings have no ability to hear such Vedic literatures. If human society gives itself to the process of hearing the Vedic literature, it will not become a victim to the impious sounds vibrated by impious men who degrade the standards of the total society. Hearing is solidified by the process of chanting. One who has perfectly heard from the perfect source becomes convinced about the all-pervading Personality of Godhead and thus becomes enthusiastic in glorifying the Lord. All the great *ācāryas*, like Rāmānuja, Madhva, Caitanya, Sarasvatī Ṭhākura or even, in other countries, Muhammad, Christ and others, have all extensively glorified the Lord by chanting always and in every place. Because the Lord is all-pervading, it is essential to glorify Him always and everywhere. In the process of glorifying the Lord there should be no restriction of time and space. This is called *sanātana-dharma* or *bhāgavata-dharma. Sanātana* means eternal, always and everywhere. *Bhāgavata* means pertaining to Bhagavān, the Lord. The Lord is the master of all time and all space, and therefore the Lord's holy name must be heard, glorified and remembered everywhere in the world. That will bring about the desired peace and prosperity so eagerly awaited by the people of the world. The word *ca* includes all the remaining processes or methods of *bhakti-yoga*, as mentioned above.

TEXT 37

पिबन्ति ये भगवत आत्मनः सतां
कथामृतं श्रवणपुटेषु सम्भृतम् ।
पुनन्ति ते विषयविदूषिताशयं
व्रजन्ति तच्चरणसरोरुहान्तिकम् ॥३७॥

pibanti ye bhagavata ātmanaḥ satāṁ
kathāmṛtaṁ śravaṇa-puṭeṣu sambhṛtam
punanti te viṣaya-vidūṣitāśayaṁ
vrajanti tac-caraṇa-saroruhāntikam

pibanti—who drink; *ye*—those; *bhagavataḥ*—of the Personality of Godhead; *ātmanaḥ*—of the most dear; *satām*—of devotees; *kathā-amṛtam*—the nectar of the messages; *śravaṇa-puṭeṣu*—within the earholes; *sambhṛtam*—fully filled; *punanti*—purify; *te*—their; *viṣaya*—material enjoyment; *vidūṣita-āśayam*—polluted aim of life; *vrajanti*—do go back; *tat*—the Lord's; *caraṇa*—feet; *saroruha-antikam*—near the lotus.

TRANSLATION

Those who drink through aural reception, fully filled with the nectarean message of Lord Kṛṣṇa, the beloved of the devotees, purify the polluted aim of life known as material enjoyment and thus go back to Godhead, to the lotus feet of Him [the Personality of Godhead].

PURPORT

The sufferings of human society are due to a polluted aim of life, namely lording it over the material resources. The more human society engages in the exploitation of undeveloped material resources for sense gratification, the more it will be entrapped by the illusory, material energy of the Lord, and thus the distress of the world will be intensified instead of diminished. The human necessities of life are fully supplied by the Lord in the shape of food grains, milk, fruit, wood, stone, sugar, silk, jewels, cotton, salt, water, vegetables, etc., in sufficient quantity to feed and care for the human race of the world as well as the living beings on each and every planet within the universe. The supply source is complete, and only a little energy by the human being is required to get his necessities into the proper channel. There is no need of machines and tools or huge steel plants for artificially creating comforts of life. Life is never made comfortable by artificial needs, but by plain living and high thinking. The highest perfectional thinking for human society is suggested here by Śukadeva Gosvāmī, namely, sufficiently hearing *Śrīmad-Bhāgavatam.* For men in this age of Kali, when they have lost the perfect vision of life, this *Śrīmad-Bhāgavatam* is the torchlight by which to see the real path. Śrīla Jīva Gosvāmī Prabhupāda has commented on the *kathāmṛtam* mentioned in this verse and has indicated *Śrīmad-*

Bhāgavatam to be the nectarean message of the Personality of Godhead. By sufficient hearing of *Śrīmad-Bhāgavatam,* the polluted aim of life, namely lording it over matter, will subside, and the people in general in all parts of the world will be able to live a peaceful life of knowledge and bliss.

For a pure devotee of the Lord, any topics in relation with His name, fame, quality, entourage, etc., are all pleasing, and because such topics have been approved by great devotees like Nārada, Hanumān, Nanda Mahārāja and other inhabitants of Vṛndāvana, certainly such messages are transcendental and pleasing to the heart and soul.

And by the constant hearing of the messages of the *Bhagavad-gītā,* and later of *Śrīmad-Bhāgavatam,* one is assured herein by Śrīla Śukadeva Gosvāmī that he will reach the Personality of Godhead and render Him transcendental loving service in the spiritual planet of the name Goloka Vṛndāvana, which resembles a huge lotus flower.

Thus by the process of *bhakti-yoga,* directly accepted, as suggested in this verse, by sufficient hearing of the transcendental message of the Lord, the material contamination is directly eliminated without one's attempting to contemplate the impersonal *virāṭ* conception of the Lord. And by practicing *bhakti-yoga,* if the performer is not purified from the material contamination, he must be a pseudodevotee. For such an imposter there is no remedy for being freed from material entanglement.

Thus end the Bhaktivedanta purports of the Second Canto, Second Chapter, of the Śrīmad-Bhāgavatam, *entitled "The Lord in the Heart."*

CHAPTER THREE

Pure Devotional Service: The Change in Heart

TEXT 1

श्रीशुक उवाच

एवमेतन्निगदितं पृष्टवान् यद्भवान् मम ।
नृणां यन्म्रियमाणानां मनुष्येषु मनीषिणाम् ॥ १ ॥

śrī-śuka uvāca
evam etan nigaditaṁ
pṛṣṭavān yad bhavān mama
nṛṇāṁ yan mriyamāṇānāṁ
manuṣyeṣu manīṣiṇām

śrī-śukaḥ uvāca—Śrī Śukadeva Gosvāmī said; *evam*—so; *etat*—all these; *nigaditam*—answered; *pṛṣṭavān*—as you inquired; *yat*—what; *bhavān*—your good self; *mama*—unto me; *nṛṇām*—of the human being; *yat*—one; *mriyamāṇānām*—on the threshold of death; *manuṣyeṣu*—amongst the human beings; *manīṣiṇām*—of the intelligent men.

TRANSLATION

Śrī Śukadeva Gosvāmī said: Mahārāja Parīkṣit, as you have inquired from me as to the duty of the intelligent man who is on the threshold of death, so I have answered you.

PURPORT

In human society all over the world there are millions and billions of men and women, and almost all of them are less intelligent because they have very little knowledge of spirit soul. Almost all of them have a wrong conception of life, for they identify themselves with the gross and subtle material bodies, which they are not, in fact. They may be situated in different high and low positions in the estimation of human society, but one should know definitely that unless one inquires about his own self beyond the body and the mind, all his activities in human life are total failures. Therefore out of thousands and thousands of men, one may inquire about his spirit self and thus consult the revealed scriptures like *Vedānta-sūtras*, *Bhagavad-gītā* and *Śrīmad-Bhāgavatam*. But in spite of reading and hearing such scriptures, unless one is in touch with a realized spiritual master, he cannot actually realize the real nature of self, etc. And out of thousands and hundreds of thousands of men, someone may know what Lord Kṛṣṇa is in fact. In the *Caitanya-caritāmṛta* (*Madhya* 20.122–123) it is said that Lord Kṛṣṇa, out of His causeless mercy, prepared the Vedic literatures in the incarnation of Vyāsadeva for reading by the intelligent class of men in a human society which is almost totally forgetful of the genuine relation with Kṛṣṇa. Even such an intelligent class of men may be forgetful in their relation with the Lord. The whole *bhakti-yoga* process is therefore a revival of the lost relation. This revival is possible in the human form of life, which is obtained only out of the evolutionary cycle of 8,400,000 species of life. The intelligent class of human being must take a serious note of this opportunity. Not all human beings are intelligent, so the importance of human life is not always understood. Therefore *manīṣiṇām*, meaning "thoughtful," is particularly used here. A *manīṣiṇām* person, like Mahārāja Parīkṣit, must therefore take to the lotus feet of Lord Kṛṣṇa and fully engage himself in devotional service, hearing, chanting, etc., of the holy name and pastimes of the Lord, which are all *hari-kathāmṛta*. This action is especially recommended when one is preparing for death.

TEXTS 2–7

ब्रह्मवर्चसकामस्तु यजेत ब्रह्मणः पतिम् ।
इन्द्रमिन्द्रियकामस्तु प्रजाकामः प्रजापतीन् ॥ २ ॥
देवीं मायां तु श्रीकामस्तेजस्कामो विभावसुम् ।
वसुकामो वसून् रुद्रान् वीर्यकामोऽथ वीर्यवान् ॥३॥
अन्नाद्यकामस्त्वदितिं स्वर्गकामोऽदितेः सुतान् ।
विश्वान्देवान् राज्यकामः साध्यान्संसाधको विशाम् ॥४॥

आयुष्कामोऽश्विनौ देवौ पुष्टिकाम इलां यजेत् ।
प्रतिष्ठाकामः पुरुषो रोदसी लोकमातरौ ॥ ५ ॥
रूपाभिकामो गन्धर्वान् स्त्रीकामोऽप्सर उर्वशीम् ।
आधिपत्यकामः सर्वेषां यजेत परमेष्ठिनम् ॥ ६ ॥
यज्ञं यजेद् यशस्कामः कोशकामः प्रचेतसम् ।
विद्याकामस्तु गिरिशं दाम्पत्यार्थ उमां सतीम् ॥ ७ ॥

brahma-varcasa-kāmas tu
yajeta brahmaṇaḥ patim
indram indriya-kāmas tu
prajā-kāmaḥ prajāpatīn

devīṁ māyāṁ tu śrī-kāmas
tejas-kāmo vibhāvasum
vasu-kāmo vasūn rudrān
vīrya-kāmo 'tha vīryavān

annādya-kāmas tv aditiṁ
svarga-kāmo 'diteḥ sutān
viśvān devān rājya-kāmaḥ
sādhyān saṁsādhako viśām

āyuṣ-kāmo 'śvinau devau
puṣṭi-kāma ilāṁ yajet
pratiṣṭhā-kāmaḥ puruṣo
rodasī loka-mātarau

rūpābhikāmo gandharvān
strī-kāmo 'psara urvaśīm
ādhipatya-kāmaḥ sarveṣāṁ
yajeta parameṣṭhinam

yajñaṁ yajed yaśas-kāmaḥ
kośa-kāmaḥ pracetasam
vidyā-kāmas tu giriśaṁ
dāmpatyārtha umāṁ satīm

brahma—the absolute; *varcasa*—effulgence; *kāmaḥ tu*—but one who desires in that way; *yajeta*—do worship; *brahmaṇaḥ*—of the *Vedas; patim*—the master; *indram*—the King of heaven; *indriya-kāmaḥ tu*—but one who desires strong sense organs; *prajā-kāmaḥ*—one who desires many offspring; *prajāpatīn*—the Prajāpatis; *devīm*—the goddess; *māyām*—unto the mistress of the material world; *tu*—but; *śrī-kāmaḥ*—one who desires beauty; *tejaḥ*—power; *kāmaḥ*—one who so desires; *vibhāvasum*—the fire-god; *vasu-kāmaḥ*—one who wants wealth; *vasūn*—the Vasu demigods; *rudrān*—the Rudra expansions of Lord Śiva; *vīrya-kāmaḥ*—one who wants to be very strongly built; *atha*—therefore; *vīryavān*—the most powerful; *anna-adya*—grains; *kāmaḥ*—one who so desires; *tu*—but; *aditim*—Aditi, mother of the demigods; *svarga*—heaven; *kāmaḥ*—so desiring; *aditeḥ sutān*—the sons of Aditi; *viśvān*—Viśvadeva; *devān*—demigods; *rājya-kāmaḥ*—those who hanker for kingdoms; *sādhyān*—the Sādhya demigods; *saṁsādhakaḥ*—what fulfills the wishes; *viśām*—of the mercantile community; *āyuḥ-kāmaḥ*—desirous of long life; *aśvinau*—the two demigods known as the Aśvinī brothers; *devau*—the two demigods; *puṣṭi-kāmaḥ*—one who desires a strongly built body; *ilām*—the earth; *yajet*—must worship; *pratiṣṭhā-kāmaḥ*—one who desires good fame, or stability in a post; *puruṣaḥ*—such men; *rodasī*—the horizon; *loka-mātarau*—and the earth; *rūpa*—beauty; *abhikāmaḥ*—positively aspiring for; *gandharvān*—the residents of the Gandharva planet, who are very beautiful and are expert in singing; *strī-kāmaḥ*—one who desires a good wife; *apsaraḥ urvaśīm*—the society girls of the heavenly kingdom; *ādhipatya-kāmaḥ*—one who desires to dominate others; *sarveṣām*—everyone; *yajeta*—must worship; *parameṣṭhinam*—Brahmā, the head of the universe; *yajñam*—the Personality of Godhead; *yajet*—must worship; *yaśaḥ-kāmaḥ*—one who desires to be famous; *kośa-kāmaḥ*—one who desires a good bank balance; *pracetasam*—the treasurer of heaven, known as Varuṇa; *vidyā-kāmaḥ tu*—but one who desires education; *giriśam*—the lord of the Himalayas, Lord Śiva; *dāmpatya-arthaḥ*—and for conjugal love; *umām satīm*—the chaste wife of Lord Śiva, known as Umā.

TRANSLATION

One who desires to be absorbed in the impersonal brahmajyoti effulgence should worship the master of the Vedas [Lord Brahmā

or Bṛhaspati, the learned priest], one who desires powerful sex should worship the heavenly King, Indra, and one who desires good progeny should worship the great progenitors called the Prajāpatis. One who desires good fortune should worship Durgādevī, the superintendent of the material world. One desiring to be very powerful should worship fire, and one who aspires only after money should worship the Vasus. One should worship the Rudra incarnations of Lord Śiva if he wants to be a great hero. One who wants a large stock of grains should worship Aditi. One who desires to attain the heavenly planets should worship the sons of Aditi. One who desires a worldly kingdom should worship Viśvadeva, and one who wants to be popular with the general mass of population should worship the Sādhya demigod. One who desires a long span of life should worship the demigods known as the Aśvinī-kumāras, and a person desiring a strongly built body should worship the earth. One who desires stability in his post should worship the horizon and the earth combined. One who desires to be beautiful should worship the beautiful residents of the Gandharva planet, and one who desires a good wife should worship the Apsarās and the Urvaśī society girls of the heavenly kingdom. One who desires domination over others should worship Lord Brahmā, the head of the universe. One who desires tangible fame should worship the Personality of Godhead, and one who desires a good bank balance should worship the demigod Varuṇa. If one desires to be a greatly learned man he should worship Lord Śiva, and if one desires a good marital relation he should worship the chaste goddess Umā, the wife of Lord Śiva.

PURPORT

There are different modes of worship for different persons desiring success in particular subjects. The conditioned soul living within the purview of the material world cannot be an expert in every type of materially enjoyable asset, but one can have considerable influence over a particular matter by worshiping a particular demigod, as mentioned above. Rāvaṇa was made a very powerful man by worshiping Lord Śiva, and he used to offer severed heads to please Lord Śiva. He became so powerful by the grace of Lord Śiva that all the demigods were afraid of him, until he at last challenged the Personality of Godhead Śrī Rāmacandra and thus ruined himself. In other words, all such persons who aspire after gaining some or all of the material objects of enjoyment, or the gross materialistic persons, are on the whole less intelligent, as confirmed in the *Bhagavad-gītā* (7.20). It is said there that those who are bereft of all good sense, or those whose intelligence is withdrawn by the deluding energy of *māyā*, aspire to achieve all sorts of material enjoyment in life by pleasing the various demigods, or by advancing in material civilization under the heading of scientific progress. The real problem of life in the material world is to solve the question of birth, death, old age and disease. No one wants to change his birthright, no one wants to meet death, no one wants to be old or invalid, and no one wants diseases. But these problems are solved neither by the grace of any demigod nor by the so-called advancement of material science. In the *Bhagavad-gītā*, as well as in the *Śrīmad-Bhāgavatam*, such less intelligent persons have been described as devoid of all good sense. Śukadeva Gosvāmī said that out of the 8,400,000 species of living entities, the human form of life is rare and valuable, and out of those rare human beings those who are conscious of the material problems are rarer still, and the still more rare persons are those who are conscious of the value of the *Śrīmad-Bhāgavatam*, which contains the messages of the Lord and His pure devotees. Death is inevitable for everyone, intelligent or foolish. But Parīkṣit Mahārāja has been addressed by the Gosvāmī as the *manīṣī*, or the man of highly developed mind, because at the time of death he left all material enjoyment and completely surrendered unto the lotus feet of the Lord by hearing His messages from the right person, Śukadeva Gosvāmī. But aspirations for material enjoyment by endeavoring persons are condemned. Such aspirations are something like the intoxication of the degraded human society. Intelligent persons should try to avoid these aspirations and seek instead the permanent life by returning home, back to Godhead.

TEXT 8

धर्मार्थ उत्तमश्लोकं तन्तुः तन्वन् पितॄन् यजेत् ।
रक्षाकामः पुण्यजनानोजस्कामो मरुद्गणान् ॥ ८ ॥

dharmārtha uttama-ślokaṁ
tantuḥ tanvan pitṝn yajet
rakṣā-kāmaḥ puṇya-janān
ojas-kāmo marud-gaṇān

dharma-arthaḥ—for spiritual advancement; *uttama-ślokam*—the Supreme Lord or persons attached to the Supreme Lord; *tantuḥ*—for offspring; *tanvan*—and for their protection; *pitṝn*—the residents of Pitṛloka; *yajet*—must worship; *rakṣā-kāmaḥ*—one who desires protection; *puṇya-janān*—pious persons; *ojaḥ-kāmaḥ*—one who desires strength should worship; *marut-gaṇān*—the demigods.

TRANSLATION

One should worship Lord Viṣṇu or His devotee for spiritual advancement in knowledge, and for protection of heredity and advancement of a dynasty one should worship the various demigods.

PURPORT

The path of religion entails making progress on the path of spiritual advancement, ultimately reviving the eternal relation with Lord Viṣṇu in His impersonal effulgence, His localized Paramātmā feature, and ultimately His personal feature by spiritual advancement in knowledge. And one who wants to establish a good dynasty and be happy in the progress of temporary bodily relations should take shelter of the Pitās and the demigods in other pious planets. Such different classes of worshipers of different demigods may ultimately reach the respective planets of those demigods within the universe, but he who reaches the spiritual planets in the *brahmajyoti* achieves the highest perfection.

TEXT 9

राज्यकामो मनून् देवान् निर्ऋतिं त्वभिचरन् यजेत् ।
कामकामो यजेत् सोममकामः पुरुषं परम् ॥ ९ ॥

rājya-kāmo manūn devān
nirṛtiṁ tv abhicaran yajet

kāma-kāmo yajet somam
akāmaḥ puruṣaṁ param

rājya-kāmaḥ—anyone desiring an empire or kingdom; *manūn*—the Manus, semi-incarnations of God; *devān*—demigods; *nirṛtim*—demons; *tu*—but; *abhicaran*—desiring victory over the enemy; *yajet*—should worship; *kāma-kāmaḥ*—one who desires sense gratification; *yajet*—should worship; *somam*—the demigod named Candra; *akāmaḥ*—one who has no material desires to be fulfilled; *puruṣam*—the Supreme Personality of Godhead; *param*—the Supreme.

TRANSLATION

One who desires domination over a kingdom or an empire should worship the Manus. One who desires victory over an enemy should worship the demons, and one who desires sense gratification should worship the moon. But one who desires nothing of material enjoyment should worship the Supreme Personality of Godhead.

PURPORT

For a liberated person, all the enjoyments listed above are considered to be absolutely useless. Only those who are conditioned by the material modes of external energy are captivated by different types of material enjoyment. In other words, the transcendentalist has no material desires to be fulfilled, whereas the materialist has all types of desires to be fulfilled. The Lord has proclaimed that the materialists, who desire material enjoyment and thus seek the favor of different demigods, as above mentioned, are not in control of their senses and so give themselves to nonsense. One should therefore not desire any sort of material enjoyment, being sensible enough to worship the Supreme Personality of Godhead. The leaders of nonsensical persons are still more nonsensical because they preach openly and foolishly that one can worship any form of demigod and get the same result. This sort of preaching is not only against the teachings of the *Bhagavad-gītā*, or those of the *Śrīmad-Bhāgavatam*, but is also foolish, just as it is foolish to claim that with the purchase of any travel ticket one may reach the same destination. No one can reach Bombay from Delhi by purchasing a ticket for Baroda. It is clearly defined herein that persons impregnated with different desires have different modes of worship, but one who has no desire for material enjoyment should worship the Supreme Lord, Śrī Kṛṣṇa, the Personality of Godhead. And this worshiping process is called devotional service. Pure devotional service means service to the Lord without any tinge of material desires, including desire for fruitive activity and empiric speculation. For fulfillment of material desires one may worship the Supreme Lord, but the result of such worship is different, as will be explained in the next verse. Generally the Lord does not fulfill anyone's material desires for sense enjoyment, but He awards such benedictions to worshipers of the Lord, for they ultimately come to the point of not desiring material enjoyment. The conclusion is that one must minimize the desires for material enjoyment, and for this one should worship the Supreme Personality of Godhead, who is described here as *param*, or beyond anything material. Śrīpāda Śaṅkarācārya has also stated, *nārāyaṇaḥ paro 'vyaktāt:* the Supreme Lord is beyond the material encirclement.

TEXT 10

अकामः सर्वकामो वा मोक्षकाम उदारधीः ।
तीव्रेण भक्तियोगेन यजेत पुरुषं परम् ॥१०॥

akāmaḥ sarva-kāmo vā
mokṣa-kāma udāra-dhīḥ
tīvreṇa bhakti-yogena
yajeta puruṣaṁ param

akāmaḥ—one who has transcended all material desires; *sarva-kāmaḥ*—one who has the sum total of material desires; *vā*—either; *mokṣa-kāmaḥ*—one who desires liberation; *udāra-dhīḥ*—with broader intelligence; *tīvreṇa*—with great force; *bhakti-yogena*—by devotional service to the Lord; *yajeta*—should worship; *puruṣam*—the Lord; *param*—the supreme whole.

TRANSLATION

A person who has broader intelligence, whether he be full of all material desire, without any material desire, or desiring liberation, must by all means worship the supreme whole, the Personality of Godhead.

PURPORT

The Supreme Personality of Godhead Lord Śrī Kṛṣṇa is described in the *Bhagavad-gītā* as *puruṣottama*, or the Supreme Personality. It is He only who can award liberation to the impersonalists by absorbing such aspirants in the *brahmajyoti*, the bodily rays of the Lord. The *brahmajyoti* is not separate from the Lord, as the glowing sun ray is not independent of the sun disc. Therefore one who desires to merge into the supreme impersonal *brahmajyoti* must also worship the Lord by *bhakti-yoga*, as recommended here in the *Śrīmad-Bhāgavatam. Bhakti-yoga* is especially stressed here as the means of all perfection. In the previous chapters it has been stated that *bhakti-yoga* is the ultimate goal of both *karma-yoga* and *jñāna-yoga*, and in the same way in this chapter it is emphatically declared that *bhakti-yoga* is the ultimate goal of the different varieties of worship of the different demigods. *Bhakti-yoga*, thus being the supreme means of self-realization, is recommended here. Everyone must therefore seriously take up the methods of *bhakti-yoga*, even though one aspires for material enjoyment or liberation from material bondage.

Akāmaḥ is one who has no material desire. A living being, naturally being the part and parcel of the supreme whole *puruṣaṁ pūrṇam*, has as his natural function to serve the Supreme Being, just as the parts and parcels of the body, or the limbs of the body, are naturally meant to serve the complete body. Desireless means, therefore, not to be inert like the stone, but to be conscious of one's actual position and thus desire satisfaction only from the Supreme Lord. Śrīla Jīva Gosvāmī has explained this desirelessness as *bhajanīya-parama-puruṣa-sukha-mātra-sva-sukhatvam* in his *Sandarbha*. This means that one should feel happy only by experiencing the happiness of the Supreme Lord. This intuition of the living being is sometimes manifested even during the conditioned stage of a living being in the material world, and such intuition is expressed in the manner of altruism, philanthropy, socialism, communism, etc., by the undeveloped minds of less intelligent persons. In the mundane field such an outlook of doing good to others in the form of society, community, family, country or humanity is a partial manifestation of the same original feeling in which a pure living entity feels happiness by the happiness of the Supreme Lord. Such superb feelings were exhibited by the damsels of Vrajabhūmi for the happiness of the Lord.

The *gopīs* loved the Lord without any return, and this is the perfect exhibition of the *akāmaḥ* spirit. *Kāma* spirit, or the desire for one's own satisfaction, is fully exhibited in the material world, whereas the spirit of *akāmaḥ* is fully exhibited in the spiritual world.

Thoughts of becoming one with the Lord, or being merged in the *brahmajyoti*, can also be exhibitions of *kāma* spirit if they are desires for one's own satisfaction to be free from the material miseries. A pure devotee does not want liberation so that he may be relieved from the miseries of life. Even without so-called liberation, a pure devotee is aspirant for the satisfaction of the Lord. Influenced by the *kāma* spirit, Arjuna declined to fight in the Kurukṣetra battlefield because he wanted to save his relatives for his own satisfaction. But being a pure devotee, he agreed to fight on the instruction of the Lord because he came to his senses and realized that satisfaction of the Lord at the cost of his own satisfaction was his prime duty. Thus he became *akāma*. That is the perfect stage of a perfect living being.

Udāra-dhīḥ means one who has a broader outlook. People with desires for material enjoyment worship small demigods, and such intelligence is condemned in the *Bhagavad-gītā* (7.20) as *hṛta-jñāna*, the intelligence of one who has lost his senses. One cannot obtain any result from demigods without getting sanction from the Supreme Lord. Therefore a person with a broader outlook can see that the ultimate authority is the Lord, even for material benefits. Under the circumstances, one with a broader outlook, even with the desire for material enjoyment or for liberation, should take to the worship of the Lord directly. And everyone, whether an *akāma* or *sakāma* or *mokṣa-kāma*, should worship the Lord with great expedience. This implies that *bhakti-yoga* may be perfectly administered without any mixture of *karma* and *jñāna*. As the unmixed sun ray is very forceful and is therefore called *tīvra*, similarly unmixed *bhakti-yoga* of hearing, chanting, etc., may be performed by one and all regardless of inner motive.

TEXT 11

एतावानेव यजतामिह निःश्रेयसोदयः ।
भगवत्यचलो भावो यद् भागवतसंगतः ॥११॥

etāvān eva yajatām
iha niḥśreyasodayaḥ
bhagavaty acalo bhāvo
yad bhāgavata-saṅgataḥ

etāvān—all these different kinds of worshipers; *eva*—certainly; *yajatām*—while worshiping; *iha*—in this life; *niḥśreyasa*—the highest benediction; *udayaḥ*—development; *bhagavati*—unto the Supreme Personality of Godhead; *acalaḥ*—unflinching; *bhāvaḥ*—spontaneous attraction; *yat*—which; *bhāgavata*—the pure devotee of the Lord; *saṅgataḥ*—association.

TRANSLATION

All the different kinds of worshipers of multidemigods can attain the highest perfectional benediction, which is spontaneous attraction unflinchingly fixed upon the Supreme Personality of Godhead, only by the association of the pure devotee of the Lord.

PURPORT

All living entities in different statuses of life within the material creation, beginning from the first demigod, Brahmā, down to the small ant, are conditioned under the law of material nature, or the external energy of the Supreme Lord. The living entity in his pure state is conscious of the fact that he is a part and parcel of the Lord, but when he is thrown into the material world on account of his desire to lord it over material energy, he becomes conditioned by the three modes of material nature and thus struggles for existence for the highest benefit. This struggle for existence is something like following the will-o'-the-wisp under the spell of material enjoyment. All plans for material enjoyment, either by worship of different demigods as described in the previous verses of this chapter or by modernized advancement of scientific knowledge without the help of God or demigod, are illusory only, for despite all such plans for happiness, the conditioned living being within the compass of material creation can never solve the problems of life, namely birth, death, old age and disease. The history of the universe is full of such planmakers, and many kings and emperors come and go, leaving a planmaking story only. But the prime problems of life remain unsolved despite all endeavors by such planmakers.

Actually human life is meant for making a solution to the problems of life. One can never solve such problems by satisfying the different demigods, by different modes of worship, or by so-called scientific advancement in knowledge without the help of God or the demigods. Apart from the gross materialists, who care very little either for God or for the demigods, the *Vedas* recommend worship of different demigods for different benefits, and so the demigods are neither false nor imaginary. The demigods are as factual as we are, but they are much more powerful due to their being engaged in the direct service of the Lord in managing different departments in the universal government. The *Bhagavad-gītā* affirms this, and the different planets of the demigods are mentioned there, including the one of the supreme demigod, Lord Brahmā. The gross materialists do not believe in the existence of God or the demigods. Nor do they believe that different planets are dominated by different demigods. They are creating a great commotion about reaching the closest celestial body, Candraloka, or the moon, but even after much mechanical research they have only very scanty information of this moon, and in spite of much false advertisement for selling land on the moon, the puffed-up scientists or gross materialists cannot live there, and what to speak of reaching the other planets, which they are unable even to count. However, the followers of the *Vedas* have a different method of acquiring knowledge. They accept the statements of the Vedic literatures as authority *in toto*, as we have already discussed in Canto One, and therefore they have full and reasonable knowledge of God and demigods and of their different residential planets situated within the compass of the material world and beyond the limit of the material sky. The most authentic Vedic literature, accepted by the great Indian *ācāryas* like Śaṅkara, Rāmānuja, Madhva, Viṣṇusvāmī, Nimbārka and Caitanya and studied by all important personalities of the world, is the *Bhagavad-gītā*, in which the worship of the demigods and their respective residential planets are mentioned. The *Bhagavad-gītā* (9.25) affirms:

yānti deva-vratā devān
pitṝn yānti pitṛ-vratāḥ

bhūtāni yānti bhūtejyā
yānti mad-yājino 'pi mām

"The worshipers of demigods reach the respective planets of the demigods, and the worshipers of forefathers reach the planets of the forefathers. The gross materialist remains in the different material planets, but the devotees of the Lord reach the kingdom of God."

We also have information from the *Bhagavad-gītā* that all the planets within the material world, including Brahmaloka, are but temporarily situated, and after a fixed period they are all annihilated. Therefore the demigods and their followers are all annihilated at the period of devastation, but one who reaches the kingdom of God gets a permanent share in eternal life. That is the verdict of Vedic literature. The worshipers of the demigods have one facility more than the unbelievers due to their being convinced of the Vedic version, by which they can get information of the benefit of worshiping the Supreme Lord in the association of the devotees of the Lord. The gross materialist, however, without any faith in the Vedic version, remains eternally in darkness, driven by a false conviction on the basis of imperfect experimental knowledge, or so-called material science, which can never reach into the realm of transcendental knowledge.

Therefore unless the gross materialists or the worshipers of the temporary demigods come in contact with a transcendentalist like the pure devotee of the Lord, their attempts are simply a waste of energy. Only by the grace of the divine personalities, the pure devotees of the Lord, can one achieve pure devotion, which is the highest perfection of human life. Only a pure devotee of the Lord can show one the right way of progressive life. Otherwise both the materialistic way of life, without any information of God or the demigods, and the life engaged in the worship of demigods, in pursuit of temporary material enjoyments, are different phases of phantasmagoria. They are nicely explained in the *Bhagavad-gītā* also, but the *Bhagavad-gītā* can be understood in the association of pure devotees only, and not by the interpretations of politicians or dry philosophical speculators.

TEXT 12

ज्ञानं यदाप्रतिनिवृत्तगुणोर्मिचक्र-
मात्मप्रसाद उत यत्र गुणेष्वसङ्गः ।

कैवल्यसम्मतपथस्त्वथ भक्तियोगः
को निर्वृतो हरिकथासु रतिं न कुर्यात् ॥१२॥

jñānaṁ yad āpratinivṛtta-guṇormi-cakram
ātma-prasāda uta yatra guṇeṣv asaṅgaḥ
kaivalya-sammata-pathas tv atha bhakti-yogaḥ
ko nirvṛto hari-kathāsu ratiṁ na kuryāt

jñānam—knowledge; *yat*—that which; *ā*—up to the limit of; *pratinivṛtta*—completely withdrawn; *guṇa-ūrmi*—the waves of the material modes; *cakram*—whirlpool; *ātma-prasādaḥ*—self-satisfaction; *uta*—moreover; *yatra*—where there is; *guṇeṣu*—in the modes of nature; *asaṅgaḥ*—no attachment; *kaivalya*—transcendental; *sammata*—approved; *pathaḥ*—path; *tu*—but; *atha*—therefore; *bhakti-yogaḥ*—devotional service; *kaḥ*—who; *nirvṛtaḥ*—absorbed in; *hari-kathāsu*—in the transcendental topics of the Lord; *ratim*—attraction; *na*—shall not; *kuryāt*—do.

TRANSLATION

Transcendental knowledge in relation with the Supreme Lord Hari is knowledge resulting in the complete suspension of the waves and whirlpools of the material modes. Such knowledge is self-satisfying due to its being free from material attachment, and being transcendental it is approved by authorities. Who could fail to be attracted?

PURPORT

According to *Bhagavad-gītā* (10.9) the characteristics of pure devotees are wonderful. The complete functional activities of a pure devotee are always engaged in the service of the Lord, and thus the pure devotees exchange feelings of ecstasy between themselves and relish transcendental bliss. This transcendental bliss is experienced even in the stage of devotional practice (*sādhana-avasthā*), if properly undertaken under the guidance of a bona fide spiritual master. And in the mature stage the developed transcendental feeling culminates in realization of the particular relationship with the Lord by which a living entity is originally constituted (up to the relationship of conjugal love with the Lord, which is estimated to be the highest transcendental bliss). Thus *bhakti-yoga*, being the only means of God realization, is called *kaivalya.* Śrīla Jīva Gosvāmī quotes the Vedic version (*eko nārāyaṇo devaḥ, parāvarāṇāṁ parama āste kaivalya-saṁjñitaḥ*) in this connection and establishes that Nārāyaṇa, the Personality of Godhead, is known as *kaivalya*, and the means which enables one to approach the Lord is called the *kaivalya-panthā*, or the only means of attainment of Godhead. This *kaivalya-panthā* begins from *śravaṇa*, or hearing those topics that relate to the Personality of Godhead, and the natural consequence of hearing such *hari-kathā* is attainment of transcendental knowledge, which causes detachment from all mundane topics, for which a devotee has no taste at all. For a devotee, all mundane activities, social and political, become unattractive, and in the mature state such a devotee becomes uninterested even in his own body, and what to speak of bodily relatives. In such a state of affairs one is not agitated by the waves of the material modes. There are different modes of material nature, and all mundane functions in which a common man is very much interested or in which he takes part become unattractive for the devotee. This state of affairs is described herein as *pratinivṛtta-guṇormi*, and it is possible by *ātma-prasāda*, or complete self-satisfaction without any material connection. The first-class devotee of the Lord attains this stage by devotional service, but despite his loftiness, for the Lord's satisfaction he may play the voluntary part of a preacher of the Lord's glory and dovetail all into devotional service, even mundane interest, just to give the neophytes a chance to transform mundane interest into transcendental bliss. Śrīla Rūpa Gosvāmī has described this action of a pure devotee as *nirbandhaḥ kṛṣṇa-sambandhe yuktaṁ vairāgyam ucyate.* Even mundane activities dovetailed with service to the Lord are also calculated to be transcendental or approved *kaivalya* affairs.

TEXT 13

शौनक उवाच
इत्यभिव्याहृतं राजा निशम्य भरतर्षभः ।
किमन्यत्पृष्टवान् भूयो वैयासकिमृषिं कविम् ॥१३॥

śaunaka uvāca
ity abhivyāhṛtaṁ rājā
niśamya bharatarṣabhaḥ

kim anyat pṛṣṭavān bhūyo
vaiyāsakim ṛṣiṁ kavim

śaunakaḥ uvāca—Śaunaka said; *iti*—thus; *abhivyāhṛtam*—all that was spoken; *rājā*—the King; *niśamya*—by hearing; *bharata-ṛṣabhaḥ*—Mahārāja Parīkṣit; *kim*—what; *anyat*—more; *pṛṣṭavān*—did he inquire from him; *bhūyaḥ*—again; *vaiyāsakim*—unto the son of Vyāsadeva; *ṛṣim*—one who is well versed; *kavim*—poetic.

TRANSLATION

Śaunaka said: The son of Vyāsadeva, Śrīla Śukadeva Gosvāmī, was a highly learned sage and was able to describe things in a poetic manner. What did Mahārāja Parīkṣit again inquire from him after hearing all that he had said?

PURPORT

A pure devotee of the Lord automatically develops all godly qualities, and some of the prominent features of those qualities are as follows: he is kind, peaceful, truthful, equable, faultless, magnanimous, mild, clean, nonpossessive, a well-wisher to all, satisfied, surrendered to Kṛṣṇa, without hankering, simple, fixed, self-controlled, a balanced eater, sane, mannerly, prideless, grave, sympathetic, friendly, *poetic*, expert and silent. Out of these twenty-six prominent features of a devotee, as described by Kṛṣṇadāsa Kavirāja in his *Caitanya-caritāmṛta*, the qualification of being poetic is especially mentioned herein in relation to Śukadeva Gosvāmī. The presentation of *Śrīmad-Bhāgavatam* by his recitation is the highest poetic contribution. He was a self-realized learned sage. In other words, he was a poet amongst the sages.

TEXT 14

एतच्छुश्रूषतां विद्वन् सूत नोऽर्हसि भाषितुम् ।
कथा हरिकथोदर्काः सतां स्युः सदसि ध्रुवम् ॥१४॥

etac chuśrūṣatāṁ vidvan
sūta no 'rhasi bhāṣitum
kathā hari-kathodarkāḥ
satāṁ syuḥ sadasi dhruvam

etat—this; *śuśrūṣatām*—of those eager to hear; *vidvan*—O learned; *sūta*—Sūta Govāmī; *naḥ*—unto us; *arhasi*—may you do it; *bhāṣitum*—just to explain it; *kathāḥ*—topics; *hari-kathā-udarkāḥ*—result in the topics of the Lord; *satām*—of the devotees; *syuḥ*—may be; *sadasi*—in the assembly of; *dhruvam*—certainly.

TRANSLATION

O learned Sūta Gosvāmī! Please continue to explain such topics to us because we are all eager to hear. Besides that, topics which result in the discussion of the Lord Hari should certainly be discussed in the assembly of devotees.

PURPORT

As we have already quoted above from the *Bhakti-rasāmṛta-sindhu* of Rūpa Gosvāmī, even mundane things, if dovetailed in the service of the Lord Śrī Kṛṣṇa, are accepted as transcendental. For example, the epics or the histories of *Rāmāyaṇa* and *Mahābhārata*, which are specifically recommended for the less intelligent classes (women, *śūdras* and unworthy sons of the higher castes), are also accepted as Vedic literature because they are compiled in connection with the activities of the Lord. *Mahābhārata* is accepted as the fifth division of the *Vedas* after its first four divisions, namely *Sāma*, *Yajur*, *Ṛg* and *Atharva*. The less intelligent do not accept *Mahābhārata* as part of the *Vedas*, but great sages and authorities accept it as the fifth division of the *Vedas*. *Bhagavad-gītā* is also part of the *Mahābhārata*, and it is full of the Lord's instruction for the less intelligent class of men. Some less intelligent men say that *Bhagavad-gītā* is not meant for householders, but such foolish men forget that *Bhagavad-gītā* was explained to Arjuna, a *gṛhastha* (family man), and spoken by the Lord in His role as a *gṛhastha*. So *Bhagavad-gītā*, although containing the high philosophy of the Vedic wisdom, is for the beginners in the transcendental science, and *Śrīmad-Bhāgavatam* is for graduates and postgraduates in the transcendental science. Therefore literatures like *Mahābhārata*, the *Purāṇas* and similar other literatures which are full of the pastimes of the Lord, are all transcendental literatures, and they should be discussed with full confidence in the society of great devotees.

The difficulty is that such literatures, when discussed by professional men, appear to be mundane literature like histories or epics because there are so many historical facts and figures. It is said here, therefore, that such literatures should be discussed in the assembly of devotees. Unless they are discussed by devotees, such literatures cannot be relished by the higher class of men. So the conclusion is that the Lord is not impersonal in the ultimate issue. He is the Supreme Person, and He has His different activities. He is the leader of all living entities, and He descends at His will and by His personal energy to reclaim the fallen souls. Thus He plays exactly like the social, political or religious leaders. Because such roles ultimately culminate in the discussion of topics of the Lord, all such preliminary topics are also transcendental. That is the way of spiritualizing the civic activities of human society. Men have inclinations for studying history and many other mundane literatures—stories, fiction, dramas, magazines, newspapers, etc.—so let them be dovetailed with the transcendental service of the Lord, and all of them will turn to the topics relished by all devotees. The propaganda that the Lord is impersonal, that He has no activity and that He is a dumb stone without any name and form has encouraged people to become godless, faithless demons, and the more they deviate from the transcendental activities of the Lord, the more they become accustomed to mundane activities that only clear their path to hell instead of return them home, back to Godhead.* *Śrīmad-Bhāgavatam* begins from the history of the Pāṇḍavas (with necessary politics and social activities), and yet *Śrīmad-Bhāgavatam* is said to be the *Pāramahaṁsa-saṁhitā*, or the Vedic literature meant for the topmost transcendentalist, and it describes *paraṁ jñānam*, the highest transcendental knowledge. Pure devotees of the Lord are all *paramahaṁsas*, and they are like the swans, who know the art of sucking milk out of a mixture of milk and water.

---

*Even fifty years ago, the social structure of all Indians was so arranged that they would not read any literature that was not connected with the activities of the Lord. They would not play any drama not connected with the Lord. They would not organize a fair or ceremony not connected with the Lord. Nor would they visit a place that was not holy and sanctified by the pastimes of the Lord. Therefore even the common man in the village would talk about *Rāmāyaṇa* and *Mahābhārata*, *Gītā* and *Bhāgavatam*, even from his very childhood. But by the influence of the age of Kali, they have been dragged to the civilization of the dogs and hogs, laboring for bread without any sense of transcendental knowledge.

TEXT 15

स वै भागवतो राजा पाण्डवेयो महारथः ।
बालक्रीडनकैः क्रीडन् कृष्णक्रीडां य आददे ॥१५॥

sa vai bhāgavato rājā
pāṇḍaveyo mahā-rathaḥ
bāla-krīḍanakaiḥ krīḍan
kṛṣṇa-krīḍāṁ ya ādade

saḥ—he; *vai*—certainly; *bhāgavataḥ*—a great devotee of the Lord; *rājā*—Mahārāja Parīkṣit; *pāṇḍaveyaḥ*—grandson of the Pāṇḍavas; *mahā-rathaḥ*—a great fighter; *bāla*—while a child; *krīḍanakaiḥ*—with play dolls; *krīḍan*—playing; *kṛṣṇa*—Lord Kṛṣṇa; *krīḍām*—activities; *yaḥ*—who; *ādade*—accepted.

TRANSLATION

Mahārāja Parīkṣit, the grandson of the Pāṇḍavas, was from his very childhood a great devotee of the Lord. Even while playing with dolls, he used to worship Lord Kṛṣṇa by imitating the worship of the family Deity.

PURPORT

In the *Bhagavad-gītā* (6.41) it is stated that even a person who has failed in the proper discharge of *yoga* practice is given a chance to take birth in the house of devout *brāhmaṇas* or in the houses of rich men like *kṣatriya* kings or rich merchants. But Mahārāja Parīkṣit was more than that because he had been a great devotee of the Lord since his previous birth, and as such he took his birth in an imperial family of the Kurus, and especially that of the Pāṇḍavas. So from the very beginning of his childhood he had the chance to know intimately the devotional service of Lord Kṛṣṇa in his own family. The Pāṇḍavas, all being devotees of the Lord, certainly venerated family Deities in the royal palace for worship. Children who appear in such families fortunately generally imitate such worship of the Deities, even in the way of childhood play. By the grace of Lord Śrī Kṛṣṇa, we had the chance of being born in a Vaiṣṇava family, and in our childhood we imitated the worship of Lord Kṛṣṇa by imitating our father. Our father encouraged us in all respects to observe all functions such as the Ratha-yātrā and Dola-yātrā ceremonies, and he used to spend money liberally for distributing *prasāda* to us children and our friends. Our spiritual master, who also took his birth in a Vaiṣṇava family, got all inspirations from his great Vaiṣṇava father, Ṭhākura Bhaktivinoda. That is the way of all lucky Vaiṣṇava families. The celebrated Mīrā Bāī was a staunch devotee of Lord Kṛṣṇa as the great lifter of Govardhana Hill.

The life history of many such devotees is almost the same because there is always symmetry between the early lives of all great devotees of the Lord. According to Jīva Gosvāmī, Mahārāja Parīkṣit must have heard about the childhood pastimes of Lord Kṛṣṇa at Vṛndāvana, for he used to imitate the pastimes with his young playmates. According to Śrīdhara Svāmī, Mahārāja Parīkṣit used to imitate the worship of the family Deity by elderly members. Śrīla Viśvanātha Cakravartī also confirms the viewpoint of Jīva Gosvāmī. So accepting either of them, Mahārāja Parīkṣit was naturally inclined to Lord Kṛṣṇa from his very childhood. He might have imitated either of the above-mentioned activities, and all of them establish his great devotion from his very childhood, a symptom of a *mahā-bhāgavata.* Such *mahā-bhāgavatas* are called *nitya-siddhas*, or souls liberated from birth. But there are also others, who may not be liberated from birth but who develop a tendency for devotional service by association, and they are called *sādhana-siddhas.* There is no difference between the two in the ultimate issue, and so the conclusion is that everyone can become a *sādhana-siddha*, a devotee of the Lord, simply by association with the pure devotees. The concrete example is our great spiritual master Śrī Nārada Muni. In his previous life he was simply a boy of a maidservant, but through association with great devotees he became a devotee of the Lord of his own standard, unique in the history of devotional service.

TEXT 16

वैयासकिश्च भगवान् वासुदेवपरायणः ।
उरुगायगुणोदाराः सतां स्युर्हि समागमे ॥१६॥

vaiyāsakiś ca bhagavān
vāsudeva-parāyaṇaḥ
urugāya-guṇodārāḥ
satāṁ syur hi samāgame

vaiyāsakiḥ—the son of Vyāsadeva; *ca*—also; *bhagavān*—full in transcendental knowledge; *vāsudeva*—Lord Kṛṣṇa; *parāyaṇaḥ*—attached to; *urugāya*—of the Personality of Godhead Śrī Kṛṣṇa, who is glorified by great philosophers; *guṇa-udārāḥ*—great qualities; *satām*—of the devotees; *syuḥ*—must have been; *hi*—as a matter of fact; *samāgame*—by the presence of.

TRANSLATION

Śukadeva Gosvāmī, the son of Vyāsadeva, was also full in transcendental knowledge and was a great devotee of Lord Kṛṣṇa, son of Vasudeva. So there must have been discussion of Lord Kṛṣṇa, who is glorified by great philosophers and in the company of great devotees.

PURPORT

The word *satām* is very important in this verse. *Satām* means the pure devotees, who have no other desire than to serve the Lord. Only in the association of such devotees are the transcendental glories of Lord Kṛṣṇa properly discussed. It is said by the Lord that His topics are all full of spiritual significance, and once one properly hears about Him in the association of the *satām*, certainly one senses the great potency and so automatically attains to the devotional stage of life. As already described, Mahārāja Parīkṣit was a great devotee of the Lord from his very birth, and so was Śukadeva Gosvāmī. Both of them were on the same level, although it appeared that Mahārāja Parīkṣit was a great king accustomed to royal facilities whereas Śukadeva Gosvāmī was a typical renouncer of the world, so much so that he did not even put a cloth on his body. Superficially, Mahārāja Parīkṣit and Śukadeva Gosvāmī might seem to be opposites, but basically they were both unalloyed pure devotees of the Lord. When such devotees are assembled together, there can be no topics save discussions of the glories of the Lord, or *bhakti-yoga*. In the *Bhagavad-*

gītā also, when there were talks between the Lord and His devotee Arjuna, there could not be any topic other than *bhakti-yoga*, however the mundane scholars may speculate on it in their own ways. The use of the word *ca* after *vaiyāsakiḥ* suggests, according to Śrīla Jīva Gosvāmī, that both Śukadeva Gosvāmī and Mahārāja Parīkṣit were of the same category, settled long before, although one was playing the part of the master and the other the disciple. Since Lord Kṛṣṇa is the center of the topics, the word *vāsudeva-parāyaṇaḥ*, or "devotee of Vāsudeva," suggests devotee of Lord Kṛṣṇa, the common aim. Although there were many others who assembled at the place where Mahārāja Parīkṣit was fasting, the natural conclusion is that there was no topic other than the glorification of Lord Kṛṣṇa, because the principal speaker was Śukadeva Gosvāmī and the chief audience was Mahārāja Parīkṣit. So *Śrīmad-Bhāgavatam*, as it was spoken and heard by two principal devotees of the Lord, is only for the glorification of the Supreme Lord, the Personality of Godhead, Śrī Kṛṣṇa.

TEXT 17

आयुर्हरति वै पुंसामुद्यन्नस्तं च यन्नसौ ।
तस्यर्ते यत्क्षणो नीत उत्तमश्लोकवार्तया ॥१७॥

āyur harati vai puṁsām
udyann astaṁ ca yann asau
tasyarte yat-kṣaṇo nīta
uttama-śloka-vārtayā

āyuḥ—duration of life; *harati*—decreases; *vai*—certainly; *puṁsām*—of the people; *udyan*—rising; *astam*—setting; *ca*—also; *yan*—moving; *asau*—the sun; *tasya*—of one who glorifies the Lord; *ṛte*—except; *yat*—by whom; *kṣaṇaḥ*—time; *nītaḥ*—utilized; *uttama-śloka*—the all-good Personality of Godhead; *vārtayā*—in the topics of.

TRANSLATION

Both by rising and by setting, the sun decreases the duration of life of everyone, except one who utilizes the time by discussing topics of the all-good Personality of Godhead.

PURPORT

This verse indirectly confirms the greater importance of utilizing the human form of life to realize our lost relationship with the Supreme Lord by acceleration of devotional service. Time and tide wait for no man. So the time indicated by the sunrise and the sunset will be uselessly wasted if such time is not properly utilized for realizing identification of spiritual values. Even a fraction of the duration of life wasted cannot be compensated by any amount of gold. Human life is simply awarded to a living entity (*jīva*) so that he can realize his spiritual identity and his permanent source of happiness. A living being, especially the human being, is seeking happiness because happiness is the natural situation of the living entity. But he is vainly seeking happiness in the material atmosphere. A living being is constitutionally a spiritual spark of the complete whole, and his happiness can be perfectly perceived in spiritual activities. The Lord is the complete spirit whole, and His name, form, quality, pastimes, entourage and personality are all identical with Him. Once a person comes into contact with any one of the above-mentioned energies of the Lord through the proper channel of devotional service, the door to perfection is immediately opened. In the *Bhagavad-gītā* (2.40) the Lord has explained such contact in the following words: "Endeavors in devotional service are never baffled. Nor is there failure. A slight beginning of such activities is sufficient even to deliver a person from the great ocean of material fears." As a highly potent drug injected intravenously acts at once on the whole body, the transcendental topics of the Lord injected through the ear of the pure devotee of the Lord can act very efficiently. Aural realization of the transcendental messages implies total realization, just as fructification of one part of a tree implies fructification of all other parts. This realization for a moment in the association of pure devotees like Śukadeva Gosvāmī prepares one's complete life for eternity. And thus the sun fails to rob the pure devotee of his duration of life, inasmuch as he is constantly busy in the devotional service of the Lord, purifying his existence. Death is a symptom of the material infection of the eternal living being; only due to material infection is the eternal living entity subjected to the law of birth, death, old age and disease.

The materialistic way of pious activities like charity is recommended in the *smṛti-śāstras* as quoted by Śrīla Viśvanātha Cakravartī Ṭhākura. Money given in charity to a suitable person is guaranteed bank balance in the next life. Such charity is recommended to be given to a *brāhmaṇa.* If the money is given in charity to a non-*brāhmaṇa* (without brahminical qualification) the money is returned in the next life in the same proportion. If it is given in charity to a half-educated *brāhmaṇa*, even then the money is returned double. If the money is given in charity to a learned and fully qualified *brāhmaṇa*, the money is returned a hundred and a thousand times, and if the money is given to a *veda-pāraga* (one who has factually realized the path of the *Vedas*), it is returned by unlimited multiplication. The ultimate end of Vedic knowledge is realization of the Personality of Godhead, Lord Kṛṣṇa, as stated in the *Bhagavad-gītā* (*vedaiś ca sarvair aham eva vedyaḥ*). There is a guarantee of money's being returned if given in charity, regardless of the proportion. Similarly, a moment passed in the association of a pure devotee by hearing and chanting the transcendental messages of the Lord is a perfect guarantee for eternal life, for returning home, back to Godhead. *Mad-dhāma gatvā punar janma na vidyate.* In other words, a devotee of the Lord is guaranteed eternal life. A devotee's old age or disease in the present life is but an impetus to such guaranteed eternal life.

TEXT 18

तरवः किं न जीवन्ति भस्त्राः किं न श्वसन्त्युत ।
न खादन्ति न मेहन्ति किं ग्रामे पशवोऽपरे ॥१८॥

taravaḥ kiṁ na jīvanti
bhastrāḥ kiṁ na śvasanty uta
na khādanti na mehanti
kiṁ grāme paśavo 'pare

taravaḥ—the trees; *kim*—whether; *na*—do not; *jīvanti*—live; *bhastrāḥ*—bellows; *kim*—whether; *na*—do not; *śvasanti*—breathe; *uta*—also; *na*—do not; *khādanti*—eat; *na*—do not; *mehanti*—discharge semen; *kim*—whether; *grāme*—in the locality; *paśavaḥ*—beastly living being; *apare*—others.

TRANSLATION

Do the trees not live? Do the bellows of the blacksmith not breathe? All around us, do the beasts not eat and discharge semen?

PURPORT

The materialistic man of the modern age will argue that life, or part of it, is never meant for discussion of theosophical or theological arguments. Life is meant for the maximum duration of existence for eating, drinking, sexual intercourse, making merry and enjoying life. The modern man wants to live forever by the advancement of material science, and there are many foolish theories for prolonging life to the maximum duration. But the *Śrīmad-Bhāgavatam* affirms that life is not meant for so-called economic development or advancement of materialistic science for the hedonistic philosophy of eating, mating, drinking and merrymaking. Life is solely meant for *tapasya,* for purifying existence so that one may enter into eternal life just after the end of the human form of life.

The materialists want to prolong life as much as possible because they have no information of the next life. They want to get the maximum comforts in this present life because they think conclusively that there is no life after death. This ignorance about the eternity of the living being and the change of covering in the material world has played havoc in the structure of modern human society. Consequently there are many problems, multiplied by various plans of modernized man. The plans for solving the problems of society have only aggravated the troubles. Even if it is possible to prolong life more than one hundred years, advancement of human civilization does not necessarily follow. The *Bhāgavatam* says that certain trees live for hundreds and thousands of years. At Vṛndāvana there is a tamarind tree (the place is known as Imlitala) which is said to have existed since the time of Lord Kṛṣṇa. In the Calcutta Botanical Garden there is a banyan tree said to be older than five hundred years, and there are many such trees all over the world. Svāmī Śaṅkarācārya lived only thirty-two years, and Lord Caitanya lived forty-eight years. Does it mean that the prolonged lives of the above-mentioned trees are more important than Śaṅkara or Caitanya? Prolonged life without spiritual value is not very important. One may doubt that trees have life because they do not breathe. But modern scientists like Bose have already proved that there is life in plants, so breathing is no sign of actual life. The *Bhāgavatam* says that the bellows of the blacksmith breathes very soundly, but that does not mean that the bellows has life. The materialist will argue that life in the tree and life in the man cannot be compared because the tree cannot enjoy life by eating palatable dishes or by enjoying sexual intercourse. In reply to this, the *Bhāgavatam* asks whether other animals like the dogs and hogs, living in the same village with human beings, do not eat and enjoy sexual life. The specific utterance of *Śrīmad-Bhāgavatam* in regard to "other animals" means that persons who are simply engaged in planning a better type of animal life consisting of eating, breathing and mating are also animals in the shape of human beings. A society of such polished animals cannot benefit suffering humanity, for an animal can easily harm another animal but rarely do good.

TEXT 19

श्वविड्वराहोष्ट्रखरैः संस्तुतः पुरुषः पशुः ।
न यत्कर्णपथोपेतो जातु नाम गदाग्रजः ॥१९॥

śva-viḍ-varāhoṣṭra-kharaiḥ
saṁstutaḥ puruṣaḥ paśuḥ
na yat-karṇa-pathopeto
jātu nāma gadāgrajaḥ

śva—a dog; *viṭ-varāha*—the village hog who eats stool; *uṣṭra*—the camel; *kharaiḥ*—and by the asses; *saṁstutaḥ*—perfectly praised; *puruṣaḥ*—a person; *paśuḥ*—animal; *na*—never; *yat*—of him; *karṇa*—ear; *patha*—path; *upetaḥ*—reached; *jātu*—at any time; *nāma*—the holy name; *gadāgrajaḥ*—Lord Kṛṣṇa, the deliver from all evils.

TRANSLATION

Men who are like dogs, hogs, camels and asses praise those men who never listen to the transcendental pastimes of Lord Śrī Kṛṣṇa, the deliverer from evils.

PURPORT

The general mass of people, unless they are trained systematically for a higher standard of life in spiritual values, are no better than animals, and in this verse they have particularly been put on the level of dogs, hogs, camels and asses. Modern university education practically prepares one to acquire a doggish mentality with which to accept the service of a greater master. After finishing a so-called education, the so-called educated persons move like dogs from door to door with applications for some service, and mostly they are driven away, informed of no vacancy. As dogs are negligible animals and serve the master faithfully for bits of bread, a man serves a master faithfully without sufficient rewards.

Persons who have no discrimination in the matter of foodstuff and who eat all sorts of rubbish are compared to hogs. Hogs are very much attached to eating stools. So stool is a kind of foodstuff for a particular type of animal. And even stones are eatables for a particular type of animal or bird. But the human being is not meant for eating everything and anything; he is meant to eat grains, vegetables, fruits, milk, sugar, etc. Animal food is not meant for the human being. For chewing solid food, the human being has a particular type of teeth meant for cutting fruits and vegetables. The human being is endowed with two canine teeth as a concession for persons who will eat animal food at any cost. It is known to everyone that one man's food is another man's poison. Human beings are expected to accept the remnants of food offered to Lord Śrī Kṛṣṇa, and the Lord accepts foodstuff from the categories of leaves, flowers, fruits, etc. (Bg. 9.26). As prescribed by Vedic scriptures, no animal food is offered to the Lord. Therefore, a human being is meant to eat a particular type of food. He should not imitate the animals to derive so-called vitamin values. Therefore, a person who has no discrimination in regard to eating is compared to a hog.

The camel is a kind of animal that takes pleasure in eating thorns. A person who wants to enjoy family life or the worldly life of so-called enjoyment is compared to the camel. Materialistic life is full of thorns, and so one should live only by the prescribed method of Vedic regulations just to make the best use of a bad bargain. Life in the material world is maintained by sucking one's own blood. The central point of attraction for material enjoyment is sex life. To enjoy sex life is to suck one's own blood, and there is not much more to be explained in this connection. The camel also sucks its own blood while chewing thorny twigs. The thorns the camel eats cut the tongue of the camel, and so blood begins to flow within the camel's mouth. The thorns, mixed with fresh blood, create a taste for the foolish camel, and so he enjoys the thorn-eating business with false pleasure. Similarly, the great business magnates, industrialists who work very hard to earn money by different ways and questionable means, eat the thorny results of their actions mixed with their own blood. Therefore the *Bhāgavatam* has situated these diseased fellows along with the camels.

The ass is an animal who is celebrated as the greatest fool, even amongst the animals. The ass works very hard and carries burdens of the maximum weight without making profit for itself.* The ass is generally

---

*Human life is meant for earning values. This life is called *arthadam*, or that which can deliver values. And what is the greatest value of life? It is to return home, back to Godhead, as indicated in the *Bhagavad-gītā* (8.15). One's selfishness must be aimed at the point of going back to Godhead. The ass does not know his self-interest, and it works very hard for others only. A person who works very hard for others only, forgetting his personal interest available in the human form of life, is compared to the ass. In the *Brahma-vaivarta Purāṇa* it is said:

aśītiṁ caturaś caiva
lakṣāṁs tāñ jīva-jātiṣu
bhramadbhiḥ puruṣaiḥ prāpyaṁ
mānuṣyaṁ janma-paryayāt

tad apy abhalatāṁ jātaḥ
teṣām ātmābhimāninām
varākāṇām anāśritya
govinda-caraṇa-dvayam

The human life is so important that even the demigods in the higher planets sometimes aspire for a human body on this earth because in the human body only can one easily go back to Godhead. In spite of having obtained such an important body, if one does not reestablish his lost eternal relation with Govinda, Lord Kṛṣṇa, he is certainly a fool who has forgotten his self-interest. This human form of material body is obtained by a gradual process of evolution to one body after another in the cycle of 8,400,000 varieties of life. And the poor man, forgetting this importance for his own interest, involves himself in so many illusory engagements for uplifting the position of others as a leader of political emancipation and economic development. There is no harm in trying for political emancipation or economic development, but one should not forget the real aim of life: all such philanthropic activities must be dovetailed to returning to Godhead. One who does not know this is compared to the ass who works only for others, without their or his own welfare in mind.

engaged by the washerman, whose social position is not very respectable. And the special qualification of the ass is that it is very much accustomed to being kicked by the opposite sex. When the ass begs for sexual intercourse, he is kicked by the fair sex, yet he still follows the female for such sexual pleasure. A henpecked man is compared, therefore, to the ass. The general mass of people work very hard, especially in the age of Kali. In this age the human being is actually engaged in the work of an ass, carrying heavy burdens and driving *ṭhelā* and rickshaws. The so-called advancement of human civilization has engaged a human being in the work of an ass. The laborers in great factories and workshops are also engaged in such burdensome work, and after working hard during the day, the poor laborer has to be again kicked by the fair sex, not only for sex enjoyment but also for so many household affairs.

So *Śrīmad-Bhāgavatam's* categorization of the common man without any spiritual enlightenment into the society of dogs, hogs, camels and asses is not at all an exaggeration. The leaders of such ignorant masses of people may feel very proud of being adored by such a number of dogs and hogs, but that is not very flattering. The *Bhāgavatam* openly declares that although a person may be a great leader of such dogs and hogs disguised as men, if he has no taste for being enlightened in the science of Kṛṣṇa, such a leader is also an animal and nothing more. He may be designated as a powerful, strong animal, or a big animal, but in the estimation of *Śrīmad-Bhāgavatam* he is never given a place in the category of man, on account of his atheistic temperament. Or, in other words, such godless leaders of dogs and hoglike men are bigger animals with the qualities of animals in greater proportion.

TEXT 20

बिले बतोरुक्रमविक्रमान् ये
न शृण्वतः कर्णपुटे नरस्य ।
जिह्वासती दार्दुरिकेव सूत
न चोपगायत्युरुगायगाथाः ॥२०॥

bile batorukrama-vikramān ye
na śṛṇvataḥ karṇa-puṭe narasya

jihvāsatī dārdurikeva sūta
na copagāyaty urugāya-gāthāḥ

bile—snake holes; *bata*—like; *urukrama*—the Lord, who acts marvelously; *vikramān*—prowess; *ye*—all these; *na*—never; *śṛṇvataḥ*—heard; *karṇa-puṭe*—the earholes; *narasya*—of the man; *jihvā*—tongue; *asatī*—useless; *dārdurikā*—of the frogs; *iva*—exactly like that; *sūta*—O Sūta Gosvāmī; *na*—never; *ca*—also; *upagāyati*—chants loudly; *urugāya*—worth singing; *gāthāḥ*—songs.

TRANSLATION

One who has not listened to the messages about the prowess and marvelous acts of the Personality of Godhead and has not sung or chanted loudly the worthy songs about the Lord is to be considered to possess earholes like the holes of snakes and a tongue like the tongue of a frog.

PURPORT

Devotional service to the Lord is rendered by all limbs or parts of the body. It is the transcendental dynamic force of the spirit soul; therefore a devotee is engaged one hundred percent in the service of the Lord. One can engage in devotional service when the senses of the body are purified in relation with the Lord, and one can render service to the Lord with the help of all the senses. As such, the senses and the action of the senses are to be considered impure or materialistic as long as they are employed only in sense gratification. The purified senses are engaged not in sense gratification but in the service of the Lord *in toto.* The Lord is the Supreme with all senses, and the servitor, who is part and parcel of the Lord, also has the same senses. Service to the Lord is the completely purified use of the senses, as described in the *Bhagavad-gītā.* The Lord imparted instructions with full senses, and Arjuna received them with full senses, and thus there was a perfect exchange of sensible and logical understanding between the master and the disciple. Spiritual understanding is nothing like an electrical charge from the master to the disciple, as foolishly claimed by some propaganda-mongers. Everything is full of sense and logic, and the exchange of views between the master and disciple is possible only when the reception is submissive and real. In the *Caitanya-caritāmṛta* it is said that one should receive the teaching of Lord Caitanya with intellect and full senses so that one can logically understand the great mission.

In the impure state of a living being, the various senses are fully engaged in mundane affairs. If the ear is not engaged in the service of the Lord by hearing about Him from *Bhagavad-gītā* or *Śrīmad-Bhāgavatam*, certainly the holes of the ear will be filled with some rubbish. Therefore the messages of *Bhagavad-gītā* and *Śrīmad-Bhāgavatam* should be preached all over the world very loudly. That is the duty of a pure devotee who has actually heard about them from the perfect sources. Many want to speak something to others, but because they are not trained to speak on the subject matter of Vedic wisdom they are all speaking nonsense, and people are receiving them with no sense. There are hundreds and thousands of sources for distributing mundane news of the world, and people of the world are also receiving it. Similarly, the people of the world should be taught to hear the transcendental topics of the Lord, and the devotee of the Lord must speak loudly so that they can hear. The frogs loudly croak, with the result that they invite the snakes to eat them. The human tongue is especially given for chanting the Vedic hymns and not for croaking like frogs. The word *asatī* used in this verse is also significant. *Asatī* means a woman who has become a prostitute. A prostitute has no reputation for good womanly qualities. Similarly, the tongue, which is given to the human being for chanting the Vedic hymns, will be considered a prostitute when engaged in chanting some mundane nonsense.

TEXT 21

भारः परं पट्टकिरीटजुष्ट-
मप्युत्तमाङ्गं न नमेन्मुकुन्दम् ।
शावौ करौ नो कुरुते सपर्यां
हरेर्लसत्काञ्चनकङ्कणौ वा ॥२१॥

bhāraḥ paraṁ paṭṭa-kirīṭa-juṣṭam
apy uttamāṅgaṁ na namen mukundam

śāvau karau no kurute saparyāṁ
harer lasat-kāñcana-kaṅkaṇau vā

bhāraḥ—a great burden; *param*—heavy; *paṭṭa*—silk; *kirīṭa*—turban; *juṣṭam*—dressed with; *api*—even; *uttama*—upper; *aṅgam*—parts of the body; *na*—never; *namet*—bow down; *mukundam*—Lord Kṛṣṇa, the deliverer; *śāvau*—dead bodies; *karau*—hands; *no*—do not; *kurute*—do; *saparyām*—worshiping; *hareḥ*—of the Personality of Godhead; *lasat*—glittering; *kāñcana*—made of gold; *kaṅkaṇau*—bangles; *vā*—even though.

TRANSLATION

The upper portion of the body, though crowned with a silk turban, is only a heavy burden if not bowed down before the Personality of Godhead who can award mukti [freedom]. And the hands, though decorated with glittering bangles, are like those of a dead man if not engaged in the service of the Personality of Godhead Hari.

PURPORT

As stated hereinbefore, there are three kinds of devotees of the Lord. The first-class devotee does not at all see anyone who is not in the service of the Lord, but the second-class devotee makes distinctions between devotees and nondevotees. The second-class devotees are therefore meant for preaching work, and as referred to in the above verse, they must loudly preach the glories of the Lord. The second-class devotee accepts disciples from the section of third-class devotees or nondevotees. Sometimes the first-class devotee also comes down to the category of the second-class devotee for preaching work. But the common man, who is expected to become at least a third-class devotee, is advised herein to visit the temple of the Lord and bow down before the Deity, even though he may be a very rich man or even a king with a silk turban or crown. The Lord is the Lord of everyone, including the great kings and emperors, and men who are rich in the estimation of mundane people must therefore make it a point to visit the temple of Lord Śrī Kṛṣṇa and regularly bow down before the Deity. The Lord in the temple in the worshipable form is never to be considered to be made of stone or wood, for the Lord in His *arcā* incarnation as the Deity in the temple shows immense favor to the fallen souls by His auspicious presence. By the hearing process, as mentioned hereinbefore, this realization of the presence of the Lord in the temple is made possible. As such, the first process in the routine work of devotional service—hearing—is the essential point. Hearing by all classes of devotees from the authentic sources like *Bhagavad-gītā* and *Śrīmad-Bhāgavatam* is essential. The common man who is puffed up with his material position and does not bow down before the Deity of the Lord in the temple, or who defies temple worship without any knowledge of the science, must know that his so-called turban or crown will only succeed in further drowning him in the water of the ocean of material existence. A drowning man with a heavy weight on his head is sure to go down more swiftly than those who have no heavy weight. A foolish, puffed-up man defies the science of God and says that God has no meaning for him, but when he is in the grip of God's law and is caught by some disease like cerebral thrombosis, that godless man sinks into the ocean of nescience by the weight of his material acquisition. Advancement of material science without God consciousness is a heavy load on the head of human society, and so one must take heed of this great warning.

The common man, if he has no time to worship the Lord, may at least engage his hands for a few seconds in washing or sweeping the Lord's temple. Mahārāja Pratāparudra, the greatly powerful king of Orissa, was always very busy with heavy state responsibilities, yet he made it a point to sweep the temple of Lord Jagannātha at Purī once a year during the festival of the Lord. The idea is that however important a man one may be he must accept the supremacy of the Supreme Lord. This God consciousness will help a man even in his material prosperity. Mahārāja Pratāparudra's subordination before Lord Jagannātha made him a powerful king, so much so that even the great Pathan in his time could not enter into Orissa on account of the powerful Mahārāja Pratāparudra. And at last Mahārāja Pratāparudra was graced by Lord Śrī Caitanya on the very grounds of his acceptance of subordination to the Lord of the universe. So even though a rich man's wife has glittering bangles made of gold on her hands, she must engage herself in rendering service to the Lord.

TEXT 22

बर्हायिते ते नयने नराणां
लिङ्गानि विष्णोर्न निरीक्षतो ये ।
पादौ नृणां तौ द्रुमजन्मभाजौ
क्षेत्राणि नानुव्रजतो हरेर्यौ ॥२२॥

barhāyite te nayane narāṇāṁ
liṅgāni viṣṇor na nirīkṣato ye
pādau nṛṇāṁ tau druma-janma-bhājau
kṣetrāṇi nānuvrajato harer yau

barhāyite—like plumes of a peacock; *te*—those; *nayane*—eyes; *narāṇām*—of men; *liṅgāni*—forms; *viṣṇoḥ*—of the Personality of Godhead; *na*—does not; *nirīkṣataḥ*—look upon; *ye*—all such; *pādau*—legs; *nṛṇām*—of men; *tau*—those; *druma-janma*—being born of the tree; *bhājau*—like that; *kṣetrāṇi*—holy places; *na*—never; *anuvrajataḥ*—goes after; *hareḥ*—of the Lord; *yau*—which.

TRANSLATION

The eyes which do not look at the symbolic representations of the Personality of Godhead Viṣṇu [His forms, name, quality, etc.] are like those printed on the plumes of the peacock, and the legs which do not move to the holy places [where the Lord is remembered] are considered to be like tree trunks.

PURPORT

Especially for the householder devotees, the path of Deity worship is strongly recommended. As far as possible, every householder, by the direction of the spiritual master, must install the Deity of Viṣṇu, forms like Rādhā-Kṛṣṇa, Lakṣmī-Nārāyaṇa or Sītā-Rāma especially, or any other form of the Lord, like Nṛsiṁha, Varāha, Gaura-Nitāi, Matsya, Kūrma, *śālagrāma-śilā* and many other forms of Viṣṇu, like Trivikrama, Keśava, Acyuta, Vāsudeva, Nārāyaṇa and Dāmodara, as recommended in the *Vaiṣṇava-tantras* or *Purāṇas*, and one's family should worship strictly following the directions and regulations of *arcana-vidhi*.

Any member of the family who is above twelve years of age should be initiated by a bona fide spiritual master, and all the members of the household should be engaged in the daily service of the Lord, beginning from morning (4 a.m.) till night (10 p.m.) by performing *maṅgala-ārātrika, nirañjana, arcanā, pūjā, kīrtana, śṛṅgāra, bhoga-vaikāli, sandhyā-ārātrika, pāṭha, bhoga* (at night), *śayana-ārātrika,* etc. Engagement in such worship of the Deity, under the direction of a bona fide spiritual master, will greatly help the householders to purify their very existence and make rapid progress in spiritual knowledge. Simple theoretical book knowledge is not sufficient for a neophyte devotee. Book knowledge is theoretical, whereas the *arcana* process is practical. Spiritual knowledge must be developed by a combination of theoretical and practical knowledge, and that is the guaranteed way for attainment of spiritual perfection. The training of devotional service for a neophyte devotee completely depends on the expert spiritual master who knows how to lead his disciple to make gradual progress towards the path back home, back to Godhead. One should not become a pseudo spiritual master as a matter of business to meet one's family expenditures; one must be an expert spiritual master to deliver the disciple from the clutches of impending death. Śrīla Viśvanātha Cakravartī Ṭhākura has defined the bona fide qualities of a spiritual master, and one of the verses in that description reads:

śrī-vigrahārādhana-nitya-nānā-
śṛṅgāra-tan-mandira-mārjanādau
yuktasya bhaktāṁś ca niyuñjato 'pi
vande guroḥ śrī-caraṇāravindam

Śrī-vigraha is the *arcā,* or suitable worshipable form of the Lord, and the disciple should be engaged in worshiping the Deity regularly by *śṛṅgāra,* by proper decoration and dressing, as also by *mandira-mārjana,* the matter of cleansing the temple. The spiritual master teaches the neophyte devotee all these kindly and personally to help him gradually in the realization of the transcendental name, quality, form, etc., of the Lord.

Only attention engaged in the service of the Lord, especially in dressing and decorating the temple, accompanied by musical *kīrtana* and spiritual instructions from scriptures, can save the common man from the hellish cinema attractions and rubbish sex-songs broadcast everywhere by radios. If one is unable to maintain a temple at home, he should go to another's temple where all the above performances are regularly executed. Visiting the temple of a devotee and looking at the profusely decorated forms of the Lord well dressed in a well-decorated, sanctified temple naturally infuse the mundane mind with spiritual inspiration. People should visit holy places like Vṛndāvana where such temples and worship of the Deity are specifically maintained. Formerly all rich men like kings and rich merchants constructed such temples under the direction of expert devotees of the Lord, like the six Gosvāmīs, and it is the duty of the common man to take advantage of these temples and festivals observed in the holy places of pilgrimage by following in the footsteps of great devotees (*anuvraja*). One should not visit all these sanctified pilgrimage places and temples with sightseeing in mind, but one must go to such temples and sanctified places immortalized by the transcendental pastimes of the Lord and be guided by proper men who know the science. This is called *anuvraja*. *Anu* means to follow. It is therefore best to follow the instruction of the bona fide spiritual master, even in visiting temples and the holy places of pilgrimage. One who does not move in that way is as good as a standing tree condemned by the Lord not to move. The moving tendency of the human being is misused by visiting places for sightseeing. The best purpose of such traveling tendencies could be fulfilled by visiting the holy places established by great *ācāryas* and thereby not being misled by the atheistic propaganda of moneymaking men who have no knowledge of spiritual matters.

TEXT 23

जीवञ्छवो भागवताङ्घ्रिरेणुं
न जातु मर्त्योऽभिलभेत यस्तु ।
श्रीविष्णुपद्या मनुजस्तुलस्याः
श्वसञ्छवो यस्तु न वेद गन्धम् ॥२३॥

jīvañ chavo bhāgavatāṅghri-reṇuṁ
na jātu martyo 'bhilabheta yas tu
śrī-viṣṇu-padyā manujas tulasyāḥ
śvasañ chavo yas tu na veda gandham

jīvan—while living; *śavaḥ*—a dead body; *bhāgavata-aṅghri-reṇum*—the dust of the feet of a pure devotee; *na*—never; *jātu*—at any time; *martyaḥ*—mortal; *abhilabheta*—particularly received; *yaḥ*—a person; *tu*—but; *śrī*—with opulence; *viṣṇu-padyāḥ*—of the lotus feet of Viṣṇu; *manu-jaḥ*—a descendant of Manu (a man); *tulasyāḥ*—leaves of the *tulasī* tree; *śvasan*—while breathing; *śavaḥ*—still a dead body; *yaḥ*—who; *tu*—but; *na veda*—never experienced; *gandham*—the aroma.

TRANSLATION

The person who has not at any time received the dust of the feet of the Lord's pure devotee upon his head is certainly a dead body. And the person who has never experienced the aroma of the tulasī leaves from the lotus feet of the Lord is also a dead body, although breathing.

PURPORT

According to Śrīla Viśvanātha Cakravartī Ṭhākura, the breathing dead body is a ghost. When a man dies, he is called dead, but when he again appears in a subtle form not visible to our present vision and yet acts, such a dead body is called a ghost. Ghosts are always very bad elements, always creating a fearful situation for others. Similarly, the ghostlike nondevotees who have no respect for the pure devotees, nor for the Viṣṇu Deity in the temples, create a fearful situation for the devotees at all times. The Lord never accepts any offering by such impure ghosts. There is a common saying that one should first love the dog of the beloved before one shows any loving sentiments for the beloved. The stage of pure devotion is attained by sincerely serving a pure devotee of the Lord. The first condition of devotional service to the Lord is therefore to be a servant of a pure devotee, and this condition is fulfilled by the statement "reception of the dust of the lotus feet of a pure devotee who has also served another pure devotee." That is the way of pure disciplic succession, or devotional *paramparā.*

Mahārāja Rahūgaṇa inquired from the great saint Jaḍa Bharata as to how he had attained such a liberated stage of a *paramahaṁsa*, and in answer the great saint replied as follows (*Bhāg.* 5.12.12):

rahūgaṇaitat tapasā na yāti
na cejyayā nirvapaṇād gṛhād vā

na cchandasā naiva jalāgni-sūryair
vinā mahat-pāda-rajo-'bhiṣekam

"O King Rahūgaṇa, the perfectional stage of devotional service, or the *paramahaṁsa* stage of life, cannot be attained unless one is blessed by *the dust of the feet of great devotees.* It is never attained by *tapasya* [austerity], the Vedic worshiping process, acceptance of the renounced order of life, the discharge of the duties of household life, the chanting of the Vedic hymns, or the performance of penances in the hot sun, within cold water or before the blazing fire."

In other words, Lord Śrī Kṛṣṇa is the property of His pure unconditional devotees, and as such only the devotees can deliver Kṛṣṇa to another devotee; Kṛṣṇa is never obtainable directly. Lord Caitanya therefore designated Himself as *gopī-bhartuḥ pada-kamalayor dāsa-dāsānudāsaḥ*, or "the most obedient servant of the servants of the Lord, who maintains the *gopī* damsels at Vṛndāvana." A pure devotee therefore never approaches the Lord directly, but tries to please the servant of the Lord's servants, and thus the Lord becomes pleased, and only then can the devotee relish the taste of the *tulasī* leaves stuck to His lotus feet. In the *Brahma-saṁhitā* it is said that the Lord is never to be found by becoming a great scholar of the Vedic literatures, but He is very easily approachable through His pure devotee. In Vṛndāvana all the pure devotees pray for the mercy of Śrīmatī Rādhārāṇī, the pleasure potency of Lord Kṛṣṇa. Śrīmatī Rādhārāṇī is a tenderhearted feminine counterpart of the supreme whole, resembling the perfectional stage of the worldly feminine nature. Therefore, the mercy of Rādhārāṇī is available very readily to the sincere devotees, and once She recommends such a devotee to Lord Kṛṣṇa, the Lord at once accepts the devotee's admittance into His association. The conclusion is, therefore, that one should be more serious about seeking the mercy of the devotee than that of the Lord directly, and by one's doing so (by the good will of the devotee) the natural attraction for the service of the Lord will be revived.

TEXT 24

तदश्मसारं हृदयं बतेदं
यद् गृह्यमाणैर्हरिनामधेयैः ।

न विक्रियेताथ यदा विकारो
नेत्रे जलं गात्ररुहेषु हर्षः ॥२४॥

tad aśma-sāraṁ hṛdayaṁ batedaṁ
yad gṛhyamāṇair hari-nāma-dheyaiḥ
na vikriyetātha yadā vikāro
netre jalaṁ gātra-ruheṣu harṣaḥ

tat—that; *aśma-sāram*—is steel-framed; *hṛdayam*—heart; *bata idam*—certainly that; *yat*—which; *gṛhyamānaiḥ*—in spite of chanting; *hari-nāma*—the holy name of the Lord; *dheyaiḥ*—by concentration of the mind; *na*—does not; *vikriyeta*—change; *atha*—thus; *yadā*—when; *vikāraḥ*—reaction; *netre*—in the eyes; *jalam*—tears; *gātra-ruheṣu*—at the pores; *harṣaḥ*—eruptions of ecstasy.

TRANSLATION

Certainly that heart is steel-framed which, in spite of one's chanting the holy name of the Lord with concentration, does not change when ecstasy takes place, tears fill the eyes and the hairs stand on end.

PURPORT

We should note with profit that in the first three chapters of the Second Canto a gradual process of development of devotional service is being presented. In the First Chapter the first step in devotional service for God consciousness by the process of hearing and chanting has been stressed, and a gross conception of the Personality of Godhead in His universal form for the beginners is recommended. By such a gross conception of God through the material manifestations of His energy, one is enabled to spiritualize the mind and the senses and gradually concentrate the mind upon Lord Viṣṇu, the Supreme, who is present as the Supersoul in every heart and everywhere, in every atom of the material universe. The system of *pañca-upāsanā*, recommending five mental attitudes for the common man, is also enacted for this purpose, namely gradual development, worship of the superior that may be in the form of fire, electricity, the sun, the mass of living beings, Lord Śiva and, at last, the impersonal Supersoul, the partial representation of Lord Viṣṇu. They are all nicely described in the Second Chapter, but in the Third Chapter further development is prescribed after one has actually reached the stage of Viṣṇu worship, or pure devotional service, and the mature stage of Viṣṇu worship is suggested herein in relation to the change of heart.

The whole process of spiritual culture is aimed at changing the heart of the living being in the matter of his eternal relation with the Supreme Lord as subordinate servant, which is his eternal constitutional position. So with the progress of devotional service, the reaction of change in the heart is exhibited by gradual detachment from the sense of material enjoyment by a false sense of lording it over the world and an increase in the attitude of rendering loving service to the Lord. *Vidhi-bhakti*, or regulated devotional service by the limbs of the body (namely the eyes, the ears, the nose, the hands and the legs, as already explained hereinbefore), is now stressed herein in relation to the mind, which is the impetus for all activities of the limbs of the body. It is expected by all means that by discharging regulated devotional service one must manifest the change of heart. If there is no such change, the heart must be considered steel-framed, for it is not melted even when there is chanting of the holy name of the Lord. We must always remember that hearing and chanting are the basic principles of discharging devotional duties, and if they are properly performed there will follow the reactional ecstasy with signs of tears in the eyes and standing of the hairs on the body. These are natural consequences and are the preliminary symptoms of the *bhāva* stage, which occurs before one reaches the perfectional stage of *prema*, love of Godhead.

If the reaction does not take place, even after continuous hearing and chanting of the holy name of the Lord, it may be considered to be due to offenses only. That is the opinion of the *Sandarbha*. In the beginning of chanting of the holy name of the Lord, if the devotee has not been very careful about evading the ten kinds of offenses at the feet of the holy name, certainly the reaction of feelings of separation will not be visible by tears in the eyes and standing of the hair on end.

The *bhāva* stage is manifested by eight transcendental symptoms, namely inertness, perspiration, standing of hairs on end, failing in the voice, trembling, paleness of the body, tears in the eyes and finally trance. *The Nectar of Devotion*, a summary study of Śrīla Rūpa

Gosvāmī's *Bhakti-rasāmṛta-sindhu*, explains those symptoms and vividly describes other transcendental developments, both in steady and accelerating manifestations.

Śrīla Viśvanātha Cakravartī Ṭhākura has very critically discussed all these *bhāva* displays in connection with some unscrupulous neophyte's imitating the above symptoms for cheap appreciation. Not only Viśvanātha Cakravartī but also Śrīla Rūpa Gosvāmī treated them very critically. Sometimes all the above eight symptoms of ecstasy are imitated by the mundane devotees (*prākṛta-sahajiyās*), but the pseudo symptoms are at once detected when one sees the pseudodevotee addicted to so many forbidden things. Even though decorated with the signs of a devotee, a person addicted to smoking, drinking or illegitimate sex with women cannot have all the above-mentioned ecstatic symptoms. But it is seen that sometimes these symptoms are willfully imitated, and for this reason Śrīla Viśvanātha Cakravartī accuses the imitators of being stonehearted men. They are sometimes even affected by the reflection of such transcendental symptoms, yet if they still do not give up the forbidden habits, then they are hopeless cases for transcendental realization.

When Lord Caitanya met Śrīla Rāmānanda Rāya of Kavaur on the bank of the Godāvarī, the Lord developed all these symptoms, but because of the presence of some nondevotee *brāhmaṇas* who were attendants of the Rāya, the Lord suppressed these symptoms. So sometimes they are not visible even in the body of the first-class devotee for certain circumstantial reasons. Therefore real, steady *bhāva* is definitely displayed in the matter of cessation of material desires (*kṣānti*), utilization of every moment in the transcendental loving service of the Lord (*avyārtha-kālatvam*), eagerness for glorifying the Lord constantly (*nāma-gāne sadā ruci*), attraction for living in the land of the Lord (*prītis tad-vasati sthale*), complete detachment from material happiness (*virakti*), and pridelessness (*māna-śūnyatā*). One who has developed all these transcendental qualities is really possessed of the *bhāva* stage, as distinguished from the stonehearted imitator or mundane devotee.

The whole process can be summarized as follows: The advanced devotee who chants the holy name of the Lord in a perfectly offenseless manner and is friendly to everyone can actually relish the transcendental taste of glorifying the Lord. And the result of such realization is reflected in the cessation of all material desires, etc., as mentioned above. The neophytes, due to their being in the lower stage of devotional service, are invariably envious, so much so that they invent their own ways and means of devotional regulations without following the *ācāryas.* As such, even if they make a show of constantly chanting the holy name of the Lord, they cannot relish the transcendental taste of the holy name. Therefore, the show of tears in the eyes, trembling, perspiration or unconsciousness, etc., is condemned. They can, however, get in touch with a pure devotee of the Lord and rectify their bad habits; otherwise they shall continue to be stonehearted and unfit for any treatment. A complete progressive march on the return path home, back to Godhead, will depend on the instructions of the revealed scriptures directed by a realized devotee.

TEXT 25

अथाभिधेह्यङ्ग मनोऽनुकूलं
प्रभाषसे भागवतप्रधानः ।
यदाह वैयासकिरात्मविद्या-
विशारदो नृपतिं साधु पृष्टः ॥२५॥

athābhidhehy aṅga mano-'nukūlaṁ
prabhāṣase bhāgavata-pradhānaḥ
yad āha vaiyāsakir ātma-vidyā-
viśārado nṛpatiṁ sādhu pṛṣṭaḥ

atha—therefore; *abhidhehi*—please explain; *aṅga*—O Sūta Gosvāmī; *manaḥ*—mind; *anukūlam*—favorable to our mentality; *prabhāṣase*—you do speak; *bhāgavata*—the great devotee; *pradhānaḥ*—the chief; *yat āha*—what he spoke; *vaiyāsakiḥ*—Śukadeva Gosvāmī; *ātma-vidyā*—transcendental knowledge; *viśāradaḥ*—expert; *nṛpatim*—unto the King; *sādhu*—very good; *pṛṣṭaḥ*—being asked.

TRANSLATION

O Sūta Gosvāmī, your words are pleasing to our minds. Please therefore explain this to us as it was spoken by the great devotee Śukadeva Gosvāmī, who is very expert in transcendental knowledge, and who spoke to Mahārāja Parīkṣit upon being asked.

PURPORT

Knowledge explained by the previous *ācārya* like Śukadeva Gosvāmī and followed by the next like Sūta Gosvāmī is always powerful transcendental knowledge, and it is therefore penetrating and useful to all submissive students.

Thus end the Bhaktivedanta purports of the Second Canto, Third Chapter, of the Śrīmad-Bhāgavatam, *entitled "Pure Devotional Service: The Change in Heart."*

CHAPTER FOUR

The Process of Creation

TEXT 1

सूत उवाच
वैयासकेरिति वचस्तत्त्वनिश्चयमात्मनः ।
उपधार्य मतिं कृष्णे औत्तरेयः सतीं व्यधात् ॥ १ ॥

sūta uvāca
vaiyāsaker iti vacas
tattva-niścayam ātmanaḥ
upadhārya matiṁ kṛṣṇe
auttareyaḥ satīṁ vyadhāt

sūtaḥ uvāca—Sūta Gosvāmī said; *vaiyāsakeḥ*—of Śukadeva Gosvāmī; *iti*—thus; *vacaḥ*—speeches; *tattva-niścayam*—that which verifies the truth; *ātmanaḥ*—in the self; *upadhārya*—just having realized; *matim*—concentration of the mind; *kṛṣṇe*—unto Lord Kṛṣṇa; *auttareyaḥ*—the son of Uttarā; *satīm*—chaste; *vyadhāt*—applied.

TRANSLATION

Sūta Gosvāmī said: Mahārāja Parīkṣit, the son of Uttarā, after hearing the speeches of Śukadeva Gosvāmī, which were all about the truth of the self, applied his concentration faithfully upon Lord Kṛṣṇa.

PURPORT

The word *satīm* is very significant. This means "existing" and "chaste". And both imports are perfectly applicable in the case of Mahārāja Parīkṣit. The whole Vedic adventure is to draw one's attention entirely unto the lotus feet of Lord Kṛṣṇa without any diversion, as instructed in the *Bhagavad-gītā* (15.15). Fortunately Mahārāja Parīkṣit had already been attracted to the Lord from the very beginning of his body, in the womb of his mother. In the womb of his mother he was struck by the *brahmāstra* atomic bomb released by Aśvatthāmā, but by the grace of the Lord he was saved from being burnt by the fiery weapon, and since then the King continuously concentrated his mind upon Lord Kṛṣṇa, which made him perfectly chaste in devotional service. So by natural sequence he was a chaste devotee of the Lord, and when he further heard from Śrīla Śukadeva Gosvāmī that one should worship the Lord only and no one else, even though full of all desires or desireless, his natural affection for Kṛṣṇa was strengthened. We have already discussed these topics.

To become a pure devotee of Lord Kṛṣṇa, two things are very much essential, namely having a chance to be born in the family of a devotee and having the blessings of a bona fide spiritual master. By the grace of Lord Kṛṣṇa, Parīkṣit Mahārāja had both opportunities. He was born in a family of such devotees as the Pāṇḍavas, and just to continue the dynasty of the Pāṇḍavas and show them special favor, the Lord specifically saved Mahārāja Parīkṣit, who later on, by the arrangement of the Lord, was cursed by the boy of a *brāhmaṇa* and was able to get the association of such a spiritual master as Śukadeva Gosvāmī. In the *Caitanya-caritāmṛta* it is said that a fortunate person, by the mercy of the spiritual master and Lord Kṛṣṇa, achieves the path of devotional service. This was perfectly applicable in the case of Mahārāja Parīkṣit. By way of being born in a family of devotees, he automatically came in touch with Kṛṣṇa, and after being so contacted he constantly remembered Him. Consequently Lord Kṛṣṇa gave the King a further chance for development in devotional service by introducing him to Śukadeva Gosvāmī, a stalwart devotee of the Lord with perfect knowledge in self-realization. And by hearing from a bona fide spiritual master, he was perfectly able to concentrate his chaste mind further upon Lord Kṛṣṇa, as a matter of course.

TEXT 2

आत्मजायासुतागारपशुद्रविणबन्धुषु ।
राज्ये चाविकले नित्यं विरूढां ममतां जहौ ॥ २ ॥

ātma-jāyā-sutāgāra-
paśu-draviṇa-bandhuṣu
rājye cāvikale nityaṁ
virūḍhāṁ mamatāṁ jahau

ātma—body; *jāyā*—wife; *suta*—son; *āgāra*—palace; *paśu*—horses and elephants; *draviṇa*—treasury house; *bandhuṣu*—unto friends and relatives; *rājye*—in the kingdom; *ca*—also; *avikale*—without being disturbed; *nityam*—constant; *virūḍhām*—deep-rooted; *mamatām*—affinity; *jahau*—gave up.

TRANSLATION

Mahārāja Parīkṣit, as a result of his wholehearted attraction for Lord Kṛṣṇa, was able to give up all deep-rooted affection for his personal body, his wife, his children, his palace, his animals like horses and elephants, his treasury house, his friends and relatives, and his undisputed kingdom.

PURPORT

To become liberated means to become free from *dehātma-buddhi,* the illusory attachment for personal bodily coverings and everything connected with the body, namely wife, children and all other entanglements. One selects a wife for bodily comforts, and the result is children. For wife and children one requires a dwelling place, and as such a residential house is also necessary. Animals like horses, elephants, cows and dogs are all household animals, and a householder has to keep them as household paraphernalia. In modern civilization the horses and elephants have been replaced by cars and conveyances with considerable horsepower. To maintain all the household affairs, one has to increase the bank balance and be careful about the treasury house, and in order to display the opulence of material assets, one has to keep good relations with friends and relatives, as well as become very careful about maintaining the status quo. This is called material civilization of material attachment. Devotion for Lord Kṛṣṇa means negation of all material attachments as detailed above. By the grace of Lord Kṛṣṇa, Mahārāja Parīkṣit was awarded all material amenities and an undisputed kingdom in which to enjoy the undisturbed position of king, but by the grace of the Lord he was able to give up all connections with material attachment. That is the position of a pure devotee. Mahārāja Parīkṣit, due to his natural affection for Lord Kṛṣṇa as a devotee of the Lord, was always executing his royal duties on behalf of the Lord, and as a responsible king of the world he was always careful to see that the influence of Kali would not enter his kingdom. A devotee of the Lord never thinks of his household paraphernalia as his own, but surrenders everything for the service of the Lord. Thereby living entities under a devotee's care get the opportunity for God realization by the management of a devotee-master.

Attachment for household paraphernalia and for Lord Kṛṣṇa go poorly together. One attachment is the path of darkness, and the other attachment is the path of light. Where there is light, there is no darkness, and where there is darkness, there is no light. But an expert devotee can turn everything to the path of light by an attitude of service to the Lord, and the best example here is the Pāṇḍavas. Mahārāja Yudhiṣṭhira and householders like him can turn everything to light by dovetailing so-called material assets in the service of the Lord, but one who is not trained or is unable to turn everything to the service of the Lord (*nirbandhaḥ kṛṣṇa-sambandhe*) must give up all material connections before he can be fit to hear and chant the glories of the Lord, or in other words, one who has seriously heard *Śrīmad-Bhāgavatam* for even one day, like Mahārāja Parīkṣit, from a fit personality like Śukadeva Gosvāmī, may be able to lose all affinity for material things. There is no utility simply in imitating Mahārāja Parīkṣit and hearing *Bhāgavatam* from professional men, even for seven hundred years. To take *Śrīmad-Bhāgavatam* as a means of maintaining family expenditure is the grossest type of *nāmāparādha* offense at the feet of the Lord (*sarva-śubha-kriyā-sāmyam api pramādaḥ*).

TEXTS 3–4

पप्रच्छ चेममेवार्थं यन्मां पृच्छथ सत्तमाः ।
कृष्णानुभावश्रवणे श्रद्दधानो महामनाः ॥ ३ ॥
संस्थां विज्ञाय संन्यस्य कर्म त्रैवर्गिकं च यत् ।
वासुदेवे भगवति आत्मभावं दृढं गतः ॥ ४ ॥

papraccha cemaṁ evārthaṁ
yan māṁ pṛcchatha sattamāḥ
kṛṣṇānubhāva-śravaṇe
śraddadhāno mahā-manāḥ

saṁsthāṁ vijñāya sannyasya
karma trai-vargikaṁ ca yat
vāsudeve bhagavati
ātma-bhāvaṁ dṛḍhaṁ gataḥ

papraccha—asked; *ca*—also; *imam*—this; *eva*—exactly like; *artham*—purpose; *yat*—that; *mām*—unto me; *pṛcchatha*—you are asking; *sattamāḥ*—O great sages; *kṛṣṇa-anubhāva*—rapt in thought of Kṛṣṇa; *śravaṇe*—in hearing; *śraddadhānaḥ*—full of faith; *mahā-manāḥ*—the great soul; *saṁsthām*—death; *vijñāya*—being informed; *sannyasya*—renouncing; *karma*—fruitive activities; *trai-vargikam*—the three principles religion, economic development and sense gratification; *ca*—also; *yat*—what it may be; *vāsudeve*—unto Lord Kṛṣṇa; *bhagavati*—the Personality of Godhead; *ātma-bhāvam*—attraction of love; *dṛḍham*—firmly fixed; *gataḥ*—achieved.

TRANSLATION

O great sages, the great soul Mahārāja Parīkṣit, constantly rapt in thought of Lord Kṛṣṇa, knowing well of his imminent death, renounced all sorts of fruitive activities, namely acts of religion, economic development and sense gratification, and thus fixed himself firmly in his natural love for Kṛṣṇa and asked all these questions, exactly as you are asking me.

PURPORT

The three activities of religion, economic development and sense gratification are generally attractive for conditioned souls struggling for existence in the material world. Such regulated activities prescribed in the *Vedas* are called the *karma-kāṇḍīya* conception of life, and householders are generally recommended to follow the rules just to enjoy material prosperity both in this life and in the next. Most people are attracted by such activities. Even in the activities of their modern godless civilization, people are more concerned with economic development and sense gratification without any religious sentiments. As a great emperor of the world, Mahārāja Parīkṣit had to observe such regulations of the Vedic *karma-kāṇḍīya* section, but by his slight association with Śukadeva Gosvāmī he could perfectly understand that Lord Kṛṣṇa, the Absolute Personality of Godhead (Vāsudeva), for whom he had a natural love since his birth, is everything, and thus he fixed his mind firmly upon Him, renouncing all modes of Vedic *karma-kāṇḍīya* activities. This perfectional stage is attained by a *jñānī* after many, many births. The *jñānīs*, or the empiric philosophers endeavoring for liberation, are thousands of times better than the fruitive workers, and out of hundreds of thousands of such *jñānīs* one is liberated factually. And out of hundreds of thousands of such liberated persons, even one person is rarely found who can firmly fix his mind unto the lotus feet of Lord Śrī Kṛṣṇa, as declared by the Lord Himself in the *Bhagavad-gītā* (7.19). Mahārāja Parīkṣit is specially qualified with the word *mahā-manāḥ*, which puts him on an equal level with the *mahātmās* described in the *Bhagavad-gītā*. In the later age also there have been many *mahātmās* of this type, and they also gave up all *karma-kāṇḍīya* conceptions of life, solely and wholly depending on the Supreme Personality of Godhead Kṛṣṇa. Lord Caitanya, who is Lord Kṛṣṇa Himself, taught us in His *Śikṣāṣṭaka* (8):

āśliṣya vā pāda-ratāṁ pinaṣṭu mām
adarśanān marma-hatāṁ karotu vā
yathā tathā vā vidadhātu lampaṭo
mat-prāṇa-nāthas tu sa eva nāparaḥ

"Lord Kṛṣṇa, who is the lover of many devotees (women), may embrace this fully surrendered maidservant or may trample me with His feet, or He may render me brokenhearted by not being present before me for a long duration of time, but still He is nothing less than the Absolute Lord of my heart."

Śrīla Rūpa Gosvāmī spoke thus:

viracaya mayi daṇḍaṁ dīna-bandho dayāmī vā
gatir iha na bhavattaḥ kācid anyā mamāsti

nipatatu śata-koṭi-nirbharaṁ vā navāmbhaḥ
tad api kila-payodaḥ stūyate cātakena

"O Lord of the poor, do what you like with me, give me either mercy or punishment, but in this world I have none to look to except Your Lordship. The *cātaka* bird always prays for the cloud, regardless of whether it showers rains or throws a thunderbolt."

Śrīla Mādhavendra Purī, the grand–spiritual master of Lord Caitanya, took leave of all *karma-kāṇḍīya* obligations in the following words:

sandhyā-vandana bhadram astu bhavato bhoḥ snāna tubhyaṁ namo
bho devāḥ pitaraś ca tarpaṇa-vidhau nāhaṁ kṣamaḥ kṣamyatām
yatra kvāpi niṣadya yādava-kulottamasya kaṁsa-dviṣaḥ
smāraṁ smāram aghaṁ harāmi tad alaṁ manye kim anyena me

"O my evening prayer, all good unto you. O my morning bath, I bid you good-bye. O demigods and forefathers, please excuse me. I am unable to perform any more offerings for your pleasure. Now I have decided to free myself from all reactions to sins simply by remembering anywhere and everywhere the great descendant of Yadu and the great enemy of Kaṁsa [Lord Kṛṣṇa]. I think that this is sufficient for me. So what is the use of further endeavors?"

Śrīla Mādhavendra Purī said further:

mugdhaṁ māṁ nigadantu nīti-nipuṇā bhrāntaṁ muhur vaidikāḥ
mandaṁ bāndhava-sañcayā jaḍa-dhiyaṁ muktādarāḥ sodarāḥ
unmattaṁ dhanino viveka-caturāḥ kāmam mahā-dāmbhikam
moktuṁ na kṣāmate manāg api mano govinda-pāda-spṛhām

"Let the sharp moralist accuse me of being illusioned; I do not mind. Experts in Vedic activities may slander me as being misled, friends and relatives may call me frustrated, my brothers may call me a fool, the wealthy mammonites may point me out as mad, and the learned philosophers may assert that I am much too proud; still my mind does not budge an inch from the determination to serve the lotus feet of Govinda, though I be unable to do it."

And also Prahlāda Mahārāja said:

dharmārtha-kāma iti yo 'bhihitas trivarga
īkṣā trayī naya-damau vividhā ca vārtā
manye tad etad akhilaṁ nigamasya satyaṁ
svātmārpaṇaṁ sva-suhṛdaḥ paramasya puṁsaḥ

"Religion, economic development and sense gratification are celebrated as three means of attaining the path of salvation. Of these, *īkṣā trayī* especially, i.e., knowledge of the self, knowledge of fruitive acts and logic and also politics and economics, are different means of livelihood. All these are different subjects of Vedic education, and therefore I consider them temporary engagements. On the other hand, surrendering unto the Supreme Lord Viṣṇu is a factual gain in life, and I consider it the ultimate truth." (*Bhāg.* 7.6.26)

The whole matter is concluded in the *Bhagavad-gītā* (2.41) as *vyavasāyātmikā buddhiḥ*, or the absolute path of perfection. Śrī Baladeva Vidyābhūṣaṇa, a great Vaiṣṇava scholar, defines this as *bhagavvad-arcanā-rūpaika-niṣkāma-karmabhir viśuddha-cittaḥ*—accepting transcendental loving service to the Lord as the prime duty, free from fruitive reaction.

So Mahārāja Parīkṣit was perfectly right when he firmly accepted the lotus feet of Lord Kṛṣṇa, renouncing all *karma-kāṇḍīya* conceptions of life.

TEXT 5

राजोवाच
समीचीनं वचो ब्रह्मन् सर्वज्ञस्य तवानघ ।
तमो विशीर्यते मह्यं हरेः कथयतः कथाम् ॥ ५ ॥

rājovāca
samīcīnaṁ vaco brahman
sarva-jñasya tavānagha
tamo viśīryate mahyaṁ
hareḥ kathayataḥ kathām

rājā uvāca—the King said; *samīcīnam*—perfectly right; *vacaḥ*—speeches; *brahman*—O learned *brāhmaṇa; sarva-jñasya*—one who knows all; *tava*—your; *anagha*—without any contamination; *tamaḥ*—

the darkness of ignorance; *viśīryate*—gradually disappearing; *mahyam*—unto me; *hareḥ*—of the Lord; *kathayataḥ*—as you are speaking; *kathām*—topics.

TRANSLATION

Mahārāja Parīkṣit said: O learned brāhmaṇa, you know everything because you are without material contamination. Therefore whatever you have spoken to me appears perfectly right. Your speeches are gradually destroying the darkness of my ignorance, for you are narrating the topics of the Lord.

PURPORT

The practical experience of Mahārāja Parīkṣit is disclosed herein, revealing that transcendental topics of the Lord act like injections when received by the sincere devotee from a person who is perfectly uncontaminated by material tinges. In other words, reception of the messages of *Śrīmad-Bhāgavatam* from professional men, heard by a *karma-kāṇḍīya* audience, never acts miraculously as stated here. Devotional hearing of the messages of the Lord is not like hearing ordinary topics; therefore the action will be felt by the sincere hearer by experience of the gradual disappearance of ignorance.

yasya deve parā bhaktir
yathā deve tathā gurau
tasyaite kathitā hy arthāḥ
prakāśante mahātmanaḥ
(*Śvetāśvatara Upaniṣad* 6.23)

When a hungry man is given food to eat, he feels satiation of hunger and the pleasure of dining simultaneously. Thus he does not have to ask whether he has actually been fed or not. The crucial test of hearing *Śrīmad-Bhāgavatam* is that one should get positive enlightenment by such an act.

TEXT 6

भूय एव विवित्सामि भगवानात्ममायया ।
यथेदं सृजते विश्वं दुर्विभाव्यमधीश्वरैः ॥ ६ ॥

bhūya eva vivitsāmi
bhagavān ātma-māyayā
yathedaṁ sṛjate viśvaṁ
durvibhāvyam adhīśvaraiḥ

bhūyaḥ—again; *eva*—also; *vivitsāmi*—I wish to learn; *bhagavān*—the Personality of Godhead; *ātma*—personal; *māyayā*—by the energies; *yathā*—as; *idam*—this phenomenal world; *sṛjate*—does create; *viśvam*—universe; *durvibhāvyam*—inconceivable; *adhīśvaraiḥ*—by the great demigods.

TRANSLATION

I beg to know from you how the Personality of Godhead, by His personal energies, creates these phenomenal universes as they are, which are inconceivable even to the great demigods.

PURPORT

In every inquisitive mind the important question of the creation of the phenomenal world arises, and therefore for a personality like Mahārāja Parīkṣit, who was to know all the activities of the Lord from his spiritual master, such an inquiry is not uncommon. For every unknown thing, we have to learn and inquire from a learned personality. The question of creation is also one of such inquiries to be made to the right person. The spiritual master, therefore, must be one who is *sarva-jña*, as stated hereinbefore in connection with Śukadeva Gosvāmī. Thus all inquiries on God which are unknown to the disciple may be made from the qualified spiritual master, and here the practical example is set by Mahārāja Parīkṣit. It was, however, already known to Mahārāja Parīkṣit that everything we see is born out of the energy of the Lord, as we have all learned in the very beginning of *Śrīmad-Bhāgavatam* (*janmādy asya yataḥ*). So Mahārāja Parīkṣit wanted to know the process of creation. The origin of creation was known to him; otherwise he would not have inquired how the Personality of Godhead, by His different energies, creates this phenomenal world. The common man also knows that the creation is made by some creator and is not created automatically. We have no experience in the practical world that a thing is created automatically. Foolish people say that the creative energy is independent and acts automatically, as electrical energy works. But the intelligent man knows that even the electrical energy is generated by an expert engineer in the localized powerhouse, and thus the energy is distributed everywhere under the resident engineer's supervision. The Lord's supervision in connection with creation is mentioned even in the *Bhagavad-gītā* (9.10), and it is clearly said there that material energy is a manifestation of one of many such energies of the Supreme (*parāsya śaktir vividhaiva śrūyate*). An inexperienced boy may be struck with wonder by seeing the impersonal actions of electronics or many other wonderful things conducted by electrical energy, but an experienced man knows that behind the action is a living man who creates such energy. Similarly the so-called scholars and philosophers of the world may, by mental speculation, present so many utopian theories about the impersonal creation of the universe, but an intelligent devotee of the Lord, by studying the *Bhagavad-gītā*, can know that behind the creation is the hand of the Supreme Lord, just as in the generating electrical powerhouse there is the resident engineer. The research scholar finds out the cause and the effect of everything, but research scholars as great as Brahmā, Śiva, Indra and many other demigods are sometimes bewildered by seeing the wonderful creative energy of the Lord, so what to speak of the tiny mundane scholars dealing in petty things. As there are differences in the living conditions of different planets of the universe, and as one planet is superior to others, the brains of the living entities in those respective planets are also of different categorical values. As stated in the *Bhagavad-gītā*, one can compare the long duration of life of the inhabitants of Brahmā's planet, which is inconceivable to the inhabitants of this planet earth, to the categorical value of the brain of Brahmājī, also inconceivable to any great scientist of this planet. And with such high brain power, even Brahmājī has described in his great *saṁhitā* (*Brahma-saṁhitā* 5.1) as follows:

īśvaraḥ paramaḥ kṛṣṇaḥ
sac-cid-ānanda-vigrahaḥ
anādir ādir govindaḥ
sarva-kāraṇa-kāraṇam

"There are many personalities possessing the qualities of Bhagavān, but Kṛṣṇa is the supreme because none can excel Him. He is the Supreme

Person, and His body is eternal, full of knowledge and bliss. He is the primeval Lord Govinda and the cause of all causes."

Brahmājī admits Lord Kṛṣṇa to be the supreme cause of all causes. But persons with tiny brains within this petty planet earth think of the Lord as one of them. Thus when the Lord says in the *Bhagavad-gītā* that He (Lord Kṛṣṇa) is all in all, the speculative philosophers and the mundane wranglers deride Him, and the Lord regretfully says:

avajānanti māṁ mūḍhā
mānuṣīṁ tanum āśritam
paraṁ bhāvam ajānanto
mama bhūta-maheśvaram

"Fools deride Me when I descend in the human form. They do not know My transcendental nature and My supreme dominion over all that be." (Bg. 9.11) Brahmā and Śiva (and what to speak of other demigods) are *bhūtas*, or powerful created demigods who manage universal affairs, much like ministers appointed by a king. The ministers may be *īśvaras*, or controllers, but the Supreme Lord is *maheśvara*, or the creator of the controllers. Persons with a poor fund of knowledge do not know this, and therefore they have the audacity to deride Him because He comes before us by His causeless mercy occasionally as a human being. The Lord is not like a human being. He is *sac-cid-ānanda-vigraha*, or the Absolute Personality of Godhead, and there is no difference between His body and His soul. He is both the power and the powerful.

Mahārāja Parīkṣit did not ask his spiritual master, Śukadeva Gosvāmī, to narrate Lord Kṛṣṇa's pastimes in Vṛndāvana; he wanted to hear first about the creation of the Lord. Śukadeva Gosvāmī did not say that the King should hear about the direct transcendental pastimes of the Lord. The time was very short, and naturally Śukadeva Gosvāmī could have gone directly to the Tenth Canto to make a shortcut of the whole thing, as generally done by the professional reciters. But neither the King nor the great speaker of *Śrīmad-Bhāgavatam* jumped up like the organizers of *Bhāgavatam;* both of them proceeded systematically, so that both future readers and hearers might take lessons from the example of the procedure of reciting *Śrīmad-Bhāgavatam.* Those who are in control of the external energy of the Lord, or in other words those who are in the material world, must first of all know how the external energy of the Lord is working under the direction of the Supreme Personality, and afterwards one may try to enter into the activities of His internal energy. The mundaners are mostly worshipers of Durgā-devī, the external energy of Kṛṣṇa, but they do not know that Durgā-devī is but the shadow energy of the Lord. Behind her astonishing display of material workings is the direction of the Lord, as confirmed in the *Bhagavad-gītā* (9.10). The *Brahma-saṁhitā* affirms that Durgā-śakti is working by the direction of Govinda, and without His sanction the powerful Durgā-śakti cannot move even a blade of grass. Therefore the neophyte devotee, instead of jumping at once to the platform of transcendental pastimes presented by the internal energy of the Lord, may know how great the Supreme Lord is by inquiring about the process of His creative energy. In the *Caitanya-caritāmṛta* also, descriptions of the creative energy and the Lord's hand in it are explained, and the author of *Caitanya-caritāmṛta* has warned the neophyte devotees to be seriously on guard against the pitfall of neglecting knowledge about Kṛṣṇa in regard to how great He is. Only when one knows Lord Kṛṣṇa's greatness can one firmly put one's unflinching faith in Him; otherwise, like the common man, even the great leaders of men will mistake Lord Kṛṣṇa for one of the many demigods, or a historical personality, or a myth only. The transcendental pastimes of the Lord in Vṛndāvana, or even at Dvārakā, are relishable for persons who have already qualified themselves in advanced spiritual techniques, and the common man may be able to attain to such a plane by the gradual process of service and inquiries, as we shall see in the behavior of Mahārāja Parīkṣit.

TEXT 7

यथा गोपायति विभुर्यथा संयच्छते पुनः ।
यां यां शक्तिमुपाश्रित्य पुरुशक्तिः परः पुमान् ।
आत्मानं क्रीडयन् क्रीडन् करोति विकरोति च ।। ७ ।।

yathā gopāyati vibhur
yathā saṁyacchate punaḥ
yāṁ yāṁ śaktim upāśritya
puru-śaktiḥ paraḥ pumān

ātmānaṁ krīḍayan krīḍan
karoti vikaroti ca

yathā—as; *gopāyati*—maintains; *vibhuḥ*—the great; *yathā*—as; *saṁyacchate*—winds up; *punaḥ*—again; *yām yām*—as; *śaktim*—energies; *upāśritya*—by employing; *puru-śaktiḥ*—the all-powerful; *paraḥ*—the Supreme; *pumān*—Personality of Godhead; *ātmānam*—plenary expansion; *krīḍayan*—having engaged them; *krīḍan*—as also personally being engaged; *karoti*—does them; *vikaroti*—and causes to be done; *ca*—and.

TRANSLATION

Kindly describe how the Supreme Lord, who is all-powerful, engages His different energies and different expansions in maintaining and again winding up the phenomenal world in the sporting spirit of a player.

PURPORT

In the *Kaṭha Upaniṣad* (2.2.13) the Supreme Lord is described as the chief eternal being amongst all other eternal individual beings (*nityo nityānāṁ cetanaś cetanānām*) and the one Supreme Lord who maintains innumerable other individual living beings (*eko bahūnāṁ yo vidadhāti kāmān*). So all living entities, both in the conditioned state and in the liberated state, are maintained by the Almighty Supreme Lord. Such maintenance is effected by the Lord through His different expansions of Self and three principal energies, namely the internal, external and marginal energies. The living entities are His marginal energies, and some of them, in the confidence of the Lord, are entrusted with the work of creation also, as are Brahmā, Marīci, etc., and the acts of creation are inspired by the Lord unto them (*tene brahma hṛdā*). The external energy (*māyā*) is also impregnated with the *jīvas*, or conditioned souls. The unconditioned marginal potency acts in the spiritual kingdom, and the Lord, by His different plenary expansions, maintains them in different transcendental relations displayed in the spiritual sky. So the one Supreme Personality of Godhead manifests Himself in many (*bahu syām*), and thus all diversities are in Him, and He is in all diversities, although He is nevertheless different from all of them. That is the inconceivable mystic power of the Lord, and as such everything is simultaneously one with and different from Him by His inconceivable potencies (*acintya-bhedābheda-tattva*).

TEXT 8

नूनं भगवतो ब्रह्मन् हरेरद्भुतकर्मणः ।
दुर्विभाव्यमिवाभाति कविभिश्चापि चेष्टितम् ॥ ८ ॥

nūnaṁ bhagavato brahman
harer adbhuta-karmaṇaḥ
durvibhāvyam ivābhāti
kavibhiś cāpi ceṣṭitam

nūnam—still insufficient; *bhagavataḥ*—of the Personality of Godhead; *brahman*—O learned *brāhmaṇa; hareḥ*—of the Lord; *adbhuta*—wonderful; *karmaṇaḥ*—one who acts; *durvibhāvyam*—inconceivable; *iva*—like that; *ābhāti*—appears; *kavibhiḥ*—even by the highly learned; *ca*—also; *api*—in spite of; *ceṣṭitam*—being endeavored for.

TRANSLATION

O learned brāhmaṇa, the transcendental activities of the Lord are all wonderful, and they appear inconceivable because even great endeavors by many learned scholars have still proved insufficient for understanding them.

PURPORT

The acts of the Supreme Lord, in the creation of just this one universe, appear inconceivably wonderful. And there are innumerable universes, and all of them aggregated together are known as the created material world. And this part of His creation is only a fractional portion of the complete creation. The material world stands as a part only (*ekāṁśena sthito jagat*). Supposing that the material world is a display of one part of His energy, the remaining three parts consist of the *vaikuṇṭha-jagat* or spiritual world described in the *Bhagavad-gītā* as *mad-dhāma* or *sanātana-dhāma*, or the eternal world. We have marked in the previous verse that He creates and again winds up the creation. This action is applicable only in the material world because the other, greater part of His creation, namely the Vaikuṇṭha world, is neither created nor annihilated; otherwise the Vaikuṇṭha-dhāma would not have been called eternal. The Lord exists with *dhāma;* His eternal name, quality, pastimes, entourage and personality are all a display of His different energies and expansions. The Lord is called *anādi*, or having no creator, and *ādi*, or the origin of all. We think in our own imperfect way that the Lord is also created, but the *Vedānta* informs us that He is not created. Rather, everything else is created by Him (*nārāyaṇaḥ paro 'vyaktāt*). Therefore, for the common man these are all very wonderful matters for consideration. Even for great scholars they are inconceivable, and thus such scholars present theories contradictory to one another. Even for the insignificant part of His creation, this particular universe, they have no complete information as to how far this limited space extends, or how many stars and planets are there, or the different conditions of those innumerable planets. Modern scientists have insufficient knowledge of all this. Some of them assert that there are one hundred million planets scattered all over space. In a news release from Moscow dated 2/21/60, the following piece of knowledge was relayed:

"Russia's well-known professor of astronomy Boris Vorontsov-Veliaminov said that there must be an infinite number of planets in the universe inhabited by beings endowed with reason.

"It could be that life similar to that on earth flourishes on such planets.

"Doctor of Chemistry Nikolai Zhirov, covering the problem of atmosphere on other planets, pointed out that the organism of a Martian, for instance, could very well adapt itself to normal existence with a low body temperature.

"He said that he felt that the gaseous composition of Martian atmosphere was quite suitable to sustain life of beings which have become adapted to it."

This adaptability of an organism to different varieties of planets is described in the *Brahma-saṁhitā* as *vibhūti-bhinnam;* i.e., each and every one of the innumerable planets within the universe is endowed with a particular type of atmosphere, and the living beings there are more perfectly advanced in science and psychology because of a better atmosphere. *Vibhūti* means "specific powers," and *bhinnam* means "variegated." Scientists who are attempting to explore outer space and are trying to reach other planets by mechanical arrangements must know for certain that organisms adapted to the atmosphere of earth cannot exist in the atmospheres of other planets (*Easy Journey to Other Planets*). One has to prepare himself, therefore, to be transferred to a different planet after being relieved of the present body, as it is said in the *Bhagavad-gītā* (9.25):

yānti deva-vratā devān
pitṝn yānti pitṛ-vratāḥ
bhūtāni yānti bhūtejyā
yānti mad-yājino 'pi mām

"Those who worship the demigods will take birth among the demigods, those who worship ghosts and spirits will take birth among such beings, and those who worship Me will live with Me."

Mahārāja Parīkṣit's statement regarding the workings of the creative energy of the Lord discloses that he knew everything of the process of creation. Why then did he ask Śukadeva Gosvāmī for such information? Mahārāja Parīkṣit, being a great emperor, a descendant of the Pāṇḍavas and a great devotee of Lord Kṛṣṇa, was quite able to know considerably about the creation of the world, but that much knowledge was not sufficient. He said therefore that even greatly learned scholars fail to know about that, even after great effort. The Lord is unlimited, and His activities are also unfathomed. With a limited source of knowledge and with imperfect senses, any living being, up to the standard of Brahmājī, the highest perfect living being within the universe, can never imagine knowing about the unlimited. We can know something of the unlimited when it is explained by the unlimited, as has been done by the Lord Himself in the unique statements of the *Bhagavad-gītā*, and it can also be known to some extent from realized souls like Śukadeva Gosvāmī, who learned it from Vyāsadeva, a disciple of Nārada, and thus the perfect knowledge can descend by the chain of disciplic succession only, and not by any form of experimental knowledge, old or modern.

TEXT 9

यथा गुणांस्तु प्रकृतेर्युगपत् क्रमशोऽपि वा ।
बिभर्ति भूरिशस्त्वेकः कुर्वन् कर्माणि जन्मभिः ॥ ९ ॥

yathā guṇāṁs tu prakṛter
yugapat kramaśo 'pi vā
bibharti bhūriśas tv ekaḥ
kurvan karmāṇi janmabhiḥ

yathā—as they are; *guṇān*—the modes of; *tu*—but; *prakṛteḥ*—of the material energy; *yugapat*—simultaneously; *kramaśaḥ*—gradually; *api*—also; *vā*—either; *bibharti*—maintains; *bhūriśaḥ*—many forms; *tu*—but; *ekaḥ*—the supreme one; *kurvan*—acting; *karmāṇi*—activities; *janmabhiḥ*—by incarnations.

TRANSLATION

The Supreme Personality of Godhead is one, whether He alone acts with the modes of material nature, or simultaneously expands in many forms, or expands consecutively to direct the modes of nature.

TEXT 10

विचिकित्सितमेतन्मे ब्रवीतु भगवान् यथा ।
शाब्दे ब्रह्मणि निष्णातः परस्मिंश्च भवान्खलु ॥१०॥

vicikitsitam etan me
bravītu bhagavān yathā
śābde brahmaṇi niṣṇātaḥ
parasmiṁś ca bhavān khalu

vicikitsitam—doubtful inquiry; *etat*—this; *me*—of me; *bravītu*—just clear up; *bhagavān*—powerful like the Lord; *yathā*—as much as; *śābde*—sound transcendental; *brahmaṇi*—Vedic literature; *niṣṇātaḥ*—fully realized; *parasmin*—in transcendence; *ca*—also; *bhavān*—your good self; *khalu*—as a matter of fact.

TRANSLATION

Kindly clear up all these doubtful inquiries, because you are not only vastly learned in the Vedic literatures and self-realized in transcendence, but are also a great devotee of the Lord and are therefore as good as the Personality of Godhead.

PURPORT

In the *Brahma-saṁhitā* it is said that the Supreme Absolute Truth, Govinda, the Personality of Godhead, although one without a second, is infallibly expanded by innumerable forms nondifferent from one another, and although He is the original person, He is still ever young with permanent youthful energy. He is very difficult to know simply by learning the transcendental science of the *Vedas*, but He is very easily realized by His pure devotees.

The expansions of different forms of the Lord, as from Kṛṣṇa to Baladeva to Saṅkarṣaṇa, from Saṅkarṣaṇa to Vāsudeva, from Vāsudeva to Aniruddha, from Aniruddha to Pradyumna and then again to second Saṅkarṣaṇa and from Him to the Nārāyaṇa *puruṣāvatāras*, and innumerable other forms, which are compared to the constant flowing of the uncountable waves of a river, are all one and the same. They are like lamps of equal power which kindle from one lamp to another. That is the transcendental potency of the Lord. The *Vedas* say that He is so complete that even though the whole complete identity emanates from Him, He still remains the same complete whole (*pūrṇasya pūrṇam ādāya pūrṇam evāvaśiṣyate*). As such, there is no validity in a material conception of the Lord produced by the mental speculator. Thus He remains always a mystery for the mundane scholar, even if he is vastly learned in the Vedic literatures (*vedeṣu durlabham adurlabham ātma-bhaktau*). Therefore, the Lord is beyond the limit of conception for mundane learned scholars, philosophers or scientists. He is easily understandable for the pure devotee because the Lord declares in the *Bhagavad-gītā* (18.54) that after surpassing the stage of knowledge, when one is able to be engaged in the devotional service of the Lord, then only can one know the true nature of the Lord. One cannot have any clear conception of the Lord or His holy name, form, attributes, pastimes, etc., unless one is engaged in His transcendental loving service. The statement of the *Bhagavad-gītā* that one must first of all surrender unto the Lord, being freed from all other engagements, means that one must become a pure, unconditional devotee of the Lord. Only then can one know Him by the strength of devotional service.

Mahārāja Parīkṣit admitted in the previous verse that the Lord is inconceivable even for the greatest learned scholars. Why then should he again request Śukadeva Gosvāmī to clarify his insufficient knowledge about the Lord? The reason is clear. Not only was Śukadeva Gosvāmī vastly learned in the Vedic literatures, but he was also a great self-realized soul and a powerful devotee of the Lord. A powerful devotee of the Lord is, by the grace of the Lord, more than the Lord Himself. The Personality of Godhead Śrī Rāmacandra attempted to bridge the Indian Ocean to reach the island of Laṅkā, but Śrī Hanumānjī, the unalloyed devotee of the Personality of Godhead, could cross the ocean simply by jumping over it. The Lord is so merciful upon His pure devotee that He presents His beloved devotee as more powerful than Himself. The Lord expressed Himself to be unable to save Durvāsā Muni, although the Muni was so powerful that he could reach the Lord directly under material conditions. But Durvāsā Muni was saved by Mahārāja Ambarīṣa, a devotee of the Lord. Therefore, not only is a devotee of the Lord more powerful than the Lord, but also worship of the devotee is considered more effective than direct worship of the Lord (*mad-bhakta-pūjābhyadhikā*).

The conclusion is, therefore, that a serious devotee must first approach a spiritual master who not only is well versed in the Vedic literatures but is also a great devotee with factual realization of the Lord and His different energies. Without the help of such a devotee spiritual master, one cannot make progress in the transcendental science of the Lord. And a bona fide spiritual master like Śukadeva Gosvāmī does not speak about the Lord only in the matter of His internal potencies, but also explains how He associates with His external potencies.

The Lord's pastimes in the internal potency are displayed in His activities in Vṛndāvana, but His external potential works are directed in His features of Kāraṇārṇavaśāyī Viṣṇu, Garbhodakaśāyī Viṣṇu and Kṣīrodakaśāyī Viṣṇu. Śrīla Viśvanātha Cakravartī offers his good counsel to the interested Vaiṣṇavas when he says that they should not be interested in hearing only about the Lord's activities (like *rāsa-līlā*), but must be keenly interested in His pastimes in His features of the *puruṣāvatāras* in connection with *sṛṣṭi-tattva*, creational functions, following the examples of Mahārāja Parīkṣit, the ideal disciple, and Śukadeva Gosvāmī, the ideal spiritual master.

TEXT 11

सूत उवाच
इत्युपामन्त्रितो राज्ञा गुणानुकथने हरेः ।
हृषीकेशमनुस्मृत्य प्रतिवक्तुं प्रचक्रमे ॥११॥

sūta uvāca
ity upāmantrito rājñā
guṇānukathane hareḥ
hṛṣīkeśam anusmṛtya
prativaktuṁ pracakrame

sūtaḥ uvāca—Sūta Gosvāmī said; *iti*—thus; *upāmantritaḥ*—being requested; *rājñā*—by the King; *guṇa-anukathane*—in describing the transcendental attributes of the Lord; *hareḥ*—of the Personality of Godhead; *hṛṣīkeśam*—the master of the senses; *anusmṛtya*—properly remembering; *prativaktum*—just to reply; *pracakrame*—executed the preliminaries.

TRANSLATION

Sūta Gosvāmī said: When Śukadeva Gosvāmī was thus requested by the King to describe the creative energy of the Personality of Godhead, he then systematically remembered the master of the senses [Śrī Kṛṣṇa], and to reply properly he spoke thus.

PURPORT

The devotees of the Lord, while delivering speeches and describing the transcendental attributes of the Lord, do not think that they can do anything independently. They think that they can speak only what they are induced to speak by the Supreme Lord, the master of the senses. The senses of the individual being are not his own; the devotee knows that such senses belong to the Supreme Lord and that they can be properly used when they are employed for the service of the Lord. The senses are instruments, and elements are ingredients, all endowed by the Lord; therefore whatever an individual can do, speak, see, etc., is under the direction of the Lord only. The *Bhagavad-gītā* (15.15) confirms this: *sarvasya cāhaṁ hṛdi sanniviṣṭo mattaḥ smṛtir jñānam apohanaṁ ca.* No one is free to act freely and independently, and as such, one should always seek the permission of the Lord to act or eat or speak, and by the blessing of the Lord everything done by a devotee is beyond the principles of the four defects typical of the conditioned soul.

TEXT 12

श्रीशुक उवाच
नमः परस्मै पुरुषाय भूयसे
सदुद्भवस्थाननिरोधलीलया ।
गृहीतशक्तित्रितयाय देहिना-
मन्तर्भवायानुपलक्ष्यवर्त्मने ॥१२॥

śrī-śuka uvāca
namaḥ parasmai puruṣāya bhūyase
sad-udbhava-sthāna-nirodha-līlayā
gṛhīta-śakti-tritayāya dehinām
antarbhavāyānupalakṣya-vartmane

śrī-śukaḥ uvaca—Śrī Śukadeva Gosvāmī said; *namaḥ*—offering obeisances; *parasmai*—the Supreme; *puruṣāya*—Personality of Godhead; *bhūyase*—unto the complete whole; *sad-udbhava*—the creation of the material world; *sthāna*—its maintenance; *nirodha*—and its winding up; *līlayā*—by the pastime of; *gṛhīta*—having accepted; *śakti*—power; *tritayāya*—three modes; *dehinām*—of all who possess material bodies; *antaḥ-bhavāya*—unto He who resides within; *anupalakṣya*—inconceivable; *vartmane*—one who has such ways.

TRANSLATION

Śukadeva Gosvāmī said: Let me offer my respectful obeisances unto the Supreme Personality of Godhead who, for the creation of the material world, accepts the three modes of nature. He is the

complete whole residing within the body of everyone, and His ways are inconceivable.

PURPORT

This material world is a manifestation of the three modes goodness, passion and ignorance, and the Supreme Lord, for the creation, maintenance and destruction of the material world, accepts three predominating forms as Brahmā, Viṣṇu and Śaṅkara (Śiva). As Viṣṇu He enters into every body materially created. As Garbhodakaśāyī Viṣṇu He enters into every universe, and as Kṣīrodakaśāyī Viṣṇu He enters the body of every living being. Lord Śrī Kṛṣṇa, being the origin of all *viṣṇu-tattvas*, is addressed here as *paraḥ pumān*, or Puruṣottama, as described in the *Bhagavad-gītā* (15.18). He is the complete whole. The *puruṣāvatāras* are therefore His plenary expansions. *Bhakti-yoga* is the only process by which one can become competent to know Him. Because the empiric philosophers and mystic *yogīs* cannot conceive of the Personality of Godhead, He is called *anupalakṣya-vartmane*, the Lord of the inconceivable way, or *bhakti-yoga*.

TEXT 13

भूयो नमः सद्वृजिनच्छिदेऽसता-
मसम्भवायाखिलसत्त्वमूर्तये ।
पुंसां पुनः पारमहंस्य आश्रमे
व्यवस्थितानामनुमृग्यदाशुषे ॥१३॥

bhūyo namaḥ sad-vṛjina-cchide 'satām
asambhavāyākhila-sattva-mūrtaye
puṁsāṁ punaḥ pāramahaṁsya āśrame
vyavasthitānām anumṛgya-dāśuṣe

bhūyaḥ—again; *namaḥ*—my obeisances; *sat*—of the devotees or the pious; *vṛjina*—distresses; *chide*—the liberator; *asatām*—of the atheists, the nondevotee-demons; *asambhavāya*—cessation of further unhappiness; *akhila*—complete; *sattva*—goodness; *mūrtaye*—unto the Personality; *puṁsām*—of the transcendentalists; *punaḥ*—again; *pāramahaṁsye*—the highest stage of spiritual perfection; *āśrame*—in the status; *vyavasthitānām*—particularly situated; *anumṛgya*—the destination; *dāśuṣe*—one who delivers.

TRANSLATION

I again offer my respectful obeisances unto the form of complete existence and transcendence, who is the liberator of the pious devotees from all distresses and the destroyer of the further advances in atheistic temperament of the nondevotee-demons. For the transcendentalists who are situated in the topmost spiritual perfection, He grants their specific destinations.

PURPORT

Lord Śrī Kṛṣṇa is the complete form of all existence, both material and spiritual. *Akhila* means complete, or that which is not *khila*, inferior. As stated in the *Bhagavad-gītā*, there are two kinds of nature (*prakṛti*), namely the material nature and the spiritual nature, or the external and internal potencies of the Lord. The material nature is called *aparā*, or inferior, and the spiritual nature is called superior or transcendental. Therefore the form of the Lord is not of the inferior, material nature. He is complete transcendence. And He is *mūrti*, or having transcendental form. The less intelligent men, who are unaware of His transcendental form, describe Him as impersonal Brahman. But Brahman is simply the rays of His transcendental body (*yasya prabhā*). The devotees, who are aware of His transcendental form, render Him service; therefore the Lord also reciprocates by His causeless mercy and thus delivers His devotees from all distresses. The pious men who follow the rulings of the *Vedas* are also dear to Him, and therefore the pious men of this world are also protected by Him. The impious and the nondevotees are against the principles of the *Vedas*, and so such persons are always hampered from making advances in their nefarious activities. Some of them, who are specially favored by the Lord, are killed by Him personally, as in the cases of Rāvana, Hiraṇyakaśipu and Kaṁsa, and thus such demons get salvation and are thereby checked from further progress in their demoniac activities. Just like a kind father, either in His favor upon the devotees or His punishment of the demons He is ever kind to everyone because He is the complete existence for all individual existence.

The *paramahaṁsa* stage of existence is the highest perfectional stage of spiritual values. According to Śrīmatī Kuntīdevī, the Lord is factually understood by the *paramahaṁsas* only. As there is gradual realization of the transcendence from impersonal Brahman to localized Paramātmā to the Personality of Godhead, Puruṣottama, Lord Kṛṣṇa, similarly there is gradual promotion of one's situation in the spiritual life of *sannyāsa. Kuṭīcaka, bahūdaka, parivrājakācārya* and *paramahaṁsa* are gradual progressive stages in the renounced order of life, *sannyāsa,* and Queen Kuntīdevī, the mother of the Pāṇḍavas, has spoken about them in her prayers for Lord Kṛṣṇa (Canto One, Chapter Eight). The *paramahaṁsas* are generally found among both the impersonalists and the devotees, but according to *Śrīmad-Bhāgavatam* (as clearly stated by Kuntīdevī), pure *bhakti-yoga* is understood by the *paramahaṁsas,* and Kuntīdevī has especially mentioned that the Lord descends (*paritrāṇāya sādhūnām*) especially to award *bhakti-yoga* to the *paramahaṁsas.* So ultimately the *paramahaṁsas,* in the true sense of the term, are unalloyed devotees of the Lord. Śrīla Jīva Gosvāmī has directly accepted that the highest destination is *bhakti-yoga,* by which one accepts the transcendental loving service of the Lord. Those who accept the path of *bhakti-yoga* are the factual *paramahaṁsas.*

Since the Lord is very kind to everyone, the impersonalists, who accept *bhakti* as the means of merging in the existence of the Lord in His impersonal *brahmajyoti,* are also awarded their desired destination. He has assured everyone in the *Bhagavad-gītā* (4.11): *ye yathā māṁ prapadyante.* According to Śrīla Viśvanātha Cakravartī, there are two classes of *paramahaṁsas,* namely the *brahmānandīs* (impersonalists) and the *premānandīs* (devotees), and both are awarded their desired destinations, although the *premānandīs* are more fortunate than the *brahmānandīs.* But both the *brahmānandīs* and the *premānandīs* are transcendentalists, and they have nothing to do with the inferior, material nature full of the existential miseries of life.

TEXT 14

नमो नमस्तेऽस्त्वृषभाय सात्वतां
विदूरकाष्ठाय मुहुः कुयोगिनाम् ।

निरस्तसाम्यातिशयेन राधसा
स्वधामनि ब्रह्मणि रंस्यते नमः ॥१४॥

namo namas te 'stv ṛṣabhāya sātvatāṁ
vidūra-kāṣṭhāya muhuḥ kuyoginām
nirasta-sāmyātiśayena rādhasā
sva-dhāmani brahmaṇi raṁsyate namaḥ

namaḥ namaḥ te—let me offer my obeisances unto You; *astu*—are; *ṛṣabhāya*—unto the great associate; *sātvatām*—of the members of the Yadu dynasty; *vidūra-kāṣṭhāya*—one who is far from mundane wranglers; *muhuḥ*—always; *ku-yoginām*—of the nondevotees; *nirasta*—vanquished; *sāmya*—equal status; *atiśayena*—by greatness; *rādhasā*—by opulence; *sva-dhāmani*—in His own abode; *brahmaṇi*—in the spiritual sky; *raṁsyate*—enjoys; *namaḥ*—I do bow down.

TRANSLATION

Let me offer my respectful obeisances unto He who is the associate of the members of the Yadu dynasty and who is always a problem for the nondevotees. He is the supreme enjoyer of both the material and spiritual worlds, yet He enjoys His own abode in the spiritual sky. There is no one equal to Him because His transcendental opulence is immeasurable.

PURPORT

There are two sides of the transcendental manifestations of the Supreme Lord, Śrī Kṛṣṇa. For the pure devotees He is the constant companion, as in the case of His becoming one of the family members of the Yadu dynasty, or His becoming the friend of Arjuna, or His becoming the associate neighbor of the inhabitants of Vṛndāvana, as the son of Nanda-Yaśodā, the friend of Sudāmā, Śrīdāmā and Madhumaṅgala, or the lover of the damsels of Vrajabhūmi, etc. That is part of His personal features. And by His impersonal feature He expands the rays of the *brahmajyoti*, which is limitless and all-pervasive. Part of this all-pervasive *brahmajyoti*, which is compared to the sun rays, is covered by the darkness of the *mahat-tattva*, and this insignificant part is known as the material world. In this material world there are innumerable universes like the one we can experience, and in each of them there are hundreds of thousands of planets like the one we are inhabiting. The mundaners are more or less captivated by the unlimited expansion of the rays of the Lord, but the devotees are concerned more with His personal form, from which everything is emanating (*janmādy asya yataḥ*). As the sun rays are concentrated in the sun disc, the *brahmajyoti* is concentrated in Goloka Vṛndāvana, the topmost spiritual planet in the spiritual sky. The immeasurable spiritual sky is full of spiritual planets, named Vaikuṇṭhas, far beyond the material sky. The mundaners have insufficient information of even the mundane sky, so what can they think of the spiritual sky? Therefore the mundaners are always far, far away from Him. Even if in the future they are able to manufacture some machine whose speed may be accelerated to the velocity of the wind or mind, the mundaners will still be unable to imagine reaching the planets in the spiritual sky. So the Lord and His residential abode will always remain a myth or a mysterious problem, but for the devotees the Lord will always be available as an associate.

In the spiritual sky His opulence is immeasurable. The Lord resides in all the spiritual planets, the innumerable Vaikuṇṭha planets, by expanding His plenary portions along with His liberated devotee associates, but the impersonalists who want to merge in the existence of the Lord are allowed to merge as one of the spiritual sparks of the *brahmajyoti*. They have no qualifications for becoming associates of the Lord either in the Vaikuṇṭha planets or in the supreme planet, Goloka Vṛndāvana, described in the *Bhagavad-gītā* as *mad-dhāma* and here in this verse as the *sva-dhāma* of the Lord.

This *mad-dhāma* or *sva-dhāma* is described in the *Bhagavad-gītā* (15.6) as follows:

na tad bhāsayate sūryo
na śaśāṅko na pāvakaḥ
yad gatvā na nivartante
tad dhāma paramaṁ mama

The Lord's *sva-dhāma* does not require any sunlight or moonlight or electricity for illumination. That *dhāma*, or place, is supreme, and whoever goes there never comes back to this material world.

The Vaikuṇṭha planets and the Goloka Vṛndāvana planet are all self-illuminating, and the rays scattered by those *sva-dhāma* of the Lord constitute the existence of the *brahmajyoti.* As further confirmed in the *Vedas* like the *Muṇḍaka* (2.2.10), *Kaṭha* (2.2.15) and *Śvetāśvatara Upaniṣads* (6.14):

na tatra sūryo bhāti na candra-tārakaṁ
nemā vidyuto bhānti kuto 'yam agniḥ
tam eva bhāntam anu bhāti sarvaṁ
tasya bhāsā sarvam idaṁ vibhāti

In the *sva-dhāma* of the Lord there is no need of sun, moon or stars for illumination. Nor is there need of electricity, so what to speak of ignited lamps? On the other hand, it is because those planets are self-illuminating that all effulgence has become possible, and whatever there is that is dazzling is due to the reflection of that *sva-dhāma.*

One who is dazzled by the effulgence of the impersonal *brahmajyoti* cannot know the personal transcendence; therefore in the *Īśopaniṣad* (15) it is prayed that the Lord shift His dazzling effulgence so that the devotee can see the real reality. It is spoken thus:

hiraṇmayena pātreṇa
satyasyāpihitaṁ mukham
tat tvaṁ pūṣann apāvṛṇu
satya-dharmāya dṛṣṭaye

"O Lord, You are the maintainer of everything, both material and spiritual, and everything flourishes by Your mercy. Your devotional service, or *bhakti-yoga,* is the actual principle of religion, *satya-dharma,* and I am engaged in that service. So kindly protect me by showing Your real face. Please, therefore, remove the veil of Your *brahmajyoti* rays so that I can see Your form of eternal bliss and knowledge."

TEXT 15

यत्कीर्तनं यत्स्मरणं यदीक्षणं
यद्वन्दनं यच्छ्रवणं यदर्हणम् ।

लोकस्य सद्यो विधुनोति कल्मषं
तस्मै सुभद्रश्रवसे नमो नमः ॥१५॥

yat-kīrtanaṁ yat-smaraṇaṁ yad-īkṣaṇaṁ
yad-vandanaṁ yac-chravaṇaṁ yad-arhaṇam
lokasya sadyo vidhunoti kalmaṣaṁ
tasmai subhadra-śravase namo namaḥ

yat—whose; *kīrtanam*—glorification; *yat*—whose; *smaraṇam*—remembrances; *yat*—whose; *īkṣaṇam*—audience; *yat*—whose; *vandanam*—prayers; *yat*—whose; *śravaṇam*—hearing about; *yat*—whose; *arhaṇam*—worshiping; *lokasya*—of all people; *sadyaḥ*—forthwith; *vidhunoti*—specifically cleanses; *kalmaṣam*—effects of sins; *tasmai*—unto Him; *subhadra*—all-auspicious; *śravase*—one who is heard; *namaḥ*—my due obeisances; *namaḥ*—again and again.

TRANSLATION

Let me offer my respectful obeisances unto the all-auspicious Lord Śrī Kṛṣṇa, about whom glorification, remembrances, audience, prayers, hearing and worship can at once cleanse the effects of all sins of the performer.

PURPORT

The sublime form of religious performances to free oneself from all reactions of sins is suggested herein by the greatest authority, Śrī Śukadeva Gosvāmī. *Kīrtanam*, or glorifying the Lord, can be performed in very many ways, such as remembering, visiting temples to see the Deity, offering prayers in front of the Lord, and hearing recitations of glorification of the Lord as they are mentioned in the *Śrīmad-Bhāgavatam* or in the *Bhagavad-gītā*. *Kīrtanam* can be performed both by singing the glories of the Lord in accompaniment with melodious music and by recitation of scriptures like *Śrīmad-Bhāgavatam* or *Bhagavad-gītā*.

The devotees need not be disappointed in the physical absence of the Lord, though they may think of not being associated with Him. The devotional process of chanting, hearing, remembering, etc., (either all or some of them, or even one of them) can give us the desired result of associating with the Lord by discharging the transcendental loving service of the Lord in the above manner. Even the very sound of the holy name of Lord Kṛṣṇa or Rāma can at once surcharge the atmosphere spiritually. We must know definitely that the Lord is present wherever such pure transcendental service is performed, and thus the performer of offenseless *kīrtanam* has positive association with the Lord. Similarly, remembrance and prayers also can give us the desired result if they are properly done under expert guidance. One should not concoct forms of devotional service. One may worship the form of the Lord in a temple, or one may impersonally offer the Lord devotional prayers in a mosque or a church. One is sure to get free from the reactions of sins provided one is very careful about not committing sins willingly in expectation of getting free from the reactions of sins by worshiping in the temple or by offering prayers in the church. This mentality of committing sins willfully on the strength of devotional service is called *nāmno balād yasya hi pāpa-buddhiḥ*, and it is the greatest offense in the discharge of devotional service. Hearing, therefore, is essential in order to keep oneself strictly on guard against such pitfalls of sins. And in order to give special stress to the hearing process, the Gosvāmī invokes all auspicious fortune in this matter.

TEXT 16

विचक्षणा यच्चरणोपसादनात्
सङ्गं व्युदस्योभयतोऽन्तरात्मनः ।
विन्दन्ति हि ब्रह्मगतिं गतक्लमा-
स्तस्मै सुभद्रश्रवसे नमो नमः ॥१६॥

vicakṣaṇā yac-caraṇopasādanāt
saṅgaṁ vyudasyobhayato 'ntar-ātmanaḥ
vindanti hi brahma-gatiṁ gata-klamās
tasmai subhadra-śravase namo namaḥ

vicakṣaṇāḥ—highly intellectual; *yat*—whose; *caraṇa-upasādanāt*—simply dedicating oneself unto the lotus feet; *saṅgam*—attachment;

vyudasya—giving up completely; *ubhayataḥ*—for present and future existence; *antaḥ-ātmanaḥ*—of the heart and soul; *vindanti*—moves progressively; *hi*—certainly; *brahma-gatim*—toward spiritual existence; *gata-klamāḥ*—without difficulty; *tasmai*—unto Him; *su-bhadra*—all-auspicious; *śravase*—unto one who is heard; *namaḥ*—my due obeisances; *namaḥ*—again and again.

TRANSLATION

Let me offer my respectful obeisances again and again unto the all-auspicious Lord Śrī Kṛṣṇa. The highly intellectual, simply by surrendering unto His lotus feet, are relieved of all attachments to present and future existences and without difficulty progress toward spiritual existence.

PURPORT

Lord Śrī Kṛṣṇa has repeatedly instructed Arjuna, or for that matter everyone concerned with becoming His unalloyed devotee. In the last phase of His instruction in the *Bhagavad-gītā* (18.64–66) He instructed most confidentially as follows:

sarva-guhyatamaṁ bhūyaḥ
śṛṇu me paramaṁ vacaḥ
iṣṭo 'si me dṛḍham iti
tato vakṣyāmi te hitam

man-manā bhava mad-bhakto
mad-yājī māṁ namaskuru
mām evaiṣyasi satyaṁ te
pratijāne priyo 'si me

sarva-dharmān parityajya
mām ekaṁ śaraṇaṁ vraja
ahaṁ tvāṁ sarva-pāpebhyo
mokṣayiṣyāmi mā śucaḥ

"My dear Arjuna, you are very dear to Me, and therefore only for your good I will disclose the most secret part of My instructions. It is simply this: become a pure devotee of Mine and give yourself unto Me only, and I promise you full spiritual existence, by which you may gain the eternal right of transcendental loving service unto Me. Just give up all other ways of religiosity and exclusively surrender unto Me and believe that I will protect you from your sinful acts, and I shall deliver you. Do not worry any more."

Persons who are intelligent take serious notice of this last instruction of the Lord. Knowledge of the self is the first step in spiritual realization, which is called confidential knowledge, and a step further is God realization, which is called more confidential knowledge. The culmination of the knowledge of *Bhagavad-gītā* is God realization, and when one attains this stage of God realization, he naturally, voluntarily becomes a devotee of the Lord to render Him loving transcendental service. This devotional service to the Lord is always based on love of God and is distinct from the nature of routine service as prescribed in *karma-yoga*, *jñāna-yoga* or *dhyāna-yoga*. In the *Bhagavad-gītā* there are different instructions for such men of different categories, and there are various descriptions for *varṇāśrama-dharma*, *sannyāsa-dharma*, *yati-dharma*, the renounced order of life, controlling the senses, meditation, perfection of mystic powers, etc., but one who fully surrenders unto the Lord to render service unto Him, out of spontaneous love for Him, factually assimilates the essence of all knowledge described in the *Vedas*. One who adopts this method very skillfully attains perfection of life at once. And this perfection of human life is called *brahma-gati*, or the progressive march in spiritual existence. As enunciated by Śrīla Jīva Gosvāmī on the basis of Vedic assurances, *brahma-gati* means to attain a spiritual form as good as that of the Lord, and in that form the liberated living being eternally lives on one of the spiritual planets situated in the spiritual sky. Attainment of this perfection of life is easily available to a pure devotee of the Lord without his undergoing any difficult method of perfection. Such a devotional life is full of *kīrtanam*, *smaraṇam*, *īkṣaṇam*, etc., as mentioned in the previous verse. One must therefore adopt this simple way of devotional life in order to attain the highest perfection available in any category of the human form of life in any part of the world. When Lord Brahmā met Lord Kṛṣṇa as a playful child at Vṛndāvana, he offered his prayer in which he said:

śreyaḥ-sṛtiṁ bhaktim udasya te vibho
kliśyanti ye kevala-bodha-labdhaye
teṣām asau kleśala eva śiṣyate
nānyad yathā sthūla-tuṣāvaghātinām
(*Bhāg.* 10.14.4)

Bhakti-yoga is the highest quality of perfection to be achieved by the intelligent person in lieu of performing a large quantity of spiritual activities. The example cited here is very appropriate. A handful of real paddy is more valuable than heaps of paddy skins without any substance within. Similarly, one should not be attracted by the jugglery of *karma-kāṇḍa* or *jñāna-kāṇḍa* or even the gymnastic performances of *yoga*, but skillfully should take to the simple performances of *kīrtanam*, *smaraṇam*, etc., under a bona fide spiritual master, and without any difficulty attain the highest perfection.

TEXT 17

तपस्विनो दानपरा यशस्विनो
मनस्विनो मन्त्रविदः सुमङ्गलाः ।
क्षेमं न विन्दन्ति विना यदर्पणं
तस्मै सुभद्रश्रवसे नमो नमः ॥१७॥

tapasvino dāna-parā yaśasvino
manasvino mantra-vidaḥ sumaṅgalāḥ
kṣemaṁ na vindanti vinā yad-arpaṇaṁ
tasmai subhadra-śravase namo namaḥ

tapasvinaḥ—the great learned sages; *dāna-parāḥ*—the great performer of charity; *yaśasvinaḥ*—the great worker of distinction; *manasvinaḥ*—the great philosophers or mystics; *mantra-vidaḥ*—the great chanter of the Vedic hymns; *su-maṅgalāḥ*—strict followers of Vedic principles; *kṣemam*—fruitful result; *na*—never; *vindanti*—attain; *vinā*—without; *yat-arpaṇam*—dedication; *tasmai*—unto Him; *subhadra*—auspicious; *śravase*—hearing about Him; *namaḥ*—my obeisances; *namaḥ*—again and again.

TRANSLATION

Let me offer my respectful obeisances unto the all-auspicious Lord Śrī Kṛṣṇa again and again because the great learned sages, the great performers of charity, the great workers of distinction, the great philosophers and mystics, the great chanters of the Vedic hymns and the great followers of Vedic principles cannot achieve any fruitful result without dedication of such great qualities to the service of the Lord.

PURPORT

Advancement of learning, a charitable disposition, political, social or religious leadership of human society, philosophical speculations, the practice of the *yoga* system, expertise in the Vedic rituals, and all similar high qualities in man serve one in the attainment of perfection only when they are employed in the service of the Lord. Without such dovetailing, all such qualities become sources of trouble for people in general. Everything can be utilized either for one's own sense gratification or in the service of one other than oneself. There are two kinds of self-interest also, namely personal selfishness and extended selfishness. But there is no qualitative difference between personal and extended selfishness. Theft for personal interest or for the family interest is of the same quality—namely, criminal. A thief pleading not guilty because of committing theft not for personal interest but for the interest of society or country has never been excused by the established law of any country. People in general have no knowledge that the self-interest of a living being attains perfection only when such an interest coincides with the interest of the Lord. For example, what is the interest of maintaining body and soul together? One earns money for maintenance of the body (personal or social), but unless there is God consciousness, unless the body is being properly maintained to realize one's relation with God, all good efforts to maintain body and soul together are similar to the attempts of the animals to maintain body and soul together. The purpose of maintaining the human body is different from that of the animals. Similarly, advancement of learning, economic development, philosophical research, study in the Vedic literature or even the execution of pious activities (like charity, opening of hospitals, and the distribution of food grains) should be done in relation with the Lord. The aim of all such acts and endeavors must be the pleasure of the Lord and not the satisfaction of any other identity, individual or collective (*saṁsiddhir hari-toṣaṇam*). In the *Bhagavad-gītā* (9.27) the same principle is confirmed where it is said that whatever we may give in charity and whatever we may observe in austerity must be given over to the Lord or be done on His account only. The expert leaders of a godless human civilization cannot bring about a fruitful result in all their different attempts at educational advancement or economic development unless they are God conscious. And to become God conscious one has to hear about the all-auspicious Lord, as He is described in literature like the *Bhagavad-gītā* and *Śrīmad-Bhāgavatam.*

TEXT 18

किरातहूणान्ध्रपुलिन्दपुल्कशा
आभीरशुम्भा यवनाः खसादयः ।
येऽन्ये च पापा यदपाश्रयाश्रयाः
शुध्यन्ति तस्मै प्रभविष्णवे नमः ॥१८॥

kirāta-hūṇāndhra-pulinda-pulkaśā
ābhīra-śumbhā yavanāḥ khasādayaḥ
ye 'nye ca pāpā yad-apāśrayāśrayāḥ
śudhyanti tasmai prabhaviṣṇave namaḥ

kirāta—a province of old Bhārata; *hūṇa*—part of Germany and Russia; *āndhra*—a province of southern India; *pulinda*—the Greeks; *pulkaśāḥ*—another province; *ābhīra*—part of old Sind; *śumbhāḥ*—another province; *yavanāḥ*—the Turks; *khasa-ādayaḥ*—the Mongolian province; *ye*—even those; *anye*—others; *ca*—also; *pāpāḥ*—addicted to sinful acts; *yat*—whose; *apāśraya-āśrayāḥ*—having taken shelter of the devotees of the Lord; *śudhyanti*—at once purified; *tasmai*—unto Him; *prabhaviṣṇave*—unto the powerful Viṣṇu; *namaḥ*—my respectful obeisances.

TRANSLATION

Kirāta, Hūṇa, Āndhra, Pulinda, Pulkaśa, Ābhīra, Śumbha, Yavana, members of the Khasa races and even others addicted to

sinful acts can be purified by taking shelter of the devotees of the Lord, due to His being the supreme power. I beg to offer my respectful obeisances unto Him.

PURPORT

Kirāta: A province of old Bhārata-varṣa mentioned in the *Bhīṣma-parva* of *Mahābhārata.* Generally the Kirātas are known as the aboriginal tribes of India, and in modern days the Santal Parganas in Bihar and Chota Nagpur might comprise the old province named Kirāta.

Hūṇa: The area of East Germany and part of Russia is known as the province of the Hūṇas. Accordingly, sometimes a kind of hill tribe is known as the Hūṇas.

Āndhra: A province in southern India mentioned in the *Bhīṣma-parva* of *Mahābhārata.* It is still extant under the same name.

Pulinda: It is mentioned in the *Mahābhārata* (*Ādi-parva* 174.38), viz., the inhabitants of the province of the name Pulinda. This country was conquered by Bhīmasena and Sahadeva. The Greeks are known as Pulindas, and it is mentioned in the *Vana-parva* of *Mahābhārata* that the non-Vedic race of this part of the world would rule over the world. This Pulinda province was also one of the provinces of Bhārata, and the inhabitants were classified amongst the *kṣatriya* kings. But later on, due to their giving up the brahminical culture, they were mentioned as *mlecchas* (just as those who are not followers of the Islamic culture are called *kafirs* and those who are not followers of the Christian culture are called heathens).

Ābhīra: This name also appears in the *Mahābhārata,* both in the *Sabhā-parva* and *Bhīṣma-parva.* It is mentioned that this province was situated on the River Sarasvatī in Sind. The modern Sind province formerly extended on the other side of the Arabian Sea, and all the inhabitants of that province were known as the Ābhīras. They were under the domination of Mahārāja Yudhiṣṭhira, and according to the statements of Mārkaṇḍeya the *mlecchas* of this part of the world would also rule over Bhārata. Later on this proved to be true, as in the case of the Pulindas. On behalf of the Pulindas, Alexander the Great conquered India, and on behalf of the Ābhīras, Muhammad Ghori conquered India. These Ābhīras were also formerly *kṣatriyas* within the brahminical culture, but they gave up the connection. The *kṣatriyas* who were afraid of Paraśurāma and had hidden themselves in the Caucasian hilly regions later on became known as the Ābhīras, and the place they inhabited was known as Ābhīradeśa.

Śumbhas or *Kaṅkas:* The inhabitants of the Kaṅka province of old Bhārata, mentioned in the *Mahābhārata.*

Yavanas: Yavana was the name of one of the sons of Mahārāja Yayāti who was given the part of the world known as Turkey to rule. Therefore the Turks are Yavanas due to being descendants of Mahārāja Yavana. The Yavanas were therefore *kṣatriyas,* and later on, by giving up the brahminical culture, they became *mleccha-yavanas.* Descriptions of the Yavanas are in the *Mahābhārata* (*Ādi-parva* 85.34). Another prince called Turvasu was also known as Yavana, and his country was conquered by Sahadeva, one of the Pāṇḍavas. The western Yavana joined with Duryodhana in the Battle of Kurukṣetra under the pressure of Karṇa. It is also foretold that these Yavanas also would conquer India, and it proved to be true.

Khasa: The inhabitants of the Khasadeśa are mentioned in the *Mahābhārata* (*Droṇa-parva*). Those who have a stunted growth of hair on the upper lip are generally called Khasas. As such, the Khasa are the Mongolians, the Chinese and others who are so designated.

The above-mentioned historical names are different nations of the world. Even those who are constantly engaged in sinful acts are all corrigible to the standard of perfect human beings if they take shelter of the devotees of the Lord. Jesus Christ and Muhammad, two powerful devotees of the Lord, have done tremendous service on behalf of the Lord on the surface of the globe. And from the version of Śrīla Śukadeva Gosvāmī it appears that instead of running a godless civilization in the present context of the world situation, if the leadership of world affairs is entrusted to the devotees of the Lord, for which a worldwide organization under the name and style of the International Society for Krishna Consciousness has already been started, then by the grace of the Almighty Lord there can be a thorough change of heart in human beings all over the world because the devotees of the Lord are able authorities to effect such a change by purifying the dust-worn minds of the people in general. The politicians of the world may remain in their respective positions because the pure devotees of the Lord are not interested in political leadership or diplomatic implications. The devotees are interested only in seeing that the people in general are not misguided by political propaganda and in seeing that the valuable life of a human being is not spoiled in following a type of civilization which is ultimately doomed. If the politicians, therefore, would be guided by the good counsel of the devotees, then certainly there would be a great change in the world situation by the purifying propaganda of the devotees, as shown by Lord Caitanya. As Śukadeva Gosvāmī began his prayer by discussing the word *yat-kīrtanam,* so also Lord Caitanya recommended that simply by glorifying the Lord's holy name, a tremendous change of heart can take place by which the complete misunderstanding between the human nations created by politicians can at once be extinguished. And after the extinction of the fire of misunderstanding, other profits will follow. The destination is to go back home, back to Godhead, as we have several times discussed in these pages.

According to the cult of devotion, generally known as the Vaiṣṇava cult, there is no bar against anyone's advancing in the matter of God realization. A Vaiṣṇava is powerful enough to turn into a Vaiṣṇava even the Kirāta, etc., as above mentioned. In the *Bhagavad-gītā* (9.32) it is said by the Lord that there is no bar to becoming a devotee of the Lord (even for those who are lowborn, or women, *śūdras* or *vaiśyas*), and by becoming a devotee everyone is eligible to return home, back to Godhead. The only qualification is that one take shelter of a pure devotee of the Lord who has thorough knowledge in the transcendental science of Kṛṣṇa (*Bhagavad-gītā* and *Śrīmad-Bhāgavatam*). Anyone from any part of the world who becomes well conversant in the science of Kṛṣṇa becomes a pure devotee and a spiritual master for the general mass of people and may reclaim them by purification of heart. Though a person be even the most sinful man, he can at once be purified by systematic contact with a pure Vaiṣṇava. A Vaiṣṇava, therefore, can accept a bona fide disciple from any part of the world without any consideration of caste and creed and promote him by regulative principles to the status of a pure Vaiṣṇava who is transcendental to brahminical culture. The system of caste, or *varṇāśrama-dharma,* is no longer regular even amongst the so-called followers of the system. Nor is it now possible to reestablish the institutional function in the present context of social, political and economic revolution. Without any reference to the particular custom of a country, one can be accepted to the Vaiṣṇava cult spiritually, and there is no hindrance in the transcendental process. So by the order of Lord Śrī Caitanya Mahāprabhu, the cult of *Śrīmad-Bhāgavatam* or the *Bhagavad-gītā* can be preached all over the world, reclaiming all persons willing to accept the transcendental cult. Such cultural propaganda by the devotees will certainly be accepted by all persons who are reasonable and inquisitive, without any particular bias for the custom of the country. The Vaiṣṇava never accepts another Vaiṣṇava on the basis of birthright, just as he never thinks of the Deity of the Lord in a temple as an idol. And to remove all doubts in this connection, Śrīla Śukadeva Gosvāmī has invoked the blessings of the Lord, who is all-powerful (*prabhaviṣṇave namaḥ*). As the all-powerful Lord accepts the humble service of His devotee in devotional activities of the *arcana*, His form as the worshipable Deity in the temple, similarly the body of a pure Vaiṣṇava changes transcendentally at once when he gives himself up to the service of the Lord and is trained by a qualified Vaiṣṇava. The injunction of Vaiṣṇava regulation in this connection runs as follows: *arcye viṣṇau śilā-dhīr guruṣu nara-matir vaiṣṇave jāti-buddhiḥ śrī-viṣṇor nāmni śabda-sāmānya-buddhiḥ*, etc. "One should not consider the Deity of the Lord as worshiped in the temple to be an idol, nor should one consider the authorized spiritual master an ordinary man. Nor should one consider a pure Vaiṣṇava to belong to a particular caste, etc." (*Padma Purāṇa*)

The conclusion is that the Lord, being all-powerful, can, under any and every circumstance, accept anyone from any part of the world, either personally or through His bona fide manifestation as the spiritual master. Lord Caitanya accepted many devotees from communities other than the varṇāśramites, and He Himself declared, to teach us, that He does not belong to any caste or social order of life, but that He is the eternal servant of the servant of the Lord who maintains the damsels of Vṛndāvana (Lord Kṛṣṇa). That is the way of self-realization.

TEXT 19

स एष आत्मात्मवतामधीश्वर-
स्त्रयीमयो धर्ममयस्तपोमयः ।

गतव्यलीकैरजशङ्करादिभि-
र्वितर्क्यलिङ्गो भगवान् प्रसीदताम् ॥१९॥

sa eṣa ātmātmavatām adhīśvaras
trayīmayo dharmamayas tapomayaḥ
gata-vyalīkair aja-śaṅkarādibhir
vitarkya-liṅgo bhagavān prasīdatām

saḥ—He; *eṣaḥ*—it is; *ātmā*—the Supersoul; *ātmavatām*—of the self-realized souls; *adhīśvaraḥ*—the Supreme Lord; *trayī-mayaḥ*—personified *Vedas; dharma-mayaḥ*—personified religious scripture; *tapaḥ-mayaḥ*—personified austerity; *gata-vyalīkaiḥ*—by those who are above all pretensions; *aja*—Brahmājī; *śaṅkara-ādibhiḥ*—by Lord Śiva and others; *vitarkya-liṅgaḥ*—one who is observed with awe and veneration; *bhagavān*—the Personality of Godhead; *prasīdatām*—be kind toward me.

TRANSLATION

He is the Supersoul and the Supreme Lord of all self-realized souls. He is the personification of the Vedas, religious scriptures and austerities. He is worshiped by Lord Brahmā and Śiva and all those who are transcendental to all pretensions. Being so revered with awe and veneration, may that Supreme Absolute be pleased with me.

PURPORT

The Supreme Lord, the Personality of Godhead, although the Lord of all followers of different paths of self-realization, is knowable only by those who are above all pretensions. Everyone is searching for eternal peace or eternal life, and with an aim to this destination everyone is either studying the Vedic scriptures or other religious scriptures or undergoing severe austerity as empiric philosophers, as mystics *yogīs* or as unalloyed devotees, etc. But the Supreme Lord is perfectly realized only by the devotees because they are above all pretensions. Those who are on the path of self-realization are generally classified as *karmīs*, *jñānīs*, *yogīs*, or devotees of the Lord. The *karmīs*, who are much attracted by the fruitive activities of the Vedic rituals, are called *bhukti-kāmī*, or those who desire material enjoyment. The *jñānīs*, who try to become one with the Supreme by mental speculation, are called *mukti-kāmī*, or those who desire liberation from material existence. The mystic *yogīs*, who practice different types of austerities for attainment of eight kinds of material perfection and who ultimately meet the Supersoul (Paramātmā) in trance, are called *siddhi-kāmī*, or those who desire the perfection of becoming finer than the finest, becoming heavier than the heaviest, getting everything desired, having control over everyone, creating everything liked, etc. All these are abilities of a powerful *yogī*. But the devotees of the Lord do not want anything like that for self-satisfaction. They want only to serve the Lord because the Lord is great and as living entities they are eternally subordinate parts and parcels of the Lord. This perfect realization of the self by the devotee helps him to become desireless, to desire nothing for his personal self, and thus the devotees are called *niṣkāmī*, without any desire. A living entity, by his constitutional position, cannot be void of all desires (the *bhukti-kāmī*, *mukti-kāmī* and *siddhi-kāmī* all desire something for personal satisfaction), but the *niṣkāmī* devotees of the Lord desire everything for the satisfaction of the Lord. They are completely dependent on the orders of the Lord and are always ready to discharge their duty for the satisfaction of the Lord.

In the beginning Arjuna placed himself as one of those who desire self-satisfaction, for he desired not to fight in the Battle of Kurukṣetra, but to make him desireless the Lord preached the *Bhagavad-gītā*, in which the ways of *karma-yoga*, *jñāna-yoga*, *haṭha-yoga* and also *bhakti-yoga* were explained. Because Arjuna was without any pretension, he changed his decision and satisfied the Lord by agreeing to fight (*kariṣye vacanaṁ tava*), and thus he became desireless.

The examples of Brahmā and Lord Śiva are specifically cited here because Brahmājī, Lord Śiva, Śrīmatī Lakṣmījī and the four Kumāras (Sanaka, Sanātana, etc.) are leaders of the four desireless Vaiṣṇava *sampradāyas*. They are all freed from all pretensions. Śrīla Jīva Gosvāmī interprets the word *gata-vyalīkaiḥ* as *projjhita-kaitavaiḥ*, or those who are freed from all pretensions (the unalloyed devotees only). In the *Caitanya-caritāmṛta* (*Madhya* 19.149) it is said:

kṛṣṇa-bhakta—niṣkāma, ata eva 'śānta'
bhukti-mukti-siddhi-kāmī, sakali 'aśānta'

Those who are after fruitive results for their pious activities, those who desire salvation and identity with the Supreme, and those who desire material perfections of mystic power are all restless because they want something for themselves, but the devotee is completely peaceful because he has no demand for himself and is always ready to serve the desire of the Lord. The conclusion is, therefore, that the Lord is for everyone because no one can achieve the result of his respective desires without His sanction, but as stated by the Lord in *Bhagavad-gītā* (8.9), all such results are awarded by Him only, for the Lord is *adhīśvara* (the original controller) of everyone, namely the Vedāntists, the great *karma-kāṇḍīyas*, the great religious leaders, the great performers of austerity and all who are striving for spiritual advancement. But ultimately He is realized by the pretensionless devotees only. Therefore special stress is given to the devotional service of the Lord by Śrīla Śukadeva Gosvāmī.

TEXT 20

श्रियः पतिर्यज्ञपतिः प्रजापति-
धियां पतिर्लोकपतिर्धरापतिः ।
पतिर्गतिश्चान्धकवृष्णिसात्वतां
प्रसीदतां मे भगवान् सतां पतिः ॥२०॥

śriyaḥ patir yajña-patiḥ prajā-patir
dhiyāṁ patir loka-patir dharā-patiḥ
patir gatiś cāndhaka-vṛṣṇi-sātvatām
prasīdatāṁ me bhagavān satāṁ patiḥ

śriyaḥ—all opulence; *patiḥ*—the owner; *yajña*—of sacrifice; *patiḥ*—the director; *prajā-patiḥ*—the leader of all living entities; *dhiyām*—of intelligence; *patiḥ*—the master; *loka-patiḥ*—the proprietor of all planets; *dharā*—earth; *patiḥ*—the supreme; *patiḥ*—head; *gatiḥ*—destination; *ca*—also; *andhaka*—one of the kings of the Yadu dynasty; *vṛṣṇi*—the first king of the Yadu dynasty; *sātvatām*—the Yadus; *prasīdatām*—be merciful; *me*—upon me; *bhagavān*—Lord Śrī Kṛṣṇa; *satām*—of all devotees; *patiḥ*—the Lord.

TRANSLATION

May Lord Śrī Kṛṣṇa, who is the worshipable Lord of all devotees, the protector and glory of all the kings like Andhaka and Vṛṣṇi of the Yadu dynasty, the husband of all goddesses of fortune, the director of all sacrifices and therefore the leader of all living entities, the controller of all intelligence, the proprietor of all planets, spiritual and material, and the supreme incarnation on the earth (the supreme all in all), be merciful upon me.

PURPORT

Since Śukadeva Gosvāmī is one of the prominent *gata-vyalīkas*, who are freed from all misconceptions, he therefore expresses his own realized perception of Lord Śrī Kṛṣṇa as being the sum total of all perfection, the Personality of Godhead. Everyone is seeking the favor of the goddess of fortune, but people do not know that Lord Śrī Kṛṣṇa is the beloved husband of all goddesses of fortune. In the *Brahma-saṁhitā* it is said that the Lord, in His transcendental abode Goloka Vṛndāvana, is accustomed to herding the *surabhi* cows and is served there by hundreds of thousands of goddesses of fortune. All these goddesses of fortune are manifestations of His transcendental pleasure potency (*hlādinī-śakti*) in His internal energy, and when the Lord manifested Himself on this earth He partially displayed the activities of His pleasure potency in His *rāsa-līlā* just to attract the conditioned souls, who are all after the phantasmagoria pleasure potency in degraded sex enjoyment. The pure devotees of the Lord like Śukadeva Gosvāmī, who was completely detached from the abominable sex life of the material world, discussed this act of the Lord's pleasure potency certainly not in relation to sex, but to relish a transcendental taste inconceivable to the mundaners who are after sex life. Sex life in the mundane world is the root-cause of being conditioned by the shackles of illusion, and certainly Śukadeva Gosvāmī was never interested in the sex life of the mundane world. Nor does the manifestation of the Lord's pleasure potency have any connection with such degraded things. Lord Caitanya was a strict *sannyāsī*, so much so that He did not allow any woman to come near Him, not even to bow down and offer respects. He never even heard the prayers of the *deva-dāsīs* offered in the temple of Jagannātha because a *sannyāsī* is forbidden to hear songs sung by the fair sex. Yet even in the rigid position of a *sannyāsī* He recommended the mode of worship preferred by the *gopīs* of Vṛndāvana as the topmost loving service possible to be rendered to the Lord. And Śrīmati Rādhārāṇī is the principal head of all such goddesses of fortune, and therefore She is the pleasure counterpart of the Lord and is nondifferent from Kṛṣṇa.

In the Vedic rituals there are recommendations for performing different types of sacrifice in order to achieve the greatest benefit in life. Such benedictions as the results of performing great sacrifices are, after all, favors given by the goddess of fortune, and the Lord, being the husband or lover of the goddess of fortune, is factually the Lord of all sacrifices also. He is the final enjoyer of all kinds of *yajña;* therefore Yajña-pati is another name of Lord Viṣṇu. It is recommended in the *Bhagavad-gītā* that everything be done for the Yajña-pati (*yajñārtāt karmaṇaḥ*), for otherwise one's acts will be the cause of conditioning by the law of material nature. Those who are not freed from all misconceptions (*vyalīkam*) perform sacrifices to please the minor demigods, but the devotees of the Lord know very well that Lord Śrī Kṛṣṇa is the supreme enjoyer of all performances of sacrifice; therefore they perform the *saṅkīrtana-yajña* (*śravaṇaṁ kīrtanaṁ viṣṇoḥ*), which is especially recommended in this age of Kali. In Kali-yuga, performance of other types of sacrifice is not feasible due to insufficient arrangements and inexpert priesthood.

We have information from the *Bhagavad-gītā* (3.10–11) that Lord Brahmā, after giving rebirth to the conditioned souls within the universe, instructed them to perform sacrifices and to lead a prosperous life. With such sacrificial performances the conditioned souls will never be in difficulty in keeping body and soul together. Ultimately they can purify their existence. They will find natural promotion into spiritual existence, the real identity of the living being. A conditioned soul should never give up the practice of sacrifice, charity and austerity, in any circumstances. The aim of all such sacrifices is to please the Yajña-pati, the Personality of Godhead; therefore the Lord is also Prajā-pati. According to the *Kaṭha Upaniṣad,* the one Lord is the leader of the innumerable living entities. The living entities are maintained by the Lord (*eko bahūnāṁ yo vidadhāti kāmān*). The Lord is therefore called the supreme Bhūta-bhṛt, or maintainer of all living beings.

Living beings are proportionately endowed with intelligence in terms of their previous activities. All living beings are not equally endowed with the same quality of intelligence because behind such development of intelligence is the control of the Lord, as declared in the *Bhagavad-gītā* (15.15). As Paramātmā, Supersoul, the Lord is living in everyone's heart, and from Him only does one's power of remembrance, knowledge and forgetfulness follow (*mattaḥ smṛtir jñānam apohanaṁ ca*). One person can sharply remember past activities by the grace of the Lord while others cannot. One is highly intelligent by the grace of the Lord, and one is a fool by the same control. Therefore the Lord is Dhiyām-pati, or the Lord of intelligence.

The conditioned souls strive to become lords of the material world. Everyone is trying to lord it over the material nature by applying his highest degree of intelligence. This misuse of intelligence by the conditioned soul is called madness. One's full intelligence should be applied to get free from the material clutches. But the conditioned soul, due to madness only, engages his full energy and intelligence in sense gratification, and to achieve this end of life he willfully commits all sorts of misdeeds. The result is that instead of attaining an unconditional life of full freedom, the mad conditioned soul is entangled again and again in different types of bondage in material bodies. Everything we see in the material manifestation is but the creation of the Lord. Therefore He is the real proprietor of everything in the universes. The conditioned soul can enjoy a fragment of this material creation under the control of the Lord, but not self-sufficiently. That is the instruction in the *Īśopaniṣad.* One should be satisfied with things awarded by the Lord of the universe. It is out of madness only that one tries to encroach upon another's share of material possessions.

The Lord of the universe, out of His causeless mercy upon the conditioned souls, descends by His own energy (*ātma-māyā*) to reestablish the eternal relation of the conditioned souls with Him. He instructs all to surrender unto Him instead of falsely claiming to be enjoyers for a certain limit under His control. When He so descends He proves how much greater is His ability to enjoy, and He exhibits His power of enjoyment by (for instance) marrying sixteen thousand wives at once. The conditioned soul is very proud of becoming the husband of even one wife, but the Lord laughs at this; the intelligent man can know who is the real husband. Factually, the Lord is the husband of all the women in His creation, but a conditioned soul under the control of the Lord feels proud to be the husband of one or two wives.

All these qualifications as the different types of *pati* mentioned in this verse are meant for Lord Śrī Kṛṣṇa, and Śukadeva Gosvāmī has therefore especially mentioned the *pati* and *gati* of the Yadu dynasty. The members of the Yadu dynasty knew that Lord Śrī Kṛṣṇa is everything, and all of them intended to return to Lord Kṛṣṇa after He had finished His transcendental pastimes on the earth. The Yadu dynasty was annihilated by the will of the Lord because its members had to return home with the Lord. The annihilation of the Yadu dynasty was a material show created by the Supreme Lord; otherwise the Lord and the members of the Yadu dynasty are all eternal associates. The Lord is therefore the guide of all devotees, and as such, Śukadeva Gosvāmī offered Him due respects with love-laden feelings.

TEXT 21

यदङ्घ्र्यभिध्यानसमाधिधौतया
धियानुपश्यन्ति हि तत्त्वमात्मनः ।
वदन्ति चैतत् कवयो यथारुचं
स मे मुकुन्दो भगवान् प्रसीदताम् ॥२१॥

yad-aṅghry-abhidhyāna-samādhi-dhautayā
dhiyānupaśyanti hi tattvam ātmanaḥ
vadanti caitat kavayo yathā-rucaṁ
sa me mukundo bhagavān prasīdatām

yat-aṅghri—whose lotus feet; *abhidhyāna*—thinking of, at every second; *samādhi*—trance; *dhautayā*—being washed off; *dhiyā*—by such clean intelligence; *anupaśyanti*—does see by following authorities; *hi*—certainly; *tattvam*—the Absolute Truth; *ātmanaḥ*—of the Supreme Lord and of oneself; *vadanti*—they say; *ca*—also; *etat*—this; *kavayaḥ*—philosophers or learned scholars; *yathā-rucam*—as he thinks; *saḥ*—He; *me*—mine; *mukundaḥ*—Lord Kṛṣṇa (who gives liberation); *bhagavān*—the Personality of Godhead; *prasīdatām*—be pleased with me.

TRANSLATION

It is the Personality of Godhead Śrī Kṛṣṇa who gives liberation. By thinking of His lotus feet at every second, following in the footsteps of authorities, the devotee in trance can see the Absolute Truth. The learned mental speculators, however, think of Him according to their whims. May the Lord be pleased with me.

PURPORT

The mystic *yogīs*, after a strenuous effort to control the senses, may be situated in a trance of *yoga* just to have a vision of the Supersoul within everyone, but the pure devotee, simply by remembering the Lord's lotus feet at every second, at once becomes established in real trance because by such realization his mind and intelligence are completely cleansed of the diseases of material enjoyment. The pure devotee thinks himself fallen into the ocean of birth and death and incessantly prays to the Lord to lift him up. He only aspires to become a speck of transcendental dust at the lotus feet of the Lord. The pure devotee, by the grace of the Lord, absolutely loses all attraction for material enjoyment, and to keep free from contamination he always thinks of the lotus feet of the Lord. King Kulaśekhara, a great devotee of the Lord, prayed:

kṛṣṇa tvadīya-pada-paṅkaja-pañjarāntam
adyaiva me viśatu mānasa-rāja-haṁsaḥ
prāṇa-prayāṇa-samaye kapha-vāta-pittaiḥ
kaṇṭhāvarodhana-vidhau smaraṇaṁ kutas te

"My Lord Kṛṣṇa, I pray that the swan of my mind may immediately sink down to the stems of the lotus feet of Your Lordship and be locked in their network; otherwise at the time of my final breath, when my throat is choked up with cough, how will it be possible to think of You?"

There is an intimate relationship between the swan and the lotus stem. So the comparison is very appropriate: without becoming a swan, or *paramahaṁsa*, one cannot enter into the network of the lotus feet of the Lord. As stated in the *Brahma-saṁhitā*, the mental speculators, even by dint of learned scholarship, cannot even dream of the Absolute Truth by speculating over it for eternity. The Lord reserves the right of not being exposed to such mental speculators. And because they cannot enter into the network stem of the lotus feet of the Lord, all mental speculators differ in conclusions, and at the end they make a useless compromise by saying "as many conclusions, as many ways," according to one's own inclination (*yathā-rucam*). But the Lord is not like a shopkeeper trying to please all sorts of customers in the mental speculator exchange. The Lord is what He is, the Absolute Personality of Godhead, and He demands absolute surrender unto Him only. The pure devotee, however, by following the ways of previous *ācāryas*, or authorities, can see the Supreme Lord through the transparent medium of a bona fide spiritual master (*anupaśyanti*). The pure devotee never tries to sec the Lord by mental speculation, but by following in the footsteps of the *ācāryas* (*mahājano yena gataḥ sa panthāḥ*). Therefore there is no difference of conclusions amongst the Vaiṣṇava *ācāryas* regarding the Lord and the devotees. Lord Caitanya asserts that the living entity (*jīva*) is eternally the servitor of the Lord and that he is simultaneously one with and different from the Lord. This *tattva* of Lord Caitanya's is shared by all four *sampradāyas* of the Vaiṣṇava school (all accepting eternal servitude to the Lord even after salvation), and there is no authorized Vaiṣṇava *ācārya* who may think of the Lord and himself as one.

This humbleness of the pure devotee, who is one hundred percent engaged in His service, puts the devotee of the Lord in a trance by which to realize everything, because to the sincere devotee of the Lord, the Lord reveals Himself, as stated in the *Bhagavad-gītā* (10.10). The Lord, being the Lord of intelligence in everyone (even in the nondevotee), favors His devotee with proper intelligence so that automatically the pure devotee is enlightened with the factual truth about the Lord and His different energies. The Lord is revealed not by one's speculative power or by one's verbal jugglery over the Absolute Truth. Rather, He reveals Himself to a devotee when He is fully satisfied by the devotee's service attitude. Śukadeva Gosvāmī is not a mental speculator or compromiser of the theory of "as many ways, as many conclusions." Rather, he prays to the Lord only, invoking His transcendental pleasure. That is the way of knowing the Lord.

TEXT 22

प्रचोदिता येन पुरा सरस्वती
वितन्वताजस्य सतीं स्मृतिं हृदि ।

स्वलक्षणा प्रादुरभूत् किलास्यतः
स मे ऋषीणामृषभः प्रसीदताम् ॥२२॥

pracoditā yena purā sarasvatī
vitanvatājasya satīṁ smṛtiṁ hṛdi
sva-lakṣaṇā prādurabhūt kilāsyataḥ
sa me ṛṣīṇām ṛṣabhaḥ prasīdatām

pracoditā—inspired; *yena*—by whom; *purā*—in the beginning of creation; *sarasvatī*—the goddess of learning; *vitanvatā*—amplified; *ajasya*—of Brahmā, the first created living being; *satīm smṛtim*—potent memory; *hṛdi*—in the heart; *sva*—in his own; *lakṣaṇā*—aiming at; *prādurabhūt*—was generated; *kila*—as if; *āsyataḥ*—from the mouth; *saḥ*—he; *me*—unto me; *ṛṣīṇām*—of the teachers; *ṛṣabhaḥ*—the chief; *prasīdatām*—be pleased.

TRANSLATION

May the Lord, who in the beginning of the creation amplified the potent knowledge of Brahmā from within his heart and inspired him with full knowledge of creation and of His own Self, and who appeared to be generated from the mouth of Brahmā, be pleased with me.

PURPORT

As we have already discussed hereinbefore, the Lord, as the Supersoul of all living beings from Brahmā to the insignificant ant, endows all with the required knowledge potent in every living being. A living being is sufficiently potent to possess knowledge from the Lord in the proportion of fifty sixty-fourths, or seventy-eight percent of the full knowledge acquirable. Since the living being is constitutionally part and parcel of the Lord, he is unable to assimilate all the knowledge that the Lord possesses Himself. In the conditioned state, the living being is subject to forget everything after a change of body known as death. This potent knowledge is again inspired by the Lord from within the heart of every living being, and it is known as the awakening of knowledge, for it is comparable to awakening from sleep or unconsciousness. This awakening of knowledge is under the full control of the Lord, and therefore we find in the practical world different grades of knowledge in different persons. This awakening of knowledge is neither an automatic nor a material interaction. The supply source is the Lord Himself (*dhiyāṁ patiḥ*), for even Brahmā is also subject to this regulation of the supreme creator. In the beginning of the creation, Brahmā is born first without any father and mother because before Brahmā there were no other living beings. Brahmā is born from the lotus which grows from the abdomen of the Garbhodakaśāyī Viṣṇu, and therefore he is known as Aja. This Brahmā, or Aja, is also a living being, part and parcel of the Lord, but being the most pious devotee of the Lord, Brahmā is inspired by the Lord to create, subsequent to the main creation by the Lord, through the agency of material nature. Therefore neither the material nature nor Brahmā is independent of the Lord. The material scientists can merely observe the reactions of the material nature without understanding the direction behind such activities, as a child can see the action of electricity without any knowledge of the powerhouse engineer. This imperfect knowledge of the material scientist is due to a poor fund of knowledge. The Vedic knowledge was therefore first impregnated within Brahmā, and it appears that Brahmā distributed the Vedic knowledge. Brahmā is undoubtedly the speaker of the Vedic knowledge, but actually he was inspired by the Lord to receive such transcendental knowledge, as it directly descends from the Lord. The *Vedas* are therefore called *apauruṣeya*, or not imparted by any created being. Before the creation the Lord was there (*nārāyaṇaḥ paro 'vyaktāt*), and therefore the words spoken by the Lord are vibrations of transcendental sound. There is a gulf of difference between the two qualities of sound, namely *prākṛta* and *aprākṛta*. The physicist can deal only with the *prākṛta* sound, or sound vibrated in the material sky, and therefore we must know that the Vedic sounds recorded in symbolic expressions cannot be understood by anyone within the universe unless and until one is inspired by the vibration of supernatural (*aprākṛta*) sound, which descends in the chain of disciplic succession from the Lord to Brahmā, from Brahmā to Nārada, from Nārada to Vyāsa and so on. No mundane scholar can translate or reveal the true import of the Vedic *mantras* (hymns). They cannot be understood unless one is inspired or initiated by the authorized spiritual master. The original spiritual master is the Lord Himself, and the succession comes down through the sources of *paramparā*, as clearly stated in the Fourth Chapter of the *Bhagavad-gītā.* So unless one receives the transcendental knowledge from the authorized *paramparā*, one should be considered useless (*viphalā matāḥ*), even though one may be greatly qualified in the mundane advancements of arts or science.

Śukadeva Gosvāmī is praying from the Lord by dint of being inspired from within by the Lord so that he could rightly explain the facts and figures of creation as inquired by Mahārāja Parīkṣit. A spiritual master is not a theoretical speculator, like the mundane scholar, but is *śrotriyaṁ brahma-niṣṭham.*

TEXT 23

भूतैर्महद्भिर्य इमाः पुरो विभु-
निर्माय शेते यदमूषु पूरुषः ।
भुङ्क्ते गुणान् षोडश षोडशात्मकः
सोऽलङ्कृषीष्ट भगवान् वचांसि मे ॥२३॥

bhūtair mahadbhir ya imāḥ puro vibhur
nirmāya śete yad amūṣu pūruṣaḥ
bhuṅkte guṇān ṣoḍaśa ṣoḍaśātmakaḥ
so 'laṅkṛṣīṣṭa bhagavān vacāṁsi me

bhūtaiḥ—by the elements; *mahadbhiḥ*—of material creation; *yaḥ*—He who; *imāḥ*—all these; *puraḥ*—bodies; *vibhuḥ*—of the Lord; *nirmāya*—for being set up; *śete*—lie down; *yat amūṣu*—one who incarnated; *pūruṣaḥ*—Lord Viṣṇu; *bhuṅkte*—causes to be subjected; *guṇān*—the three modes of nature; *ṣoḍaśa*—in sixteen divisions; *ṣoḍaśa-ātmakaḥ*—being the generator of these sixteen; *saḥ*—He; *alaṅkṛṣīṣṭa*—may decorate; *bhagavān*—the Personality of Godhead; *vacāṁsi*—statements; *me*—mine.

TRANSLATION

May the Supreme Personality of Godhead, who enlivens the materially created bodies of the elements by lying down within the universe, and who in His puruṣa incarnation causes the living being to be subjected to the sixteen divisions of material modes which are his generator, be pleased to decorate my statements.

PURPORT

As a fully dependent devotee, Śukadeva Gosvāmī (unlike a mundane man who is proud of his own capability) invokes the pleasure of the Personality of Godhead so that his statements may be successful and be appreciated by the hearers. The devotee always thinks of himself as instrumental for anything successfully carried out, and he declines to take credit for anything done by himself. The godless atheist wants to take all credit for activities, not knowing that even a blade of grass cannot move without the sanction of the Supreme Spirit, the Personality of Godhead. Śukadeva Gosvāmī therefore wants to move by the direction of the Supreme Lord, who inspired Brahmā to speak the Vedic wisdom. The truths described in the Vedic literatures are not theories of mundane imagination, nor are they fictitious, as the less intelligent class of men sometimes think. The Vedic truths are all perfect descriptions of the factual truth without any mistake or illusion, and Śukadeva Gosvāmī wants to present the truths of creation not as a metaphysical theory of philosophical speculation, but as the actual facts and figures of the subject, since he would be dictated to by the Lord exactly in the same manner as Brahmājī was inspired. As stated in the *Bhagavad-gītā* (15.15), the Lord is Himself the father of the *Vedānta* knowledge, and it is He only who knows the factual purport of the *Vedānta* philosophy. So there is no greater truth than the principles of religion mentioned in the *Vedas*. Such Vedic knowledge or religion is disseminated by authorities like Śukadeva Gosvāmī because he is a humble devotional servitor of the Lord who has no desire to become a self-appointed interpreter without authority. That is the way of explaining the Vedic knowledge, technically known as the *paramparā* system, or descending process.

The intelligent man can see without mistake that any material creation (whether one's own body or a fruit or flower) cannot beautifully grow up without the spiritual touch. The greatest intelligent man of the world or the greatest man of science can present everything very beautifully only insofar as the spirit life is there or insomuch as the spiritual touch is there. Therefore the source of all truths is the Supreme Spirit, and not gross matter as wrongly conceived by the gross materialist. We get information from the Vedic literature that the Lord Himself first entered the vacuum of the material universe, and thus all things gradually developed one after another. Similarly, the Lord is situated as localized Paramātmā in every individual being; hence everything is done by Him very beautifully. The sixteen principal creative elements, namely earth, water, fire, air, sky, and the eleven sense organs, first developed from the Lord Himself and were thereby shared by the living entities. Thus the material elements were created for the enjoyment of the living entities. The beautiful arrangement behind all material manifestations is therefore made possible by the energy of the Lord, and the individual living entity can only pray to the Lord to understand it properly. Since the Lord is the supreme entity, different from Śukadeva Gosvāmī, the prayer can be offered to Him. The Lord helps the living entity to enjoy material creation, but He is aloof from such false enjoyment. Śukadeva prays for the mercy of the Lord, not only for being helped personally in presenting the truth, but also for helping others to whom he would like to speak.

TEXT 24

नमस्तस्मै भगवते वासुदेवाय वेधसे ।
पपुर्ज्ञानमयं सौम्या यन्मुखाम्बुरुहासवम् ॥२४॥

namas tasmai bhagavate
vāsudevāya vedhase
papur jñānam ayaṁ saumyā
yan-mukhāmburuhāsavam

namaḥ—my obeisances; *tasmai*—unto Him; *bhagavate*—unto the Personality of Godhead; *vāsudevāya*—unto Vāsudeva or His incarnations; *vedhase*—the compiler of the Vedic literatures; *papuḥ*—drunk; *jñānam*—knowledge; *ayam*—this Vedic knowledge; *saumyāḥ*—the devotees, especially the consorts of Lord Kṛṣṇa; *yat*—from whose; *mukha-amburuha*—the lotuslike mouth; *āsavam*—nectar from His mouth.

TRANSLATION

I offer my respectful obeisances unto Śrīla Vyāsadeva, the incarnation of Vāsudeva who compiled the Vedic scriptures. The pure devotees drink up the nectarean transcendental knowledge dropping from the lotuslike mouth of the Lord.

PURPORT

In pursuance of the specific utterance *vedhase*, or "the compiler of the system of transcendental knowledge," Śrīla Śrīdhara Svāmī has commented that the respectful obeisances are offered to Śrīla Vyāsadeva, who is the incarnation of Vāsudeva. Śrīla Jīva Gosvāmī has agreed to this, but Śrīla Viśvanātha Cakravartī Ṭhākura has made a further advance, namely that the nectar from the mouth of Lord Kṛṣṇa is transferred to His different consorts, and thus they learn the finer arts of music, dance, dressing, decorations and all such things which are relished by the Lord. Such music, dance and decorations enjoyed by the Lord are certainly not anything mundane, because the Lord is addressed in the very beginning as *para*, or transcendental. This transcendental knowledge is unknown to the forgotten conditioned souls. Śrīla Vyāsadeva, who is the incarnation of the Lord, thus compiled the Vedic literatures to revive the lost memory of the conditioned souls about their eternal relation with the Lord. One should therefore try to understand the Vedic scriptures, or the nectar transferred by the Lord to His consorts in the conjugal humor, from the lotuslike mouth of Vyāsadeva or Śukadeva. By gradual development of transcendental knowledge, one can rise to the stage of the transcendental arts of music and dance displayed by the Lord in His *rāsa-līlā*. But without having the Vedic knowledge one can hardly understand the transcendental nature of the Lord's *rāsa* dance and music. The pure devotees of the Lord, however, can equally relish the nectar in the form of the profound philosophical discourses and in the form of kissing by the Lord in the *rāsa* dance, as there is no mundane distinction between the two.

TEXT 25

एतदेवात्मभू राजन् नारदाय विपृच्छते ।
वेदगर्भोऽभ्यधात् साक्षाद् यदाह हरिरात्मनः ॥२५॥

etad evātma-bhū rājan
nāradāya vipṛcchate
veda-garbho 'bhyadhāt sākṣād
yad āha harir ātmanaḥ

etat—on this matter; *eva*—exactly; *ātma-bhūḥ*—the firstborn (Brahmājī); *rājan*—my dear King; *nāradāya*—unto Nārada Muni; *viprcchate*—having inquired about it from; *veda-garbhaḥ*—one who is impregnated with Vedic knowledge from birth; *abhyadhāt*—apprised; *sākṣāt*—directly; *yat āha*—what he spoke; *hariḥ*—the Lord; *ātmanaḥ* —unto His own (Brahmā).

TRANSLATION

My dear King, Brahmā, the firstborn, on being questioned by Nārada, exactly apprised him on this subject, as it was directly spoken by the Lord to His own son, who was impregnated with Vedic knowledge from his very birth.

PURPORT

As soon as Brahmā was born of the abdominal lotus petals of Viṣṇu, he was impregnated with Vedic knowledge, and therefore he is known as *veda-garbha*, or a Vedāntist from the embryo. Without Vedic knowledge, or perfect, infallible knowledge, no one can create anything. All scientific knowledge and perfect knowledge are Vedic. One can get all types of information from the *Vedas*, and as such, Brahmā was impregnated with all-perfect knowledge so that it was possible for him to create. Thus Brahmā knew the perfect description of creation, as it was exactly apprised to him by the Supreme Lord Hari. Brahmā, on being questioned by Nārada, told Nārada exactly what he had heard directly from the Lord. Nārada again told exactly the same thing to Vyāsa, and Vyāsa also told Śukadeva exactly what he heard from Nārada. And Śukadeva was going to repeat the same statements as he had heard them from Vyāsa. That is the way of Vedic understanding. The language of the *Vedas* can be revealed only by the above-mentioned disciplic succession, and not otherwise.

There is no use in theories. Knowledge must be factual. There are many things that are complicated, and one cannot understand them unless they are explained by one who knows. The Vedic knowledge is also very difficult to know and must be learned by the above-mentioned system; otherwise it is not at all understood.

Śukadeva Gosvāmī, therefore, prayed for the mercy of the Lord so that he might be able to repeat the very same message that was spoken directly by the Lord to Brahmā, or what was directly spoken by Brahmā to Nārada. Therefore the statements of creation explained by Śukadeva Gosvāmī are not at all, as the mundaners suggest, theoretical, but are perfectly correct. One who hears these messages and tries to assimilate them gets perfect information of the material creation.

Thus end the Bhaktivedanta purports of the Second Canto, Fourth Chapter, of the Śrīmad-Bhāgavatam, *entitled "The Process of Creation."*

CHAPTER FIVE

The Cause of All Causes

TEXT 1

नारद उवाच
देवदेव नमस्तेऽस्तु भूतभावन पूर्वज ।
तद् विजानीहि यज्ज्ञानमात्मतत्त्वनिदर्शनम् ॥ १ ॥

nārada uvāca
deva-deva namas te 'stu
bhūta-bhāvana pūrvaja
tad vijānīhi yaj jñānam
ātma-tattva-nidarśanam

nāradaḥ uvāca—Śrī Nārada said; *deva*—of all demigods; *deva*—the demigod; *namaḥ*—obeisances; *te*—unto you as; *astu*—are; *bhūta-bhāvana*—the generator of all living beings; *pūrva-ja*—the firstborn; *tat vijānīhi*—please explain that knowledge; *yat jñānam*—which knowledge; *ātma-tattva*—transcendental; *nidarśanam*—specifically directs.

TRANSLATION

Śrī Nārada Muni asked Brahmājī: O chief amongst the demigods, O firstborn living entity, I beg to offer my respectful obeisances unto you. Please tell me that transcendental knowledge which specifically directs one to the truth of the individual soul and the Supersoul.

PURPORT

The perfection of the *paramparā* system, or the path of disciplic succession, is further confirmed. In the previous chapter it has been established that Brahmājī, the firstborn living entity, received knowledge directly from the Supreme Lord, and the same knowledge was imparted to Nārada, the next disciple. Nārada asked to receive the knowledge, and Brahmājī imparted it upon being asked. Therefore, asking for transcendental knowledge from the right person and receiving it properly is the regulation of the disciplic succession. This process is recommended in the *Bhagavad-gītā* (4.2). The inquisitive student must approach a qualified spiritual master to receive transcendental knowledge by surrender, submissive inquiries and service. Knowledge received by submissive inquiries and service is more effective than knowledge received in exchange for money. A spiritual master in the line of disciplic succession from Brahmā and Nārada has no demand for dollars and cents. A bona fide student has to satisfy him by sincere service to obtain knowledge of the relation and nature of the individual soul and the Supersoul.

TEXT 2

यद्रूपं यदधिष्ठानं यतः सृष्टमिदं प्रभो ।
यत्संस्थं यत्परं यच्च तत् तत्त्वं वद तत्त्वतः ॥ २ ॥

yad rūpaṁ yad adhiṣṭhānaṁ
yataḥ sṛṣṭam idaṁ prabho
yat saṁsthaṁ yat paraṁ yac ca
tat tattvaṁ vada tattvataḥ

yat—what; *rūpam*—the symptoms of manifestation; *yat*—what; *adhiṣṭhānam*—background; *yataḥ*—from where; *sṛṣṭam*—created; *idam*—this world; *prabho*—O my father; *yat*—in which; *saṁstham*—conserved; *yat*—what; *param*—under control; *yat*—what are; *ca*—and; *tat*—of this; *tattvam*—the symptoms; *vada*—please describe; *tattvataḥ*—factually.

TRANSLATION

My dear father, please describe factually the symptoms of this manifest world. What is its background? How is it created? How is it conserved? And under whose control is all this being done?

PURPORT

The inquiries by Nārada Muni on the basis of factual cause and effect appear very reasonable. The atheists, however, put forward many self-made theories without any touch of cause and effect. The manifested world, as well as the spirit soul, is still unexplained by the godless atheists through the medium of experimental knowledge, although they have put forward many theories manufactured by their fertile brains. Contrary to such mental speculative theories of creation, however, Nārada Muni wanted to know all the facts of creation in truth, and not by theories.

Transcendental knowledge regarding the soul and the Supersoul includes knowledge of the phenomenal world and the basis of its creation. In the phenomenal world three things are factually observed by any intelligent man: the living beings, the manifest world, and the ultimate control over them. The intelligent man can see that neither the living entity nor the phenomenal world are creations of chance. The symmetry of creation and its regulative actions and reactions suggests the plan of an intelligent brain behind them, and by genuine inquiry one may find out the ultimate cause with the help of one who knows them factually.

TEXT 3

सर्वं ह्येतद् भवान् वेद भूतभव्यभवत्प्रभुः ।
करामलकवद् विश्वं विज्ञानावसितं तव ॥ ३ ॥

sarvaṁ hy etad bhavān veda
bhūta-bhavya-bhavat-prabhuḥ
karāmalaka-vad viśvaṁ
vijñānāvasitaṁ tava

sarvam—all and everything; *hi*—certainly; *etat*—this; *bhavān*—your good self; *veda*—know; *bhūta*—all that is created or born; *bhavya*—all that will be created or born; *bhavat*—all that is being created; *prabhuḥ*—you, the master of everything; *kara-āmalaka-vat*—just like a walnut within your grip; *viśvam*—the universe; *vijñāna-avasitam*—within your knowledge scientifically; *tava*—your.

TRANSLATION

My dear father, all this is known to you scientifically because whatever was created in the past, whatever will be created in the future, or whatever is being created at present, as well as everything within the universe, is within your grip, just like a walnut.

PURPORT

Brahmā is the direct creator of the manifested universe and everything within the universe. He therefore knows what happened in the past, what will happen in the future, and what is happening at present. Three principal items, namely the living being, the phenomenal world and the controller, are all in continuous action—past, present and future—and the direct manager is supposed to know everything of such actions and reactions, as one knows about a walnut within the grip of one's palm. The direct manufacturer of a particular thing is supposed to know how he learned the art of manufacturing, where he got the ingredients, how he set it up and how the products in the manufacturing process are being turned out. Because Brahmā is the firstborn living being, naturally he is supposed to know everything about creative functions.

TEXT 4

यद्विज्ञानो यदाधारो यत्परस्त्वं यदात्मकः ।
एकः सृजसि भूतानि भूतैरेवात्ममायया ॥ ४ ॥

yad-vijñāno yad-ādhāro
yat-paras tvaṁ yad-ātmakaḥ
ekaḥ sṛjasi bhūtāni
bhūtair evātma-māyayā

yat-vijñānaḥ—the source of knowledge; *yat-ādhāraḥ*—under whose protection; *yat-paraḥ*—under whose subordination; *tvam*—you; *yat-ātmakaḥ*—in what capacity; *ekaḥ*—alone; *sṛjasi*—you are creating; *bhūtāni*—the living entities; *bhūtaiḥ*—with the help of the material elements; *eva*—certainly; *ātma*—self; *māyayā*—by potency.

TRANSLATION

My dear father, what is the source of your knowledge? Under whose protection are you standing? And under whom are you working? What is your real position? Do you alone create all entities with material elements by your personal energy?

PURPORT

It was known to Śrī Nārada Muni that Lord Brahmā attained creative energy by undergoing severe austerities. As such, he could understand that there was someone else superior to Brahmājī who invested Brahmā with the power of creation. Therefore he asked all the above questions. Discoveries of progressive scientific achievements are therefore not independent. The scientist has to attain the knowledge of a thing already existing by means of the wonderful brain made by someone else. A scientist can work with the help of such an awarded brain, but it is not possible for the scientist to create his own or a similar brain. Therefore no one is independent in the matter of any creation, nor is such creation automatic.

TEXT 5

आत्मन् भावयसे तानि न पराभावयन् स्वयम् ।
आत्मशक्तिमवष्टभ्य ऊर्णनाभिरिवाक्लमः ॥ ५ ॥

ātman bhāvayase tāni
na parābhāvayan svayam
ātma-śaktim avaṣṭabhya
ūrṇanābhir ivāklamaḥ

ātman (*ātmani*)—by self; *bhāvayase*—manifest; *tāni*—all those; *na*—not; *parābhāvayan*—being defeated; *svayam*—yourself; *ātma-śaktim*—self-sufficient power; *avaṣṭabhya*—being employed; *ūrṇanābhiḥ*—the spider; *iva*—like; *aklamaḥ*—without help.

TRANSLATION

As the spider very easily creates the network of its cobweb and manifests its power of creation without being defeated by others,

so also you yourself, by employment of your self-sufficient energy, create without any other's help.

PURPORT

The best example of self-sufficiency is the sun. The sun does not require to be illuminated by any other body. Rather, it is the sun which helps all other illuminating agents, for in the presence of the sun no other illuminating agent becomes prominent. Nārada compared the position of Brahmā to the self-sufficiency of the spider, who creates its own field of activities without any other's help by employment of its own energetic creation of saliva.

TEXT 6

नाहं वेद परं ह्यस्मिन्नापरं न समं विभो ।
नामरूपगुणैर्भाव्यं सदसत् किञ्चिदन्यतः ॥ ६ ॥

nāhaṁ veda paraṁ hy asmin
nāparaṁ na samaṁ vibho
nāma-rūpa-guṇair bhāvyaṁ
sad-asat kiñcid anyataḥ

na—do not; *aham*—myself; *veda*—know; *param*—superior; *hi*—for; *asmin*—in this world; *na*—neither; *aparam*—inferior; *na*—nor; *samam*—equal; *vibho*—O great one; *nāma*—name; *rūpa*—characteristics; *guṇaiḥ*—by qualification; *bhāvyam*—all that is created; *sat*—eternal; *asat*—temporary; *kiñcit*—or anything like that; *anyataḥ*—from any other source.

TRANSLATION

Whatever we can understand by the nomenclature, characteristics and features of a particular thing—superior, inferior or equal, eternal or temporary—is not created from any source other than that of Your Lordship, thou so great.

PURPORT

The manifested world is full of varieties of created beings in 8,400,000 species of life, and some of them are superior and inferior to others. In human society the human being is considered to be the superior living being, and amongst the human beings there are also different varieties: good, bad, equal, etc. But Nārada Muni took for granted that none of them has any source of generation besides his father, Brahmājī. Therefore he wanted to know all about them from Lord Brahmā.

TEXT 7

स भवानचरद् घोरं यत् तपः सुसमाहितः ।
तेन खेदयसे नस्त्वं पराशङ्कां च यच्छसि ॥ ७ ॥

sa bhavān acarad ghoraṁ
yat tapaḥ susamāhitaḥ
tena khedayase nas tvaṁ
parā-śaṅkāṁ ca yacchasi

saḥ—he; *bhavān*—your good self; *acarat*—undertook; *ghoram*—severe; *yat tapaḥ*—meditation; *su-samāhitaḥ*—in perfect discipline; *tena*—for that reason; *khedayase*—gives pain; *naḥ*—ourselves; *tvam*—your good self; *parā*—the ultimate truth; *śaṅkām*—doubts; *ca*—and; *yacchasi*—giving us a chance.

TRANSLATION

Yet we are moved to wonder about the existence of someone more powerful than you when we think of your great austerities in perfect discipline, although your good self is so powerful in the matter of creation.

PURPORT

Following in the footsteps of Śrī Nārada Muni, one should not blindly accept his spiritual master as God Himself. A spiritual master is duly respected on a par with God, but a spiritual master claiming to be God Himself should at once be rejected. Nārada Muni accepted Brahmā as the Supreme due to Lord Brahmā's wonderful acts in creation, but doubts arose in him when he saw that Lord Brahmā also worshiped some superior authority. The Supreme is supreme, and He has no worshipable superior. The *ahaṅgrahopāsitā*, or the one who worships himself with the idea of becoming God Himself, is misleading, but the intelligent disciple can at once detect that the Supreme God does not need to worship anyone, including Himself, in order to become God. *Ahaṅgrahopāsanā* may be one of the processes for transcendental realization, but the *ahaṅgrahopāsitā* can never be God Himself. No one becomes God by undergoing a process of transcendental realization. Nārada Muni thought of Brahmājī as the Supreme Person, but when he saw Brahmājī engaged in the process of transcendental realization, doubts arose in him. So he wanted to be clearly informed.

TEXT 8

एतन्मे पृच्छतः सर्वं सर्वज्ञ सकलेश्वर ।
विजानीहि यथैवेदमहं बुध्येऽनुशासितः ॥ ८ ॥

etan me pṛcchataḥ sarvaṁ
sarva-jña sakaleśvara
vijānīhi yathaivedam
ahaṁ budhye 'nuśāsitaḥ

etat—all those; *me*—unto me; *pṛcchataḥ*—inquisitive; *sarvam*—all that is inquired; *sarva-jña*—one who knows everything; *sakala*—over all; *īśvara*—the controller; *vijānīhi*—kindly explain; *yathā*—as; *eva*—they are; *idam*—this; *aham*—myself; *budhye*—can understand; *anuśāsitaḥ*—just learning from you.

TRANSLATION

My dear father, you know everything, and you are the controller of all. Therefore may all that I have inquired from you be kindly instructed to me so that I may be able to understand it as your student.

PURPORT

The inquiries made by Nārada Muni are very important for everyone concerned, and as such Nārada requested Brahmājī to deem them suitable so that all others who may come in the line of disciplic succession of the Brahma-sampradāya may also know them properly without any difficulty.

TEXT 9

ब्रह्मोवाच
सम्यक् कारुणिकस्येदं वत्स ते विचिकित्सितम् ।
यदहं चोदितः सौम्य भगवद्वीर्यदर्शने ॥ ९ ॥

brahmovāca
samyak kāruṇikasyedaṁ
vatsa te vicikitsitam
yad ahaṁ coditaḥ saumya
bhagavad-vīrya-darśane

brahmā uvāca—Lord Brahmā said; *samyak*—perfectly; *kāruṇikasya*—of you, who are very kind; *idam*—this; *vatsa*—my dear boy; *te*—your; *vicikitsitam*—inquisitiveness; *yat*—by which; *aham*—myself; *coditaḥ*—inspired; *saumya*—O gentle one; *bhagavat*—of the Personality of Godhead; *vīrya*—prowess; *darśane*—in the matter of.

TRANSLATION

Lord Brahmā said: My dear boy Nārada, being merciful to all (including me) you have asked all these questions because I have been inspired to see into the prowess of the Almighty Personality of Godhead.

PURPORT

Brahmājī, being so questioned by Nāradajī, congratulated him, for it is usual for the devotees to become very enthusiastic whenever they are questioned concerning the Almighty Personality of Godhead. That is the sign of a pure devotee of the Lord. Such discourses on the transcendental activities of the Lord purify the atmosphere in which such discussions are held, and the devotees thus become enlivened while answering such questions. It is purifying both for the questioners and for one who answers the questions. The pure devotees are not only satisfied by knowing everything about the Lord, but are also eager to broadcast the information to others, for they want to see that the glories of the Lord are known to everyone. Thus the devotee feels satisfied when such an opportunity is offered to him. This is the basic principle of missionary activities.

TEXT 10

नानृतं तव तच्चापि यथा मां प्रब्रवीषि भोः ।
अविज्ञाय परं मत्त एतावत्त्वं यतो हि मे ॥१०॥

nānṛtaṁ tava tac cāpi
yathā māṁ prabravīṣi bhoḥ
avijñāya paraṁ matta
etāvat tvaṁ yato hi me

na—not; *anṛtam*—false; *tava*—of yours; *tat*—that; *ca*—also; *api*—as you have stated; *yathā*—in the matter of; *mām*—of myself; *prabravīṣi*—as you describe; *bhoḥ*—O my son; *avijñāya*—without knowing; *param*—the Supreme; *mattaḥ*—beyond myself; *etāvat*—all that you have spoken; *tvam*—yourself; *yataḥ*—for the reason of; *hi*—certainly; *me*—about me.

TRANSLATION

Whatever you have spoken about me is not false because unless and until one is aware of the Personality of Godhead, who is the ultimate truth beyond me, one is sure to be illusioned by observing my powerful activities.

PURPORT

"The frog in the well" logic illustrates that a frog residing in the atmosphere and boundary of a well cannot imagine the length and breadth of the gigantic ocean. Such a frog, when informed of the gigantic length and breadth of the ocean, first of all does not believe that there is such an ocean, and if someone assures him that factually there is such a thing, the frog then begins to measure it by imagination by means of pumping its belly as far as possible, with the result that the tiny abdomen of the frog bursts and the poor frog dies without any experience of the actual ocean. Similarly, the material scientists also want to challenge the inconceivable potency of the Lord by measuring Him with their froglike brains and their scientific achievements, but at the end they simply die unsuccessfully, like the frog.

Sometimes a materially powerful man is accepted as God or the incarnation of God without any knowledge of the factual God. Such a material assessment may be gradually extended, and the attempt may reach to the highest limit of Brahmājī, who is the topmost living being within the universe and has a duration of life unimaginable to the material scientist. As we get information from the most authentic book of knowledge, the *Bhagavad-gītā* (8.17), Brahmājī's one day and night is calculated to be some hundreds of thousands of years on our planet. This long duration of life may not be believed by "the frog in the well," but persons who have a realization of the truths mentioned in the *Bhagavad-gītā* accept the existence of a great personality who creates the variegatedness of the complete universe. It is understood from the revealed scriptures that the Brahmājī of this universe is younger than all the other Brahmās in charge of the many, many universes beyond this, but none of them can be equal to the Personality of Godhead.

Nāradajī is one of the liberated souls, and after his liberation he was known as Nārada; otherwise, before his liberation, he was simply a son of a maidservant. The questions may be asked why Nāradajī was not aware of the Supreme Lord and why he misconceived Brahmājī to be the Supreme Lord, although factually he was not. A liberated soul is never bewildered by such a mistaken idea, so why did Nāradajī ask all those questions just like an ordinary man with a poor fund of knowledge? There was such bewilderment in Arjuna also, although he is eternally the associate of the Lord. Such bewilderment in Arjuna or in Nārada takes place by the will of the Lord so that other, nonliberated persons may realize the real truth and knowledge of the Lord. The doubt arising in the mind of Nārada about Brahmājī's becoming all-powerful is a lesson for the frogs in the well, that they may not be bewildered in misconceiving the identity of the Personality of Godhead (even by comparison to a personality like Brahmā, so what to speak of ordinary men who falsely pose themselves as God or an incarnation of God). The Supreme Lord is always the Supreme, and as we have tried to establish many times in these purports, no living being, even up to the standard of Brahmā, can claim to be one with the Lord. One should not be misled when people worship a great man as God after his death as a matter of hero worship. There were many kings like Lord Rāmacandra, the King of Ayodhyā, but none of them are mentioned as God in the revealed scriptures. To be a good king is not necessarily the qualification for being Lord Rāma, but to be a great personality like Kṛṣṇa is the qualification for being the Personality of Godhead. If we scrutinize the characters who took part in the Battle of Kurukṣetra, we may find that Mahārāja Yudhiṣṭhira was no less a pious king than Lord Rāmacandra, and by character study Mahārāja Yudhiṣṭhira was a better moralist than Lord Kṛṣṇa. Lord Kṛṣṇa asked Mahārāja Yudhiṣṭhira to lie, but Mahārāja Yudhiṣṭhira protested. But that does not mean that Mahārāja Yudhiṣṭhira could be equal to Lord Rāmacandra or Lord Kṛṣṇa. The great authorities have estimated Mahārāja Yudhiṣṭhira to be a pious man, but they have accepted Lord Rāma or Kṛṣṇa as the Personality of Godhead. The Lord is therefore a different identity in all circumstances, and no idea of anthropomorphism can be applied to Him. The Lord is always the Lord, and a common living being can never be equal to Him.

TEXT 11

येन स्वरोचिषा विश्वं रोचितं रोचयाम्यहम् ।
यथार्कोऽग्निर्यथा सोमो यथर्क्षग्रहतारकाः ॥११॥

yena sva-rociṣā viśvaṁ
rocitaṁ rocayāmy aham
yathārko 'gnir yathā somo
yatharkṣa-graha-tārakāḥ

yena—by whom; *sva-rociṣā*—by His own effulgence; *viśvam*—all the world; *rocitam*—already created potentially; *rocayāmi*—do manifest; *aham*—I; *yathā*—as much; *arkaḥ*—the sun; *agniḥ*—fire; *yathā*—as; *somaḥ*—the moon; *yathā*—as also; *ṛkṣa*—the firmament; *graha*—the influential planets; *tārakāḥ*—the stars.

TRANSLATION

I create after the Lord's creation by His personal effulgence [known as the brahmajyoti], just as when the sun manifests its fire, the moon, the firmament, the influential planets and the twinkling stars also manifest their brightness.

PURPORT

Lord Brahmājī said to Nārada that his impression that Brahmā was not the supreme authority in the creation was correct. Sometimes less intelligent men have the foolish impression that Brahmā is the cause of all causes. But Nārada wanted to clear the matter by the statements of Brahmājī, the supreme authority in the universe. As the decision of the supreme court of a state is final, similarly the judgment of Brahmājī, the supreme authority in the universe, is final in the Vedic process of acquiring knowledge. As we have already affirmed in the previous verse, Nāradajī was a liberated soul; therefore, he was not one of the less intelligent men who accept a false god or gods in their own ways. He represented himself as less intelligent and yet intelligently presented a doubt to be cleared by the supreme authority so that the uninformed might take note of it and be rightly informed about the intracacies of the creation and the creator.

In this verse Brahmājī clears up the wrong impression held by the less intelligent and affirms that he creates the universal variegatedness after the potential creation by the glaring effulgence of Lord Śrī Kṛṣṇa. Brahmājī has also separately given this statement in the *saṁhitā* known as the *Brahma-saṁhitā* (5.40), where he says:

yasya prabhā prabhavato jagad-aṇḍa-koṭi-
koṭiṣv aśeṣa-vasudhādi-vibhūti-bhinnam
tad brahma niṣkalam anantam aśeṣa-bhūtaṁ
govindam ādi-puruṣaṁ tam ahaṁ bhajāmi

"I serve the Supreme Personality of Godhead Govinda, the primeval Lord, whose transcendental bodily effulgence, known as the *brahmajyoti*, which is unlimited, unfathomed and all-pervasive, is the cause of the creation of unlimited numbers of planets, etc., with varieties of climates and specific conditions of life."

The same statement is in the *Bhagavad-gītā* (14.27). Lord Kṛṣṇa is the background of the *brahmajyoti* (*brahmaṇo hi pratiṣṭhāham*). In the *Nirukti*, or Vedic dictionary, the import of *pratiṣṭhā* is mentioned as "that which establishes." So the *brahmajyoti* is not independent or self-sufficient. Lord Śrī Kṛṣṇa is ultimately the creator of the *brahmajyoti*, mentioned in this verse as *sva-rociṣā*, or the effulgence of the transcendental body of the Lord. This *brahmajyoti* is all-pervading, and all creation is made possible by its potential power; therefore the Vedic hymns declare that everything that exists is being sustained by the *brahmajyoti* (*sarvaṁ khalv idaṁ brahma*). Therefore the potential seed of all creation is the *brahmajyoti*, and the same *brahmajyoti*, unlimited and unfathomed, is established by the Lord. Therefore the Lord (Śrī Kṛṣṇa) is ultimately the supreme cause of all creation (*ahaṁ sarvasya prabhavaḥ*).

One should not expect the Lord to create like a blacksmith with a hammer and other instruments. The Lord creates by His potencies. He has His multifarious potencies (*parāsya śaktir vividhaiva śrūyate*). Just as the small seed of a banyan fruit has the potency to create a big banyan tree, the Lord disseminates all varieties of seeds by His potential *brahmajyoti* (*sva-rociṣā*), and the seeds are made to develop by the watering process of persons like Brahmā. Brahmā cannot create the seeds, but he can manifest the seed into a tree, just as a gardener helps plants and orchards to grow by the watering process. The example cited here of the sun is very appropriate. In the material world the sun is the cause of all illumination: fire, electricity, the rays of the moon, etc. All luminaries in the sky are creations of the sun, the sun is the creation of the *brahmajyoti*, and the *brahmajyoti* is the effulgence of the Lord. Thus the ultimate cause of creation is the Lord.

TEXT 12

तस्मै नमो भगवते वासुदेवाय धीमहि ।
यन्मायया दुर्जयया मां वदन्ति जगद्गुरुम् ॥१२॥

tasmai namo bhagavate
vāsudevāya dhīmahi
yan-māyayā durjayayā
māṁ vadanti jagad-gurum

tasmai—unto Him; *namaḥ*—offer my obeisances; *bhagavate*—unto the Personality of Godhead; *vāsudevāya*—unto Lord Kṛṣṇa; *dhīmahi*—

do meditate upon Him; *yat*—by whose; *māyayā*—potencies; *durjayayā*—invincible; *mām*—unto me; *vadanti*—they say; *jagat*—the world; *gurum*—the master.

TRANSLATION

I offer my obeisances and meditate upon Lord Kṛṣṇa [Vāsudeva], the Personality of Godhead, whose invincible potency influences them [the less intelligent class of men] to call me the supreme controller.

PURPORT

As will be more clearly explained in the next verse, the illusory potency of the Lord bewilders the less intelligent to accept Brahmājī, or for that matter any other person, as the Supreme Lord. Brahmājī, however, refuses to be called this, and he directly offers his respectful obeisances unto Lord Vāsudeva, or Śrī Kṛṣṇa, the Personality of Godhead, as he has already offered the same respects to Him in the *Brahma-saṁhitā* (5.1):

īśvaraḥ paramaḥ kṛṣṇaḥ
sac-cid-ānanda-vigrahaḥ
anādir ādir govindaḥ
sarva-kāraṇa-kāraṇam

"The Supreme Lord is the Personality of Godhead Śrī Kṛṣṇa, the primeval Lord in His transcendental body, the ultimate cause of all causes. I worship that primeval Lord Govinda."

Brahmājī is conscious of his actual position, and he knows how less intelligent persons, bewildered by the illusory energy of the Lord, whimsically accept anyone and everyone as God. A responsible personality like Brahmājī refuses to be addressed as the Supreme Lord by his disciples or subordinates, but foolish persons praised by men of the nature of dogs, hogs, camels and asses feel flattered to be addressed as the Supreme Lord. Why such persons take pleasure in being addressed as God, or why such persons are addressed as God by foolish admirers, is explained in the following verse.

TEXT 13

विलज्जमानया यस्य स्थातुमीक्षापथेऽमुया ।
विमोहिता विकत्थन्ते ममाहमिति दुर्धियः ॥१३॥

vilajjamānayā yasya
sthātum īkṣā-pathe 'muyā
vimohitā vikatthante
mamāham iti durdhiyaḥ

vilajjamānayā—by one who is ashamed; *yasya*—whose; *sthātum*—to stay; *īkṣā-pathe*—in front; *amuyā*—by the bewildering energy; *vimohitāḥ*—those who are bewildered; *vikatthante*—talk nonsense; *mama*—it is mine; *aham*—I am everything; *iti*—thus vituperating; *durdhiyaḥ*—thus ill conceived.

TRANSLATION

The illusory energy of the Lord cannot take precedence, being ashamed of her position, but those who are bewildered by her always talk nonsense, being absorbed in thoughts of "It is I" and "It is mine."

PURPORT

The invincibly powerful deluding energy of the Personality of God, or the third energy, representing nescience, can bewilder the entire world of animation, but still she is not strong enough to be able to stand in front of the Supreme Lord. Nescience is behind the Personality of Godhead, where she is powerful enough to mislead the living beings, and the primary symptom of bewildered persons is that they talk nonsense. Nonsensical talks are not supported by the principles of Vedic literatures, and first-grade nonsense talk is "It is I, it is mine." A godless civilization is exclusively conducted by such false ideas, and such persons, without any factual realization of God, accept a false God or falsely declare themselves to be God to mislead persons who are already bewildered by the deluding energy. Those who are before the Lord, however, and who surrender unto Him, cannot be influenced by the deluding energy; therefore they are free from the misconception of "It is I, it is mine," and therefore they do not accept a false God or pose themselves as equal to the Supreme Lord. Identification of the bewildered person is distinctly given in this verse.

TEXT 14

द्रव्यं कर्म च कालश्च स्वभावो जीव एव च ।
वासुदेवात्परो ब्रह्मन्न चान्योऽर्थोऽस्ति तत्त्वतः ॥१४॥

dravyaṁ karma ca kālaś ca
svabhāvo jīva eva ca
vāsudevāt paro brahman
na cānyo 'rtho 'sti tattvataḥ

dravyam—the ingredients (earth, water, fire, air and sky); *karma*—the interaction; *ca*—and; *kālaḥ*—eternal time; *ca*—also; *sva-bhāvaḥ*—intuition or nature; *jīvaḥ*—the living being; *eva*—certainly; *ca*—and; *vāsudevāt*—from Vāsudeva; *paraḥ*—differentiated parts; *brahman*—O *brāhmaṇa; na*—never; *ca*—also; *anyaḥ*—separate; *arthaḥ*—value; *asti*—there is; *tattvataḥ*—in truth.

TRANSLATION

The five elementary ingredients of creation, the interaction thereof set up by eternal time, and the intuition or nature of the individual living beings are all differentiated parts and parcels of the Personality of Godhead, Vāsudeva, and in truth there is no other value in them.

PURPORT

This phenomenal world is impersonally the representation of Vāsudeva because the ingredients of its creation, their interaction and the enjoyer of the resultant action, the living being, are all produced by the external and internal energies of Lord Kṛṣṇa. This is confirmed in the *Bhagavad-gītā* (7.4–5). The ingredients, namely earth, water, fire, air and sky, as well as the conception of material identity, intelligence and the mind, are produced of the external energy of the Lord. The living entity who enjoys the interaction of the above gross and subtle ingredients, as set up by eternal time, is an offshoot of internal potency, with freedom to remain either in the material world or in the spiritual world. In the material world the living entity is enticed by deluding nescience, but in the spiritual world he is in the normal condition of spiritual existence without any delusion. The living entity is known as the marginal potency of the Lord. But in all circumstances, neither the material ingredients nor the spiritual parts and parcels are independent of the Personality of Godhead Vāsudeva, for all things, whether products of the external, internal or marginal potencies of the Lord, are simply displays of the same effulgence of the Lord, just as light, heat and smoke are displays of fire. None of them are separate from the fire—all of them combine together to be called fire; similarly, all phenomenal manifestations, as well as the effulgence of the body of Vāsudeva, are His impersonal features, whereas He eternally exists in His transcendental form called *sac-cid-ānanda-vigrahaḥ*, distinct from all conceptions of the material ingredients mentioned above.

TEXT 15

नारायणपरा वेदा देवा नारायणाङ्गजाः ।
नारायणपरा लोका नारायणपरा मखाः ॥१५॥

nārāyaṇa-parā vedā
devā nārāyaṇāṅgajāḥ
nārāyaṇa-parā lokā
nārāyaṇa-parā makhāḥ

nārāyaṇa—the Supreme Lord; *parāḥ*—is the cause and is meant for; *vedāḥ*—knowledge; *devāḥ*—the demigods; *nārāyaṇa*—the Supreme Lord; *aṅga-jāḥ*—assisting hands; *nārāyaṇa*—the Personality of Godhead; *parāḥ*—for the sake of; *lokāḥ*—the planets; *nārāyaṇa*—the Supreme Lord; *parāḥ*—just to please Him; *makhāḥ*—all sacrifices.

TRANSLATION

The Vedic literatures are made by and are meant for the Supreme Lord, the demigods are also meant for serving the Lord

as parts of His body, the different planets are also meant for the sake of the Lord, and different sacrifices are performed just to please Him.

PURPORT

According to the *Vedānta-sūtras* (*śāstra-yonitvāt*), the Supreme Lord is the author of all revealed scriptures, and all revealed scriptures are for knowing the Supreme Lord. *Veda* means knowledge that leads to the Lord. The *Vedas* are made just to revive the forgotten consciousness of the conditioned souls, and any literature not meant for reviving God consciousness is rejected at once by the *nārāyaṇa-para* devotees. Such deluding books of knowledge, not having Nārāyaṇa as their aim, are not at all knowledge, but are the playgrounds for crows who are interested in the rejected refuse of the world. Any book of knowledge (science or art) must lead to the knowledge of Nārāyaṇa; otherwise it must be rejected. That is the way of advancement of knowledge. The supreme worshipable Deity is Nārāyaṇa. The demigods are recommended secondarily for worship in relation to Nārāyaṇa because the demigods are assisting hands in the management of the universal affairs. As the officers of a kingdom are respected due to their relation to the king, the demigods are worshiped due to their relation to the Lord. Without the Lord's relation, worship of the demigods is unauthorized (*avidhi-pūrvakam*), just as it is improper to water the leaves and branches of a tree without watering its root. Therefore the demigods are also dependent on Nārāyaṇa. The *lokas*, or different planets, are attractive because they have different varieties of life and bliss partially representing the *sac-cid-ānanda-vigraha*. Everyone wants the eternal life of bliss and knowledge. In the material world such an eternal life of bliss and knowledge is progressively realized in the upper planets, but after reaching there one is inclined to achieve further progress along the path back to Godhead. Duration of life, with a proportionate quantity of bliss and knowledge, may be increased from one planet to another. One can increase the duration of life to thousands and hundreds of thousands of years in different planets, but nowhere is there eternal life. But one who can reach the highest planet, that of Brahmā, can aspire to reach the planets in the spiritual sky, where life is eternal. Therefore, the progressive journey from one planet to another culminates in reaching the supreme planet of the Lord (*mad-dhāma*), where life is eternal and full of bliss and knowledge. All different kinds of sacrifice are performed just to satisfy Lord Nārāyaṇa with a view to reach Him, and the best sacrifice recommended in this age of Kali is *saṅkīrtana-yajña*, the mainstay of the devotional service of a *nārāyaṇa-para* devotee.

TEXT 16

नारायणपरो योगो नारायणपरं तपः ।
नारायणपरं ज्ञानं नारायणपरा गतिः ॥१६॥

nārāyaṇa-paro yogo
nārāyaṇa-paraṁ tapaḥ
nārāyaṇa-paraṁ jñānaṁ
nārāyaṇa-parā gatiḥ

nārāyaṇa-paraḥ—just to know Nārāyaṇa; *yogaḥ*—concentration of mind; *nārāyaṇa-param*—just with an aim to achieve Nārāyaṇa; *tapaḥ*—austerity; *nārāyaṇa-param*—just to realize a glimpse of Nārāyaṇa; *jñānam*—culture of transcendental knowledge; *nārāyaṇa-parā*—the path of salvation ends by entering the kingdom of Nārāyaṇa; *gatiḥ*—progressive path.

TRANSLATION

All different types of meditation or mysticism are means for realizing Nārāyaṇa. All austerities are aimed at achieving Nārāyaṇa. Culture of transcendental knowledge is for getting a glimpse of Nārāyaṇa, and ultimately salvation is entering the kingdom of Nārāyaṇa.

PURPORT

In meditation, there are two systems of *yoga*, namely *aṣṭāṅga-yoga* and *sāṅkhya-yoga. Aṣṭāṅga-yoga* is practice in concentrating the mind, releasing oneself from all engagements by the regulative processes of meditation, concentration, sitting postures, blocking the movements of the internal circulation of air, etc. *Sāṅkhya-yoga* is meant to distinguish the truth from ephemerals. But ultimately both the systems are meant for realizing the impersonal Brahman, which is but a partial representation of Nārāyaṇa, the Personality of Godhead. As we have explained before, the impersonal Brahman effulgence is only a part of the Personality of Godhead. Impersonal Brahman is situated on the person of the Supreme Personality of Godhead, and as such, Brahman is the glorification of the Personality of the Godhead. This is confirmed both in the *Bhagavad-gītā* and in the *Matsya Purāṇa. Gati* refers to the ultimate destination, or the last word in liberation. Oneness with the impersonal *brahmajyoti* is not ultimate liberation; superior to that is the sublime association of the Personality of Godhead in one of the innumerable spiritual planets in the Vaikuṇṭha sky. Therefore the conclusion is that Nārāyaṇa, or the Personality of Godhead, is the ultimate destination for all kinds of *yoga* systems as well as all kinds of liberation.

TEXT 17

तस्यापि द्रष्टुरीशस्य कूटस्थस्याखिलात्मनः ।
सृज्यं सृजामि सृष्टोऽहमीक्षयैवाभिचोदितः ॥१७॥

tasyāpi draṣṭur īśasya
kūṭa-sthasyākhilātmanaḥ
sṛjyaṁ sṛjāmi sṛṣṭo 'ham
īkṣayaivābhicoditaḥ

tasya—His; *api*—certainly; *draṣṭuḥ*—of the seer; *īśasya*—of the controller; *kūṭa-sthasya*—of the one who is over everyone's intelligence; *akhila-ātmanaḥ*—of the Supersoul; *sṛjyam*—that which is already created; *sṛjāmi*—do I discover; *sṛṣṭaḥ*—created; *aham*—myself; *īkṣayā*—by glance over; *eva*—exactly; *abhicoditaḥ*—being inspired by Him.

TRANSLATION

Inspired by Him only, I discover what is already created by Him [Nārāyaṇa] under His vision as the all-pervading Supersoul, and I also am created by Him only.

PURPORT

Even Brahmā, the creator of the universe, admits that he is not the actual creator but is simply inspired by the Lord Nārāyaṇa and therefore creates under His superintendence those things already created by Him, the Supersoul of all living entities. Two identities of soul, the Supersoul and the individual soul, are admitted to be in the living entity, even by the greatest authority of the universe. The Supersoul is the Supreme Lord, the Personality of Godhead, whereas the individual soul is the eternal servitor of the Lord. The Lord inspires the individual soul to create what is already created by the Lord, and by the good will of the Lord a discoverer of something in the world is accredited as the discoverer. It is said that Columbus discovered the Western Hemisphere, but actually the tract of land was not created by Columbus. The vast tract of land was already there by the omnipotency of the Supreme Lord, and Columbus, by dint of his past service unto the Lord, was blessed with the credit of discovering America. Similarly, no one can create anything without the sanction of the Lord, since everyone sees according to his ability. This ability is also awarded by the Lord according to one's willingness to render service unto the Lord. One must therefore be voluntarily willing to render service unto the Lord, and thus the Lord will empower the doer in proportion to his surrender unto the lotus feet of the Lord. Lord Brahmā is a great devotee of the Lord; therefore he has been empowered or inspired by the Lord to create such a universe as the one manifested before us. The Lord also inspired Arjuna to fight in the field of Kurukṣetra as follows:

tasmāt tvam uttiṣṭha yaśo labhasva
jitvā śatrūn bhuṅkṣva rājyaṁ samṛddham
mayaivaite nihatāḥ pūrvam eva
nimitta-mātraṁ bhava savyasācin
(Bg. 11.33)

The Battle of Kurukṣetra, or any other battle at any place or at any time, is made by the will of the Lord, for no one can arrange such mass annihilation without the sanction of the Lord. The party of Duryodhana insulted Draupadī, a great devotee of Kṛṣṇa, and she appealed to the Lord as well as to all the silent observers of this unwarranted insult. Arjuna was then advised by the Lord to fight and take credit; otherwise the party of Duryodhana would be killed anyway by the will of the Lord.

So Arjuna was advised just to become the agent and take the credit for killing great generals like Bhīṣma and Karṇa.

In the Vedic writings such as the *Kaṭha Upaniṣad*, the Lord is described as the *sarva-bhūta-antarātmā*, or the Personality of Godhead who resides in everyone's body and who directs everything for one who is a soul surrendered unto Him. Those who are not surrendered souls are put under the care of the material nature (*bhrāmayan sarva-bhūtāni yantrārūḍhāni māyayā*); therefore, they are allowed to do things on their own account and suffer the consequences themselves. Devotees like Brahmā and Arjuna do not do anything on their own account, but as fully surrendered souls they always await indications from the Lord; therefore they attempt to do something which appears very wonderful to ordinary vision. One of the Lord's names is Urukrama, or one whose actions are very wonderful and are beyond the imagination of the living being, so the actions of His devotees sometimes appear very wonderful due to the direction of the Lord. Beginning from Brahmā, the topmost intelligent living entity within the universe, down to the smallest ant, every living entity's intelligence is overseen by the Lord in His transcendental position as the witness of all actions. The subtle presence of the Lord is felt by the intelligent man who can study the psychic effects of thinking, feeling and willing.

TEXT 18

सत्त्वं रजस्तम इति निर्गुणस्य गुणास्त्रयः ।
स्थितिसर्गनिरोधेषु गृहीता मायया विभोः ॥१८॥

sattvaṁ rajas tama iti
nirguṇasya guṇās trayaḥ
sthiti-sarga-nirodheṣu
gṛhītā māyayā vibhoḥ

sattvam—the mode of goodness; *rajaḥ*—the mode of passion; *tamaḥ*—the mode of ignorance; *iti*—all these; *nirguṇasya*—of the Transcendence; *guṇāḥ trayaḥ*—are three qualities; *sthiti*—maintenance; *sarga*—creation; *nirodheṣu*—in destruction; *gṛhītāḥ*—accepted; *māyayā*—by the external energy; *vibhoḥ*—of the Supreme.

TRANSLATION

The Supreme Lord is pure spiritual form, transcendental to all material qualities, yet for the sake of the creation of the material world and its maintenance and annihilation, He accepts through His external energy the material modes of nature called goodness, passion and ignorance.

PURPORT

The Supreme Lord is the master of the external energy manifested by the three material modes, namely goodness, passion and ignorance, and as master of this energy He is ever unaffected by the influence of such bewildering energy. The living entities, the *jīvas*, however, are affected by or susceptible to being influenced by such modes of material nature—that is the difference between the Lord and the living entities. The living entities are subjected by those qualities, although originally the living entities are qualitatively one with the Lord. In other words, the material modes of nature, being products of the energy of the Lord, are certainly connected with the Lord, but the connection is just like that between the master and the servants. The Supreme Lord is the controller of the material energy, whereas the living entities, who are entangled in the material world, are neither masters nor controllers. Rather, they become subordinate to or controlled by such energy. Factually the Lord is eternally manifested by His internal potency or spiritual energy just like the sun and its rays in the clear sky, but at times He creates the material energy, as the sun creates a cloud in the clear sky. As the sun is ever increasingly unaffected by a spot of cloud, so also the unlimited Lord is unaffected by the spot of material energy manifested at times in the unlimited span of the Lord's rays of *brahmajyoti.*

TEXT 19

कार्यकारणकर्तृत्वे द्रव्यज्ञानक्रियाश्रयाः ।
बध्नन्ति नित्यदा मुक्तं मायिनं पुरुषं गुणाः ॥१९॥

kārya-kāraṇa-kartṛtve
dravya-jñāna-kriyāśrayāḥ

badhnanti nityadā muktaṁ
māyinaṁ puruṣaṁ guṇāḥ

kārya—effect; *kāraṇa*—cause; *kartṛtve*—in activities; *dravya*—material; *jñāna*—knowledge; *kriyā-āśrayāḥ*—manifested by such symptoms; *badhnanti*—conditions; *nityadā*—eternally; *muktam*—transcendental; *māyinam*—affected by material energy; *puruṣam*—the living entity; *guṇāḥ*—the material modes.

TRANSLATION

These three modes of material nature, being further manifested as matter, knowledge and activities, put the eternally transcendental living entity under conditions of cause and effect and make him responsible for such activities.

PURPORT

Because they are between the internal and external potencies, the eternally transcendental living entities are called the marginal potency of the Lord. Factually, the living entities are not meant to be so conditioned by material energy, but due to their being affected by the false sense of lording it over the material energy, they come under the influence of such potency and thus become conditioned by the three modes of material nature. This external energy of the Lord covers up the pure knowledge of the living entity's eternally existing with Him, but the covering is so constant that it appears that the conditioned soul is eternally ignorant. Such is the wonderful action of *māyā*, or external energy manifested as if materially produced. By the covering power of the material energy, the material scientist cannot look beyond the material causes, but factually, behind the material manifestations, there are *adhibhūta*, *adhyātma* and *adhidaiva* actions, which the conditioned soul in the mode of ignorance cannot see. The *adhibhūta* manifestation entails repetitions of births and deaths with old age and diseases, the *adhyātma* manifestation conditions the spirit soul, and the *adhidaiva* manifestation is the controlling system. These are the material manifestations of cause and effect and the sense of responsibility of the conditioned actors. They are, after all, manifestations of the conditioned state, and the human being's freedom from such a conditioned state is the highest perfectional attainment.

TEXT 20

स एष भगवाल्लिँङ्गैस्त्रिभिरेतैरधोक्षजः ।
स्वलक्षितगतिर्ब्रह्मन् सर्वेषां मम चेश्वरः ॥२०॥

sa eṣa bhagavāl̐ liṅgais
tribhir etair adhokṣajaḥ
svalakṣita-gatir brahman
sarveṣāṁ mama ceśvaraḥ

saḥ—He; *eṣaḥ*—this; *bhagavān*—the Personality of Godhead; *liṅgaiḥ*—by the symptoms; *tribhiḥ*—by the three; *etaiḥ*—by all these; *adhokṣajaḥ*—the Superseer Transcendence; *su-alakṣita*—veritably unseen; *gatiḥ*—movement; *brahman*—O Nārada; *sarveṣām*—of everyone; *mama*—mine; *ca*—as also; *īśvaraḥ*—the controller.

TRANSLATION

O Brāhmaṇa Nārada, the Superseer, the transcendent Lord, is beyond the perception of the material senses of the living entities because of the above-mentioned three modes of nature. But He is the controller of everyone, including me.

PURPORT

In the *Bhagavad-gītā* (7.24–25) the Lord has declared very clearly that the impersonalist, who gives more importance to the transcendental rays of the Lord as *brahmajyoti* and who concludes that the Absolute Truth is ultimately impersonal and only manifests a form at a time of necessity, is less intelligent than the personalist, however much the impersonalist may be engaged in studying the *Vedānta.* The fact is that such impersonalists are covered by the above-mentioned three modes of material nature; therefore, they are unable to approach the transcendental Personality of the Lord. The Lord is not approachable by everyone because He is curtained by His *yogamāyā* potency. But one should not wrongly conclude that the Lord was formerly unmanifested and has now manifested Himself in the human form. This misconception of the formlessness of the Supreme Personality of Godhead is due to the *yogamāyā* curtain of the Lord and can be removed only by the Supreme Will, as soon as the conditioned soul surrenders unto Him. The devotees of the Lord who are transcendental to the above-mentioned three modes of material nature can see the all-blissful transcendental form of the Lord with their vision of love in the attitude of pure devotional service.

TEXT 21

कालं कर्म स्वभावं च मायेशो मायया स्वया ।
आत्मन् यदृच्छया प्राप्तं विबुभूषुरुपाददे ॥२१॥

kālaṁ karma svabhāvaṁ ca
māyeśo māyayā svayā
ātman yadṛcchayā prāptaṁ
vibubhūṣur upādade

kālam—eternal time; *karma*—the fate of the living entity; *svabhāvam*—nature; *ca*—also; *māyā*—potency; *īśaḥ*—the controller; *māyayā*—by the energy; *svayā*—of His own; *ātman (ātmani)*—unto His Self; *yadṛcchayā*—independently; *prāptam*—being merged in; *vibubhūṣuḥ*—appearing differently; *upādade*—accepted for being created again.

TRANSLATION

The Lord, who is the controller of all energies, thus creates, by His own potency, eternal time, the fate of all living entities, and their particular nature, for which they were created, and He again merges them independently.

PURPORT

The creation of the material world, wherein the conditioned souls are allowed to act subordinately by the Supreme Lord, takes place again and again after being repeatedly annihilated. The material creation is something like a cloud in the unlimited sky. The real sky is the spiritual sky, eternally filled with the rays of the *brahmajyoti*, and a portion of this unlimited sky is covered by the *mahat-tattva* cloud of the material creation, in which the conditioned souls, who want to lord it against the will of the Lord, are put into play as they desire under the control of the Lord by the agency of His external energy. As the rainy season appears and disappears regularly, the creation takes place and is again annihilated under the control of the Lord, as confirmed in the *Bhagavad-gītā* (8.19). So the creation and annihilation of the material worlds is a regular action of the Lord just to allow the conditioned souls to play as they like and thereby create their own fate of being differently created again in terms of their independent desires at the time of annihilation. The creation, therefore, takes place at a historical date (as we are accustomed to think of everything which has a beginning in our tiny experience). The process of creation and annihilation is called *anādi,* or without reference to date regarding the time the creation first took place, because the duration of even a partial creation is 8,640,000,000 years. The law of creation is, however, as mentioned in the Vedic literatures, that it is created at certain intervals and is again annihilated by the will of the Lord. The whole material or even the spiritual creation is a manifestation of the energy of the Lord, just as the light and heat of a fire are different manifestations of the fire's energy. The Lord therefore exists in His impersonal form by such expansion of energy, and the complete creation rests on His impersonal feature. Nonetheless He keeps Himself distinct from such creation as the *pūrṇam* (or complete), and so no one should wrongly think that His personal feature is not existent due to His impersonal unlimited expansions. The impersonal expansion is a manifestation of His energy, and He is always in His personal feature despite His innumerable unlimited expansions of impersonal energies (Bg. 9.5–7). For human intelligence it is very difficult to conceive how the whole creation rests on His expansion of energy, but the Lord has given a very good example in the *Bhagavad-gītā.* It is said that although the air and the atoms rest within the huge expansion of the sky, which is like the resting reservoir of everything materially created, still the sky remains separate and unaffected. Similarly although the Supreme Lord maintains everything created by His expansion of energy, He always remains separate. This is accepted even by Śaṅkarācārya, the great advocate of the impersonal form of the Absolute. He says *nārāyaṇaḥ paro 'vyaktāt,* or Nārāyaṇa exists separately, apart from the impersonal creative energy. The whole creation thus merges within the body of transcendental Nārāyaṇa at the time of annihilation, and the creation emanates from His body again with the same unchanging categories of fate and individual nature. The individual living entities, being parts and parcels of the Lord, are sometimes described as *ātmā*, qualitatively one in spiritual constitution. But because such living entities are apt to be attracted to the material creation, actively and subjectively, they are therefore different from the Lord.

TEXT 22

कालाद् गुणव्यतिकरः परिणामः स्वभावतः ।
कर्मणो जन्म महतः पुरुषाधिष्ठितादभूत् ॥२२॥

kālād guṇa-vyatikaraḥ
pariṇāmaḥ svabhāvataḥ
karmaṇo janma mahataḥ
puruṣādhiṣṭhitād abhūt

kālāt—from eternal time; *guṇa-vyatikaraḥ*—transformation of the modes by reaction; *pariṇāmaḥ*—transformation; *svabhāvataḥ*—from the nature; *karmaṇaḥ*—of activities; *janma*—creation; *mahataḥ*—of the *mahat-tattva; puruṣa-adhiṣṭhitāt*—because of the *puruṣa* incarnation of the Lord; *abhūt*—it took place.

TRANSLATION

After the incarnation of the first puruṣa [Kāraṇārṇavaśāyī Viṣṇu], the mahat-tattva, or the principles of material creation, take place, and then time is manifested, and in course of time the three qualities appear. Nature means the three qualitative appearances. They transform into activities.

PURPORT

By the omnipotency of the Supreme Lord, the whole material creation evolves by the process of transformation and reactions one after another, and by the same omnipotency, they are wound up again one after another and conserved in the body of the Supreme. *Kāla*, or time, is the synonym of nature and is the transformed manifestation of the principles of material creation. As such, *kāla* may be taken as the first cause of all creation, and by transformation of nature different activities of the material world become visible. These activities may be taken up as the natural instinct of each and every living being, or even of the inert objects, and after the manifestation of activities there are varieties of products and by-products of the same nature. Originally these are all due to the Supreme Lord. The *Vedānta-sūtras* and the *Bhāgavatam* thus begin with the Absolute Truth as the beginning of all creations (*janmādy asya yataḥ*).

TEXT 23

महतस्तु विकुर्वाणाद्रजःसत्त्वोपबृंहितात् ।
तमःप्रधानस्त्वभवद् द्रव्यज्ञानक्रियात्मकः ॥२३॥

mahatas tu vikurvāṇād
rajaḥ-sattvopabṛṁhitāt
tamaḥ-pradhānas tv abhavad
dravya-jñāna-kriyātmakaḥ

mahataḥ—of the *mahat-tattva; tu*—but; *vikurvāṇāt*—being transformed; *rajaḥ*—the material mode of passion; *sattva*—the mode of goodness; *upabṛṁhitāt*—because of being increased; *tamaḥ*—the mode of darkness; *pradhānaḥ*—being prominent; *tu*—but; *abhavat*—took place; *dravya*—matter; *jñāna*—material knowledge; *kriyā-ātmakaḥ*—predominantly material activities.

TRANSLATION

Material activities are caused by the mahat-tattva's being agitated. At first there is transformation of the modes of goodness and passion, and later—due to the mode of ignorance—matter, its knowledge, and different activities of material knowledge come into play.

PURPORT

Material creations of every description are more or less due to the development of the mode of passion (*rajas*). The *mahat-tattva* is the principle of material creation, and when it is agitated by the will of the Supreme at first the modes of passion and goodness are prominent, and afterwards the mode of passion, being generated in due course by material activities of different varieties, becomes prominent, and the living entities are thus involved more and more in ignorance. Brahmā is the representation of the mode of passion, and Viṣṇu is the representation of the mode of goodness, while the mode of ignorance is represented by Lord Śiva, the father of material activities. Material nature is called the mother, and the initiator for materialistic life is the father, Lord Śiva. All material creation by the living entities is therefore initiated by the mode of passion. With the advancement of the duration of life in a particular millennium, the different modes act by gradual development. In the age of Kali (when the mode of passion is most prominent) material activities of different varieties, in the name of advancement of human civilization, take place, and the living entities become more and more involved in forgetting their real identity—the spiritual nature. By a slight cultivation of the mode of goodness, a glimpse of spiritual nature is perceived, but due to the prominence of the mode of passion, the mode of goodness becomes adulterated. Therefore one cannot transcend the limits of the material modes, and therefore realization of the Lord, who is always transcendental to the modes of material nature, becomes very difficult for the living entities, even though prominently situated in the mode of goodness through cultivation of the various methods. In other words, the gross matters are *adhibhūtam*, their maintenance is *adhidaivam*, and the initiator of material activities is called *adhyātmam*. In the material world these three principles act as prominent features, namely as raw material, its regular supplies, and its use in different varieties of material creations for sense enjoyment by the bewildered entities.

TEXT 24

सोऽहङ्कार इति प्रोक्तो विकुर्वन् समभूत्त्रिधा ।
वैकारिकस्तैजसश्च तामसश्चेति यद्भिदा ।
द्रव्यशक्तिः क्रियाशक्तिर्ज्ञानशक्तिरिति प्रभो ॥२४॥

so 'haṅkāra iti prokto
vikurvan samabhūt tridhā

vaikārikas taijasaś ca
tāmasaś ceti yad-bhidā
dravya-śaktiḥ kriyā-śaktir
jñāna-śaktir iti prabho

saḥ—the very same thing; *ahaṅkāraḥ*—ego; *iti*—thus; *proktaḥ*—said; *vikurvan*—being transformed; *samabhūt*—became manifested; *tridhā*—in three features; *vaikārikaḥ*—in the mode of goodness; *taijasaḥ*—in the mode of passion; *ca*—and; *tāmasaḥ*—in the mode of ignorance; *ca*—also; *iti*—thus; *yat*—what is; *bhidā*—divided; *dravya-śaktiḥ*—powers that evolve matter; *kriyā-śaktiḥ*—initiation that creates; *jñāna-śaktiḥ*—intelligence that guides; *iti*—thus; *prabho*—O master.

TRANSLATION

The self-centered materialistic ego, thus being transformed into three features, becomes known as the modes of goodness, passion and ignorance in three divisions, namely the powers that evolve matter, knowledge of material creations, and the intelligence that guides such materialistic activities. Nārada, you are quite competent to understand this.

PURPORT

Materialistic ego, or the sense of identification with matter, is grossly self-centered, devoid of clear knowledge of the existence of God. And this self-centered egoism of the materialistic living entities is the cause of their being conditioned by the other paraphernalia and continuing their bondage of material existence. In the *Bhagavad-gītā* this self-centered egoism is very nicely explained in the Seventh Chapter (verses 24 through 27). The self-centered impersonalist, without a clear conception of the Personality of Godhead, concludes in his own way that the Personality of Godhead takes a material shape from His original impersonal spiritual existence for a particular mission. And this misleading conception of the Supreme Lord by the self-centered impersonalist continues, even though he is seen to be very interested in the Vedic literatures such as the *Brahma-sūtras* and other highly intellectual sources of knowledge. This ignorance of the personal feature of the Lord is due simply to ignorance of the mixture of different modes. The impersonalist thus cannot conceive of the Lord's eternal spiritual form of eternal knowledge, bliss and existence. The reason is that the Lord reserves the right of not exposing Himself to the nondevotee who, even after a thorough study of literature like the *Bhagavad-gītā*, remains an impersonalist simply by obstinacy. This obstinacy is due to the action of *yogamāyā*, a personal energy of the Lord that acts like an aide-de-camp by covering the vision of the obstinate impersonalist. Such a bewildered human being is described as *mūḍha*, or grossly ignorant, because he is unable to understand the transcendental form of the Lord as being unborn and unchangeable. If the Lord takes a form or material shape from His original impersonal feature, then it means that He is born and changeable from impersonal to personal. But He is not changeable. Nor does He ever take a new birth like a conditioned soul. The conditioned soul may take a form birth after birth due to his conditional existence in matter, but the self-centered impersonalists, by their gross ignorance, accept the Lord as one of them because of self-centered egoism, even after so-called advancement of knowledge in the *Vedānta*. The Lord, being situated in the heart of every individual living entity, knows very well the tendency of such conditioned souls in terms of past, present and future, but the bewildered conditioned soul hardly can know Him in His eternal form. By the will of the Lord, therefore, the impersonalist, even after knowing the Brahman and Paramātmā features of the Lord, remains ignorant of His eternal personal feature as ever-existent Nārāyaṇa, transcendental to all material creation.

The cause of such gross ignorance is constant engagement by the materialistic man in the matter of artificially increasing material demands. To realize the Supreme Personality of Godhead, one has to purify the materialistic senses by devotional service. The mode of goodness, or the brahminical culture recommended in the Vedic literatures, is helpful to such spiritual realization, and thus the *jñāna-śakti* stage of the conditioned soul is comparatively better than the other two stages, namely *dravya-śakti* and *kriyā-śakti*. The whole material civilization is manifested by a huge accumulation of materials, or, in other words, raw materials for industrial purposes, and the industrial enterprises (*kriyā-śakti*) are all due to gross ignorance of spiritual life. In order to rectify this great anomaly of materialistic civilization, based on the principles of *dravya-śakti* and *kriyā-śakti*, one has to adopt the process of devotional service of the Lord by adoption of the principles of *karma-yoga*, mentioned in the *Bhagavad-gītā* (9.27) as follows:

yat karoṣi yad aśnāsi
yaj juhoṣi dadāsi yat
yat tapasyasi kaunteya
tat kuruṣva mad-arpaṇam

"O son of Kuntī, all that you do, all that you eat, all that you offer and give away, as well as all austerities that you may perform, should be done as an offering unto Me."

TEXT 25

तामसादपि भूतादेर्विकुर्वाणादभून्नभः ।
तस्य मात्रा गुणः शब्दो लिङ्गं यद् द्रष्टृदृश्ययोः ॥२५॥

tāmasād api bhūtāder
vikurvāṇād abhūn nabhaḥ
tasya mātrā guṇaḥ śabdo
liṅgaṁ yad draṣṭṛ-dṛśyayoḥ

tāmasāt—from the darkness of false ego; *api*—certainly; *bhūta-ādeḥ*—of the material elements; *vikurvāṇāt*—because of transformation; *abhūt*—generated; *nabhaḥ*—the sky; *tasya*—its; *mātrā*—subtle form; *guṇaḥ*—quality; *śabdaḥ*—sound; *liṅgam*—characteristics; *yat*—as its; *draṣṭṛ*—the seer; *dṛśyayoḥ*—of what is seen.

TRANSLATION

From the darkness of false ego, the first of the five elements, namely the sky, is generated. Its subtle form is the quality of sound, exactly as the seer is in relationship with the seen.

PURPORT

The five elements, namely sky, air, fire, water and earth, are all but different qualities of the darkness of false ego. This means that the false ego in the sum total form of *mahat-tattva* is generated from the marginal potency of the Lord, and due to this false ego of lording it over the material creation, ingredients are generated for the false enjoyment of the living being. The living being is practically the dominating factor over the material elements as the enjoyer, though the background is the Supreme Lord. Factually, save and except the Lord, no one can be called the enjoyer, but the living entity falsely desires to become the enjoyer. This is the origin of false ego. When the bewildered living being desires this, the shadow elements are generated by the will of the Lord, and the living entities are allowed to run after them as after a phantasmagoria.

It is said that first the *tan-mātrā* sound is created and then the sky, and in this verse it is confirmed that actually it is so, but sound is the subtle form of the sky, and the distinction is like that between the seer and the seen. The sound is the representation of the actual object, as the sound produced speaking of the object gives an idea of the description of the object. Therefore sound is the subtle characteristic of the object. Similarly, sound representation of the Lord, in terms of His characteristics, is the complete form of the Lord, as was seen by Vasudeva and Mahārāja Daśaratha, the fathers of Lord Kṛṣṇa and Lord Rāma. The sound representation of the Lord is nondifferent from the Lord Himself because the Lord and His representation in sound are absolute knowledge. Lord Caitanya has instructed us that in the holy name of the Lord, as sound representation of the Lord, all the potencies of the Lord are invested. Thus one can immediately enjoy the association of the Lord by the pure vibration of the sound representation of His holy name, and the concept of the Lord is immediately manifested before the pure devotee. A pure devotee, therefore, is not aloof from the Lord even for a moment. The holy name of the Lord, as recommended in the *śāstras*—Hare Kṛṣṇa, Hare Kṛṣṇa, Kṛṣṇa Kṛṣṇa, Hare Hare/ Hare Rāma, Hare Rāma, Rāma Rāma, Hare Hare—may therefore be constantly chanted by the devotee aspiring to be constantly in touch with the Supreme Lord. One who is thus able to associate with the Lord is sure to be delivered from the darkness of the created world, which is a product of false ego (*tamasi mā jyotir gama*).

TEXTS 26–29

नभसोऽथ विकुर्वाणादभूत् स्पर्शगुणोऽनिलः ।
परान्वयाच्छब्दवांश्च प्राण ओजः सहो बलम् ॥२६॥

वायोरपि विकुर्वाणात् कालकर्मस्वभावतः ।
उदपद्यत तेजो वै रूपवत् स्पर्शशब्दवत् ॥२७॥
तेजसस्तु विकुर्वाणादासीदम्भो रसात्मकम् ।
रूपवत् स्पर्शवच्चाम्भो घोषवच्च परान्वयात् ॥२८॥
विशेषस्तु विकुर्वाणादम्भसो गन्धवानभूत् ।
परान्वयाद् रसस्पर्शशब्दरूपगुणान्वितः ॥२९॥

nabhaso 'tha vikurvāṇād
abhūt sparśa-guṇo 'nilaḥ
parānvayāc chabdavāṁś ca
prāṇa ojaḥ saho balam

vāyor api vikurvāṇāt
kāla-karma-svabhāvataḥ
udapadyata tejo vai
rūpavat sparśa-śabdavat

tejasas tu vikurvāṇād
āsīd ambho rasātmakam
rūpavat sparśavac cāmbho
ghoṣavac ca parānvayāt

viśeṣas tu vikurvāṇād
ambhaso gandhavān abhūt
parānvayād rasa-sparśa-
śabda-rūpa-guṇānvitaḥ

nabhasaḥ—of the sky; *atha*—thus; *vikurvāṇāt*—being transformed; *abhūt*—generated; *sparśa*—touch; *guṇaḥ*—quality; *anilaḥ*—air; *para*—previous; *anvayāt*—by succession; *śabdavān*—full of sound; *ca*—also; *prāṇaḥ*—life; *ojaḥ*—sense perception; *sahaḥ*—fat; *balam*—strength; *vāyoḥ*—of the air; *api*—also; *vikurvāṇāt*—by transformation; *kāla*—time; *karma*—reaction of the past; *svabhāvataḥ*—on the basis of nature; *udapadyata*—generated; *tejaḥ*—fire; *vai*—duly; *rūpavat*—with form; *sparśa*—touch; *śabdavat*—with sound also; *tejasaḥ*—of the fire;

tu—but; *vikurvāṇāt*—on being transformed; *āsīt*—it so happened; *ambhaḥ*—water; *rasa-ātmakam*—composed of juice; *rūpavat*—with form; *sparśavat*—with touch; *ca*—and; *ambhaḥ*—water; *ghoṣavat*—with sound; *ca*—and; *para*—previous; *anvayāt*—by succession; *viśeṣaḥ*—variegatedness; *tu*—but; *vikurvāṇāt*—by transformation; *ambhasaḥ*—of water; *gandhavān*—odorous; *abhūt*—became; *para*—previous; *anvayāt*—by succession; *rasa*—juice; *sparśa*—touch; *śabda*—sound; *rūpa-guṇa-anvitaḥ*—qualitative.

TRANSLATION

Because the sky is transformed, the air is generated with the quality of touch, and by previous succession the air is also full of sound and the basic principles of duration of life: sense perception, mental power and bodily strength. When the air is transformed in course of time and nature's course, fire is generated, taking shape with the sense of touch and sound. Since fire is also transformed, there is a manifestation of water, full of juice and taste. As previously, it also has form and touch and is also full of sound. And water, being transformed from all variegatedness on earth, appears odorous and, as previously, becomes qualitatively full of juice, touch, sound and form respectively.

PURPORT

The whole process of creation is an act of gradual evolution and development from one element to another, reaching up to the variegatedness of the earth as so many trees, plants, mountains, rivers, reptiles, birds, animals and varieties of human beings. The quality of sense perception is also evolutionary, namely generated from sound, then touch, and from touch to form. Taste and odor are also generated along with the gradual development of sky, air, fire, water and earth. They are all mutually the cause and effect of one another, but the original cause is the Lord Himself in plenary portion, as Mahā-Viṣṇu lying in the causal water of the *mahat-tattva*. As such, Lord Kṛṣṇa is described in the *Brahma-saṁhitā* as the cause of all causes, and this is confirmed in the *Bhagavad-gītā* (10.8) as follows:

ahaṁ sarvasya prabhavo
mattaḥ sarvaṁ pravartate
iti matvā bhajante māṁ
budhā bhāva-samanvitāḥ

The qualitites of sense perception are fully represented in the earth, and they are manifested in other elements to a lesser extent. In the sky there is sound only, whereas in the air there are sound and touch. In the fire there are sound, touch and shape, and in the water there is taste also, along with the other perceptions, namely sound, touch and shape. In the earth, however, there are all the above-mentioned qualities with an extra development of odor also. Therefore on the earth there is a full display of variegatedness of life, which is originally started with the basic principle of air. Diseases of the body take place due to derangement of air within the earthly body of the living beings. Mental diseases result from special derangement of the air within the body, and as such, yogic exercise is especially beneficial to keep the air in order so that diseases of the body become almost nil by such exercises. When they are properly done the duration of life also increases, and one can have control over death also by such practices. A perfect *yogī* can have command over death and quit the body at the right moment, when he is competent to transfer himself to a suitable planet. The *bhakti-yogī,* however, surpasses all the *yogīs* because, by dint of his devotional service, he is promoted to the region beyond the material sky and is placed in one of the planets in the spiritual sky by the supreme will of the Lord, the controller of everything.

TEXT 30

वैकारिकान्मनो जज्ञे देवा वैकारिका दश ।
दिग्वातार्कप्रचेतोऽश्विवह्नीन्द्रोपेन्द्रमित्रकाः ॥३०॥

vaikārikān mano jajñe
devā vaikārikā daśa
dig-vātārka-praceto 'śvi-
vahnīndropendra-mitra-kāḥ

vaikārikāt—from the mode of goodness; *manaḥ*—the mind; *jajñe*—generated; *devāḥ*—demigods; *vaikārikāḥ*—in the mode of goodness;

daśa—ten; *dik*—the controller of directions; *vāta*—the controller of air; *arka*—the sun; *pracetaḥ*—Varuṇa; *aśvi*—the Aśvinī-kumāras; *vahni*—the fire-god; *indra*—the King of heaven; *upendra*—the deity in heaven; *mitra*—one of the twleve Ādityas; *kāḥ*—Prajāpati Brahmā.

TRANSLATION

From the mode of goodness the mind is generated and becomes manifest, as also the ten demigods controlling the bodily movements. Such demigods are known as the controller of directions, the controller of air, the sun-god, the father of Dakṣa Prajāpati, the Aśvinī-kumāras, the fire-god, the King of heaven, the worshipable deity in heaven, the chief of the Ādityas, and Brahmājī, the Prajāpati. All come into existence.

PURPORT

Vaikārika is the neutral stage of creation, and *tejas* is the initiative of creation, while *tamas* is the full display of material creation under the spell of the darkness of ignorance. Manufacture of the "necessities of life" in factories and workshops, excessively prominent in the age of Kali, or in the age of the machine, is the summit stage of the quality of darkness. Such manufacturing enterprises by human society are in the mode of darkness because factually there is no necessity for the commodities manufactured. Human society primarily requires food for subsistance, shelter for sleeping, defense for protection, and commodities for satisfaction of the senses. The senses are the practical signs of life, as will be explained in the next verse. Human civilization is meant for purifying the senses, and objects of sense satisfaction should be supplied as much as absolutely required, but not for aggravating artificial sensory needs. Food, shelter, defense and sense gratification are all needs in material existence. Otherwise, in his pure, uncontaminated state of original life, the living entity has no such needs. The needs are therefore artificial, and in the pure state of life there are no such needs. As such, increasing the artificial needs, as is the standard of material civilization, or advancing the economic development of human society, is a sort of engagement in darkness, without knowledge. By such engagement, human energy is spoiled, because human energy is primarily meant for purifying the senses in order to engage them in satisfying the senses of the Supreme Lord. The Supreme Lord, being the supreme possessor of spiritual senses, is the master of the senses, Hṛṣīkeśa. *Hṛṣīka* means the senses, and *īśa* means the master. The Lord is not the servant of the senses, or, in other words, He is not directed by the dictation of the senses, but the conditioned souls or the individual living entities *are* servants of the senses. They are conducted by the direction or dictation of the senses, and therefore material civilization is a kind of engagement in sense gratification only. The standard of human civilization should be to cure the disease of sense gratification, and one can do this simply by becoming an agent for satisfying the spiritual senses of the Lord. The senses are never to be stopped in their engagements, but one should purify them by engaging them in the pure service of sense gratification of the master of the senses. This is the instruction of the whole *Bhagavad-gītā*. Arjuna wanted first of all to satisfy his own senses by his decision not to fight with his kinsmen and friends, but Lord Śrī Kṛṣṇa taught him the *Bhagavad-gītā* just to purify Arjuna's decision for sense gratification. Therefore Arjuna agreed to satisfy the senses of the Lord, and thus he fought the Battle of Kurukṣetra, as the Lord desired.

The *Vedas* instruct us to get out of the existence of darkness and go forward on the path of light (*tamasi mā jyotir gama*). The path of light is therefore to satisfy the senses of the Lord. Misguided men, or less intelligent men, follow the path of self-realization without any attempt to satisfy the transcendental senses of the Lord by following the path shown by Arjuna and other devotees of the Lord. On the contrary, they artificially try to stop the activities of the senses (*yoga* system), or they deny the transcendental senses of the Lord (*jñāna* system). The devotees, however, are above the *yogīs* and the *jñānīs* because pure devotees do not deny the senses of the Lord; they want to satisfy the senses of the Lord. Only because of the darkness of ignorance do the *yogīs* and *jñānīs* deny the senses of the Lord and thus artificially try to control the activities of the diseased senses. In the diseased condition of the senses there is too much engagement of the senses in increasing material needs. When one comes to see the disadvantage of aggravating the sense activities, one is called a *jñānī*, and when one tries to stop the activities of the senses by the practice of yogic principles, he is called a *yogī*, but when one is fully aware of the transcendental senses of the Lord and tries to satisfy His senses, one is called a devotee of the Lord. The devotees of the Lord do not try to deny the senses of the Lord, nor do they artificially stop the actions of the senses. But they do voluntarily engage the purified senses in the service of the master of the senses, as was done by Arjuna, thereby easily attaining the perfection of satisfying the Lord, the ultimate goal of all perfection.

TEXT 31

तैजसात् तु विकुर्वाणादिन्द्रियाणि दशाभवन् ।
ज्ञानशक्तिः क्रियाशक्तिर्बुद्धिः प्राणश्च तैजसौ ।
श्रोत्रं त्वग्घ्राणदृग्जिह्वा वाग्दोर्मेढ्राङ्घ्रिपायवः॥३१॥

taijasāt tu vikurvāṇād
indriyāṇi daśābhavan
jñāna-śaktiḥ kriyā-śaktir
buddhiḥ prāṇaś ca taijasau
śrotraṁ tvag-ghrāṇa-dṛg-jihvā
vāg-dor-meḍhrāṅghri-pāyavaḥ

taijasāt—by the passionate egoism; *tu*—but; *vikurvāṇāt*—transformation of; *indriyāṇi*—the senses; *daśa*—ten; *abhavan*—generated; *jñāna-śaktiḥ*—the five senses for acquiring knowledge; *kriyā-śaktiḥ*—the five senses of activities; *buddhiḥ*—intelligence; *prāṇaḥ*—the living energy; *ca*—also; *taijasau*—all products of the mode of passion; *śrotram*—the sense for hearing; *tvak*—the sense for touching; *ghrāṇa*—the sense for smelling; *dṛk*—the sense for seeing; *jihvāḥ*—the sense for tasting; *vāk*—the sense for speaking; *doḥ*—the sense for handling; *meḍhra*—the genitals; *aṅghri*—the legs; *pāyavaḥ*—the sense for evacuating.

TRANSLATION

By further transformation of the mode of passion, the sense organs like the ear, skin, nose, eyes, tongue, mouth, hands, genitals, legs, and the outlet for evacuating, together with intelligence and living energy, are all generated.

PURPORT

The living condition in material existence depends more or less on one's intelligence and powerful living energy. Intelligence to counteract the hard struggle for existence is assisted by the senses for acquiring knowledge, and the living energy maintains himself by manipulating the active organs, like the hands and legs. But on the whole, the struggle for existence is an exertion of the mode of passion. Therefore all the sense organs, headed by intelligence and the living energy, *prāṇa*, are different products and by-products of the second mode of nature, called passion. This mode of passion, however, is the product of the air element, as described before.

TEXT 32

यदैतेऽसङ्गता भावा भूतेन्द्रियमनोगुणाः ।
यदायतननिर्माणे न शेकुर्ब्रह्मवित्तम ॥३२॥

yadaite 'saṅgatā bhāvā
bhūtendriya-mano-guṇāḥ
yadāyatana-nirmāṇe
na śekur brahma-vittama

yadā—as long as; *ete*—all these; *asaṅgatāḥ*—without being assembled; *bhāvāḥ*—remained so situated; *bhūta*—elements; *indriya*—senses; *manaḥ*—mind; *guṇāḥ*—modes of nature; *yadā*—so long; *āyatana*—the body; *nirmāṇe*—in being formed; *na śekuḥ*—was not possible; *brahma-vit-tama*—O Nārada, the best knower of transcendental knowledge.

TRANSLATION

O Nārada, best of the transcendentalists, the forms of the body cannot take place as long as these created parts, namely the elements, senses, mind and modes of nature, are not assembled.

PURPORT

The different types of bodily construction of the living entities are exactly like different types of motorcars manufactured by assembling the allied motor parts. When the car is ready, the driver sits in the car and moves it as he desires. This is also confirmed in the *Bhagavad-gītā* (18.61): the living entity is as if seated on the machine of the body, and the car of the body is moving by the control of material nature, just as the railway trains are moving under the direction of the controller. The living entities, however, are not the bodies; they are separate from the cars of the body. But the less intelligent material scientist cannot understand the process of assembling the parts of the body, namely the senses, the mind and the qualities of the material modes. Every living entity is a spiritual spark, part and parcel of the Supreme Being, and by the kindness of the Lord, for the Father is kind to His sons, the individual living beings are given a little freedom to act according to their will to lord it over the material nature. Just as a father gives some playthings to the crying child to satisfy him, the whole material creation is made possible by the will of the Lord to allow the bewildered living entities to lord it over things as they desire, although under the control of the agent of the Lord. The living entities are exactly like small children playing the material field under the control of the maidservant of the Lord (nature). They accept the *māyā*, or the maidservant, as all in all and thus wrongly conceive the Supreme Truth to be feminine (goddess Durgā, etc.). The foolish, childlike materialists cannot reach beyond the conception of the maidservant, material nature, but the intelligent grown-up sons of the Lord know well that all the acts of material nature are controlled by the Lord, just as a maidservant is under the control of the master, the father of the undeveloped children.

The parts of the body, such as the senses, are the creation of the *mahat-tattva*, and when they are assembled by the will of the Lord, the material body comes into existence, and the living entity is allowed to use it for further activities. This is explained as follows.

TEXT 33

तदा संहत्य चान्योन्यं भगवच्छक्तिचोदिताः ।
सदसत्त्वमुपादाय चोभयं ससृजुर्ह्यदः ॥३३॥

tadā saṁhatya cānyonyaṁ
bhagavac-chakti-coditāḥ

sad-asattvam upādāya
cobhayaṁ sasṛjur hy adaḥ

tadā—all those; *saṁhatya*—being assembled; *ca*—also; *anyonyam*—one another; *bhagavat*—by the Personality of Godhead; *śakti*—energy; *coditāḥ*—being applied; *sat-asattvam*—primarily and secondarily; *upādāya*—accepting; *ca*—also; *ubhayam*—both; *sasṛjuḥ*—came into existence; *hi*—certainly; *adaḥ*—this universe.

TRANSLATION

Thus when all these became assembled by force of the energy of the Supreme Personality of Godhead, this universe certainly came into being by accepting both the primary and secondary causes of creation.

PURPORT

In this verse it is clearly mentioned that the Supreme Personality of Godhead exerts His different energies in the creation; it is not that He Himself is transformed into material creations. He expands Himself by His different energies, as well as by His plenary portions. In a corner of the spiritual sky of *brahmajyoti* a spiritual cloud sometimes appears, and the covered portion is called the *mahat-tattva.* The Lord then, by His plenary portion as Mahā-Viṣṇu, lies down within the water of the *mahat-tattva,* and the water is called the Causal Ocean (Kāraṇa-jala). While Mahā-Viṣṇu sleeps within the Causal Ocean, innumerable universes are generated along with His breathing. These universes are floating, and they are scattered all over the Causal Ocean. They stay only during the breathing period of Mahā-Viṣṇu. In each and every universal globe, the same Mahā-Viṣṇu enters again as Garbhodakaśāyī Viṣṇu and lies there on the serpentlike Śeṣa incarnation. From His navel sprouts a lotus stem, and on the lotus, Brahmā, the lord of the universe, is born. Brahmā creates all forms of living beings of different shapes in terms of different desires within the universe. He also creates the sun, moon and other demigods.

Therefore the chief engineer of the material creation is the Lord Himself, as confirmed in the *Bhagavad-gītā* (9.10). It is He only who directs the material nature to produce all sorts of moving and nonmoving creations.

There are two modes of material creation: the creation of the collective universes, as stated above, done by the Mahā-Viṣṇu, and the creation of the single universe. Both are done by the Lord, and thus the universal shape, as we can see, takes place.

TEXT 34

वर्षपूगसहस्रान्ते तदण्डमुदकेशयम् ।
कालकर्मस्वभावस्थो जीवोऽजीवमजीवयत् ॥३४॥

varṣa-pūga-sahasrānte
tad aṇḍam udake śayam
kāla-karma-svabhāva-stho
jīvo 'jīvam ajīvayat

varṣa-pūga—many years; *sahasra-ante*—of thousands of years; *tat*—that; *aṇḍam*—the universal globe; *udake*—in the causal water; *śayam*—being drowned; *kāla*—eternal time; *karma*—action; *svabhāva-sthaḥ*—according to the modes of nature; *jīvaḥ*—the Lord of the living beings; *ajīvam*—nonanimated; *ajīvayat*—caused to be animated.

TRANSLATION

Thus all the universes remained thousands of aeons within the water [the Causal Ocean], and the Lord of living beings, entering in each of them, caused them to be fully animated.

PURPORT

The Lord is described here as the *jīva* because He is the leader of all other *jīvas* (living entities). In the *Vedas* He is described as the *nitya*, the leader of all other *nityas*. The Lord's relation with the living entities is like that of the father with the sons. The sons and the father are qualitatively equal, but the father is never the son, nor is the son ever the father who begets. So, as described above, the Lord as Garbhodakaśāyī Viṣṇu or Hiraṇyagarbha Supersoul enters into each and every universe and causes it to be animated by begetting the living entities within the womb of the material nature, as confirmed in the *Bhagavad-gītā* (14.3). After each annihilation of the material creation, all the living entities are merged within the body of the Lord, and after creation they are again impregnated within the material energy. In material existence, therefore, the material energy is seemingly the mother of the living entities, and the Lord is the father. When, however, the animation takes place, the living entities revive their own natural activities under the spell of time and energy, and thus the varieties of living beings are manifested. The Lord, therefore, is ultimately the cause of all animation in the material world.

TEXT 35

स एव पुरुषस्तस्मादण्डं निर्भिद्य निर्गतः ।
सहस्रोर्वङ्घ्रिबाह्वक्षः सहस्राननशीर्षवान् ॥३५॥

sa eva puruṣas tasmād
aṇḍaṁ nirbhidya nirgataḥ
sahasrorv-aṅghri-bāhv-akṣaḥ
sahasrānana-śīrṣavān

saḥ—He (the Lord); *eva*—Himself; *puruṣaḥ*—the Supreme Personality of Godhead; *tasmāt*—from within the universe; *aṇḍam*—Hiraṇyagarbha; *nirbhidya*—dividing; *nirgataḥ*—came out; *sahasra*—thousands; *ūru*—thighs; *aṅghri*—legs; *bāhu*—arms; *akṣaḥ*—eyes; *sahasra*—thousands of; *ānana*—mouths; *śīrṣavān*—with heads also.

TRANSLATION

The Lord [Mahā-Viṣṇu], although lying in the Causal Ocean, came out of it, and dividing Himself as Hiraṇyagarbha, He entered into each universe and assumed the virāṭ-rūpa, with thousands of legs, arms, mouths, heads, etc.

PURPORT

The expansions of the planetary systems within each and every universe are situated in the different parts of the *virāṭ-rūpa* (universal form) of the Lord, and they are described as follows.

TEXT 36

यस्येहावयवैर्लोकान् कल्पयन्ति मनीषिणः ।
कट्यादिभिरधः सप्त सप्तोर्ध्वं जघनादिभिः ॥३६॥

yasyehāvayavair lokān
kalpayanti manīṣiṇaḥ
kaṭya-ādibhir adhaḥ sapta
saptordhvaṁ jaghanādibhiḥ

yasya—whose; *iha*—in the universe; *avayavaiḥ*—by the limbs of the body; *lokān*—all the planets; *kalpayanti*—imagine; *manīṣiṇaḥ*—great philosophers; *kaṭi-ādibhiḥ*—down from the waist; *adhaḥ*—downwards; *sapta*—seven systems; *sapta ūrdham*—and seven systems upwards; *jaghana-ādibhiḥ*—front portion.

TRANSLATION

Great philosophers imagine that the complete planetary systems in the universe are displays of the different upper and lower limbs of the universal body of the Lord.

PURPORT

The word *kalpayanti*, or "imagine," is significant. The *virāṭ* universal form of the Absolute is an imagination of the speculative philosophers who are unable to adjust to the eternal two-handed form of Lord Śrī Kṛṣṇa. Although the universal form, as imagined by the great philosophers, is one of the features of the Lord, it is more or less imaginary. It is said that the seven upper planetary systems are situated above the waist of the universal form, whereas the lower planetary systems are situated below His waist. The idea impressed herein is that the Supreme Lord is conscious of every part of His body, and nowhere in the creation is there anything beyond His control.

TEXT 37

पुरुषस्य मुखं ब्रह्म क्षत्रमेतस्य बाहवः ।
ऊर्वोर्वैश्यो भगवतः पद्भ्यां शूद्रो व्यजायत ॥३७॥

puruṣasya mukhaṁ brahma
kṣatram etasya bāhavaḥ
ūrvor vaiśyo bhagavataḥ
padbhyāṁ śūdro vyajāyata

puruṣasya—of the Supreme Personality of Godhead; *mukham*—mouth; *brahma*—is the *brāhmaṇas; kṣatram*—the royal order; *etasya*—of Him; *bāhavaḥ*—the arms; *ūrvoḥ*—the thighs; *vaiśyaḥ*—are the mercantile men; *bhagavataḥ*—of the Personality of Godhead; *padbhyām*—from His legs; *śūdraḥ*—the laborer class; *vyajāyata*—became manifested.

TRANSLATION

The brāhmaṇas represent His mouth, the kṣatriyas His arms, the vaiśyas His thighs, and the śūdras are born of His legs.

PURPORT

All living beings are stated to be the parts and parcels of the Supreme Lord, and how they are so is explained in this verse. The four divisions of human society, namely the intelligent class (the *brāhmaṇas*), the administrative class (the *kṣatriyas*), the mercantile class (the *vaiśyas*), and the laborer class (the *śūdras*), are all in different parts of the body of the Lord. As such, no one is different from the Lord. The mouth of the body and the legs of the body are nondifferent constitutionally, but the mouth or the head of the body is qualitatively more important than the legs. At the same time, the mouth, the legs, the arms and the thighs are all component parts of the body. These limbs of the body of the Lord are meant to serve the complete whole. The mouth is meant for speaking and eating, the arms are meant for the protection of the body, the legs are meant for carrying the body, and the waist of the body is meant for maintaining the body. The intelligent class in society, therefore, must speak on behalf of the body, as well as accept foodstuff to satisfy the hunger of the body. The hunger of the Lord is to accept the fruits of sacrifice. The *brāhmaṇas*, or the intelligent class, must be very expert in performing such sacrifices, and the subordinate classes must join in such sacrifices. To speak for the Supreme Lord means to glorify the Lord by means of propagating the knowledge of the Lord as it is, broadcasting the factual nature of the Lord and the factual position of all other parts of the whole body. The *brāhmaṇas,* therefore, are required to know the *Vedas,* or the ultimate source of knowledge. *Veda* means knowledge, and *anta* means the end of it. According to *Bhagavad-gītā,* the Lord is the source of everything (*ahaṁ sarvasya prabhavaḥ*), and thus the end of all knowledge (*Vedānta*) is to know the Lord, to know our relationship with Him and to act according to that relationship only. The parts of the body are related to the body; similarly, the living being must know his relationship with the Lord. The human life is especially meant for this purpose, namely to know the factual relationship of every living being with the Supreme Lord. Without knowing this relationship, the human life is spoiled. The intelligent class of men, the *brāhmaṇas,* are therefore especially responsible for broadcasting this knowledge of our relationship with the Lord and leading the general mass of people to the right path. The administrative class is meant for protecting the living beings so that they can serve this purpose; the mercantile class is meant for producing food grains and distributing them to the complete human society so that the whole population is given a chance to live comfortably and discharge the duties of human life. The mercantile class is also required to give protection to the cows in order to get sufficient milk and milk products, which alone can give the proper health and intelligence to maintain a civilization perfectly meant for knowledge of the ultimate truth. And the laborer class, who are neither intelligent nor powerful, can help by physical services to the other higher classes and thus be benefited by their cooperation. Therefore the universe is a complete unit in relationship with the Lord, and without this relationship with the Lord the whole human society is disturbed and is without any peace and prosperity. This is confirmed in the *Vedas: brāhmaṇo 'sya mukham āsīd, bāhū rājanyaḥ kṛtaḥ.*

TEXT 38

भूर्लोकः कल्पितः पद्भ्यां भुवर्लोकोऽस्य नाभितः ।
हृदा स्वर्लोक उरसा महर्लोको महात्मनः ॥३८॥

bhūrlokaḥ kalpitaḥ padbhyāṁ
bhuvarloko 'sya nābhitaḥ

hṛdā svarloka urasā
maharloko mahātmanaḥ

bhūḥ—the lower planetary systems up to the stratum of the earth; *lokaḥ*—the planets; *kalpitaḥ*—it is so imagined or said; *padbhyām*—out of the legs; *bhuvaḥ*—the upper; *lokaḥ*—the planetary system; *asya*—of Him (the Lord); *nābhitaḥ*—from the navel abdomen; *hṛdā*—by the heart; *svarlokaḥ*—the planetary systems occupied by the demigods; *urasā*—by the chest; *maharlokaḥ*—the planetary system occupied by great sages and saints; *mahā-ātmanaḥ*—of the Supreme Personality of Godhead.

TRANSLATION

The lower planetary systems, up to the limit of the earthly stratum, are said to be situated in His legs. The middle planetary systems, beginning from Bhuvarloka, are situated in His navel. And the still higher planetary systems, occupied by the demigods and highly cultured sages and saints, are situated in the chest of the Supreme Lord.

PURPORT

There are fourteen spheres of planetary systems within this universe. The lower systems are called Bhūrloka, the middle systems are called Bhuvarloka, and the higher planetary systems, up to Brahmaloka, the highest planetary system of the universe, are called Svarloka. And all of them are situated on the body of the Lord. In other words, no one within this universe is without a relationship with the Lord.

TEXT 39

ग्रीवायां जनलोकोऽस्य तपोलोकः स्तनद्वयात् ।
मूर्धभिः सत्यलोकस्तु ब्रह्मलोकः सनातनः ॥३९॥

grīvāyāṁ janaloko 'sya
tapolokaḥ stana-dvayāt
mūrdhabhiḥ satyalokas tu
brahmalokaḥ sanātanaḥ

grīvāyām—up to the neck; *janalokaḥ*—the Janaloka planetary system; *asya*—of Him; *tapolokaḥ*—the Tapoloka planetary system; *stana-dvayāt*—beginning from the breast; *mūrdhabhiḥ*—by the head; *satyalokaḥ*—the Satyaloka planetary system; *tu*—but; *brahmalokaḥ*—the spiritual planets; *sanātanaḥ*—eternal.

TRANSLATION

From the forefront of the chest up to the neck of the universal form of the Lord are situated the planetary systems named Janaloka and Tapoloka, whereas Satyaloka, the topmost planetary system, is situated on the head of the form. The spiritual planets, however, are eternal.

PURPORT

Many times in these pages we have discussed the spiritual planets situated beyond the material sky, and the description is corroborated in this verse . The word *sanātana* is significant. This very idea of eternity is expressed in the *Bhagavad-gītā* (8.20), where it is said that beyond the material creation is the spiritual sky, where everything is eternal. Sometimes Satyaloka, the planet in which Brahmā resides, is also called Brahmaloka. But the Brahmaloka mentioned here is not the same as the Satyaloka planetary system. This Brahmaloka is eternal, whereas the Satyaloka planetary system is not eternal. And to distinguish between the two, the adjective *sanātana* has been used in this case. According to Śrīla Jīva Gosvāmī, this Brahmaloka is the *loka* or abode of Brahman, or the Supreme Lord. In the spiritual sky all the planets are as good as the Lord Himself. The Lord is all spirit, and His name, fame, glories, qualities, pastimes, etc., are all nondifferent from Him because He is absolute. As such, the planets in the kingdom of God are also nondifferent from Him. In those planets there is no difference between the body and the soul, nor is there any influence of time as we experience it in the material world. And in addition to there being no influence of time, the planets in Brahmaloka, duc to being spiritual, are never annihilated. All variegatedness in the spiritual planets is also one with the Lord, and therefore the Vedic aphorism *ekam evādvitīyam* is fully realized in that *sanātana* atmosphere of spiritual variegatedness. This material world is only a shadow phantasmagoria of the spiritual kingdom of the Lord, and because it is a shadow it is never eternal; the variegatedness in the material world of duality (spirit and matter) cannot be compared to that of the spiritual world. Because of a poor fund of knowledge, less intelligent persons sometimes mistake the conditions of the shadow world to be equivalent to those of the spiritual world, and thus they mistake the Lord and His pastimes in the material world to be one with the conditioned souls and their activities. The Lord condemns such less intelligent persons in the *Bhagavad-gītā* (9.11):

avajānanti māṁ mūḍhā
mānuṣīṁ tanum āśritam
paraṁ bhāvam ajānanto
mama bhūta-maheśvaram

Whenever the Lord incarnates, He does so in His full internal potency (*ātma-māyā*), and less intelligent persons mistake Him to be one of the material creations. Śrīla Śrīdhara Svāmī, therefore, rightly commenting on this verse, says that the Brahmaloka mentioned here is Vaikuṇṭha, the kingdom of God, which is *sanātana*, or eternal, and is therefore not exactly like the material creations described above. The *virāṭ* universal form of the Lord is an imagination for the material world. It has nothing to do with the spiritual world, or the kingdom of God.

TEXTS 40–41

तत्कट्यां चातलं क्लृप्तमूरुभ्यां वितलं विभोः ।
जानुभ्यां सुतलं शुद्धं जङ्घाभ्यां तु तलातलम् ॥४०॥
महातलं तु गुल्फाभ्यां प्रपदाभ्यां रसातलम् ।
पातालं पादतलत इति लोकमयः पुमान् ॥४१॥

tat-kaṭyāṁ cātalaṁ kḷptam
ūrubhyāṁ vitalaṁ vibhoḥ
jānubhyāṁ sutalaṁ śuddhaṁ
jaṅghābhyāṁ tu talātalam

mahātalaṁ tu gulphābhyāṁ
prapadābhyāṁ rasātalam

pātālaṁ pāda-talata
iti lokamayaḥ pumān

tat—in His; *kaṭyām*—waist; *ca*—also; *atalam*—the first planetary system below the earth; *kḷptam*—situated; *ūrubhyām*—on the thighs; *vitalam*—the second planetary system below; *vibhoḥ*—of the Lord; *jānubhyām*—on the ankles; *sutalam*—the third planetary system below; *śuddham*—purified; *jaṅghābhyām*—on the joints; *tu*—but; *talātalam*—the fourth planetary system below; *mahātalam*—the fifth planetary system below; *tu*—but; *gulphābhyām*—situated on the calves; *prapadābhyām*—on the upper or front portion of the feet; *rasātalam*—the sixth planetary system below; *pātālam*—the seventh planetary system below; *pāda-talataḥ*—on the bottom or soles of the feet; *iti*—thus; *loka-mayaḥ*—full of planetary systems; *pumān*—the Lord.

TRANSLATION

My dear son Nārada, know from me that there are seven lower planetary systems out of the total fourteen. The first planetary system, known as Atala, is situated on the waist; the second, Vitala, is situated on the thighs; the third, Sutala, on the knees; the fourth, Talātala, on the shanks; the fifth, Mahātala, on the ankles; the sixth, Rasātala, on the upper portion of the feet; and the seventh, Pātāla, on the soles of the feet. Thus the virāṭ form of the Lord is full of all planetary systems.

PURPORT

Modern enterprisers (the astronauts who travel in space) may take information from *Śrīmad-Bhāgavatam* that in space there are fourteen divisions of planetary systems. The situation is calculated from the earthly planetary system, which is called Bhūrloka. Above Bhūrloka is Bhuvarloka, and the topmost planetary system is called Satyaloka. These are the upper seven *lokas*, or planetary systems. And similarly, there are seven lower planetary systems, known as Atala, Vitala, Sutala, Talātala, Mahātala, Rasātala and Pātāla *lokas*. All these planetary systems are scattered over the complete universe, which occupies an area of two billion times two billion square miles. The modern astronauts can travel only a few thousand miles away from the earth, and therefore their attempt to travel in the sky is something like child's play on the shore of an expansive ocean. The moon is situated in the third status of the upper planetary system, and in the Fifth Canto of *Śrīmad-Bhāgavatam* we shall be able to know the distant situation of the various planets scattered over the vast material sky. There are innumerable universes beyond the one in which we are put, and all these material universes cover only an insignificant portion of the spiritual sky, which is described above as *sanātana* Brahmaloka. The Supreme Lord very kindly invites the intelligent human beings to return home, back to Godhead, in the following verse of the *Bhagavad-gītā* (8.16):

ābrahma-bhuvanāl lokāḥ
punar āvartino 'rjuna
mām upetya tu kaunteya
punar janma na vidyate

Beginning from Satyaloka, the topmost planet of the universe, situated just below the eternal Brahmaloka, as described above, all the planets are material. And one's situation in any of the many material planets is still subject to the laws of material nature, namely birth, death, old age and disease. But one can get complete liberation from all the abovementioned material pangs when one enters into the eternal Brahmaloka *sanātana* atmosphere, the kingdom of God. Therefore liberation, as contemplated by the speculative philosophers and the mystics, is possible only when one becomes a devotee of the Lord. Anyone who is not a devotee cannot enter into the kingdom of God. Only by attainment of a service attitude in the transcendental position can one enter into the kingdom of Godhead. Therefore the speculative philosophers, as well as the mystics, must first of all be attracted to the devotional cult before they can factually attain liberation.

TEXT 42

भूर्लोकः कल्पितः पद्भ्यां भुवर्लोकोऽस्य नाभितः ।
स्वर्लोकः कल्पितो मूर्ध्ना इति वा लोककल्पना ॥४२॥

bhūrlokaḥ kalpitaḥ padbhyāṁ
bhuvarloko 'sya nābhitaḥ
svarlokaḥ kalpito mūrdhnā
iti vā loka-kalpanā

bhūrlokaḥ—the entire planetary system from Pātāla to the earthly planetary system; *kalpitaḥ*—imagined; *padbhyām*—situated on the legs; *bhuvarlokaḥ*—the Bhuvarloka planetary system; *asya*—of the universal form of the Lord; *nābhitaḥ*—out of the navel abdomen; *svarlokaḥ*—the higher planetary system, beginning with the heavenly planets; *kalpitaḥ*—imagined; *mūrdhnā*—from the chest to the head; *iti*—thus; *vā*—either; *loka*—the planetary systems; *kalpanā*—imagination.

TRANSLATION

Others may divide the whole planetary system into three divisions, namely the lower planetary systems on the legs [up to the earth], the middle planetary systems on the navel, and the upper planetary systems [Svarloka] from the chest to the head of the Supreme Personality.

PURPORT

The three divisions of the complete planetary systems are here mentioned; fourteen are imagined by others, and that is also explained.

Thus end the Bhaktivedanta purports of the Second Canto, Fifth Chapter, of the Śrīmad-Bhāgavatam, *entitled "The Cause of All Causes."*

CHAPTER SIX

Puruṣa-sūkta Confirmed

TEXT 1

ब्रह्मोवाच
वाचां वह्नेर्मुखं क्षेत्रं छन्दसां सप्त धातवः ।
हव्यकव्यामृतान्नानां जिह्वा सर्वरसस्य च ॥ १ ॥

brahmovāca
vācāṁ vahner mukhaṁ kṣetraṁ
chandasāṁ sapta dhātavaḥ
havya-kavyāmṛtānnānāṁ
jihvā sarva-rasasya ca

brahmā uvāca—Lord Brahmā said; *vācām*—of the voice; *vahneḥ*—of fire; *mukham*—the mouth; *kṣetram*—the generating center; *chandasām*—of the Vedic hymns, such as Gāyatrī; *sapta*—seven; *dhātavaḥ*—skin and six other layers; *havya-kavya*—offerings for the demigods and the forefathers; *amṛta*—food for human beings; *annānām*—of all sorts of foodstuffs; *jihvā*—the tongue; *sarva*—all; *rasasya*—of all delicacies; *ca*—also.

TRANSLATION

Lord Brahmā said: The mouth of the virāṭ-puruṣa [the universal form of the Lord] is the generating center of the voice, and the controlling deity is Fire. His skin and six other layers are the generating centers of the Vedic hymns, and His tongue is the productive center of different foodstuffs and delicacies for offering to the demigods, the forefathers and the general mass of people.

PURPORT

The opulences of the universal form of the Lord are described herein. It is said that His mouth is the generating center of all kinds of voices, and its controlling deity is the fire demigod. And His skin and other six layers of bodily construction are the representative generating centers of the seven kinds of Vedic hymns, like the Gāyatrī. Gāyatrī is the beginning of all Vedic *mantras*, and it is explained in the first volume of *Śrīmad-Bhāgavatam*. Since the generating centers are the different parts of the universal form of the Lord, and since the form of the Lord is transcendental to the material creation, it is to be understood that the voice, the tongue, the skin, etc., suggest that the Lord in His transcendental form is not without them. The material voice, or the energy of taking in foodstuff, is generated originally from the Lord; such actions are but perverted reflections of the original reservoirs—the transcendental situation is not without spiritual variegatedness. In the spiritual world, all the perverted forms of material variegatedness are fully represented in their original spiritual identity. The only difference is that material activities are contaminated by the three modes of material nature, whereas the potencies in the spiritual world are all pure because they are engaged in the unalloyed transcendental loving service of the Lord. In the spiritual world, the Lord is the sublime enjoyer of everything, and the living entities there are all engaged in His transcendental loving service without any contamination of the modes of material nature. The activities in the spiritual world are without any of the inebrieties of the material world, but there is no question of impersonal voidness on the spiritual platform, as suggested by the impersonalists. Devotional service is defined in the *Nārada-pañcarātra* as follows:

sarvopādhi-vinirmuktaṁ
tat-paratvena nirmalam
hṛṣīkeṇa hṛṣīkeśa-
sevanaṁ bhaktir ucyate

Originally, since all the senses are produced of the Lord's reservoir of senses, the sensual activities of the material world are to be purified by the process of devotional service, and thus the perfection of life can be attained simply by purifying the present position of our material activities. And the purifying process begins from the stage of being liberated from the conception of different designations. Every living entity is engaged in some sort of service, either for the self, or for the family, or for the society, country, etc., but, unfortunately, all such services are rendered due to material attachment. The attachments of the material affinity may be simply changed to the service of the Lord, and thus the treatment of being freed from material attachment begins automatically. The process of liberation is therefore easier through devotional service than by any other methods, for in the *Bhagavad-gītā* (12.5) it is said that one is subjected to various kinds of tribulations if one is impersonally attached: *kleśo 'dhikataras teṣām avyaktāsakta-cetasām.*

TEXT 2

सर्वासूनां च वायोश्च तन्नासे परमायणे ।
अश्विनोरोषधीनां च घ्राणो मोदप्रमोदयोः ॥ २ ॥

sarvāsūnāṁ ca vāyoś ca
tan-nāse paramāyaṇe
aśvinor oṣadhīnāṁ ca
ghrāṇo moda-pramodayoḥ

sarva—all; *asūnām*—different kinds of life air; *ca*—and; *vāyoḥ*—of the air; *ca*—also; *tat*—His; *nāse*—in the nose; *parama-āyaṇe*—in the transcendental generating center; *aśvinoḥ*—of the Aśvinī-kumāra demigods; *oṣadhīnām*—of all medicinal herbs; *ca*—also; *ghrāṇaḥ*—His smelling power; *moda*—pleasure; *pramodayoḥ*—specific sport.

TRANSLATION

His two nostrils are the generating centers of our breathing and of all other airs, His smelling powers generate the Aśvinī-kumāra demigods and all kinds of medicinal herbs, and His breathing energies produce different kinds of fragrance.

TEXT 3

रूपाणां तेजसां चक्षुर्दिवः सूर्यस्य चाक्षिणी ।
कर्णौ दिशां च तीर्थानां श्रोत्रमाकाशशब्दयोः ॥ ३ ॥

rūpāṇāṁ tejasāṁ cakṣur
divaḥ sūryasya cākṣiṇī

karṇau diśāṁ ca tīrthānāṁ
śrotram ākāśa-śabdayoḥ

rūpāṇām—for all kinds of forms; *tejasām*—of all that is illuminating; *cakṣuḥ*—the eyes; *divaḥ*—that which glitters; *sūryasya*—of the sun; *ca*—also; *akṣiṇī*—the eyeballs; *karṇau*—the ears; *diśām*—of all directions; *ca*—and; *tīrthānām*—of all the *Vedas; śrotram*—the sense of hearing; *ākāśa*—the sky; *śabdayoḥ*—of all sounds.

TRANSLATION

His eyes are the generating centers of all kinds of forms, and they glitter and illuminate. His eyeballs are like the sun and the heavenly planets. His ears hear from all sides and are receptacles for all the Vedas, and His sense of hearing is the generating center of the sky and of all kinds of sound.

PURPORT

The word *tīrthānām* is sometimes interpreted to mean the places of pilgrimage, but Śrīla Jīva Gosvāmī says that it means the reception of the Vedic transcendental knowledge. The propounders of the Vedic knowledge are also known as the *tīrthas.*

TEXT 4

तद्गात्रं वस्तुसाराणां सौभगस्य च भाजनम् ।
त्वगस्य स्पर्शवायोश्च सर्वमेधस्य चैव हि ॥ ४ ॥

tad-gātraṁ vastu-sārāṇāṁ
saubhagasya ca bhājanam
tvag asya sparśa-vāyoś ca
sarva-medhasya caiva hi

tat—His; *gātram*—bodily surface; *vastu-sārāṇām*—of the active principles of all articles; *saubhagasya*—of all auspicious opportunities; *ca*—and; *bhājanam*—the field of production; *tvak*—skin; *asya*—His; *sparśa*—touch; *vāyoḥ*—of the moving airs; *ca*—also; *sarva*—all kinds of; *medhasya*—of sacrifices; *ca*—also; *eva*—certainly; *hi*—exactly.

TRANSLATION

His bodily surface is the breeding ground for the active principles of everything and for all kinds of auspicious opportunities. His skin, like the moving air, is the generating center for all kinds of sense of touch and is the place for performing all kinds of sacrifice.

PURPORT

The air is the moving agent of all the planets, and as such the generating centers for promotion to the deserving planets, the sacrifices, are His bodily surface and are naturally the origin of all auspicious opportunities.

TEXT 5

रोमाण्युद्भिज्जजातीनां यैर्वा यज्ञस्तु सम्भृतः ।
केशश्मश्रुनखान्यस्य शिलालोहाभ्रविद्युताम् ॥ ५ ॥

romāṇy udbhijja-jātīnāṁ
yair vā yajñas tu sambhṛtaḥ
keśa-śmaśru-nakhāny asya
śilā-lohābhra-vidyutām

romāṇi—hairs on the body; *udbhijja*—vegetables; *jātīnām*—of the kingdoms; *yaiḥ*—by which; *vā*—either; *yajñaḥ*—sacrifices; *tu*—but; *sambhṛtaḥ*—particularly served; *keśa*—hairs on the head; *śmaśru*—facial hair; *nakhāni*—nails; *asya*—of Him; *śilā*—stones; *loha*—iron ores; *abhra*—clouds; *vidyutām*—electricity.

TRANSLATION

The hairs on His body are the cause of all vegetation, particularly of those trees which are required as ingredients for sacrifice. The hairs on His head and face are reservoirs for the clouds, and His nails are the breeding ground of electricity, stones and iron ores.

PURPORT

The polished nails of the Lord generate electricity, and the clouds rest on the hairs of His head. One can therefore collect all sorts of necessities of life from the person of the Lord, and therefore the *Vedas* affirm that everything that is produced is caused by the Lord. The Lord is the supreme cause of all causes.

TEXT 6

बाहवो लोकपालानां प्रायशः क्षेमकर्मणाम् ॥ ६ ॥

bāhavo loka-pālānāṁ
prāyaśaḥ kṣema-karmaṇām

bāhavaḥ—arms; *loka-pālānām*—of the governing deities of the planets, the demigods; *prāyaśaḥ*—almost always; *kṣema-karmaṇām*—of those who are leaders and protectors of the general mass.

TRANSLATION

The Lord's arms are the productive fields for the great demigods and other leaders of the living entities who protect the general mass.

PURPORT

This important verse of *Śrīmad-Bhāgavatam* is corroborated and nicely explained in the *Bhagavad-gītā* (10.41–42) as follows:

yad yad vibhūtimat sattvaṁ
śrīmad ūrjitam eva vā
tat tad evāvagaccha tvaṁ
mama tejo-'ṁśa-sambhavam

athavā bahunaitena
kiṁ jñātena tavārjuna
viṣṭabhyāham idaṁ kṛtsnam
ekāṁśena sthito jagat

There are many powerful kings, leaders, learned scholars, scientists, artists, engineers, inventors, excavators, archaeologists, industrialists, politicians, economists, business magnates, and many more powerful deities or demigods like Brahmā, Śiva, Indra, Candra, Sūrya, Varuṇa and Marut, who are all protecting the interest of the universal affairs of maintenance, in different positions, and all of them are different powerful parts and parcels of the Supreme Lord. The Supreme Lord Śrī Kṛṣṇa is the father of all living entities, who are placed in different high and low positions according to their desires or aspirations. Some of them, as particularly mentioned above, are specifically endowed with powers by the will of the Lord. A sane person must know for certain that a living being, however powerful he may be, is neither absolute nor independent. All living beings must accept the origin of their specific power as mentioned in this verse. And if they act accordingly, then simply by discharging their respective occupational duties they can achieve the highest perfection of life, namely eternal life, complete knowledge and inexhaustible blessings. As long as the powerful men of the world do not accept the origin of their respective powers, namely the Personality of Godhead, the actions of *māyā* (illusion) will continue to act. The actions of *māyā* are such that a powerful person, misled by the illusory, material energy, wrongly accepts himself as all in all and does not develop God consciousness. As such, the false sense of egoism (namely myself and mine) has become overly prominent in the world, and there is a hard struggle for existence in human society. The intelligent class of men, therefore, must admit the Lord as the ultimate source of all energies and thus pay tribute to the Lord for His good blessings. Simply by accepting the Lord as the supreme proprietor of everything, since He is actually so, one can achieve the highest perfection of life. Whatever a person may be in the estimation of the social order of things, if a person tries to reciprocate a feeling of love towards the Supreme Personality of Godhead and is satisfied with the blessings of the Lord, he will at once feel the highest peace of mind for which he is hankering life after life. Peace of mind, or in other words the healthy state of mind, can be achieved only when the mind is situated in the transcendental loving service of the Lord. The parts and parcels of the Lord are endowed with specific powers for rendering service unto the Lord, just as a big business magnate's sons are empowered with specific powers of administration. The obedient son of the father never goes against the will of the father and therefore passes life very peacefully in concurrence with the head of the family, the father. Similarly, the Lord being the father, all living beings should fully and satisfactorily discharge the duty and will of the father, as faithful sons. This very mentality will at once bring peace and prosperity to human society.

TEXT 7

विक्रमो भूर्भुवः स्वश्च क्षेमस्य शरणस्य च ।
सर्वकामवरस्यापि हरेश्चरण आस्पदम् ॥ ७ ॥

vikramo bhūr bhuvaḥ svaś ca
kṣemasya śaraṇasya ca
sarva-kāma-varasyāpi
hareś caraṇa āspadam

vikramaḥ—forward steps; *bhūḥ bhuvaḥ*—of the lower and upper planets; *svaḥ*—as well as of heaven; *ca*—also; *kṣemasya*—of protection of all that we have; *śaraṇasya*—of fearlessness; *ca*—also; *sarva-kāma*—all that we need; *varasya*—of all benedictions; *api*—exactly; *hareḥ*—of the Lord; *caraṇaḥ*—the lotus feet; *āspadam*—shelter.

TRANSLATION

Thus the forward steps of the Lord are the shelter for the upper, lower and heavenly planets, as well as for all that we need. His lotus feet serve as protection from all kinds of fear.

PURPORT

For absolute protection from all sorts of fear, as well as for all our needs of life, we must take shelter of the lotus feet of the Lord, not only in this planet but also in all the upper, lower and heavenly planets. This absolute dependence on the lotus feet of the Lord is called pure devotional service, and it is directly hinted at within this passage. No one should have any kind of doubt in this matter, nor should one be inclined to seek the help of any other demigods, because all of them are dependent on Him only. Everyone, except the Lord Himself, is dependent on the mercy of the Lord; even the all-pervading Supersoul is also dependent on the supreme aspect of Bhagavān, the Personality of Godhead.

TEXT 8

अपां वीर्यस्य सर्गस्य पर्जन्यस्य प्रजापतेः ।
पुंसः शिश्न उपस्थस्तु प्रजात्यानन्दनिर्वृतेः ॥ ८ ॥

apāṁ vīryasya sargasya
parjanyasya prajāpateḥ
puṁsaḥ śiśna upasthas tu
prajāty-ānanda-nirvṛteḥ

apām—of water; *vīryasya*—of the semen; *sargasya*—of the generative; *parjanyasya*—of rains; *prajāpateḥ*—of the creator; *puṁsaḥ*—of the Lord; *śiśnaḥ*—the genitals; *upasthaḥ tu*—the place where the genitals are situated; *prajāti*—due to begetting; *ānanda*—pleasure; *nirvṛteḥ*—cause.

TRANSLATION

From the Lord's genitals originate water, semen, generatives, rains, and the procreators. His genitals are the cause of a pleasure that counteracts the distress of begetting.

PURPORT

The genitals and the pleasure of begetting counteract the distresses of family encumbrances. One would cease to generate altogether if there were not, by the grace of the Lord, a coating, a pleasure-giving substance, on the surface of the generative organs. This substance gives a pleasure so intense that it counteracts fully the distress of family encumbrances. A person is so captivated by this pleasure-giving substance that he is not satisfied by begetting a single child, but increases the number of children, with great risk in regard to maintaining them, simply for this pleasure-giving substance. This pleasure-giving substance is not false, however, because it originates from the transcendental body of the Lord. In other words, the pleasure-giving substance is a reality, but it has taken on an aspect of pervertedness on account of material contamination. In the material world, sex life is the cause of many distresses on account of material contact. Therefore, the sex life in the material world should not be encouraged beyond the necessity. There is a necessity for generating progency even in the material world, but such generation of children must be carried out with full responsibility for spiritual values. The spiritual values of life can be realized in the human form of material existence, and the human being must adopt family planning with reference to the context of spiritual values, and not otherwise. The degraded form of family restriction by use of contraceptives, etc., is the grossest type of material contamination. Materialists who use these devices want to fully utilize the pleasure potency of the coating on the genitals by artificial means, without knowing the spiritual importance. And without knowledge of spiritual values, the less intelligent man tries to utilize only the material sense pleasure of the genitals.

TEXT 9

पायुर्यमस्य मित्रस्य परिमोक्षस्य नारद ।
हिंसाया निरृतेर्मृत्योर्निरयस्य गुदं स्मृतः ॥ ९ ॥

pāyur yamasya mitrasya
parimokṣasya nārada
hiṁsāyā nirṛter mṛtyor
nirayasya gudaṁ smṛtaḥ

pāyuḥ—the evacuating outlet; *yamasya*—the controlling deity of death; *mitrasya*—of Mitra; *parimokṣasya*—of the evacuating hole; *nārada*—O Nārada; *hiṁsāyāḥ*—of envy; *nirṛteḥ*—of misfortune; *mṛtyoḥ*—of death; *nirayasya*—of hell; *gudam*—the rectum; *smṛtaḥ*—is understood.

TRANSLATION

O Nārada, the evacuating outlet of the universal form of the Lord is the abode of the controlling deity of death, Mitra, and the evacuating hole and the rectum of the Lord is the place of envy, misfortune, death, hell, etc.

TEXT 10

पराभूतेरधर्मस्य तमसश्चापि पश्चिमः ।
नाड्यो नदनदीनां च गोत्राणामस्थिसंहतिः ॥१०॥

parābhūter adharmasya
tamasaś cāpi paścimaḥ
nāḍyo nada-nadīnāṁ ca
gotrāṇām asthi-saṁhatiḥ

parābhūteḥ—of frustration; *adharmasya*—of immorality; *tamasaḥ*—of ignorance; *ca*—and; *api*—as also; *paścimaḥ*—the back; *nāḍyaḥ*—of the intestines; *nada*—of the great rivers; *nadīnām*—of the rivulets; *ca*—also; *gotrāṇām*—of the mountains; *asthi*—bones; *saṁhatiḥ*—accumulation.

TRANSLATION

The back of the Lord is the place for all kinds of frustration and ignorance, as well as for immorality. From His veins flow the great rivers and rivulets, and on His bones are stacked the great mountains.

PURPORT

In order to defy the impersonal conception of the Supreme Personality of Godhead, a systematic analysis of the physiological and anatomical constitution of His transcendental body is given here. It is clear from the available description of the body of the Lord (His universal form) that the form of the Lord is distinct from the forms of ordinary mundane conception. In any case, He is never a formless void. Ignorance is the back of the Lord, and therefore the ignorance of the less intelligent class of men is also not separate from His bodily conception. Since His body is the complete whole of everything that be, one cannot assert that He is impersonal only. On the contrary, the perfect description of the Lord holds that He is both impersonal and personal simultaneously. The Personality of Godhead is the original feature of the Lord, and His impersonal emanation is but the reflection of His transcendental body. Those who are fortunate enough to have a view of the Lord from the front can realize His personal feature, whereas those who are frustrated and are thus kept on the ignorance side of the Lord, or, in other words, those who have the view of the Lord from the back, realize Him in His impersonal feature.

TEXT 11

अव्यक्तरससिन्धूनां भूतानां निधनस्य च ।
उदरं विदितं पुंसो हृदयं मनसः पदम् ॥११॥

avyakta-rasa-sindhūnāṁ
bhūtānāṁ nidhanasya ca
udaraṁ viditaṁ puṁso
hṛdayaṁ manasaḥ padam

avyakta—the impersonal feature; *rasa-sindhūnām*—of the seas and oceans of water; *bhūtānām*—of those who take birth in the material world; *nidhanasya*—of the annihilation; *ca*—also; *udaram*—His belly; *viditam*—is known by the intelligent class of men; *puṁsaḥ*—of the great personality; *hṛdayam*—the heart; *manasaḥ*—of the subtle body; *padam*—the place.

TRANSLATION

The impersonal feature of the Lord is the abode of great oceans, and His belly is the resting place for the materially annihilated living entities. His heart is the abode of the subtle material bodies of living beings. Thus it is known by the intelligent class of men.

PURPORT

In the *Bhagavad-gītā* (8.17–18) it is stated that according to human calculations one day of Brahmā is equal to one thousand ages of four millenniums (4,300,000 years) each, and the same period is calculated to be his night also. A Brahmā lives for one hundred such years and then dies. A Brahmā, who is generally a great devotee of the Lord, attains liberation after such a downfall. The universe (called the *brahmāṇḍa*, or the round football-like domain controlled by a Brahmā) is thus annihilated, and thus the inhabitants of a particular planet, or of the whole universe, are also annihilated. *Avyakta*, mentioned here in this verse, means the night of Brahmā, when partial annihilation takes place and the living entities of that particular *brahmāṇḍa*, up to the planets of Brahmaloka, along with the big oceans, etc., all repose in the belly of the *virāṭ-puruṣa*. At the end of a Brahmā's night, the creation again takes place, and the living entities, reserved within the belly of the Lord, are let loose to play their respective parts as if being awakened from a deep slumber. Since the living entities are never destroyed, the annihilation of the material world does not annihilate the existence of the living entities, but until liberation is attained one has to accept one material body after another, again and again. The human life is meant for making a solution to this repeated change of bodies and thereby attaining a place in the spiritual sky, where everything is eternal, blissful and full of knowledge. In other words, the subtle forms of the living entities take place in the heart of the Supreme Being, and such forms take tangible shape at the time of creation.

TEXT 12

धर्मस्य मम तुभ्यं च कुमाराणां भवस्य च ।
विज्ञानस्य च सत्त्वस्य परस्यात्मा परायणम् ॥१२॥

dharmasya mama tubhyaṁ ca
kumārāṇāṁ bhavasya ca
vijñānasya ca sattvasya
parasyātmā parāyaṇam

dharmasya—of religious principles, or of Yamarāja; *mama*—mine; *tubhyam*—of yours; *ca*—and; *kumārāṇām*—of the four Kumāras; *bhavasya*—Lord Śiva; *ca*—and also; *vijñānasya*—of transcendental knowledge; *ca*—also; *sattvasya*—of truth; *parasya*—of the great personality; *ātmā*—consciousness; *parāyaṇam*—dependent.

TRANSLATION

Also, the consciousness of that great personality is the abode of religious principles—mine, yours, and those of the four bachelors Sanaka, Sanātana, Sanat-kumāra and Sanandana. That consciousness is also the abode of truth and transcendental knowledge.

TEXTS 13–16

अहं भवान् भवश्चैव त इमे मुनयोऽग्रजाः ।
सुरासुरनरा नागाः खगा मृगसरीसृपाः ॥१३॥

गन्धर्वाप्सरसो यक्षा रक्षोभूतगणोरगाः ।
पशवः पितरः सिद्धा विद्याध्राश्चारणा द्रुमाः ॥१४॥
अन्ये च विविधा जीवा जलस्थलनभौकसः ।
ग्रहर्क्षकेतवस्तारास्तडितः स्तनयित्नवः ॥१५॥
सर्वं पुरुष एवेदं भूतं भव्यं भवच्च यत् ।
तेनेदमावृतं विश्वं वितस्तिमधितिष्ठति ॥१६॥

aham bhavān bhavaś caiva
ta ime munayo 'grajāḥ
surāsura-narā nāgāḥ
khagā mṛga-sarīsṛpāḥ

gandharvāpsaraso yakṣā
rakṣo-bhūta-gaṇoragāḥ
paśavaḥ pitaraḥ siddhā
vidyādhrāś cāraṇā drumāḥ

anye ca vividhā jīvā
jala-sthala-nabhaukasaḥ
graharkṣa-ketavas tārās
taḍitaḥ stanayitnavaḥ

sarvam puruṣa evedam
bhūtam bhavyam bhavac ca yat
tenedam āvṛtam viśvam
vitastim adhitiṣṭhati

aham—myself; *bhavān*—yourself; *bhavaḥ*—Lord Śiva; *ca*—also; *eva*—certainly; *te*—they; *ime*—all; *munayaḥ*—the great sages; *agra-jāḥ*—born before you; *sura*—the demigods; *asura*—the demons; *narāḥ*—the human beings; *nāgāḥ*—the inhabitants of the Nāga planet; *khagāḥ*—birds; *mṛga*—beasts; *sarīsṛpāḥ*—reptiles; *gandharva-apsarasaḥ, yakṣāḥ, rakṣaḥ-bhūta-gaṇa-uragāḥ, paśavaḥ, pitaraḥ, siddhāḥ, vidyādhrāḥ, cāraṇāḥ*—all inhabitants of different planets; *drumāḥ*—the vegetable kingdom; *anye*—many others; *ca*—also; *vividhāḥ*—of different varieties; *jīvāḥ*—living entities; *jala*—water; *sthala*—land; *nabha-okasaḥ*—the inhabitants of the sky, or the birds; *graha*—the asteroids; *ṛkṣa*—the influential stars; *ketavaḥ*—the comets; *tārāḥ*—the luminaries; *taḍitaḥ*—the lightning; *stanayitnavaḥ*—the sound of the clouds; *sarvam*—everything; *puruṣaḥ*—the Personality of Godhead; *eva idam*—certainly all these; *bhūtam*—whatever is created; *bhavyam*—whatever will be created; *bhavat*—and whatever was created in the past; *ca*—also; *yat*—whatever; *tena idam*—it is all by Him; *āvṛtam*—covered; *viśvam*—universally comprehending; *vitastim*—half a cubit; *adhitiṣṭhati*—situated.

TRANSLATION

Beginning from me [Brahmā] down to you and Bhava [Śiva], all the great sages who were born before you, the demigods, the demons, the Nāgas, the human beings, the birds, the beasts, as well as the reptiles, etc., and all phenomenal manifestations of the universes, namely the planets, stars, asteroids, luminaries, lightning, thunder, and the inhabitants of the different planetary systems, namely the Gandharvas, Apsarās, Yakṣas, Rakṣas, Bhūtagaṇas, Uragas, Paśus, Pitās, Siddhas, Vidyādharas, Cāraṇas, and all other different varieties of living entities, including the birds, beasts, trees and everything that be, are all covered by the universal form of the Lord at all times, namely past, present and future, although He is transcendental to all of them, eternally existing in a form not exceeding nine inches.

PURPORT

The Supreme Personality of Godhead, by His partial representation, measuring not more than nine inches as Supersoul, expands by His potential energy in the shape of the universal form, which includes everything manifested in different varieties of organic and inorganic materials. The manifested varieties of the universe are therefore not different from the Lord, just as golden ornaments of different shapes and forms are nondifferent from the original stock reserve of gold. In other words, the Lord is the Supreme Person who controls everything within the creation, and still He remains the supreme separate identity, distinct from all manifested material creation. In the *Bhagavad-gītā* (9.4–5) He is therefore said to be Yogeśvara. Everything rests on the potency of Lord Śrī Kṛṣṇa, and still the Lord is different from and transcendental to all such identities. In the Vedic *Puruṣa-sūkta* of the *Ṛg mantra*, this is also confirmed. This philosophical truth of simultaneous oneness and difference was propounded by Lord Śrī Caitanya Mahāprabhu, and it is known as *acintya-bhedābheda-tattva*. Brahmā, Nārada and all others are simultaneously one with the Lord and different from the Supreme Lord. We are all one with Him, just as the gold ornaments are one in quality with the stock gold, but the individual gold ornament is never equal in quantity with the stock gold. The stock gold is never exhausted even if there are innumerable ornaments emanating from the stock because the stock is *pūrṇam*, complete; even if *pūrṇam* is deducted from the *pūrṇam*, still the supreme *pūrṇam* remains the same *pūrṇam*. This fact is inconceivable to our present imperfect senses. Lord Caitanya therefore defined His theory of philosophy as *acintya* (inconceivable), and as confirmed in the *Bhagavad-gītā* as well as in the *Bhāgavatam*, Lord Caitanya's theory of *acintya-bhedābheda-tattva* is the perfect philosophy of the Absolute Truth.

TEXT 17

स्वधिष्ण्यं प्रतपन् प्राणो बहिश्च प्रतपत्यसौ ।
एवं विराजं प्रतपंस्तपत्यन्तर्बहिः पुमान् ॥१७॥

sva-dhiṣṇyaṁ pratapan prāṇo
bahiś ca pratapaty asau
evaṁ virājaṁ pratapaṁs
tapaty antar bahiḥ pumān

sva-dhiṣṇyam—radiation; *pratapan*—by expansion; *prāṇaḥ*—living energy; *bahiḥ*—external; *ca*—also; *pratapati*—illuminated; *asau*—the sun; *evam*—in the same way; *virājam*—the universal form; *pratapan*—by expansion of; *tapati*—enlivens; *antaḥ*—internally; *bahiḥ*—externally; *pumān*—the Supreme Personality.

TRANSLATION

The sun illuminates both internally and externally by expanding its radiation; similarly, the Supreme Personality of Godhead,

by expanding His universal form, maintains everything in the creation both internally and externally.

PURPORT

The universal form of the Lord, or the impersonal feature of the Lord known as the *brahmajyoti*, is clearly explained here and compared to the radiation of the sun. The sunshine may expand all over the universe, but the source of the sunshine, namely the sun planet or the deity known as Sūrya-nārāyaṇa, is the basis of such radiation. Similarly, the Supreme Personality of Godhead Lord Kṛṣṇa is the basis of the impersonal *brahmajyoti* radiation, or the impersonal feature of the Lord. This is confirmed in the *Bhagavad-gītā* (14.27). So the universal form of the Lord is the secondary imagination of the impersonal form of the Lord, but the primary form of the Lord is Śyāmasundara, with two hands, playing on His eternal flute. Seventy-five percent of the expansive radiation of the Lord is manifested in the spiritual sky (*tripād-vibhūti*), and twenty-five percent of His personal radiation comprehends the entire expansion of the material universes. This is also explained and stated in the *Bhagavad-gītā* (10.42). Thus the seventy-five percent expansion of His radiation is called His internal energy, whereas the twenty-five percent expansion is called the external energy of the Lord. The living entities, who are residents of the spiritual as well as the material expansions, are His marginal energy (*taṭastha-śakti*), and they are at liberty to live in either of the energies, external or internal. Those who live within the spiritual expansion of the Lord are called liberated souls, whereas the residents of the external expansion are called the conditioned souls. We can just make an estimate of the number of the residents of the internal expansions in comparison with the number of residents in the external energy and may easily conclude that the liberated souls are far more numerous than the conditioned souls.

TEXT 18

सोऽमृतस्याभयस्येशो मर्त्यमन्नं यदत्यगात् ।
महिमैष ततो ब्रह्मन् पुरुषस्य दुरत्ययः ॥१८॥

so 'mṛtasyābhayasyeśo
martyam annaṁ yad atyagāt

mahimaiṣa tato brahman
puruṣasya duratyayaḥ

saḥ—He (the Lord); *amṛtasya*—of deathlessness; *abhayasya*—of fearlessness; *īśaḥ*—the controller; *martyam*—dying; *annam*—fruitive action; *yat*—one who has; *atyagāt*—has transcended; *mahimā*—the glories; *eṣaḥ*—of Him; *tataḥ*—therefore; *brahman*—O *brāhmaṇa* Nārada; *puruṣasya*—of the Supreme Personality; *duratyayaḥ*—immeasurable.

TRANSLATION

The Supreme Personality of Godhead is the controller of immortality and fearlessness, and He is transcendental to death and the fruitive actions of the material world. O Nārada, O brāhmaṇa, it is therefore difficult to measure the glories of the Supreme Person.

PURPORT

The glories of the Lord, in the transcendental seventy-five percent of the Lord's internal potency, are stated in the *Padma Purāṇa* (*Uttara-khaṇḍa*). It is said there that those planets in the spiritual sky, which comprises the seventy-five percent expansion of the internal potency of the Lord, are far, far greater than those planets in the total universes composed of the external potency of the Lord. In the *Caitanya-caritāmṛta*, the total universes in the external potency of the Lord are compared to a bucketful of mustard seeds. One mustard seed is calculated to be a universe itself. In one of the universes, in which we are now living, the number of planets cannot be counted by human energy, and so how can we think of the sum total in all the universes, which are compared to a bucketful of mustard seeds? And the planets in the spiritual sky are at least three times the number of those in the material sky. Such planets, being spiritual, are in fact transcendental to the material modes; therefore they are constituted in the mode of unalloyed goodness only. The conception of spiritual bliss (*brahmānanda*) is fully present in those planets. Each of them is eternal, indestructible and free from all kinds of inebrieties experienced in the material world. Each of them is self-illuminating and more powerfully dazzling than (if we can imagine) the total sunshine of millions of mundane suns. The inhabitants of those planets are liberated from birth, death, old age and diseases and have full knowledge of everything; they are all godly and free from all sorts of material hankerings. They have nothing to do there except to render transcendental loving service to the Supreme Lord Nārāyaṇa, who is the predominating Deity of such Vaikuṇṭha planets. Those liberated souls are engaged incessantly in singing songs mentioned in the *Sāma Veda* (*vedaiḥ sāṅga-pada-kramopaniṣadair gāyanti yaṁ sāmagāḥ*). All of them are personifications of the five *Upaniṣads. Tripād-vibhūti*, or the seventy-five percent known as the internal potency of the Lord, is to be understood as the kingdom of God far beyond the material sky; and when we speak of *pāda-vibhūti*, or the twenty-five percent comprising His external energy, we should understand that this refers to the sphere of the material world. It is also said in the *Padma Purāṇa* that the kingdom of *tripād-vibhūti* is transcendental, whereas the *pāda-vibhūti* is mundane; *tripād-vibhūti* is eternal, whereas the *pāda-vibhūti* is transient. The Lord and His eternal servitors in the transcendental kingdom all have eternal forms which are auspicious, infallible, spiritual and eternally youthful. In other words, there is no birth, death, old age and disease. That eternal land is full of transcendental enjoyment and full of beauty and bliss. This very fact is also corroborated in this verse of *Śrīmad-Bhāgavatam*, and the transcendental nature is described as *amṛta*. As described in the *Vedas*, *utāmṛtatvasyeśānaḥ:* the Supreme Lord is the Lord of immortality, or in other words, the Lord is immortal, and because He is the Lord of immortality He can award immortality to His devotees. In the *Bhagavad-gītā* (8.16) the Lord also assures that whoever may go to His abode of immortality shall never return to this mortal land of threefold miseries. The Lord is not like the mundane lord. The mundane master or lord never enjoys equally with his subordinates, nor is a mundane lord immortal, nor can he award immortality to his subordinate. The Supreme Lord, who is the leader of all living entities, can award all the qualities of His personality unto His devotees, including immortality and spiritual bliss. In the material world there is always anxiety or fearfulness in the hearts of all living entities, but the Lord, being Himself the supreme fearless, also awards the same quality of fearlessness to His pure devotees. Mundane existence is itself a kind of fear because in all mundane bodies the effects of birth, death, old age and disease always keep a living being compact in fear. In the mundane world, there is always the influence of time, which changes things from one stage to another, and the living entity, originally being *avikāra*, or unchangeable, suffers a great deal on account of changes due to the influence of time. The changing effects of eternal time are conspicuously absent in the immortal kingdom of God, which should therefore be understood to have no influence of time and therefore no fear whatsoever. In the material world, so-called happiness is the result of one's own work. One can become a rich man by dint of one's own hard labor, and there are always fear and doubts as to the duration of such acquired happiness. But in the kingdom of God, no one has to endeavor to attain a standard of happiness. Happiness is the nature of the spirit, as stated in the *Vedānta-sūtras: ānandamayo 'bhyāsāt*—the spirit is by nature full of happiness. Happiness in spiritual nature always increases in volume with a new phase of appreciation; there is no question of decreasing the bliss. Such unalloyed spiritual bliss is nowhere to be found within the orbit of the material universe, including the Janaloka planets, or, for that matter, the Maharloka or Satyaloka planets, because even Lord Brahmā is subject to the laws of fruitive actions and the law of birth and death. It is therefore stated here: *duratyayaḥ*, or, in other words, spiritual happiness in the eternal kingdom of God cannot be imagined even by the great *brahmacārīs* or *sannyāsīs* who are eligible to be promoted to the planets beyond the region of heaven. Or, the greatness of the Supreme Lord is so great that it cannot be imagined even by the great *brahmacārīs* or *sannyāsīs*, but such happiness is factually attained by the unalloyed devotees of the Lord, by His divine grace.

TEXT 19

पादेषु सर्वभूतानि पुंसः स्थितिपदो विदुः ।
अमृतं क्षेममभयं त्रिमूर्ध्नोऽधायि मूर्धसु ॥१९॥

pādeṣu sarva-bhūtāni
puṁsaḥ sthiti-pado viduḥ
amṛtaṁ kṣemam abhayaṁ
tri-mūrdhno 'dhāyi mūrdhasu

pādeṣu—in the one fourth; *sarva*—all; *bhūtāni*—living entities; *puṁsaḥ*—of the Supreme Person; *sthiti-padaḥ*—the reservoir of all material opulence; *viduḥ*—you should know; *amṛtam*—deathlessness; *kṣemam*—all happiness, free from the anxiety of old age, diseases, etc.; *abhayam*—fearlessness; *tri-mūrdhnaḥ*—beyond the three higher planetary systems; *adhāyi*—exist; *mūrdhasu*—beyond the material coverings.

TRANSLATION

The Supreme Personality of Godhead is to be known as the supreme reservoir of all material opulences by the one fourth of His energy in which all the living entities exist. Deathlessness, fearlessness and freedom from the anxieties of old age and disease exist in the kingdom of God, which is beyond the three higher planetary systems and beyond the material coverings.

PURPORT

Out of the total manifestations of the *sandhinī* energy of the Lord, one fourth is displayed in the material world, and three fourths are displayed in the spiritual world. The Lord's energy is divided into three component parts, namely *sandhinī, saṁvit* and *hlādinī;* in other words, He is the full manifestation of existence, knowledge and bliss. In the material world such a sense of existence, knowledge and pleasure is meagerly exhibited, and all living entities, who are minute parts and parcels of the Lord, are eligible to relish such consciousness of existence, knowledge and bliss very minutely in the liberated stage, whereas in the conditioned stage of material existence they can hardly appreciate what is the factual, existential, cognizable and pure happiness of life. The liberated souls, who exist in far greater numerical strength than those souls in the material world, can factually experience the potency of the above-mentioned *sandhinī, saṁvit* and *hlādinī* energies of the Lord in the matter of deathlessness, fearlessness and freedom from old age and disease.

In the material world, the planetary systems are arranged in three spheres, called *triloka,* or Svarga, Martya and Pātāla, and all of them constitute only one fourth of the total *sandhinī* energy. Beyond that is the spiritual sky where the Vaikuṇṭha planets exist beyond the coverings of seven material strata. In none of the *triloka* planetary systems can one experience the status of immortality, full knowledge and full bliss. The upper three planetary systems are called *sāttvika* planets because they provide facilities for a long duration of life and relative freedom from disease and old age, as well as a sense of fearlessness. The great sages and saints are promoted beyond the heavenly planets to Maharloka, but that also is not the place of complete fearlessness because at the end of one *kalpa* the Maharloka is annihilated and the inhabitants have to transport themselves to still higher planets. Yet even on these planets no one is immune to death. There may be a comparative extension of life, expansion of knowledge and sense of full bliss, but factual deathlessness, fearlessness and freedom from old age, diseases, etc., are possible only beyond the material spheres of the coverings of the material sky. Such things are situated on the head (*adhāyi mūrdhasu*).

TEXT 20

पादास्त्रयो बहिश्चासन्नप्रजानां य आश्रमाः ।
अन्तस्त्रिलोक्यास्त्वपरो गृहमेधोऽबृहद्व्रतः ॥२०॥

pādās trayo bahiś cāsann
aprajānāṁ ya āśramāḥ
antas tri-lokyās tv aparo
gṛha-medho 'bṛhad-vrataḥ

pādāḥ trayaḥ—the cosmos of three fourths of the Lord's energy; *bahiḥ*—thus situated beyond; *ca*—and for all; *āsan*—were; *aprajānām*—of those who are not meant for rebirth; *ye*—those; *āśramāḥ*—status of life; *antaḥ*—within; *tri-lokyāḥ*—of the three worlds; *tu*—but; *aparaḥ*—others; *gṛha-medhaḥ*—attached to family life; *abṛhat-vrataḥ*—without strictly following a vow of celibacy.

TRANSLATION

The spiritual world, which consists of three fourths of the Lord's energy, is situated beyond this material world, and it is especially meant for those who will never be reborn. Others, who are

attached to family life and who do not strictly follow celibacy vows, must live within the three material worlds.

PURPORT

The climax of the system of *varṇāśrama-dharma,* or *sanātana-dharma,* is clearly expressed here in this particular verse of *Śrīmad-Bhāgavatam.* The highest benefit that can be awarded to a human being is to train him to be detached from sex life, particularly because it is only due to sex indulgence that the conditioned life of material existence continues birth after birth. Human civilization in which there is no control of sex life is a fourth-class civilization because in such an atmosphere there is no liberation of the soul encaged in the material body. Birth, death, old age and disease are related to the material body, and they have nothing to do with the spirit soul. But as long as the bodily attachment for sensual enjoyment is encouraged, the individual spirit soul is forced to continue the repetition of birth and death on account of the material body, which is compared to garments subjected to the law of deterioration.

In order to award the highest benefit of human life, the *varṇāśrama* system trains the follower to adopt the vow of celibacy beginning from the order of *brahmacārī.* The *brahmacārī* life is for students who are educated to follow strictly the vow of celibacy. Youngsters who have had no taste of sex life can easily follow the vow of celibacy, and once fixed in the principle of such a life, one can very easily continue to the highest perfectional stage, attaining the kingdom of the three-fourths energy of the Lord. It is already explained that in the cosmos of three-fourths energy of the Lord there is neither death nor fear, and one is full of the blissful life of happiness and knowledge. A householder attached to family life can easily give up such a life of sex indulgence if he has been trained in the principles of the life of a *brahmacārī.* A householder is recommended to quit home at the end of fifty years (*pañcāśordhvaṁ vanaṁ vrajet*) and live a life in the forest; then, being fully detached from family affection, he may accept the order of renunciation as a *sannyāsī* fully engaged in the service of the Lord. Any form of religious principles in which the followers are trained to pursue the vow of celibacy is good for the human being because only those who are trained in that way can end the miserable life of material existence. The principles of *nirvāṇa*, as recommended by Lord Buddha, are also meant for ending the miserable life of material existence. And this process, in the highest degree, is recommended here in the *Śrīmad-Bhāgavatam*, with clear perception of ideal perfection, although basically there is no difference between the process of Buddhists, Śaṅkarites and Vaiṣṇavites. For promotion to the highest status of perfection, namely freedom from birth and death, anxiety and fearfulness, not one of these processes allows the follower to break the vow of celibacy.

The householders and persons who have deliberately broken the vow of celibacy cannot enter into the kingdom of deathlessness. The pious householders or the fallen *yogīs* or the fallen transcendentalists can be promoted to the higher planets within the material world (one fourth of the energy of the Lord), but they will fail to enter into the kingdom of deathlessness. *Abṛhad-vratas* are those who have broken the vow of celibacy. The *vānaprasthas*, or those retired from family life, and the *sannyāsīs*, or the renounced persons, cannot break the vow of celibacy if they want success in the process. The *brahmacārīs*, *vānaprasthas* and *sannyāsīs* do not intend to take rebirth (*apraja*), nor are they meant for secretly indulging in sex life. Such a falldown by the spiritualist may be compensated by another chance for human life in good families of learned *brāhmaṇas* or of rich merchants for another term of elevation, but the best thing is to attain the highest perfection of deathlessness as soon as the human form of life is attained; otherwise the whole policy of human life will prove to be a total failure. Lord Caitanya was very strict in advising His followers in this matter of celibacy. One of His personal attendants, Choṭa Haridāsa, was severly punished by Lord Caitanya because of his failure to observe the vow of celibacy. For a transcendentalist, therefore, who at all wants to be promoted to the kingdom beyond material miseries, it is worse than suicide to deliberately indulge in sex life, especially in the renounced order of life. Sex life in the renounced order of life is the most perverted form of religious life, and such a misguided person can only be saved if, by chance, he meets a pure devotee.

TEXT 21

सृती विचक्रमे विश्वङ् साशनानशने उभे ।
यदविद्या च विद्या च पुरुषस्तूभयाश्रयः ॥२१॥

sṛtī vicakrame viśvaṅ
sāśanānaśane ubhe
yad avidyā ca vidyā ca
puruṣas tūbhayāśrayaḥ

sṛtī—the destination of the living entities; *vicakrame*—exists comprehensively; *viśvaṅ*—the all-pervading Personality of Godhead; *sāśana*—activities of lording it over; *anaśane*—activities in devotional service; *ubhe*—both; *yat*—what is; *avidyā*—nescience; *ca*—as well as; *vidyā*—factual knowledge; *ca*—and; *puruṣaḥ*—the Supreme Person; *tu*—but; *ubhaya*—for both of them; *āśrayaḥ*—the master.

TRANSLATION

By His energies, the all-pervading Personality of Godhead is thus comprehensively the master in the activities of controlling and in devotional service. He is the ultimate master of both nescience and factual knowledge of all situations.

PURPORT

The word *viśvaṅ* is significant in this verse. One who travels perfectly in every field of activity is called the *puruṣa* or *kṣetrajña.* These two terms, *kṣetrajña* and *puruṣa,* are equally applicable to both the individual self and the Supreme Self, the Lord. In the *Bhagavad-gītā* (13.3) the matter is explained as follows:

kṣetrajñaṁ cāpi māṁ viddhi
sarva-kṣetreṣu bhārata
kṣetra-kṣetrajñayor jñānaṁ
yat taj jñānaṁ mataṁ mama

Kṣetra means the place, and one who knows the place is called the *kṣetrajña.* The individual self knows about his limited field of activities, but the Supreme Self, the Lord, knows about the unlimited field of activities. The individual soul knows about his own thinking, feeling and willing activities, but the Supersoul, or the Paramātmā, the supreme controller, being present everywhere, knows everyone's thinking, feeling and willing activities, and as such the individual living entity is the minute master of his personal affairs whereas the Supreme Personality of Godhead is the master of everyone's affairs, past, present and future (*vedāhaṁ samatītāni*, etc.). Only the ignorant person does not know this difference between the Lord and the living entities. The living entities, as distinguished from incognizant matter, may be qualitatively equal to the Lord in cognizance, but the living entity can never be equal to the Lord in full knowledge of past, present and future.

And because the living entity is partially cognizant, he is therefore sometimes forgetful of his own identity. This forgetfulness is specifically manifested in the field of the *ekapād-vibhūti* of the Lord, or in the material world, but in the *tripād-vibhūti* field of actions, or in the spiritual world, there is no forgetfulness by the living entities, who are free from all kinds of contaminations resulting from the forgetful state of existence. The material body is the symbol of the gross and subtle form of forgetfulness; therefore the whole atmosphere of the material world is called *avidyā*, or nescience, whereas the whole atmosphere of the spiritual world is called *vidyā*, or full of knowledge. There are different stages of *avidyā*, and they are called *dharma*, *artha* and *mokṣa*. The idea of *mokṣa*, or liberation, held by the monist in the matter of oneness of the living entity and the Lord by ultimate merging in one, is also the last stage of materialism or forgetfulness. Knowledge of the qualitative oneness of the self and Superself is partial knowledge and ignorance also because there is no knowledge of quantitative difference, as explained above. The individual self can never be equal to the Lord in cognizance; otherwise he could not be placed in the state of forgetfulness. So, because there is a stage of forgetfulness of the individual selves, or the living entities, there is always a gulf of difference between the Lord and the living entity, as between the part and the whole. The part is never equal to the whole. So the conception of one hundred percent equality of the living being with the Lord is also nescience.

In the field of nescience, activities are directed toward lording it over the creation. In the material world, therefore, everyone is engaged in acquiring material opulence to lord it over the material world. Therefore there is always clash and frustration, which are the symptoms of nescience. But in the field of knowledge, there is devotional service to the Lord (*bhakti*). Therefore there is no chance of being contaminated by the influence of nescience or forgetfulness (*avidyā*) in the liberated stage of devotional activities. The Lord is thus the proprietor of the fields both of nescience and of cognition, and it remains the choice of the living entity to exist in either of the above regions.

TEXT 22

यस्मादण्डं विराड् जज्ञे भूतेन्द्रियगुणात्मकः ।
तद् द्रव्यमत्यगाद् विश्वं गोभिः सूर्य इवातपन् ॥२२॥

yasmād aṇḍaṁ virāḍ jajñe
bhūtendriya-guṇātmakaḥ
tad dravyam atyagād viśvaṁ
gobhiḥ sūrya ivātapan

yasmāt—from whom; *aṇḍam*—the universal globes; *virāṭ*—and the gigantic universal form; *jajñe*—appeared; *bhūta*—elements; *indriya*—senses; *guṇa-ātmakaḥ*—qualitative; *tat dravyam*—the universes and the universal form, etc.; *atyagāt*—surpassed; *viśvam*—all the universes; *gobhiḥ*—by the rays; *sūryaḥ*—the sun; *iva*—like; *ātapan*—distributed rays and heat.

TRANSLATION

From that Personality of Godhead, all the universal globes and the universal form with all material elements, qualities and senses are generated. Yet He is aloof from such material manifestations, like the sun, which is separate from its rays and heat.

PURPORT

The supreme truth has been ascertained in the previous verse as *puruṣa* or the *puruṣottama*, the Supreme Person. The Absolute Person is the *īśvara*, or the supreme controller, by His different energies. The *ekapād-vibhūti* manifestation of the material energy of the Lord is just like one of the many mistresses of the Lord, by whom the Lord is not so much attracted, as indicated in the language of the *Gītā* (*bhinnā prakṛtiḥ*). But the region of the *tripād-vibhūti*, being a pure spiritual manifestation of the energy of the Lord, is, so to speak, more attractive to

Him. The Lord, therefore, generates the material manifestations by impregnating the material energy, and then, within the manifestation, He expands Himself as the gigantic form of the *viśva-rūpa.* The *viśva-rūpa,* as it was shown to Arjuna, is not the original form of the Lord. The original form of the Lord is the transcendental form of Puruṣottama, or Kṛṣṇa Himself. It is very nicely explained herein that He expands Himself just like the sun. The sun expands itself by its terrible heat and rays, yet the sun is always aloof from such rays and heat. The impersonalist takes into consideration the rays of the Lord without any information of the tangible, transcendental, eternal form of the Lord, known as Kṛṣṇa. Therefore Kṛṣṇa, in His supreme personal form, with two hands and flute, is bewildering for the impersonalists who can accommodate only the gigantic *viśva-rūpa* of the Lord. They should know that the rays of the sun are secondary to the sun, and similarly the impersonal gigantic form of the Lord is also secondary to the personal form as Puruṣottama. The *Brahma-saṁhitā* (5.37) confirms this statement as follows:

ānanda-cinmaya-rasa-pratibhāvitābhis
tābhir ya eva nija-rūpatayā kalābhiḥ
goloka eva nivasaty akhilātma-bhūto
govindam ādi-puruṣaṁ tam ahaṁ bhajāmi

"The Supreme Personality of Godhead, Govinda, the one who enlivens the senses of everyone by His personal bodily rays, resides in His transcendental abode, called Goloka. Yet He is present in every nook and corner of His creation by expansion of happy spiritual rays, equal in power to His personal potency of bliss." He is therefore simultaneously personal and impersonal by His inconceivable potency, or He is the one without a second, displaying complete unity in a diversity of material and spiritual manifestations. He is separate from everything, and still nothing is different from Him.

TEXT 23

यदास्य नाभ्यान्नलिनादहमासं महात्मनः ।
नाविदं यज्ञसम्भारान् पुरुषावयवानृते ॥२३॥

yadāsya nābhyān nalinād
aham āsaṁ mahātmanaḥ
nāvidaṁ yajña-sambhārān
puruṣāvayavān ṛte

yadā—at the time of; *asya*—His; *nābhyāt*—from the abdomen; *nalināt*—from the lotus flower; *aham*—myself; *āsam*—took my birth; *mahā-ātmanaḥ*—of the great person; *na avidam*—did not know; *yajña*—sacrificial; *sambhārān*—ingredients; *puruṣa*—of the Lord; *avayavān*—personal bodily limbs; *ṛte*—except.

TRANSLATION

When I was born from the abdominal lotus flower of the Lord [Mahā-Viṣṇu], the great person, I had no ingredients for sacrificial performances except the bodily limbs of the great Personality of Godhead.

PURPORT

Lord Brahmā, the creator of the cosmic manifestation, is known as Svayambhū, or one who is born without father and mother. The general process is that a living creature is born out of the sex combination of the male father and the female mother. But Brahmā, the firstborn living being, is born out of the abdominal lotus flower of the Mahā-Viṣṇu plenary expansion of Lord Kṛṣṇa. The abdominal lotus flower is part of the Lord's bodily limbs, and Brahmā is born out of the lotus flower. Therefore Lord Brahmā is also a part of the Lord's body. Brahmā, after his appearance in the gigantic hollow of the universe, saw darkness and nothing else. He felt perplexity, and from his heart he was inspired by the Lord to undergo austerity, thereby acquiring the ingredients for sacrificial performances. But there was nothing besides the two of them, namely the Personality of Mahā-Viṣṇu and Brahmā himself, born of the bodily part of the Lord. For sacrificial performances many ingredients were in need, especially animals. The animal sacrifice is never meant for killing the animal, but for achieving the successful result of the sacrifice.

The animal offered in the sacrificial fire is, so to speak, destroyed, but the next moment it is given a new life by dint of the Vedic hymns chanted by the expert priest. When such an expert priest is not available, the animal sacrifice in the fire of the sacrificial altar is forbidden. Thus Brahmā created even the sacrificial ingredients out of the bodily limbs of the Garbhodakaśāyī Viṣṇu, which means that the cosmic order was created by Brahmā himself. Also, nothing is created out of nothing, but everything is created from the person of the Lord. The Lord says in the *Bhagavad-gītā* (10.8), *ahaṁ sarvasya prabhavo mattaḥ sarvaṁ pravartate.* "Everything is made from My bodily limbs, and I am therefore the original source of all creations."

The impersonalists argue that there is no use in worshiping the Lord when everything is nothing but the Lord Himself. The personalist, however, worships the Lord out of a great sense of gratitude, utilizing the ingredients born out of the bodily limbs of the Lord. The fruits and flowers are available from the body of the earth, and yet mother earth is worshiped by the sensible devotee with ingredients born from the earth. Similarly, mother Ganges is worshiped by the water of the Ganges, and yet the worshiper enjoys the result of such worship. Worship of the Lord is also performed by the ingredients born from the bodily limbs of the Lord, and yet the worshiper, who is himself a part of the Lord, achieves the result of devotional service to the Lord. While the impersonalist wrongly concludes that he is the Lord himself, the personalist, out of a great gratitude, worships the Lord in devotional service, knowing perfectly well that nothing is different from the Lord. The devotee therefore endeavors to apply everything in the service of the Lord because he knows that everything is the property of the Lord and that no one can claim anything as one's own. This perfect conception of oneness helps the worshiper in being engaged in His loving service, whereas the impersonalist, being falsely puffed up, remains a nondevotee forever, without being recognized by the Lord.

TEXT 24

तेषु यज्ञस्य पशवः सवनस्पतयः कुशाः ।
इदं च देवयजनं कालश्चोरुगुणान्वितः ॥२४॥

teṣu yajñasya paśavaḥ
savanaspatayaḥ kuśāḥ
idaṁ ca deva-yajanaṁ
kālaś coru-guṇānvitaḥ

teṣu—in such sacrifices; *yajñasya*—of the sacrificial performance; *paśavaḥ*—the animals or the sacrificial ingredients; *sa-vanaspatayaḥ*—along with flowers and leaves; *kuśāḥ*—the straw; *idam*—all these; *ca*—as also; *deva-yajanam*—the sacrificial altar; *kālaḥ*—a suitable time; *ca*—as also; *uru*—great; *guṇa-anvitaḥ*—qualified.

TRANSLATION

For performing sacrificial ceremonies, one requires sacrificial ingredients, such as flowers, leaves and straw, along with the sacrificial altar and a suitable time [spring].

TEXT 25

वस्तून्योषधयः स्नेहा रसलोहमृदो जलम् ।
ऋचो यजूंषि सामानि चातुर्होत्रं च सत्तम ॥२५॥

vastūny oṣadhayaḥ snehā
rasa-loha-mṛdo jalam
ṛco yajūṁṣi sāmāni
cātur-hotraṁ ca sattama

vastūni—utensils; *oṣadhayaḥ*—grains; *snehāḥ*—clarified butter; *rasa-loha-mṛdaḥ*—honey, gold and earth; *jalam*—water; *ṛcaḥ*—the *Ṛg Veda; yajūṁsi*—the *Yajur Veda; sāmāni*—the *Sāma Veda; cātuḥ-hotram*—four persons conducting the performance; *ca*—all these; *sattama*—O most pious one.

TRANSLATION

Other requirements are utensils, grains, clarified butter, honey, gold, earth, water, the Ṛg Veda, Yajur Veda and Sāma Veda and four priests to perform the sacrifice.

PURPORT

To perform a sacrifice successfully, at least four expert priests are needed: one who can offer (*hotā*), one who can chant (*udgātā*), one who can kindle the sacrificial fire without the aid of separate fire (*adhvaryu*), and one who can supervise (*brahmā*). Such sacrifices were conducted from the birth of Brahmā, the first living creature, and were carried on till the reign of Mahārāja Yudhiṣṭhira. But such expert *brāhmaṇa* priests are very rare in this age of corruption and quarrel, and therefore in the present age only the *yajña* of chanting the holy name of the Lord is recommended. The scriptures enjoin:

harer nāma harer nāma
harer nāmaiva kevalam
kalau nāsty eva nāsty eva
nāsty eva gatir anyathā

TEXT 26

नामधेयानि मन्त्राश्च दक्षिणाश्च व्रतानि च ।
देवतानुक्रमः कल्पः सङ्कल्पस्तन्त्रमेव च ॥२६॥

nāma-dheyāni mantrāś ca
dakṣiṇāś ca vratāni ca
devatānukramaḥ kalpaḥ
saṅkalpas tantram eva ca

nāma-dheyāni—invoking the names of the demigods; *mantrāḥ*—specific hymns to offer to a particular demigod; *ca*—also; *dakṣiṇāḥ*—reward; *ca*—and; *vratāni*—vows; *ca*—and; *devatā-anukramaḥ*—one demigod after another; *kalpaḥ*—the specific scripture; *saṅkalpaḥ*—the specific purpose; *tantram*—a particular process; *eva*—as they are; *ca*—also.

TRANSLATION

Other necessities include invoking the different names of the demigods by specific hymns and vows of recompense, in accor-

dance with the particular scripture, for specific purposes and by specific processes.

PURPORT

The whole process of offering sacrifice is under the category of fruitive action, and such activities are extremely scientific. They mainly depend on the process of vibrating sounds with a particular accent. It is a great science, and due to being out of proper use for more than four thousand years, for want of qualified *brāhmaṇas*, such performances of sacrifice are no longer effective. Nor are they recommended in this fallen age. Any such sacrifice undertaken in this age as a matter of show may simply be a cheating process by the clever priestly order. But such a show of sacrifices cannot be effective at any stage. Fruitive action is being carried on by the help of material science and to a little extent by gross material help, but the materialists await a still more subtle advancement in the process of vibrating sounds on which the Vedic hymns are established. Gross material science cannot divert the real purpose of human life. They can only increase the artificial needs of life without any solution to the problems of life; therefore the way of materialistic life leads to the wrong type of human civilization. Since the ultimate aim of life is spiritual realization, the direct way of invoking the holy name of the Lord, as mentioned above, is precisely recommended by Lord Caitanya, and people of the modern age can easily take advantage of this simple process, which is tenable for the condition of the complicated social structure.

TEXT 27

गतयो मतयश्चैव प्रायश्चित्तं समर्पणम् ।
पुरुषावयवैरेते सम्भाराः सम्भृता मया ॥२७॥

gatayo matayaś caiva
prāyaścittaṁ samarpaṇam
puruṣāvayavair ete
sambhārāḥ sambhṛtā mayā

gatayaḥ—progress to the ultimate goal (Viṣṇu); *matayaḥ*—worshiping the demigods; *ca*—as also; *eva*—certainly; *prāyaścittam*—

compensation; *samarpaṇam*—ultimate offering; *puruṣa*—the Personality of Godhead; *avayavaiḥ*—from the parts of the body of the Personality of Godhead; *ete*—these; *sambhārāḥ*—the ingredients; *sambhṛtāḥ*—were arranged; *mayā*—by me.

TRANSLATION

Thus I had to arrange all these necessary ingredients and paraphernalia of sacrifice from the personal bodily parts of the Personality of Godhead. By invocation of the demigods' names, the ultimate goal, Viṣṇu, was gradually attained, and thus compensation and ultimate offering were complete.

PURPORT

In this verse, special stress is given to the person of the Supreme Lord, and not to His impersonal *brahmajyoti,* as being the source of all supplies. Nārāyaṇa, the Supreme Lord, is the goal of sacrificial results, and therefore the Vedic hymns are ultimately meant for attaining this goal. Human life is thus made successful by pleasing Nārāyaṇa and getting entrance into the direct association of Nārāyaṇa in the spiritual kingdom of Vaikuṇṭha.

TEXT 28

इति सम्भृतसम्भारः पुरुषावयवैरहम् ।
तमेव पुरुषं यज्ञं तेनैवायजमीश्वरम् ॥२८॥

iti sambhṛta-sambhāraḥ
puruṣāvayavair aham
tam eva puruṣaṁ yajñaṁ
tenaivāyajam īśvaram

iti—thus; *sambhṛta*—executed; *sambhāraḥ*—equipped myself well; *puruṣa*—the Personality of Godhead; *avayavaiḥ*—by the parts and parcels; *aham*—I; *tam eva*—unto Him; *puruṣam*—the Personality of Godhead; *yajñam*—the enjoyer of all sacrifices; *tena eva*—by all those; *ayajam*—worshiped; *īśvaram*—the supreme controller.

TRANSLATION

Thus I created the ingredients and paraphernalia for offering sacrifice out of the parts of the body of the Supreme Lord, the enjoyer of the sacrifice, and I performed the sacrifice to satisfy the Lord.

PURPORT

People in general are always anxious to have peace of mind or peace in the world, but they do not know how to achieve such a standard of peace in the world. Such peace in the world is obtainable by performances of sacrifice and by practice of austerity. In the *Bhagavad-gītā* (5.29) the following prescription is recommended:

bhoktāraṁ yajña-tapasāṁ
sarva-loka-maheśvaram
suhṛdaṁ sarva-bhūtānāṁ
jñātvā māṁ śāntim ṛcchati

"The *karma-yogīs* know that the Supreme Lord is the factual enjoyer and maintainer of all sacrifices and of the austere life. They also know that the Lord is the ultimate proprietor of all the planets and is the factual friend of all living entities. Such knowledge gradually converts the *karma-yogīs* into pure devotees of the Lord through the association of unalloyed devotees, and thus they are able to be liberated from material bondage."

Brahmā, the original living being within the material world, taught us the way of sacrifice. The word "sacrifice" suggests dedication of one's own interests for satisfaction of a second person. That is the way of all activities. Every man is engaged in sacrificing his interests for others, either in the form of family, society, community, country or the entire human society. But perfection of such sacrifices is attained when they are performed for the sake of the Supreme Person, the Lord. Because the Lord is the proprietor of everything, because the Lord is the friend of all living creatures, and because He is the maintainer of the performer of sacrifice, as well as the supplier of the ingredients of sacrifices, it is He only and no one else who should be satisfied by all sacrifices.

The whole world is engaged in sacrificing energy for advancement of learning, social upliftment, economic development and plans for total improvement of the human condition, but no one is interested in sacrificing for the sake of the Lord, as it is advised in the *Bhagavad-gītā.* Therefore, there is no peace in the world. If men at all want peace in the world, they must practice sacrifice in the interest of the supreme proprietor and friend of all.

TEXT 29

ततस्ते भ्रातर इमे प्रजानां पतयो नव ।
अयजन् व्यक्तमव्यक्तं पुरुषं सुसमाहिताः ॥२९॥

tatas te bhrātara ime
prajānāṁ patayo nava
ayajan vyaktam avyaktaṁ
puruṣaṁ su-samāhitāḥ

tataḥ—thereafter; *te*—your; *bhrātaraḥ*—brothers; *ime*—these; *prajānām*—of the living creatures; *patayaḥ*—masters; *nava*—nine; *ayajan*—performed; *vyaktam*—manifested; *avyaktam*—nonmanifested; *puruṣam*—personalities; *su-samāhitāḥ*—with proper rituals.

TRANSLATION

My dear son, thereafter your nine brothers, who are the masters of living creatures, performed the sacrifice with proper rituals to satisfy both the manifested and nonmanifested personalities.

PURPORT

The manifested personalities are the demigods like the ruler of the heavenly kingdom, Indra, and his associates; and the nonmanifested personality is the Lord Himself. The manifested personalities are mundane controllers of the material affairs, whereas the nonmanifested Personality of Godhead is transcendental, beyond the range of the material atmosphere. In this age of Kali the manifested demigods are also not to be seen, for space travel has completely stopped. So both the powerful demigods and the Supreme Personality of Godhead are nonmanifested to the covered eyes of the modern man. Modern men want to see everything with their eyes, although they are not sufficiently qualified. Consequently, they disbelieve in the existence of the demigods or of the Supreme God. They should see through the pages of authentic scriptures and should not simply believe their unqualified eyes. Even in these days, God can also be seen by qualified eyes tinged with the ointment of love of God.

TEXT 30

ततश्च मनवः काले ईजिरे ऋषयोऽपरे ।
पितरो विबुधा दैत्या मनुष्याः क्रतुभिर्विभुम् ॥३०॥

tataś ca manavaḥ kāle
ījire ṛṣayo 'pare
pitaro vibudhā daityā
manuṣyāḥ kratubhir vibhum

tataḥ—thereafter; *ca*—also; *manavaḥ*—the Manus, the fathers of mankind; *kāle*—in due course of time; *ījire*—worshiped; *ṛṣayaḥ*—great sages; *apare*—others; *pitaraḥ*—the forefathers; *vibudhāḥ*—the learned scholars; *daityāḥ*—great devotees of the demigods; *manuṣyāḥ*—mankind; *kratubhiḥ vibhum*—by performance of sacrifices to please the Supreme Lord.

TRANSLATION

Thereafter, the Manus, the fathers of mankind, the great sages, the forefathers, the learned scholars, the Daityas and mankind performed sacrifices meant to please the Supreme Lord.

PURPORT

The *daityas* are devotees of the demigods because they want to derive the greatest possible material facilities from them. The devotees of the Lord are *eka-niṣṭha*, or absolutely attached to the devotional service of the Lord. Therefore they have practically no time to seek the benefits of material facilities. Because of their realization of their spiritual identity, they are more concerned with spiritual emancipation than with material comforts.

TEXT 31

नारायणे भगवति तदिदं विश्वमाहितम् ।
गृहीतमायोरुगुणः सर्गादावगुणः स्वतः ॥३१॥

nārāyaṇe bhagavati
tad idaṁ viśvam āhitam
gṛhīta-māyoru-guṇaḥ
sargādāv aguṇaḥ svataḥ

nārāyaṇe—unto Nārāyaṇa; *bhagavati*—the Personality of Godhead; *tat idam*—all these material manifestations; *viśvam*—all the universes; *āhitam*—situated; *gṛhīta*—having accepted; *māyā*—material energies; *uru-guṇaḥ*—greatly powerful; *sarga-ādau*—in creation, maintenance and destruction; *aguṇaḥ*—without affinity for the material modes; *svataḥ*—self-sufficiently.

TRANSLATION

All the material manifestations of the universes are therefore situated in His powerful material energies, which He accepts self-sufficiently, although He is eternally without affinity for the material modes.

PURPORT

The question put by Nārada before Brahmā concerning the sustenance of the material creation is thus answered. Material actions and reactions, as the material scientist can superficially observe, are not basically ultimate truth in regard to creation, maintenance and destruction. The material energy is a potency of the Lord which is displayed in time, accepting the three qualities of goodness, passion and ignorance in the forms of Viṣṇu, Brahmā and Śiva. The material energy thus works under the supreme spell of His Lordship, although He is always transcendental to all such material activities. A rich man constructs a big house by spending his energy in the shape of resources, and similarly he destroys a big house by his resources, but the maintenance is always under his personal care. The Lord is the richest of the rich because He is always fully complete in six opulences. Therefore He is not required to do anything personally, but everything in the material world is carried out by His wishes and direction; therefore, the entire material manifestation is situated in Nārāyaṇa, the Supreme Personality of Godhead. The impersonal conception of the supreme truth is due to lack of knowledge only, and this fact is clearly explained by Brahmājī, who is supposed to be the creator of the universal affairs. Brahmājī is the highest authority in Vedic wisdom, and his assertion in this connection is therefore the supreme information.

TEXT 32

सृजामि तन्नियुक्तोऽहं हरो हरति तद्वशः ।
विश्वं पुरुषरूपेण परिपाति त्रिशक्तिधृक् ॥३२॥

sṛjāmi tan-niyukto 'haṁ
haro harati tad-vaśaḥ
viśvaṁ puruṣa-rūpeṇa
paripāti tri-śakti-dhṛk

sṛjāmi—do create; *tat*—by His; *niyuktaḥ*—appointment; *aham*—I; *haraḥ*—Lord Śiva; *harati*—destroys; *tat-vaśaḥ*—under His subordination; *viśvam*—the whole universe; *puruṣa*—the Personality of Godhead; *rūpeṇa*—by His eternal form; *paripāti*—maintains; *tri-śakti-dhṛk*—the controller of three energies.

TRANSLATION

By His will, I create, Lord Śiva destroys, and He Himself, in His eternal form as the Personality of Godhead, maintains everything. He is the powerful controller of these three energies.

PURPORT

The conception of one without a second is clearly confirmed here. The one is Lord Vāsudeva, and only by His different energies and expansions are different manifestations, both in the material and in the spiritual worlds, maintained. In the material world also, Lord Vāsudeva is everything, as stated in the *Bhagavad-gītā* (7.19). *Vāsudevaḥ sarvam iti:* everything is Vāsudeva only. In the Vedic hymns also the same Vāsudeva is held to be supreme. It is said in the *Vedas, vāsudevāt paro brahman na cānyo 'rtho 'sti tattvataḥ:* in fact there is no greater truth than Vāsudeva. And Lord Kṛṣṇa affirms the same truth in the *Bhagavad-gītā* (7.7). *Mattaḥ parataraṁ nānyat:* "There is nothing above Me [Lord Kṛṣṇa]." So the conception of oneness, as overly stressed by the impersonalist, is also accepted by the personalist devotee of the Lord. The difference is that the impersonalist denies personality in the ultimate issue, whereas the devotee gives more importance to the Personality of Godhead. *Śrīmad-Bhāgavatam* explains this truth in the verse under discussion: Lord Vāsudeva is one without a second, but because He is all-powerful, He can expand Himself as well as display His omnipotencies. The Lord is described here as omnipotent by three energies (*tri-śakti-dhṛk*). So primarily His three energies are internal, marginal and external. This external energy is also displayed in the three modes of goodness, passion and ignorance. Similarly, the internal potency is also displayed in three spiritual modes—*saṁvit, sandhinī* and *hlādinī.* The marginal potency, or the living entities, is also spiritual (*prakṛtiṁ viddhi me parām*), but the living entities are never equal to the Lord. The Lord is *nirasta-sāmya-atiśaya;* in other words, no one is greater than or equal to the Supreme Lord. So the living entities, including even such great personalities as Lord Brahmā and Lord Śiva, are all subordinate to the Lord. In the material world also, in His eternal form of Viṣṇu, He maintains and controls all the affairs of the demigods, including Brahmā and Śiva.

TEXT 33

इति तेऽभिहितं तात यथेदमनुपृच्छसि ।
नान्यद्भगवतः किंचिद्भाव्यं सदसदात्मकम् ॥३३॥

iti te 'bhihitaṁ tāta
yathedam anupṛcchasi
nānyad bhagavataḥ kiñcid
bhāvyaṁ sad-asad-ātmakam

iti—thus; *te*—unto you; *abhihitam*—explained; *tāta*—my dear son; *yathā*—as; *idam*—all these; *anupṛcchasi*—as you have inquired; *na*—

never; *anyat*—anything else; *bhagavataḥ*—beyond the Personality of Godhead; *kiñcit*—nothing; *bhāvyam*—to be thought ever; *sat*—cause; *asat*—effect; *ātmakam*—in the matter of.

TRANSLATION

My dear son, whatever you inquired from me I have thus explained unto you, and you must know for certain that whatever there is (either as cause or as effect, both in the material and spiritual worlds) is dependent on the Supreme Personality of Godhead.

PURPORT

The complete cosmic situation, both in the material and in the spiritual manifestations of the energies of the Lord, is working and moving first as the cause and then as the effect. But the original cause is the Supreme Personality of Godhead. Effects of the original cause become the causes of other effects, and thus everything, either permanent or temporary, is working as cause and effect. And because the Lord is the primeval cause of all persons and all energies, He is called the cause of all causes, as confirmed in the *Brahma-saṁhitā* as well as in the *Bhagavad-gītā.* The *Brahma-saṁhitā* (5.1) affirms:

īśvaraḥ paramaḥ kṛṣṇaḥ
sac-cid-ānanda-vigrahaḥ
anādir ādir govindaḥ
sarva-kāraṇa-kāraṇam

And in the *Bhagavad-gītā* (10.8) it is said:

ahaṁ sarvasya prabhavo
mattaḥ sarvaṁ pravartate
iti matvā bhajante māṁ
budhā bhāva-samanvitāḥ

So the original primeval cause is *vigraha,* the personal, and the impersonal spiritual effulgence, *brahmajyoti,* is also an effect of the Supreme Brahman (*brahmaṇo hi pratiṣṭhāham*), Lord Kṛṣṇa.

TEXT 34

न भारती मेऽङ्ग मृषोपलक्ष्यते
न वै क्वचिन्मे मनसो मृषा गतिः ।
न मे हृषीकाणि पतन्त्यसत्पथे
यन्मे हृदौत्कण्ठ्यवता धृतो हरिः ॥३४॥

na bhāratī me 'ṅga mṛṣopalakṣyate
na vai kvacin me manaso mṛṣā gatiḥ
na me hṛṣīkāṇi patanty asat-pathe
yan me hṛdautkaṇṭhyavatā dhṛto hariḥ

na—never; *bhāratī*—statements; *me*—mind; *aṅga*—O Nārada; *mṛṣā*—untruth; *upalakṣyate*—prove to be; *na*—never; *vai*—certainly; *kvacit*—at any time; *me*—mine; *manasaḥ*—of the mind; *mṛṣā*—untruth; *gatiḥ*—progress; *na*—nor; *me*—mine; *hṛṣīkāṇi*—senses; *patanti*—degrades; *asat-pathe*—in temporary matter; *yat*—because; *me*—mine; *hṛdā*—heart; *autkaṇṭhyavatā*—by great earnestness; *dhṛtaḥ*—caught hold of; *hariḥ*—the Supreme Personality of Godhead.

TRANSLATION

O Nārada, because I have caught hold of the lotus feet of the Supreme Personality of Godhead, Hari, with great zeal, whatever I say has never proved to have been false. Nor is the progress of my mind ever deterred. Nor are my senses ever degraded by temporary attachment to matter.

PURPORT

Lord Brahmā is the original speaker of Vedic wisdom to Nārada, and Nārada is the distributor of transcendental knowledge all over the world through his various disciples, like Vyāsadeva and others. The followers of Vedic wisdom accept the statements of Brahmājī as gospel truth, and transcendental knowledge is thus being distributed all over the world by the process of disciplic succession from time immemorial, since the beginning of the creation. Lord Brahmā is the perfect liberated living being within the material world, and any sincere student of transcendental knowledge must accept the words and statements of Brahmājī as infallible. The Vedic knowledge is infallible because it comes down directly from the Supreme Lord unto the heart of Brahmā, and since he is the most perfect living being, Brahmājī is always correct to the letter. And this is because Lord Brahmā is a great devotee of the Lord who has earnestly accepted the lotus feet of the Lord as the supreme truth. In the *Brahma-saṁhitā*, which is compiled by Brahmājī, he repeats the aphorism *govindam ādi-puruṣaṁ tam ahaṁ bhajāmi:* "I am a worshiper of the original Personality of Godhead, Govinda, the primeval Lord." So whatever he says, whatever he thinks, and whatever he does normally in his mood are to be accepted as truth because of his direct and very intimate connection with Govinda, the primeval Lord. Śrī Govinda, who pleasingly accepts the loving transcendental service of His devotees, gives all protection to the words and actions of His devotees. The Lord declares in the *Bhagavad-gītā* (9.31), *kaunteya pratijānīhi:* "O son of Kuntī, please declare it." The Lord asks Arjuna to declare, and why? Because sometimes the declaration of Govinda Himself may seem contradictory to mundane creatures, but the mundaner will never find any contradiction in the words of the Lord's devotees. The devotees are especially protected by the Lord so that they may remain infallible. Therefore the process of devotional service always begins in the service of the devotee who appears in disciplic succession. The devotees are always liberated, but that does not mean that they are impersonal. The Lord is a person eternally, and the devotee of the Lord is also a person eternally. Because the devotee has his sense organs even at the liberated stage, he is therefore a person always. And because the devotee's service is accepted by the Lord in full reciprocation, the Lord is also a person in His complete spiritual embodiment. The devotee's senses, being engaged in the service of the Lord, never go astray under the attraction of false material enjoyment. The plans of the devotee never go in vain, and all this is due to the faithful attachment of the devotee for the service of the Lord. This is the standard of perfection and liberation. Anyone, beginning from Brahmājī down to the human being, is at once put on the path of liberation simply by his attachment in great earnestness for the Supreme Lord, Śrī Kṛṣṇa, the primeval Lord. The Lord affirms this in the *Bhagavad-gītā* (14.26):

māṁ ca yo 'vyabhicāreṇa
bhakti-yogena sevate
sa guṇān samatītyaitān
brahma-bhūyāya kalpate

Anyone, therefore, who is earnestly serious in heart and soul about being in intimate touch with the Personality of Godhead in the relationship of transcendental loving service will always be infallible in words and action. The reason is that the Supreme Lord is Absolute Truth, and anything earnestly dovetailed with the Absolute Truth attains the same transcendental quality. On the other hand, any amount of mental speculation on the strength of material science and knowledge without any bona fide touch with the Absolute Truth is sure to be a mundane untruth and failure, simply due to not being in touch with the Absolute Truth. Such godless, unfaithful words and actions, however materially enriched, are never to be trusted. That is the purport of this important verse. A grain of devotion is more valuable than tons of faithlessness.

TEXT 35

सोऽहं समाम्नायमयस्तपोमयः
प्रजापतीनामभिवन्दितः पतिः ।
आस्थाय योगं निपुणं समाहित-
स्तं नाध्यगच्छं यत आत्मसम्भवः ॥३५॥

so 'haṁ samāmnāyamayas tapomayaḥ
prajāpatīnām abhivanditaḥ patiḥ
āsthāya yogaṁ nipuṇaṁ samāhitas
taṁ nādhyagacchaṁ yata ātma-sambhavaḥ

saḥ aham—myself (the great Brahmā); *samāmnāya-mayaḥ*—in the chain of disciplic succession of Vedic wisdom; *tapaḥ-mayaḥ*—successfully having undergone all austerities; *prajāpatīnām*—of all the forefathers of living entities; *abhivanditaḥ*—worshipable; *patiḥ*—master; *āsthāya*—successfully practiced; *yogam*—mystic powers; *nipuṇam*—very expert; *samāhitaḥ*—self-realized; *tam*—the Supreme

Lord; *na*—did not; *adhyagaccham*—properly understood; *yataḥ*—from whom; *ātma*—self; *sambhavaḥ*—generated.

TRANSLATION

Although I am known as the great Brahmā, perfect in the disciplic succession of Vedic wisdom, and although I have undergone all austerities and am an expert in mystic powers and self-realization, and although I am recognized as such by the great forefathers of the living entities, who offer me respectful obeisances, still I cannot understand Him, the Lord, the very source of my birth.

PURPORT

Brahmā, the greatest of all living creatures within the universe, is admitting his failure to know the Supreme Lord despite his vast learning in the Vedic wisdom, despite his austerity, penance, mystic powers and self-realization, and despite being worshiped by the great Prajāpatis, the forefathers of the living entities. So these qualifications are not sufficient to know the Supreme Lord. Brahmājī could understand the Lord to a little extent only when he was trying to serve Him by the eagerness of his heart (*hṛdautkaṇṭhyavatā*), which is the devotional service mood. Therefore, the Lord can be known only by the sincere mood of eagerness for service, and not by any amount of material qualification as scientist or speculative philosopher or by attainment of mystic powers. This fact is clearly corroborated in the *Bhagavad-gītā* (18.54–55):

brahma-bhūtaḥ prasannātmā
na śocati na kāṅkṣati
samaḥ sarveṣu bhūteṣu
mad-bhaktiṁ labhate parām

bhaktyā mām abhijānāti
yāvān yaś cāsmi tattvataḥ
tato māṁ tattvato jñātvā
viśate tad anantaram

Only self-realization, by attainment of the above high qualifications of Vedic wisdom, austerity, etc., can help one on the path of devotional service. But failing in devotional service, one remains still imperfect because even in that position of self-realization one cannot factually know the Supreme Lord. By self-realization, one is qualified to become a devotee, and the devotee, by service mood (*bhaktyā*) only, can gradually know the Personality of Godhead. One should not, however, misunderstand the import of *viśate* ("enters into") as referring to merging into the existence of the Supreme. Even in material existence, one is merged in the existence of the Lord. No materialist can disentangle self from matter, for the self is merged in the external energy of the Lord. As no layman can separate butter from milk, no one can extricate the merged self from matter by acquiring some material qualification. This *viśate* by devotion (*bhaktyā*) means to be able to participate in the association of the Lord in person. *Bhakti*, or devotional service to the Lord, means to become free from material entanglement and then to enter into the kingdom of God, becoming one like Him. Losing one's individuality is not the aim of *bhakti-yoga* or of the devotees of the Lord. There are five types of liberation, one of which is called *sāyujya-mukti*, or being merged into the existence or body of the Lord. The other forms of liberation maintain the individuality of the particle soul and involve being always engaged in the transcendental loving service of the Lord. The word *viśate*, used in the verses of the *Bhagavad-gītā*, is thus meant for the devotees who are not at all anxious for any kind of liberation. The devotees are satisfied simply in being engaged in the service of the Lord, regardless of the situation.

Lord Brahmā is the first living being, who directly learned the Vedic wisdom from the Lord (*tene brahma hṛdā ya ādi-kavaye*). Therefore, who can be a more learned Vedāntist than Lord Brahmā? He admits that in spite of his perfect knowledge in the *Vedas*, he was unable to know the glories of the Lord. Since no one can be more than Lord Brahmā, how can a so-called Vedāntist be perfectly cognizant of the Absolute Truth? The so-called Vedāntist, therefore, cannot enter into the existence of the Lord without being trained in the matter of *bhakti-vedānta*, or *Vedānta* plus *bhakti*. *Vedānta* means self-realization, and *bhakti* means realization of the Personality of Godhead, to some extent. No one can know the Personality of Godhead in full, but at least to a certain extent one can know the Absolute Truth, the Personality of Godhead, by self-surrender and a devotional attitude, and by nothing else. In the *Brahma-saṁhitā* also, it is said, *vedeṣu durlabham*, or simply by study of Vedānta one can hardly find out the existence of the Personality of Godhead, but the Lord is *adurlabham ātma-bhaktau*, very easily available to His devotee. Śrīla Vyāsadeva, therefore, was not satisfied simply with compiling the *Vedānta-sūtras*, but over and above this, by the advice of his spiritual master, Nārada, he compiled the *Śrīmad-Bhāgavatam* in order to understand the real import of *Vedānta*. *Śrīmad-Bhāgavatam* therefore, is the absolute medium by which to understand the Absolute Truth.

TEXT 36

नतोऽस्म्यहं तच्चरणं समीयुषां
भवच्छिदं स्वस्त्ययनं सुमङ्गलम् ।
यो ह्यात्ममायाविभवं स्म पर्यगाद्
यथा नभः स्वान्तमथापरे कुतः ॥३६॥

nato 'smy ahaṁ tac-caraṇaṁ samīyuṣāṁ
bhavac-chidaṁ svasty-ayanaṁ sumaṅgalam
yo hy ātma-māyā-vibhavaṁ sma paryagād
yathā nabhaḥ svāntam athāpare kutaḥ

nataḥ—let me offer my obeisances; *asmi*—am; *aham*—I; *tat*—the Lord's; *caraṇam*—feet; *samīyuṣām*—of the surrendered soul; *bhavat-chidam*—that which stops repetition of birth and death; *svasti-ayanam*—perception of all happiness; *su-maṅgalam*—all-auspicious; *yaḥ*—one who; *hi*—exactly; *ātma-māyā*—personal energies; *vibhavam*—potency; *sma*—certainly; *paryagāt*—cannot estimate; *yathā*—as much as; *nabhaḥ*—the sky; *sva-antam*—its own limit; *atha*—therefore; *apare*—others; *kutaḥ*—how.

TRANSLATION

Therefore it is best for me to surrender unto His feet, which alone can deliver one from the miseries of repeated birth and death. Such surrender is all-auspicious and allows one to perceive all happiness. Even the sky cannot estimate the limits of its own

expansion. So what can others do when the Lord Himself is unable to estimate His own limits?

PURPORT

Lord Brahmā, the greatest of all learned living beings, the greatest sacrificer, the greatest observer of the austere life, and the greatest self-realized mystic, advises us, as the supreme spiritual master of all living beings, that one should simply surrender unto the lotus feet of the Lord in order to achieve all success, even up to the limit of being liberated from the miseries of material life and being endowed with all-auspicious spiritual existence. Lord Brahmā is known as the *pitāmaha,* or the father's father. A young man consults his experienced father about discharging his duties. So the father is naturally a good advisor. But Lord Brahmā is the father of all fathers. He is the father of the father of Manu, who is the father of mankind all over the universal planets. Therefore the men of this insignificant planet should kindly accept the instruction of Brahmājī and would do well to surrender unto the lotus feet of the Lord rather than try to estimate the length and breadth of the Lord's potencies. His potencies are immeasurable, as confirmed in the *Vedas. Parāsya śaktir vividhaiva śrūyate svābhāvikī jñāna-bala-kriyā ca* (*Śvetāśvatara Up.* 6.8). He is the greatest of all, and all others, even the greatest of all living beings, namely Brahmājī, admits that the best thing for us is to surrender unto Him. Therefore only those persons with a very poor fund of knowledge claim that they themselves are lords of all that they survey. And what can they survey? They cannot survey even the length and breadth of a small sky in one small universe. The so-called material scientist says that he would need to live forty thousand years to reach the highest planet of the universe, being carried by a sputnik. This is also utopian because no one can be expected to live forty thousand years. Besides, when the space pilot returned from his travel, none of his friends would be present to receive him back as the greatest astronaut, as has become fashionable for modern bewildered scientific men. One scientific man, who had no belief in God, was very much enthusiastic in making plans for his material existence and therefore opened a hospital to save the living. But after opening the hospital, he himself died within six months. So one should not spoil his human life, which is obtained after many, many changes of bodies in 8,400,000 species of life, simply for the concocted material happiness of life through increasing artificial needs in the name of advancement of economic development and scientific knowledge. Rather, one should simply surrender unto the feet of the Lord to make a solution to all miseries of life. That is the instruction of Lord Kṛṣṇa directly in the *Bhagavad-gītā*, and that is the instruction of *Śrīmad-Bhāgavatam* by Brahmājī, the supreme father of all living beings.

Anyone denying this surrendering process as recommended both in the *Bhagavad-gītā* and in the *Śrīmad-Bhāgavatam*—and, for that matter, in all authorized scriptures—will be forced to surrender unto the laws of material nature. The living entity, by his constitutional position, is not independent. He must surrender, either unto the Lord or unto material nature. Material nature is also not independent of the Lord, since the Lord Himself has claimed material nature as *mama māyā*, or "My energy" (Bg. 7.14), and as *me bhinnā prakṛtir aṣṭadhā*, or "My separated energy in eight divisions" (Bg. 7.4). Therefore material nature is also controlled by the Lord, as He has claimed in *Bhagavad-gītā* (9.10). *Mayādhyakṣeṇa prakṛtiḥ sūyate sacarācaram:* "Under My direction only is material nature working, and thus are all things moving." And the living entities, being superior energy to matter, have choice and discrimination either to surrender unto the Lord or to surrender unto material nature. By surrendering unto the Lord, one is happy and liberated, but by surrendering unto material nature the living entity suffers. So the end of all suffering means surrendering unto the Lord because the surrendering process itself is *bhava-cchidam* (liberation from all material miseries), *svasty-ayanam* (perception of all happiness), and *sumaṅgalam* (the source of everything auspicious).

Therefore liberty, happiness and all good fortune can be attained only by surrendering unto the Lord because He is full liberty, full happiness and full auspiciousness. Such liberation and happiness are also unlimited, and they have been compared to the sky, although such liberation and happiness are infinitely greater than the sky. In our present position we can simply understand the magnitude of greatness when it is compared to the sky. We fail to measure the sky, but the happiness and liberty obtained in association with the Lord are far greater than the sky. That spiritual happiness is so great that it cannot be measured, even by the Lord Himself, not to speak of others.

It is said in the scriptures, *brahma-saukhyaṁ tv anantam:* spiritual happiness is unlimited. Here it is said that even the Lord cannot measure such happiness. This does not mean that the Lord cannot measure it and is therefore imperfect in that sense. The actual position is that the Lord can measure it, but the happiness in the Lord is also identical with the Lord on account of absolute knowledge. So the happiness derived from the Lord may be measured by the Lord, but the happiness increases again, and the Lord measures it again, and then again the happiness increases more and more, and the Lord measures it more and more, and as such there is eternally a competition between increment and measurement, so much so that the competition is never stopped, but goes on unlimitedly *ad infinitum.* Spiritual happiness is *ānandāmbudhi-vardhanam*, or the ocean of happiness which increases. The material ocean is stagnant, but the spiritual ocean is dynamic. In the *Caitanya-caritāmṛta,* (*Ādi-līlā*, Fourth Chapter) Kavirāja Gosvāmī has very nicely described this dynamic increment of the ocean of spiritual happiness in the transcendental person of Śrīmatī Rādhārāṇī, the pleasure potency of Lord Kṛṣṇa.

TEXT 37

नाहं न यूयं यदृतां गतिं विदु-
र्न वामदेवः किमुतापरे सुराः ।
तन्मायया मोहितबुद्धयस्त्विदं
विनिर्मितं चात्मसमं विचक्ष्महे ॥३७॥

nāhaṁ na yūyaṁ yad-ṛtāṁ gatiṁ vidur
na vāmadevaḥ kim utāpare surāḥ
tan-māyayā mohita-buddhayas tv idaṁ
vinirmitaṁ cātma-samaṁ vicakṣmahe

na—neither; *aham*—I; *yūyam*—all you sons; *yat*—whose; *ṛtām*—factual; *gatim*—movements; *viduḥ*—do know; *na*—nor; *vāmadevaḥ*—Lord Śiva; *kim*—what; *uta*—else; *apare*—others; *surāḥ*—demigods;

tat—by His; *māyayā*—by the illusory energy; *mohita*—bewildered; *buddhayaḥ*—with such intelligence; *tu*—but; *idam*—this; *vinirmitam*—what is created; *ca*—also; *ātma-samam*—by dint of one's personal ability; *vicakṣmahe*—observe.

TRANSLATION

Since neither Lord Śiva nor you nor I could ascertain the limits of spiritual happiness, how can other demigods know it? And because all of us are bewildered by the illusory external energy of the Supreme Lord, we can see only this manifested cosmos according to our individual ability.

PURPORT

We have many times mentioned the names of twelve selected authorities (*dvādaśa-mahājana*), of which Brahmā, Nārada and Lord Śiva head the list as the first, second and third in order of merit of those who know something of the Supreme Lord. Other demigods, semi-demigods, Gandharvas, Cāraṇas, Vidyādharas, human beings or *asuras* cannot possibly know fully about the potencies of the Absolute Lord, Śrī Kṛṣṇa. The demigods, semi-demigods, Gandharvas, etc., are all highly intelligent persons in the upper planets, the human beings are inhabitants of the intermediate planets, and the *asuras* are inhabitants of the lower planets. All of them have their respective conceptions and estimations of the Absolute Truth, as does the scientist or the empiric philosopher in human society. All such living entities are creatures of the material nature, and consequently they are bewildered by the wonderful display of the three modes of material nature. Such bewilderment is mentioned in the *Bhagavad-gītā* (7.13). *Tribhir guṇamayair bhāvair ebhiḥ sarvam idaṁ jagat:* every entity, beginning from Brahmā down to the ant, is individually bewildered by the three modes of material nature, namely goodness, passion and ignorance. Everyone thinks, in terms of individual capacity, that this universe, which is manifested before us, is all in all. And so the scientist in the human society of the twentieth century calculates the beginning and end of the universe in his own way. But what can the scientists know? Even Brahmā himself was once bewildered, thinking himself the only one Brahmā favored by the Lord, but later on, by the grace of the Lord, he came to know that there are innumerable more powerful Brahmās as well, in far bigger universes beyond this universe, and all of these universes combined together form *ekapād-vibhūti*, or one fourth of the manifestation of the Lord's creative energy. The other three fourths of His energy are displayed in the spiritual world, and so what can the tiny scientist with a tiny brain know of the Absolute Personality of Godhead, Lord Kṛṣṇa? The Lord says, therefore, *mohitaṁ nābhijānāti mām ebhyaḥ param avyayam:* bewildered by such modes of material nature, they cannot understand that beyond these manifestations is a Supreme Person who is the absolute controller of everything. Brahmā, Nārada and Lord Śiva know about the Lord to a considerable extent, and therefore one should follow the instructions of these great personalities instead of being satisfied with a tiny brain and its playful discoveries such as spacecraft and similar products of science. As the mother is the only authority to identify the father of a child, so the mother *Vedas*, presented by the recognized authority such as Brahmā, Nārada or Śiva, is the only authority to inform us about the Absolute Truth.

TEXT 38

यस्यावतारकर्माणि गायन्ति ह्यस्मदादयः ।
न यं विदन्ति तत्त्वेन तस्मै भगवते नमः ॥३८॥

yasyāvatāra-karmāṇi
gāyanti hy asmad-ādayaḥ
na yaṁ vidanti tattvena
tasmai bhagavate namaḥ

yasya—whose; *avatāra*—incarnation; *karmāṇi*—activities; *gāyanti*—chant in glorification; *hi*—indeed; *asmat-ādayaḥ*—persons like us; *na*—do not; *yam*—whom; *vidanti*—know; *tattvena*—cent percent as He is; *tasmai*—unto Him; *bhagavate*—unto the Personality of Godhead Śrī Kṛṣṇa; *namaḥ*—respectful obeisances.

TRANSLATION

Let us offer our respectful obeisances unto that Supreme Personality of Godhead, whose incarnations and activities are chanted

by us for glorification, though He can hardly be fully known as He is.

PURPORT

It is said that the transcendental name, form, quality, pastimes, paraphernalia, personality, etc., cannot possibly be perceived by the gross materialistic senses. But when the senses are purified by the process of hearing, chanting, remembering, and worshiping the lotus feet of the holy Deity, etc., the Lord reveals Himself proportionately to the advancement of the quality of devotional service (*ye yathā māṁ prapadyante*). One should not expect the Lord to be an order-supplying agent who must be present before us as soon as we desire to see Him. We must be ready to undergo the prescribed devotional duties, following the path shown by the predecessors in the disciplic succession from Brahmā, Nārada and similar authorities. As the senses are progressively purified by bona fide devotional service, the Lord reveals His identity according to the spiritual advancement of the devotee. But one who is not in the line of devotional service can hardly perceive Him simply by calculations and philosophical speculations. Such a hard worker can present a jugglery of words before an audience, but can never know the Supreme Personality of Godhead in His personal feature. The Lord has clearly stated in the *Bhagavad-gītā* that one can know Him only by devotional service. No one can know the Lord by any puffed-up material process of challenge, but the humble devotee can please the Lord by his earnest devotional activities. Thus the Lord reveals Himself proportionately before the devotee. Lord Brahmā therefore offers his respectful obeisances as a bona fide spiritual master and advises us to follow the process of *śravaṇa* and *kīrtana.* Simply by this process, or simply by hearing and chanting the glories of the activities of the Lord's incarnation, one can certainly see within himself the identity of the Lord. We have already discussed this subject in volume one of *Śrīmad-Bhāgavatam*, in connection with this verse:

tac chraddadhānā munayo
jñāna-vairāgya-yuktayā
paśyanty ātmani cātmānaṁ
bhaktyā śruta-gṛhītayā
(*Bhāg.* 1.2.12)

The conclusion is that one cannot know the Supreme Personality of Godhead fully by any method, but He can be seen and felt partially by the devotional service process of hearing, chanting, etc.

TEXT 39

स एष आद्यः पुरुषः कल्पे कल्पे सृजत्यजः ।
आत्मात्मन्यात्मनात्मानं स संयच्छति पाति च ॥३९॥

sa eṣa ādyaḥ puruṣaḥ
kalpe kalpe sṛjaty ajaḥ
ātmātmany ātmanātmānaṁ
sa saṁyacchati pāti ca

saḥ—He; *eṣaḥ*—the very; *ādyaḥ*—the original Personality of Godhead; *puruṣaḥ*—the Mahā-Viṣṇu incarnation, a plenary portion of Govinda, Lord Kṛṣṇa; *kalpe kalpe*—in each and every millennium; *sṛjati*—creates; *ajaḥ*—the unborn; *ātmā*—self; *ātmani*—upon the self; *ātmanā*—by His own self; *ātmānam*—own self; *saḥ*—He; *saṁyacchati*—absorbs; *pāti*—maintains; *ca*—also.

TRANSLATION

That supreme original Personality of Godhead, Lord Śrī Kṛṣṇa, expanding His plenary portion as Mahā-Viṣṇu, the first incarnation, creates this manifested cosmos, but He is unborn. The creation, however, takes place in Him, and the material substance and manifestations are all Himself. He maintains them for some time and absorbs them into Himself again.

PURPORT

The creation is nondifferent from the Lord, and still He is not in the creation. This is explained in the *Bhagavad-gītā* (9.4) as follows:

mayā tatam idaṁ sarvaṁ
jagad avyakta-mūrtinā
mat-sthāni sarva-bhūtāni
na cāhaṁ teṣv avasthitaḥ

The impersonal conception of the Absolute Truth is also a form of the Lord called *avyakta-mūrti. Mūrti* means "form," but because His impersonal feature is inexplicable to our limited senses, He is the *avyakta-mūrti* form, and in that inexplicable form of the Lord the whole creation is resting; or, in other words, the whole creation is the Lord Himself, and the creation is also nondifferent from Him, but simultaneously He, as the original Personality of Godhead Śrī Kṛṣṇa, is aloof from the created manifestation. The impersonalist gives stress to the impersonal form or feature of the Lord and does not believe in the original personality of the Lord, but the Vaiṣṇavas accept the original form of the Lord, of whom the impersonal form is merely one of the features. The impersonal and personal conceptions of the Lord are existing simultaneously, and this fact is clearly described both in the *Bhagavad-gītā* and in the *Śrīmad-Bhāgavatam*, and also in other Vedic scriptures. Inconceivable to human intelligence, the idea must simply be accepted on the authority of the scriptures, and it can only be practically realized by the progress of devotional service unto the Lord, and never by mental speculation or inductive logic. The impersonalists depend more or less on inductive logic, and therefore they always remain in darkness about the original Personality of Godhead Śrī Kṛṣṇa. Their conception of Kṛṣṇa is not clear, although everything is clearly mentioned in all the Vedic scriptures. A poor fund of knowledge cannot comprehend the existence of an original personal form of the Lord when He is expanded in everything. This imperfectness is due, more or less, to the material conception that a substance distributed widely in parts can no longer exist in the original form.

The original Personality of Godhead (*ādyaḥ*), Govinda, expands Himself as the Mahā-Viṣṇu incarnation and rests in the Causal Ocean, which He Himself creates. The *Brahma-saṁhitā* (5.47) confirms this as follows:

yaḥ kāraṇārṇava-jale bhajati sma yoga-
nidrām ananta-jagad-aṇḍa-saroma-kūpaḥ
ādhāra-śaktim avalambya parāṁ sva-mūrtiṁ
govindam ādi-puruṣaṁ tam ahaṁ bhajāmi

Lord Brahmājī says in his *Brahma-saṁhitā*, "I worship the primeval Lord Govinda, who lies down in the Causal Ocean in His plenary portion as Mahā-Viṣṇu, with all the universes generating from the pores of hair on His transcendental body, and who accepts the mystic slumber of eternity."

So this Mahā-Viṣṇu is the first incarnation in the creation, and from Him all the universes are generated and all material manifestations are produced, one after another. The Causal Ocean is created by the Lord as the *mahat-tattva,* as a cloud in the spiritual sky, and is only a part of His different manifestations. The spiritual sky is an expansion of His personal rays, and He is the *mahat-tattva* cloud also. He lies down and generates the universes by His breathing, and again, by entering into each universe as Garbhodakaśāyī Viṣṇu, He creates Brahmā, Śiva and many other demigods for maintenance of the universe and again absorbs the whole thing into His person as confirmed in the *Bhagavad-gītā* (9.7):

sarva-bhūtāni kaunteya
prakṛtiṁ yānti māmikām
kalpa-kṣaye punas tāni
kalpādau visṛjāmy aham

"O son of Kuntī, when the *kalpa,* or the duration of the life of Brahmā, is ended, then all the created manifestations enter into My *prakṛti,* or energy, and again, when I desire, the same creation takes place by My personal energy."

The conclusion is that these are all but displays of the Lord's inconceivable personal energies, of which no one can have any full information. This point we have already discussed.

TEXTS 40–41

विशुद्धं केवलं ज्ञानं प्रत्यक् सम्यगवस्थितम् ।
सत्यं पूर्णमनाद्यन्तं निर्गुणं नित्यमद्वयम् ॥४०॥
ऋषे विदन्ति मुनयः प्रशान्तात्मेन्द्रियाशयाः ।
यदा तदेवासत्तर्कैस्तिरोधीयेत विप्लुतम् ॥४१॥

viśuddhaṁ kevalaṁ jñānaṁ
pratyak samyag avasthitam

satyaṁ pūrṇam anādy-antaṁ
nirguṇaṁ nityam advayam

ṛṣe vidanti munayaḥ
praśāntātmendriyāśayāḥ
yadā tad evāsat-tarkais
tirodhīyeta viplutam

viśuddham—without any material tinge; *kevalam*—pure and perfect; *jñānam*—knowledge; *pratyak*—all-pervading; *samyak*—in fullness; *avasthitam*—situated; *satyam*—truth; *pūrṇam*—absolute; *anādi*—without any beginning; *antam*—and so also without any end; *nirguṇam*—devoid of material modes; *nityam*—eternal; *advayam*—without any rival; *ṛṣe*—O Nārada, O great sage; *vidanti*—they can only understand; *munayaḥ*—the great thinkers; *praśānta*—pacified; *ātma*—self; *indriya*—senses; *āśayāḥ*—sheltered; *yadā*—while; *tat*—that; *eva*—certainly; *asat*—untenable; *tarkaiḥ*—arguments; *tiraḥ-dhīyeta*—disappears; *viplutam*—distorted.

TRANSLATION

The Personality of Godhead is pure, being free from all contaminations of material tinges. He is the Absolute Truth and the embodiment of full and perfect knowledge. He is all-pervading, without beginning or end, and without rival. O Nārada, O great sage, the great thinkers can know Him when completely freed from all material hankerings and when sheltered under undisturbed conditions of the senses. Otherwise, by untenable arguments, all is distorted, and the Lord disappears from our sight.

PURPORT

Here is an estimation of the Lord apart from His transcendental activities in the temporary, material creations. Māyāvāda philosophy tries to designate the Lord as contaminated by a material body when He accepts forms of incarnation. This sort of interpolation is completely denied herein by the explanation that the Lord's position is pure and unalloyed in all circumstances. According to Māyāvāda philosophy, the spirit soul, when covered by nescience, is designated as *jīva*, but when freed from such ignorance or nescience he merges in the impersonal existence of the Absolute Truth. But here it is said that the Lord is eternally the symbol of full and perfect knowledge. This is His speciality: perpetual freedom from all material contaminations. This distinguishes the Lord from the individual, common living entities who have the aptitude for being subordinated by nescience and thus becoming materially designated. In the *Vedas* it is said that the Lord is *vijñānam ānandam*, full of bliss and knowledge. The conditioned souls are never to be compared to Him because such individual souls have the tendency to become contaminated. Although after liberation the living entity can become one with the same quality of existence as the Lord, his very tendency to become contaminated, which the Lord never has, makes the individual living entity different from the Lord. In the *Vedas* it is said, *śuddham apāpa-viddham:* the individual *ātmā* becomes polluted by sin, but the Lord is never contaminated by sins. The Lord is compared to the powerful sun. The sun is never contaminated by anything infectious because it is so powerful. On the contrary, infected things are sterilized by the rays of the sun. Similarly, the Lord is never contaminated by sins; on the contrary, the sinful living entities become sterilized by contact with the Lord. This means that the Lord is also all-pervading like the sun, and as such the word *pratyak* is used in this verse. Nothing is excluded from the existence of the Lord's potential expansions. The Lord is within everything, and He is all-covering also, without being disturbed by the activities of the individual souls. He is therefore infinite, and the living entities are infinitesimal. In the *Vedas* it is said that only the Lord alone exists, and all others' existences depend on Him. He is the generating reservoir for everyone's existential capacity; He is the Supreme Truth of all other categorical truths. He is the source of everyone's opulence, and therefore no one can equal Him in opulence. Being full of all opulences, namely wealth, fame, strength, beauty, knowledge and renunciation, certainly He is the Supreme Person. And because He is a person, He has many personal qualities, although He is transcendental to the material modes. We have already discussed the statement, *itthaṁ-bhūta-guṇo hariḥ* (*Bhāg.* 1.7.10). His transcendental qualities are so attractive that even the liberated souls (*ātmārāmas*) are also attracted by them. Although possessed of all personal qualities, He is nevertheless omnipotent. Therefore, personally He has nothing to do, for everything is being carried out by His omnipotent energies. This is confirmed by the Vedic *mantras: parāsya śaktir vividhaiva śrūyate svābhāvikī jñāna-bala-kriyā ca.* This suggests His specific spiritual form, which can never be experienced by the material senses. He can be seen only when the senses are purified by devotional service (*yam evaiṣa vṛṇute tena labhyaḥ*). As such, there are basic differences between the Lord and the living entities, in so many respects. No one can be compared to the Lord, as the *Vedas* declare (*ekam evādvitīyaṁ brahma, dvaitād vai bhayaṁ bhavati*). The Lord has no competitor, and He has nothing to fear from any other being, nor can anyone be equal to Him. Although He is the root of all other beings, there are basic differences between Him and other beings. Otherwise there would have been no necessity for the statement in the previous verse that no one can know Him one hundred percent as He is (*na yaṁ vidanti tattvena*). That no one can fully understand Him is explained also in this verse, but the qualification for understanding to some degree is mentioned here. Only the *praśāntas*, or the unalloyed devotees of the Lord, can know Him to a greater extent. The reason is that the devotees have no demands in their lives but to be obedient servants of the Lord, while all others, namely the empiric philosophers, the mystics and the fruitive workers, all basically have some demand, and as such they cannot be pacified. The fruitive worker wants reward for his work, the mystic wants some perfection of life, and the empiric philosopher wants to merge in the existence of the Lord. Somehow or other, as long as there is a demand for sense satisfaction, there is no chance for pacification; on the contrary, by unnecessary dry speculative arguments, the whole matter becomes distorted, and thus the Lord moves still further away from our understanding. The dry speculators, however, because of their following the principles of austerity and penance, can have knowledge of the impersonal features of the Lord to some extent, but there is no chance of their understanding His ultimate form as Govinda because only the *amalātmanas*, or the completely sinless persons, can accept pure devotional service to the Lord, as confirmed in the *Bhagavad-gītā* (7.28):

yeṣāṁ tv anta-gataṁ pāpaṁ
janānāṁ puṇya-karmaṇām
te dvandva-moha-nirmuktā
bhajante māṁ dṛḍha-vratāḥ

TEXT 42

आद्योऽवतारः पुरुषः परस्य
कालः स्वभावः सदसन्मनश्च ।
द्रव्यं विकारो गुण इन्द्रियाणि
विराट् स्वराट् स्थास्नु चरिष्णु भूम्नः ॥४२॥

ādyo 'vatāraḥ puruṣaḥ parasya
kālaḥ svabhāvaḥ sad-asan-manaś ca
dravyaṁ vikāro guṇa indriyāṇi
virāṭ svarāṭ sthāsnu cariṣṇu bhūmnaḥ

ādyaḥ—first; *avatāraḥ*—incarnation; *puruṣaḥ*—Kāraṇārṇavaśāyī Viṣṇu; *parasya*—of the Lord; *kālaḥ*—time; *svabhāvaḥ*—space; *sat*—result; *asat*—cause; *manaḥ*—mind; *ca*—also; *dravyam*—elements; *vikāraḥ*—material ego; *guṇaḥ*—modes of nature; *indriyāṇi*—senses; *virāṭ*—the complete whole body; *svarāṭ*—Garbhodakaśāyī Viṣṇu; *sthāsnu*—immovable; *cariṣṇu*—movable; *bhūmnaḥ*—of the Supreme Lord.

TRANSLATION

Kāraṇārṇavaśāyī Viṣṇu is the first incarnation of the Supreme Lord, and He is the master of eternal time, space, cause and effects, mind, the elements, the material ego, the modes of nature, the senses, the universal form of the Lord, Garbhodakaśāyī Viṣṇu, and the sum total of all living beings, both moving and nonmoving.

PURPORT

That the material creation is not permanent has been discussed many times hereinbefore. The material creation is but a temporary exhibition of the material energy of the Almighty God. This material manifestation is necessary to give a chance to the conditioned souls who are unwilling to associate with the Lord in the relationship of loving transcendental service. Such unwilling conditioned souls are not allowed to enter into the liberated life of spiritual existence because at heart they are not willing to serve. Instead, they want to enjoy themselves as imitation Gods.

The living entities are constitutionally eternal servitors of the Lord, but some of them, because of misusing their independence, do not wish to serve; therefore they are allowed to enjoy the material nature, which is called *māyā*, or illusion. It is called illusion because the living beings under the clutches of *māyā* are not factually enjoyers, although they think that they are, being illusioned by *māyā*. Such illusioned living entities are given a chance at intervals to rectify their perverted mentality of becoming false masters of the material nature, and they are imparted lessons from the *Vedas* about their eternal relationship with the Supreme Lord Kṛṣṇa (*vedaiś ca sarvair aham eva vedyaḥ*). So the temporary creation of the material manifestation is an exhibition of the material energy of the Lord, and to manage the whole show the Supreme Lord incarnates Himself as the Kāraṇārṇavaśāyī Viṣṇu just as a magistrate is deputed by the government to manage affairs temporarily. This Kāraṇodakaśāyī Viṣṇu causes the manifestation of material creation by looking over His material energy (*sa aikṣata*). In the first volume of this book we have already discussed to some extent the explanation of the verse *jagṛhe pauruṣaṁ rūpam*. The duration of the illusory play of material creation is called a *kalpa*, and we have already discussed the creation's taking place in *kalpa* after *kalpa*. By His incarnation and potential activities, the complete ingredients of creation, namely time, space, cause, result, mind, the gross and subtle elements and their interactional modes of nature—goodness, passion and ignorance—and then the senses and their reservoir source, the gigantic universal form as the second incarnation Garbhodakaśāyī Viṣṇu, and all living beings, both moving and standing, which come out of the second incarnation, all became manifested. Ultimately, all these creative elements and the creation itself are but potential manifestations of the Supreme Lord; nothing is independent of the control of the Supreme Being. This first incarnation in the material creation, namely Kāraṇārṇavaśāyī Viṣṇu, is the plenary part of the original Personality of Godhead, Śrī Kṛṣṇa, described in the *Brahma-saṁhitā* (5.48) as follows:

yasyaika-niśvasita-kālam athāvalambya
jīvanti loma-vilajā jagad-aṇḍa-nāthāḥ
viṣṇur mahān sa iha yasya kalā-viśeṣo
govindam ādi-puruṣaṁ tam ahaṁ bhajāmi

All the innumerable universes are maintained only during the breathing period of Mahā-Viṣṇu, or Kāraṇārṇavaśāyī Viṣṇu, who is only a plenary part of Govinda, the original Personality of Godhead Lord Kṛṣṇa.

TEXTS 43–45

अहं भवो यज्ञ इमे प्रजेशा
दक्षादयो ये भवदादयश्च ।
स्वर्लोकपालाः खगलोकपाला
नृलोकपालास्तललोकपालाः ॥४३॥
गन्धर्वविद्याधरचारणेशा
ये यक्षरक्षोरगनागनाथाः ।
ये वा ऋषीणामृषभाः पितॄणां
दैत्येन्द्रसिद्धेश्वरदानवेन्द्राः ।
अन्ये च ये प्रेतपिशाचभूत-
कूष्माण्डयादोमृगपक्ष्यधीशाः ॥४४॥
यत्किंच लोके भगवन्महस्व-
दोजःसहस्वद् बलवत् क्षमावत् ।
श्रीह्रीविभूत्यात्मवदद्भुतार्णं
तत्त्वं परं रूपवदस्वरूपम् ॥४५॥

ahaṁ bhavo yajña ime prajeśā
dakṣādayo ye bhavad-ādayaś ca
svarloka-pālāḥ khagaloka-pālā
nṛloka-pālās talaloka-pālāḥ

gandharva-vidyādhara-cāraṇeśā
ye yakṣa-rakṣoraga-nāga-nāthāḥ
ye vā ṛṣīṇām ṛṣabhāḥ pitṝṇāṁ
daityendra-siddheśvara-dānavendrāḥ
anye ca ye preta-piśāca-bhūta-
kūṣmāṇḍa-yādo-mṛga-pakṣy-adhīśāḥ

yat kiñca loke bhagavan mahasvad
ojaḥ-sahasvad balavat kṣamāvat
śrī-hrī-vibhūty-ātmavad adbhutārṇaṁ
tattvaṁ paraṁ rūpavad asva-rūpam

aham—myself (Brahmājī); *bhavaḥ*—Lord Śiva; *yajñaḥ*—Lord Viṣṇu; *ime*—all these; *prajā-īśāḥ*—the father of the living beings; *dakṣa-ādayaḥ*—Dakṣa, Marīci, Manu, etc.; *ye*—those; *bhavat*—yourself; *ādayaḥ ca*—and the bachelors (Sanat-kumāra and his brothers); *svarloka-pālāḥ*—the leaders of the heavenly planets; *khagaloka-pālāḥ*—the leaders of space travelers; *nṛloka-pālāḥ*—the leaders of mankind; *talaloka-pālāḥ*—the leaders of the lower planets; *gandharva*—the residents of Gandharvaloka; *vidyādhara*—the residents of the Vidyādhara planet; *cāraṇa-īśāḥ*—the leaders of the Cāraṇas; *ye*—as also others; *yakṣa*—the leaders of the Yakṣas; *rakṣa*—demons; *uraga*—snakes; *nāga-nāthāḥ*—the leaders of Nāgaloka (below the earth); *ye*—others; *vā*—also; *ṛṣīṇām*—of the sages; *ṛṣabhāḥ*—the chief; *pitṝṇām*—of the forefathers; *daitya-indra*—leaders of the atheists; *siddha-īśvara*—leaders of the Siddhaloka planets (spacemen); *dānava-indrāḥ*—leaders of the non-Āryans; *anye*—besides them; *ca*—also; *ye*—those; *preta*—dead bodies; *piśāca*—evil spirits; *bhūta*—jinn; *kūṣmāṇḍa*—a special type of evil spirit; *yādaḥ*—aquatics; *mṛga*—animals; *pakṣi-adhīśāḥ*—giant eagles; *yat*—anything; *kim ca*—and everything; *loke*—in the world; *bhagavat*—possessed of *bhaga*, or extraordinary power; *mahasvat*—of a special degree; *ojaḥ-sahasvat*—specific mental and sensual dexterity; *balavat*—possessed of strength; *kṣamāvat*—possessed of forgiveness; *śrī*—beauty; *hrī*—ashamed of impious acts; *vibhūti*—riches; *ātmavat*—possessed of intelligence; *adbhuta*—wonderful; *arṇam*—race; *tattvam*—specific truth; *param*—transcendental; *rūpavat*—as if the form of; *asva-rūpam*—not the form of the Lord.

TRANSLATION

I myself [Brahmā], Lord Śiva, Lord Viṣṇu, great generators of living beings like Dakṣa and Prajāpati, yourselves [Nārada and the Kumāras], heavenly demigods like Indra and Candra, the leaders

of the Bhūrloka planets, the leaders of the earthly planets, the leaders of the lower planets, the leaders of the Gandharva planets, the leaders of the Vidyādhara planets, the leaders of the Cāraṇaloka planets, the leaders of the Yakṣas, Rakṣas and Uragas, the great sages, the great demons, the great atheists and the great spacemen, as well as the dead bodies, evil spirits, satans, jinn, kūṣmāṇḍas, great aquatics, great beasts and great birds, etc.—in other words, anything and everything which is exceptionally possessed of power, opulence, mental and perceptual dexterity, strength, forgiveness, beauty, modesty, opulence, and breeding, whether in form or formless—may appear to be the specific truth and the form of the Lord, but actually they are not so. They are only a fragment of the transcendental potency of the Lord.

PURPORT

Those in the list given above, beginning from the name Brahmājī, the first living creature within the universe, down to Lord Śiva, Lord Viṣṇu, Nārada and other powerful demigods, men, supermen, sages, *ṛṣis,* and other lower creatures of extraordinary strength and opulence, including the dead bodies, satans, evil spirits, jinn, aquatics, birds and beasts, may appear to be the Supreme Lord, but factually none of them is the Supreme Lord; every one of them possesses only a fragment of the great potencies of the Supreme Lord. The less intelligent man is surprised to see the wonderful actions of material phenomena, as the aborigines are fearful of a great thunderbolt, a great and gigantic banyan tree, or a great lofty mountain in the jungle. For such undeveloped human beings, merely the slight display of the Lord's potency is captivating. A still more advanced person is captivated by the powers of the demigods and goddesses. Therefore, those who are simply astonished by the powers of anything in the creation of the Lord, without any factual information of the Lord Himself, are known as *śaktas,* or worshipers of the great powers. The modern scientist is also captivated by the wonderful actions and reactions of natural phenomena and therefore is also a *śakta.* These lower-grade persons gradually rise to become *saurīyas* (worshipers of the sun-god) or *gāṇapatyas* (worshipers of the mass of people as *janatā-janārdana* or *daridra-nārāyaṇa,* etc., in the form of Gaṇapati) and then rise to the platform of worshiping Lord Śiva in search for the ever-existing soul, and then to the stage of worshiping Lord Viṣṇu, the Supersoul, etc., without any information of Govinda, Lord Kṛṣṇa, who is the original Lord Viṣṇu. In other ways some are worshipers of race, nationality, birds, beasts, evil spirits, satans, etc. The general worship of Śanideva, the lord of distressful condition, and Sītalādevī, the goddess of smallpox, is also common to the mass of people, and there are many foolish men who worship the mass of people or the poor class of men. So different persons, societies and communities, etc., worship some of the potent manifestations of the Lord, wrongly accepting the powerful object as God. But in this verse it is advised by Brahmājī that none of them is the Supreme Lord; they are only borrowed plumes from the original Almighty Lord Śrī Kṛṣṇa. When the Lord advises in *Bhagavad-gītā* to worship Him alone, it is to be understood that worshiping Lord Kṛṣṇa includes worshiping all that is mentioned, because He, Lord Kṛṣṇa, includes everyone.

When the Lord is described as formless in the Vedic literatures, it is to be understood that all these forms mentioned above, within the experience of universal knowledge, are different exhibitions of the Lord's transcendental potencies only, and none of them factually represents the transcendental form of the Lord. But when the Lord actually descends on the earth or anywhere within the universe, the less intelligent class of men also mistake Him to be one of them, and thus they imagine the Transcendence to be formless or impersonal. Factually, the Lord is not formless, nor does He belong to any of the multiforms experienced within the universal forms. One should try to know the truth about the Lord by following the instruction of Brahmājī.

TEXT 46

प्राधान्यतो यानृष आमनन्ति
लीलावतारान् पुरुषस्य भूम्नः ।
आपीयतां कर्णकषायशोषा-
ननुक्रमिष्ये त इमान् सुपेशान् ॥४६॥

prādhānyato yān ṛṣa āmananti
līlāvatārān puruṣasya bhūmnaḥ

āpīyatāṁ karṇa-kaṣāya-śoṣān
anukramiṣye ta imān supeśān

prādhānyataḥ—chiefly; *yān*—all those; *ṛṣe*—O Nārada; *āmananti*—worship; *līlā*—pastimes; *avatārān*—incarnations; *puruṣasya*—of the Personality of Godhead; *bhūmnaḥ*—the Supreme; *āpīyatām*—in order to be relished by you; *karṇa*—ears; *kaṣāya*—foul matter; *śoṣān*—that which evaporates; *anukramiṣye*—shall state one after another; *te*—they; *imān*—as they are in my heart; *su-peśān*—all pleasing to hear.

TRANSLATION

O Nārada, now I shall state, one after another, the transcendental incarnations of the Lord known as līlā-avatāras. Hearing of their activities counteracts all foul matters accumulated in the ear. These pastimes are pleasing to hear and are to be relished. Therefore they are in my heart.

PURPORT

As it was said in the beginning of *Śrīmad-Bhāgavatam* (1.5.8), one cannot be fully satisfied by hearing unless and until one is given a chance to hear of the transcendental activities of the Lord. So Brahmājī is also trying, in this verse, to stress the importance of narrating the transcendental pastimes of the Lord as He comes and manifests Himself here on the surface of the material planets. Every living entity has a tendency to hear pleasing messages, and as such almost every one of us is inclined to hear news and talks broadcast by the radio stations. But the difficulty is that no one is satisfied at heart by hearing all those messages. The cause of such dissatisfaction is the imcompatibility of the message with the innermost stratum of the living soul. This transcendental literature is especially prepared by Śrīla Vyāsadeva to give the utmost satisfaction to the people in general by narration of the activities of the Lord, as instructed by Śrī Nārada Muni to Śrīla Vyāsadeva. Such activities of the Lord are principally of two varieties. One concerns the mundane manifestation of the material creative force, and the other deals with His pastimes in the form of different incarnations in terms of the time and place. There are innumerable incarnations of the Lord, like the waves of the river flowing constantly in and out. Less intelligent persons take more interest in the creative forces of the Lord in the material world, and, being disconnected from their relationship with the Lord, they put forward many theories of the creation in the name of scientific research. The devotees of the Lord, however, know well how the creative forces work concurrently by the action and reaction of the material energy of the Lord. Therefore they take more interest in the transcendental activities of the Lord as He incarnates Himself on the surface of the material world. *Śrīmad-Bhāgavatam* is the history of such activities of the Lord, and people who take interest in hearing *Śrīmad-Bhāgavatam* clear their hearts of accumulated mundane filth. There are a thousand and one rash literatures on the market, but one who has taken interest in the *Śrīmad-Bhāgavatam* loses all interest in such filthy literatures. Śrī Brahmājī is thus attempting to narrate the principal incarnations of the Lord so that they may be drunk by Nārada as transcendental nectar.

Thus end the Bhaktivedanta purports of the Second Canto, Sixth Chapter, of the Śrīmad-Bhāgavatam, *entitled* "Puruṣa-sūkta *Confirmed.*"

CHAPTER SEVEN

Scheduled Incarnations with Specific Functions

TEXT 1

ब्रह्मोवाच
यत्रोद्यतः क्षितितलोद्धरणाय बिभ्रत्
क्रौडीं तनुं सकलयज्ञमयीमनन्तः ।
अन्तर्महार्णव उपागतमादिदैत्यं
तं दंष्ट्रयाद्रिमिव वज्रधरो ददार ॥ १ ॥

brahmovāca
yatrodyataḥ kṣiti-taloddharaṇāya bibhrat
krauḍīṁ tanuṁ sakala-yajña-mayīm anantaḥ
antar-mahārṇava upāgatam ādi-daityaṁ
taṁ daṁṣṭrayādrim iva vajra-dharo dadāra

brahmā uvāca—Lord Brahmā said; *yatra*—at that time (when); *udyataḥ*—attempted; *kṣiti-tala*—the planet earth; *uddharaṇāya*—for the matter of lifting; *bibhrat*—assumed; *krauḍīm*—pastimes; *tanum*—form; *sakala*—total; *yajña-mayīm*—all-inclusive sacrifices; *anantaḥ*—the Unlimited; *antar*—within the universe; *mahā-arṇave*—the great Garbha Ocean; *upāgatam*—having arrived at; *ādi*—the first; *daityam*—demon; *tam*—him; *daṁṣṭrayā*—by the tusk; *adrim*—the flying mountains; *iva*—like; *vajra-dharaḥ*—the controller of the thunderbolts; *dadāra*—pierced.

TRANSLATION

Lord Brahmā said: When the unlimitedly powerful Lord assumed the form of a boar as a pastime, just to lift the planet earth, which was drowned in the great ocean of the universe called the Garbhodaka, the first demon [Hiraṇyākṣa] appeared, and the Lord pierced him with His tusk.

PURPORT

Since the beginning of creation, the demons and the demigods, or the Vaiṣṇavas, are always the two classes of living beings to dominate the planets of the universes. Lord Brahmā is the first demigod, and Hiraṇyākṣa is the first demon in this universe. Only under certain conditions do the planets float as weightless balls in the air, and as soon as these conditions are disturbed, the planets may fall down in the Garbhodaka Ocean, which covers half the universe. The other half is the spherical dome within which the innumerable planetary systems exist. The floating of the planets in the weightless air is due to the inner constitution of the globes, and the modernized drilling of the earth to exploit oil from within is a sort of disturbance by the modern demons and can result in a greatly harmful reaction to the floating condition of the earth. A similar disturbance was created formerly by the demons headed by Hiraṇyākṣa (the great exploiter of the gold rush), and the earth was detached from its weightless condition and fell down into the Garbhodaka Ocean. The Lord, as maintainer of the whole creation of the material world, therefore assumed the gigantic form of a boar with a proportionate snout and picked up the earth from within the water of Garbhodaka. Śrī Jayadeva Gosvāmī, the great Vaiṣṇava poet, sang as follows:

vasati daśana-śikhare dharaṇī tava lagnā
śaśini kalaṅka-kaleva nimagnā
keśava dhṛta-śūkara-rūpa
jaya jagadīśa hare

"O Keśava! O Supreme Lord who have assumed the form of a boar! O Lord! The planet earth rested on Your tusks, and it appeared like the moon engraved with spots."

Such is the symptom of an incarnation of the Lord. The incarnation of the Lord is not the concocted idea of fanciful men who create an incarnation out of imagination. The incarnation of the Lord appears under certain extraordinary circumstances like the above-mentioned occasion, and the incarnation performs a task which is not even imaginable by the tiny brain of mankind. The modern creators of the many cheap incarnations may take note of the factual incarnation of God as the gigantic boar with a suitable snout to carry the planet earth.

When the Lord appeared to pick up the earth, the demon of the name Hiraṇyākṣa tried to create a disturbance in the methodical functions of the Lord, and therefore he was killed by being pierced by the Lord's tusk. According to Śrīla Jīva Gosvāmī, the demon Hiraṇyākṣa was killed by the hand of the Lord. Therefore his version is that after being killed by the hand of the Lord, the demon was pierced by the tusk. Śrīla Viśvanātha Cakravartī Ṭhākura confirms this version.

TEXT 2

जातो रुचेरजनयत् सुयमान् सुयज्ञ
आकूतिसूनुरमरानथ दक्षिणायाम् ।
लोकत्रयस्य महतीमहरद् यदार्तिं
स्वायम्भुवेन मनुना हरिरित्यनूक्तः ॥ २ ॥

jāto rucer ajanayat suyamān suyajña
ākūti-sūnur amarān atha dakṣiṇāyām
loka-trayasya mahatīṁ aharad yad ārtiṁ
svāyambhuvena manunā harir ity anūktaḥ

jātaḥ—was born; *ruceḥ*—of the wife of Prajāpati; *ajanayat*—gave birth; *suyamān*—headed by Suyama; *suyajñaḥ*—Suyajña; *ākūti-sūnuḥ*—of the son of Ākūti; *amarān*—the demigods; *atha*—thus; *dakṣiṇāyām*—unto the wife of the name Dakṣiṇā; *loka*—the planetary systems; *trayasya*—of the three; *mahatīm*—very great; *aharat*—diminished; *yat*—all those; *ārtim*—distresses; *svāyambhuvena*—by the Manu named Svāyambhuva; *manunā*—by the father of mankind; *hariḥ*—Hari; *iti*—thus; *anūktaḥ*—named.

TRANSLATION

The Prajāpati first begot Suyajña, in the womb of his wife Ākūti, and then Suyajña begot demigods, headed by Suyama, in the womb of his wife Dakṣiṇā. Suyajña, as the Indradeva, diminished very great miseries in the three planetary systems [upper, lower and intermediate], and because he so diminished the miseries of the universe, he was later called Hari by the great father of mankind, namely Svāyambhuva Manu.

PURPORT

In order to guard against the invention of unauthorized incarnations of God by the fanciful, less intelligent persons, the name of the father of the bona fide incarnation is also mentioned in the authorized revealed scriptures. No one, therefore, can be accepted as an incarnation of the Lord if his father's name, as well as the name of the village or place in which he appears, is not mentioned by the authorized scriptures. In the *Bhāgavata Purāṇa* the name of the Kalki incarnation, which is to take place in almost four hundred thousand years, is mentioned along with the name of His father and the name of the village in which He will appear. A sane man, therefore, does not accept any cheap edition of an incarnation without reference to the authorized scriptures.

TEXT 3

जज्ञे च कर्दमगृहे द्विज देवहूत्यां
स्त्रीभिः समं नवभिरात्मगतिं स्वमात्रे ।
ऊचे ययात्मशमलं गुणसङ्गपङ्क-
मस्मिन् विधूय कपिलस्य गतिं प्रपेदे ॥ ३ ॥

jajñe ca kardama-gṛhe dvija devahūtyāṁ
strībhiḥ samaṁ navabhir ātma-gatiṁ sva-mātre
ūce yayātma-śamalaṁ guṇa-saṅga-paṅkam
asmin vidhūya kapilasya gatiṁ prapede

jajñe—took birth; *ca*—also; *kardama*—the Prajāpati named Kardama; *gṛhe*—in the house of; *dvija*—O *brāhmaṇa; devahūtyām*—in the womb of Devahūti; *strībhiḥ*—by women; *samam*—accompanied by; *navabhiḥ*—by nine; *ātma-gatim*—spiritual realization; *sva-mātre*—unto His own mother; *ūce*—uttered; *yayā*—by which; *ātma-śamalam*—coverings of the spirit soul; *guṇa-saṅga*—associated with the modes of nature; *paṅkam*—mud; *asmin*—this very life; *vidhūya*—being washed off; *kapilasya*—of Lord Kapila; *gatim*—liberation; *prapede*—achieved.

TRANSLATION

The Lord then appeared as the Kapila incarnation, being the son of the prajāpati brāhmaṇa Kardama and his wife, Devahūti, along with nine other women [sisters]. He spoke to His mother about self-realization, by which, in that very lifetime, she became fully cleansed of the mud of the material modes and thereby achieved liberation, the path of Kapila.

PURPORT

The instructions of Lord Kapila to His mother Devahūti are fully described in the Third Canto (Chapters 25–32) of the *Śrīmad-Bhāgavatam*, and anyone who follows the instructions can achieve the same liberation obtained by Devahūti. The Lord spoke *Bhagavad-gītā*, and thereby Arjuna achieved self-realization, and even today anyone who follows the path of Arjuna can also attain the same benefit as Śrī Arjuna. The scriptures are meant for this purpose. Foolish, unintelligent persons make their own interpretations by imagination and thus mislead their followers, causing them to remain in the dungeon of material existence. However, simply by following the instructions imparted by Lord Kṛṣṇa or Lord Kapila, one can obtain the highest benefit, even today.

The word *ātma-gatim* is significant in the sense of perfect knowledge of the Supreme. One should not be satisfied simply by knowing the qualitative equality of the Lord and the living being. One should know the Lord as much as can be known by our limited knowledge. It is impossible for the Lord to be known perfectly as He is, even by such liberated persons as Śiva or Brahmā, so what to speak of other demigods or men in this world. Still, by following the principles of the great devotees and the instructions available in the scriptures, one can know to a considerable extent the features of the Lord. His Lordship Kapila, the incarnation of the Lord, instructed His mother fully about the personal form of the Lord, and thereby she realized the personal form of the Lord and was able to achieve a place in the Vaikuṇṭhaloka where Lord Kapila predominates. Every incarnation of the Lord has His own abode in the spiritual sky. Therefore Lord Kapila also has His separate Vaikuṇṭha planet. The spiritual sky is not void. There are innumerable Vaikuṇṭha planets, and in each of them the Lord, by His innumerable expansions, predominates, and the pure devotees who are there also live in the same style as the Lord and His eternal associates.

When the Lord descends personally or by His personal plenary expansions, such incarnations are called *aṁśa*, *kalā*, *guṇa*, *yuga* and *manvantara* incarnations, and when the Lord's associates descend by the order of the Lord, such incarnations are called *śaktyāveśa* incarnations. But in all cases all the incarnations are supported by the invulnerable statements of the authorized scriptures, and not by any imagination of some self-interested propagandist. Such incarnations of the Lord, in either of the above categories, always declare the Supreme Personality of Godhead to be the ultimate truth. The impersonal conception of the supreme truth is just a process of negation of the form of the Lord from the mundane conception of the supreme truth.

The living entities, by their very constitution, are spiritually as good as the Lord, and the only difference between them is that the Lord is always supreme and pure, without contamination by the modes of material nature, whereas the living entities are apt to be contaminated by association with the material modes of goodness, passion and ignorance. This contamination by the material modes can be washed off completely by knowledge, renunciation and devotional service. Devotional service to the Lord is the ultimate issue, and therefore those who are directly engaged in the devotional service of the Lord not only acquire the necessary knowledge in spiritual science, but also attain detachment from material connection and are thus promoted to the kingdom of God by complete liberation, as stated in the *Bhagavad-gītā* (14.26):

māṁ ca yo 'vyabhicāreṇa
bhakti-yogena sevate
sa guṇān samatītyaitān
brahma-bhūyāya kalpate

Even in the nonliberated stage, a living entity can be directly engaged in the transcendental loving service of the Personality of Godhead Lord Kṛṣṇa or His plenary expansions like Rāma and Narasiṁha. Thus, with the proportionate improvement of such transcendental devotional service, the devotee makes definite progress toward *brahma-gatim* or *ātma-*

gatim, and ultimately attains *kapilasya gatim*, or the abode of the Lord, without difficulty. The antiseptic potency of devotional service to the Lord is so great that it can neutralize the material infection even in the present life of a devotee. A devotee does not need to wait for his next birth for complete liberation.

TEXT 4

अत्रेरपत्यमभिकाङ्क्षत आह तुष्टो
दत्तो मयाहमिति यद् भगवान् स दत्तः ।
यत्पादपङ्कजपरागपवित्रदेहा
योगर्द्धिमापुरुभयीं यदुहैहयाद्याः ॥ ४ ॥

atrer apatyam abhikāṅkṣata āha tuṣṭo
datto mayāham iti yad bhagavān sa dattaḥ
yat-pāda-paṅkaja-parāga-pavitra-dehā
yogarddhim āpur ubhayīṁ yadu-haihayādyāḥ

atreḥ—of the sage Atri; *apatyam*—issue; *abhikāṅkṣataḥ*—having prayed for; *āha*—said it; *tuṣṭaḥ*—being satisfied; *dattaḥ*—given over; *mayā*—by me; *aham*—myself; *iti*—thus; *yat*—because; *bhagavān*—the Personality of Godhead; *saḥ*—He; *dattaḥ*—Dattātreya; *yat-pāda*—one whose feet; *paṅkaja*—lotus; *parāga*—dust; *pavitra*—purified; *dehāḥ*—body; *yoga*—mystic; *ṛddhim*—opulence; *āpuḥ*—got; *ubhayīm*—for both the worlds; *yadu*—the father of the Yadu dynasty; *haihaya-ādyāḥ*—and others, like King Haihaya.

TRANSLATION

The great sage Atri prayed for offspring, and the Lord, being satisfied with him, promised to incarnate as Atri's son, Dattātreya [Datta, the son of Atri]. And by the grace of the lotus feet of the Lord, many Yadus, Haihayas, etc., became so purified that they obtained both material and spiritual blessings.

PURPORT

Transcendental relations between the Personality of Godhead and the living entities are eternally established in five different affectionate humors, which are known as *śānta*, *dāsya*, *sakhya*, *vātsalya* and *mādhurya.* The sage Atri was related with the Lord in the affectionate *vātsalya* humor, and therefore, as a result of his devotional perfection, he was inclined to have the Personality of Godhead as his son. The Lord accepted his prayer, and He gave Himself as the son of Atri. Such a relation of sonhood between the Lord and His pure devotees can be cited in many instances. And because the Lord is unlimited, He has an unlimited number of father-devotees. Factually the Lord is the father of all living entities, but out of transcendental affection and love between the Lord and His devotees, the Lord takes more pleasure in becoming the son of a devotee than in becoming one's father. The father actually serves the son, whereas the son only demands all sorts of services from the father; therefore a pure devotee who is always inclined to serve the Lord wants Him as the son, and not as the father. The Lord also accepts such service from the devotee, and thus the devotee becomes more than the Lord. The impersonalists desire to become one with the Supreme, but the devotee becomes more than the Lord, surpassing the desire of the greatest monist. Parents and other relatives of the Lord achieve all mystic opulences automatically because of their intimate relationship with the Lord. Such opulences include all details of material enjoyment, salvation and mystic powers. Therefore, the devotee of the Lord does not seek them separately, wasting his valuable time in life. The valuable time of one's life must therefore be fully engaged in the transcendental loving service of the Lord. Then other desirable achievements are automatically gained. But even after obtaining such achievements, one should be on guard against the pitfall of offenses at the feet of the devotees. The vivid example is Haihaya, who achieved all such perfection in devotional service but, because of his offense at the feet of a devotee, was killed by Lord Paraśurāma. The Lord became the son of the great sage Atri and became known as Dattātreya.

TEXT 5

तप्तं तपो विविधलोकसिसृक्षया मे
आदौ सनात् स्वतपसः स चतुःसनोऽभूत्।
प्राक्कल्पसम्प्लवविनष्टमिहात्मतत्त्वं
सम्यग् जगाद मुनयो यदचक्षतात्मन् ॥५॥

taptaṁ tapo vividha-loka-sisṛkṣayā me
ādau sanāt sva-tapasaḥ sa catuḥ-sano 'bhūt
prāk-kalpa-samplava-vinaṣṭam ihātma-tattvaṁ
samyag jagāda munayo yad acakṣatātman

taptam—having undergone austerities; *tapaḥ*—penance; *vividha-loka*—different planetary systems; *sisṛkṣayā*—desiring to create; *me*—of mine; *ādau*—at first; *sanāt*—from the Personality of Godhead; *sva-tapasaḥ*—by dint of my own penances; *saḥ*—He (the Lord); *catuḥ-sanaḥ*—the four bachelors named Sanat-kumāra, Sanaka, Sanandana and Sanātana; *abhūt*—appeared; *prāk*—previous; *kalpa*—creation; *samplava*—in the inundation; *vinaṣṭam*—devastated; *iha*—in this material world; *ātma*—the spirit; *tattvam*—truth; *samyak*—in complete; *jagāda*—became manifested; *munayaḥ*—sages; *yat*—that which; *acakṣata*—saw clearly; *ātman*—the spirit.

TRANSLATION

To create different planetary systems I had to undergo austerities and penance, and the Lord, thus being pleased with me, incarnated in four sanas [Sanaka, Sanatkumāra, Sanandana and Sanātana]. In the previous creation the spiritual truth was devastated, but the four sanas explained it so nicely that the truth at once became clearly perceived by the sages.

PURPORT

The *Viṣṇu-sahasra-nāma* prayers mention the Lord's name as *sanāt* and *sanātanatama.* The Lord and the living entities are both qualitatively *sanātana*, or eternal, but the Lord is *sanātana-tama* or the eternal in the superlative degree. The living entities are positively *sanātana,* but not superlatively, because the living entities are apt to fall to the atmosphere of noneternity. Therefore, the living entities are quantitatively different from the superlative *sanātana,* the Lord.

The word *san* is also used in the sense of charity; therefore when everything is given up in charity unto the Lord, the Lord reciprocates by giving Himself unto the devotee. This is also confirmed in the *Bhagavad-gītā* (4.11): *ye yathā māṁ prapadyante.* Brahmājī wanted to create the whole cosmic situation as it was in the previous millennium, and because, in the last devastation, knowledge of the Absolute Truth was altogether erased from the universe, he desired that the same knowledge again be renovated; otherwise there would be no meaning in the creation. Because transcendental knowledge is a prime necessity, the ever-conditioned souls are given a chance for liberation in every millennium of creation. This mission of Brahmājī was fulfilled by the grace of the Lord when the four *sanas*, namely Sanaka, Sanatkumāra, Sanandana and Sanātana, appeared as his four sons. These four *sanas* were incarnations of the knowledge of the Supreme Lord, and as such they explained transcendental knowledge so explicitly that all the sages could at once assimilate this knowledge without the least difficulty. By following in the footsteps of the four Kumāras, one can at once see the Supreme Personality of Godhead within oneself.

TEXT 6

धर्मस्य दक्षदुहितर्यजनिष्ट मूर्त्यां
नारायणो नर इति स्वतपःप्रभावः ।
दृष्ट्वात्मनो भगवतो नियमावलोपं
देव्यस्त्वनङ्गपृतना घटितुं न शेकुः ॥ ६ ॥

dharmasya dakṣa-duhitary ajaniṣṭa mūrtyāṁ
nārāyaṇo nara iti sva-tapaḥ-prabhāvaḥ
dṛṣṭvātmano bhagavato niyamāvalopaṁ
devyas tv anaṅga-pṛtanā ghaṭituṁ na śekuḥ

dharmasya—of Dharma (the controller of religious principles); *dakṣa*—Dakṣa, one of the Prajāpatis; *duhitari*—unto the daughter; *ajaniṣṭa*—took birth; *mūrtyām*—of the name Mūrti; *nārāyaṇaḥ*—Nārāyaṇa; *naraḥ*—Nara; *iti*—thus; *sva-tapaḥ*—personal penances; *prabhāvaḥ*—strength; *dṛṣṭvā*—by seeing; *ātmanaḥ*—of His own; *bhagavataḥ*—of the Personality of Godhead; *niyama-avalopam*—breaking the vow; *devyaḥ*—celestial beauties; *tu*—but; *anaṅga-pṛtanāḥ*—companion of Cupid; *ghaṭitum*—to happen; *na*—never; *śekuḥ*—made possible.

TRANSLATION

To exhibit His personal way of austerity and penance, He appeared in twin forms as Nārāyaṇa and Nara in the womb of Mūrti, the wife of Dharma and the daughter of Dakṣa. Celestial beauties, the companions of Cupid, went to try to break His vows, but they were unsuccessful, for they saw that many beauties like them were emanating from Him, the Personality of Godhead.

PURPORT

The Lord, being the source of everything that be, is the origin of all austerities and penances also. Great vows of austerity are undertaken by sages to achieve success in self-realization. Human life is meant for such *tapasya,* with the great vow of celibacy, or *brahmacarya. In the rigid life of* tapasya, *there is no place for the association of women.* And because human life is meant for *tapasya,* for self-realization, factual human civilization, as conceived by the system of *sanātana-dharma* or the school of four castes and four orders of life, prescribes rigid dissociation from woman in three stages of life. In the order of gradual cultural development, one's life may be divided into four divisions: celibacy, household life, retirement, and renunciation. During the first stage of life, up to twenty-five years of age, a man may be trained as a *brahmacārī* under the guidance of a bona fide spiritual master just to understand that woman is the real binding force in material existence. If one wants to get freedom from the material bondage of conditional life, he must get free from the attraction for the form of woman. Woman, or the fair sex, is the enchanting principle for the living entities, and the male form, especially in the human being, is meant for self-realization. The whole world is moving under the spell of womanly attraction, and as soon as a man becomes united with a woman, he at once becomes a victim of material bondage under a tight knot. The desires for lording it over the material world, under the intoxication of a false sense of lordship, specifically begin just after the man's unification with a woman. The desires for acquiring a house, possessing land, having children and becoming prominent in society, the affection for community and the place of birth, and the hankering for wealth, which are all like phantasmagoria or illusory dreams, encumber a human being, and he is thus impeded in his progress toward self-realization, the real aim of life. The *brahmacārī*, or a boy from the age of five years, especially from the higher castes, namely from the scholarly parents (the *brāhmaṇas)*, the administrative parents (the *kṣatriyas)*, or the mercantile or productive parents (the *vaiśyas)*, is trained until twenty-five years of age under the care of a bona fide *guru* or teacher, and under strict observance of discipline he comes to understand the values of life along with taking specific training for a livelihood. The *brahmacārī* is then allowed to go home and enter householder life and get married to a suitable woman. But there are many *brahmacārīs* who do not go home to become householders but continue the life of *naiṣṭhika-brahmacārīs*, without any connection with women. They accept the order of *sannyāsa*, or the renounced order of life, knowing well that combination with women is an unnecessary burden that checks self-realization. Since sex desire is very strong at a certain stage of life, the *guru* may allow the *brahmacārī* to marry; this license is given to a *brahmacārī* who is unable to continue the way of *naiṣṭhika-brahmacarya*, and such discriminations are possible for the bona fide *guru*. A program of so-called family planning is needed. The householder who associates with woman under scriptural restrictions, after a thorough training of *brahmacarya*, cannot be a householder like cats and dogs. Such a householder, after fifty years of age, would retire from the association of woman as a *vānaprastha* to be trained to live alone without the association of woman. When the practice is complete, the same retired householder becomes a *sannyāsī*, strictly separate from woman, even from his married wife. Studying the whole scheme of disassociation from women, it appears that a woman is a stumbling block for self-realization, and the Lord appeared as Nārāyaṇa to teach the principle of womanly disassociation with a vow in life. The demigods, being envious of the austere life of the rigid *brahmacārīs*, would try to cause them to break their vows by dispatching soldiers of Cupid. But in the case of the Lord, it became an unsuccessful attempt when the celestial beauties saw that the Lord can produce innumerable such beauties by His mystic internal potency and that there was consequently no need to be attracted by others externally. There is a common proverb that a confectioner is never attracted by sweetmeats. The confectioner, who is always manufacturing sweetmeats, has very little desire to eat them; similarly, the Lord, by His pleasure potential powers, can produce innumerable spiritual beauties and not be the least attracted by the false beauties of material creation. One who does not know alleges foolishly that Lord Kṛṣṇa enjoyed women in His *rāsa-līlā* in Vṛndāvana, or with His sixteen thousand married wives at Dvārakā.

TEXT 7

कामं दहन्ति कृतिनो ननु रोषदृष्ट्या
रोषं दहन्तमुत ते न दहन्त्यसह्यम् ।
सोऽयं यदन्तरमलं प्रविशन् बिभेति
कामः कथं नु पुनरस्य मनः श्रयेत ॥ ७ ॥

kāmaṁ dahanti kṛtino nanu roṣa-dṛṣṭyā
roṣaṁ dahantam uta te na dahanty asahyam
so 'yaṁ yad antaram alaṁ praviśan bibheti
kāmaḥ kathaṁ nu punar asya manaḥ śrayeta

kāmam—lust; *dahanti*—chastise; *kṛtinaḥ*—great stalwarts; *nanu*—but; *roṣa-dṛṣṭyā*—by wrathful glance; *roṣam*—wrath; *dahantam*—being overwhelmed; *uta*—although; *te*—they; *na*—cannot; *dahanti*—subjugate; *asahyam*—intolerable; *saḥ*—that; *ayam*—Him; *yat*—because; *antaram*—within; *alam*—however; *praviśan*—entering; *bibheti*—is afraid of; *kāmaḥ*—lust; *katham*—how; *nu*—as a matter of fact; *punaḥ*—again; *asya*—His; *manaḥ*—mind; *śrayeta*—take shelter of.

TRANSLATION

Great stalwarts like Lord Śiva can, by their wrathful glances, overcome lust and vanquish him, yet they cannot be free from the overwhelming effects of their own wrath. Such wrath can never enter into the heart of Him [the Lord], who is above all this. So how can lust take shelter in His mind?

PURPORT

When Lord Śiva was engaged in severely austere meditation, Cupid, the demigod of lust, threw his arrow of sex desire. Lord Śiva, thus being angry at him, glanced at Cupid in great wrath, and at once the body of Cupid was annihilated. Although Lord Śiva was so powerful, he was unable to get free from the effects of such wrath. But in the behavior of Lord Viṣṇu there is no incident of such wrath at any time. On the contrary, Bhṛgu Muni tested the tolerance of the Lord by purposely kicking His chest, but instead of being angry at Bhṛgu Muni the Lord begged his pardon, saying that Bhṛgu Muni's leg might have been badly hurt because His chest is too hard. The Lord has the sign of the foot of *bhṛgu-pāda* as the mark of tolerance. The Lord, therefore, is never affected by any kind of wrath, so how can there be any place for lust, which is less strong than wrath? When lust or desire is not fulfilled, there is the appearance of wrath, but in the absence of wrath how can there be any place for lust? The Lord is known as *āpta-kāma*, or one who can fulfill His desires by Himself. He does not require anyone's help to satisfy His desires. The Lord is unlimited, and therefore His desires are also unlimited. All living entities but the Lord are limited in every respect; how then can the limited satisfy the desires of the unlimited? The conclusion is that the Absolute Personality of Godhead has neither lust nor anger, and even if there is sometimes a show of lust and anger by the Absolute, it should be considered an absolute benediction.

TEXT 8

विद्धः सपत्न्युदितपत्रिभिरन्ति राज्ञो
बालोऽपि सन्नुपगतस्तपसे वनानि ।
तस्मा अदाद् ध्रुवगतिं गृणते प्रसन्नो
दिव्याः स्तुवन्ति मुनयो यदुपर्यधस्तात् ॥ ८ ॥

viddhaḥ sapatny-udita-patribhir anti rājño
bālo 'pi sann upagatas tapase vanāni
tasmā adād dhruva-gatiṁ gṛṇate prasanno
divyāḥ stuvanti munayo yad upary-adhastāt

viddhaḥ—pinched by; *sapatni*—a co-wife; *udita*—uttered by; *patribhiḥ*—by sharp words; *anti*—just before; *rājñaḥ*—of the king; *bālaḥ*—a boy; *api*—although; *san*—being so; *upagataḥ*—took to;

tapase—severe penances; *vanāni*—in a great forest; *tasmai*—therefore; *adāt*—gave as a reward; *dhruva-gatim*—a path to the Dhruva planet; *gṛṇate*—on being prayed for; *prasannaḥ*—being satisfied; *divyāḥ*—denizens of higher planets; *stuvanti*—do pray; *munayaḥ*—great sages; *yat*—thereupon; *upari*—up; *adhastāt*—down.

TRANSLATION

Being insulted by sharp words spoken by the co-wife of the king, even in his presence, Prince Dhruva, though only a boy, took to severe penances in the forest. And the Lord, being satisfied by his prayer, awarded him the Dhruva planet, which is worshiped by great sages, both upward and downward.

PURPORT

When he was only five years old, Prince Dhruva, a great devotee and the son of Mahārāja Uttānapāda, was sitting on the lap of his father. His stepmother did not like the King's patting her stepson, so she dragged him out, saying that he could not claim to sit on the lap of the King because he was not born out of her womb. The little boy felt insulted by this act of his stepmother. Nor did his father make any protest, for he was too attached to his second wife. After this incident, Prince Dhruva went to his own mother and complained. His real mother also could not take any step against this insulting behavior, and so she wept. The boy inquired from his mother how he could sit on the royal throne of his father, and the poor queen replied that only the Lord could help him. The boy inquired where the Lord could be seen, and the queen replied that it is said that the Lord is sometimes seen by great sages in the dense forest. The child prince decided to go into the forest to perform severe penances in order to achieve his objective.

Prince Dhruva performed a stringent type of penance under the instruction of his spiritual master, Śrī Nārada Muni, who was specifically deputed for this purpose by the Personality of Godhead. Prince Dhruva was initiated by Nārada into chanting the hymn composed of eighteen letters, namely *oṁ namo bhagavate vāsudevāya,* and Lord Vāsudeva incarnated Himself as Pṛśnigarbha, the Personality of Godhead with four hands, and awarded the prince a specific planet above the seven stars.

Prince Dhruva, after achieving success in his undertakings, saw the Lord face to face, and he was satisfied that all his needs were fulfilled.

The planet awarded to Prince Dhruva Mahārāja is a fixed Vaikuṇṭha planet, installed in the material atmosphere by the will of the Supreme Lord, Vāsudeva. This planet, although within the material world, will not be annihilated at the time of devastation, but will remain fixed in its place. And because it is a Vaikuṇṭha planet never to be annihilated, it is worshiped even by the denizens of the seven stars situated below the Dhruva planet, as well as by the planets which are even above the Dhruva planet. Maharṣi Bhṛgu's planet is situated above the Dhruva planet.

So the Lord incarnated Himself as Pṛśnigarbha just to satisfy a pure devotee of the Lord. And Prince Dhruva achieved this perfection simply by chanting the hymn mentioned above, after being initiated by another pure devotee, Nārada. A serious personality can thus achieve the highest perfection of meeting the Lord and attain his objective simply by being guided by a pure devotee, who automatically approaches by dint of one's serious determination to meet the Lord by all means.

The description of Prince Dhruva's activities can be read in detail in the Fourth Canto of *Śrīmad-Bhāgavatam.*

TEXT 9

यद्वेनमुत्पथगतं द्विजवाक्यवज्र-
निष्प्लुष्टपौरुषभगं निरये पतन्तम् ।
त्रात्वार्थितो जगति पुत्रपदं च लेभे
दुग्धा वसूनि वसुधा सकलानि येन ॥ ९ ॥

yad venam utpatha-gataṁ dvija-vākya-vajra-
niṣpluṣṭa-pauruṣa-bhagaṁ niraye patantam
trātvārthito jagati putra-padaṁ ca lebhe
dugdhā vasūni vasudhā sakalāni yena

yat—when; *venam*—unto King Vena; *utpatha-gatam*—going astray from the righteous path; *dvija*—of the *brāhmaṇas; vākya*—words of cursing; *vajra*—thunderbolt; *niṣpluṣṭa*—being burnt by; *pauruṣa*—

great deeds; *bhagam*—opulence; *niraye*—into hell; *patantam*—going down; *trātvā*—by delivering; *arthitaḥ*—so being prayed for; *jagati*—on the world; *putra-padam*—the position of the son; *ca*—as well as; *lebhe*—achieved; *dugdhā*—exploited; *vasūni*—produce; *vasudhā*—the earth; *sakalāni*—all kinds of; *yena*—by whom.

TRANSLATION

Mahārāja Vena went astray from the path of righteousness, and the brāhmaṇas chastised him by the thunderbolt curse. By this King Vena was burnt with his good deeds and opulence and was en route to hell. The Lord, by His causeless mercy, descended as his son, by the name of Pṛthu, delivered the condemned King Vena from hell, and exploited the earth by drawing all kinds of crops as produce.

PURPORT

According to the system of *varṇāśrama-dharma*, the pious and learned *brāhmaṇas* were the natural guardians of society. The *brāhmaṇas*, by their learned labor of love, would instruct the administrator-kings how to rule the country in complete righteousness, and thus the process would go on as a perfect welfare state. The kings or the *kṣatriya* administrators would always consult the council of learned *brāhmaṇas*. They were never autocratic monarchs. The scriptures like *Manu-saṁhitā* and other authorized books of the great sages were guiding principles for ruling the subjects, and there was no need for less intelligent persons to manufacture a code of law in the name of democracy. The less intelligent mass of people have very little knowledge of their own welfare, as a child has very little knowledge of its future well-being. The experienced father guides the innocent child towards the path of progress, and the childlike mass of people need similar guidance. The standard welfare codes are already there in the *Manu-saṁhitā* and other Vedic literatures. The learned *brāhmaṇas* would advise the king in terms of those standard books of knowledge and with reference to the particular situation of time and place. Such *brāhmaṇas* were not paid servants of the king, and therefore they had the strength to dictate to the king on the principles of scriptures. This system continued even up to the time of

Mahārāja Candragupta, and the *brāhmaṇa* Cāṇakya was his unpaid prime minister.

Mahārāja Vena did not adhere to this principle of ruling, and he disobeyed the learned *brāhmaṇas.* The broad-minded *brāhmaṇas* were not self-interested, but looked to the interest of complete welfare for all the subjects. They wanted to chastise King Vena for his misconduct and so prayed to the Almighty Lord as well as cursed the king.

Long life, obedience, good reputation, righteousness, prospects of being promoted to higher planets, and blessings of great personalities are all vanquished simply by disobedience to a great soul. One should strictly try to follow in the footsteps of great souls. Mahārāja Vena became a king, undoubtedly due to his past deeds of righteousness, but because he willfully neglected the great souls, he was punished by the loss of all the above-mentioned acquisitions. In the *Vāmana Purāṇa* the history of Mahārāja Vena and his degradation are fully described. When Mahārāja Pṛthu heard about the hellish condition of his father, Vena, who was suffering from leprosy in the family of a *mleccha,* he at once brought the former king to Kurukṣetra for his purification and relieved him of all sufferings.

Mahārāja Pṛthu, the incarnation of God, descended by the prayer of the *brāhmaṇas* to rectify the disorders on earth. He produced all kinds of crops. But, at the same time, he performed the duty of a son who delivers his father from hellish conditions. The word *putra* means one who delivers from hell, called *put.* That is a worthy son.

TEXT 10

नाभेरसावृषभ आस सुदेविसूनु-
र्यो वै चचार समदृग् जडयोगचर्याम् ।
यत्पारमहंस्यमृषयः पदमामनन्ति
स्वस्थः प्रशान्तकरणः परिमुक्तसङ्गः ॥१०॥

nābher asāv ṛṣabha āsa sudevi-sūnur
yo vai cacāra sama-dṛg jaḍa-yoga-caryām
yat pāramahaṁsyam ṛṣayaḥ padam āmananti
svasthaḥ praśānta-karaṇaḥ parimukta-saṅgaḥ

nābheḥ—by Mahārāja Nābhi; *asau*—the Personality of Godhead; *ṛṣabhaḥ*—Ṛṣabha; *āsa*—became; *sudevi*—Sudevī; *sūnuḥ*—the son of; *yaḥ*—who; *vai*—certainly; *cacāra*—performed; *sama-dṛk*—equibalanced; *jaḍa*—material; *yoga-caryām*—performance of *yoga; yat*—which; *pāramahaṁsyam*—the highest stage of perfection; *ṛṣayaḥ*—the learned sages; *padam*—situation; *āmananti*—do accept; *svasthaḥ*—self-reposed; *praśānta*—suspended; *karaṇaḥ*—the material senses; *parimukta*—perfectly liberated; *saṅgaḥ*—material contamination.

TRANSLATION

The Lord appeared as the son of Sudevī, the wife of King Nābhi, and was known as Ṛṣabhadeva. He performed materialistic yoga to equibalance the mind. This stage is also accepted as the highest perfectional situation of liberation, wherein one is situated in one's self and is completely satisfied.

PURPORT

Out of many types of mystic performances for self-realization, the process of *jaḍa-yoga* is also one accepted by authorities. This *jaḍa-yoga* involves practicing becoming like a dumb stone and not being affected by material reactions. Just as a stone is indifferent to all kinds of attacks and reattacks of external situations, similarly one practices *jaḍa-yoga* by tolerating voluntary infliction of pain upon the material body. Such *yogīs*, out of many self-infliction methods, practice plucking out the hairs on their heads, without shaving and without any instrumental help. But the real purpose of such *jaḍa-yoga* practice is to get free from all material affection and to be completely situated in the self. At the last stage of his life, Emperor Ṛṣabhadeva wandered like a dumb madman, unaffected by all kinds of bodily mistreatment. Seeing him like a madman, wandering naked with long hair and a long beard, less intelligent children and men in the street used to spit on him and urinate on his body. He used to lie in his own stool and never move. But the stool of his body was fragrant like the smell of fragrant flowers, and a saintly person would recognize him as a *paramahaṁsa*, one in the highest state of human perfection. One who is not able to make his stool fragrant should not, however, imitate Emperor Ṛṣabhadeva. The practice of *jaḍa-yoga* was possible for Ṛṣabhadeva and others on the same level of perfection, but such an uncommon practice is impossible for an ordinary man.

The real purpose of *jaḍa-yoga*, as mentioned here in this verse, is *praśānta-karaṇaḥ*, or subduing the senses. The whole process of *yoga*, under whatever heading it may be, is to control the unbridled material senses and thus prepare oneself for self-realization. In this age specifically, this *jaḍa-yoga* cannot be of any practical value, but on the other hand the practice of *bhakti-yoga* is feasible because it is just suitable for this age. The simple method of hearing from the right source, *Śrīmad-Bhāgavatam*, will lead one to the highest perfectional stage of *yoga*. Ṛṣabhadeva was the son of King Nābhi and the grandson of King Āgnīdhra, and he was the father of King Bharata, after whose name this planet earth was called *Bhārata-varṣa*. Ṛṣabhadeva's mother was also known as Merudevī, although her name is mentioned here as Sudevī. It is sometimes proposed that Sudevī was another wife of King Nābhi, but since King Ṛṣabhadeva is mentioned elsewhere as the son of Merudevī, it is clear that Merudevī and Sudevī are the same person under different names.

TEXT 11

सत्रे ममास भगवान् हयशीरषाथो
साक्षात् स यज्ञपुरुषस्तपनीयवर्णः ।
छन्दोमयो मखमयोऽखिलदेवतात्मा
वाचो बभूवुरुशतीः श्वसतोऽस्य नस्तः ॥११॥

satre mamāsa bhagavān haya-śīraṣātho
sākṣāt sa yajña-puruṣas tapanīya-varṇaḥ
chandomayo makhamayo 'khila-devatātmā
vāco babhūvur uśatīḥ śvasato 'sya nastaḥ

satre—in the sacrificial ceremony; *mama*—of mine; *āsa*—appeared; *bhagavān*—the Personality of Godhead; *haya-śīraṣā*—with His horselike head; *atha*—thus; *sākṣāt*—directly; *saḥ*—He; *yajña-puruṣaḥ*—the person who is pleased by performances of sacrifice; *tapanīya*—golden; *varṇaḥ*—hue; *chandaḥ-mayaḥ*—personified Vedic hymns; *makha-mayaḥ*—personified sacrifices; *akhila*—all that be; *devatā-ātmā*—the soul of the demigods; *vācaḥ*—sounds; *babhūvuḥ*—become audible; *uśatīḥ*—very pleasing to hear; *śvasataḥ*—while breathing; *asya*—His; *nastaḥ*—through the nostrils.

TRANSLATION

The Lord appeared as the Hayagrīva incarnation in a sacrifice performed by me [Brahmā]. He is the personified sacrifices, and the hue of His body is golden. He is the personified Vedas as well, and the Supersoul of all demigods. When He breathed, all the sweet sounds of the Vedic hymns came out of His nostrils.

PURPORT

The Vedic hymns are generally meant for sacrifices performed by fruitive workers who also want to satisfy the demigods to achieve their fruitive result. But the Lord is the personified sacrifices and personified Vedic hymns. Therefore one who is directly a devotee of the Lord is a person who has automatically both served the purposes of sacrifices and pleased the demigods. The devotees of the Lord may not perform any sacrifice or may not please the demigods as per Vedic injunctions, and still the devotees are on a higher level than the fruitive workers or the worshipers of different demigods.

TEXT 12

मत्स्यो युगान्तसमये मनुनोपलब्धः
क्षोणीमयो निखिलजीवनिकायकेतः।
विस्रंसितानुरुभये सलिले मुखान्मे
आदाय तत्र विजहार ह वेदमार्गान् ॥१२॥

matsyo yugānta-samaye manunopalabdhaḥ
kṣoṇīmayo nikhila-jīva-nikāya-ketaḥ
visraṁsitān uru-bhaye salile mukhān me
ādāya tatra vijahāra ha veda-mārgān

matsyaḥ—incarnation of the fish; *yuga-anta*—at the end of the millennium; *samaye*—at the time of; *manunā*—the would-be Vaivasvata Manu; *upalabdhaḥ*—seen; *kṣoṇīmayaḥ*—up to the earthly planets; *nikhila*—all; *jīva*—living entities; *nikāya-ketaḥ*—shelter for; *visraṁsitān*—emanating from; *uru*—great; *bhaye*—out of fear; *salile*—in the water; *mukhāt*—from the mouth; *me*—mine; *ādāya*—having taken to; *tatra*—there; *vijahāra*—enjoyed; *ha*—certainly; *veda-mārgān*—all the *Vedas.*

TRANSLATION

At the end of the millennium, the would-be Vaivasvata Manu, of the name Satyavrata, would see that the Lord in the fish incarnation is the shelter of all kinds of living entities, up to those in the earthly planets. Because of my fear of the vast water at the end of the millennium, the Vedas come out of my [Brahmā's] mouth, and the Lord enjoys those vast waters and protects the Vedas.

PURPORT

During one day of Brahmā there are fourteen Manus, and at the end of each Manu there is devastation up to the earthly planets, and the vast water is fearful even to Brahmā. So in the beginning of the would-be Vaivasvata Manu, such devastation would be seen by him. There would be many other incidents also, such as the killing of the famous Śaṅkhāsura. This foretelling is by the past experience of Brahmājī, who knew that in that fearful devastating scene, the *Vedas* would come out of his mouth, but the Lord in His fish incarnation not only would save all living entities, namely the demigods, animals, men and great sages, but would also save the *Vedas.*

TEXT 13

क्षीरोदधावमरदानवयूथपाना-
मुन्मथ्नताममृतलब्धय आदिदेवः ।
पृष्ठेन कच्छपवपुर्विदधार गोत्रं
निद्राक्षणोऽद्रिपरिवर्तकषाणकण्डूः ॥१३॥

kṣīrodadhāv amara-dānava-yūthapānām
unmathnatām amṛta-labdhaya ādi-devaḥ
pṛṣṭhena kacchapa-vapur vidadhāra gotraṁ
nidrākṣaṇo 'dri-parivarta-kaṣāṇa-kaṇḍūḥ

kṣīra—milk; *udadhau*—in the ocean of; *amara*—the demigods; *dānava*—the demons; *yūtha-pānām*—of the leaders of both hosts; *unmathnatām*—while churning; *amṛta*—nectar; *labdhaya*—for gaining; *ādi-devaḥ*—the primeval Lord; *pṛṣṭhena*—by the backbone; *kacchapa*—tortoise; *vapuḥ*—body; *vidadhāra*—assumed; *gotram*—the Mandara Hill; *nidrākṣaṇaḥ*—while partly sleeping; *adri-parivarta*—rolling the hill; *kaṣāṇa*—scratching; *kaṇḍūḥ*—itching.

TRANSLATION

The primeval Lord then assumed the tortoise incarnation in order to serve as a resting place [pivot] for the Mandara Mountain, which was acting as a churning rod. The demigods and demons were churning the ocean of milk with the Mandara Mountain in order to extract nectar. The mountain moved back and forth, scratching the back of Lord Tortoise, who, while partially sleeping, was experiencing an itching sensation.

PURPORT

Although it is not in our experience, there is a milk ocean within this universe. Even the modern scientist accepts that there are hundreds and hundreds of thousands of planets hovering over our heads, and each of them has different kinds of climatic conditions. *Śrīmad-Bhāgavatam* gives much information which may not tally with our present experience. But as far as Indian sages are concerned, knowledge is received from the Vedic literatures, and the authorities accept without any hesitation that we should look through the pages of authentic books of knowledge (*śāstra-cakṣurvat*). So we cannot deny the existence of the ocean of milk as stated in the *Śrīmad-Bhāgavatam* unless and until we have experimentally seen all the planets hovering in space. Since such an experiment is not possible, naturally we have to accept the statement of *Śrīmad-Bhāgavatam* as it is because it is so accepted by spiritual leaders like Śrīdhara Svāmī, Jīva Gosvāmī, Viśvanātha Cakravartī and others. The Vedic process is to follow in the footsteps of great authorities, and that is the only process for knowing that which is beyond our imagination.

The primeval Lord, being all-powerful, can do whatever He likes, and therefore His assuming the incarnation of a tortoise or a fish for serving a particular purpose is not at all astonishing. Therefore we should not have any hesitation whatsoever in accepting the statements of the authentic scriptures like *Śrīmad-Bhāgavatam.*

The gigantic work of churning the milk ocean by the combined effort of the demigods and the demons required a gigantic resting ground or pivot for the gigantic Mandara Hill. Thus to help the attempt of the demigods the primeval Lord assumed the incarnation of a gigantic tortoise, swimming in the ocean of milk. At the same time, the mountain scratched His backbone as He was partially sleeping and thus relieved His itching sensation.

TEXT 14

त्रैपिष्टपोरुभयहा स नृसिंहरूपं
कृत्वा भ्रमद्भ्रुकुटिदंष्ट्रकरालवक्त्रम् ।
दैत्येन्द्रमाशु गदयाभिपतन्तमारा-
दूरौ निपात्य विददार नखैः स्फुरन्तम्॥१४॥

trai-piṣṭaporu-bhaya-hā sa nṛsiṁha-rūpaṁ
kṛtvā bhramad-bhrukuṭi-daṁṣṭra-karāla-vaktram
daityendram āśu gadayābhipatantam ārād
ūrau nipātya vidadāra nakhaiḥ sphurantam

trai-piṣṭapa—the demigods; *uru-bhaya-hā*—one who vanquishes great fears; *saḥ*—He (the Personality of Godhead); *nṛsiṁha-rūpam*—assuming the incarnation Nṛsiṁha; *kṛtvā*—doing so; *bhramat*—by rolling; *bhru-kuṭi*—eyebrows; *daṁṣṭra*—teeth; *karāla*—greatly fearful; *vaktram*—mouth; *daitya-indram*—the king of the demons; *āśu*—immediately; *gadayā*—with club in hand; *abhipatantam*—while falling down; *ārāt*—nearby; *ūrau*—on the thighs; *nipātya*—placing on;

vidadāra—pierced; *nakhaiḥ*—by the nails; *sphurantam*—while challenging.

TRANSLATION

The Personality of Godhead assumed the incarnation of Nṛsiṁhadeva in order to vanquish the great fears of the demigods. He killed the king of the demons [Hiraṇyakaśipu], who challenged the Lord with a club in his hand, by placing the demon on His thighs and piercing him with His nails, rolling His eyebrows in anger and showing His fearful teeth and mouth.

PURPORT

The history of Hiraṇyakaśipu and his great devotee-son Prahlāda Mahārāja is narrated in the Seventh Canto of *Śrīmad-Bhāgavatam.* Hiraṇyakaśipu became very powerful by material achievements and thought himself to be immortal by the grace of Brahmājī. Brahmājī declined to award him the benediction of immortality because he himself is not an immortal being. But Hiraṇyakaśipu derived Brahmājī's benediction in a roundabout way, almost equal to becoming an immortal being. Hiraṇyakaśipu was sure that he would not be killed by any man or demigod or by any kind of known weapon, nor would he die in day or night. The Lord, however, assumed the incarnation of half-man and half-lion, which was beyond the imagination of a materialistic demon like Hiraṇyakaśipu, and thus, keeping pace with the benediction of Brahmājī, the Lord killed him. He killed him on His lap, so that he was killed neither on the land nor on the water nor in the sky. The demon was pierced by Nṛsiṁha's nails, which were beyond the human weapons imaginable by Hiraṇyakaśipu. The literal meaning of Hiraṇyakaśipu is one who is after gold and soft bedding, the ultimate aim of all materialistic men. Such demonic men, who have no relationship with God, gradually become puffed up by material acquisitions and begin to challenge the authority of the Supreme Lord and torture those who are devotees of the Lord. Prahlāda Mahārāja happened to be the son of Hiraṇyakaśipu, and because the boy was a great devotee, his father tortured him to the best of his ability. In this extreme situation, the Lord assumed the incarnation of Nṛsiṁhadeva, and just to finish the enemy of the demigods, the Lord killed Hiraṇyakaśipu in a manner beyond the demon's imagination. Materialistic plans of godless demons are always frustrated by the all-powerful Lord.

TEXT 15

अन्तःसरस्युरुबलेन पदे गृहीतो
ग्राहेण यूथपतिरम्बुजहस्त आर्तः ।
आहेदमादिपुरुषाखिललोकनाथ
तीर्थश्रवः श्रवणमङ्गलनामधेय ॥१५॥

antaḥ-sarasy uru-balena pade gṛhīto
grāheṇa yūtha-patir ambuja-hasta ārtaḥ
āhedam ādi-puruṣākhila-loka-nātha
tīrtha-śravaḥ śravaṇa-maṅgala-nāmadheya

antaḥ-sarasi—within the river; *uru-balena*—by superior strength; *pade*—leg; *gṛhītaḥ*—being taken up; *grāheṇa*—by the crocodile; *yūtha-patiḥ*—of the leader of the elephants; *ambuja-hastaḥ*—with a lotus flower in the hand; *ārtaḥ*—greatly aggrieved; *āha*—addressed; *idam*—like this; *ādi-puruṣa*—the original enjoyer; *akhila-loka-nātha*—the Lord of the universe; *tīrtha-śravaḥ*—as famous as a place of pilgrimage; *śravaṇa-maṅgala*—all good simply by hearing the name; *nāma-dheya*—whose holy name is worth chanting.

TRANSLATION

The leader of the elephants, whose leg was attacked in a river by a crocodile of superior strength, was much aggrieved. Taking a lotus flower in his trunk, he addressed the Lord, saying, "O original enjoyer, Lord of the universe! O deliverer, as famous as a place of pilgrimage! All are purified simply by hearing Your holy name, which is worthy to be chanted."

PURPORT

The history of delivering the leader of the elephants, whose leg was attacked in the river by the superior strength of a crocodile, is described in the Eighth Canto of *Śrīmad-Bhāgavatam.* Since the Lord is absolute knowledge, there is no difference between His holy name and the Personality of Godhead. The leader of the elephants was much distressed when he was attacked by the crocodile. Although the elephant is always stronger than the crocodile, the latter is stronger than the elephant when it is in the water. And because the elephant was a great devotee of the Lord in his previous birth, he was able to chant the holy name of the Lord by dint of his past good deeds. Every living entity is always distressed in this material world because this place is such that at every step one has to meet with some kind of distress. But one who is supported by his past good deeds engages himself in the devotional service of the Lord, as confirmed in the *Bhagavad-gītā* (7.16). Those who are supported by impious acts cannot be engaged in the devotional service of the Lord, even though they are distressed. This is also confirmed in the *Bhagavad-gītā* (7.15). The Personality of Godhead Hari appeared at once on the back of His eternal bearer, Garuḍa, and delivered the elephant.

The elephant was conscious of his relation with the Supreme Lord. He addressed the Lord as *ādi-puruṣa,* or the original enjoyer. Both the Lord and the living beings are conscious and are therefore enjoyers, but the Lord is the original enjoyer because He is the creator of everything. In a family, both the father and his sons are undoubtedly enjoyers but the father is the original enjoyer, and the sons are subsequent enjoyers. A pure devotee knows well that everything in the universe is the property of the Lord and that a living entity can enjoy a thing as ordained by the Lord. A living being cannot even touch a thing which is not allotted to him. This idea of the original enjoyer is explained very nicely in the *Īśopaniṣad.* One who knows this difference between the Lord and himself never accepts anything without first offering it to the Lord.

The elephant addressed the Lord as *akhila-loka-nātha,* or the Lord of the universe, who is therefore the Lord of the elephant also. The elephant, being a pure devotee of the Lord, specifically deserved to be saved from the attack of the crocodile, and because it is a promise of the Lord that His devotee will never be vanquished, it was quite befitting that the elephant called upon the Lord to protect him, and the merciful Lord also at once responded. The Lord is the protector of everyone, but He is the first protector of one who acknowledges the superiority of the Lord instead of being so falsely proud as to deny the superiority of the

Lord or to claim to be equal to Him. He is ever superior. A pure devotee of the Lord knows this difference between the Lord and himself. Therefore a pure devotee is given first preference because of his full dependence, whereas the person who denies the existence of the Lord and declares himself the Lord is called *asura,* and as such he is given protection by the strength of limited power subject to the sanction of the Lord. Since the Lord is superior to everyone, His perfection is also superior. No one can imagine it.

The elephant addressed the Lord as *tīrtha-śravaḥ,* or "as famous as a place of pilgrimage." People go to places of pilgrimage in order to be delivered from the reactions of unknown sinful acts. But one can be freed from all sinful reactions simply by remembering His holy name. The Lord is therefore as good as the holy places of pilgrimage. One can be free from all sinful reactions after reaching a place of pilgrimage, but one can have the same benefit at home or at any place simply by chanting the holy name of the Lord. For a pure devotee, there is no need to go to the holy place of pilgrimage. He can be delivered from all sinful acts simply by remembering the Lord in earnestness. A pure devotee of the Lord never commits any sinful acts, but because the whole world is full of the sinful atmosphere, even a pure devotee may commit a sin unconsciously, as a matter of course. One who commits sinful acts consciously cannot be worthy of being a devotee of the Lord, but a pure devotee who unconsciously does something sinful is certainly delivered by the Lord because a pure devotee remembers the Lord always.

The Lord's holy name is called *śravaṇa-maṅgala.* This means that one receives everything auspicious simply by hearing the holy name. In another place in *Śrīmad-Bhāgavatam,* His holy name is described as *puṇya-śravaṇa-kīrtana.* It is a pious act simply to chant and hear all about the Lord. The Lord descends on this earth and acts like others in connection with the activities of the world just to create subject matters for hearing about Him; otherwise the Lord has nothing to do in this world, nor has He any obligation to do anything. He comes out of His own causeless mercy and acts as He desires, the *Vedas* and *Purāṇas* are full of descriptions of His different activities so that people in general may naturally be eager to hear and read something about His activities. Generally, however, the modern fictions and novels of the world occupy a greater part of people's valuable time. Such literatures cannot do good to anyone; on the contrary, they agitate the young mind unnecessarily and increase the modes of passion and ignorance, leading to increasing bondage to the material conditions. The same aptitude for hearing and reading is better utilized in hearing and reading of the Lord's activities. This will give one all-around benefit.

It is concluded, therefore, that the holy name of the Lord and topics in relation with Him are always worth hearing, and therefore He is called here in this verse *nāma-dheya,* or one whose holy name is worth chanting.

TEXT 16

श्रुत्वा हरिस्तमरणार्थिनमप्रमेय-
श्चक्रायुधः पतगराजभुजाधिरूढः ।
चक्रेण नक्रवदनं विनिपाट्य तस्मा-
द्धस्ते प्रगृह्य भगवान् कृपयोज्जहार ॥१६॥

śrutvā haris tam araṇārthinam aprameyaś
cakrāyudhaḥ patagarāja-bhujādhirūḍhaḥ
cakreṇa nakra-vadanaṁ vinipāṭya tasmād
dhaste pragṛhya bhagavān kṛpayojjahāra

śrutvā—by hearing; *hariḥ*—the Personality of Godhead; *tam*—him; *araṇa-arthinam*—one who is in need of help; *aprameyaḥ*—the unlimitedly powerful Lord; *cakra*—wheel; *āyudhaḥ*—equipped with His weapon; *pataga-rāja*—the king of the birds (Garuḍa); *bhuja-adhirūḍhaḥ*—being seated on the wings of; *cakreṇa*—by the wheel; *nakra-vadanam*—the mouth of the crocodile; *vinipāṭya*—cutting in two; *tasmāt*—from the mouth of the crocodile; *haste*—in the hands; *pragṛhya*—taking hold of the trunk; *bhagavān*—the Personality of Godhead; *kṛpayā*—out of causeless mercy; *ujjahāra*—delivered him.

TRANSLATION

The Personality of Godhead, after hearing the elephant's plea, felt that the elephant needed His immediate help, for he was in

great distress. Thus at once the Lord appeared there on the wings of the king of birds, Garuḍa, fully equipped with His weapon, the wheel [cakra]. With the wheel He cut to pieces the mouth of the crocodile to save the elephant, and He delivered the elephant by lifting him by his trunk.

PURPORT

The Lord resides in His Vaikuṇṭha planet. No one can estimate how far away this planet is situated. It is said, however, that anyone trying to reach that planet by airships or by mindships, traveling for millions of years, will find it still unknown. Modern scientists have invented airships which are material, and the *yogīs* make a still finer material attempt to travel by mindships. The *yogīs* can reach any distant place very quickly with the help of mindships. But neither the airship nor the mindship has access to the kingdom of God in the Vaikuṇṭhaloka, situated far beyond the material sky. Since this is the situation, how was it possible for the prayers of the elephant to be heard from such an unlimitedly distant place, and how could the Lord at once appear on the spot? These things cannot be calculated by human imagination. All this was possible by the unlimited power of the Lord, and therefore the Lord is described here as *aprameya*, for not even the best human brain can estimate His powers and potencies by mathematical calculation. The Lord can hear from such a distant place, He can eat from there, and He can appear simultaneously in all places at a moment's notice. Such is the omnipotency of the Lord.

TEXT 17

ज्यायान् गुणैरवरजोऽप्यदितेः सुतानां
लोकान् विचक्रम इमान् यदथाधियज्ञः।
क्ष्मां वामनेन जगृहे त्रिपदच्छलेन
याच्ञामृते पथि चरन् प्रभुभिर्न चाल्यः ॥१७॥

jyāyān guṇair avarajo 'py aditeḥ sutānāṁ
lokān vicakrama imān yad athādhiyajñaḥ
kṣmāṁ vāmanena jagṛhe tripada-cchalena
yācñām ṛte pathi caran prabhubhir na cālyaḥ

jyāyān—the greatest; *guṇaiḥ*—by qualities; *avarajaḥ*—transcendental; *api*—although He is so; *aditeḥ*—of Aditi; *sutānām*—of all the sons (known as Ādityas); *lokān*—all the planets; *vicakrame*—surpassed; *imān*—in this universe; *yat*—one who; *atha*—therefore; *adhiyajñaḥ*—the Supreme Personality of Godhead; *kṣmām*—all the lands; *vāmanena*—in the incarnation of Vāmana; *jagṛhe*—accepted; *tri-pada*—three steps; *chalena*—by pretention; *yācñām*—begging; *ṛte*—without; *pathi caran*—passing over the right path; *prabhubhiḥ*—by authorities; *na*—never to be; *cālyaḥ*—to be bereft of.

TRANSLATION

The Lord, although transcendental to all material modes, still surpassed all the qualities of the sons of Aditi, known as the Ādityas. The Lord appeared as the youngest son of Aditi. And because He surpassed all the planets of the universe, He is the Supreme Personality of Godhead. On the pretense of asking for a measurement of three footsteps of land, He took away all the lands of Bali Mahārāja. He asked simply because without begging, no authority can take one's rightful possession.

PURPORT

The history of Bali Mahārāja and his charity to Vāmanadeva is described in the Eighth Canto of *Śrīmad-Bhāgavatam.* Bali Mahārāja conquered all the planets of the universe by rightful possession. A king can conquer other kings by strength, and such possession is considered to be rightful. So Bali Mahārāja possessed all the lands of the universe, and he happened to be charitably disposed toward the *brāhmaṇas.* The Lord therefore pretended to be a beggar *brāhmaṇa,* and He asked Bali Mahārāja for a measurement of three footsteps of land. The Lord, as the proprietor of everything, could take from Bali Mahārāja all the land he possessed, but he did not do so because Bali Mahārāja possessed all those lands by king's rights. When Bali Mahārāja was asked by Lord Vāmana for such small charity, Bali Mahārāja's spiritual master, namely Śukrācārya, objected to this proposal because he knew that Vāmanadeva was Viṣṇu Himself, pretending to be a beggar. Bali Mahārāja did not agree to abide by the order of his spiritual master when he understood that the beggar was Viṣṇu Himself, and he at once agreed to give Him in charity the land requested. By this agreement Lord Vāmana covered all the lands of the universe with His first two steps and then asked Bali Mahārāja where to place the third step. Bali Mahārāja was very glad to receive the Lord's remaining step upon his head, and thus Bali Mahārāja, instead of losing everything he possessed, was blessed by the Lord's becoming his constant companion and doorman. So, by giving everything to the cause of the Lord, one does not lose anything, but he gains everything that he could never otherwise expect.

TEXT 18

नार्थो बलेरयमुरुक्रमपादशौच-
मापः शिखा धृतवतो विबुधाधिपत्यम्।
यो वै प्रतिश्रुतमृते न चिकीर्षदन्य-
दात्मानमङ्ग मनसा हरयेऽभिमेने ॥१८॥

nārtho baler ayam urukrama-pāda-śaucam
āpaḥ śikhā-dhṛtavato vibudhādhipatyam
yo vai pratiśrutam ṛte na cikīrṣad anyad
ātmānam aṅga manasā haraye 'bhimene

na—never; *arthaḥ*—of any value in comparison with; *baleḥ*—of strength; *ayam*—this; *urukrama-pāda-śaucam*—the water washed from the feet of the Personality of Godhead; *āpaḥ*—water; *śikhā-dhṛtavataḥ*—of one who has kept it on his head; *vibudha-adhipatyam*—supremacy over the kingdom of the demigods; *yaḥ*—one who; *vai*—certainly; *pratiśrutam*—what was duly promised; *ṛte na*—besides that; *cikīrṣat*—tried for; *anyat*—anything else; *ātmānam*—even his personal body; *aṅga*—O Nārada; *manasā*—within his mind; *haraye*—unto the Supreme Lord; *abhimene*—dedicated.

TRANSLATION

Bali Mahārāja, who put on his head the water washed from the lotus feet of the Lord, did not think of anything besides his promise, in spite of being forbidden by his spiritual master. The king

dedicated his own personal body to fulfill the measurement of the Lord's third step. For such a personality, even the kingdom of heaven, which he conquered by his strength, was of no value.

PURPORT

Bali Mahārāja, by gaining the transcendental favor of the Lord in exchange for his great material sacrifice, was able to have a place in Vaikuṇṭhaloka with equal or greater facilities of eternal enjoyment; therefore he was not at all the loser by sacrificing the kingdom of heaven, which he had possessed by his material strength. In other words, when the Lord snatches away one's hard-earned material possessions and favors one with His personal transcendental service for eternal life, bliss and knowledge, such taking away by the Lord should be considered a special favor upon such a pure devotee.

Material possessions, however alluring they may be, cannot be permanent possessions. Therefore one has to voluntarily give up such possessions, or one has to leave such possessions at the time of quitting this material body. The sane man knows that all material possessions are temporary and that the best use of such possessions is to engage them in the service of the Lord so that the Lord may be pleased with him and award him a permanent place in His *paraṁ dhāma.*

In the *Bhagavad-gītā* (15.5–6), the *paraṁ dhāma* of the Lord is described as follows:

nirmāna-mohā jita-saṅga-doṣā
adhyātma-nityā vinivṛtta-kāmāḥ
dvandvair vimuktāḥ sukha-duḥkha-saṁjñair
gacchanty amūḍhāḥ padam avyayaṁ tat

na tad bhāsayate sūryo
na śaśāṅko na pāvakaḥ
yad gatvā na nivartante
tad dhāma paramaṁ mama

One who possesses more in this material world, in the shape of houses, land, children, society, friendship and wealth, possesses these things only for the time being. One cannot possess all this illusory paraphernalia, created by *māyā*, permanently. Such a possessor is more illusioned in the matter of his self-realization; therefore one should possess less or nothing, so that one may be free from artificial prestige. We are contaminated in the material world by association with the three modes of material nature. Therefore, the more one spiritually advances by devotional service to the Lord, in exchange for his temporary possessions, the more one is freed from the attachment of material illusion. To achieve this stage of life one must be firmly convinced about spiritual existence and its permanent effects. To know exactly the permanency of spiritual existence, one must voluntarily practice possessing less or only the minimum to maintain one's material existence without difficulty. One should not create artificial needs. That will help one be satisfied with the minimum. Artificial needs of life are activities of the senses. The modern advancement of civilization is based on these activities of the senses, or, in other words, it is a civilization of sense gratification. Perfect civilization is the civilization of *ātmā*, or the soul proper. The civilized man of sense gratification is on an equal level with animals because animals cannot go beyond the activities of the senses. Above the senses is the mind. The civilization of mental speculation is also not the perfect stage of life because above the mind is the intelligence, and the *Bhagavad-gītā* gives us information of the intellectual civilization. The Vedic literatures give different directions for the human civilization, including the civilization of the senses, of the mind, of the intelligence, and of the soul proper. The *Bhagavad-gītā* primarily deals with the intelligence of man, leading one to the progressive path of civilization of the spirit soul. And *Śrīmad-Bhāgavatam* is the complete human civilization dealing with the subject matter of the soul proper. As soon as a man is raised to the status of the civilization of the soul, he is fit to be promoted to the kingdom of God, which is described in the *Bhagavad-gītā* as per the above verses.

The primary information of the kingdom of God informs us that there is no need of sun, moon or electricity, which are all necessary in this material world of darkness. And the secondary information of the kingdom of God explains that anyone able to reach that kingdom by adoption of the civilization of the soul proper, or, in other words, by the method of *bhakti-yoga*, attains the highest perfection of life. One is then situated in the permanent existence of the soul, with full knowledge of transcendental loving service for the Lord. Bali Mahārāja accepted this civilization of the soul in exchange for his great material possessions and thus became fit for promotion to the kingdom of God. The kingdom of heaven, which he achieved by dint of his material power, was considered most insignificant in comparison with the kingdom of God.

Those who have attained the comforts of a material civilization made for sense gratification should try to attain the kingdom of God by following in the footsteps of Bali Mahārāja, who exchanged his acquired material strength, adopting the process of *bhakti-yoga* as recommended in the *Bhagavad-gītā* and further explained in the *Śrīmad-Bhāgavatam.*

TEXT 19

तुभ्यं च नारद भृशं भगवान् विवृद्ध-
भावेन साधुपरितुष्ट उवाच योगम् ।
ज्ञानं च भागवतमात्मसतत्त्वदीपं
यद्वासुदेवशरणा विदुरञ्जसैव ॥१९॥

tubhyaṁ ca nārada bhṛśaṁ bhagavān vivṛddha-
bhāvena sādhu parituṣṭa uvāca yogam
jñānaṁ ca bhāgavatam ātma-satattva-dīpaṁ
yad vāsudeva-śaraṇā vidur añjasaiva

tubhyam—unto you; *ca*—also; *nārada*—O Nārada; *bhṛśam*—very nicely; *bhagavān*—the Personality of Godhead; *vivṛddha*—developed; *bhāvena*—by transcendental love; *sādhu*—your goodness; *parituṣṭaḥ*—being satisfied; *uvāca*—described; *yogam*—service; *jñānam*—knowledge; *ca*—also; *bhāgavatam*—the science of God and His devotional service; *ātma*—the self; *sa-tattva*—with all details; *dīpam*—just like the light in the darkness; *yat*—that which; *vāsudeva-śaraṇāḥ*—those who are souls surrendered unto Lord Vāsudeva; *viduḥ*—know them; *añjasā*—perfectly well; *eva*—as it is.

TRANSLATION

O Nārada, you were taught about the science of God and His transcendental loving service by the Personality of Godhead in His

incarnation of Haṁsāvatāra. He was very much pleased with you, due to your intense proportion of devotional service. He also explained unto you, lucidly, the full science of devotional service, which is especially understandable by persons who are souls surrendered unto Lord Vāsudeva, the Personality of Godhead.

PURPORT

The devotee and devotional service are two correlative terms. Unless one is inclined to be a devotee of the Lord, he cannot enter into the intricacies of devotional service. Lord Śrī Kṛṣṇa wanted to explain the *Bhagavad-gītā*, which is the science of devotional service, unto Śrī Arjuna because Arjuna was not only His friend but a great devotee as well. The whole process is that all living entities, being constitutionally parts and parcels of the supreme living being, the Absolute Personality of Godhead, have proportionately minute independence of action also. So the preliminary qualification for entering into the devotional service of the Lord is that one become a willing cooperator, and as such one should voluntarily cooperate with persons who are already engaged in the transcendental devotional service of the Lord. By cooperating with such persons, the prospective candidate will gradually learn the techniques of devotional service, and with the progress of such learning one becomes proportionately free from the contamination of material association. Such a purificatory process will establish the prospective candidate in firm faith and gradually elevate him to the stage of transcendental taste for such devotional service. Thus he acquires a genuine attachment for the devotional service of the Lord, and his conviction carries him on to the point of ecstasy, just prior to the stage of transcendental love.

Such knowledge of devotional service may be divided into two sections, namely preliminary knowledge of the nature of devotional service and the secondary knowledge of its execution. *Bhāgavatam* is in relation with the Personality of Godhead, His beauty, fame, opulence, dignity, attraction and transcendental qualities which attract one towards Him for exchanges of love and affection. There is a natural affinity of the living entity for the loving service of the Lord. This affinity becomes artificially covered by the influence of material association, and *Śrīmad-Bhāgavatam* helps one very genuinely remove that artificial covering.

Therefore it is particularly mentioned herein that *Śrīmad-Bhāgavatam* acts like the lamp of transcendental knowledge. These two sections of transcendental knowledge in devotional service become revealed to a person who is a soul surrendered unto Vāsudeva; as it is said in the *Bhagavad-gītā* (7.19), such a great soul, fully surrendered unto the lotus feet of Vāsudeva, is very, very rare.

TEXT 20

चक्रं च दिक्ष्वविहतं दशसु स्वतेजो
मन्वन्तरेषु मनुवंशधरो बिभर्ति ।
दुष्टेषु राजसु दमं व्यदधात् स्वकीर्तिं
सत्ये त्रिपृष्ठ उशतीं प्रथयंश्चरित्रैः ॥२०॥

cakraṁ ca dikṣv avihataṁ daśasu sva-tejo
manvantareṣu manu-vaṁśa-dharo bibharti
duṣṭeṣu rājasu damaṁ vyadadhāt sva-kīrtiṁ
satye tri-pṛṣṭha uśatīṁ prathayaṁś caritraiḥ

cakram—the Sudarśana wheel of the Lord; *ca*—as well as; *dikṣu*—in all directions; *avihatam*—without being deterred; *daśasu*—ten sides; *sva-tejaḥ*—personal strength; *manvantareṣu*—in different incarnations of Manu; *manu-vaṁśa-dharaḥ*—as the descendant of the Manu dynasty; *bibharti*—rules over; *duṣṭeṣu*—unto the miscreants; *rājasu*—upon the kings of that type; *damam*—subjection; *vyadadhāt*—performed; *sva-kīrtim*—personal glories; *satye*—in the Satyaloka planet; *tri-pṛṣṭhe*—the three planetary systems; *uśatīm*—glorious; *prathayan*—established; *caritraiḥ*—characteristics.

TRANSLATION

As the incarnation of Manu, the Lord became the descendant of the Manu dynasty and ruled over the miscreant kingly order, subduing them by His powerful wheel weapon. Undeterred in all circumstances, His rule was characterized by His glorious fame, which spread over the three lokas, and above them to the planetary system of Satyaloka, the topmost in the universe.

PURPORT

We have already discussed the incarnations of Manu in the First Canto. In one day of Brahmā there are fourteen Manus, changing one after another. In that way there are 420 Manus in a month of Brahmā and 5,040 Manus in one year of Brahmā. Brahmā lives for one hundred years according to his calculation, and as such there are 504,000 Manus in the jurisdiction of one Brahmā. There are innumerable Brahmās, and all of them live only during one breathing period of Mahā-Viṣṇu. So we can just imagine how the incarnations of the Supreme Lord work all over the material worlds, which comprehend only one-fourth of the total energy of the Supreme Personality of Godhead.

The *manvantara* incarnation chastises all the miscreant rulers of different planets with as much power as that of the Supreme Personality of Godhead, who punishes the miscreants with His wheel weapon. The *manvantara* incarnations disseminate the transcendental glories of the Lord.

TEXT 21

धन्वन्तरिश्च भगवान् स्वयमेव कीर्ति-
नाम्ना नृणां पुरुरुजां रुज आशु हन्ति ।
यज्ञे च भागममृतायुरवावरुन्ध
आयुष्यवेदमनुशास्त्यवतीर्य लोके ॥२१॥

dhanvantariś ca bhagavān svayam eva kīrtir
nāmnā nṛṇāṁ puru-rujāṁ ruja āśu hanti
yajñe ca bhāgam amṛtāyur-avāvarundha
āyuṣya-vedam anuśāsty avatīrya loke

dhanvantariḥ—the incarnation of God named Dhanvantari; *ca*—and; *bhagavān*—the Personality of Godhead; *svayam eva*—personally Himself; *kīrtiḥ*—fame personified; *nāmnā*—by the name; *nṛṇām puru-rujām*—of the diseased living entities; *rujaḥ*—diseases; *āśu*—very soon; *hanti*—cures; *yajñe*—in the sacrifice; *ca*—also; *bhāgam*—share; *amṛta*—nectar; *āyuḥ*—duration of life; *ava*—from; *avarundhe*—obtains; *āyuṣya*—of duration of life; *vedam*—knowledge; *anuśāsti*—directs; *avatīrya*—incarnating; *loke*—in the universe.

TRANSLATION

The Lord in His incarnation of Dhanvantari very quickly cures the diseases of the ever-diseased living entities simply by his fame personified, and only because of him do the demigods achieve long lives. Thus the Personality of Godhead becomes ever glorified. He also exacted a share from the sacrifices, and it is he only who inaugurated the medical science or the knowledge of medicine in the universe.

PURPORT

As stated in the beginning of the *Śrīmad-Bhāgavatam*, everything emanates from the ultimate source of the Personality of Godhead; it is therefore understood in this verse that medical science or knowledge in medicine was also inaugurated by the Personality of Godhead in His incarnation Dhanvantari, and thus the knowledge is recorded in the *Vedas*. The *Vedas* are the source of all knowledge, and thus knowledge in medical science is also there for the perfect cure of the diseases of the living entity. The embodied living entity is diseased by the very construction of his body. The body is the symbol of diseases. The disease may differ from one variety to another, but disease must be there just as there is birth and death for everyone. So, by the grace of the Personality of Godhead, not only are diseases of the body and mind cured, but also the soul is relieved of the constant repetition of birth and death. The name of the Lord is also called *bhavauṣadhi*, or the source of curing the disease of material existence.

TEXT 22

क्षत्रं क्षयाय विधिनोपभृतं महात्मा
ब्रह्मध्रुगुज्झितपथं नरकार्तिलिप्सु ।
उद्धन्त्यसाववनिकण्टकमुग्रवीर्य-
स्त्रिःसप्तकृत्व उरुधारपरश्वधेन ॥२२॥

kṣatraṁ kṣayāya vidhinopabhṛtaṁ mahātmā
brahma-dhrug ujjhita-pathaṁ narakārti-lipsu
uddhanty asāv avanikaṇṭakam ugra-vīryas
triḥ-sapta-kṛtva urudhāra-paraśvadhena

kṣatram—the royal order; *kṣayāya*—for the sake of diminishing; *vidhinā*—by destination; *upabhṛtam*—increased in proportion; *mahātmā*—the Lord in the form of the great sage Paraśurāma; *brahmadhruk*—the ultimate truth in Brahman; *ujjhita-patham*—those who have given up the path of the Absolute Truth; *naraka-ārti-lipsu*—desirous to suffer pain in hell; *uddhanti*—exacts; *asau*—all those; *avanikaṇṭakam*—thorns of the world; *ugra-vīryaḥ*—awfully powerful; *triḥ-satpa*—thrice seven times; *kṛtvaḥ*—performed; *urudhāra*—very sharp; *paraśvadhena*—by the great chopper.

TRANSLATION

When the ruling administrators, who are known as the kṣatriyas, turned astray from the path of the Absolute Truth, being desirous to suffer in hell, the Lord, in His incarnation as the sage Paraśurāma, uprooted those unwanted kings, who appeared as the thorns of the earth. Thus He thrice seven times uprooted the kṣatriyas with His keenly sharpened chopper.

PURPORT

The *kṣatriyas*, or the ruling administrators of any part of the universe, either on this planet or on other planets, are factually the representatives of the Almighty Personality of Godhead, and they are meant to lead the subjects towards the path of God realization. Every state and its administrators, regardless of the nature of the administration—monarchy or democracy, oligarchy or dictatorship or autocracy—have the prime responsibility to lead the citizens toward God realization. This is essential for all human beings, and it is the duty of the father, spiritual master, and ultimately the state to take up the responsibility of leading the citizens towards this end. The whole creation of material existence is made for this purpose, just to give a chance to the fallen souls who rebelled against the will of the Supreme Father and thus became conditioned by material nature. The force of material nature gradually leads one to a hellish condition of perpetual pains and miseries. Those going against the prescribed rules and regulations of conditional life are called *brahmojjhita-pathas*, or persons going against the path of the Absolute Truth, and they are liable to be punished. Lord Paraśurāma, the incarnation of the Personality of Godhead, appeared in such a state of worldly affairs and killed all the miscreant kings twenty-one times. Many *kṣatriya* kings fled from India to other parts of the world at that time, and according to the authority of the *Mahābhārata*, the kings of Egypt originally migrated from India because of Paraśurāma's program of chastisement. The kings or administrators are similarly chastised in all circumstances whenever they become godless and plan a godless civilization. That is the order of the Almighty.

TEXT 23

अस्मत्प्रसादसुमुखः कलया कलेश
इक्ष्वाकुवंश अवतीर्य गुरोर्निदेशे ।
तिष्ठन् वनं सदयितानुज आविवेश
यस्मिन् विरुध्य दशकन्धर आर्तिमार्च्छत् ॥२३॥

asmat-prasāda-sumukhaḥ kalayā kaleśa
ikṣvāku-vaṁśa avatīrya guror nideśe
tiṣṭhan vanaṁ sa-dayitānuja āviveśa
yasmin virudhya daśa-kandhara ārtim ārcchat

asmat—unto us, beginning from Brahmā down to the insignificant ant; *prasāda*—causeless mercy; *sumukhaḥ*—so inclined; *kalayā*—with His plenary extensions; *kaleśaḥ*—the Lord of all potencies; *ikṣvāku*—Mahārāja Ikṣvāku, in the dynasty of the sun; *vaṁśe*—family; *avatīrya*—by descending in; *guroḥ*—of the father or spiritual master; *nideśe*—under the order of; *tiṣṭhan*—being situated in; *vanam*—in the forest; *sa-dayitā-anujaḥ*—along with His wife and younger brother; *āviveśa*—entered; *yasmin*—unto whom; *virudhya*—being rebellious; *daśa-kandharaḥ*—Rāvaṇa, who had ten heads; *ārtim*—great distress; *ārcchat*—achieved.

TRANSLATION

Due to His causeless mercy upon all living entities within the universe, the Supreme Personality of Godhead, along with His plenary extensions, appeared in the family of Mahārāja Ikṣvāku as the Lord of His internal potency, Sītā. Under the order of His father, Mahārāja Daśaratha, He entered the forest and lived there

for considerable years with His wife and younger brother. Rāvaṇa, who was very materially powerful, with ten heads on his shoulders, committed a great offense against Him and was thus ultimately vanquished.

PURPORT

Lord Rāma is the Supreme Personality of Godhead, and His brothers, namely Bharata, Lakṣmaṇa and Śatrughna, are His plenary expansions. All four brothers are *viṣṇu-tattva* and were never ordinary human beings. There are many unscrupulous and ignorant commentators on *Rāmāyaṇa* who present the younger brothers of Lord Rāmacandra as ordinary living entities. But here in the *Śrīmad-Bhāgavatam,* the most authentic scripture on the science of Godhead, it is clearly stated that His brothers were His plenary expansions. Originally Lord Rāmacandra is the incarnation of Vāsudeva, Lakṣmaṇa is the incarnation of Saṅkarṣaṇa, Bharata is the incarnation of Pradyumna, and Śatrughna is the incarnation of Aniruddha, expansions of the Personality of Godhead. Lakṣmījī Sītā is the internal potency of the Lord and is neither an ordinary woman nor the external potency incarnation of Durgā. Durgā is the external potency of the Lord, and she is associated with Lord Śiva.

As stated in the *Bhagavad-gītā* (4.7), the Lord appears when there are discrepancies in the discharge of factual religion. Lord Rāmacandra also appeared under the same circumstances, accompanied by His brothers, who are expansions of the Lord's internal potency, and by Lakṣmījī Sītādevī.

Lord Rāmacandra was ordered by His father, Mahārāja Daśaratha, to leave home for the forest under awkward circumstances, and the Lord, as the ideal son of His father, carried out the order, even on the occasion of His being declared the King of Ayodhyā. One of His younger brothers, Lakṣmaṇajī, desired to go with Him, and so also His eternal wife, Sītājī, desired to go with Him. The Lord agreed to both of them, and all together they entered the Daṇḍakāraṇya Forest, to live there for fourteen years. During their stay in the forest, there was some quarrel between Rāmacandra and Rāvaṇa, and the latter kidnapped the Lord's wife, Sītā. The quarrel ended in the vanquishing of the greatly powerful Rāvaṇa, along with all his kingdom and family.

Sītā is Lakṣmījī, or the goddess of fortune, but she is never to be enjoyed by any living being. She is meant for being worshiped by the living being along with her husband, Śrī Rāmacandra. A materialistic man like Rāvaṇa does not understand this great truth, but on the contrary he wants to snatch Sītādevī from the custody of Rāma and thus incurs great miseries. The materialists, who are after opulence and material prosperity, may take lessons from the *Rāmāyaṇa* that the policy of exploiting the nature of the Lord without acknowledging the supremacy of the Supreme Lord is the policy of Rāvaṇa. Rāvaṇa was very advanced materially, so much so that he turned his kingdom, Laṅkā, into pure gold, or full material wealth. But because he did not recognize the supremacy of Lord Rāmacandra and defied Him by stealing His wife, Sītā, Rāvaṇa was killed, and all his opulence and power were destroyed.

Lord Rāmacandra is a full incarnation with six opulences in full, and He is therefore mentioned in this verse as *kaleśaḥ*, or master of all opulence.

TEXT 24

यस्मा अदादुदधिरूढभयाङ्गवेपो
मार्गं सपद्यरिपुरं हरवद् दिधक्षोः ।
दूरे सुहृन्मथितरोषसुशोणदृष्ट्या
तातप्यमानमकरोरगनक्रचक्रः ॥२४॥

yasmā adād udadhir ūḍha-bhayāṅga-vepo
mārgaṁ sapady ari-puraṁ haravad didhakṣoḥ
dūre suhṛn-mathita-roṣa-suśoṇa-dṛṣṭyā
tātapyamāna-makaroraga-nakra-cakraḥ

yasmai—unto whom; *adāt*—gave; *udadhiḥ*—the great Indian Ocean; *ūḍha-bhaya*—affected by fear; *aṅga-vepaḥ*—bodily trembling; *mārgam*—way; *sapadi*—quickly; *ari-puram*—the city of the enemy; *hara-vat*—like that of Hara (Mahādeva); *didhakṣoḥ*—desiring to burn to ashes; *dūre*—at a long distance; *su-hṛt*—intimate friend; *mathita*—being aggrieved by; *roṣa*—in anger; *su-śoṇa*—red-hot; *dṛṣṭyā*—by such a glance; *tātapyamāna*—burning in heat; *makara*—sharks; *uraga*—snakes; *nakra*—crocodiles; *cakraḥ*—circle.

TRANSLATION

The Personality of Godhead Rāmacandra, being aggrieved for His distant intimate friend [Sītā], glanced over the city of the enemy Rāvaṇa with red-hot eyes like those of Hara [who wanted to burn the kingdom of heaven]. The great ocean, trembling in fear, gave Him His way because its family members, the aquatics like the sharks, snakes and crocodiles, were being burnt by the heat of the angry red-hot eyes of the Lord.

PURPORT

The Personality of Godhead has every sentiment of a sentient being, like all other living beings, because He is the chief and original living entity, the supreme source of all other living beings. He is the *nitya*, or the chief eternal amongst all other eternals. He is the chief one, and all others are the dependent many. The many eternals are supported by the one eternal, and thus both the eternals are qualitatively one. Due to such oneness, both the eternals constitutionally have a complete range of sentiments, but the difference is that the sentiments of the chief eternal are different in quantity from the sentiments of the dependent eternals. When Rāmacandra was angry and showed His red-hot eyes, the whole ocean became heated with that energy, so much so that the aquatics within the great ocean felt the heat, and the personified ocean trembled in fear and offered the Lord an easy path for reaching the enemy's city. The impersonalists will see havoc in this red-hot sentiment of the Lord because they want to see negation in perfection. Because the Lord is absolute, the impersonalists imagine that in the Absolute the sentiment of anger, which resembles mundane sentiments, must be conspicuous by absence. Due to a poor fund of knowledge, they do not realize that the sentiment of the Absolute Person is transcendental to all mundane concepts of quality and quantity. Had Lord Rāmacandra's sentiment been of mundane origin, how could it disturb the whole ocean and its inhabitants? Can any mundane red-hot eye generate heat in the great ocean? These are factors to be distinguished in terms of the personal and impersonal conceptions of the Absolute Truth. As it is said in the beginning of the *Śrīmad-Bhāgavatam*, the Absolute Truth is the source of everything, so the Absolute Person cannot be devoid of the sentiments that are reflected in the temporary mundane world. Rather, the different sentiments found in the Absolute, either in anger or in mercy, have the same qualitative influence, or, in other words, there is no mundane difference of value because these sentiments are all on the absolute plane. Such sentiments are definitely not absent in the Absolute, as the impersonalists think, making their mundane estimation of the transcendental world.

TEXT 25

वक्षःस्थलस्पर्शरुग्नमहेन्द्रवाह-
दन्तैर्विडम्बितककुब्जुष ऊढहासम् ।
सद्योऽसुभिः सह विनेष्यति दारहर्तु-
र्विस्फूर्जितैर्धनुष उच्चरतोऽधिसैन्ये ॥२५॥

vakṣaḥ-sthala-sparśa-rugna-mahendra-vāha-
dantair viḍambita-kakubjuṣa ūḍha-hāsam
sadyo 'subhiḥ saha vineṣyati dāra-hartur
visphūrjitair dhanuṣa uccarato 'dhisainye

vakṣaḥ-sthala—chest; *sparśa*—touched by; *rugna*—broken; *mahā-indra*—the King of heaven; *vāha*—the conveyor; *dantaiḥ*—by the trunk; *viḍambita*—illuminated; *kakup-juṣaḥ*—all directions thus being served; *ūḍha-hāsam*—overtaken by laughter; *sadyaḥ*—within no time; *asubhiḥ*—by the life; *saha*—along with; *vineṣyati*—was killed; *dāra-hartuḥ*—of the one who kidnapped the wife; *visphūrjitaiḥ*—by the tingling of the bow; *dhanuṣaḥ*—bow; *uccarataḥ*—strolling fast; *adhisainye*—in the midst of the fighting soldiers of both sides.

TRANSLATION

When Rāvaṇa was engaged in the battle, the trunk of the elephant which carried the King of heaven, Indra, broke in pieces, having collided with the chest of Rāvaṇa, and the scattered broken parts illuminated all directions. Rāvaṇa therefore felt proud of his prowess and began to loiter in the midst of the fighting soldiers, thinking himself the conqueror of all directions. But his laughter, overtaken by joy, along with his very air of life, suddenly ceased

with the tingling sound of the bow of Rāmacandra, the Personality of Godhead.

PURPORT

However powerful a living being may be, when he is condemned by God no one can save him, and, similarly, however weak one may be, if he is protected by the Lord no one can annihilate him.

TEXT 26

भूमेः सुरेतरवरूथविमर्दितायाः
क्लेशव्ययाय कलया सितकृष्णकेशः ।
जातः करिष्यति जनानुपलक्ष्यमार्गः
कर्माणि चात्ममहिमोपनिबन्धनानि ॥२६॥

bhūmeḥ suretara-varūtha-vimarditāyāḥ
kleśa-vyayāya kalayā sita-kṛṣṇa-keśaḥ
jātaḥ kariṣyati janānupalakṣya-mārgaḥ
karmāṇi cātma-mahimopanibandhanāni

bhūmeḥ—of the entire world; *sura-itara*—other than godly persons; *varūtha*—soldiers; *vimarditāyāḥ*—distressed by the burden; *kleśa*—miseries; *vyayāya*—for the matter of diminishing; *kalayā*—along with His plenary expansion; *sita-kṛṣṇa*—not only beautiful but also black; *keśaḥ*—with such hairs; *jātaḥ*—having appeared; *kariṣyati*—would act; *jana*—people in general; *anupalakṣya*—rarely to be seen; *mārgaḥ*—path; *karmāṇi*—activities; *ca*—also; *ātma-mahimā*—glories of the Lord Himself; *upanibandhanāni*—in relation to.

TRANSLATION

When the world is overburdened by the fighting strength of kings who have no faith in God, the Lord, just to diminish the distress of the world, descends with His plenary portion. The Lord comes in His original form, with beautiful black hair. And just to expand His transcendental glories, He acts extraordinarily. No one can properly estimate how great He is.

PURPORT

This verse is especially describing the appearance of Lord Kṛṣṇa and His immediate expansion, Lord Baladeva. Both Lord Kṛṣṇa and Lord Baladeva are one Supreme Personality of Godhead. The Lord is omnipotent, and He expands Himself in innumerable forms and energies, and the whole unit is known as the one Supreme Brahman. Such extensions of the Lord are divided into two divisions, namely personal and differential. The personal expansions are called the *viṣṇu-tattvas*, and the differential expansions are called the *jīva-tattvas*. And in such expansional activity, Lord Baladeva is the first personal expansion of Kṛṣṇa, the Supreme Personality of Godhead.

In the *Viṣṇu Purāṇa*, as well as in the *Mahābhārata*, both Kṛṣṇa and Baladeva are mentioned as having beautiful black hair, even in Their advanced age. The Lord is called *anupalakṣya-mārgaḥ* or, in still more technical Vedic terms, *avāṅ-manasā gocaraḥ:* one who is never to be seen or realized by the limited sense perception of the people in general. In the *Bhagavad-gītā* (7.25) it is said by the Lord, *nāhaṁ prakāśaḥ sarvasya yogamāyā-samāvṛtaḥ.* In other words, He reserves the right of not being exposed to anyone and everyone. Only the bona fide devotees can know Him by His specific symptoms, and out of many, many such symptoms, one symptom is mentioned here in this verse, that the Lord is *sita-kṛṣṇa-keśaḥ*, or one who is observed always with beautiful black hair. Both Lord Kṛṣṇa and Lord Baladeva have such hair on Their heads, and thus even in advanced age They appeared like young boys sixteen years old. That is the particular symptom of the Personality of Godhead. In the *Brahma-saṁhitā* it is stated that although He is the oldest personality among all living entities, He always looks like a new, youthful boy. That is the characteristic of a spiritual body. The material body is symptomized by birth, death, old age and diseases, but the spiritual body is conspicuous by the absence of those symptoms. Living entities who reside in the Vaikuṇṭhalokas in eternal life and bliss have the same type of spiritual body, without being affected by any signs of old age. It is described in the *Bhāgavatam* (Canto Six) that the party of Viṣṇudūtas who came to deliver Ajāmila from the clutches of the party of Yamarāja appeared like youthful boys, corroborating the description in this verse. It is ascertained thus that the spiritual bodies in the Vaikuṇṭhalokas, either of the Lord or of the other inhabitants, are completely distinct from the material bodies of this world. Therefore, when the Lord descends from that world to this world, He descends in His spiritual body of *ātma-māyā*, or internal potency, without any touch of the *bahiraṅgā-māyā*, or external, material energy. The allegation that the impersonal Brahman appears in this material world by accepting a material body is quite absurd. Therefore the Lord, when He comes here, has not a material body, but a spiritual body. The impersonal *brahmajyoti* is only the glaring effulgence of the body of the Lord, and there is no difference in quality between the body of the Lord and the impersonal ray of the Lord, called *brahmajyoti.*

Now the question is why the Lord, who is omnipotent, comes here to diminish the burden created upon the world by the unscrupulous kingly order. Certainly the Lord does not need to come here personally for such purposes, but He actually descends to exhibit His transcendental activities in order to encourage His pure devotees, who want to enjoy life by chanting the glories of the Lord. In the *Bhagavad-gītā* (9.13–14) it is stated that the *mahātmās*, great devotees of the Lord, take pleasure in chanting of the activities of the Lord. All Vedic literatures are meant for turning one's attention towards the Lord and His transcendental activities. Thus the activities of the Lord, in His dealings with worldly people, create a subject matter for discussion by His pure devotees.

TEXT 27

तोकेन जीवहरणं यदुलूकिकाया-
त्रैमासिकस्य च पदा शकटोऽपवृत्तः ।
यद् रिङ्गतान्तरगतेन दिविस्पृशोर्वा
उन्मूलनं त्वितरथार्जुनयोर्न भाव्यम्॥२७॥

tokena jīva-haraṇaṁ yad ulūki-kāyās
trai-māsikasya ca padā śakaṭo 'pavṛttaḥ
yad riṅgatāntara-gatena divi-spṛśor vā
unmūlanaṁ tv itarathārjunayor na bhāvyam

tokena—by a child; *jīva-haraṇam*—killing a living being; *yat*—one which; *ulūki-kāyāḥ*—assumed the giant body of a demon; *trai-*

māsikasya—of one who is only three months old; *ca*—also; *padā*—by the leg; *śakaṭaḥ apavṛttaḥ*—turned over the cart; *yat*—one who; *riṅgatā*—while crawling; *antara-gatena*—being overtaken; *divi*—high in the sky; *spṛśoḥ*—touching; *vā*—either; *unmūlanam*—uprooting; *tu*—but; *itarathā*—anyone else than; *arjunayoḥ*—of the two *arjuna* trees; *na bhāvyam*—was not possible.

TRANSLATION

There is no doubt about Lord Kṛṣṇa's being the Supreme Lord, otherwise how was it possible for Him to kill a giant demon like Pūtanā when He was just on the lap of His mother, to overturn a cart with His leg when He was only three months old, to uproot a pair of arjuna trees, so high that they touched the sky, when He was only crawling? All these activities are impossible for anyone other than the Lord Himself.

PURPORT

One cannot manufacture a God by one's mental speculation or by numerical votes, as has become a practice for the less intelligent class of men. God is God eternally, and an ordinary living entity is eternally a part and parcel of God. God is one without a second, and the ordinary living entities are many without number. All such living entities are maintained by God Himself, and that is the verdict of the Vedic literatures. When Kṛṣṇa was on the lap of His mother, the demon Pūtanā appeared before His mother and prayed to nurture the child in her lap. Mother Yaśodā agreed, and the child was transferred onto the lap of Pūtanā, who was in the garb of a respectable lady. Pūtanā wanted to kill the child by smearing poison on the nipple of her breast. But when everything was complete, the Lord sucked her breast along with her very air of life, and the demon's gigantic body, said to be as long as six miles, fell down. But Lord Kṛṣṇa did not need to expand Himself to the length of the she-demon Pūtanā, although He was quite competent to cxtend IIimself more than six miles long. In His Vāmana incarnation He posed Himself as a dwarf *brāhmaṇa*, but when He took possession of His land, promised by Bali Mahārāja, He expanded His footstep to the top of the universe, extending over thousands and millions of miles. So it was not very difficult for Kṛṣṇa to perform a miracle by extending His bodily feature, but He had no desire to do it because of His deep filial love for His mother, Yaśodā. If Yaśodā had seen Kṛṣṇa in her lap extending six miles to cope with the she-demon Pūtanā, then the natural filial love of Yaśodā would have been hurt because in that way Yaśodā would have come to know that her so-called son, Kṛṣṇa, was God Himself. And with the knowledge of the Godhood of Kṛṣṇa, Yaśodāmayī would have lost the temper of her love for Kṛṣṇa as a natural mother. But as far as Lord Kṛṣṇa is concerned, He is God always, either as a child on the lap of His mother, or as the coverer of the universe, Vāmanadeva. He does not require to become God by undergoing severe penances, although some men think of becoming God in that way. By undergoing severe austerities and penances, one cannot become one or equal with God, but one can attain most of the godly qualities. A living being can attain godly qualities to a large extent, but he cannot become God, whereas Kṛṣṇa, without undergoing any type of penance, is God always, either in the lap of His mother or growing up or at any stage of growth.

So at the age of only three months He killed the Śakaṭāsura, who had remained hidden behind a cart in the house of Yaśodāmayī. And when He was crawling and was disturbing His mother from doing household affairs, the mother tied Him with a grinding pestle, but the naughty child dragged the pestle up to a pair of very high *arjuna* trees in the yard of Yaśodāmayī, and when the pestle was stuck between the pair of trees, they fell down with a horrible sound. When Yaśodāmayī came to see the happenings, she thought that her child had been saved from the falling trees by the mercy of the Lord, without knowing that the Lord Himself, crawling in her yard, had wreaked the havoc. So that is the way of reciprocation of love affairs between the Lord and His devotees. Yaśodāmayī wanted to have the Lord as her child, and the Lord played exactly like a child in her lap, but at the same time played the part of the Almighty Lord whenever it was so required. The beauty of such pastimes was that the Lord fulfilled everyone's desire. In the case of felling the gigantic *arjuna* trees, the Lord's mission was to deliver the two sons of Kuvera, who were condemned to become trees by the curse of Nārada, as well as to play like a crawling child in the yard of Yaśodā, who took transcendental pleasure in seeing such activities of the Lord in the very yard of her home.

The Lord in any condition is Lord of the universe, and He can act as such in any form, gigantic or small, as He likes.

TEXT 28

यद् वै व्रजे व्रजपशून् विषतोयपीतान्
पालांस्त्वजीवयदनुग्रहदृष्टिवृष्ट्या ।
तच्छुद्धयेऽतिविषवीर्यविलोलजिह्व-
मुच्चाटयिष्यदुरगं विहरन् ह्रदिन्याम् ॥२८॥

yad vai vraje vraja-paśūn viṣatoya-pītān
pālāṁs tv ajīvayad anugraha-dṛṣṭi-vṛṣṭyā
tac-chuddhaye 'ti-viṣa-vīrya-vilola-jihvam
uccāṭayiṣyad uragaṁ viharan hradinyām

yat—one who; *vai*—certainly; *vraje*—at Vṛndāvana; *vraja-paśūn*—the animals thereof; *viṣa-toya*—poisoned water; *pītān*—those who drank; *pālān*—the cowherd men; *tu*—also; *ajīvayat*—brought to life; *anugraha-dṛṣṭi*—merciful glance; *vṛṣṭyā*—by the showers of; *tat*—that; *śuddhaye*—for purification; *ati*—exceedingly; *viṣa-vīrya*—highly potent poison; *vilola*—lurking; *jihvam*—one who has such a tongue; *uccāṭayiṣyat*—severely punished; *uragam*—unto the snake; *viharan*—taking it as a pleasure; *hradinyām*—in the river.

TRANSLATION

Then also when the cowherd boys and their animals drank the poisoned water of the River Yamunā, and after the Lord [in His childhood] revived them by His merciful glance, just to purify the water of the River Yamunā He jumped into it as if playing and chastised the venomous Kāliya snake, which was lurking there, its tongue emitting waves of poison. Who can perform such herculean tasks but the Supreme Lord?

TEXT 29

तत् कर्म दिव्यमिव यन्निशि निःशयानं
दावाग्निना शुचिवने परिदह्यमाने ।

उन्नेष्यति व्रजमतोऽवसितान्तकालं
नेत्रे पिधाप्य सबलोऽनधिगम्यवीर्यः॥२९॥

tat karma divyam iva yan niśi niḥśayānaṁ
dāvāgninā śuci-vane paridahyamāne
unneṣyati vrajam ato 'vasitānta-kālaṁ
netre pidhāpya sabalo 'nadhigamya-vīryaḥ

tat—that; *karma*—activity; *divyam*—superhuman; *iva*—like; *yat*—which; *niśi*—at night; *niḥśayānam*—sleeping carefreely; *dāva-agninā*—by the glare of the forest fire; *śuci-vane*—in the dry forest; *paridahyamāne*—being set ablaze; *unneṣyati*—would deliver; *vrajam*—all the inhabitants of Vraja; *ataḥ*—hence; *avasita*—surely; *anta-kālam*—last moments of life; *netre*—on the eyes; *pidhāpya*—simply by closing; *sa-balaḥ*—along with Baladeva; *anadhigamya*—unfathomable; *vīryaḥ*—prowess.

TRANSLATION

On the very night of the day of the chastisement of the Kāliya snake, when the inhabitants of Vrajabhūmi were sleeping carefreely, there was a forest fire ablaze due to dry leaves, and it appeared that all the inhabitants were sure to meet their death. But the Lord, along with Balarāma, saved them simply by closing His eyes. Such are the superhuman activities of the Lord.

PURPORT

Although in this verse the Lord's activity has been described as superhuman, it should be noted that the Lord's activities are always superhuman, and that distinguishes Him from the ordinary living being. Uprooting a gigantic banyan or *arjuna* tree and extinguishing a blazing forest fire simply by closing one's eyes are certainly impossible by any kind of human endeavor. But not only are these activities amazing to hear, but in fact all other activities of the Lord, whatever He may do, are all superhuman, as confirmed in the *Bhagavad-gītā* (4.9). Whoever knows the superhuman activities of the Lord, due to their very transcendental nature, becomes eligible to enter the kingdom of Kṛṣṇa, and as such, after quitting this present material body, the knower of the transcendental activities of the Lord goes back home, back to Godhead.

TEXT 30

गृह्णीत यद् यदुपबन्धममुष्य माता
शुल्बं सुतस्य न तु तत् तदमुष्य माति ।
यज्जृम्भतोऽस्य वदने भुवनानि गोपी
संवीक्ष्य शङ्कितमनाः प्रतिबोधितासीत् ॥३०॥

gṛhṇīta yad yad upabandham amuṣya mātā
śulbaṁ sutasya na tu tat tad amuṣya māti
yaj jṛmbhato 'sya vadane bhuvanāni gopī
saṁvīkṣya śaṅkita-manāḥ pratibodhitāsīt

gṛhṇīta—by taking up; *yat yat*—whatsoever; *upabandham*—ropes for tying; *amuṣya*—His; *mātā*—mother; *śulbam*—ropes; *sutasya*—of her son; *na*—not; *tu*—however; *tat tat*—by and by; *amuṣya*—His; *māti*—was sufficient; *yat*—that which; *jṛmbhataḥ*—opening the mouth; *asya*—of Him; *vadane*—in the mouth; *bhuvanāni*—the worlds; *gopī*—the cowherd woman; *saṁvīkṣya*—so seeing it; *śaṅkita-manāḥ*—doubtful in mind; *pratibodhitā*—convinced in a different way; *āsīt*—was so done.

TRANSLATION

When the cowherd woman [Kṛṣṇa's foster mother, Yaśodā] was trying to tie the hands of her son with ropes, she found the rope to be always insufficient in length, and when she finally gave up, Lord Kṛṣṇa, by and by, opened His mouth, wherein the mother found all the universes situated. Seeing this, she was doubtful in her mind, but she was convinced in a different manner of the mystic nature of her son.

PURPORT

One day Lord Kṛṣṇa as the naughty child disturbed His mother Yaśodā, and she began to tie up the child with ropes just to punish Him.

But no matter how much rope she used, she found it always insufficient. Thus she became fatigued, but in the meantime the Lord opened His mouth, and the affectionate mother saw within the mouth of her son all the universes situated together. The mother was astonished, but out of her deep affection for Kṛṣṇa she thought that the Almighty Godhead Nārāyaṇa had kindly looked after her son just to protect Him from all the continuous calamities happening to Him. Because of her deep affection for Kṛṣṇa, she could never think that her very son was Nārāyaṇa, the Personality of Godhead Himself. That is the action of *yogamāyā*, the internal potency of the Supreme Lord, which acts to perfect all the pastimes of the Lord with His different types of devotees. Who could play such wonders without being God?

TEXT 31

नन्दं च मोक्ष्यति भयाद् वरुणस्य पाशाद्
गोपान् बिलेषु पिहितान् मयसूनुना च।
अह्न्याप‍ृतं निशि शयानमतिश्रमेण
लोकं विकुण्ठमुपनेष्यति गोकुलं स्म ॥३१॥

nandaṁ ca mokṣyati bhayād varuṇasya pāśād
gopān bileṣu pihitān maya-sūnunā ca
ahny āpṛtaṁ niśi śayānam atiśrameṇa
lokaṁ vikuṇṭham upaneṣyati gokulaṁ sma

nandam—unto Nanda (the father of Kṛṣṇa); *ca*—also; *mokṣyati*—saves; *bhayāt*—from the fear of; *varuṇasya*—of Varuṇa, the demigod of water; *pāśāt*—from the clutches of; *gopān*—the cowherd men; *bileṣu*—in the caves of the mountain; *pihitān*—placed; *maya-sūnunā*—by the son of Maya; *ca*—also; *ahni āpṛtam*—being very engaged during the daytime; *niśi*—at night; *śayānam*—lying down; *atiśrameṇa*—because of hard labor; *lokam*—planet; *vikuṇṭham*—the spiritual sky; *upaneṣyati*—He awarded; *gokulam*—the highest planet; *sma*—certainly.

TRANSLATION

Lord Kṛṣṇa saved His foster father, Nanda Mahārāja, from the fear of the demigod Varuṇa and released the cowherd boys from

the caves of the mountain, for they were placed there by the son of Maya. Also, to the inhabitants of Vṛndāvana, who were busy working during daytime and sleeping soundly at night because of their hard labor in the day, Lord Kṛṣṇa awarded promotion to the highest planet in the spiritual sky. All these acts are transcendental and certainly prove without any doubt His Godhood.

PURPORT

Nanda Mahārāja, the foster father of Lord Kṛṣṇa, went to take his bath in the River Yamunā in the dead of night, mistakenly thinking that the night was already over; thus the demigod Varuṇa took him to the Varuṇa planet just to have a look at the Personality of Godhead Lord Kṛṣṇa, who appeared there to release His father. Actually there was no arrest of Nanda Mahārāja by Varuṇa because the inhabitants of Vṛndāvana were always engaged in thinking of Kṛṣṇa, in constant meditation on the Personality of Godhead in a particular form of *samādhi,* or trance of *bhakti-yoga.* They had no fear of the miseries of material existence. In the *Bhagavad-gītā* it is confirmed that to be in association with the Supreme Personality of Godhead by full surrender in transcendental love frees one from the miseries inflicted by the laws of material nature. Here it is clearly mentioned that the inhabitants of Vṛndāvana were extensively busy in the hard labor of their day's work, and due to the day's hard labor they were engaged in sound sleep at night. So practically they had very little time to devote to meditation or to the other paraphernalia of spiritual activities. But factually they were engaged in the highest spiritual activities only. Everything done by them was spiritualized because everything was dovetailed in their relationship with Lord Śrī Kṛṣṇa. The central point of activities was Kṛṣṇa, and as such the so-called activities in the material world were saturated with spiritual potency. That is the advantage of the way of *bhakti-yoga.* One should discharge one's duty on Lord Kṛṣṇa's behalf, and all one's actions will be saturated with Kṛṣṇa thought, the highest pattern of trance in spiritual realization.

TEXT 32

गोपैर्मखे प्रतिहते व्रजविप्लवाय
देवेऽभिवर्षति पशून् कृपया रिरक्षुः ।

धर्तोच्छिलीन्ध्रमिव सप्तदिनानि सप्त-
वर्षो महीध्रमनघैककरे सलीलम् ॥३२॥

gopair makhe pratihate vraja-viplavāya
deve 'bhivarṣati paśūn kṛpayā rirakṣuḥ
dhartocchilīndhram iva sapta-dināni sapta-
varṣo mahīdhram anaghaika-kare salīlam

gopaiḥ—by the cowherd men; *makhe*—in offering a sacrifice to the King of heaven; *pratihate*—being hampered; *vraja-viplavāya*—for devastating the whole existence of Vrajabhūmi, the land of Kṛṣṇa's pastimes; *deve*—by the King of heaven; *abhivarṣati*—having poured down heavy rain; *paśūn*—the animals; *kṛpayā*—by causeless mercy upon them; *rirakṣuḥ*—desired to protect them; *dharta*—held up; *ucchilīndhram*—uprooted as an umbrella; *iva*—exactly like that; *sapta-dināni*—continuously for seven days; *sapta-varṣaḥ*—although He was only seven years old; *mahīdhram*—the Govardhana Hill; *anagha*—without being tired; *eka-kare*—in one hand only; *salīlam*—playfully.

TRANSLATION

When the cowherd men of Vṛndāvana, under instruction of Kṛṣṇa, stopped offering sacrifice to the heavenly King, Indra, the whole tract of land known as Vraja was threatened with being washed away by constant heavy rains for seven days. Lord Kṛṣṇa, out of His causeless mercy upon the inhabitants of Vraja, held up the hill known as Govardhana with one hand only, although He was only seven years old. He did this to protect the animals from the onslaught of water.

PURPORT

Children play with an umbrella generally known as a frog's umbrella, and Lord Kṛṣṇa, when He was only seven years old, could snatch the great hill known as the Govardhana Parvata at Vṛndāvana and hold it for seven days continuously with one hand, just to protect the animals and the inhabitants of Vṛndāvana from the wrath of Indra, the heavenly King, who had been denied sacrificial offerings by the inhabitants of Vrajabhūmi.

Factually there is no need of offering sacrifices to the demigods for their services if one is engaged in the service of the Supreme Lord. Sacrifices recommended in the Vedic literature for satisfaction of the demigods are a sort of inducement to the sacrificers to realize the existence of higher authorities. The demigods are engaged by the Lord as controlling deities of material affairs, and according to the *Bhagavad-gītā*, when a demigod is worshiped the process is accepted as the indirect method for worshiping the Supreme Lord. But when the Supreme Lord is worshiped directly there is no need of worshiping the demigods or offering them sacrifices as recommended in particular circumstances. Lord Kṛṣṇa therefore advised the inhabitants of Vrajabhūmi not to offer any sacrifices to the heavenly King Indra. But Indra, not knowing Lord Kṛṣṇa in Vrajabhūmi, was angry at the inhabitants of Vrajabhūmi and tried to avenge the offense. But, competent as the Lord was, He saved the inhabitants and animals of Vrajabhūmi by His personal energy and proved definitely that anyone directly engaged as a devotee of the Supreme Lord need not satisfy any other demigods, however great, even to the level of Brahmā, or Śiva. Thus this incident definitely proved without a doubt that Lord Kṛṣṇa is the Personality of Godhead and that He was so in all circumstances, as a child on the lap of His mother, as a boy 7 years old, and as an old man of 125 years of age. In either case He was never on the level of the ordinary man, and even in His advanced age He appeared a young boy 16 years old. These are the particular features of the transcendental body of the Lord.

TEXT 33

क्रीडन् वने निशि निशाकररश्मिगौर्यां
रासोन्मुखः कलपदायतमूर्च्छितेन ।
उद्दीपितस्मररुजां व्रजभृद्वधूनां
हर्तुर्हरिष्यति शिरो धनदानुगस्य ॥३३॥

krīḍan vane niśi niśākara-raśmi-gauryāṁ
rāsonmukhaḥ kala-padāyata-mūrcchitena
uddīpita-smara-rujāṁ vraja-bhṛd-vadhūnāṁ
hartur hariṣyati śiro dhanadānugasya

krīḍan—while engaged in His pastimes; *vane*—in the forest of Vṛndāvana; *niśi*—nocturnal; *niśākara*—the moon; *raśmi-gauryām*—white moonshine; *rāsa-unmukhaḥ*—desiring to dance with; *kala-padāyata*—accompanied by sweet songs; *mūrcchitena*—and melodious music; *uddīpita*—awakened; *smara-rujām*—sexual desires; *vraja-bhṛt*—the inhabitants of Vrajabhūmi; *vadhūnām*—of the wives; *hartuḥ*—of the kidnappers; *hariṣyati*—will vanquish; *śiraḥ*—the head; *dhanada-anugasya*—of the follower of the rich Kuvera.

TRANSLATION

When the Lord was engaged in His pastimes of the rāsa dance in the forest of Vṛndāvana, enlivening the sexual desires of the wives of the inhabitants of Vṛndāvana by sweet and melodious songs, a demon of the name Śaṅkhacūḍa, a rich follower of the treasurer of heaven [Kuvera], kidnapped the damsels, and the Lord severed his head from his trunk.

PURPORT

We should carefully note that the statements described herein are the statements of Brahmājī to Nārada, and he was speaking to Nārada of events that would happen in the future, during the advent of Lord Kṛṣṇa. The pastimes of the Lord are known to the experts who are able to see past, present and future, and Brahmājī, being one of them, foretold what would happen in the future. The killing of Śaṅkhacūḍa by the Lord is a more recent incident, after the *rāsa-līlā,* and not exactly a simultaneous affair. In the previous verses we have seen also that the Lord's engagement in the affairs of the forest fire was described along with His pastimes of punishing the Kāliya snake, and similarly the pastimes of the *rāsa* dance and the killing of Śaṅkhacūḍa are also described herein. The adjustment is that all these incidents would take place in the future, after the time when it was being foretold by Brahmājī to Nārada. The demon Śaṅkhacūḍa was killed by the Lord during His pastimes at Horikā in the month of Phālguna, and the same ceremony is still observed in India by the burning of the effigy of Śaṅkhacūḍa one day prior to the Lord's pastimes at Horikā, generally known as Holi.

Generally the future appearance and the activities of the Lord or His incarnations are foretold in the scriptures, and thus the pseudo-incarnations are unable to cheat persons who are in knowledge of the events as they are described in the authoritative scriptures.

TEXTS 34–35

ये च प्रलम्बखरदर्दुरकेश्यरिष्ट-
मल्लेभकंसयवनाः कपिपौण्ड्रकाद्याः ।
अन्ये च शाल्वकुजबल्वलदन्तवक्र-
सप्तोक्षशम्बरविदूरथरुक्मिमुख्याः ॥३४॥
ये वा मृधे समितिशालिन आत्तचापाः
काम्बोजमत्स्यकुरुसृञ्जयकैकयाद्याः ।
यास्यन्त्यदर्शनमलं बलपार्थभीम-
व्याजाह्वयेन हरिणा निलयं तदीयम् ॥३५॥

ye ca pralamba-khara-dardura-keśy-ariṣṭa-
mallebha-kaṁsa-yavanāḥ kapi-pauṇḍrakādyāḥ
anye ca śālva-kuja-balvala-dantavakra-
saptokṣa-śambara-vidūratha-rukmi-mukhyāḥ

ye vā mṛdhe samiti-śālina ātta-cāpāḥ
kāmboja-matsya-kuru-sṛñjaya-kaikayādyāḥ
yāsyanty adarśanam alaṁ bala-pārtha-bhīma-
vyājāhvayena hariṇā nilayaṁ tadīyam

ye—all those; *ca*—totally; *pralamba*—the demon named Pralamba; *khara*—Dhenukāsura; *dardura*—Bakāsura; *keśī*—the Keśī demon; *ariṣṭa*—the demon Ariṣṭāsura; *malla*—a wrestler in the court of Kaṁsa; *ibha*—Kuvalayāpīḍa; *kaṁsa*—the King of Mathurā and maternal uncle of Kṛṣṇa; *yavanāḥ*—the kings of Persia and other adjoining places; *kapi*—Dvivida; *pauṇḍraka-ādyāḥ*—Pauṇḍraka and others; *anye*—others; *ca*—as much as; *śālva*—King Śālva; *kuja*—Narakāsura; *balvala*—King Balvala; *dantavakra*—the brother of Śiśupāla, a dead rival of Kṛṣṇa's; *saptokṣa*—King Saptokṣa; *śambara*—King Śambara; *vidūratha*—King Vidūratha; *rukmi-mukhyāḥ*—the brother of Rukmiṇī, the first queen of Kṛṣṇa at Dvārakā; *ye*—all those; *vā*—either; *mṛdhe*—in the battlefield; *samiti-śālinaḥ*—all very powerful; *ātta-cāpāḥ*—well equipped with bows and arrows; *kāmboja*—the King of Kāmboja; *matsya*—the King of Dvarbhaṅga; *kuru*—the sons of Dhṛtarāṣṭra; *sṛñjaya*—King Sṛñjaya; *kaikaya-ādyāḥ*—the King of Kekaya and others; *yāsyanti*—would attain; *adarśanam*—impersonal merging within the *brahmajyoti; alam*—what to speak of; *bala*—Baladeva, the elder brother of Kṛṣṇa; *pārtha*—Arjuna; *bhīma*—the second Pāṇḍava; *vyāja-āhvayena*—by the false names; *hariṇā*—by Lord Hari; *nilayam*—the abode; *tadīyam*—of Him.

TRANSLATION

All demonic personalities like Pralamba, Dhenuka, Baka, Keśī, Ariṣṭa, Cāṇūra, Muṣṭika, Kuvalayāpīḍa elephant, Kaṁsa, Yavana, Narakāsura and Pauṇḍraka, great marshals like Śālva, Dvivida monkey and Balvala, Dantavakra, the seven bulls, Śambara, Vidūratha and Rukmī, as also great warriors like Kāmboja, Matsya, Kuru, Sṛñjaya and Kekaya, would all fight vigorously, either with the Lord Hari directly or with Him under His names of Baladeva, Arjuna, Bhīma, etc. And the demons, thus being killed, would attain either the impersonal brahmajyoti or His personal abode in the Vaikuṇṭha planets.

PURPORT

All manifestations, in both the material and spiritual worlds, are demonstrations of the different potencies of Lord Kṛṣṇa. The Personality of Godhead Baladeva is His immediate personal expansion, and Bhīma, Arjuna, etc., are His personal associates. The Lord would appear (and He does so whenever He appears) with all His associates and potencies. Therefore the rebellious souls, like the demons and demoniac men, mentioned by names like Pralamba, would be killed either by the Lord Himself or by His associates. All these affairs will be clearly explained in the Tenth Canto. But we should know well that all the above-mentioned living entities killed would attain salvation either by being merged in the *brahmajyoti* of the Lord or being allowed to enter into the abodes of the

Lord called Vaikuṇṭhas. This has already been explained by Bhīṣmadeva (First Canto). All persons who participated in the Battlefield of Kurukṣetra or otherwise with the Lord or with Baladeva, etc., would benefit by attaining spiritual existence according to the situation of their minds at the time of death. Those who recognized the Lord would enter Vaikuṇṭha, and those who estimated the Lord as only a powerful being would attain salvation by merging into the spiritual existence of the impersonal *brahmajyoti* of the Lord. But every one of them would get release from material existence. Since such is the benefit of those who played with the Lord inimically, one can imagine what would be the position of those who devoutly served the Lord in transcendental relationship with Him.

TEXT 36

कालेन मीलितधियामवमृश्य नृणां
स्तोकायुषां स्वनिगमो बत दूरपारः ।
आविर्हितस्त्वनुयुगं स हि सत्यवत्यां
वेदद्रुमं विटपशो विभजिष्यति स्म ॥३६॥

kālena mīlita-dhiyām avamṛśya nṝṇāṁ
stokāyuṣāṁ sva-nigamo bata dūra-pāraḥ
āvirhitas tv anuyugaṁ sa hi satyavatyāṁ
veda-drumaṁ viṭa-paśo vibhajiṣyati sma

kālena—in course of time; *mīlita-dhiyām*—of the less intelligent persons; *avamṛśya*—considering the difficulties; *nṝṇām*—of humanity at large; *stoka-āyuṣām*—of the short-living persons; *sva-nigamaḥ*—the Vedic literatures compiled by Him; *bata*—exactly; *dūra-pāraḥ*—greatly difficult; *āvirhitaḥ*—having appeared as; *tu*—but; *anuyugam*—in terms of the age; *saḥ*—He (the Lord); *hi*—certainly; *satyavatyām*—in the womb of Satyavatī; *veda-drumam*—the desire tree of the *Vedas; viṭa-paśaḥ*—by division of branches; *vibhajiṣyati*—will divide; *sma*—as it were.

TRANSLATION

The Lord Himself in His incarnation as the son of Satyavatī [Vyāsadeva] will consider his compilation of the Vedic literature to

be very difficult for the less intelligent persons with short life, and thus He will divide the tree of Vedic knowledge into different branches, according to the circumstances of the particular age.

PURPORT

Herein Brahmā mentions the future compilation of *Śrīmad-Bhāgavatam* for the short-lived persons of the Kali age. As explained in the First Canto, the less intelligent persons of the age of Kali would be not only short-lived, but also perplexed with so many problems of life due to the awkward situation of the godless human society. Advancement of material comforts of the body is activity in the mode of ignorance according to the laws of material nature. Real advancement of knowledge means progress of knowledge in self-realization. But in the age of Kali the less intelligent men mistakenly consider the short lifetime of one hundred years (now factually reduced to about forty or sixty years) to be all in all. They are less intelligent because they have no information of the eternity of life; they identify with the temporary material body existing for forty years and consider it the only basic principle of life. Such persons are described as equal to the asses and bulls. But the Lord, as the compassionate father of all living beings, imparts unto them the vast Vedic knowledge in short treatises like the *Bhagavad-gītā* and, for the graduates, the *Śrīmad-Bhāgavatam.* The *Purāṇas* and the *Mahābhārata* are also similarly made by Vyāsadeva for the different types of men in the modes of material nature. But none of them are independent of the Vedic principles.

TEXT 37

देवद्विषां निगमवर्त्मनि निष्ठितानां
पूर्भिर्मयेन विहिताभिरदृश्यतूर्भिः ।
लोकान् घ्नतां मतिविमोहमतिप्रलोभं
वेषं विधाय बहु भाष्यत औपधर्म्यम् ॥३७॥

deva-dviṣāṁ nigama-vartmani niṣṭhitānāṁ
pūrbhir mayena vihitābhir adṛśya-tūrbhiḥ
lokān ghnatāṁ mati-vimoham atipralobhaṁ
veṣaṁ vidhāya bahu bhāṣyata aupadharmyam

deva-dviṣām—of those who were envious of the devotees of the Lord; *nigama*—the *Vedas; vartmani*—on the path of; *niṣṭhitānām*—of the well situated; *pūrbhiḥ*—by rockets; *mayena*—made by the great scientist Maya; *vihitābhiḥ*—made by; *adṛśya-tūrbhiḥ*—unseen in the sky; *lokān*—the different planets; *ghnatām*—of the killers; *mati-vimoham*—bewilderment of the mind; *atipralobham*—very attractive; *veṣam*—dress; *vidhāya*—having done so; *bahu bhāṣyate*—will talk very much; *aupadharmyam*—subreligious principles.

TRANSLATION

When the atheists, after being well versed in the Vedic scientific knowledge, annihilate inhabitants of different planets, flying unseen in the sky on well-built rockets prepared by the great scientist Maya, the Lord will bewilder their minds by dressing Himself attractively as Buddha and will preach on subreligious principles.

PURPORT

This incarnation of Lord Buddha is not the same Buddha incarnation we have in the present history of mankind. According to Śrīla Jīva Gosvāmī, the Buddha incarnation mentioned in this verse appeared in a different Kali age. In the duration of life of one Manu there are more than seventy-two Kali-yugas, and in one of them the particular type of Buddha mentioned here would appear. Lord Buddha incarnates at a time when the people are most materialistic and preaches commonsense religious principles. Such *ahiṁsā* is not a religious principle itself, but it is an important quality for persons who are actually religious. It is a commonsense religion because one is advised to do no harm to any other animal or living being because such harmful actions are equally harmful to he who does the harm. But before learning these principles of nonviolence one has to learn two other principles, namely to be humble and to be prideless. Unless one is humble and prideless, one cannot be harmless and nonviolent. And after being nonviolent one has to learn tolerance and simplicity of living. One must offer respects to the great religious preachers and spiritual leaders and also train the senses for controlled action, learning to be unattached to family and home, and enacting devotional service to the Lord, etc. At the ultimate stage one has to accept the Lord and become His devotee; otherwise there is no religion. In religious principles there must be God in the center; otherwise simple moral instructions are merely subreligious principles, generally known as *upadharma*, or nearness to religious principles.

TEXT 38

यर्ह्यालयेष्वपि सतां न हरेः कथाः स्युः
पाषण्डिनो द्विजजना वृषला नृदेवाः ।
स्वाहा स्वधा वषडिति स्म गिरो न यत्र
शास्ता भविष्यति कलेर्भगवान् युगान्ते ॥३८॥

yarhy ālayeṣv api satāṁ na hareḥ kathāḥ syuḥ
pāṣaṇḍino dvija-janā vṛṣalā nṛdevāḥ
svāhā svadhā vaṣaḍ iti sma giro na yatra
śāstā bhaviṣyati kaler bhagavān yugānte

yarhi—when it happens; *ālayeṣu*—in the residence of; *api*—even; *satām*—civilized gentlemen; *na*—no; *hareḥ*—of the Personality of Godhead; *kathāḥ*—topics; *syuḥ*—will take place; *pāṣaṇḍinaḥ*—atheists; *dvija-janāḥ*—persons declaring themselves to be the higher three classes (*brāhmaṇas, kṣatriyas* and *vaiśyas*); *vṛṣalāḥ*—the lower class *śūdras; nṛ-devāḥ*—ministers of the government; *svāhā*—hymns to perform sacrifices; *svadhā*—the ingredients to perform sacrifices; *vaṣaṭ*—the altar of sacrifice; *iti*—all these; *sma*—shall; *giraḥ*—words; *na*—never; *yatra*—anywhere; *śāstā*—the chastiser; *bhaviṣyati*—will appear; *kaleḥ*—of the Kali age; *bhagavān*—the Personality of Godhead; *yuga-ante*—at the end of.

TRANSLATION

Thereafter, at the end of Kali-yuga, when there exist no topics on the subject of God, even at the residences of so-called saints and respectable gentlemen of the three higher castes, and when the power of government is transferred to the hands of ministers elected from the lowborn śūdra class or those less than them, and when nothing is known of the techniques of sacrifice, even by word, at that time the Lord will appear as the supreme chastiser.

PURPORT

The symptoms of the worst conditions of the material world, at the last stage of this age, called Kali-yuga, are stated herein. The sum and substance of such conditions is godlessness. Even the so-called saints and higher castes of the social orders, generally known as the *dvija-janas* or the twice-born, will become atheists. As such, all of them will practically forget even the holy name of the Lord, and what to speak of His activities. The higher castes of society, namely the intelligent class of men guiding the destinies of the social orders, the administrative class of men guiding the law and order of the society, and the productive class of men guiding the economic development of the society, must all be properly well versed in knowledge of the Supreme Lord, knowing factually His name, quality, pastimes, entourage, paraphernalia and personalities. The saints and the higher castes or orders of the society are judged by their proportion of knowledge in the science of God, or *tattva-jñāna*, and not by any kind of birthright or bodily designations. Such designations, without any knowledge of the science of God and practical knowledge of devotional service, are considered to be all decorations of dead bodies. And when there is too much inflation of these decorated dead bodies in society, there develop so many anomalies in the progressive, peaceful life of the human being. Because of the lack of training or culture in the upper section of the social orders, they are no more to be designated as the *dvija-janas*, or the twice-born. The significance of being twice-born has been explained in many places in these great literatures, and again one is reminded herewith that birth, executed by the sex life of the father and the mother, is called animal birth. But such animal birth and progress of life on the animal principles of eating, sleeping, fearing and mating (without any scientific culture of spiritual life) is called the *śūdra* life, or, to be more explicit, the uncultured life of the lower class of men. It is stated herein that the governmental power of society in the Kali-yuga will be passed over to the uncultured, godless laborer classes of men, and thus the *nṛdevas* (or the ministers of the government) will be the *vṛṣalas*, or the uncultured lower-class men of society. No one can expect any peace and prosperity in a human society full of uncultured lower classes of men. The symptoms of such uncultured social animals are already in vogue, and it is the duty of the leaders of men to take note of it and try to reform the social order by introducing the principles of twice-born men trained in the science of God consciousness. This can be done by expanding the culture of *Śrīmad-Bhāgavatam* all over the world. In the degraded condition of human society, the Lord incarnates as the Kalki *avatāra* and kills all the demonic without mercy.

TEXT 39

सर्गे तपोऽहमृषयो नव ये प्रजेशाः
स्थानेऽथ धर्ममखमन्वमरावनीशाः ।
अन्ते त्वधर्महरमन्युवशासुराद्या
मायाविभूतय इमाः पुरुशक्तिभाजः ॥३९॥

sarge tapo 'ham ṛṣayo nava ye prajeśāḥ
sthāne 'tha dharma-makha-manv-amarāvanīśāḥ
ante tv adharma-hara-manyu-vaśāsurādyā
māyā-vibhūtaya imāḥ puru-śakti-bhājaḥ

sarge—in the beginning of the creation; *tapaḥ*—penance; *aham*—myself; *ṛṣayaḥ*—sages; *nava*—nine; *ye prajeśāḥ*—those who would generate; *sthāne*—in the middle while maintaining the creation; *atha*—certainly; *dharma*—religion; *makha*—Lord Viṣṇu; *manu*—the father of mankind; *amara*—the demigods deputed to control the affairs of maintenance; *avanīśāḥ*—and the kings of different planets; *ante*—at the end; *tu*—but; *adharma*—irreligion; *hara*—Lord Śiva; *manyu-vaśa*—subjected to anger; *asura-ādyāḥ*—atheists, the enemies of the devotees; *māyā*—energy; *vibhūtayaḥ*—powerful representatives; *imāḥ*—all of them; *puru-śakti-bhājaḥ*—of the supreme powerful Lord.

TRANSLATION

At the beginning of creation there are penance, myself [Brahmā], and the Prajāpatis, the great sages who generate; then, during the maintenance of the creation, there are Lord Viṣṇu, the demigods with controlling powers, and the kings of different planets. But at the end there is irreligion, and then Lord Śiva and the atheists full of anger, etc. All of them are different representative manifestations of the energy of the supreme power, the Lord.

PURPORT

The material world is created by the energy of the Lord, which is manifested in the beginning of the creation by the penance of Brahmājī, the first living being in the creation, and then there are the nine Prajāpatis, known as great sages. In the stage when the creation is maintained, there are devotional service to Lord Viṣṇu, or factual religion, the different demigods, and the kings of different planets who maintain the world. At last, when the creation is preparing to wind up, there is first the principle of irreligion, then Lord Śiva along with the atheists, full of anger. But all of them are but different manifestations of the Supreme Lord. Therefore Brahmā, Viṣṇu and Mahādeva (Śiva) are different incarnations of the different modes of material nature. Viṣṇu is the Lord of the mode of goodness. Brahmā is the lord of the mode of passion, and Śiva is the lord of the mode of ignorance. Ultimately, the material creation is but a temporary manifestation meant to give the chance of liberation to the conditioned souls, who are entrapped in the material world, and one who develops the mode of goodness under the protection of Lord Viṣṇu has the greatest chance of being liberated by following the Vaiṣṇava principles and thus being promoted to the kingdom of God, no more to return to this miserable material world.

TEXT 40

विष्णोर्नु वीर्यगणनां कतमोऽर्हतीह
यः पार्थिवान्यपि कविर्विममे रजांसि ।
चस्कम्भ यः स्वरहसास्खलता त्रिपृष्ठं
यस्मात् त्रिसाम्यसदनादुरुकम्पयानम् ॥४०॥

viṣṇor nu vīrya-gaṇanāṁ katamo 'rhatīha
yaḥ pārthivāny api kavir vimame rajāṁsi
caskambha yaḥ sva-rahasāskhalatā tri-pṛṣṭhaṁ
yasmāt tri-sāmya-sadanād uru-kampayānam

viṣṇoḥ—of Lord Viṣṇu; *nu*—but; *vīrya*—prowess; *gaṇanām*—in the matter of accounting; *katamaḥ*—who else; *arhati*—is able to do it; *iha*—in this world; *yaḥ*—one who; *pārthivāni*—the atoms; *api*—also;

kaviḥ—great scientist; *vimame*—might have counted; *rajāṁsi*—particles; *caskambha*—could catch; *yaḥ*—one who; *sva-rahasā*—by His own leg; *askhalatā*—without being hampered; *tri-pṛṣṭham*—the topmost planetary space; *yasmāt*—by which; *tri-sāmya*—the neutral state of the three modes; *sadanāt*—up to that place; *uru-kampayānam*—moving very greatly.

TRANSLATION

Who can describe completely the prowess of Viṣṇu? Even the scientist, who might have counted the particles of the atoms of the universe, cannot do so. Because it is He only who in His form of Trivikrama moved His leg effortlessly beyond the topmost planet, Satyaloka, up to the neutral state of the three modes of material nature. And all were moved.

PURPORT

The highest scientific advancement of the material scientists is atomic energy. But the material scientist is not able to have an estimation of the particles of atoms contained in the whole universe. But even if one is able to count such atomic particles or is able to roll up the sky like one's bedding, even then one is unable to estimate the extent of the prowess and energy of the Supreme Lord. He is known as Trivikrama because once, in His incarnation of Vāmana, He expanded His leg beyond the highest planetary system, Satyaloka, and reached the neutral state of the modes of nature called the covering of the material world. There are seven layers of material coverings over the material sky, and the Lord could penetrate even those coverings. With His toe He made a hole through which the water of the Causal Ocean filters into the material sky, and the current is known as the sacred Ganges, which purifies the planets of the three worlds. In other words, no one is equal to the transcendentally powerful Viṣṇu. He is omnipotent, and no one is equal to or greater than Him.

TEXT 41

नान्तं विदाम्यहममी मुनयोऽग्रजास्ते
मायाबलस्य पुरुषस्य कुतोऽवरा ये ।

गायन् गुणान् दशशताननं आदिदेवः
शेषोऽधुनापि समवस्यति नास्य पारम्॥४१॥

nāntaṁ vidāmy aham amī munayo 'gra-jās te
māyā-balasya puruṣasya kuto 'varā ye
gāyan guṇān daśa-śatānana ādi-devaḥ
śeṣo 'dhunāpi samavasyati nāsya pāram

na—never; *antam*—end; *vidāmi*—do I know; *aham*—myself; *amī*—and all those; *munayaḥ*—great sages; *agra-jāḥ*—born prior to you; *te*—you; *māyā-balasya*—of the omnipotent; *puruṣasya*—of the Personality of Godhead; *kutaḥ*—what to speak of others; *avarāḥ*—born after us; *ye*—those; *gāyan*—by singing; *guṇān*—the qualities; *daśa-śata-ānanaḥ*—one who has ten hundred faces; *ādi-devaḥ*—the first incarnation of the Lord; *śeṣaḥ*—known as Śeṣa; *adhunā*—until now; *api*—even; *samavasyati*—can achieve; *na*—not; *asya*—of Him; *pāram*—limit.

TRANSLATION

Neither I nor all the sages born before you know fully the omnipotent Personality of Godhead. So what can others, who are born after us, know about Him? Even the first incarnation of the Lord, namely Śeṣa, has not been able to reach the limit of such knowledge, although He is describing the qualities of the Lord with ten hundred faces.

PURPORT

The omnipotent Personality of Godhead has primarily three potential manifestations, namely internal, external, and marginal potencies, with unlimited expansions of these three energies. As such, the potential expansions can never be calculated by anyone because even the Personality of God Himself, as the incarnation of Śeṣa, cannot estimate the potencies, although He has been describing them continuously with His one thousand faces.

TEXT 42

येषां स एष भगवान् दययेदनन्तः
सर्वात्मनाश्रितपदो यदि निर्व्यलीकम्।

ते दुस्तरामतितरन्ति च देवमायां
नैषां ममाहमिति धीः श्वशृगालभक्ष्ये ॥४२॥

yeṣāṁ sa eṣa bhagavān dayayed anantaḥ
sarvātmanāśrita-pado yadi nirvyalīkam
te dustarām atitaranti ca deva-māyāṁ
naiṣāṁ mamāham iti dhīḥ śva-sṛgāla-bhakṣye

yeṣām—unto those only; *saḥ*—the Lord; *eṣaḥ*—the; *bhagavān*—the Personality of Godhead; *dayayet*—does bestow His mercy; *anantaḥ*—the unlimited potential; *sarva-ātmanā*—by all means, without reservation; *āśrita-padaḥ*—surrendered soul; *yadi*—if such surrender; *nirvyalīkam*—without pretention; *te*—those only; *dustarām*—insurmountable; *atitaranti*—can overcome; *ca*—and the paraphernalia; *deva-māyām*—diverse energies of the Lord; *na*—not; *eṣām*—of them; *mama*—mine; *aham*—myself; *iti*—thus; *dhīḥ*—conscious; *śva*—dogs; *sṛgāla*—jackals; *bhakṣye*—in the matter of eating.

TRANSLATION

But anyone who is specifically favored by the Supreme Lord, the Personality of Godhead, due to unalloyed surrender unto the service of the Lord, can overcome the insurmountable ocean of illusion and can understand the Lord. But those who are attached to this body, which is meant to be eaten at the end by dogs and jackals, cannot do so.

PURPORT

The unalloyed devotees of the Lord know the glories of the Lord in the sense that they can understand how great the Lord is and how great is His expansion of diverse energy. Those who are attached to the perishable body can hardly enter into the realm of the science of Godhead. The whole materialistic world, based on the conception of the material body as the self, is ignorant of the science of God. The materialist is always busy working for the welfare of the material body, not only his own but also those of his children, kinsmen, communitymen, countrymen, etc. The materialists have many branches of philanthropic and altruistic activities from a political, national and international angle of vision, but none of the field work can go beyond the jurisdiction of the misconception of identifying the material body with the spirit soul. Unless, therefore, one is saved from the wrong conception of the body and the soul, there is no knowledge of Godhead, and unless there is knowledge of God, all advancement of material civilization, however dazzling, should be considered a failure.

TEXTS 43–45

वेदाहमङ्ग परमस्य हि योगमायां
यूयं भवश्च भगवानथ दैत्यवर्यः ।
पत्नी मनोः स च मनुश्च तदात्मजाश्च
प्राचीनबर्हिर्ऋभुरङ्ग उत ध्रुवश्च ॥४३॥
इक्ष्वाकुरैलमुचुकुन्दविदेहगाधि-
रघ्वम्बरीषसगरा गयनाहुषाद्याः ।
मान्धात्रलर्कशतधन्वनुरन्तिदेवा
देवव्रतो बलिरमूर्त्तरयो दिलीपः ॥४४॥
सौभर्युतङ्कशिबिदेवलपिप्पलाद-
सारस्वतोद्धवपराशरभूरिषेणाः ।
येऽन्ये विभीषणहनूमदुपेन्द्रदत्त-
पार्थार्ष्टिषेणविदुरश्रुतदेववर्याः ॥४५॥

vedāham aṅga paramasya hi yoga-māyāṁ
yūyaṁ bhavaś ca bhagavān atha daitya-varyaḥ
patnī manoḥ sa ca manuś ca tad-ātmajāś ca
prācīnabarhir ṛbhur aṅga uta dhruvaś ca

ikṣvākur aila-mucukunda-videha-gādhi-
raghv-ambarīṣa-sagarā gaya-nāhuṣādyāḥ
māndhātr-alarka-śatadhanv-anu-rantidevā
devavrato balir amūrttarayo dilīpaḥ

saubhary-utaṅka-śibi-devala-pippalāda-
sārasvatoddhava-parāśara-bhūriṣeṇāḥ

ye 'nye vibhīṣaṇa-hanūmad-upendradatta-
pārthārṣṭiṣeṇa-vidura-śrutadeva-varyāḥ

veda—know it; *aham*—myself; *aṅga*—O Nārada; *paramasya*—of the Supreme; *hi*—certainly; *yoga-māyām*—potency; *yūyam*—yourself; *bhavaḥ*—Śiva; *ca*—and; *bhagavān*—the great demigod; *atha*—as also; *daitya-varyaḥ*—Prahlāda Mahārāja, the great devotee of the Lord born in the family of an atheist; *patnī*—Śatarūpā; *manoḥ*—of Manu; *saḥ*—he; *ca*—also; *manuḥ*—Svāyambhuva; *ca*—and; *tat-ātma-jāḥ ca*—and his children like Priyavrata, Uttānapāda, Devahūti, etc.; *prācīnabarhiḥ*—Prācīnabarhi; *ṛbhuḥ*—Ṛbhu; *aṅgaḥ*—Aṅga; *uta*—even; *dhruvaḥ*—Dhruva; *ca*—and; *ikṣvākuḥ*—Ikṣvāku; *aila*—Aila; *mucukunda*—Mucukunda; *videha*—Mahārāja Janaka; *gādhi*—Gādhi; *raghu*—Raghu; *ambarīṣa*—Ambarīṣa; *sagarāḥ*—Sagara; *gaya*—Gaya; *nāhuṣa*—Nāhuṣa; *ādyāḥ*—and so on; *māndhātṛ*—Māndhātā; *alarka*—Alarka; *śatadhanu*—Śatadhanu; *anu*—Anu; *rantidevāḥ*—Rantideva; *devavrataḥ*—Bhīṣma; *baliḥ*—Bali; *amūrttarayaḥ*—Amūrttaraya; *dilīpaḥ*—Dilīpa; *saubhari*—Saubhari; *utaṅka*—Utaṅka; *śibi*—Śibi; *devala*—Devala; *pippalāda*—Pippalāda; *sārasvata*—Sārasvata; *uddhava*—Uddhava; *parāśara*—Parāśara; *bhūriṣeṇāḥ*—Bhūriṣeṇa; *ye*—those who; *anye*—others; *vibhīṣaṇa*—Vibhīṣaṇa; *hanūmat*—Hanumān; *upendra-datta*—Śukadeva Gosvāmī; *pārtha*—Arjuna; *ārṣṭiṣeṇa*—Arṣṭiṣeṇa; *vidura*—Vidura; *śrutadeva*—Śrutadeva; *varyāḥ*—the foremost.

TRANSLATION

O Nārada, although the potencies of the Lord are unknowable and immeasurable, still, because we are all surrendered souls, we know how He acts through yogamāyā potencies. And, similarly, the potencies of the Lord are also known to the all-powerful Śiva, the great king of the atheist family, namely Prahlāda Mahārāja, Svāyambhuva Manu, his wife Śatarūpā, his sons and daughters like Priyavrata, Uttānapāda, Ākūti, Devahūti and Prasūti, Prācīnabarhi, Ṛbhu, Aṅga the father of Vena, Mahārāja Dhruva, Ikṣvāku, Aila, Mucukunda, Mahārāja Janaka, Gādhi, Raghu, Ambarīṣa, Sagara, Gaya, Nāhuṣa, Māndhātā, Alarka, Śatadhanve, Anu, Rantideva, Bhīṣma, Bali, Amūrttaraya, Dilīpa, Saubhari, Utaṅka,

Śibi, Devala, Pippalāda, Sārasvata, Uddhava, Parāśara, Bhūriṣeṇa, Vibhīṣaṇa, Hanumān, Śukadeva Gosvāmī, Arjuna, Ārṣṭiṣeṇa, Vidura, Śrutadeva, etc.

PURPORT

All the great devotees of the Lord, as mentioned above, who flourished in the past or present, and all the devotees of the Lord who will come in the future, are aware of the different potencies of the Lord along with the potency of His name, quality, pastimes, entourage, personality, etc. And how do they know? Certainly it is not by mental speculation, nor by any attempt by dint of limited instruments of knowledge. By the limited instruments of knowledge (either the senses or the material instruments like microscopes and telescopes) one cannot even fully know the Lord's material potencies, which are manifested before our eyes. For example there are many millions and billions of planets far, far beyond the scientist's calculation. But these are only the manifestations of the Lord's material energy. What can the scientist hope to know of the spiritual potency of the Lord by such material efforts? Mental speculations, by adding some dozens of "if's" and "maybe's," cannot aid the advancement of knowledge—on the contrary, such mental speculations will only end in despair by dismissing the case abruptly and declaring the nonexistence of God. The sane person, therefore, ceases to speculate on subjects beyond the jurisdiction of his tiny brain, and as a matter of course he tries to learn to surrender unto the Supreme Lord, who alone can lead one to the platform of real knowledge. In the *Upaniṣads* it is clearly said that the Supreme Personality of Godhead can never be known simply by working very hard and taxing the good brain, nor can He be known simply by mental speculation and jugglery of words. The Lord is knowable only by one who is a surrendered soul. Herein Brahmājī, the greatest of all material living beings, acknowledges this truth. Therefore, the fruitless spoiling of energy by pursuing the path of experimental knowledge must be given up. One should gain knowledge by surrendering unto the Lord and by acknowledging the authority of the persons mentioned herein. The Lord is unlimited and, by the grace of the *yogamāyā*, helps the surrendered soul to know Him proportionately with the advance of one's surrender.

TEXT 46

ते वै विदन्त्यतितरन्ति च देवमायां
स्त्रीशूद्रहूणशबरा अपि पापजीवाः ।
यद्यद्भुतक्रमपरायणशीलशिक्षा-
स्तिर्यग्जना अपि किमु श्रुतधारणा ये ॥४६॥

te vai vidanty atitaranti ca deva-māyām
strī-śūdra-hūṇa-śabarā api pāpa-jīvāḥ
yady adbhuta-krama-parāyaṇa-śīla-śikṣās
tiryag-janā api kim u śruta-dhāraṇā ye

te—such persons; *vai*—undoubtedly; *vidanti*—do know; *atitaranti*—surpass; *ca*—also; *deva-māyām*—the covering energy of the Lord; *strī*—such as women; *śūdra*—the laborer class of men; *hūṇa*—the mountaineers; *śabarāḥ*—the Siberians, or those lower than the *śūdras; api*—although; *pāpa-jīvāḥ*—sinful living beings; *yadi*—provided; *adbhuta-krama*—one whose acts are so wonderful; *parāyaṇa*—those who are devotees; *śīla*—behavior; *śikṣāḥ*—trained by; *tiryak-janāḥ*—even those who are not human beings; *api*—also; *kim*—what; *u*—to speak of; *śruta-dhāraṇāḥ*—those who have taken to the idea of the Lord by hearing about Him; *ye*—those.

TRANSLATION

Surrendered souls, even from groups leading sinful lives, such as women, the laborer class, the mountaineers and the Siberians, or even the birds and beasts, can also know about the science of Godhead and become liberated from the clutches of the illusory energy by surrendering unto the pure devotees of the Lord and by following in their footsteps in devotional service.

PURPORT

Sometimes there are inquiries as to how one can surrender unto the Supreme Lord. In the *Bhagavad-gītā* (18.66) the Lord asked Arjuna to surrender unto Him, and therefore persons unwilling to do so question where God is and to whom they should surrender. The answer to such questions or inquiries is given herein very properly. The Personality of Godhead may not be present before one's eyes, but if one is sincere in wanting such guidance the Lord will send a bona fide person who can guide one properly back home, back to Godhead. There is no need of material qualifications for making progress on the path of spiritual realization. In the material world, when one accepts some particular type of service, he is required to possess some particular type of qualification also. Without this one is unfit for such service. But in the devotional service of the Lord the only qualification required is surrender. Surrendering oneself is in one's own hand. If one likes, he can surrender immediately, without delay, and that begins his spiritual life. The bona fide representative of God is as good as God Himself. Or, in other words, the loving representative of the Lord is more kind and more easy to approach. A sinful soul cannot approach the Lord directly, but such a sinful man can very easily approach a pure devotee of the Lord. And if one agrees to put himself under the guidance of such a devotee of the Lord, he can also understand the science of God and can also become like the transcendental pure devotee of the Lord and thus get his liberation back to Godhead, back home for eternal happiness.

So realization of the science of Godhead and relief from the unnecessary, useless struggle for existence are not at all difficult for the willing candidate. But they are very difficult for persons who are not surrendered souls but only simple, profitless speculators.

TEXT 47

शश्वत् प्रशान्तमभयं प्रतिबोधमात्रं
शुद्धं समं सदसतः परमात्मतत्त्वम् ।
शब्दो न यत्र पुरुकारकवान् क्रियार्थो
माया परैत्यभिमुखे च विलज्जमाना
तद् वै पदं भगवतः परमस्य पुंसो
ब्रह्मेति यद् विदुरजस्रसुखं विशोकम् ॥४७॥

śaśvat praśāntam abhayaṁ pratibodha-mātraṁ
śuddhaṁ samaṁ sad-asataḥ paramātma-tattvam

śabdo na yatra puru-kārakavān kriyārtho
māyā paraity abhimukhe ca vilajjamānā
tad vai padaṁ bhagavataḥ paramasya puṁso
brahmeti yad vidur ajasra-sukhaṁ viśokam

śaśvat—eternal; *praśāntam*—without disturbance; *abhayam*—without fear; *pratibodha-mātram*—a consciousness opposed to the material counterpart; *śuddham*—uncontaminated; *samam*—without distinction; *sat-asataḥ*—of the cause and effect; *paramātma-tattvam*—the principle of primeval cause; *śabdaḥ*—speculative sound; *na*—not; *yatra*—where there is; *puru-kārakavān*—resulting in fruitive action; *kriyā-arthaḥ*—for the matter of sacrifice; *māyā*—illusion; *paraiti*—flies away; *abhimukhe*—in front of; *ca*—also; *vilajjamānā*—being ashamed of; *tat*—that; *vai*—is certainly; *padam*—ultimate phase; *bhagavataḥ*—of the Personality of Godhead; *paramasya*—of the Supreme; *puṁsaḥ*—of the person; *brahma*—the Absolute; *iti*—thus; *yat*—which; *viduḥ*—known as; *ajasra*—unlimited; *sukham*—happiness; *viśokam*—without grief.

TRANSLATION

What is realized as the Absolute Brahman is full of unlimited bliss without grief. That is certainly the ultimate phase of the supreme enjoyer, the Personality of Godhead. He is eternally void of all disturbances and fearless. He is complete consciousness as opposed to matter. Uncontaminated and without distinctions, He is the principle primeval cause of all causes and effects, in whom there is no sacrifice for fruitive activities and in whom the illusory energy does not stand.

PURPORT

The supreme enjoyer, the Personality of Godhead, is the Supreme Brahman or the *summum bonum* because of His being the supreme cause of all causes. The conception of impersonal Brahman realization is the first step, due to His distinction from the illusory conception of material existence. In other words, impersonal Brahman is a feature of the Absolute distinct from the material variegatedness, just as light is a conception distinct from its counterpart, darkness. But the light has its variegatedness, which is seen by those who further advance in the light, and thus the ultimate realization of Brahman is the source of the Brahman light, the Supreme Personality of Godhead, the *summum bonum* or the ultimate source of everything. Therefore, meeting the Personality of Godhead includes the realization of the impersonal Brahman as realized at first in contrast with material inebriety. The Personality of Godhead is the third step of Brahman realization. As explained in the First Canto, one must understand all three features of the Absolute—Brahman, Paramātmā and Bhagavān.

Pratibodha-mātram is just the opposite conception of material existence. In matter there are material miseries, and thus in the first realization of Brahman there is the negation of such material inebrieties, and there is a feeling of eternal existence distinct from the pangs of birth and death, disease and old age. That is the primary conception of impersonal Brahman.

The Supreme Lord is the Supreme Soul of everything, and therefore in the supreme conception affection is realized. The conception of affection is due to the relationship of soul to soul. A father is affectionate to his son because there is some relationship of nearness between the son and the father. But that sort of affection in the material world is full of inebriety. When the Personality of Godhead is met, the fullness of affection becomes manifested because of the reality of the affectionate relationship. He is not the object of affection by material tinges of body and mind, but He is the full, naked, uncontaminated object of affection for all living entities because He is the Supersoul, or Paramātmā, within everyone's heart. In the liberated state of affairs, the full-fledged affection for the Lord is awakened.

As such, there is an unlimited flow of everlasting happiness, without the fear of its being broken as we have experienced here in the material world. The relationship with the Lord is never broken; thus there is no grief and no fear. Such happiness is inexplicable by words, and there can be no attempt to generate such happiness by fruitive activities by arrangements and sacrifices. But we must also know that happiness, unbroken happiness exchanged with the Supreme Person, the Personality of Godhead as described in this verse, transcends the impersonal conception of the *Upaniṣads*. In the *Upaniṣads* the description is more or less negation of the material conception of things, but this is not denial of the transcendental senses of the Supreme Lord. Herein also the same is affirmed in the statements about the material elements; they are all transcendental, free from all contamination of material identification. And also the liberated souls are not devoid of senses; otherwise there cannot be any reciprocation of unhampered spiritual happiness exchanged between them in spontaneous unbroken joy. All the senses, both of the Lord and of the devotees, are without material contamination. They are so because they are beyond the material cause and effects, as clearly mentioned herein (*sad-asataḥ param*). The illusory, material energy cannot work there, being ashamed before the Lord and His transcendental devotees. In the material world the sense activities are not without grief, but here it is clearly said that the senses of the Lord and the devotees are without any grief. There is a distinct difference between the material and spiritual senses. And one should understand it without denying the spiritual senses because of a material conception.

The senses in the material world are surcharged with material ignorance. In every way, the authorities have recommended purification of the senses from the material conception. In the material world the senses are manipulated for individual and personal satisfaction, whereas in the spiritual world the senses are properly used for the purpose for which they were originally meant, namely the satisfaction of the Supreme Lord. Such sensual activities are natural, and therefore sense gratification there is uninterrupted and unbroken by material contamination because the senses are spiritually purified. And such satisfaction of the senses is equally shared by the transcendental reciprocators. Since the activities are unlimited and constantly increasing, there is no scope for material attempts or artificial arrangements. Such happiness of transcendental quality is called *brahma-saukhyam*, which will be clearly described in the Fifth Canto.

TEXT 48

सध्र्यङ् नियम्य यतयो यमकर्तहेतिं
जह्युः स्वराडिव निपानखनित्रमिन्द्रः ॥४८॥

sadhryaṅ niyamya yatayo yama-karta-hetiṁ
jahyuḥ svarāḍ iva nipāna-khanitram indraḥ

sadhryak—artificial mental speculation or meditation; *niyamya*—controlling; *yatayaḥ*—the mystics; *yama-karta-hetim*—the process of spiritual culture; *jahyuḥ*—are given up; *svarāṭ*—fully independent; *iva*—as; *nipāna*—well; *khanitram*—trouble for digging; *indraḥ*—the controlling demigod supplying rains.

TRANSLATION

In such a transcendental state there is no need of artificial control of the mind, mental speculation or meditation, as performed by the jñānīs and yogīs. One gives up such processes, as the heavenly King, Indra, forgoes the trouble to dig a well.

PURPORT

A poor man in want of water digs a well and undertakes the trouble of digging. Similarly, those who are poor in transcendental realization speculate on the mind or meditate by controlling the senses. But they do not know that such control of the senses and achievement of spiritual perfection are simultaneously made possible as soon as one is factually engaged in the transcendental loving service of the Supreme Person, the Personality of Godhead. It is for this reason that the great liberated souls also desire to be associated in hearing and chanting the activities of the Lord. The example of Indra is very appropriate in this connection. King Indra of heaven is the controlling deity or demigod for arranging clouds and supplying rains in the universe, and as such he does not have to take the trouble to dig a well for his personal water supply. For him, digging a well for a water supply is simply ludicrous. Similarly, those who are factually engaged in the loving service of the Lord have attained the ultimate goal of life, and for them there is no need of mental speculation to find out the true nature of God or His activities. Nor do such devotees have to meditate upon the imaginary or real identity of the Lord. Because they are factually engaged in the transcendental loving service of the Lord, the Lord's pure devotees have already achieved the results of mental speculation and meditation. The real perfection of life is therefore to be engaged in the transcendental loving service of the Lord.

TEXT 49

स श्रेयसामपि विभुर्भगवान् यतोऽस्य
भावस्वभावविहितस्य सतः प्रसिद्धिः ।

देहे स्वधातुविगमेऽनुविशीर्यमाणे
व्योमेव तत्र पुरुषो न विशीर्यतेऽजः ॥४९॥

sa śreyasām api vibhur bhagavān yato 'sya
bhāva-svabhāva-vihitasya sataḥ prasiddhiḥ
dehe sva-dhātu-vigame 'nuviśīryamāṇe
vyomeva tatra puruṣo na viśīryate 'jaḥ

saḥ—He; *śreyasām*—all auspiciousness; *api*—also; *vibhuḥ*—the master; *bhagavān*—the Personality of Godhead; *yataḥ*—because; *asya*—of the living entity; *bhāva*—natural modes; *sva-bhāva*—own constitution; *vihitasya*—performances; *sataḥ*—all good work; *prasiddhiḥ*—ultimate success; *dehe*—of the body; *sva-dhātu*—forming elements; *vigame*—being vanquished; *anu*—after; *viśīryamāṇe*—having given up; *vyoma*—sky; *iva*—like; *tatra*—thereupon; *puruṣaḥ*—the living entity; *na*—never; *viśīryate*—becomes vanquished; *ajaḥ*—due to being unborn.

TRANSLATION

The Personality of Godhead is the supreme master of everything auspicious because the results of whatever actions are performed by the living being, in either the material or spiritual existence, are awarded by the Lord. As such, He is the ultimate benefactor. Every individual living entity is unborn, and therefore even after the annihilation of the material elementary body, the living entity exists, exactly like the air within the body.

PURPORT

The living entity is unborn and eternal, and as confirmed in the *Bhagavad-gītā* (2.30), the living entity is not exhausted even though the material elementary body is vanquished. As long as the living entity is in material existence, actions performed by him are rewarded in the next life, or even in the present life. Similarly, in his spiritual life also actions are rewarded by the Lord by the five kinds of liberation. Even the impersonalist cannot achieve the desired merging into the existence of the Supreme without being favored by the Supreme Personality of Godhead. It is confirmed in the *Bhagavad-gītā* (4.11) that the Lord awards similar results, as one desires, in one's present life. The living entities are given freedom to make their choice, and the Lord awards them accordingly.

It is the duty of everyone, therefore, to worship devoutly only the Personality of Godhead to achieve his desired goal. The impersonalist, instead of speculating or meditating, can directly execute the routine devotional service of the Lord and thus easily obtain the desired goal.

The devotees, however, are naturally inclined to become associates of the Lord and not merge in the spiritual existence, as conceived by the impersonalist. The devotees, therefore, following their constitutional instincts, achieve the desired goal of becoming servitors, friends, fathers, mothers or conjugal lovers of the Lord. The devotional service of the Lord involves nine transcendental processes, such as hearing and chanting, and by performing such easy and natural devotional services the devotees achieve the highest perfectional results, far, far superior to merging into the existence of Brahman. The devotees are therefore never advised to indulge in speculating upon the nature of the Supreme or artificially meditating on the the void.

One should not, however, mistakenly think that after the annihilation of this present body there is no body by which one can associate with the Lord face to face. The living entity is unborn. It is not that he is manifest with the creation of the material body. On the other hand, it is true that the material body develops only by the desire of the living entity. The evolution of the material body is due to the desires of the living being. According to the desires of the living being, the material body develops. So from the spirit soul the material body comes into existence, generated from the living force. Since the living being is eternal, he exists just like the air within the body. Air is within and without the body. Therefore when the external covering, the material body, is vanquished, the living spark, like the air within the body, continues to exist. And by the direction of the Lord, because He is the ultimate benefactor, the living entity is at once awarded the necessary spiritual body befitting his association with the Lord in the manner of *sārūpya* (equal bodily feature), *sālokya* (equal facility to live on the same planet with the Lord), *sārṣṭi* (equal possession of opulence like the Lord), and *sāmīpya* (equal association with the Lord).

The Lord is so kind that even if a devotee of the Lord cannot fulfill the complete course of devotional service unalloyed and uncontaminated by material association, he is given another chance in the next life by being awarded a birth in the family of a devotee or rich man so that without being engaged in the struggle for material existence the devotee can finish the remaining purification of his existence and thus immediately, after relinquishing the present body, go back home, back to Godhead. This is confirmed in the *Bhagavad-gītā.*

In this connection detailed information is available in the *Bhagavat-sandarbha* of Śrīla Jīva Gosvāmī Prabhupāda. Once achieving the spiritual existence, the devotee is eternally situated there, as already discussed in the previous verse.

TEXT 50

सोऽयं तेऽभिहितस्तात भगवान् विश्वभावनः ।
समासेन हरेर्नान्यदन्यस्मात् सदसच्च यत् ॥५०॥

so 'yaṁ te 'bhihitas tāta
bhagavān viśva-bhāvanaḥ
samāsena harer nānyad
anyasmāt sad-asac ca yat

saḥ—that; *ayam*—the same; *te*—unto you; *abhihitaḥ*—explained by me; *tāta*—my dear son; *bhagavān*—the Personality of Godhead; *viśva-bhāvanaḥ*—the creator of the manifested worlds; *samāsena*—in brief; *hareḥ*—without Hari, the Lord; *na*—never; *anyat*—anything else; *anyasmāt*—being the cause of; *sat*—manifested or phenomenal; *asat*—noumenal; *ca*—and; *yat*—whatever there may be.

TRANSLATION

My dear son, I have now explained in brief the Supreme Personality of Godhead, who is creator of the manifested worlds. Without Him, Hari, the Lord, there are no other causes of the phenomenal and noumenal existences.

PURPORT

Since we generally have the experience of the temporary, material world and conditioned souls trying to lord it over the material worlds,

Brahmājī explained to Nāradadeva that this temporary world is the work of the external potency of the Lord and that the conditioned souls struggling here for existence are the marginal potency of the Supreme Lord, the Personality of Godhead. There is no cause for all these phenomenal activities but Him, Hari, the Supreme Lord, who is the primeval cause of all causes. This does not mean, however, that the Lord Himself is distributed impersonally. He is aloof from all these interactions of the external and marginal potencies. In the *Bhagavad-gītā* (9.4) it is confirmed that by His potencies alone He is present everywhere and anywhere. Everything that is manifested rests on His potency only, but He, as the Supreme Personality of Godhead, is always aloof from everything. The potency and the potent are simultaneously one and different from one another.

One should not deprecate the Supreme Lord for the creation of this miserable world, just as one should not blame the king for creating a prisonhouse in the government. The prisonhouse is a necessary institution of the governmental establishment for those who are disobedient to the laws of the government. Similarly, this material world, full of miseries, is a temporary creation of the Lord for those who have forgotten Him and are trying to lord it over the false manifestation. He, however, is always anxious to get the fallen souls back home, back to Godhead, and for this He has given so many chances to the conditioned souls via the authoritative scriptures, His representatives, and personal incarnations also. Since He has no direct attachment to this material world, He is not to be blamed for its creation.

TEXT 51

इदं भागवतं नाम यन्मे भगवतोदितम् ।
संग्रहोऽयं विभूतीनां त्वमेतद् विपुलीकुरु ।।५१।।

idaṁ bhāgavataṁ nāma
yan me bhagavatoditam
saṅgraho 'yaṁ vibhūtīnāṁ
tvam etad vipulī kuru

idam—this; *bhāgavatam*—the science of Godhead; *nāma*—of the name; *yat*—that which; *me*—unto me; *bhagavatā*—by the Personality of Godhead; *uditam*—enlightened; *saṅgrahaḥ*—is the accumulation of; *ayam*—His; *vibhūtīnām*—of the diverse potencies; *tvam*—your good self; *etat*—this science of Godhead; *vipulī*—expand; *kuru*—do it.

TRANSLATION

O Nārada, this science of God, Śrīmad-Bhāgavatam, was spoken to me in summary by the Supreme Personality of Godhead, and it was spoken as the accumulation of His diverse potencies. Please expand this science yourself.

PURPORT

The *Bhāgavatam* in a nutshell, spoken by the Personality of Godhead in about half a dozen verses, which will appear ahead, is the science of God, and it is the potent representation of the Personality of Godhead. He, being absolute, is nondifferent from the science of God, *Śrīmad-Bhāgavatam.* Brahmājī received this science of Godhead from the Lord directly, and he handed over the same to Nārada, who in his turn ordered Śrīla Vyāsadeva to expand it. So the transcendental knowledge of the Supreme Lord is not mental speculation by the mundane wranglers, but is uncontaminated, eternal, perfect knowledge beyond the jurisdiction of material modes. The *Bhāgavata Purāṇa* is therefore the direct incarnation of the Lord in the form of transcendental sound, and one should receive this transcendental knowledge from the bona fide representative of the Lord in the chain of disciplic succession from the Lord to Brahmājī, from Brahmājī to Nārada, from Nārada to Vyāsa, from Vyāsadeva to Śukadeva Gosvāmī, from Śukadeva Gosvāmī to Sūta Gosvāmī. The ripened fruit of the Vedic tree drops from one hand to another without being broken by falling suddenly from a high branch down to the earth. Therefore unless one hears the science of Godhead from the bona fide representative of the disciplic succession, as above mentioned, for one to understand the theme of the science of Godhead will be a difficult job. It should never be heard from the professional *Bhāgavatam* reciters who earn their livelihood by gratifying the senses of the audience.

TEXT 52

यथा हरौ भगवति नृणां भक्तिर्भविष्यति ।
सर्वात्मन्यखिलाधारे इति सङ्कल्प्य वर्णय ॥५२॥

yathā harau bhagavati
nṛṇāṁ bhaktir bhaviṣyati
sarvātmany akhilādhāre
iti saṅkalpya varṇaya

yathā—as much as; *harau*—unto the Personality of Godhead; *bhagavati*—unto the Lord; *nṛṇām*—for human beings; *bhaktiḥ*—devotional service; *bhaviṣyati*—become enlightened; *sarva-ātmani*—the Absolute Whole; *akhila-ādhāre*—unto the *summum bonum; iti*—thus; *saṅkalpya*—by determination; *varṇaya*—describe.

TRANSLATION

Please describe the science of Godhead with determination and in a manner by which it will be quite possible for the human being to develop transcendental devotional service unto the Personality of Godhead Hari, the Supersoul of every living being and the summum bonum source of all energies.

PURPORT

Śrīmad-Bhāgavatam is the philosophy of devotional service and the scientific presentation of man's relationship with the Supreme Personality of Godhead. Prior to the age of Kali there was no need for such a book of knowledge to know the Lord and His potential energies, but with the beginning of the age of Kali human society gradually became influenced by four sinful principles, namely illegitimate connection with women, intoxication, gambling and unnecessary killing of animals. Because of these basic sinful acts, man gradually became forgetful of his eternal relation with God. Therefore man became blind, so to speak, to his ultimate goal of life. The ultimate goal of life is not to pass a life of irresponsibility like the animals and indulge in a polished way in the four animal principles, namely eating, sleeping, fearing and mating. For such a blind human society in the darkness of ignorance, *Śrīmad-Bhāgavatam* is the torchlight to see things in proper perspective. Therefore it was necessary to describe the science of God from the very beginning, or from the very birth of the phenomenal world.

As we have already explained, *Śrīmad-Bhāgavatam* is so scientifically presented that any sincere student of this great science will be able to understand the science of God simply by reading it with attention or simply by regularly hearing it from the bona fide speaker. Everyone is hankering after happiness in life, but in this age the members of human society, blind as they are, do not have the proper vision that the Personality of Godhead is the reservoir of all happiness because He is the ultimate source of everything (*janmādy asya yataḥ*). Happiness in complete perfection without hindrance can be achieved only by our devotional relationship with Him. And it is only by His association that we can get free of distressful material existence. Even those who are after the enjoyment of this material world can also take shelter of the great science of *Śrīmad-Bhāgavatam*, and they will be successful at the end. Nārada is therefore requested or ordered by his spiritual master to present this science with determination and in good plan. Nārada was never advised to preach the principles of *Bhāgavatam* to earn a livelihood; he was ordered by his spiritual master to take the matter very seriously in a missionary spirit.

TEXT 53

मायां वर्णयतोऽमुष्य ईश्वरस्यानुमोदतः ।
शृण्वतः श्रद्धया नित्यं माययात्मा न मुह्यति ॥५३॥

māyāṁ varṇayato 'muṣya
īśvarasyānumodataḥ
śṛṇvataḥ śraddhayā nityaṁ
māyayātmā na muhyati

māyām—affairs of the external energy; *varṇayataḥ*—while describing; *amuṣya*—of the Lord; *īśvarasya*—of the Personality of Godhead; *anumodataḥ*—thus appreciating; *śṛṇvataḥ*—thus hearing; *śraddhayā*—with devotion; *nityam*—regularly; *māyayā*—by the illusory energy; *ātmā*—the living entity; *na*—never; *muhyati*—becomes illusioned.

TRANSLATION

The Lord's activities in association with His different energies should be described, appreciated and heard in accordance with the teachings of the Supreme Lord. If this is done regularly with devotion and respect, one is sure to get out of the illusory energy of the Lord.

PURPORT

The science of learning a subject matter seriously is different from the sentiments of fanatics. Fanatics or fools may consider the Lord's activities in relation with the external energy to be useless for them, and they may falsely claim to be higher participants in the internal energy of the Lord, but factually the Lord's activities in relation with the external energy and the internal energy are equally good. On the other hand, those who are not completely free from the clutches of the Lord's external energy should devoutly hear regularly about the activities of the Lord in relation with the external energy. They should not foolishly jump up to the activities of the internal energy, falsely attracted by the Lord's internal potential activities like His *rāsa-līlā.* The cheap reciters of the *Bhāgavatam* are very much enthusiastic about the Lord's internal potential activities, and the pseudodevotees, absorbed in material sense enjoyment, falsely jump to the stage of liberated souls and thus fall down deeply into the clutches of external energy.

Some of them think that to hear about the pastimes of the Lord means to hear about His activities with the *gopīs* or about His pastimes like lifting the Govardhana Hill, and they have nothing to do with the Lord's plenary expansions as the *puruṣāvatāras* and Their pastimes of the creation, maintenance or annihilation of the material worlds. But a pure devotee knows that there is no difference between the pastimes of the Lord, either in *rāsa-līlā* or in creation, maintenance or destruction of the material world. Rather, the descriptions of such activities of the Lord as the *puruṣāvatāras* are specifically meant for persons who are in the clutches of the external energy. Topics like the *rāsa-līlā* are meant for the liberated souls and not for the conditioned souls. The conditioned souls, therefore, must hear with appreciation and devotion the Lord's pastimes in relationship with the external energy, and such acts are as good as the hearing of *rāsa-līlā* in the liberated stage. A conditioned soul should not imitate the activities of liberated souls. Lord Śrī Caitanya never indulged in hearing the *rāsa-līla* with ordinary men.

In the *Śrīmad-Bhāgavatam*, the science of God, the first nine cantos prepare the ground for hearing the Tenth Canto. This will be further explained in the last chapter of this canto. In the Third Canto it will be more explicit. A pure devotee of the Lord, therefore, must begin reading or hearing *Śrīmad-Bhāgavatam* from the very beginning, and not from the Tenth Canto. We have several times been requested by some so-called devotees to take up the Tenth Canto immediately, but we have refrained from such an action because we wish to present *Śrīmad-Bhāgavatam* as the science of Godhead and not as a sensuous understanding for the conditioned souls. This is forbidden by such authorities as Śrī Brahmājī. By reading and hearing *Śrīmad-Bhāgavatam* as a scientific presentation, the conditioned souls will gradually be promoted to the higher status of transcendental knowledge after being freed from the illusory energy based on sense enjoyment.

Thus end the Bhaktivedanta purports of the Second Canto, Seventh Chapter, of the Śrīmad-Bhāgavatam, *entitled "Scheduled Incarnations with Specific Functions."*

CHAPTER EIGHT

Questions by King Parīkṣit

TEXT 1

राजोवाच
ब्रह्मणा चोदितो ब्रह्मन् गुणाख्यानेऽगुणस्य च ।
यस्मै यस्मै यथा प्राह नारदो देवदर्शनः ॥ १ ॥

rājovāca
brahmaṇā codito brahman
guṇākhyāne 'guṇasya ca
yasmai yasmai yathā prāha
nārado deva-darśanaḥ

rājā—the King; *uvāca*—inquired; *brahmaṇā*—by Lord Brahmā; *coditaḥ*—being instructed; *brahman*—O learned *brāhmaṇa* (Śukadeva Gosvāmī); *guṇa-ākhyāne*—in narrating the transcendental qualities; *aguṇasya*—of the Lord, who is without material qualities; *ca*—and; *yasmai yasmai*—and whom; *yathā*—as much as; *prāha*—explained; *nāradaḥ*—Nārada Muni; *deva-darśanaḥ*—one whose audience is as good as that of any demigod.

TRANSLATION

King Parīkṣit inquired from Śukadeva Gosvāmī: How did Nārada Muni, whose hearers are as fortunate as those instructed by Lord Brahmā, explain the transcendental qualities of the Lord, who is without material qualities, and before whom did he speak?

PURPORT

Devarṣi Nārada was directly instructed by Brahmājī, who was also directly instructed by the Supreme Lord; therefore the instructions imparted by Nārada to his various disciples are as good as those of the Supreme Lord. That is the way of understanding Vedic knowledge. It comes down from the Lord by disciplic succession, and this transcendental knowledge is distributed to the world by this descending process. There is no chance, however, to receive the Vedic knowledge from mental speculators. Therefore, wherever Nārada Muni goes, he represents himself as authorized by the Lord, and his appearance is as good as that of the Supreme Lord. Similarly, the disciplic succession which strictly follows the transcendental instruction is the bona fide chain of disciplic succession, and the test for such bona fide spiritual masters is that there should be no difference between the instruction of the Lord originally imparted to His devotee and that which is imparted by the authority in the line of disciplic succession. How Nārada Muni distributed the transcendental knowledge of the Lord will be explained in later cantos.

It will appear also that the Lord existed prior to the material creation, and therefore His transcendental name, quality, etc., do not represent any material quality. Whenever, therefore, the Lord is described as *aguṇa*, or without any quality, it does not mean that He has no quality, but that He has no material quality, such as the modes of goodness, passion or ignorance, as the conditioned souls have. He is transcendental to all material conceptions, and thus He is described as *aguṇa*.

TEXT 2

एतद् वेदितुमिच्छामि तत्त्वं तत्त्वविदां वर ।
हरेरद्भुतवीर्यस्य कथा लोकसुमङ्गलाः ॥ २ ॥

etad veditum icchāmi
tattvaṁ tattva-vidāṁ vara
harer adbhuta-vīryasya
kathā loka-sumaṅgalāḥ

etat—this; *veditum*—to understand; *icchāmi*—I wish; *tattvam*—truth; *tattva-vidām*—of those who are well versed in the Absolute Truth; *vara*—O best; *hareḥ*—of the Lord; *adbhuta-vīryasya*—of the one who possesses wonderful potencies; *kathāḥ*—narrations; *loka*—for all planets; *su-maṅgalāḥ*—auspicious.

TRANSLATION

The King said: I wish to know. Narrations concerning the Lord, who possesses wonderful potencies, are certainly auspicious for living beings in all planets.

PURPORT

Śrīmad-Bhāgavatam, which is full of narrations of the activities of the Supreme Lord, is auspicious for all living beings residing in every planet. One who takes it as belonging to a particular sect is certainly mistaken. *Śrīmad-Bhāgavatam* is certainly a very dear scripture for all the devotees of the Lord, but it is auspicious even for the nondevotees also because it explains that even the nondevotees hovering under the spell of material energy can be delivered from such clutches if they hear the narration of the *Śrīmad-Bhāgavatam* with devotion and attention from the right source representing the Lord by disciplic succession.

TEXT 3

कथयस्व महाभाग यथाहमखिलात्मनि ।
कृष्णे निवेश्य निःसङ्गं मनस्त्यक्ष्ये कलेवरम् ॥ ३ ॥

kathayasva mahābhāga
yathāham akhilātmani
kṛṣṇe niveśya niḥsaṅgaṁ
manas tyakṣye kalevaram

kathayasva—please continue speaking; *mahābhāga*—O greatly fortunate one; *yathā*—as much as; *aham*—I; *akhila-ātmani*—unto the Supreme Soul; *kṛṣṇe* —unto Lord Śrī Kṛṣṇa; *niveśya*—having placed; *niḥsaṅgam*—being freed from material qualities; *manaḥ*—mind; *tyakṣye*—may relinquish; *kalevaram*—body.

TRANSLATION

O greatly fortunate Śukadeva Gosvāmī, please continue narrating Śrīmad-Bhāgavatam so that I can place my mind upon the Supreme Soul, Lord Kṛṣṇa, and, being completely freed from material qualities, thus relinquish this body.

PURPORT

To be fully engaged in hearing the transcendental narration described in the text of *Śrīmad-Bhāgavatam* means to constantly associate with the Supreme Soul, Śrī Kṛṣṇa. And to constantly associate with the Supreme Lord Kṛṣṇa means to be liberated from the qualities of matter. Lord Kṛṣṇa is like the sun, and material contamination is like darkness. As the presence of the sun dissipates darkness, constant engagement in the association of the Lord Śrī Kṛṣṇa frees one from the contamination of the material qualities. Contamination by the material qualities is the cause of repeated birth and death, and liberation from material qualities is transcendence. Mahārāja Parīkṣit was now a realized soul by this secret of liberation, through the grace of Śukadeva Gosvāmī, for the latter had informed the King that the highest perfection of life is to be in remembrance of Nārāyaṇa at the end of life. Mahārāja Parīkṣit was destined to give up his body at the end of seven days, and thus he decided to continue remembering the Lord by His association with the topics of *Śrīmad-Bhāgavatam,* and thus to quit his body in full consciousness of the presence of the Lord Śrī Kṛṣṇa, the Supreme Soul.

The hearing of *Śrīmad-Bhāgavatam* performed by professional men is different from the transcendental hearing of Mahārāja Parīkṣit. Mahārāja Parīkṣit was a soul realized in the Absolute Truth, Śrī Kṛṣṇa, the Personality of Godhead. The fruitive materialist is not a realized soul; he wants to derive some material benefit from his so-called hearing of *Śrīmad-Bhāgavatam.* Undoubtedly such an audience, hearing *Śrīmad-Bhāgavatam* from the professional men, can derive some material benefit as they desire, but that does not mean that such a pretense of hearing *Śrīmad-Bhāgavatam* for a week is as good as the hearing of Mahārāja Parīkṣit.

It is the duty of the sane to hear *Śrīmad-Bhāgavatam* from a self-realized soul and not be duped by professional men. One should continue such hearing till the end of one's life so that one can actually have the transcendental association of the Lord and thus be liberated simply by hearing *Śrīmad-Bhāgavatam.*

Mahārāja Parīkṣit had already given up all his connections with his kingdom and family, the most attractive features of materialism, but still he was conscious of his material body. He wanted to be free of such bondage also by the constant association of the Lord.

TEXT 4

शृण्वतः श्रद्धया नित्यं गृणतश्च स्वचेष्टितम् ।
कालेन नातिदीर्घेण भगवान् विशते हृदि ॥ ४ ॥

śṛṇvataḥ śraddhayā nityaṁ
gṛṇataś ca sva-ceṣṭitam
kālena nātidīrgheṇa
bhagavān viśate hṛdi

śṛṇvataḥ—of those who hear; *śraddhayā*—in earnestness; *nityam*—regularly, always; *gṛṇataḥ*—taking the matter; *ca*—also; *sva-ceṣṭitam*—seriously by one's own endeavor; *kālena*—duration; *na*—not; *ati-dīrgheṇa*—very prolonged time; *bhagavān*—the Personality of Godhead Śrī Kṛṣṇa; *viśate*—becomes manifest; *hṛdi*—within one's heart.

TRANSLATION

Persons who hear Śrīmad-Bhāgavatam regularly and are always taking the matter very seriously will have the Personality of Godhead Śrī Kṛṣṇa manifested in their hearts within a short time.

PURPORT

Cheap devotees or materialistic devotees of the Lord are very much desirous to see the Lord personally without meeting the requisite qualifications. Such third-grade devotees should know well that material attachment and seeing the Lord face to face cannot go together. It is not such a mechanical process that the professional *Bhāgavatam* reciters can do the job on behalf of the third-grade materialistic pseudo-devotee. The professional men are useless in this connection because they are neither self-realized nor interested in the liberation of the audience. They are simply interested in maintaining the material establishment of family attachment and earning some material benefits out of the profession. Mahārāja Parīkṣit had no more than seven days to live, but for others Mahārāja Parīkṣit personally recommends that one hear *Śrīmad-Bhāgavatam* regularly, *nityam,* always by one's own effort and with serious devotion also. That will help one to see the Lord Śrī Kṛṣṇa manifested in one's heart within no time.

The pseudo-devotee, however, is very anxious to see the Lord according to his whims, not making any serious effort to hear *Śrīmad-Bhāgavatam* regularly and without detachment from material benefit. That is not the way recommended by an authority like Mahārāja Parīkṣit, who heard and benefited by hearing *Śrīmad-Bhāgavatam.*

TEXT 5

प्रविष्टः कर्णरन्ध्रेण स्वानां भावसरोरुहम् ।
धुनोति शमलं कृष्णः सलिलस्य यथा शरत् ॥ ५ ॥

praviṣṭaḥ karṇa-randhreṇa
svānāṁ bhāva-saroruham
dhunoti śamalaṁ kṛṣṇaḥ
salilasya yathā śarat

praviṣṭaḥ—thus being entered; *karṇa-randhreṇa*—through the holes of the ears; *svānām*—according to one's liberated position; *bhāva*—constitutional relationship; *saraḥ-ruham*—the lotus flower; *dhunoti*—cleanses; *śamalam*—material qualities like lust, anger, avarice and hankering; *kṛṣṇaḥ*—Lord Kṛṣṇa, the Supreme Personality of Godhead; *salilasya*—of the reservoir of waters; *yathā*—as it were; *śarat*—the autumn season.

TRANSLATION

The sound incarnation of Lord Kṛṣṇa, the Supreme Soul [i.e. Śrīmad-Bhāgavatam], enters into the heart of a self-realized devotee, sits on the lotus flower of his loving relationship, and thus cleanses the dust of material association, such as lust, anger and hankering. Thus it acts like autumnal rains upon pools of muddy water.

PURPORT

It is said that a single pure devotee of the Lord can deliver all the fallen souls of the world. Thus one who is actually in the confidence of a pure devotee like Nārada or Śukadeva Gosvāmī and thus is empowered by one's spiritual master, as Nārada was by Brahmājī, can not only deliver himself from the clutches of *māyā*, or illusion, but can deliver the whole world by his pure and empowered devotional strength. The comparison to the autumnal rain that falls on muddy reservoirs of water is very appropriate. During the rainy season, all the waters of the rivers become muddy, but in the month of July-August, the autumn season, when there is a slight rainfall, the muddy waters of the rivers all over the world become at once clear. By addition of some chemical, a small reservoir of water like that of a metropolitan waterworks tank can be cleared, but by such a tiny effort it is not possible to clear up all the reservoirs of water like the rivers. A powerful pure devotee of the Lord, however, can deliver not only his personal self but also many others in his association.

In other words, the cleansing of the polluted heart by other methods (like the culture of empiric knowledge or mystic gymnastics) can simply cleanse one's own heart, but devotional service to the Lord is so powerful that it can cleanse the hearts of the people in general, by the devotional service of the pure, empowered devotee. A true representative of the Lord like Nārada, Śukadeva Gosvāmī, Lord Caitanya, the six Gosvāmīs and later Śrīla Bhaktivinoda Ṭhākura and Śrīmad Bhaktisiddhānta Sarasvatī Ṭhākura, etc., can deliver all people by their empowered devotional service.

By sincere efforts to hear *Śrīmad-Bhāgavatam* one realizes his constitutional relationship with the Lord in the transcendental humor of servitude, friendship, paternal affection or conjugal love, and by such self-realization one becomes situated at once in the transcendental loving service of the Lord. Not only were all the pure devotees like Nārada self-realized souls, but they were engaged in preaching work automatically by spiritual impetus, and thus they delivered many poor souls entangled in the material modes. They became so powerful because they sincerely followed the *Bhāgavatam* principles by regular hearing and worshiping. By such actions the accumulated material lusts, etc., become cleansed by the personal endeavor of the Lord within the heart. The Lord is always within the heart of the living being, but He becomes manifested by one's devotional service.

Purification of the heart by culture of knowledge or mystic *yoga* may be all right for the time being for an individual person, but it is like the cleansing of a small quantity of stagnant water by chemical processes. Such clarification of water may stand for the time being and the sediments settle down, but by a slight agitation everything becomes muddy.

The idea is that devotional service to the Lord is the only method of cleansing the heart for good. Whereas other methods may be superficially good for the time being, there is a risk of becoming muddy again due to agitation of the mind. Devotional service to the Lord, with specific attention for hearing *Śrīmad-Bhāgavatam* regularly and always, is the best recommended method for liberation from the clutches of illusion.

TEXT 6

धौतात्मा पुरुषः कृष्णपादमूलं न मुञ्चति ।
मुक्तसर्वपरिक्लेशः पान्थः स्वशरणं यथा ॥ ६ ॥

dhautātmā puruṣaḥ kṛṣṇa-
pāda-mūlaṁ na muñcati
mukta-sarva-parikleśaḥ
pānthaḥ sva-śaraṇaṁ yathā

dhauta-ātmā—whose heart has been cleansed; *puruṣaḥ*—the living being; *kṛṣṇa*—the Supreme Personality of Godhead; *pāda-mūlam*—the shelter of the lotus feet; *na*—never; *muñcati*—gives up; *mukta*—liberated; *sarva*—all; *parikleśaḥ*—of all miseries of life; *pānthaḥ*—the traveler; *sva-śaraṇam*—in his own abode; *yathā*—as it were.

TRANSLATION

A pure devotee of the Lord whose heart has once been cleansed by the process of devotional service never relinquishes the lotus feet of Lord Kṛṣṇa, for they fully satisfy him, as a traveler is satisfied at home after a troubled journey.

PURPORT

One who is not a pure devotee of the Supreme Lord Kṛṣṇa is not completely cleansed in the heart. But a perfectly cleansed person never quits the devotional service of the Lord. In discharging such devotional service, as ordered by Brahmājī to Nārada in the preaching of *Śrīmad-Bhāgavatam*, sometimes a representative of the Lord engaged in preaching work meets various so-called difficulties. This was exhibited by Lord

Nityānanda when He delivered the two fallen souls Jagāi and Mādhāi, and similarly Lord Jesus Christ was crucified by the nonbelievers. But such difficulties are very gladly suffered by the devotees in preaching because in such activities, although apparently very severe, the devotees of the Lord feel transcendental pleasure because the Lord is satisfied. Prahlāda Mahārāja suffered greatly, but still he never forgot the lotus feet of the Lord. This is because a pure devotee of the Lord is so purified in his heart that he cannot leave the shelter of Lord Kṛṣṇa in any circumstances. There is no self-interest in such service. The progress of culturing knowledge by the *jñānīs* or the bodily gymnastics by the *yogīs* are ultimately given up by the respective performers, but a devotee of the Lord cannot give up the service of the Lord, for he is ordered by his spiritual master. Pure devotees like Nārada and Nityānanda Prabhu take up the order of the spiritual master as the sustenance of life. They do not mind what becomes of the future of their lives. They take the matter very seriously as the order comes from the higher authority, from the representative of the Lord, or from the Lord Himself.

The example set herein is very appropriate. A traveler leaves home to search for wealth in far distant places, sometimes in the forest and sometimes on the ocean and sometimes on hilltops. Certainly there are many troubles for the traveler when he is in such unknown places. But all such troubles are at once mitigated as soon as the sense of his family affection is remembered, and as soon as he returns home he forgets all such troubles on the way.

A pure devotee of the Lord is exactly in a family tie with the Lord, and therefore he is undeterred in discharging his duty in a full affectionate tie with the Lord.

TEXT 7

यदधातुमतो ब्रह्मन् देहारम्भोऽस्य धातुभिः ।
यदृच्छया हेतुना वा भवन्तो जानते यथा ॥ ७ ॥

yad adhātu-mato brahman
dehārambho 'sya dhātubhiḥ
yadṛcchayā hetunā vā
bhavanto jānate yathā

yat—as it is; *adhātu-mataḥ*—without being materially constituted; *brahman*—O learned *brāhmaṇa; deha*—the material body; *ārambhaḥ*—the beginning of; *asya*—of the living being; *dhātubhiḥ*—by matter; *yadṛcchayā*—without cause, accidental; *hetunā*—due to some cause; *vā*—either; *bhavantaḥ*—your good self; *jānate*—as you may know it; *yathā*—so you inform me.

TRANSLATION

O learned brāhmaṇa, the transcendental spirit soul is different from the material body. Does he acquire the body accidentally or by some cause? Will you kindly explain this, for it is known to you.

PURPORT

Mahārāja Parīkṣit, being a typical devotee, is not only satisfied by confirming the importance of hearing the *Śrīmad-Bhāgavatam* from the representative of Brahmājī by disciplic succession, but he is still more anxious to establish the philosophical basis of *Śrīmad-Bhāgavatam. Śrīmad-Bhāgavatam* is the science of the Supreme Personality of Godhead, and as such all questions that may arise in the mind of a serious student must be cleared by the statements of the authority. A person on the path of devotional service may inquire from his spiritual master all about the spiritual position of God and the living beings. From the *Bhagavad-gītā,* as well as from the *Śrīmad-Bhāgavatam,* it is known that qualitatively the Lord and the living beings are one. The living being in the conditioned state of material existence is subjected to many transmigrations by continuous changing of the material body. But what are the causes of the material embodiment of the part and parcel of the Lord? Mahārāja Parīkṣit inquires about this very important matter for the benefit of all classes of candidates on the path of self-realization and devotional service to the Lord.

Indirectly it is confirmed that the Supreme Being, the Lord, makes no such material changes of body. He is spiritually whole, with no difference between His body and His soul, unlike the conditioned soul. The liberated living beings, who associate with the Lord in person, are also exactly like the Lord. Only the conditioned souls awaiting liberation are subjected to change of bodies. How was the process first begun?

In the process of devotional service, the first step is to take shelter of the spiritual master and then inquire from the spiritual master all about the process. This inquiry is essential for immunity to all kinds of offenses on the path of devotional service. Even if one is fixed in devotional service like Mahārāja Parīkṣit, he must still inquire from the realized spiritual master all about this. In other words, the spiritual master must also be well versed and learned so that he may be able to answer all these inquiries from the devotees. Thus one who is not well versed in the authorized scriptures and not able to answer all such relevant inquiries should not pose as a spiritual master for the matter of material gain. It is illegal to become a spiritual master if one is unable to deliver the disciple.

TEXT 8

आसीद् यदुदरात् पद्मं लोकसंस्थानलक्षणम् ।
यावानयं वै पुरुष इयत्तावयवैः पृथक् ।
तावानसाविति प्रोक्तः संस्थावयववानिव ॥ ८ ॥

āsīd yad-udarāt padmaṁ
loka-saṁsthana-lakṣaṇam
yāvān ayaṁ vai puruṣa
iyattāvayavaiḥ pṛthak
tāvān asāv iti proktaḥ
saṁsthāvayavavān iva

āsīt—as it grew; *yat-udarāt*—from whose abdomen; *padmam*—lotus flower; *loka*—world; *saṁsthāna*—situation; *lakṣaṇam*—possessed of; *yāvān*—as it were; *ayam*—this; *vai*—certainly; *puruṣaḥ*—the Supreme Personality of Godhead; *iyattā*—measurement; *avayavaiḥ*—by embodiments; *pṛthak*—different; *tāvān*—so; *asau*—that; *iti proktaḥ*—it is so said; *saṁsthā*—situation; *avayavavān*—embodiment; *iva*—like.

TRANSLATION

If the Supreme Personality of Godhead, from whose abdomen the lotus stem sprouted, is possessed of a gigantic body according

to His own caliber and measurement, then what is the specific difference between the body of the Lord and those of common living entities?

PURPORT

One should note how Mahārāja Parīkṣit intelligently put questions before his spiritual master for scientific understanding of the transcendental body of the Lord. It has been described in many places before this that the Lord assumed a gigantic body, like that of Kāraṇodakaśāyī Viṣṇu, from whose hair pores innumerable universes have generated. The body of Garbhodakaśāyī Viṣṇu is described as sprouting the lotus stem within which all the planets of the universe remain, and at the top of the stem is the lotus flower on which Lord Brahmā is born. In the creation of the material world the Supreme Lord undoubtedly assumes a gigantic body, and living entities also get bodies, big or small, according to necessity. For example, an elephant gets a gigantic body according to its needs, and so also an ant gets its body according to its needs. Similarly, if the Personality of Godhead assumes a gigantic body to accommodate the universes or the planets of a particular universe, there is no difference in the principle of assuming or accepting a particular type of body in terms of necessity. A living being and the Lord cannot be distinguished simply by the difference in the magnitude of the body. So the answer depends on the specific significance of the body of the Lord, as distinguished from the body of the common living being.

TEXT 9

अजः सृजति भूतानि भूतात्मा यदनुग्रहात् ।
ददृशे येन तद्रूपं नाभिपद्मसमुद्भवः ॥ ९ ॥

ajaḥ sṛjati bhūtāni
bhūtātmā yad-anugrahāt
dadṛśe yena tad-rūpaṁ
nābhi-padma-samudbhavaḥ

ajaḥ—one who is born without a material source; *sṛjati*—creates; *bhūtāni*—all those materially born; *bhūta-ātmā*—having a body of matter; *yat*—whose; *anugrahāt*—by the mercy of; *dadṛśe*—could see;

yena—by whom; *tat-rūpam*—His form of body; *nābhi*—navel; *padma*—lotus flower; *samudbhavaḥ*—being born of.

TRANSLATION

Brahmā, who was not born of a material source but of the lotus flower coming out of the navel abdomen of the Lord, is the creator of all those who are materially born. Of course, by the grace of the Lord, Brahmā was able to see the form of the Lord.

PURPORT

The first living creature, Brahmā, is called *ajaḥ* because he did not take his birth from the womb of a mother materially born. He was directly born from the bodily expansion of the lotus flower of the Lord. Thus it is not readily understandable whether the body of the Lord and that of Brahmā are of the same quality or different. This must also be clearly understood. One thing is, however, certain: Brahmā was completely dependent on the mercy of the Lord because after his birth he could create living beings by the Lord's grace only, and he could see the form of the Lord. Whether the form seen by Brahmā is of the same quality as that of Brahmā is a bewildering question, and Mahārāja Parīkṣit wanted to get clear answers from Śrīla Śukadeva Gosvāmī.

TEXT 10

स चापि यत्र पुरुषो विश्वस्थित्युद्भवाप्ययः ।
मुक्त्वात्ममायां मायेशः शेते सर्वगुहाशयः ॥१०॥

sa cāpi yatra puruṣo
viśva-sthity-udbhavāpyayaḥ
muktvātma-māyāṁ māyeśaḥ
śete sarva-guhāśayaḥ

saḥ—He; *ca*—also; *api*—as He is; *yatra*—where; *puruṣaḥ*—the Personality of Godhead; *viśva*—the material worlds; *sthiti*—maintenance; *udbhava*—creation; *apyayaḥ*—annihilation; *muktvā*—without being touched; *ātma-māyām*—own energy; *māyā-īśaḥ*—the Lord of all energies; *śete*—does lie on; *sarva-guhā-śayaḥ*—one who lies in everyone's heart.

TRANSLATION

Please also explain the Personality of Godhead, who lies in every heart as the Supersoul, and as the Lord of all energies, but is untouched by His external energy.

PURPORT

Undoubtedly the form of the Lord who was seen by Brahmā must be transcendental, otherwise how could He simply look upon the creative energy without being touched? It is understood also that the same *puruṣa* lies in the heart of every living entity. This also requires proper explanation.

TEXT 11

पुरुषावयवैर्लोकाः सपालाः पूर्वकल्पिताः ।
लोकैरमुष्यावयवाः सपालैरिति शुश्रुम ॥११॥

puruṣāvayavair lokāḥ
sapālāḥ pūrva-kalpitāḥ
lokair amuṣyāvayavāḥ
sa-pālair iti śuśruma

puruṣa—the universal form of the Lord (*virāṭ-puruṣaḥ*); *avayavaiḥ*—by different parts of the body; *lokāḥ*—the planetary system; *sa-pālāḥ*—with respective governors; *pūrva*—formerly; *kalpitāḥ*—discussed; *lokaiḥ*—by the different planetary systems; *amuṣya*—His; *avayavāḥ*—different parts of the body; *sa-pālaiḥ*—with the governors; *iti*—thus; *śuśruma*—I heard.

TRANSLATION

O learned brāhmaṇa, it was formerly explained that all the planets of the universe with their respective governors are situated in the different parts of the gigantic body of the virāṭ-puruṣa. I have also heard that the different planetary systems are supposed to be

in the gigantic body of the virāṭ-puruṣa. But what is their actual position? Will you please explain that?

TEXT 12

यावान् कल्पोविकल्पो वा यथा कालोऽनुमीयते ।
भूतभव्यभवच्छब्द आयुर्मानं च यत् सतः ॥१२॥

yāvān kalpo vikalpo vā
yathā kālo 'numīyate
bhūta-bhavya-bhavac-chabda
āyur-mānaṁ ca yat sataḥ

yāvān—as it is; *kalpaḥ*—the duration of time between creation and annihilation; *vikalpaḥ*—subsidiary creation and annihilation; *vā*—either; *yathā*—as also; *kālaḥ*—the time; *anumīyate*—is measured; *bhūta*—past; *bhavya*—future; *bhavat*—present; *śabdaḥ*—sound; *āyuḥ*—duration of life; *mānam*—measurement; *ca*—also; *yat*—which; *sataḥ*—of all living beings in all planets.

TRANSLATION

Also please explain the duration of time between creation and annihilation, and that of other subsidiary creations, as well as the nature of time, indicated by the sound of past, present and future. Also, please explain the duration and measurement of life of the different living beings known as the demigods, the human beings, etc., in different planets of the universe.

PURPORT

Past, present and future are different features of time to indicate the duration of life for the universe and all its paraphernalia, including the different living beings in different planets.

TEXT 13

कालस्यानुगतिर्या तु लक्ष्यतेऽण्वी बृहत्यपि ।
यावत्यः कर्मगतयो यादृशीर्द्विजसत्तम ॥१३॥

kālasyānugatir yā tu
lakṣyate 'ṇvī bṛhaty api
yāvatyaḥ karma-gatayo
yādṛśīr dvija-sattama

kālasya—of eternal time; *anugatiḥ*—beginning; *yā tu*—as they are; *lakṣyate*—experienced; *aṇvī*—small; *bṛhatī*—great; *api*—even; *yāvatyaḥ*—as long as; *karma-gatayaḥ*—in terms of the work performed; *yādṛśīḥ*—as it may; *dvija-sattama*—O purest of all *brāhmaṇas.*

TRANSLATION

O purest of the brāhmaṇas, please also explain the cause of the different durations of time, both short and long, as well as the beginning of time, following the course of action.

TEXT 14

यस्मिन् कर्मसमावायो यथा येनोपगृह्यते ।
गुणानां गुणिनां चैव परिणाममभीप्सताम् ॥१४॥

yasmin karma-samāvāyo
yathā yenopagṛhyate
guṇānāṁ guṇināṁ caiva
pariṇāmam abhīpsatām

yasmin—in which; *karma*—actions; *samāvāyaḥ*—accumulation; *yathā*—as far as; *yena*—by which; *upagṛhyate*—takes over; *guṇānām*—of the different modes of material nature; *guṇinām*—of the living beings; *ca*—also; *eva*—certainly; *pariṇāmam*—resultant; *abhīpsatām*—of the desires.

TRANSLATION

Then again, kindly describe how the proportionate accumulation of the reactions resulting from the different modes of material nature act upon the desiring living being, promoting or degrading him among the different species of life, beginning from the demigods down to the most insignificant creatures.

PURPORT

The actions and reactions of all works in the material modes of nature, either in the minute form or in the gigantic form, are accumulated, and thus the result of such accumulated actions and reactions of *karma*, or work, become manifested in the same proportion. How such actions and reactions take place, what the different procedures are, and in what proportion they act are all subject matters of Mahārāja Parīkṣit's inquiries from the great *brāhmaṇa* Śukadeva Gosvāmī.

Life in the higher planets, known as the abodes of the denizens of heaven, is obtained not by the strength of spacecraft (as is now being contemplated by the inexperienced scientists), but by works done in the mode of goodness.

Even on the very planet where we are now living, there are restrictions upon the entrance of foreigners into a country where the citizens are more prosperous. For example, the American government has many restrictions for the entrance of foreigners from less prosperous countries. The reason is that the Americans do not wish to share their prosperity with any foreigner who has not qualified himself as a citizen of America. Similarly, the same mentality is prevailing in every other planet where there are more intelligent living beings residing. The higher planetary living conditions are all in the mode of goodness, and anyone desiring to enter the higher planets like the moon, sun and Venus must qualify thoroughly by activity in complete goodness.

Mahārāja Parīkṣit's inquiries are on the basis of proportionate actions of goodness which qualify one in this planet to be promoted to the highest regions of the universe.

Even on this planet of our present residence, one cannot achieve a good position within the social order without being qualified with proportionate good work. One cannot forcibly sit on the chair of a high-court judge without being qualified for the post. Similarly, one cannot enter into the higher planetary systems without being qualified by good works in this life. Persons addicted to the habits of passion and ignorance have no chance of entering the higher planetary systems simply by an electronic mechanism.

According to the statement of the *Bhagavad-gītā* (9.25), persons trying to qualify themselves for promotion to the higher, heavenly planets can go there; similarly, persons trying for the Pitṛlokas can go there;

similarly, persons trying to improve the conditions on this earth can also do that, and persons who are engaged in going back home, back to Godhead, can achieve that result. The various actions and reactions of work in the mode of goodness are generally known as pious work with devotional service, culture of knowledge with devotional service, mystic powers with devotional service and (at last) devotional service unmixed with any other varieties of goodness. This unmixed devotional service is transcendental and is called *parā bhakti.* It alone can promote a person to the transcendental kingdom of God. Such a transcendental kingdom is not a myth, but is as factual as the moon. One must have transcendental qualities to understand the kingdom of God and God Himself.

TEXT 15

भूपातालककुब्व्योमग्रहनक्षत्रभूभृताम् ।
सरित्समुद्रद्वीपानां सम्भवश्चैतदोकसाम् ॥१५॥

bhū-pātāla-kakub-vyoma-
graha-nakṣatra-bhūbhṛtām
sarit-samudra-dvīpānāṁ
sambhavaś caitad-okasām

bhū-pātāla—underneath the land; *kakup*—the four sides of the heavens; *vyoma*—the sky; *graha*—the planets; *nakṣatra*—the stars; *bhūbhṛtām*—of the hills; *sarit*—the river; *samudra*—the sea; *dvīpānām*—of the islands; *sambhavaḥ*—appearance; *ca*—also; *etat*—their; *okasām*—of the inhabitants.

TRANSLATION

O best of the brāhmaṇas, please also describe how the creation of the globes throughout the universe, the four directions of the heavens, the sky, the planets, the stars, the mountains, the rivers, the seas and the islands, as well as their different kinds of inhabitants, takes place.

PURPORT

The inhabitants of different varieties of land, etc., are differently situated, and not all of them are equal in all respects. The inhabitants of the land are different from the inhabitants of the water or the sky, and similarly the inhabitants of the different planets and stars in the sky are also different from one another. By the laws of the Lord, no place is vacant, but the creatures of one particular place are different from those of other places. Even in human society the inhabitants of the jungles or the deserts are different from those of the cities and villages. They are so made according to different qualities of the modes of nature. Such adjustment by the laws of nature is not blind. There is a great plan behind the arrangement. Mahārāja Parīkṣit requests the great sage Śukadeva Gosvāmī to explain all these authoritatively, in accordance with proper understanding.

TEXT 16

प्रमाणमण्डकोशस्य बाह्याभ्यन्तरभेदतः ।
महतां चानुचरितं वर्णाश्रमविनिश्चयः ॥१६॥

pramāṇam aṇḍa-kośasya
bāhyābhyantara-bhedataḥ
mahatāṁ cānucaritaṁ
varṇāśrama-viniścayaḥ

pramāṇam—extent and measurement; *aṇḍa-kośasya*—of the universe; *bāhya*—outer space; *abhyantara*—inner space; *bhedataḥ*—by division of; *mahatām*—of the great souls; *ca*—also; *anucaritam*—character and activities; *varṇa*—castes; *āśrama*—orders of life; *viniścayaḥ*—specifically describe.

TRANSLATION

Also, please describe the inner and outer space of the universe by specific divisions, as well as the character and activities of the great souls, and also the characteristics of the different classifications of the castes and orders of social life.

PURPORT

Mahārāja Parīkṣit is a typical devotee of Lord Kṛṣṇa, and as such he is anxious to know the complete significance of the creation of the Lord. He wants to know the inner and outer space of the universal form. It is quite fitting for the real searcher of knowledge to know all about this. Those who are of the opinion that the devotees of the Lord are satisfied with mere sentiments can find in the inquiries of Mahārāja Parīkṣit good lessons as to how inquisitive a pure devotee is to know things in their true perfection. The modern scientist is unable to know about the inner space of the universal horizon, and what to speak of the space which covers the universe.

Mahārāja Parīkṣit is not satisfied with only material knowledge. He is inquisitive about the character and activities of the great souls, the devotees of the Lord. The glories of the Lord and the glories of His devotees, combined together, comprise the complete knowledge of *Śrīmad-Bhāgavatam.* Lord Kṛṣṇa showed His mother the complete universal creation within His mouth, while she, completely charmed by her son, wanted to look inside the mouth of the Lord just to see how much earth the child had eaten. By the grace of the Lord the devotees are able to see everything in the universe within the mouth of the Lord.

The very idea of the scientific divisions of four classes of human society and four orders of life is also inquired about herewith on the basis of individual personal quality. The four divisions are exactly like the four divisions of one's personal body. The parts and parcels of the body are nondifferent from the body, but by themselves they are only parts. That is the significance of the whole scientific system of four castes and four social orders. The value of such scientific divisions of human society can be ascertained only in terms of the proportionate development of devotional service to the Lord. Any person employed in government service, including the president, is a part and parcel of the entire government. Everyone is a government servant, but no one is the government himself. That is the position of all living entities in the government of the Supreme Lord. No one can artificially claim the supreme position of the Lord, but everyone is meant to serve the purpose of the supreme whole.

TEXT 17

युगानि युगमानं च धर्मो यश्च युगे युगे ।
अवतारानुचरितं यदाश्चर्यतमं हरेः ॥१७॥

yugāni yuga-mānaṁ ca
dharmo yaś ca yuge yuge
avatārānucaritaṁ
yad āścaryatamaṁ hareḥ

yugāni—the different ages; *yuga-mānam*—the duration of each age; *ca*—as well as; *dharmaḥ*—the particular occupational duty; *yaḥ ca*—and which; *yuge yuge*—in each and every *yuga*, or particular age; *avatāra*—the incarnation; *anucaritam*—and the activities of the incarnation; *yat*—which; *āścaryatamam*—the most wonderful activities; *hareḥ*—of the Supreme Lord.

TRANSLATION

Please explain all the different ages in the duration of the creation, and also the duration of such ages. Also tell me about the different activities of the different incarnations of the Lord in different ages.

PURPORT

Lord Kṛṣṇa is the original Personality of Godhead, and all the incarnations of the Supreme Lord, although nondifferent from Him, are emanations from the Supreme. Mahārāja Parīkṣit inquired from the great and learned sage Śukadeva Gosvāmī about the different activities of such incarnations so that the incarnation of the Lord might be confirmed by His activities in the authoritative scriptures. Mahārāja Parīkṣit was not to be carried away by the sentiments of the common man to accept an incarnation of the Lord very cheaply. Instead he wished to accept the incarnation of the Lord by symptoms mentioned in the Vedic literatures and confirmed by an *ācārya* like Śukadeva Gosvāmī. The Lord descends by His internal energy without any obligation to the laws of material nature, and thus His activities are also uncommon. The specific activities of the Lord are mentioned, and one should know that the activities of the Lord and the Lord Himself are identical due to being on the absolute plane. Thus to hear the activities of the Lord means to associate with the Lord directly, and association with the Lord directly means purification from material contamination. We have already discussed this point in the previous volume.

TEXT 18

नृणां साधारणो धर्मः सविशेषश्च यादृशः ।
श्रेणीनां राजर्षीणां च धर्मः कृच्छ्रेषु जीवताम् ॥१८॥

nṛṇāṁ sādhāraṇo dharmaḥ
saviśeṣaś ca yādṛśaḥ
śreṇīnāṁ rājarṣīṇāṁ ca
dharmaḥ kṛcchreṣu jīvatām

nṛṇām—of human society; *sādhāraṇaḥ*—general; *dharmaḥ*—religious affiliation; *sa-viśeṣaḥ*—specific; *ca*—also; *yādṛśaḥ*—as they are; *śreṇīnām*—of the particular three classes; *rājarṣīṇām*—of the saintly royal order; *ca*—also; *dharmaḥ*—occupational duty; *kṛcchreṣu*—in the matter of distressed conditions; *jīvatām*—of the living beings.

TRANSLATION

Please also explain what may generally be the common religious affiliations of human society, as well as their specific occupational duties in religion, the classification of the social orders as well as the administrative royal orders, and the religious principles for one who may be in distress.

PURPORT

The common religion of all classes of human beings, regardless of whosoever and whatsoever one may be, is devotional service. Even the animals may be included in devotional service to the Lord, and the best example is set by Śrī Vajrāṅgajī, or Hanumān, the great devotee of Lord Śrī Rāma. As we have already discussed, even the aborigines and cannibals can also be engaged in the devotional service of the Lord if they happen to be under the guidance of a genuine devotee of the Lord. In the *Skanda Purāṇa* there is a narration that a hunter in the jungle became the most enlightened devotee of the Lord by the guidance of Śrī Nārada Muni. Therefore devotional service to the Lord can be equally shared by every living being.

Religious affiliation in terms of different countries and cultural circumstances is obviously not the common religion of the human being;

rather, the basic principle is devotional service. Even if a particular type of religious principle does not recognize the supremacy of the Supreme Personality of Godhead, the followers still have to obey the disciplinary principles laid down by a particular leader. Such a leader of a religious sect is never the supreme leader because such a circumstantial leader comes to the position of leadership after undergoing some penance. The Supreme Personality of Godhead does not, however, require to be under disciplinary action to become leader, as we see in the activities of Lord Kṛṣṇa.

The occupational duties of the castes and the orders of society, following the principles of livelihood, also depend on the principle of devotional service. In the *Bhagavad-gītā* it is stated that a person can achieve the highest perfection of life simply by awarding the results of his occupational duty unto the devotional service of the Lord. People following the principles of devotional service to the Lord can never be put into difficulty, and thus there cannot be any question of *āpad-dharma*, or religion in distress. As will be explained in this book by the greatest authority, Śrīla Śukadeva Gosvāmī, there is no religion save and except the devotional service of the Lord, though this may be presented in different forms.

TEXT 19

तत्त्वानां परिसंख्यानं लक्षणं हेतुलक्षणम् ।
पुरुषाराधनविधिर्योगस्याध्यात्मिकस्य च ॥१९॥

tattvānāṁ parisaṅkhyānaṁ
lakṣaṇaṁ hetu-lakṣaṇam
puruṣārādhana-vidhir
yogasyādhyātmikasya ca

tattvānām—of the elements that constitute the creation; *parisaṅkhyānam*—of the number of such elements; *lakṣaṇam*—symptoms; *hetu-lakṣaṇam*—the symptoms of the causes; *puruṣa*—of the Lord; *ārādhana*—of devotional service; *vidhiḥ*—rules and regulations; *yogasya*—of cultivation of the *yoga* system; *adhyātmikasya*—spiritual methods leading to devotional service; *ca*—also.

TRANSLATION

Kindly explain all about the elementary principles of creation, the number of such elementary principles, their causes, and their development, and also the process of devotional service and the method of mystic powers.

TEXT 20

योगेश्वरैश्वर्यगतिर्लिङ्गभङ्गस्तु योगिनाम् ।
वेदोपवेदधर्माणामितिहासपुराणयोः ॥२०॥

yogeśvaraiśvarya-gatir
liṅga-bhaṅgas tu yoginām
vedopaveda-dharmāṇām
itihāsa-purāṇayoḥ

yoga-īsvara—of the master of the mystic powers; *aiśvarya*—opulence; *gatiḥ*—advancement; *liṅga*—astral body; *bhaṅgaḥ*—detachment; *tu*—but; *yoginām*—of the mystics; *veda*—transcendental knowledge; *upaveda*—knowledge in pursuance of the *Veda* indirectly; *dharmāṇām*—of the religiosities; *itihāsa*—history; *purāṇayoḥ*—of the *Purāṇas.*

TRANSLATION

What are the opulences of the great mystics, and what is their ultimate realization? How does the perfect mystic become detached from the subtle astral body? What is the basic knowledge of the Vedic literatures, including the branches of history and the supplementary Purāṇas?

PURPORT

The *yogeśvara,* or the master of mystic powers, can exhibit eight kinds of wonders of perfection by becoming smaller than the atom or lighter than a feather, getting anything and everything he desires, going anywhere and everywhere he likes, creating even a planet in the sky, etc. There are many *yogeśvaras* having different proficiencies in these wonderful powers, and the topmost of all of them is Lord Śiva. Lord Śiva is the greatest *yogī,* and he can perform such wonderful things, far beyond the ordinary living beings. The devotees of the Lord, the Supreme Personality of Godhead, do not directly practice the process of mystic powers, but, by the grace of the Lord, His devotee can defeat even a great *yogeśvara* like Durvāsā Muni, who picked a quarrel with Mahārāja Ambarīṣa and wanted to show the wonderful achievements of his mystic powers. Mahārāja Ambarīṣa was a pure devotee of the Lord, and thus without any effort on his part the Lord saved him from the wrath of Yogeśvara Durvāsā Muni, and the latter was obliged to beg pardon from the King. Similarly, at the time of Draupadī's precarious position, when she was attacked by the Kurus who wanted to see her naked in the open assembly of the royal order, the Lord saved her from being stripped by supplying an unlimited length of sari to cover her. And Draupadī knew nothing of mystic powers. Therefore the devotees are also *yogeśvaras* by the unlimited power of the Lord, just as a child is powerful by the strength of the parents. They do not try to protect themselves by any artificial means, but are saved by the mercy of the parents.

Mahārāja Parīkṣit inquired from the learned *brāhmaṇa* Śukadeva Gosvāmī about the ultimate destination of such great mystics or how they attain such extraordinary powers by their own efforts or by the grace of the Lord. He inquired also about their detachment from the subtle and gross material bodies. He inquired also about the purports of the Vedic knowledge. As stated in the *Bhagavad-gītā* (15.15), the whole purport of all the *Vedas* is to know the Supreme Personality of Godhead and thus become a transcendental loving servant of the Lord.

TEXT 21

सम्प्लवः सर्वभूतानां विक्रमः प्रतिसंक्रमः ।
इष्टापूर्तस्य काम्यानां त्रिवर्गस्य च यो विधिः ॥२१॥

samplavaḥ sarva-bhūtānāṁ
vikramaḥ pratisaṅkramaḥ
iṣṭā-pūrtasya kāmyānāṁ
tri-vargasya ca yo vidhiḥ

samplavaḥ—the perfect means or complete devastation; *sarva-bhūtānām*—of all living beings; *vikramaḥ*—specific power or situation; *pratisaṅkramaḥ*—ultimate destruction; *iṣṭā*—performance of Vedic rituals; *pūrtasya*—pious acts in terms of religion; *kāmyānām*—rituals for economic development; *tri-vargasya*—the three means of religion, economic development and sense satisfaction; *ca*—also; *yaḥ*—whatsoever; *vidhiḥ*—procedures.

TRANSLATION

Please explain unto me how the living beings are generated, how they are maintained, and how they are annihilated. Tell me also of the advantages and disadvantages of discharging devotional service unto the Lord. What are the Vedic rituals and injunctions of the supplementary Vedic rites, and what are the procedures of religion, economic development and sense satisfaction?

PURPORT

Samplavaḥ, in the sense of "perfect means," is employed to denote the discharging of devotional service, and *pratisamplavaḥ* means just the opposite, or that which destroys the progress of devotional service. One who is firmly situated in the devotional service of the Lord can very easily execute the function of conditional life. Living the conditional life is just like plying a boat in the middle of the ocean. One is completely at the mercy of the ocean, and at every moment there is every chance of being drowned in the ocean by slight agitation. If the atmosphere is all right, the boat can ply very easily, undoubtedly, but if there is some storm, fog, wind or cloud, there is every possibility of being drowned in the ocean. No one can control the whims of the ocean, however one may be materially well equipped. One who has crossed the oceans by ship may have sufficient experience of such dependence upon the mercy of the ocean. But one can ply over the ocean of material existence by the grace of the Lord very easily, without any fear of storm or fog. It all depends on the will of the Lord; no one can help if there is some unfortunate danger in the state of conditional life. The devotees of the Lord, however, cross the ocean of material existence without anxiety because a pure devotee is always protected by the Lord (Bg. 9.13). The Lord gives special attention to His devotees in their activities within material, conditional life (Bg. 9.29). Therefore everyone should take shelter of the lotus feet of the Lord and be a pure devotee of the Lord by all means.

One should know, therefore, from the expert spiritual master, the advantages and disadvantages of discharging devotional service, just as Mahārāja Parīkṣit asked his spiritual master, Śrīla Śukadeva Gosvāmī. According to *Bhakti-rasāmṛta-sindhu*, the science of devotional service, one should not eat more than what he requires to maintain body and soul together. Vegetable diets and milk are sufficient for maintenance of the human body, and therefore one has no need to eat anything more to satisfy the palate. One should also not accumulate money to become puffed up in the material world. One should earn his livelihood easily and honestly, for it is better to become a coolie for an honest livelihood than to become a great man in society by hook and crook. There is no harm if one becomes the richest man in the world by honest dealings, but one should not sacrifice the honest means of livelihood simply to accumulate wealth. Such an endeavor is harmful to devotional service. One should not talk nonsense. A devotee's business is to earn the favor of the Lord. Therefore a devotee should always glorify the Lord in His wonderful creations. A devotee should not decry the creation of the Lord, defying Him by saying that He has created a false world. The world is not false. Factually we have to take so many things from the world for our maintenance, so how we can say that the world is false? Similarly, how can one think of the Lord as being without form? How can one become formless and at the same time have all intelligence and consciousness, direct and indirect? So there are many things for a pure devotee to learn, and he should learn them perfectly from a bona fide personality like Śukadeva Gosvāmī.

The favorable conditions for discharging devotional service are that one should be very enthusiastic in serving the Lord. The Lord in His form of Śrī Caitanya Mahāprabhu wanted the cult of devotional service to the Lord to be preached all over the world, in every nook and corner, and therefore a pure devotee's duty is to discharge this order as far as possible. Every devotee should be very enthusiastic, not only in performing his daily rituals of devotional service, but in trying to preach the cult peacefully by following in the footsteps of Lord Caitanya. If he is not superficially successful in such an attempt, he should not be deterred from the discharge of his duty. Success or failure has no meaning for a pure devotee because he is a soldier in the field. Preaching the cult of devotional service is something like declaring war against materialistic life. There are different kinds of materialists, such as the fruitive workers, the mental speculators, the mystic jugglers, and so many others. All of them are against the existence of Godhead. They would declare that they are themselves God, although in every step and in every action they are dependent on the mercy of the Lord. Therefore a pure devotee may not associate with such gangs of atheists. A strong devotee of the Lord will not be misled by such atheistic propaganda of the nondevotees, but a neophyte devotee should be very cautious about them. A devotee should see to the right discharge of devotional service under the guidance of a bona fide spiritual master and should not stick only to the formalities. Under the direction of the bona fide spiritual master, one should see how much service is being executed, and not simply in the matter of rituals. A devotee should not hanker after anything, but he should be satisfied with things that may automatically come to him by the will of the Lord. That should be the principle of a devotional life. And all these principles are easily learned under the guidance of a spiritual master like Śukadeva Gosvāmī. Mahārāja Parīkṣit inquired from Śukadeva correctly, and one should follow his example.

Mahārāja Parīkṣit inquired about the process of creation, maintenance and destruction of the material world, the process of Vedic rituals and the method of executing pious activities in terms of the supplementary *Vedas* like the *Purāṇas* and *Mahābhārata.* As explained before, the *Mahābhārata* is the history of ancient India, and so also are the *Purāṇas.* Pious acts are prescribed in the supplementary *Vedas* (*smṛtis*), which specifically mention digging tanks and wells for the water supply of the people in general. To plant trees on the public roads, to construct public temples and places of worship of God, to establish places of charity where the poor destitutes can be provided with foodstuff, and similar activities are called *pūrta.*

Similarly, the process of fulfilling the natural desires for sense gratification was also inquired about by the King for the benefit of all concerned.

TEXT 22

यो वानुशायिनां सर्गः पाषण्डस्य च सम्भवः ।
आत्मनो बन्धमोक्षौ च व्यवस्थानं स्वरूपतः ॥२२॥

yo vānuśāyināṁ sargaḥ
pāṣaṇḍasya ca sambhavaḥ

ātmano bandha-mokṣau ca
vyavasthānaṁ sva-rūpataḥ

yaḥ—all those; *vā*—either; *anuśāyinām*—merged into the body of the Lord; *sargaḥ*—creation; *pāṣaṇḍasya*—of the infidels; *ca*—and; *sambhavaḥ*—appearance; *ātmanaḥ*—of the living beings; *bandha*—conditioned; *mokṣau*—being liberated; *ca*—also; *vyavasthānam*—being situated; *sva-rūpataḥ*—in an unconditioned state.

TRANSLATION

Please also explain how, merged in the body of the Lord, living beings are created, and how the infidels appear in the world. Also please explain how the unconditioned living entities exist.

PURPORT

The progressive devotee of the Lord must inquire from the bona fide spiritual master how living entities merged in the body of the Lord again come back at the time of creation. There are two kinds of living entities. There are the ever-liberated, unconditioned living beings as well as the ever-conditioned living beings. Of the ever-conditioned living beings, there are two divisions. They are the faithful and the infidels. Of the faithful there are again two divisions, namely the devotees and the mental speculators. The mental speculators desire to merge into the existence of the Lord, or to become one with the Lord, whereas the devotees of the Lord desire to keep separate identities and constantly engage in the service of the Lord. The devotees who are not fully purified, as well as the empiric philosophers, become conditioned again during the next creation for further purification. Such conditioned souls become liberated by further progress of devotional service to the Lord. Mahārāja Parīkṣit asked all these questions from the bona fide spiritual master in order to become fully equipped in the science of God.

TEXT 23

यथात्मतन्त्रो भगवान् विक्रीडत्यात्ममायया ।
विसृज्य वा यथा मायामुदास्ते साक्षिवद् विभुः॥२३॥

yathātma-tantro bhagavān
vikrīḍaty ātma-māyayā
visṛjya vā yathā māyām
udāste sākṣivad vibhuḥ

yathā—as; *ātma-tantraḥ*—independent; *bhagavān*—the Personality of Godhead; *vikrīḍati*—enjoys His pastimes; *ātma-māyayā*—by His internal potency; *visṛjya*—giving up; *vā*—as also; *yathā*—as He desires; *māyām*—the external potency; *udāste*—remains; *sākṣivat*—just as the witness; *vibhuḥ*—the almighty.

TRANSLATION

The independent Personality of Godhead enjoys His pastimes by His internal potency and at the time of annihilation gives them up to the external potency, and He remains a witness to it all.

PURPORT

Lord Śrī Kṛṣṇa, being the Supreme Personality of Godhead and fountainhead of all other incarnations, is the only independent person. He enjoys His pastimes by creation as He desires and gives them up to the external energy at the time of annihilation. By His internal potency only, He kills the demon Pūtanā, even though enjoying His pastimes in the lap of His mother Yaśodā. And when He desires to leave this world He creates the pastimes of killing His own family members (Yadu-kula) and remains unaffected by such annihilation. He is the witness of everything that is happening, and yet He has nothing to do with anything. He is independent in every respect. Mahārāja Parīkṣit desired to know more perfectly, for a pure devotee ought to know well.

TEXT 24

सर्वमेतच्च भगवन् पृच्छतो मेऽनुपूर्वशः ।
तत्त्वतोऽर्हस्युदाहर्तुं प्रपन्नाय महामुने ॥२४॥

sarvam etac ca bhagavan
pṛcchato me 'nupūrvaśaḥ

tattvato 'rhasy udāhartuṁ
prapannāya mahā-mune

sarvam—all these; *etat*—inquiries; *ca*—also that I have not been able to ask; *bhagavan*—O great sage; *pṛcchataḥ*—of the inquisitive; *me*—myself; *anupūrvaśaḥ*—from the beginning; *tattvataḥ*—just in accordance with the truth; *arhasi*—may kindly be explained; *udāhartum*—as you will let know; *prapannāya*—one who is surrounded; *mahā-mune*—O great sage.

TRANSLATION

O great sage, representative of the Lord, kindly satisfy my inquisitiveness in all that I have inquired from you and all that I may not have inquired from you from the very beginning of my questionings. Since I am a soul surrendered unto you, please impart full knowledge in this connection.

PURPORT

The spiritual master is always prepared to impart knowledge to the disciple and specifically when the disciple is very inquisitive. Inquisitiveness on the part of a disciple is greatly necessary for the progressive disciple. Mahārāja Parīkṣit is a typical disciple because he is perfectly inquisitive. If one is not very inquisitive about self-realization, one need not approach a spiritual master simply to make a show of discipleship. Not only is Mahārāja Parīkṣit inquisitive concerning all he has inquired about, but he is also anxious to know about what he has not been able to inquire. Factually it is not possible for a man to inquire about everything from the spiritual master, but the bona fide spiritual master is able to enlighten the disciple in every way for the disciple's benefit.

TEXT 25

अत्र प्रमाणं हि भवान् परमेष्ठी यथात्मभूः ।
अपरे चानुतिष्ठन्ति पूर्वेषां पूर्वजैः कृतम् ॥२५॥

atra pramāṇaṁ hi bhavān
parameṣṭhī yathātma-bhūḥ

apare cānutiṣṭhanti
pūrveṣāṁ pūrva-jaiḥ kṛtam

atra—in this matter; *pramāṇam*—evidential facts; *hi*—certainly; *bhavān*—yourself; *parameṣṭhī*—Brahmā, the creator of the universe; *yathā*—as; *ātma-bhūḥ*—born directly from the Lord; *apare*—others; *ca*—only; *anutiṣṭhanti*—just to follow; *pūrveṣām*—as a matter of custom; *pūrva-jaiḥ*—knowledge suggested by a previous philosopher; *kṛtam*—having been done.

TRANSLATION

O great sage, you are as good as Brahmā, the original living being. Others follow custom only, as followed by the previous philosophical speculators.

PURPORT

It may be argued that Śukadeva Gosvāmī is not the only authority of perfect knowledge in transcendence because there are many other sages and their followers. Contemporary to Vyāsadeva or even prior to him there were many other great sages, such as Gautama, Kaṇāda, Jaimini, Kapila and Aṣṭāvakra, and all of them have presented a philosophical path by themselves. Patañjali is also one of them, and all these six great *ṛṣis* have their own way of thinking, exactly like the modern philosophers and mental speculators. The difference between the six philosophical paths put forward by the renowned sages above mentioned and that of Śukadeva Gosvāmī, as presented in the *Śrīmad-Bhāgavatam,* is that all the six sages mentioned above speak the facts according to their own thinking, but Śukadeva Gosvāmī presents the knowledge which comes down directly from Brahmājī, who is known as *ātma-bhūḥ,* or born of and educated by the Almighty Personality of Godhead.

Vedic transcendental knowledge descends directly from the Personality of Godhead. By His mercy, Brahmā, the first living being in the universe, was enlightened, and from Brahmājī, Nārada was enlightened, and from Nārada, Vyāsa was enlightened. Śukadeva Gosvāmī received such transcendental knowledge directly from his father, Vyāsadeva. Thus the knowledge, being received from the chain of disciplic succession, is perfect. One cannot be a spiritual master in perfection unless and until one has received the same by disciplic succession. That is the secret of receiving transcendental knowledge. The six great sages mentioned above may be great thinkers, but their knowledge by mental speculation is not perfect. However perfect an empiric philosopher may be in presenting a philosophical thesis, such knowledge is never perfect because it is produced by an imperfect mind. Such great sages also have their disciplic successions, but they are not authorized because such knowledge does not come directly from the independent Supreme Personality of Godhead, Nārāyaṇa. No one can be independent except Nārāyaṇa; therefore no one's knowledge can be perfect, for everyone's knowledge is dependent on the flickering mind. Mind is material and thus knowledge presented by material speculators is never transcendental and can never become perfect. Mundane philosophers, being imperfect in themselves, disagree with other philosophers because a mundane philosopher is not a philosopher at all unless he presents his own theory. Intelligent persons like Mahārāja Parīkṣit do not recognize such mental speculators, however great they may be, but hear from the authorities like Śukadeva Gosvāmī, who is nondifferent from the Supreme Personality of Godhead by the *paramparā* system, as is specially stressed in the *Bhagavad-gītā*.

TEXT 26

न मेऽसवः परायन्ति ब्रह्मन्ननशनादमी ।
पिबतोऽच्युतपीयूषम् तद् वाक्याब्धिविनिःसृतम् ॥२६॥

na me 'savaḥ parāyanti
brahmann anaśanād amī
pibato 'cyuta-pīyūṣam
tad vākya-abdhi-viniḥsṛtam

na—never; *me*—mine; *asavaḥ*—life; *parāyanti*—becomes exhausted; *brahman*—O learned *brāhmaṇa; anaśanāt amī*—because of fasting; *pibataḥ*—because of my drinking; *acyuta*—of the Infallible; *pīyūṣam*—nectar; *tat*—your; *vākya-abdhi*—ocean of speech; *viniḥsṛtam*—flowing down from.

TRANSLATION

O learned brāhmaṇa, because of my drinking the nectar of the message of the infallible Personality of Godhead, which is flowing

down from the ocean of your speeches, I do not feel any sort of exhaustion due to my fasting.

PURPORT

The disciplic succession from Brahmā, Nārada, Vyāsa and Śukadeva Gosvāmī is particularly different from others. The disciplic successions from other sages are simply a waste of time, being devoid of *acyuta-kathā*, or the message of the infallible Lord. The mental speculators can present their theories very nicely by reason and arguments, but such reasons and arguments are not infallible, for they are defeated by better mental speculators. Mahārāja Parīkṣit was not interested in the dry speculation of the flickering mind, but he was interested in the topics of the Lord because factually he felt that by hearing such a nectarean message from the mouth of Śukadeva Gosvāmī he was not feeling any exhaustion, even though he was fasting because of his imminent death.

One can indulge in hearing the mental speculators, but such hearing cannot endure for any length of time. One will be exhausted very soon from hearing such hackneyed ways of thinking, and no one in the world can be satisfied simply by hearing such useless speculations. The message of the Lord, especially from a personality like Śukadeva Gosvāmī, can never be tiring, even though one may be exhausted from other causes.

In some editions of the *Śrīmad-Bhāgavatam*, the text of the last line of this verse reads *anyatra kupitād dvijāt*, which means that the King might be overwhelmed by the thought of his imminent death by snakebite. The snake is also twice-born, and its anger is compared to the cursing *brāhmaṇa* boy who was without good intelligence. Mahārāja Parīkṣit was not at all afraid of death, for he was fully encouraged by the message of the Lord. One who is fully absorbed in *acyuta-kathā* can never be afraid of anything in this world.

TEXT 27

सूत उवाच

स उपामन्त्रितो राज्ञा कथायामिति सत्पतेः ।
ब्रह्मरातो भृशं प्रीतो विष्णुरातेन संसदि ॥२७॥

sūta uvāca
sa upāmantrito rājñā
kathāyām iti sat-pateḥ
brahmarāto bhṛśaṁ prīto
viṣṇurātena saṁsadi

sūtaḥ uvāca—Śrīla Sūta Gosvāmī said; *saḥ*—he (Śukadeva Gosvāmī); *upāmantritaḥ*—thus being inquired; *rājñā*—by the King; *kathāyām*—in the topics, *iti*—thus; *sat-pateḥ*—of the highest truth; *brahma-rātaḥ*—Śukadeva Gosvāmī; *bhṛśam*—very much; *prītaḥ*—pleased; *viṣṇu-rātena*—by Mahārāja Parīkṣit; *saṁsadi*—in the meeting.

TRANSLATION

Sūta Gosvāmī said: Thus Śukadeva Gosvāmī, being invited by Mahārāja Parīkṣit to speak on topics of the Lord Śrī Kṛṣṇa with the devotees, was very much pleased.

PURPORT

Śrīmad-Bhāgavatam can be legitimately discussed only among the devotees of the Lord. As the *Bhagavad-gītā* was authoritatively discussed between Lord Kṛṣṇa and Arjuna (the Lord and the devotee respectively), similarly *Śrīmad-Bhāgavatam,* which is the postgraduate study of the *Bhagavad-gītā,* can also be discussed between the scholars and devotees like Śukadeva Gosvāmī and Mahārāja Parīkṣit. Otherwise the real taste of the nectar cannot be relished. Śukadeva Gosvāmī was pleased with Mahārāja Parīkṣit because he was not at all tired of hearing the topics of the Lord and was more and more anxious to hear them on and on with interest. Foolish interpreters unnecessarily tackle the *Bhagavad-gītā* and *Śrīmad-Bhāgavatam* when they have no access to the subject matter. There is no use in nondevotees' meddling with the two topmost Vedic literatures, and therefore Śaṅkarācārya did not touch *Śrīmad-Bhāgavatam* for commentation. In his commentation on the *Bhagavad-gītā,* Śrīpāda Śaṅkarācārya accepted Lord Kṛṣṇa as the Supreme Personality of Godhead, but later on he commented from the impersonalist's view. But, being conscious of his position, he did not comment on the *Śrīmad-Bhāgavatam.*

Śrīla Śukadeva Gosvāmī was protected by Lord Kṛṣṇa (vide *Brahma-vaivarta Purāṇa)*, and therefore he is known as Brahmarāta, and Śrīmān Parīkṣit Mahārāja was protected by Viṣṇu, and thus he is known as Viṣṇurāta. As devotees of the Lord, they are always protected by the Lord. It is clear also in this connection that a Viṣṇurāta should hear *Śrīmad-Bhāgavatam* from Brahmarāta and no one else because others misrepresent the transcendental knowledge and thus spoil one's valuable time.

TEXT 28

प्राह भागवतं नाम पुराणं ब्रह्मसम्मितम् ।
ब्रह्मणे भगवत्प्रोक्तं ब्रह्मकल्प उपागते ॥२८॥

prāha bhāgavataṁ nāma
purāṇaṁ brahma-sammitam
brahmaṇe bhagavat-proktaṁ
brahma-kalpa upāgate

prāha—he said; *bhāgavatam*—the science of the Personality of Godhead; *nāma*—of the name; *purāṇam*—the supplement of the *Vedas; brahma-sammitam*—just in pursuance of the *Vedas; brahmaṇe*—unto Lord Brahmā; *bhagavat-proktam*—was spoken by the Personality of Godhead; *brahma-kalpe*—the millennium in which Brahmā was first generated; *upāgate*—just in the beginning.

TRANSLATION

He began to reply to the inquiries of Mahārāja Parīkṣit by saying that the science of the Personality of Godhead was spoken first by the Lord Himself to Brahmā when he was first born. Śrīmad-Bhāgavatam is the supplementary Vedic literature, and it is just in pursuance of the Vedas.

PURPORT

Śrīmad-Bhāgavatam is the science of the Personality of Godhead. The impersonalist always tries to misrepresent the personal feature of the Lord, not knowing the science of this great knowledge, and *Śrīmad-*

Bhāgavatam is in pursuance of the *Vedas* and scientific knowledge of the Personality of Godhead. To learn this science one should take shelter of the representative of Śrī Śukadeva and follow in the footsteps of Mahārāja Parīkṣit without foolishly attempting to interpret, thereby committing a great offense at the feet of the Lord. The dangerous ways of interpretations by the nondevotee class of men have played havoc in understanding the *Śrīmad-Bhāgavatam*, and the careful student should be always alert in this matter if he at all wants to learn the science of Godhead.

TEXT 29

यद् यत् परीक्षिदृषभः पाण्डूनामनुपृच्छति ।
आनुपूर्व्येण तत्सर्वमाख्यातुमुपचक्रमे ॥२९॥

yad yat parīkṣid ṛṣabhaḥ
pāṇḍūnām anupṛcchati
ānupūrvyeṇa tat sarvam
ākyātum upacakrame

yat yat—whatsoever; *parīkṣit*—the King; *ṛṣabhaḥ*—the best; *pāṇḍūnām*—in the dynasty of Pāṇḍu; *anupṛcchati*—goes on inquiring; *ānupūrvyeṇa*—the beginning to the end; *tat*—all those; *sarvam*—fully; *ākhyātum*—to describe; *upacakrame*—he just prepared himself.

TRANSLATION

He also prepared himself to reply to all that King Parīkṣit had inquired from him. Mahārāja Parīkṣit was the best in the dynasty of the Pāṇḍus, and thus he was able to ask the right questions from the right person.

PURPORT

Mahārāja Parīkṣit asked many questions, some of them very curiously, to know things as they are, but it is not necessary for the master to answer them in the order of the disciple's inquiries, one after the other. But Śukadeva Gosvāmī, experienced teacher that he was, answered all the questions in a systematic way as they were received from the chain of disciplic succession. And he answered all of them without exception.

Thus end the Bhaktivedanta purports of the Second Canto, Eighth Chapter, of the Śrīmad-Bhāgavatam, *entitled "Questions by King Parīkṣit."*

CHAPTER NINE

Answers by Citing the Lord's Version

TEXT 1

श्रीशुक उवाच
आत्ममायामृते राजन् परस्यानुभवात्मनः ।
न घटेतार्थसम्बन्धः स्वप्नद्रष्टुरिवाञ्जसा ॥ १ ॥

śrī-śuka uvāca
ātma-māyām ṛte rājan
parasyānubhavātmanaḥ
na ghaṭetārtha-sambandhaḥ
svapna-draṣṭur ivāñjasā

śrī-śukaḥ uvāca—Śrī Śukadeva Gosvāmī said; *ātma*—the Supreme Personality of Godhead; *māyām*—energy; *ṛte*—without; *rājan*—O King; *parasya*—of the pure soul; *anubhava-ātmanaḥ*—of the purely conscious; *na*—never; *ghaṭeta*—it can so happen; *artha*—meaning; *sambandhaḥ*—relation with the material body; *svapna*—dream; *draṣṭuḥ*—of the seer; *iva*—like; *añjasā*—completely.

TRANSLATION

Śrī Śukadeva Gosvāmī said: O King, unless one is influenced by the energy of the Supreme Personality of Godhead, there is no meaning to the relationship of the pure soul in pure consciousness with the material body. That relationship is just like a dreamer's seeing his own body working.

PURPORT

Mahārāja Parīkṣit's question as to how a living entity began his material life, although he is apart from the material body and mind, is perfectly answered. The spirit soul is distinct from the material conception of his life, but he is absorbed in such a material conception because of being influenced by the external energy of the Lord, called *ātma-māyā.* This has already been explained in the First Canto in connection with Vyāsadeva's realization of the Supreme Lord and His external energy. The external energy is controlled by the Lord, and the living entities are controlled by the external energy—by the will of the Lord. Therefore, although the living entity is purely conscious in his pure state, he is subordinate to the will of the Lord in being influenced by the external energy of the Lord. In the *Bhagavad-gītā* (15.15) also the same thing is confirmed; the Lord is present within the heart of every living entity, and all the living entity's consciousness and forgetfulness are influenced by the Lord.

Now the next question automatically made will be why the Lord influences the living entity to such consciousness and forgetfulness. The answer is that the Lord clearly wishes that every living entity be in his pure consciousness as a part and parcel of the Lord and thus be engaged in the loving service of the Lord as he is constitutionally made; but because the living entity is partially independent also, he may not be willing to serve the Lord, but may try to become as independent as the Lord is. All the nondevotee living entities are desirous of becoming equally as powerful as the Lord, although they are not fit to become so. The living entities are illusioned by the will of the Lord because they wanted to become like Him. Like a person who thinks of becoming a king without possessing the necessary qualification, when the living entity desires to become the Lord Himself, he is put in a condition of dreaming that he is a king. Therefore the first sinful will of the living entity is to become the Lord, and the consequent will of the Lord is that the living entity forget his factual life and thus dream of the land of utopia where he may become one like the Lord. The child cries to have the moon from the mother, and the mother gives the child a mirror to satisfy the crying and disturbing child with the reflection of the moon. Similarly, the crying child of the Lord is given over to the reflection, the material world, to lord it over as *karmī* and to give this up in frustration to become one with the Lord. Both these stages are dreaming illusions only. There is no necessity of tracing out the history of when the living entity desired this. But the fact is that as soon as he desired it, he was put under the control of *ātma-māyā* by the direction of the Lord. Therefore the living entity in his material condition is dreaming falsely that this is "mine" and this is "I." The dream is that the conditioned soul thinks of his material body as "I" or falsely thinks that he is the Lord and that everything in connection with that material body is "mine." Thus only in dream does the misconception of "I" and "mine" persist life after life. This continues life after life, as long as the living entity is not purely conscious of his identity as the subordinate part and parcel of the Lord.

In his pure consciousness, however, there is no such misconceived dream, and in that pure conscious state the living entity does not forget that he is never the Lord, but that he is eternally the servitor of the Lord in transcendental love.

TEXT 2

बहुरूप इवाभाति मायया बहुरूपया ।
रममाणो गुणेष्वस्या ममाहमिति मन्यते ॥ २ ॥

bahu-rūpa ivābhāti
māyayā bahu-rūpayā
ramamāṇo guṇeṣv asyā
mamāham iti manyate

bahu-rūpaḥ—multiforms; *iva*—as it were; *ābhāti*—manifested; *māyayā*—by the influence of the exterior energy; *bahu-rūpayā*—in multifarious forms; *ramamāṇaḥ*—enjoying as it were; *guṇeṣu*—in the modes of different qualities; *asyāḥ*—of the external energy; *mama*—mine; *aham*—I; *iti*—thus; *manyate*—thinks.

TRANSLATION

The illusioned living entity appears in so many forms offered by the external energy of the Lord. While enjoying in the modes of material nature, the encaged living entity misconceives, thinking in terms of "I" and "mine."

PURPORT

The different forms of the living entities are different dresses offered by the illusory, external energy of the Lord according to the modes of nature the living being desires to enjoy. The external, material energy is represented by her three modes, namely goodness, passion and ignorance. So even in the material nature there is a chance of an independent choice by the living entity, and according to his choice the material energy offers him different varieties of material bodies. There are 900,000 varieties of material bodies in the water, 2,000,000 vegetable bodies, 1,100,000 worms and reptiles, 1,000,000 forms of birds, 3,000,000 different bodies of beasts, and 400,000 human forms. Altogether there are 8,400,000 varieties of bodies in different planets of the universe, and the living entity is traveling by so many transmigrations according to different modes of enjoying spirit within himself. Even in one particular body the living entity changes from childhood to boyhood, from boyhood to youth, from youth to old age and from old age to another body created by his own action. The living entity creates his own body by his personal desires, and the external energy of the Lord supplies him the exact form by which he can enjoy his desires to the fullest extent. The tiger wanted to enjoy the blood of another animal, and therefore, by the grace of the Lord, the material energy supplied him the body of the tiger with facilities for enjoying blood from another animal. Similarly, a living entity desiring to get the body of a demigod in a higher planet can also get it by the grace of the Lord. And if he is intelligent enough, he can desire to get a spiritual body to enjoy the company of the Lord, and he will get it. So the minute freedom of the living entity can be fully utilized, and the Lord is so kind that He will award the living entity the same type of body he desires. The living entity's desiring is like dreaming of a golden mountain. A person knows what a mountain is, and he knows also what gold is. Out of his desire only, he dreams of a golden mountain, and when the dream is over he sees something else in his presence. He finds in his awakened state that there is neither gold nor a mountain, and what to speak of a golden mountain.

The different positions of the living entities in the material world under multifarious manifestations of bodies are due to the misconception of "mine" and "I." The *karmī* thinks of this world as "mine," and the *jñānī* thinks "I am" everything. The whole material conception of politics, sociology, philanthropy, altruism, etc., conceived by the conditioned souls is on the basis of this misconceived "I" and "mine," which are products of a strong desire to enjoy material life. Identification with the body and the place where the body is obtained under different conceptions of socialism, nationalism, family affection, and so on and so forth is all due to forgetfulness of the real nature of the living entity, and the whole misconception of the bewildered living entity can be removed by the association of Śukadeva Gosvāmī and Mahārāja Parīkṣit, as all this is explained in the *Śrīmad-Bhāgavatam.*

TEXT 3

यर्हि वाव महिम्नि स्वे परस्मिन् कालमाययोः ।
रमेत गतसम्मोहस्त्यक्त्वोदास्ते तदोभयम् ॥ ३ ॥

yarhi vāva mahimni sve
parasmin kāla-māyayoḥ
rameta gata-sammohas
tyaktvodāste tadobhayam

yarhi—at any time; *vāva*—certainly; *mahimni*—in the glory; *sve*—of himself; *parasmin*—in the Supreme; *kāla*—time; *māyayoḥ*—of the material energy; *rameta*—enjoys; *gata-sammohaḥ*—being freed from the misconception; *tyaktvā*—giving up; *udāste*—in fullness; *tadā*—then; *ubhayam*—both (the misconceptions of I and mine).

TRANSLATION

As soon as the living entity becomes situated in his constitutional glory and begins to enjoy the transcendence beyond time and material energy, he at once gives up the two misconceptions of life [I and mine] and thus becomes fully manifested as the pure self.

PURPORT

The two misconceptions of life, namely "I" and "mine," are verily manifested in two classes of men. In the lower state the conception of "mine" is very prominent, and in the higher state the misconception of "I" is prominent. In the animal state of life the misconception of "mine" is perceivable even in the category of cats and dogs, who fight with one another with the same misconception of "mine." In the lower stage of human life the same misconception is also prominent in the shape of "It is my body," "It is my house," "It is my family," "It is my caste," "It is my nation," "It is my country," and so on. And in the higher stage of speculative knowledge, the same misconception of "mine" is transformed into "I am," or "It is all I am," etc. There are many classes of men comprehending the same misconception of "I" and "mine" in different colors. But the real significance of "I" can be realized only when one is situated in the consciousness of "*I am the eternal servitor of the Lord.*" This is pure consciousness, and the whole Vedic literatures teach us this conception of life.

The misconception of "I am the Lord," or "I am the Supreme," is more dangerous than the misconception of "mine." Although there are sometimes directions in the Vedic literatures to think oneself one with the Lord, that does not mean that one becomes identical with the Lord in every respect. Undoubtedly there is oneness of the living entity with the Lord in many respects, but ultimately the living entity is subordinate to the Lord, and he is constitutionally meant for satisfying the senses of the Lord. The Lord therefore asks the conditioned souls to surrender unto Him. Had the living entities not been subordinate to the supreme will, why would the living entity be asked to surrender? Had the living being been equal in all respects, then why was he put under the influence of *māyā?* We have already discussed many times that the material energy is controlled by the Lord. The *Bhagavad-gītā* (9.10) confirms this controlling power of the Lord over the material nature. Can a living entity who claims to be as good as the Supreme Being control the material nature? The foolish "I" would reply that he will do so in the future. Even accepting that in the future one will be as good a controller of material nature as the Supreme Being, then why is one now under the control of material nature? The *Bhagavad-gītā* says that one can be freed from the control of the material nature by surrendering unto the Supreme Lord, but if there is no surrender, then the living entity will never be able to control the material nature. So one must also give up this misconception of "I" by practicing the way of devotional service or firmly being situated in the transcendental loving service of the Lord. A poor man without any employment or occupation may undergo so many troubles in life, but if by chance the same man gets a good service under the government, he at once becomes happy. There is no profit in denying the supremacy of the

Lord, who is the controller of all energies, but one should be constitutionally situated in one's own glory, namely to be situated in the pure consciousness of being the eternal servitor of the Lord. In his conditional life the living entity is servant of the illusory *māyā,* and in his liberated state he is the pure, unqualified servant of the Lord. To become untinged by the modes of material nature is the qualification for entering into the service of the Lord. As long as one is a servant of mental concoctions, one cannot be completely free from the disease of "I" and "mine."

The Supreme Truth is uncontaminated by the illusory energy because He is the controller of that energy. The relative truths are apt to be engrossed in illusory energy. The best purpose is served, however, when one is directly facing the Supreme Truth, as when one faces the sun. The sun overhead in the sky is full of light, but when the sun is not in the visible sky, all is in darkness. Similarly, when one is face to face with the Supreme Lord, he is freed from all illusions, and one who is not so is in the darkness of illusory *māyā.* The *Bhagavad-gītā* (14.26) confirms this as follows:

māṁ ca yo 'vyabhicāreṇa
bhakti-yogena sevate
sa guṇān samatītyaitān
brahma-bhūyāya kalpate

So the science of *bhakti-yoga,* of worshiping the Lord, glorifying the Lord, hearing the *Śrīmad-Bhāgavatam* from the right sources (not from the professional man but from a person who is *Bhāgavatam* in life) and being always in the association of pure devotees, should be adopted in earnestness. One should not be misled by misconceptions of "I" and "mine." The *karmīs* are fond of the conception of "mine," the *jñānīs* are fond of the conception of "I," and both of them are unqualified to be free from the bondage of the illusory energy. *Śrīmad-Bhāgavatam* and, primarily, the *Bhagavad-gītā* are both meant for delivering a person from the misconception of "I" and "mine," and Śrīla Vyāsadeva transcribed them for the deliverance of the fallen souls. The living entity has to be situated in the transcendental position where there is no more influence of time nor of the material energy. In conditioned life the living entity is subjected to the influence of time in the dream of past, present and future. The mental speculator tries to conquer the influence of time by future speculations of becoming Vāsudeva or the Supreme Lord himself by means of culturing knowledge and conquering over ego. But the process is not perfect. The perfect process is to accept Lord Vāsudeva as the Supreme in everything, and the best perfection in culturing knowledge is to surrender unto Him because He is the source of everything. Only in that conception can one get rid of the misconception of I and mine. Both *Bhagavad-gītā* and the *Śrīmad-Bhāgavatam* confirm it. Śrīla Vyāsadeva has specifically contributed to the illusioned living entities the science of God and the process of *bhakti-yoga* in his great literature *Śrīmad-Bhāgavatam,* and the conditioned soul should fully take advantage of this great science.

TEXT 4

आत्मतत्त्वविशुद्ध्यर्थं यदाह भगवानृतम् ।
ब्रह्मणे दर्शयन् रूपमव्यलीकव्रतादृतः ॥ ४ ॥

ātma-tattva-viśuddhy-arthaṁ
yad āha bhagavān ṛtam
brahmaṇe darśayan rūpam
avyalīka-vratādṛtaḥ

ātma-tattva—the science of God or that of the living entity; *viśuddhi*—purification; *artham*—goal; *yat*—that which; *āha*—said; *bhagavān*—the Personality of Godhead; *ṛtam*—in reality; *brahmaṇe*—unto Lord Brahmā; *darśayan*—by showing; *rūpam*—eternal form; *avyalīka*—without any deceptive motive; *vrata*—vow; *ādṛtaḥ*—worshiped.

TRANSLATION

O King, the Personality of Godhead, being very much pleased with Lord Brahmā because of his nondeceptive penance in bhakti-yoga, presented His eternal and transcendental form before Brahmā. And that is the objective goal for purifying the conditioned soul.

PURPORT

Ātma-tattva is the science of both God and the living entity. Both the Supreme Lord and the living entity are known as *ātmā.* The Supreme

Lord is called Paramātmā, and the living entity is called the *ātmā*, the *brahma* or the *jīva.* Both the Paramātmā and the *jīvātmā*, being transcendental to the material energy, are called *ātmā.* So Śukadeva Gosvāmī explains this verse with the aim of purifying the truth of both the Paramātmā and the *jīvātmā.* Generally people have many wrong conceptions about both of them. The wrong conception of the *jīvātmā* is to identify the material body with the pure soul, and the wrong conception of Paramātmā is to think Him on an equal level with the living entity. But both misconceptions can be removed by one stroke of *bhakti-yoga*, just as in the sunlight both the sun and the world and everything within the sunlight are properly seen. In the darkness one cannot see the sun, nor himself, nor the world. But in the sunlight one can see the sun, himself and the world around him. Śrīla Śukadeva Gosvāmī therefore says that for purification of both wrong conceptions, the Lord presented His eternal form before Brahmājī, being fully satisfied by Brahmā's nondeceptive vow of discharging *bhakti-yoga.* Except for *bhakti-yoga*, any method for realization of *ātma-tattva*, or the science of *ātmā*, will prove deceptive in the long run.

In the *Bhagavad-gītā*, the Lord says that only by *bhakti-yoga* can one know Him perfectly, and then one can enter into the science of God. Brahmājī undertook great penance in performing *bhakti-yoga*, and thus he was able to see the transcendental form of the Lord. His transcendental form is one hundred percent spiritual, and one can see Him only by spiritualized vision after proper discharge of *tapasya* or penance, in pure *bhakti-yoga.* The form of the Lord manifested before Brahmā is not one of the forms with which we have experience in the material world. Brahmājī did not perform such severe types of penance just to see a form of material production. Therefore the question by Mahārāja Parīkṣit about the form of the Lord is answered. The form of the Lord is *sac-cid-ānanda*, or eternal, full of knowledge and full of bliss. But the material form of the living being is neither eternal, nor full of knowledge, nor blissful. That is the distinction between the form of the Lord and that of the conditioned soul. The conditioned soul, however, can regain his form of eternal knowledge and bliss simply by seeing the Lord by means of *bhakti-yoga.*

The summary is that due to ignorance the conditioned soul is encaged in the temporary varieties of material forms. But the Supreme Lord has no such temporary form like the conditioned souls. He is always possessed of an eternal form of knowledge and bliss, and that is the difference between the Lord and the living entity. One can understand this difference by the process of *bhakti-yoga*. Brahmā was then told by the Lord the gist of *Śrīmad-Bhāgavatam* in four original verses. Thus *Śrīmad-Bhāgavatam* is not a creation of the mental speculators. The sound of *Śrīmad-Bhāgavatam* is transcendental, and the resonance of *Śrīmad-Bhāgavatam* is as good as that of the *Vedas*. Thus the topic of the *Śrīmad-Bhāgavatam* is the science of both the Lord and the living entity. Regular reading or hearing of *Śrīmad-Bhāgavatam* is also performance of *bhakti-yoga*, and one can attain the highest perfection simply by the association of *Śrīmad-Bhāgavatam*. Both Śukadeva Gosvāmī and Mahārāja Parīkṣit attained perfection through the medium of *Śrīmad-Bhāgavatam*.

TEXT 5

स आदिदेवो जगतां परो गुरुः
स्वधिष्ण्यमास्थाय सिसृक्षयैक्षत ।
तां नाध्यगच्छद् दृशमत्र सम्मतां
प्रपञ्चनिर्माणविधिर्यया भवेत् ॥ ५ ॥

sa ādi-devo jagatāṁ paro guruḥ
svadhiṣṇyam āsthāya sisṛkṣayaikṣata
tāṁ nādhyagacchad dṛśam atra sammatāṁ
prapañca-nirmāṇa-vidhir yayā bhavet

saḥ—he; *ādi-devaḥ*—the first demigod; *jagatām*—of the universe; *paraḥ*—supreme; *guruḥ*—spiritual master; *svadhiṣṇyam*—his lotus seat; *āsthāya*—to find the source of it; *sisṛkṣayā*—for the matter of creating the universal affairs; *aikṣata*—began to think; *tām*—in that matter; *na*—could not; *adhyagacchat*—understand; *dṛśam*—the direction; *atra*—therein; *sammatām*—just the proper way; *prapañca*—material; *nirmāṇa*—construction; *vidhiḥ*—process; *yayā*—as much as; *bhavet*—should be.

TRANSLATION

Lord Brahmā, the first spiritual master, supreme in the universe, could not trace out the source of his lotus seat, and while thinking of creating the material world, he could not understand the proper direction for such creative work, nor could he find out the process for such creation.

PURPORT

This verse is the prelude for explaining the transcendental nature of the form and the abode of the Lord. In the beginning of *Śrīmad-Bhāgavatam* it has already been said that the Supreme Absolute Truth exists in His own abode without any touch of the deluding energy. Therefore the kingdom of God is not a myth but factually a different and transcendental sphere of planets known as the Vaikuṇṭhas. This will also be explained in this chapter.

Such knowledge of the spiritual sky far above this material sky and its paraphernalia can be known only by dint of devotional service, or *bhakti-yoga.* The power of creation by Lord Brahmā was also achieved by *bhakti-yoga.* Brahmāji was bewildered in the matter of creation, and he could not even trace out the source of his own existence. But all this knowledge was fully achieved by him through the medium of *bhakti-yoga.* By *bhakti-yoga* one can know the Lord, and by knowing the Lord as the Supreme, one is able to know everything else. One who knows the Supreme knows everything else. That is the version of all *Vedas.* Even the first spiritual master of the universe was enlightened by the grace of the Lord, so who else can attain perfect knowledge of everything without the mercy of the Lord? If anyone desires to seek perfect knowledge of everything, he must seek the mercy of the Lord, and there is no other means. To seek knowledge on the strength of one's personal attempt is a sheer waste of time.

TEXT 6

स चिन्तयन् द्व्यक्षरमेकदाम्भ-
स्युपाशृणोद् द्विर्गदितं वचो विभुः ।

स्पर्शेषु यत्षोडशमेकविंशं
निष्किञ्चनानां नृप यद् धनं विदुः ॥ ६ ॥

sa cintayan dvy-akṣaram ekadāmbhasy
upāśṛṇod dvir-gaditaṁ vaco vibhuḥ
sparśeṣu yat ṣoḍaśam ekaviṁśaṁ
niṣkiñcanānāṁ nṛpa yad dhanaṁ viduḥ

saḥ—he; *cintayan*—while thus thinking; *dvi*—two; *akṣaram*—syllables; *ekadā*—once upon a time; *ambhasi*—in the water; *upāśṛṇot*—heard it nearby; *dviḥ*—twice; *gaditam*—uttered; *vacaḥ*—words; *vibhuḥ*—the great; *sparśeṣu*—in the *sparśa* letters; *yat*—which; *ṣoḍaśam*—the sixteenth; *ekaviṁśam*—and the twenty-first; *niṣkiñcanānām*—of the renounced order of life; *nṛpa*—O King; *yat*—what is; *dhanam*—wealth; *viduḥ*—as it is known.

TRANSLATION

While thus engaged in thinking, in the water, Brahmājī heard twice from nearby two syllables joined together. One of the syllables was taken from the sixteenth and the other from the twenty-first of the sparśa alphabets, and both joined to become the wealth of the renounced order of life.

PURPORT

In Sanskrit language, the consonant alphabets are divided into two divisions, namely the *sparśa-varṇas* and the *tālavya-varṇas.* From *ka* to *ma* the letters are known as the *sparśa-varṇas,* and the sixteenth of the group is called *ta,* whereas the twenty-first letter is called *pa.* So when they are joined together, the word *tapa,* or penance, is constructed. This penance is the beauty and wealth of the *brāhmaṇas* and the renounced order of life. According to *Bhāgavata* philosophy, every human being is meant simply for this *tapa* and for no other business, because by penance only can one realize his self; and self-realization, not sense gratification, is the business of human life. This *tapa,* or penance, was begun from the very beginning of the creation, and it was first adopted by the supreme spiritual master, Lord Brahmā. By *tapasya* only can one get the profit of human life, and not by a polished civilization of animal life. The animal does not know anything except sense gratification in the jurisdiction of eat, drink, be merry and enjoy. But the human being is made to undergo *tapasya* for going back to Godhead, back home.

When Lord Brahmā was perplexed about how to construct the material manifestations in the universe and went down within the water to find out the means and the source of his lotus seat, he heard the word *tapa* vibrated twice. Taking the path of *tapa* is the second birth of the desiring disciple. The word *upāśṛṇot* is very significant. It is similar to *upanayana*, or bringing the disciple nearer to the spiritual master for the path of *tapa*. So Brahmājī was thus initiated by Lord Kṛṣṇa, and this fact is corroborated by Brahmājī himself in his book the *Brahma-saṁhitā*. In the *Brahma-saṁhitā* Lord Brahmā has sung in every verse *govindam ādi-puruṣaṁ tam ahaṁ bhajāmi*. Thus Brahmā was initiated by the Kṛṣṇa *mantra*, by Lord Kṛṣṇa Himself, and thus he became a Vaiṣṇava, or a devotee of the Lord, before he was able to construct the huge universe. It is stated in the *Brahma-saṁhitā* that Lord Brahmā was initiated into the eighteen-letter Kṛṣṇa *mantra*, which is generally accepted by all the devotees of Lord Kṛṣṇa. We follow the same principle because we belong to the Brahmā *sampradāya*, directly in the disciplic chain from Brahmā to Nārada, from Nārada to Vyāsa, from Vyāsa to Madhva Muni, from Madhva Muni to Mādhavendra Purī, from Mādhavendra Purī to Īśvara Purī, from Īśvara Purī to Lord Caitanya and gradually to His Divine Grace Bhaktisiddhānta Sarasvatī, our divine master.

One who is thus initiated in the disciplic succession is able to achieve the same result or power of creation. Chanting of this holy *mantra* is the only shelter of the desireless pure devotee of the Lord. Simply by such *tapasya*, or penance, the devotee of the Lord achieves all perfections like Lord Brahmā.

TEXT 7

निशम्य तद्वक्तृदिदृक्षया दिशो
विलोक्य तत्रान्यदपश्यमानः ।
स्वधिष्ण्यमास्थाय विमृश्य तद्धितं
तपस्युपादिष्ट इवादधे मनः ॥ ७ ॥

niśamya tad-vaktṛ-didṛkṣayā diśo
vilokya tatrānyad apaśyamānaḥ
svadhiṣṇyam āsthāya vimṛśya tad-dhitaṁ
tapasy upādiṣṭa ivādadhe manaḥ

niśamya—after hearing; *tat*—that; *vaktṛ*—the speaker; *didṛkṣayā*—just to find out who spoke; *diśaḥ*—all sides; *vilokya*—seeing; *tatra*—there; *anyat*—any other; *apaśyamānaḥ*—not to be found; *svadhiṣṇyam*—on his lotus seat; *āsthāya*—sit down; *vimṛśya*—thinking; *tat*—it; *hitam*—welfare; *tapasi*—in penance; *upādiṣṭaḥ*—as he was instructed; *iva*—in pursuance of; *ādadhe*—gave; *manaḥ*—attention.

TRANSLATION

When he heard the sound, he tried to find the speaker, searching on all sides. But when he was unable to find anyone besides himself, he thought it wise to sit down on his lotus seat firmly and give his attention to the execution of penance, as he was instructed.

PURPORT

To achieve success in life, one should follow the example of Lord Brahmā, the first living creature in the beginning of creation. After being initiated by the Supreme Lord to execute *tapasya*, he was fixed in his determination to do it, and although he could not find anyone besides himself, he could rightly understand that the sound was transmitted by the Lord Himself. Brahmā was the only living being at that time because there was no other creation and none could be found there except himself. In the beginning of the First Canto, in the First Chapter, first verse, of the *Śrīmad-Bhāgavatam*, it has already been mentioned that Brahmā was initiated by the Lord from within. The Lord is within every living entity as the Supersoul, and He initiated Brahmā because Brahmā was willing to receive the initiation. The Lord can similarly initiate everyone who is inclined to have it.

As already stated, Brahmā is the original spiritual master for the universe, and since he was initiated by the Lord Himself, the message of *Śrīmad-Bhāgavatam* is coming down by disciplic succession, and in order to receive the real message of *Śrīmad-Bhāgavatam* one should approach the current link, or spiritual master, in the chain of disciplic succession. After being initiated by the proper spiritual master in that chain of succession, one should engage himself in the discharge of *tapasya* in the execution of devotional service. One should not, however, think himself on the level of Brahmā to be initiated directly by the Lord from inside because in the present age no one can be accepted to be as pure as Brahmā. The post of Brahmā to officiate in the creation of the universe is offered to the most pure living being, and unless one is so qualified one cannot expect to be treated like Brahmājī directly. But one can have the same facility through unalloyed devotees of the Lord, through scriptural instructions (as revealed in the *Bhagavad-gītā* and *Śrīmad-Bhāgavatam* especially), and also through the bona fide spiritual master available to the sincere soul. The Lord Himself appears as the spiritual master to a person who is sincere in heart about serving the Lord. Therefore the bona fide spiritual master who happens to meet the sincere devotee should be accepted as the most confidential and beloved representative of the Lord. If a person is posted under the guidance of such a bona fide spiritual master, it may be accepted without any doubt that the desiring person has achieved the grace of the Lord.

TEXT 8

दिव्यं सहस्राब्दममोघदर्शनो
जितानिलात्मा विजितोभयेन्द्रियः।
अतप्यत स्माखिललोकतापनं
तपस्तपीयांस्तपतां समाहितः ॥ ८ ॥

divyaṁ sahasrābdam amogha-darśano
jitānilātmā vijitobhayendriyaḥ
atapyata smākhila-loka-tāpanaṁ
tapas tapīyāṁs tapatāṁ samāhitaḥ

divyam—pertaining to the demigods in the higher planets; *sahasra*—one thousand; *abdam*—years; *amogha*—spotless, without a tinge of impurity; *darśanaḥ*—one who has such a vision of life; *jita*—controlled;

anila—life; *ātmā*—mind; *vijita*—controlled over; *ubhaya*—both; *indriyaḥ*—one who has such senses; *atapyata*—executed penance; *sma*—in the past; *akhila*—all; *loka*—planet; *tāpanam*—enlightening; *tapaḥ*—penance; *tapīyān*—extremely hard penance; *tapatām*—of all the executors of penances; *samāhitaḥ*—thus situated.

TRANSLATION

Lord Brahmā underwent penances for one thousand years by the calculations of the demigods. He heard this transcendental vibration from the sky, and he accepted it as divine. Thus he controlled his mind and senses, and the penances he executed were a great lesson for the living entities. Thus he is known as the greatest of all ascetics.

PURPORT

Lord Brahmā heard the occult sound *tapa*, but he did not see the person who vibrated the sound. And still he accepted the instruction as beneficial for him, and therefore he engaged himself in meditation for one thousand celestial years. One celestial year is equal to 6 X 30 X 12 X 1000 of our years. His acceptance of the sound was due to his pure vision of the absolute nature of the Lord. And due to his correct vision, he made no distinction between the Lord and the Lord's instruction. There is no difference between the Lord and sound vibration coming from Him, even though He is not personally present. The best way of understanding is to accept such divine instruction, and Brahmā, the prime spiritual master of everyone, is the living example of this process of receiving transcendental knowledge. The potency of transcendental sound is never minimized because the vibrator is apparently absent. Therefore *Śrīmad-Bhāgavatam* or *Bhagavad-gītā* or any revealed scripture in the world is never to be accepted as an ordinary mundane sound without transcendental potency.

One has to receive the transcendental sound from the right source, accept it as a reality and prosecute the direction without hesitation. The secret of success is to receive the sound from the right source of a bona fide spiritual master. Mundane manufactured sound has no potency, and as such, seemingly transcendental sound received from an unauthorized person also has no potency. One should be qualified enough to discern such transcendental potency, and either by discriminating or by fortunate chance if one is able to receive the transcendental sound from the bona fide spiritual master, his path of liberation is guaranteed. The disciple, however, must be ready to execute the order of the bona fide spiritual master as Lord Brahmā executed the instruction of his spiritual master, the Lord Himself. Following the order of the bona fide spiritual master is the only duty of the disciple, and this completely faithful execution of the order of the bona fide spiritual master is the secret of success.

Lord Brahmā controlled his two grades of senses by means of sense perception and sense organs because he had to engage such senses in the execution of the order of the Lord. Therefore controlling the senses means engaging them in the transcendental service of the Lord. The Lord's order descends in disciplic succession through the bona fide spiritual master, and thus execution of the order of the bona fide spiritual master is factual control of the senses. Such execution of penance in full faith and sincerity made Brahmājī so powerful that he became the creator of the universe. And because he was able to attain such power, he is called the best amongst all the *tapasvīs*.

TEXT 9

तस्मै स्वलोकं भगवान् सभाजितः
सन्दर्शयामास परं न यत्परम् ।
व्यपेतसंक्लेशविमोहसाध्वसं
स्वदृष्टवद्भिर्पुरुषैरभिष्टुतम् ॥ ९ ॥

tasmai sva-lokaṁ bhagavān sabhājitaḥ
sandarśayām āsa paraṁ na yat-param
vyapeta-saṅkleśa-vimoha-sādhvasaṁ
sva-dṛṣṭavadbhir puruṣair abhiṣṭutam

tasmai—unto him; *sva-lokam*—His own planet or abode; *bhagavān*—the Personality of Godhead; *sabhājitaḥ*—being pleased by the penance of Brahmā; *sandarśayām āsa*—manifested; *param*—the supreme; *na*—

not; *yat*—of which; *param*—further supreme; *vyapeta*—completely given up; *saṅkleśa*—five kinds of material afflictions; *vimoha*—without illusion; *sādhvasam*—fear of material existence; *sva-dṛṣṭa-vadbhiḥ*—by those who have perfectly realized the self; *puruṣaih*—by persons; *abhiṣṭutam*—worshiped by.

TRANSLATION

The Personality of Godhead, being thus very much satisfied with the penance of Lord Brahmā, was pleased to manifest His personal abode, Vaikuṇṭha, the supreme planet above all others. This transcendental abode of the Lord is adored by all self-realized persons freed from all kinds of miseries and fear of illusory existence.

PURPORT

The troubles of penance accepted by Lord Brahmā were certainly in the line of devotional service (*bhakti*). Otherwise there was no chance that Vaikuṇṭha or *svalokam*, the Lord's personal abodes, would become visible to Brahmājī. The personal abodes of the Lord, known as Vaikuṇṭhas, are neither mythical nor material, as conceived by the impersonalists. But realization of the transcendental abodes of the Lord is possible only through devotional service, and thus the devotees enter into such abodes. There is undoubtedly trouble in executing penance. But the trouble accepted in executing *bhakti-yoga* is transcendental happiness from the very beginning, whereas the trouble of penance in other processes of self-realization (*jñāna-yoga, dhyāna-yoga*, etc.), without any Vaikuṇṭha realization, ends in trouble only and nothing more. There is no profit in biting husks without grains. Similarly, there is no profit in executing troublesome penances other than *bhakti-yoga* for self-realization.

Executing *bhakti-yoga* is exactly like sitting on the lotus sprouted out of the abdomen of the transcendental Personality of Godhead, for Lord Brahmā was seated there. Brahmājī was able to please the Lord, and the Lord was also pleased to show Brahmājī His personal abode. Śrīla Jīva Gosvāmī, in the comments of his *Krama-sandarbha* annotation of *Śrīmad-Bhāgavatam*, cites quotations from the *Garga Upaniṣad*, Vedic evidence. It is said that Yājñavalkya described the transcendental abode of the Lord to Gārgī, and that the abode of the Lord is situated above the highest planet of the universe, namely Brahmaloka. This abode of the Lord, although described in revealed scriptures like the *Bhagavad-gītā* and the *Śrīmad-Bhāgavatam*, remains only a myth for the less intelligent class of men with a poor fund of knowledge. Herein the word *sva-dṛṣṭavadbhiḥ* is very significant. One who has actually realized his self realizes the transcendental form of one's self. Impersonal realization of self and the Supreme is not complete, because it is just an opposite conception of material personalities. The Personality of Godhead and the personalities of devotees of the Lord are all transcendental; they do not have material bodies. The material body is overcast with five kinds of miserable conditions, namely ignorance, material conception, attachment, hatred and absorption. As long as one is overwhelmed by these five kinds of material miseries, there is no question of entering into the Vaikuṇṭhalokas. The impersonal conception of one's self is just the negation of material personality and is far from the positive existence of personal form. The personal forms of the transcendental abode will be explained in the following verses. Brahmājī also described the highest planet of the Vaikuṇṭhaloka as Goloka Vṛndāvana, where the Lord resides as a cowherd boy keeping transcendental *surabhi* cows and surrounded by hundreds and thousands of goddesses of fortune.

cintāmaṇi-prakara-sadmasu kalpavṛkṣa-
lakṣāvṛteṣu surabhīr abhipālayantam
lakṣmī-sahasra-śata-sambhrama-sevyamānaṁ
govindam ādi-puruṣaṁ tam ahaṁ bhajāmi
(*Brahma-saṁhitā* 5.29)

The statement of the *Bhagavad-gītā*, *yad gatvā na nivartante tad dhāma paramaṁ mama*, is also confirmed herewith. *Param* means transcendental Brahman. Therefore, the abode of the Lord is also Brahman, nondifferent from the Supreme Personality of Godhead. The Lord is known as Vaikuṇṭha, and His abode is also known as Vaikuṇṭha. Such Vaikuṇṭha realization and worship can be made possible by transcendental form and sense.

TEXT 10

प्रवर्तते यत्र रजस्तमस्तयोः
सत्त्वं च मिश्रं न च कालविक्रमः ।
न यत्र माया किमुतापरे हरे-
रनुव्रता यत्र सुरासुरार्चिताः ॥१०॥

pravartate yatra rajas tamas tayoḥ
sattvaṁ ca miśraṁ na ca kāla-vikramaḥ
na yatra māyā kim utāpare harer
anuvratā yatra surāsurārcitāḥ

pravartate—prevail; *yatra*—wherein; *rajaḥ tamaḥ*—the modes of passion and ignorance; *tayoḥ*—of both of them; *sattvam*—the mode of goodness; *ca*—and; *miśram*—mixture; *na*—never; *ca*—and; *kāla*—time; *vikramaḥ*—influence; *na*—neither; *yatra*—therein; *māyā*—illusory, external energy; *kim*—what; *uta*—there is; *apare*—others; *hareḥ*—of the Personality of Godhead; *anuvratāḥ*—devotees; *yatra*—wherein; *sura*—by the demigods; *asura*—and the demons; *arcitāḥ*—worshiped.

TRANSLATION

In that personal abode of the Lord, the material modes of ignorance and passion do not prevail, nor is there any of their influence in goodness. There is no predominance of the influence of time, so what to speak of the illusory, external energy; it cannot enter that region. Without discrimination, both the demigods and the demons worship the Lord as devotees.

PURPORT

The kingdom of God, or the atmosphere of the Vaikuṇṭha nature, which is called the *tripād-vibhūti*, is three times bigger than the material universes and is described here, as also in the *Bhagavad-gītā*, in a nutshell. This universe, containing billions of stars and planets, is one of the billions of such universes clustered together within the compass of the *mahat-tattva*. And all these millions and billions of universes combined together constitute only one fourth of the magnitude of the whole creation of the Lord. There is the spiritual sky also; beyond this sky are the spiritual planets under the names of Vaikuṇṭha, and all of them constitute three fourths of the entire creation of the Lord. God's creations are always innumerable. Even the leaves of a tree cannot be counted by a man, nor can the hairs on his head. However, foolish men are puffed up with the idea of becoming God Himself, though unable to create a hair of their own bodies. Man may discover so many wonderful vehicles of journey, but even if he reaches the moon by his much advertised spacecraft, he cannot remain there. The sane man, therefore, without being puffed up, as if he were the God of the universe, abides by the instructions of the Vedic literature, the easiest way to acquire knowledge in transcendence. So let us know through the authority of *Śrīmad-Bhāgavatam* of the nature and constitution of the transcendental world beyond the material sky. In that sky the material qualities, especially the modes of ignorance and passion, are completely absent. The mode of ignorance influences a living entity to the habit of lust and hankering, and this means that in the Vaikuṇṭhalokas the living entities are free from these two things. As confirmed in the *Bhagavad-gītā*, in the *brahma-bhūta* stage of life one becomes free from hankering and lamentation. Therefore the conclusion is that the inhabitants of the Vaikuṇṭha planets are all *brahma-bhūta* living entities, as distinguished from the mundane creatures who are all compact in hankering and lamentation. When one is not in the modes of ignorance and passion, one is supposed to be situated in the mode of goodness in the material world. Goodness in the material world also at times becomes contaminated by touches of the modes of passion and ignorance. In the Vaikuṇṭhaloka, it is unalloyed goodness only.

The whole situation there is one of freedom from the illusory manifestation of the external energy. Although illusory energy is also part and parcel of the Supreme Lord, illusory energy is differentiated from the Lord. The illusory energy is not, however, false, as claimed by the monist philosophers. The rope accepted as a snake may be an illusion to a particular person, but the rope is a fact, and the snake is also a fact. The illusion of water on the hot desert may be illusion for the ignorant animal searching for water in the desert, but the desert and water are actual facts. Therefore the material creation of the Lord may be an illusion to the nondevotee, but to a devotee even the material creation of the Lord is a fact, as the manifestation of His external energy. But this energy of the Lord is not all. The Lord has His internal energy also, which has another creation known to be the Vaikuṇṭhalokas, where there is no ignorance, no passion, no illusion and no past and present. With a poor fund of knowledge one may be unable to understand the existence of such things as the Vaikuṇṭha atmosphere, but that does not nullify its existence. That spacecraft cannot reach these planets does not mean that there are no such planets, for they are described in the revealed scriptures.

As quoted by Śrīla Jīva Gosvāmī, we can know from the *Nārada-pañcarātra* that the transcendental world or Vaikuṇṭha atmosphere is enriched with transcendental qualities. These transcendental qualities, as revealed through the devotional service of the Lord, are distinct from the mundane qualities of ignorance, passion and goodness. Such qualities are not attainable by the nondevotee class of men. In the *Padma Purāṇa, Uttara-khaṇḍa,* it is stated that beyond the one-fourth part of God's creation is the three-fourths manifestation. The marginal line between the material manifestation and the spiritual manifestation is the Virajā River, and beyond the Virajā, which is a transcendental current flowing from the perspiration of the body of the Lord, there is the three-fourths manifestation of God's creation. This part is eternal, everlasting, without deterioration, and unlimited, and it contains the highest perfectional stage of living conditions. In the *Sāṅkhya-kaumudī* it is stated that unalloyed goodness or transcendence is just opposite to the material modes. All living entities there are eternally associated without any break, and the Lord is the chief and prime entity. In the *Āgama Purāṇas* also, the transcendental abode is described as follows: The associated members there are free to go everywhere within the creation of the Lord, and there is no limit to such creation, particularly in the region of the three-fourths magnitude. Since the nature of that region is unlimited, there is no history of such association, nor is there end of it.

The conclusion may be drawn that because of the complete absence of the mundane qualities of ignorance and passion, there is no question of creation nor of annihilation. In the material world everything is created, and everything is annihilated, and the duration of life between the creation and annihilation is temporary. In the transcendental realm there is no creation and no destruction, and thus the duration of life is eternal unlimitedly. In other words, everything in the transcendental world is everlasting, full of knowledge and bliss without deterioration. Since there is no deterioration, there is no past, present and future in the estimation of time. It is clearly stated in this verse that the influence of time is conspicuous by its absence. The whole material existence is manifested by actions and reactions of elements which make the influence of time prominent in the matter of past, present and future. There are no such actions and reactions of cause and effects there, so the cycle of birth, growth, existence, transformations, deterioration and annihilation—the six material changes—are not existent there. It is the unalloyed manifestation of the energy of the Lord, without illusion as experienced here in the material world. The whole Vaikuṇṭha existence proclaims that everyone there is a follower of the Lord. The Lord is the chief leader there, without any competition for leadership, and the people in general are all followers of the Lord. It is confirmed in the *Vedas*, therefore, that the Lord is the chief leader and all other living entities are subordinate to Him, for only the Lord satisfies all the needs of all other living entities.

TEXT 11

श्यामावदाताः शतपत्रलोचनाः
पिशङ्गवस्त्राः सुरुचः सुपेशसः ।
सर्वे चतुर्बाहव उन्मिषन्मणि-
प्रवेकनिष्काभरणाः सुवर्चसः ॥११॥

śyāmāvadātāḥ śata-patra-locanāḥ
piśaṅga-vastrāḥ surucaḥ supeśasaḥ
sarve catur-bāhava unmiṣan-maṇi-
praveka-niṣkābharaṇāḥ suvarcasaḥ

śyāma—sky-bluish; *avadātāḥ*—glowing; *śata-patra*—lotus flower; *locanāḥ*—eyes; *piśaṅga*—yellowish; *vastrāḥ*—clothing; *su-rucaḥ*—greatly attractive; *su-peśasaḥ*—growing youthful; *sarve*—all of them; *catuḥ*—four; *bāhavaḥ*—hands; *unmiṣan*—rising luster; *maṇi*—pearls; *praveka*—superior quality; *niṣka-ābharaṇāḥ*—ornamental medallions; *su-varcasaḥ*—effulgent.

TRANSLATION

The inhabitants of the Vaikuṇṭha planets are described as having a glowing sky-bluish complexion. Their eyes resemble lotus flowers, their dress is of yellowish color, and their bodily features very attractive. They are just the age of growing youths, they all have four hands, they are all nicely decorated with pearl necklaces with ornamental medallions, and they all appear to be effulgent.

PURPORT

The inhabitants in Vaikuṇṭhaloka are all personalities with spiritual bodily features not to be found in the material world. We can find the descriptions in the revealed scriptures like *Śrīmad-Bhāgavatam.* Impersonal descriptions of transcendence in the scriptures indicate that the bodily features in Vaikuṇṭhaloka are never to be seen in any part of the universe. As there are different bodily features in different places of a particular planet, or as there are different bodily features between bodies in different planets, similarly the bodily features of the inhabitants in Vaikuṇṭhaloka are completely different from those in the material universe. For example, the four hands are distinct from the two hands in this world.

TEXT 12

प्रवालवैदूर्यमृणालवर्चसः
परिस्फुरत्कुण्डलमौलिमालिनः ॥१२॥

pravāla-vaidūrya-mṛṇāla-varcasaḥ
parisphurat-kuṇḍala-mauli-mālinaḥ

pravāla—coral; *vaidūrya*—a special diamond; *mṛṇāla*—celestial lotus; *varcasaḥ*—rays; *parisphurat*—blooming; *kuṇḍala*—earring; *mauli*—heads; *mālinaḥ*—with garlands.

TRANSLATION

Some of them are effulgent like coral and diamonds in complexion and have garlands on their heads, blooming like lotus flowers, and some wear earrings.

PURPORT

There are some inhabitants who have attained the liberation of *sārūpya*, or possessing bodily features like those of the Personality of Godhead. The *vaidūrya* diamond is especially meant for the Personality of Godhead, but one who achieves the liberation of bodily equality with the Lord is especially favored with such diamonds on his body.

TEXT 13

भ्राजिष्णुभिर्यः परितो विराजते
लसद्विमानावलिभिर्महात्मनाम् ।
विद्योतमानः प्रमदोत्तमाद्युभिः
सविद्युदभ्रावलिभिर्यथा नभः ॥१३॥

bhrājiṣṇubhir yaḥ parito virājate
lasad-vimānāvalibhir mahātmanām
vidyotamānaḥ pramadottamādyubhiḥ
savidyud abhrāvalibhir yathā nabhaḥ

bhrājiṣṇubhiḥ—by the glowing; *yaḥ*—the Vaikuṇṭhalokas; *paritaḥ*—surrounded by; *virājate*—thus situated; *lasat*—brilliant; *vimāna*—airplanes; *avalibhiḥ*—assemblage; *mahā-ātmanām*—of the great devotees of the Lord; *vidyotamānaḥ*—beautiful like lightning; *pramada*—ladies; *uttama*—celestial; *adyubhiḥ*—by complexion; *sa-vidyut*—with electric lightning; *abhrāvalibhiḥ*—with clouds in the sky; *yathā*—as it were; *nabhaḥ*—the sky.

TRANSLATION

The Vaikuṇṭha planets are also surrounded by various airplanes, all glowing and brilliantly situated. These airplanes belong to the great mahātmās or devotees of the Lord. The ladies are as beautiful as lightning because of their celestial complexions, and all these combined together appear just like the sky decorated with both clouds and lightning.

PURPORT

It appears that in the Vaikuṇṭha planets there are also airplanes brilliantly glowing, and they are occupied by the great devotees of the Lord with ladies of celestial beauty as brilliant as lightning. As there are airplanes, so there must be different types of carriages like airplanes, but they may not be driven machines, as we have experience in this world. Because everything is of the same nature of eternity, bliss and knowledge, the airplanes and carriages are of the same quality as Brahman. Although there is nothing except Brahman, one should not mistakenly think that there is only void and no variegatedness. Thinking like that is due to a poor fund of knowledge; otherwise no one would have such a misconception of voidness in Brahman. As there are airplanes, ladies and gentlemen, so there must be cities and houses and everything else just suitable to the particular planets. One should not carry the ideas of imperfection from this world to the transcendental world and not take into consideration the nature of the atmosphere, as completely free from the influence of time, etc., as described previously.

TEXT 14

श्रीर्यत्र रूपिण्युरुगायपादयोः
करोति मानं बहुधा विभूतिभिः ।
प्रेङ्खं श्रिता या कुसुमाकरानुगै-
र्विगीयमाना प्रियकर्म गायती ॥१४॥

śrīr yatra rūpiṇy urugāya-pādayoḥ
karoti mānaṁ bahudhā vibhūtibhiḥ
preṅkhaṁ śritā yā kusumākarānugair
vigīyamānā priya-karma gāyatī

śrīḥ—the goddess of fortune; *yatra*—in the Vaikuṇṭha planets; *rūpiṇī*—in her transcendental form; *urugāya*—the Lord, who is sung of by the great devotees; *pādayoḥ*—under the lotus feet of the Lord; *karoti*—does; *mānam*—respectful services; *bahudhā*—in diverse paraphernalia; *vibhūtibhiḥ*—accompanied by her personal associates; *preṅkham*—movement of enjoyment; *śritā*—taken shelter of; *yā*—who;

kusumākara—spring; *anugaiḥ*—by the black bees; *vigīyamānā*—being followed by the songs; *priya-karma*—activities of the dearmost; *gāyatī*—singing.

TRANSLATION

The goddess of fortune in her transcendental form is engaged in the loving service of the Lord's lotus feet, and being moved by the black bees, followers of spring, she is not only engaged in variegated pleasure—service to the Lord, along with her constant companions—but is also engaged in singing the glories of the Lord's activities.

TEXT 15

ददर्श तत्राखिलसात्वतां पतिं
श्रियः पतिं यज्ञपतिं जगत्पतिम् ।
सुनन्दनन्दप्रबलार्हणादिभिः
स्वपार्षदाग्रैः परिसेवितं विभुम् ॥१५॥

dadarśa tatrākhila-sātvatāṁ patiṁ
śriyaḥ patiṁ yajña-patiṁ jagat-patim
sunanda-nanda-prabalārhaṇādibhiḥ
sva-pārṣadāgraiḥ parisevitaṁ vibhum

dadarśa—Brahmā saw; *tatra*—there (in Vaikuṇṭhaloka); *akhila*—entire; *sātvatām*—of the great devotees; *patim*—the Lord; *śriyaḥ*—of the goddess of fortune; *patim*—the Lord; *yajña*—of sacrifice; *patim*—the Lord; *jagat*—of the universe; *patim*—the Lord; *sunanda*—Sunanda; *nanda*—Nanda; *prabala*—Prabala; *arhaṇa*—Arhaṇa; *ādibhiḥ*—by them; *sva-pārṣada*—own associates; *agraiḥ*—by the foremost; *parisevitam*—being served in transcendental love; *vibhum*—the great Almighty.

TRANSLATION

Lord Brahmā saw in the Vaikuṇṭha planets the Personality of Godhead, who is the Lord of the entire devotee community, the

Lord of the goddess of fortune, the Lord of all sacrifices, and the Lord of the universe, and who is served by the foremost servitors like Nanda, Sunanda, Prabala and Arhaṇa, His immediate associates.

PURPORT

When we speak of a king it is naturally understood that the king is accompanied by his confidential associates, like his secretary, private secretary, aide-de-camp, ministers and advisers. So also when we see the Lord we see Him with His different energies, associates, confidential servitors, etc. So the Supreme Lord, who is the leader of all living entities, the Lord of all devotee sects, the Lord of all opulences, the Lord of sacrifices and the enjoyer of everything in His entire creation, is not only the Supreme Person, but also is always surrounded by His immediate associates, all engaged in their loving transcendental service to Him.

TEXT 16

भृत्यप्रसादाभिमुखं दृगासवं
प्रसन्नहासारुणलोचनाननम् ।
किरीटिनं कुण्डलिनं चतुर्भुजं
पीतांशुकं वक्षसि लक्षितं श्रिया ॥१६॥

bhṛtya-prasādābhimukhaṁ dṛg-āsavaṁ
prasanna-hāsāruṇa-locanānanam
kirīṭinaṁ kuṇḍalinaṁ catur-bhujaṁ
pītāṁśukaṁ vakṣasi lakṣitaṁ śriyā

bhṛtya—the servitor; *prasāda*—affection; *abhimukham*—favorably facing; *dṛk*—the very sight; *āsavam*—an intoxication; *prasanna*—very much pleased; *hāsa*—smile; *aruṇa*—reddish; *locana*—eyes; *ānanam*—face; *kirīṭinam*—with helmet; *kuṇḍalinam*—with earrings; *catuḥ-bhujam*—with four hands; *pīta*—yellow; *aṁśukam*—dress; *vakṣasi*—on the chest; *lakṣitam*—marked; *śriyā*—with the goddess of fortune.

TRANSLATION

The Personality of Godhead, seen leaning favorably towards His loving servitors, His very sight intoxicating and attractive, ap-

peared to be very much satisfied. He had a smiling face decorated with an enchanting reddish hue. He was dressed in yellow robes and wore earrings and a helmet on his head. He had four hands, and His chest was marked with the lines of the goddess of fortune.

PURPORT

In the *Padma Purāṇa, Uttara-khaṇḍa,* there is a full description of the *yoga-pīṭha,* or the particular place where the Lord is in audience to His eternal devotees. In that *yoga-pīṭha,* the personifications of religion, knowledge, opulence and renunciation are all seated at the lotus feet of the Lord. The four *Vedas,* namely *Ṛk, Sāma, Yajur* and *Atharva,* are present there personally to advise the Lord. The sixteen energies headed by Caṇḍa are all present there. Caṇḍa and Kumuda are the first two doorkeepers, at the middle door are the doorkeepers named Bhadra and Subhadra, and at the last door are Jaya and Vijaya. There are other doorkeepers also, named Kumuda, Kumudākṣa, Puṇḍarīka, Vāmana, Śaṅkukarṇa, Sarvanetra, Sumukha, etc. The Lord's palace is well decorated and protected by the above-mentioned doorkeepers.

TEXT 17

अध्यर्हणीयासनमास्थितं परं
वृतं चतुःषोडशपञ्चशक्तिभिः ।
युक्तं भगैः स्वैरितरत्र चाध्रुवैः
स्व एव धामन् रममाणमीश्वरम् ॥१७॥

adhyarhaṇīyāsanam āsthitaṁ paraṁ
vṛtaṁ catuḥ-ṣoḍaśa-pañca-śaktibhiḥ
yuktaṁ bhagaiḥ svair itaratra cādhruvaiḥ
sva eva dhāman ramamāṇam īśvaram

adhyarhaṇīya—greatly worshipable; *āsanam*—throne; *āsthitam*—seated on it; *param*—the Supreme; *vṛtam*—surrounded by; *catuḥ*—four, namely *prakṛti, puruṣa, mahat* and ego; *ṣoḍaśa*—the sixteen; *pañca*—the five; *śaktibhiḥ*—by the energies; *yuktam*—empowered with; *bhagaiḥ*—His opulences; *svaiḥ*—personal; *itaratra*—other minor prowesses; *ca*—also; *adhruvaiḥ*—temporary; *sve*—own; *eva*—certainly; *dhāman*—abode; *ramamāṇam*—enjoying; *īśvaram*—the Supreme Lord.

TRANSLATION

The Lord was seated on His throne and was surrounded by different energies like the four, the sixteen, the five, and the six natural opulences, along with other insignificant energies of the temporary character. But He was the factual Supreme Lord, enjoying His own abode.

PURPORT

The Lord is naturally endowed with His six opulences. Specifically, He is the richest, He is the most powerful, He is the most famous, He is the most beautiful, He is the greatest in knowledge, and He is the greatest renouncer as well. And for His material creative energies, He is served by four, namely the principles of *prakṛti, puruṣa, mahat-tattva* and ego. He is also served by the sixteen, namely the five elements (earth, water, air, fire and sky), the five perceptive sense organs (the eye, ear, nose, tongue and skin), and the five working sense organs (the hand, the leg, the stomach, the evacuation outlet and the genitals), and the mind. The five includes the sense objects, namely form, taste, smell, sound and touch. All these twenty-five items serve the Lord in the material creation, and all of them are personally present to serve the Lord. The insignificant opulences numbering eight (the *aṣṭa-siddhis*, attained by *yogīs* for temporary overlordship) are also under His control, but He is naturally full with all such powers without any effort, and therefore He is the Supreme Lord.

The living being, by severe penance and performance of bodily exercises, can temporarily attain some wonderful power, but that does not make him the Supreme Lord. The Supreme Lord, by His own potency, is unlimitedly more powerful than any *yogī*, He is unlimitedly more learned than any *jñānī*, He is unlimitedly richer than any wealthy person, He is unlimitedly more beautiful than any beautiful living being, and He is unlimitedly more charitable than any philanthropist. He is above all; no one is equal to or greater than Him. Nor can anyone reach His level of perfection in any of the above powers by any amount of penance or yogic demonstrations. The *yogīs* are dependent on His mercy.

Out of His immensely charitable disposition He can award some temporary powers to the *yogīs* because of the *yogīs'* hankering after them, but to His unalloyed devotees, who do not want anything from the Lord save and except His transcendental service, the Lord is so pleased that He gives Himself in exchange for unalloyed service.

TEXT 18

तद्दर्शनाह्लादपरिप्लुतान्तरो
हृष्यत्तनुः प्रेमभराश्रुलोचनः ।
ननाम पादाम्बुजमस्य विश्वसृग्
यत् पारमहंस्येन पथाधिगम्यते ॥१८॥

tad-darśanāhlāda-pariplutāntaro
hṛṣyat-tanuḥ prema-bharāśru-locanaḥ
nanāma pādāmbujam asya viśva-sṛg
yat pāramahaṁsyena pathādhigamyate

tat—by that audience of the Lord; *darśana*—audience; *āhlāda*—joy; *paripluta*—overwhelmed; *antaraḥ*—within the heart; *hṛṣyat*—full in ecstasy; *tanuḥ*—body; *prema-bhara*—in full transcendental love; *aśru*—tears; *locanaḥ*—in the eyes; *nanāma*—bowed down; *pāda-ambujam*—under the lotus feet; *asya*—of the Lord; *viśva-sṛk*—the creator of the universe; *yat*—which; *pāramahaṁsyena*—by the great liberated soul; *pathā*—the path; *adhigamyate*—is followed.

TRANSLATION

Lord Brahmā, thus seeing the Personality of Godhead in His fullness, was overwhelmed with joy within his heart, and thus in full transcendental love and ecstasy, his eyes filled with tears of love. He thus bowed down before the Lord. That is the way of the highest perfection for the living being [paramahaṁsa].

PURPORT

In the beginning of the *Śrīmad-Bhāgavatam* it is stated that this great literature is meant for the *paramahaṁsas. Paramo nirmatsarāṇāṁ satām*, i.e. the *Śrīmad-Bhāgavatam* is meant for persons completely free from malice. In the conditioned life the malicious life begins from the top, namely bearing malice against the Supreme Personality of Godhead. The Personality of Godhead is an established fact in all the revealed scriptures, and in the *Bhagavad-gītā* the personal feature of the Supreme Lord is especially mentioned, so much so that the last portion of the great literature has emphatically stressed that one should surrender unto the Personality of Godhead to be saved from the miseries of life. Unfortunately, persons with impious backgrounds do not believe in the Personality of Godhead, and everyone wants to become God himself without any qualification. This malicious nature in the conditioned soul continues even up to the stage when a person wants to be one with the Lord, and thus even the greatest of the empiric philosophers speculating on becoming one with the Supreme Lord cannot become a *paramahaṁsa* because the malicious mind is there. Therefore the *paramahaṁsa* stage of life can be attained only by those who are fixed in the practice of *bhakti-yoga*. This *bhakti-yoga* begins if a person has the firm conviction that simply discharging devotional service to the Lord in full transcendental love can elevate him to the highest perfectional stage of life. Brahmājī believed in this art of *bhakti-yoga;* he believed in the instruction of the Lord to execute *tapa*, and he discharged the function with great penance and thus achieved the great success of seeing the Vaikuṇṭhalokas and the Lord also by personal experience. No one can reach the abode of the Supreme Lord by any mechanical means of the mind or machine, but one can reach the abode of the Vaikuṇṭhalokas simply by following the process of *bhakti-yoga* because the Lord can be realized only through the *bhakti-yoga* process. Lord Brahmājī was actually sitting on his lotus seat, and from there, by executing the process of *bhakti-yoga* in great seriousness, he could see the Vaikuṇṭhalokas with all variegatedness as well as the Lord in person and His associates.

Following in the footsteps of Lord Brahmā, any person, even up to this day, can attain the same perfection by following the path of the *paramahaṁsa* as recommended herein. Lord Caitanya also approved of this method of self-realization for men in this age. One should first, with all conviction, believe in the Personality of Godhead Śrī Kṛṣṇa, and without making efforts to realize Him by speculative philosophy, one should prefer to hear about Him from the *Śrīmad Bhagavad-gītā* and later from the text of the *Śrīmad-Bhāgavatam*. One should hear such discourses from a person *Bhāgavatam* and not from the professional man, or from the *karmī, jñānī* or *yogī*. That is the secret of learning the science. One does not need to be in the renounced order of life; he can remain in his present condition of life, but he must search out the association of a bona fide devotee of the Lord and hear from him the transcendental message of the Lord with faith and conviction. That is the path of the *paramahaṁsa* recommended herein. Amongst various holy names of the Lord, He is also called *ajita*, or one who can never be conquered by anyone else. Yet He can be conquered by the *paramahaṁsa* path, as practically realized and shown by the great spiritual master Lord Brahmā. Lord Brahmā has personally recommended this *paramahaṁsa-panthāḥ* in his own words as follows:

jñāne prayāsam udapāsya namanta eva
jīvanti sanmukharitāṁ bhavadīya vārtām
sthāne sthitāḥ śruti-gatāṁ tanu-vāṅ-manobhir
ye prāyaśo 'jita jito 'py asi tais trilokyām

Lord Brahmā said, "O my Lord Kṛṣṇa, a devotee who abandons the path of empiric philosophical speculation aimed at merging in the existence of the Supreme and engages himself in *hearing* Your glories and activities from a bona fide *sādhu*, or saint, and who lives an honest life in the occupational engagement of his social life, can conquer Your sympathy and mercy even though You are *ajita*, or unconquerable." (*Bhāg.* 10.14.3) That is the path of the *paramahaṁsas*, which was personally followed by Lord Brahmā and later recommended by him for attaining perfect success in life

TEXT 19

तं प्रीयमाणं समुपस्थितं कविं
प्रजाविसर्गे निजशासनार्हणम् ।
बभाष ईषत्स्मितशोचिषा गिरा
प्रियः प्रियं प्रीतमनाः करे स्पृशन् ॥१९॥

taṁ prīyamāṇaṁ samupasthitaṁ kaviṁ
prajā-visarge nija-śāsanārhaṇam

babhāṣa īṣat-smita-śociṣā girā
priyaḥ priyaṁ prīta-manāḥ kare spṛśan

tam—unto Lord Brahmā; *prīyamāṇam*—worthy of being dear; *samupasthitam*—present before; *kavim*—the great scholar; *prajā*—living entities; *visarge*—in the matter of creation; *nija*—His own; *śāsana*—control; *arhaṇam*—just suitable; *babhāṣe*—addressed; *īṣat*—mild; *smita*—smiling; *śociṣā*—with enlightening; *girā*—words; *priyaḥ*—the beloved; *priyam*—the counterpart of love; *prīta-manāḥ*—being very much pleased; *kare*—by the hand; *spṛśan*—shaking.

TRANSLATION

And seeing Brahmā present before Him, the Lord accepted him as worthy to create living beings, to be controlled as He desired, and thus being much satisfied with him, the Lord shook hands with Brahmā and, slightly smiling, addressed him thus.

PURPORT

The creation of the material world is not blind or accidental. The living entities who are ever conditioned, or *nitya-baddha*, are thus given a chance for liberation under the guidance of His own representative like Brahmā. The Lord instructs Brahmā in Vedic knowledge in order to diffuse this knowledge to the conditioned souls. The conditioned souls are forgetful souls in their relationship with the Lord, and thus a period of creation and the process of dissemination of Vedic knowledge are necessary activities of the Lord. Lord Brahmā has a great responsibility in delivering the conditioned souls, and therefore he is very dear to the Lord.

Brahmā also does his duty very perfectly, not only by generating the living entities but also by spreading his party for reclaiming the fallen souls. The party is called the Brahma-sampradāya, and any member of this party to date is naturally engaged in reclaiming the fallen souls back to Godhead, back home. The Lord is very much anxious to get back His parts and parcels, as stated in the *Bhagavad-gītā*. No one is more dear than the one who takes the task of reclaiming the fallen souls back to Godhead.

There are many renegades from the Brahma-sampradāya whose only business is to make men more forgetful of the Lord and thus entangle them more and more in material existence. Such persons are never dear to the Lord, and the Lord sends them deeper into the darkest region of matter so that such envious demons may not be able to know the Supreme Lord.

Anyone, however, preaching the mission of the Lord in the line of the Brahma-sampradāya is always dear to the Lord, and the Lord, being satisfied with such a preacher of the authorized *bhakti* cult, shakes hands with him in great satisfaction.

TEXT 20

श्रीभगवानुवाच
त्वयाहं तोषितः सम्यग् वेदगर्भ सिसृक्षया ।
चिरं भृतेन तपसा दुस्तोषः कूटयोगिनाम् ॥२०॥

śrī-bhagavān uvāca
tvayāhaṁ toṣitaḥ samyag
veda-garbha sisṛkṣayā
ciraṁ bhṛtena tapasā
dustoṣaḥ kūṭa-yoginām

śrī-bhagavān uvāca—the all-beautiful Personality of Godhead said; *tvayā*—by you; *aham*—I am; *toṣitaḥ*—pleased; *samyak*—complete; *veda-garbha*—impregnated with the *Vedas; sisṛksayā*—for creating; *ciram*—for a long time; *bhṛtena*—accumulated; *tapasā*—by penance; *dustoṣaḥ*—very hard to please; *kūṭa-yoginām*—for the pseudo mystics.

TRANSLATION

The beautiful Personality of Godhead addressed Lord Brahmā: O Brahmā, impregnated with the Vedas, I am very much pleased with your long accumulated penance with the desire for creation. Hardly am I pleased with the pseudo mystics.

PURPORT

There are two kinds of penance: one for sense gratification and the other for self-realization. There are many pseudo mystics who undergo severe penances for their own satisfaction, and there are others who undergo severe penances for the satisfaction of the senses of the Lord. For example, the penances undertaken to discover nuclear weapons will never satisfy the Lord because such a penance is never satisfactory. By nature's own way, everyone has to meet death, and if such a process of death is accelerated by anyone's penances, there is no satisfaction for the Lord. The Lord wants every one of His parts and parcels to attain eternal life and bliss by coming home to Godhead, and the whole material creation is meant for that objective. Brahmā underwent severe penances for that purpose, namely to regulate the process of creation so that the Lord might be satisfied. Therefore the Lord was very much pleased with him, and for this Brahmā was impregnated with Vedic knowledge. The ultimate purpose of Vedic knowledge is to know the Lord and not to misuse the knowledge for any other purposes. Those who do not utilize Vedic knowledge for that purpose are known as *kūṭa-yogīs*, or pseudo transcendentalists who spoil their lives with ulterior motives.

TEXT 21

वरं वरय भद्रं ते वरेशं माभिवाञ्छितम् ।
ब्रह्मञ्छ्रेयःपरिश्रामः पुंसां मद्दर्शनावधिः ॥२१॥

varaṁ varaya bhadraṁ te
vareśaṁ mābhivāñchitam
brahmañ chreyaḥ-pariśrāmaḥ
puṁsāṁ mad-darśanāvadhiḥ

varam—benediction; *varaya*—just ask from; *bhadram*—auspicious; *te*—unto you; *vara-īśam*—the giver of all benediction; *mā (mām)*—from Me; *abhivāñchitam*—wishing; *brahman*—O Brahmā; *śreyaḥ*—the ultimate success; *pariśrāmaḥ*—for all penances; *puṁsām*—for everyone; *mat*—My; *darśana*—realization; *avadhiḥ*—up to the limit of.

TRANSLATION

I wish you good luck. O Brahmā, you may ask from Me, the giver of all benediction, all that you may desire. You may know that the ultimate benediction, as the result of all penances, is to see Me by realization.

PURPORT

The ultimate realization of the Supreme Truth is knowing and seeing face to face the Personality of Godhead. Realization of the impersonal Brahman and localized Paramātmā features of the Personality of Godhead is not ultimate realization. When one realizes the Supreme Lord, one does not struggle hard to perform such penances. The next stage of life is to discharge devotional service to the Lord just to satisfy Him. In other words, one who has realized and seen the Supreme Lord has attained all perfection because everything is included in that highest perfectional stage. The impersonalists and the pseudo mystics, however, cannot reach this state.

TEXT 22

मनीषितानुभावोऽयं मम लोकावलोकनम् ।
यदुपश्रुत्य रहसि चकर्थ परमं तपः ॥२२॥

manīṣitānubhāvo 'yaṁ
mama lokāvalokanam
yad upaśrutya rahasi
cakartha paramaṁ tapaḥ

manīṣita—ingenuity; *anubhāvaḥ*—perception; *ayam*—this; *mama*—My; *loka*—abode; *avalokanam*—seeing by actual experience; *yat*—because; *upaśrutya*—hearing; *rahasi*—in great penance; *cakartha*—having performed; *paramam*—highest; *tapaḥ*—penance.

TRANSLATION

The highest perfectional ingenuity is the personal perception of My abodes, and this has been possible because of your submissive

attitude in the performance of severe penance according to My order.

PURPORT

The highest perfectional stage of life is to know the Lord by actual perception, by the grace of the Lord. This can be attained by everyone who is willing to discharge the act of devotional service to the Lord as enjoined in the revealed scriptures that are standard and accepted by the bona fide *ācāryas*, spiritual masters. For example, the *Bhagavad-gītā* is the approved Vedic literature accepted by all the great *ācāryas*, such as Śaṅkara, Rāmānuja, Madhva, Caitanya, Viśvanātha, Baladeva, Siddhānta Sarasvatī and many others. In that *Bhagavad-gītā* the Personality of Godhead, Śrī Kṛṣṇa, asks that one always be mindful of Him, always be His devotee, always worship Him only, and always bow down before the Lord. And by doing so one is sure to go back home, back to Godhead, without any doubt. In other places also the same order is there, that one give up all other engagements and fully surrender unto the Lord without hesitation. And the Lord will give such a devotee all protection. These are the secrets of attaining the highest perfectional stage. Lord Brahmā exactly followed these principles without any superiority complex, and thus he attained the highest perfectional stage of experiencing the abode of the Lord and the Lord Himself with all His paraphernalia. Impersonal realization of the effulgence of the Lord's body is not the highest perfectional stage, nor is the stage of Paramātmā realization. The word *manīṣita* is significant. Everyone is falsely or factually proud of his so-called learning. But the Lord says that the highest perfectional stage of learning is to know Him and His abode, devoid of all illusion.

TEXT 23

प्रत्यादिष्टं मया तत्र त्वयि कर्मविमोहिते ।
तपो मे हृदयं साक्षादात्माहं तपसोऽनघ ॥२३॥

pratyādiṣṭaṁ mayā tatra
tvayi karma-vimohite
tapo me hṛdayaṁ sākṣād
ātmāhaṁ tapaso 'nagha

pratyādiṣṭam—ordered; *mayā*—by Me; *tatra*—because of; *tvayi*—unto you; *karma*—duty; *vimohite*—being perplexed; *tapaḥ*—penance; *me*—Me; *hṛdayam*—heart; *sākṣāt*—directly; *ātmā*—life and soul; *aham*—Myself; *tapasaḥ*—of one who is engaged in penance; *anagha*—O sinless one.

TRANSLATION

O sinless Brahmā, you may know from Me that it was I who first ordered you to undergo penance when you were perplexed in your duty. Such penance is My heart and soul, and therefore penance and I are nondifferent.

PURPORT

The penance by which one can see the Personality of Godhead face to face is to be understood as devotional service to the Lord and nothing else because only by discharging devotional service in transcendental love can one approach the Lord. Such penance is the internal potency of the Lord and is nondifferent from Him. Such acts of internal potency are exhibited by nonattachment for material enjoyment. The living entities are encaged in the conditions of material bondage because of their propensity for overlordship. But by engagement in the devotional service of the Lord one becomes detached from this enjoying spirit. The devotees automatically become detached from worldly enjoyment, and this detachment is the result of perfect knowledge. Therefore the penance of devotional service includes knowledge and detachment, and that is the manifestation of the transcendental potency.

One cannot enjoy material illusory prosperity if he desires to return home, back to Godhead. One who has no information of the transcendental bliss in the association of the Lord foolishly desires to enjoy this temporary material happiness. In the *Caitanya-caritāmṛta* it is said that if someone sincerely wants to see the Lord and at the same time wants to enjoy this material world, he is considered to be a fool only. One who wants to remain here in the material world for material enjoyment has no business entering into the eternal kingdom of God. The Lord favors such a foolish devotee by snatching all that he may possess in the material world. If such a foolish devotee of the Lord tries to recoup his position, then the merciful Lord again snatches away all that he may have possessed. By such repeated failures in material prosperity he becomes very unpopular with his family members and friends. In the material world the family members and friends honor persons who are very successful in accumulating wealth by any means. The foolish devotee of the Lord is thus put into forcible penance by the grace of the Lord, and at the end the devotee becomes perfectly happy, being engaged in the service of the Lord. Therefore penance in devotional service of the Lord, either by voluntary submission or by being forced by the Lord, is necessary for attaining perfection, and thus such penance is the internal potency of the Lord.

One cannot, however, be engaged in the penance of devotional service without being completely free from all sins. As stated in the *Bhagavad-gītā*, only a person who is completely free from all reactions of sins can engage himself in the worship of the Lord. Brahmājī was sinless, and therefore he faithfully discharged the advice of the Lord, "*tapa tapa*," and the Lord, being satisfied with him, awarded him the desired result. Therefore only love and penance combined can please the Lord, and thus one is able to attain His complete mercy. He directs the sinless, and the sinless devotee attains the highest perfection of life.

TEXT 24

सृजामि तपसैवेदं ग्रसामि तपसा पुनः ।
बिभर्मि तपसा विश्वं वीर्यं मे दुश्चरं तपः ॥२३॥

sṛjāmi tapasaivedaṁ
grasāmi tapasā punaḥ
bibharmi tapasā viśvaṁ
vīryaṁ me duścaraṁ tapaḥ

sṛjāmi—I create; *tapasā*—by the same energy of penance; *eva*—certainly; *idam*—this; *grasāmi tapasā*—I do withdraw also by the same energy; *punaḥ*—again; *bibharmi*—do maintain; *tapasā*—by penance; *viśvam*—the cosmos; *vīryam*—potency; *me*—My; *duścaram*—severe; *tapaḥ*—penance.

TRANSLATION

I create this cosmos by such penance, I maintain it by the same energy, and I withdraw it all by the same energy. Therefore the potential power is penance only.

PURPORT

In executing penance, one must be determined to return home, back to Godhead, and must decide to undergo all types of tribulations for that end. Even for material prosperity, name and fame, one has to undergo severe types of penance, otherwise no one can become an important figure in this material world. Why, then, are there severe types of penance for the perfection of devotional service? An easygoing life and attainment of perfection in transcendental realization cannot go together. The Lord is more clever than any living entity; therefore He wants to see how painstaking the devotee is in devotional service. The order is received from the Lord, either directly or through the bona fide spiritual master, and to execute that order, however painstaking, is the severe type of penance. One who follows the principle rigidly is sure to achieve success in attaining the Lord's mercy.

TEXT 25

ब्रह्मोवाच
भगवन् सर्वभूतानामध्यक्षोऽवस्थितो गुहाम् ।
वेद ह्यप्रतिरुद्धेन प्रज्ञानेन चिकीर्षितम् ॥२४॥

brahmovāca
bhagavan sarva-bhūtānām
adhyakṣo 'vasthito guhām
veda hy apratiruddhena
prajñānena cikīrṣitam

brahmā uvāca—Lord Brahmā said; *bhagavan*—O my Lord; *sarva bhūtānām*—of all living entities; *adhyakṣaḥ*—director; *avasthitaḥ*—situated; *guhām*—within the heart; *veda*—know; *hi*—certainly; *apratiruddhena*—without hindrance; *prajñānena*—by superintelligence; *cikīrṣitam*—endeavors.

TRANSLATION

Lord Brahmā said: O Personality of Godhead, You are situated in every living entity's heart as the supreme director, and

therefore You are aware of all endeavors by Your superior intelligence, without any hindrance whatsoever.

PURPORT

The *Bhagavad-gītā* confirms that the Lord is situated in everyone's heart as the witness, and as such He is the supreme director of sanction. The director is not the enjoyer of the fruits of action, for without the Lord's sanction no one can enjoy. For example, in a prohibited area a habituated drunkard puts forward his application to the director of drinking, and the director, considering his case, sanctions only a certain amount of liquor for drinking. Similarly, the whole material world is full of many drunkards, in the sense that each and every one of the living entities has something in his mind to enjoy, and everyone desires the fulfillment of his desires very strongly. The almighty Lord, being very kind to the living entity, as the father is kind to the son, fulfills the living entity's desire for his childish satisfaction. With such desires in mind, the living entity does not actually enjoy, but he serves the bodily whims unnecessarily, without profit. The drunkard does not derive any profit out of drinking, but because he has become a servant of the drinking habit and does not wish to get out of it, the merciful Lord gives him all facilities to fulfill such desires.

The impersonalists recommend that one should become desireless, and others recommend banishing desires altogether. That is impossible; no one can banish desires altogether because desiring is the living symptom. Without having desires a living entity would be dead, which he is not. Therefore, living conditions and desire go together. Perfection of desires may be achieved when one desires to serve the Lord, and the Lord also desires that every living entity banish all personal desires and cooperate with His desires. That is the last instruction of the *Bhagavad-gītā*. Brahmājī agreed to this proposal, and therefore he is given the responsible post of creating generations in the vacant universe. Oneness with the Lord therefore consists of dovetailing one's desires with the desires of the Supreme Lord. That makes for the perfection of all desires.

The Lord, as the Supersoul in the heart of every living being, knows what is in the mind of each living entity, and no one can do anything without the knowledge of the Lord within. By His superior intelligence, the Lord gives everyone the chance to fulfill his desires to the fullest extent, and the resultant reaction is also awarded by the Lord.

TEXT 26

तथापि नाथमानस्य नाथ नाथय नाथितम् ।
परावरे यथा रूपे जानीयां ते त्वरूपिणः ॥२६॥

tathāpi nāthamānasya
nātha nāthaya nāthitam
parāvare yathā rūpe
jānīyāṁ te tv arūpiṇaḥ

tathā api—in spite of that; *nāthamānasya*—of the one who is asking for; *nātha*—O Lord; *nāthaya*—please award; *nāthitam*—as it is desired; *para-avare*—in the matter of mundane and transcendental; *yathā*—as it is; *rūpe*—in the form; *jānīyām*—may it be known; *te*—Your; *tu*—but; *arūpiṇaḥ*—one who is formless.

TRANSLATION

In spite of that, my Lord, I am praying to You to kindly fulfill my desire. May I please be informed how, in spite of Your transcendental form, You assume the mundane form, although You have no such form at all.

TEXT 27

यथात्ममायायोगेन नानाशक्त्युपबृंहितम् ।
विलुम्पन् विसृजन् गृह्णन् बिभ्रदात्मानमात्मना ॥२७॥

yathātma-māyā-yogena
nānā-śakty-upabṛṁhitam
vilumpan visṛjan gṛhṇan
bibhrad ātmānam ātmanā

yathā—as much as; *ātma*—own; *māyā*—potency; *yogena*—by combination; *nānā*—various; *śakti*—energy; *upabṛṁhitam*—by combination and permutation; *vilumpan*—in the matter of annihilation; *visṛjan*—in the matter of generation; *gṛhṇan*—in the matter of acceptance; *bibhrat*—in the matter of maintenance; *ātmānam*—own self; *ātmanā*—by the self.

TRANSLATION

And [please inform me] how You, by Your own Self, manifest different energies for annihilation, generation, acceptance and maintenance by combination and permutation.

PURPORT

The whole manifestation is the Lord Himself by diffusion of His different energies only, namely the internal, external and marginal, just as the sunlight is the manifestation of the energy of the sun planet. Such energy is simultaneously one with and different from the Lord, just as the sunshine is simultaneously one with and different from the sun planet. The energies are acting by combination and permutation by the indication of the Lord, and the acting agents, like Brahmā, Viṣṇu and Śiva, are also different incarnations of the Lord. In other words, there is nothing but the Lord, and still the Lord is different from all such manifestive activities. How it is so will be explained later on.

TEXT 28

क्रीडस्यमोघसङ्कल्प ऊर्णनाभिर्यथोर्णुते ।
तथा तद्विषयां धेहि मनीषां मयि माधव ॥२८॥

krīḍasy amogha-saṅkalpa
ūrṇanābhir yathorṇute
tathā tad-viṣayāṁ dhehi
manīṣāṁ mayi mādhava

krīḍasi—as You play; *amogha*—infallible; *saṅkalpa*—determination; *ūrṇanābhiḥ*—the spider; *yathā*—as much as; *ūrṇute*—covers; *tathā*—so and so; *tat-viṣayām*—in the subject of all those; *dhehi*—do let me know; *manīṣām*—philosophically; *mayi*—unto me; *mādhava*—O master of all energies.

TRANSLATION

O master of all energies, please tell me philosophically all about them. You play like a spider that covers itself by its own energy, and Your determination is infallible.

PURPORT

By the inconceivable energy of the Lord, every creative element has its own potencies, known as the potency of the element, potency of knowledge and potency of different actions and reactions. By a combination of such potential energies of the Lord there is the manifestation of creation, maintenance and annihilation in due course of time and by different agents like Brahmā, Viṣṇu and Maheśvara. Brahmā creates, Viṣṇu maintains, and Lord Śiva destroys. But all such agents and creative energies are emanations from the Lord, and as such there is nothing except the Lord, or the one supreme source of different diversities. The exact example is the spider and spider's web. The web is created by the spider, and it is maintained by the spider, and as soon as the spider likes, the whole thing is wound up within the spider. The spider is covered within the web. If an insignificant spider is so powerful as to act according to its will, why can't the Supreme Being act by His supreme will in the creation, maintenance and destruction of the cosmic manifestations? By the grace of the Lord, a devotee like Brahmā, or one in his chain of disciplic succession, can understand the almighty Personality of Godhead eternally engaged in His transcendental pastimes in the region of different energies.

TEXT 29

भगवच्छिक्षितमहं करवाणि ह्यतन्द्रितः ।
नेहमानः प्रजासर्गं बध्येयं यदनुग्रहात् ॥२९॥

bhagavac-chikṣitam ahaṁ
karavāṇi hy atandritaḥ
nehamānaḥ prajā-sargaṁ
badhyeyaṁ yad-anugrahāt

bhagavat—by the Personality of Godhead; *śikṣitam*—taught; *aham*—myself; *karavāṇi*—by acting; *hi*—certainly; *atandritaḥ*—instrumental; *na*—never; *ihamānaḥ*—although acting; *prajā-sargam*—generation of the living entities; *badhyeyam*—be conditioned; *yat*—as a matter of fact; *anugrahāt*—by the mercy of.

TRANSLATION

Please tell me so that I may be taught in the matter by the instruction of the Personality of Godhead and may thus act instrumentally to generate living entities, without being conditioned by such activities.

PURPORT

Brahmājī does not want to become a speculator dependent on the strength of his personal knowledge and conditioned to material bondage. Everyone should know in clear consciousness that one is, in the execution of all activities, an instrument. A conditioned soul is instrumental in the hands of the external energy, *guṇamayī māyā*, or the illusory energy of the Lord, and in the liberated stage the living entity is instrumental to the will of the Personality of Godhead directly. To be instrumental to the direct will of the Lord is the natural constitutional position of the living entity, whereas to be an instrument in the hands of the illusory energy of the Lord is material bondage for the living entity. In that conditioned state, the living entity speculates on the Absolute Truth and His different activities. But in the unconditioned stage the living entity directly receives knowledge from the Lord, and such a liberated soul acts flawlessly, without any speculative habit. The *Bhagavad-gītā* (10.10–11) confirms emphatically that the pure devotees, who are constantly engaged in the loving transcendental service of the Lord, are directly advised by the Lord, so much so that the devotee unwaveringly makes progress on the path home, back to Godhead. Pure devotees of the Lord are therefore not proud of their definite progress, whereas the nondevotee speculator is in the darkness of illusory energy and is very much proud of his misleading knowledge based on speculation without any definite path. Lord Brahmā wanted to be saved from that pitfall of pride, although he was posted in the most exalted position within the universe.

TEXT 30

यावत् सखा सख्युरिवेश ते कृतः
प्रजाविसर्गे विभजामि भो जनम् ।
अविक्लवस्ते परिकर्मणि स्थितो
मा मे समुन्नद्धमदोऽजमानिनः ॥३०॥

yāvat sakhā sakhyur iveśa te kṛtaḥ
prajā-visarge vibhajāmi bho janam
aviklavas te parikarmaṇi sthito
mā me samunnaddha-mado 'ja māninaḥ

yāvat—as it is; *sakhā*—friend; *sakhyuḥ*—unto the friend; *iva*—like that; *īśa*—O Lord; *te*—You; *kṛtaḥ*—have accepted; *prajā*—the living entities; *visarge*—in the matter of creation; *vibhajāmi*—as I shall do it differently; *bhoḥ*—O my Lord; *janam*—those who are born; *aviklavaḥ*—without being perturbed; *te*—Your; *parikarmaṇi*—in the matter of service; *sthitaḥ*—thus situated; *mā*—may it never be; *me*—unto me; *samunnaddha*—resulting arise; *madaḥ*—madness; *aja*—O unborn one; *māninaḥ*—thus being thought of.

TRANSLATION

O my Lord, the unborn, You have shaken hands with me just as a friend does with a friend [as if equal in position]. I shall be engaged in the creation of different types of living entities, and I shall be occupied in Your service. I shall have no perturbation, but I pray that all this may not give rise to pride, as if I were the Supreme.

PURPORT

Lord Brahmā is definitely situated in the humor of friendship with the Lord. Every living being is eternally related with the Personality of Godhead in one of five different transcendental humors, namely *śānta*, *dāsya*, *sakhya*, *vātsalya* and *mādhurya*. We have already discussed these five kinds of humors in relationship with the Personality of Godhead. It is clearly exhibited herein that Lord Brahmā is related to the Personality of Godhead in the transcendental humor of friendship. A pure devotee may be related with the Lord in any one of the transcendental humors, even in the humor of parenthood, but the devotee of the Lord is always a transcendental servitor. No one is equal to or greater than the Lord. That is the version of the *Bhagavad-gītā*. Brahmājī, although eternally related with the Lord in the transcendental humor of friendship, and although entrusted with the most exalted post of creating different grades of living entities, is still conscious of his position, that he is neither the Supreme Lord nor supremely powerful. It is possible that some extremely powerful personality, within or without the universe, may sometimes show more power than the Lord Himself. Still the pure devotee knows that this power is a *vibhūti* delegated by the Lord, and such a delegated powerful living entity is never independent. Śrī Hanumānjī crossed the Indian Ocean by jumping over the sea, and Lord Śrī Rāmacandra engaged Himself in marching over the bridge, but this does not mean that Hanumānjī was more powerful than the Lord. Sometimes the Lord gives extraordinary powers to His devotee, but the devotee knows always that the power belongs to the Personality of Godhead and that the devotee is only an instrument. The pure devotee is never puffed up like the nondevotee class of men who falsely think that they are God. It is astonishing to see how a person who is being kicked by the laws of the Lord's illusory energy at every step can falsely think of becoming one with the Lord. Such thinking is the last snare of the illusory energy offered to the conditioned soul. The first illusion is that he wants to become Lord of the material world by accumulating wealth and power, but when he is frustrated in that attempt he wants to be one with the Lord. So both becoming the most powerful man in the material world and desiring to become one with the Lord are different illusory snares. And because the pure devotees of the Lord are surrendered souls, they are above the illusory snares of *māyā*. Because Lord Brahmā is a pure devotee, even though the first dominating deity in the material world and therefore able to do many wonderful things, he would never, like the nondevotee with a poor fund of knowledge, have the audacity to think of becoming one with the Lord. People with a poor fund of knowledge should take lessons from Brahmā when they are puffed up with the false notion of becoming God.

Factually Lord Brahmā does not create the living entities. In the beginning of the creation he is empowered to give different bodily shapes to the living entities according to their work during the last millennium. Brahmājī's duty is just to wake the living entities from their slumber and to engage them in their proper duty. The different grades of living entities are not created by Brahmājī by his capricious whims, but he is entrusted with the task of giving the living entities different grades of body so that they can work accordingly. And still he is conscious that he is only instrumental, so that he may not think of himself as the Supreme Powerful Lord.

Devotees of the Lord are engaged in the specific duty offered by the Lord, and such duties are successfully carried out without hindrance because they are ordained by the Lord. The credit of success goes not to the doer but to the Lord. But persons with a poor fund of knowledge take the credit of success into their own accounts and give nothing to the credit of the Lord. That is the symptom of the nondevotee class of men.

TEXT 31

श्रीभगवानुवाच
ज्ञानं परमगुह्यं मे यद् विज्ञानसमन्वितम् ।
सरहस्यं तदङ्गं च गृहाण गदितं मया ॥३१॥

śrī-bhagavān uvāca
jñānaṁ parama-guhyaṁ me
yad vijñāna-samanvitam
sarahasyaṁ tad-aṅgaṁ ca
gṛhāṇa gaditaṁ mayā

śrī-bhagavān uvāca—the Personality of Godhead said; *jñānam*—knowledge acquired; *parama*—extremely; *guhyam*—confidential; *me*—of Me; *yat*—which is; *vijñāna*—realization; *samanvitam*—coordinated; *sa-rahasyam*—with devotional service; *tat*—of that; *aṅgam ca*—necessary paraphernalia; *gṛhāṇa*—just try to take up; *gaditam*—explained; *mayā*—by Me.

TRANSLATION

The Personality of Godhead said: Knowledge about Me as described in the scriptures is very confidential, and it has to be

realized in conjunction with devotional service. The necessary paraphernalia for that process is being explained by Me. You may take it up carefully.

PURPORT

Lord Brahmā is the topmost devotee of the Lord within the universe, and therefore the Personality of Godhead replied to his four principal inquiries in four important statements, which are known as the original *Bhāgavatam* in four verses. These were Brahmā's questions: (1) What are the forms of the Lord both in matter and in transcendence? (2) How are the different energies of the Lord working? (3) How does the Lord play with His different energies? (4) How may Brahmā be instructed to discharge the duty entrusted to Him? The prelude to the answers is this verse under discussion, wherein the Lord informs Brahmā that knowledge of Him, the Supreme Absolute Truth, as it is stated in the revealed scriptures, is very subtle and cannot be understood unless one is self-realized by the grace of the Lord. The Lord says that Brahmā may take the answers as He explains them. This means that transcendental knowledge of the absolute Supreme Being can be known if it is made known by the Lord Himself. By the mental speculation of the greatest mundane thinkers, the Absolute Truth cannot be understood. The mental speculators can reach up to the standard of impersonal Brahman realization, but, factually, complete knowledge of transcendence is beyond the knowledge of impersonal Brahman. Thus it is called the supreme confidential wisdom. Out of many liberated souls, someone may be qualified to know the Personality of Godhead. In the *Bhagavad-gītā* it is also said by the Lord Himself that out of many hundreds of thousands of people, one may try for perfection in human life, and out of many liberated souls, one may know Him as He is. Therefore, the knowledge of the Personality of Godhead may be attained by devotional service only. *Rahasyam* means devotional service. Lord Kṛṣṇa instructed Arjuna in the *Bhagavad-gītā* because He found Arjuna to be a devotee and friend. Without such qualifications, one cannot enter into the mystery of the *Bhagavad-gītā*. Therefore, one cannot understand the Personality of Godhead unless one becomes a devotee and discharges devotional service. This mystery is *love of Godhead.* Therein lies the main qualification for knowing the mystery of the Personality of Godhead. And to attain the stage of transcendental love of Godhead, regulative principles of devotional service must be followed. The regulative principles are called *vidhi-bhakti*, or the devotional service of the Lord, and they can be practiced by a neophyte with his present senses. Such regulative principles are mainly based on hearing and chanting of the glories of the Lord. And such hearing and chanting of the glories of the Lord can be made possible in the association of devotees only. Lord Caitanya therefore recommended five main principles for attaining perfection in the devotional service of the Lord. The first is association with devotees (hearing); second is chanting the glories of the Lord; third, hearing *Śrīmad-Bhāgavatam* from the pure devotee; fourth, residing in a holy place connected with the Lord; and fifth, worshiping the Deity of the Lord with devotion. Such rules and regulations are parts of devotional service. So, as requested by Lord Brahmā, the Personality of Godhead will explain all about the four questions put forward by Brahmā, and others also which are parts and parcels of the same questions.

TEXT 32

यावानहं यथाभावो यद्रूपगुणकर्मकः ।
तथैव तत्त्वविज्ञानमस्तु ते मदनुग्रहात् ॥३२॥

yāvān ahaṁ yathā-bhāvo
yad-rūpa-guṇa-karmakaḥ
tathaiva tattva-vijñānam
astu te mad-anugrahāt

yāvān—as I am in eternal form; *aham*—Myself; *yathā*—as much as; *bhāvaḥ*—transcendental existence; *yat*—those; *rūpa*—various forms and colors; *guṇa*—qualities; *karmakaḥ*—activities; *tathā*—so and so; *eva*—certainly; *tattva-vijñānam*—factual realization; *astu*—let it be; *te*—unto you; *mat*—My; *anugrahāt*—by causeless mercy.

TRANSLATION

All of Me, namely My actual eternal form and My transcendental existence, color, qualities and activities—let all be awakened within you by factual realization, out of My causeless mercy.

PURPORT

The secret of success in understanding the intricacies of knowledge of the Absolute Truth, the Personality of Godhead, is the causeless mercy of the Lord. Even in the material world, the father of many sons discloses the secret of his position to the pet sons. The father discloses the confidence unto the son whom he thinks worthy. An important man in the social order can be known by his mercy only. Similarly, one must be very dear to the Lord in order to know the Lord. The Lord is unlimited; no one can know Him completely, but one's advancement in the transcendental loving service of the Lord can make one eligible to know the Lord. Here we can see that the Lord is sufficiently pleased with Brahmājī, and therefore He offers His causeless mercy to him so that Brahmājī may have the factual realization of the Lord by His mercy only.

In the *Vedas* also it is said that a person cannot know the Absolute Truth Personality of Godhead simply by dint of mundane education or intellectual gymnastics. One can know the Supreme Truth if one has unflinching faith in the bona fide spiritual master as well as in the Lord. Such a faithful person, even though illiterate in the mundane sense, can know the Lord automatically by the mercy of the Lord. In the *Bhagavad-gītā* also, it is said that the Lord reserves the right of not being exposed to everyone, and He keeps Himself concealed from the faithless by His *yoga-māyā* potency.

To the faithful the Lord reveals Himself in His form, quality and pastimes. The Lord is not formless, as wrongly conceived by the impersonalist, but His form is not like one that we have experienced. The Lord discloses His form, even to the extent of measurement, to His pure devotees, and that is the meaning of *yāvān,* as explained by Śrīla Jīva Gosvāmī, the greatest scholar of *Śrīmad-Bhāgavatam.*

The Lord discloses the transcendental nature of His existence. The mundane wranglers make mundane conceptions of the form of the Lord. It is said in the revealed scriptures that the Lord has no mundane form; therefore persons with a poor fund of knowledge conclude that He must be formless. They cannot distinguish between the mundane form and the spiritual form. According to them, without a mundane form one must be formless. This conclusion is also mundane because formlessness is the opposite conception of form. Negation of the mundane conception does not establish a transcendental fact. In the *Brahma-saṁhitā* it is said that the Lord has a transcendental form and that He can utilize any one of His senses for any purpose. For example, He can eat with His eyes, and He can see with His leg. In the mundane conception of form, one cannot eat with one's eyes or see with his leg. That is the difference between the mundane body and the spiritual body of *sac-cid-ānanda.* A spiritual body is not formless; it is a different type of body, of which we cannot conceive with our present mundane senses. Formless therefore means devoid of mundane form, or possessing a spiritual body of which the nondevotee can have no conception by the speculative method.

The Lord discloses to the devotee His unlimited varieties of transcendental bodies, all identical with one another with different kinds of bodily features. Some of the transcendental bodies of the Lord are blackish, and some of them are whitish. Some of them are reddish, and some are yellowish. Some of them are four-handed and some of them two-handed. Some of them are like the fish, and some are like the lion. All these different transcendental bodies of the Lord, without any differential category, are disclosed to the devotees of the Lord by the mercy of the Lord, and thus the impersonalists' false arguments claiming the formlessness of the Supreme Truth do not appeal to a devotee of the Lord, even though such a devotee may not be very advanced in devotional service.

The Lord has unlimited numbers of transcendental qualities, and one of them is His affection for His unalloyed devotee. In the history of the mundane world we can appreciate His transcendental qualities. The Lord incarnates Himself for the protection of His devotees and for the annihilation of the faithless. His activities are in relationship with His devotees. *Śrīmad-Bhāgavatam* is full of such activities of the Lord in relationship with His devotees, and the nondevotees have no knowledge of such pastimes. The Lord lifted the Govardhana Hill when He was only seven years old and protected His pure devotees at Vṛndāvana from the wrath of Indra, who was overflooding the place with rain. Now this lifting of the Govardhana Hill by a seven-year-old boy may be unbelievable for the faithless, but for the devotees it is absolutely believable. The devotee believes in the almighty potency of the Lord, while the faithless say that the Lord is almighty but do not believe it. Such men with a poor fund of knowledge do not know that the Lord is the Lord eternally and that one cannot become the Lord by meditation for millions of years or by mental speculation for billions of years.

The impersonal interpretation of the mundane wranglers is completely refuted in this verse because it is clearly stated here that the Supreme Lord has His qualities, form, pastimes and everything that a person has. All these descriptions of the transcendental nature of the Personality of Godhead are factual realizations by the devotee of the Lord, and by the causeless mercy of the Lord they are revealed to His pure devotee, and to no one else.

TEXT 33

अहमेवासमेवाग्रे नान्यद् यत् सदसत् परम् ।
पश्चादहं यदेतच्च योऽवशिष्येत सोऽस्म्यहम् ॥३३॥

aham evāsam evāgre
nānyad yat sad-asat param
paścād ahaṁ yad etac ca
yo 'vaśiṣyeta so 'smy aham

aham—I, the Personality of Godhead; *eva*—certainly; *āsam*—existed; *eva*—only; *agre*—before the creation; *na*—never; *anyat*—anything else; *yat*—all those; *sat*—the effect; *asat*—the cause; *param*—the supreme; *paścāt*—at the end; *aham*—I, the Personality of Godhead; *yat*—all these; *etat*—creation; *ca*—also; *yaḥ*—everything; *avaśiṣyeta*—remains; *saḥ*—that; *asmi*—I am; *aham*—I, the Personality of Godhead.

TRANSLATION

Brahmā, it is I, the Personality of Godhead, who was existing before the creation, when there was nothing but Myself. Nor was there the material nature, the cause of this creation. That which you see now is also I, the Personality of Godhead, and after annihilation what remains will also be I, the Personality of Godhead.

PURPORT

We should note very carefully that the Personality of Godhead is addressing Lord Brahmā and specifying with great emphasis Himself, pointing out that it is He, the Personality of Godhead, who existed before the creation, it is He only who maintains the creation, and it is He only who remains after the annihilation of the creation. Brahmā is also a creation of the Supreme Lord. The impersonalist puts forth the theory of oneness in the sense that Brahmā, also being the same principle of "I" because he is an emanation from the I, the Absolute Truth, is identical with the Lord, the principle of I, and that there is thus nothing more than the principle of I, as explained in this verse. Accepting the argument of the impersonalist, it is to be admitted that the Lord is the creator I and that the Brahmā is the created I. Therefore there is a difference between the two "I's," namely the predominator I and the predominated I. Therefore there are still two I's, even accepting the argument of the impersonalist. But we must note carefully that these two I's are accepted in the Vedic literature (*Kaṭhopaniṣad*) in the sense of quality. The *Kaṭhopaniṣad* says:

nityo nityānāṁ cetanaś cetanānām
eko bahūnāṁ yo vidadhāti kāmān

The creator "I" and the created "I" are both accepted in the *Vedas* as qualitatively one because both of them are *nityas* and *cetanas*. But the singular "I" is the creator "I," and the created "I's" are of plural number because there are many "I's" like Brahmā and those generated by Brahmā. It is the simple truth. The father creates or begets a son, and the son also creates many other sons, and all of them may be one as human beings, but at the same time from the father, the son and the grandsons are all different. The son cannot take the place of the father, nor can the grandsons. Simultaneously the father, the son and the grandson are one and different also. As human beings they are one, but as relativities they are different. Therefore the relativities of the creator and the created or the predominator and the predominated have been differentiated in the *Vedas* by saying that the predominator "I" is the feeder of the predominated "I's," and thus there is a vast difference between the two principles of "I."

In another feature of this verse, no one can deny the personalities of both the Lord and Brahmā. Therefore in the ultimate issue both the predominator and predominated are persons. This conclusion refutes the conclusion of the impersonalist that in the ultimate issue everything is impersonal. This impersonal feature stressed by the less intelligent impersonalist school is refuted by pointing out that the predominator "I" is the Absolute Truth and that He is a person. The predominated "I," Brahmā, is also a person, but he is not the Absolute. For realization of one's self in spiritual psychology it may be convenient to assume oneself to be the same principle as the Absolute Truth, but there is always the difference of the predominated and the predominator, as clearly pointed out here in this verse, which is grossly misused by the impersonalists. Brahmā is factually seeing face to face his predominator Lord, who exists in His transcendental eternal form, even after the annihilation of the material creation. The form of the Lord, as seen by Brahmā, existed before the creation of Brahmā, and the material manifestation with all the ingredients and agents of material creation are also energetic expansions of the Lord, and after the exhibition of the Lord's energy comes to a close, what remains is the same Personality of Godhead. Therefore the form of the Lord exists in all circumstances of creation, maintenance and annihilation. The Vedic hymns confirm this fact in the statement *vāsudevo vā idam agra āsīn na brahmā na ca śaṅkara eko nārāyaṇa āsīn na brahmā neśāna*, etc. Before the creation there was none except Vāsudeva. There was neither Brahmā nor Śaṅkara. Only Nārāyaṇa was there and no one else, neither Brahmā nor Īśāna. Śrīpāda Śaṅkarācārya also confirms in his comments on the *Bhagavad-gītā* that Nārāyaṇa, or the Personality of Godhead, is transcendental to all creation, but that the whole creation is the product of *avyakta*. Therefore the difference between the created and the creator is always there, although both the creator and created are of the same quality.

The other feature of the statement is that the supreme truth is Bhagavān, or the Personality of Godhead. The Personality of Godhead and His kingdom have already been explained. The kingdom of Godhead is not void as conceived by the impersonalists. The Vaikuṇṭha planets are full of transcendental variegatedness, including the four-handed residents of those planets, with great opulence of wealth and prosperity, and there are even airplanes and other amenities required for high-grade personalities. Therefore the Personality of Godhead exists before the creation, and He exists with all transcendental variegatedness in the Vaikuṇṭhalokas. The Vaikuṇṭhalokas, also accepted in the *Bhagavad-gītā* as being of the *sanātana* nature, are not annihilated even after the annihilation of the manifested cosmos. Those transcendental planets are of a different nature altogether, and that nature is not subjected to the rules and regulations of material creation, maintenance or annihilation. The existence of the Personality of Godhead implies the existence of the Vaikuṇṭhalokas, as the existence of a king implies the existence of a kingdom.

In various places in *Śrīmad-Bhāgavatam* and in other revealed scriptures the existence of the Personality of Godhead is mentioned. For example, in *Śrīmad-Bhāgavatam* (2.8.10), Mahārāja Parīkṣit asks:

sa cāpi yatra puruṣo
viśva-sthity-udbhavāpyayaḥ
muktvātma-māyāṁ māyeśaḥ
śete sarva-guhāśayaḥ

"How does the Personality of Godhead, the cause of creation, maintenance and annihilation, who is always freed from the influence of the illusory energy and is the controller of the same, lie in everyone's heart?" Similar also is a question of Vidura's:

tattvānāṁ bhagavaṁs teṣāṁ
katidhā pratisaṅkramaḥ
tatremaṁ ka upāsīran
ka u svid anuśerate
(*Bhāg.* 3.7.37)

Śrīdhara Svāmī explains this in his notes: "During the annihilation of the creation, who serves the Lord lying on the Śeṣa, etc." This means that the transcendental Lord with all His name, fame, quality and paraphernalia exists eternally. The same confirmation is also in the *Kāśī-khaṇḍa* of the *Skanda Purāṇa* in connection with *dhruva-carita*. It is said there:

na cyavante 'pi yad-bhaktā
mahatyāṁ pralayāpadi
ato 'cyuto 'khile loke
sa ekaḥ sarvago 'vyayaḥ

Even the devotees of the Personality of Godhead are not annihilated during the period of the entire annihilation of the material world, not to speak of the Lord Himself. The Lord is ever-existent in all three stages of material change.

The impersonalist adduces no activity in the Supreme, but in this discussion between Brahmā and the Supreme Personality of Godhead the Lord is said to have activities also, as He has His form and quality. The activities of Brahmā and other demigods during the maintenance of the creation are to be understood as the activities of the Lord. The king, or the head executive of a state, may not be seen in the government offices, for he may be engaged in royal comforts. Yet it should be understood that everything is being done under his direction and everything is at his command. The Personality of Godhead is never formless. In the material world He may not be visible in His personal form to the less intelligent class of men, and therefore He may sometimes be called formless. But actually He is always in His eternal form in His Vaikuṇṭha planets as well as in other planets of the universes as different incarnations. The example of the sun is very appropriate in this connection. The sun in the night may not be visible to the eyes of men in the darkness, but the sun is visible wherever it has risen. That the sun is not visible to the eyes of the inhabitants of a particular part of the earth does not mean that the sun has no form.

In the *Bṛhad-āraṇyaka Upaniṣad* (1.4.1) there is the hymn *ātmaivedam agra āsīt puruṣa-vidhaḥ.* This *mantra* indicates the Supreme Personality of Godhead (Kṛṣṇa) even before the appearance of the *puruṣa* incarnation. In the *Bhagavad-gītā* (15.18) it is said that Lord Kṛṣṇa is Puruṣottama because He is the supreme *puruṣa*, transcendental even to the *puruṣa-akṣara* and the *puruṣa-kṣara.* The *akṣara-puruṣa*, or the Mahā-Viṣṇu, throws His glance over *prakṛti*, or material nature, but the Puruṣottama existed even before that. The *Bṛhad-āraṇyaka Upaniṣad* therefore confirms the statement of the *Bhagavad-gītā* that Lord Kṛṣṇa is the Supreme Person (Puruṣottama).

In some of the *Vedas* it is also said that in the beginning only the impersonal Brahman existed. However, according to this verse, the impersonal Brahman, which is the glowing effulgence of the body of the Supreme Lord, may be called the immediate cause, but the cause of all causes, or the remote cause, is the Supreme Personality of Godhead. The

Lord's impersonal feature is existent in the material world because by material senses or material eyes the Lord cannot be seen or perceived. One has to spiritualize the senses before one can expect to see or perceive the Supreme Lord. But He is always engaged in His personal capacity, and He is eternally visible to the inhabitants of Vaikuṇṭhaloka, eye to eye. Therefore He is materially impersonal, just as the executive head of the state may be impersonal in the government offices, although he is not impersonal in the government house. Similarly, the Lord is not impersonal in His abode, which is always *nirasta-kuhakam*, as stated in the very beginning of the *Bhāgavatam.* Therefore both the impersonal and personal features of the Lord are acceptable, as mentioned in the revealed scriptures. This Personality of Godhead is very emphatically explained in the *Bhagavad-gītā* in connection with the verse *brahmaṇo hi pratiṣṭhāham* (Bg. 14.27). Therefore in all ways the confidential part of spiritual knowledge is realization of the Personality of Godhead, and not His impersonal Brahman feature. One should therefore have his ultimate aim of realization not in the impersonal feature but in the personal feature of the Absolute Truth. The example of the sky within the pot and the sky outside the pot may be helpful to the student for his realization of the all-pervading quality of the cosmic consciousness of the Absolute Truth. But that does not mean that the individual part and parcel of the Lord becomes the Supreme by a false claim. It means only that the conditioned soul is a victim of the illusory energy in her last snare. To claim to be one with the cosmic consciousness of the Lord is the last trap set by the illusory energy, or *daivī māyā.* Even in the impersonal existence of the Lord, as it is in the material creation, one should aspire for personal realization of the Lord, and that is the meaning of *paścād ahaṁ yad etac ca yo 'vaśiṣyeta so 'smy aham.*

Brahmājī also accepted the same truth when he was instructing Nārada. He said:

so 'yaṁ te 'bhihitas tāta
bhagavān viśva-bhāvanaḥ
(*Bhāg.* 2.7.50)

There is no other cause of all causes than the Supreme Personality of Godhead, Hari. Therefore this verse *aham eva* never indicates anything other than the Supreme Lord, and one should therefore follow the path of the Brahma-sampradāya, or the path from Brahmājī to Nārada, to Vyāsadeva, etc., and make it a point in life to realize the Supreme Personality of Godhead, Hari, or Lord Kṛṣṇa. This very confidential instruction to the pure devotees of the Lord was also given to Arjuna and to Brahmā in the beginning of the creation. The demigods like Brahmā, Viṣṇu, Maheśvara, Indra, Candra and Varuṇa are undoubtedly different forms of the Lord for execution of different functions; the different elemental ingredients of material creation, as well as the multifarious energies, also may be of the same Personality of Godhead, but the root of all of them is the Supreme Personality of Godhead, Śrī Kṛṣṇa. One should be attached to the root of everything rather than bewildered by the branches and leaves. That is the instruction given in this verse.

TEXT 34

ऋतेऽर्थं यत् प्रतीयेत न प्रतीयेत चात्मनि ।
तद्विद्यादात्मनो मायां यथाभासो यथा तमः ॥३४॥

ṛte 'rthaṁ yat pratīyeta
na pratīyeta cātmani
tad vidyād ātmano māyāṁ
yathābhāso yathā tamaḥ

ṛte—without; *artham*—value; *yat*—that which; *pratīyeta*—appears to be; *na*—not; *pratīyeta*—appears to be; *ca*—and; *ātmani*—in relation to Me; *tat*—that; *vidyāt*—you must know; *ātmanaḥ*—My; *māyām*—illusory energy; *yathā*—just as; *ābhāsaḥ*—the reflection; *yathā*—as; *tamaḥ*—the darkness.

TRANSLATION

O Brahmā, whatever appears to be of any value, if it is without relation to Me, has no reality. Know it as My illusory energy, that reflection which appears to be in darkness.

PURPORT

In the previous verse it has already been concluded that in any stage of the cosmic manifestation—its appearance, its sustenance, its growth, its interactions of different energies, its deterioration and its disappearance—all has its basic relation with the existence of the Personality of Godhead. And as such, whenever there is forgetfulness of this prime relation with the Lord, and whenever things are accepted as real without being related to the Lord, that conception is called a product of the illusory energy of the Lord. Because nothing can exist without the Lord, it should be known that the illusory energy is also an energy of the Lord. The right conclusion of dovetailing everything in relationship with the Lord is called *yoga-māyā*, or the energy of union, and the wrong conception of detaching a thing from its relationship with the Lord is called the Lord's *daivī māyā*, or *mahā-māyā*. Both the *māyās* also have connections with the Lord because nothing can exist without being related to Him. As such, the wrong conception of detaching relationships from the Lord is not false but illusory.

Misconceiving one thing for another thing is called illusion. For example, accepting a rope as a snake is illusion, but the rope is not false. The rope, as it exists in the front of the illusioned person, is not at all false, but the acceptance is illusory. Therefore the wrong conception of accepting this material manifestation as being divorced from the energy of the Lord is illusion, but it is not false. And this illusory conception is called the reflection of the reality in the darkness of ignorance. Anything that appears as apparently not being "produced out of My energy" is called *māyā*. The conception that the living entity is formless or that the Supreme Lord is formless is also illusion. In the *Bhagavad-gītā* (2.12) it was said by the Lord in the midst of the battlefield that the warriors standing in front of Arjuna, Arjuna himself, and even the Lord had all existed before, they were existing on the Battlefield of Kurukṣetra, and they would all continue to be individual personalities in the future also, even after the annihilation of the present body and even after being liberated from the bondage of material existence. In all circumstances, the Lord and the living entities are individual personalities, and the personal features of both the Lord and living beings are never abolished; only the influence of the illusory energy, the reflection of light in the darkness, can, by the mercy of the Lord, be removed. In the material world, the light of the sun is also not independent, nor is that of the moon. The real source of light is the *brahmajyoti*, which diffuses light from the transcendental body of the Lord, and the same light is reflected in varieties of light: the light of the sun, the light of the moon, the light of fire, or the light of electricity. So the identity of the self as being unconnected with the Supreme Self, the Lord, is also illusion, and the false claim "*I am the Supreme*" is the last illusory snare of the same *māyā*, or the external energy of the Lord.

The *Vedānta-sūtra* in the very beginning affirms that everything is born from the Supreme, and thus, as explained in the previous verse, all individual living entities are born from the energy of the supreme living being, the Personality of Godhead. Brahmā himself was born from the energy of the Lord, and all other living entities are born from the energy of the Lord through the agency of Brahmā; none of them has any existence without being dovetailed with the Supreme Lord.

The independence of the individual living entity is not real independence, but is just the reflection of the real independence existing in the Supreme Being, the Lord. The false claim of supreme independence by the conditioned souls is illusion, and this conclusion is admitted in this verse.

Persons with a poor fund of knowledge become illusioned, and therefore the so-called scientists, physiologists, empiric philosophers, etc., become dazzled by the glaring reflection of the sun, moon, electricity, etc., and deny the existence of the Supreme Lord, putting forward theories and different speculations about the creation, maintenance and annihilation of everything material. The medical practitioner may deny the existence of the soul in the physiological bodily construction of an individual person, but he cannot give life to a dead body, even though all the mechanisms of the body exist even after death. The psychologist makes a serious study of the physiological conditions of the brain, as if the construction of the cerebral lump were the machine of the functioning mind, but in the dead body the psychologist cannot bring back the function of the mind. These scientific studies of the cosmic manifestation or the bodily construction independent of the Supreme Lord are different reflective intellectual gymnastics only, but at the end they are all illusion and nothing more. All such advancement of science and knowledge in the present context of material civilization is but an action of the covering influence of the illusory energy. The illusory energy has two phases of existence, namely the covering influence and the throwing influence. By the throwing influence the illusory energy throws the living entities into the darkness of ignorance, and by the covering influence she covers the eyes of men with a poor fund of knowledge about the existence of the Supreme Person who enlightened the supreme individual living being, Brahmā. The identity of Brahmā with the Supreme Lord is never claimed herein, and therefore such a foolish claim by the man with a poor fund of knowledge is another display of the illusory energy of the Lord. The Lord says in the *Bhagavad-gītā* (16.18–20) that demoniac persons who deny the existence of the Lord are thrown more and more into the darkness of ignorance, and thus such demoniac persons transmigrate life after life without any knowledge of the Supreme Personality of Godhead.

The sane man, however, is enlightened in the disciplic succession from Brahmājī, who was personally instructed by the Lord, or in the disciplic succession from Arjuna, who was personally instructed by the Lord in the *Bhagavad-gītā*. He accepts this statement of the Lord:

ahaṁ sarvasya prabhavo
mattaḥ sarvaṁ pravartate
iti matvā bhajante māṁ
budhā bhāva-samanvitāḥ
(Bg. 10.8)

The Lord is the original source of all emanations, and everything that is created, maintained and annihilated exists by the energy of the Lord. The sane man who knows this is actually learned, and therefore he becomes a pure devotee of the Lord, engaged in the transcendental loving service of the Lord.

Although the reflectory energy of the Lord displays various illusions to the eyes of persons with a poor fund of knowledge, the sane person knows clearly that the Lord can act, even from far, far beyond our vision, by His different energies, just as fire can diffuse heat and light from a distant place. In the medical science of the ancient sages, known as the *Āyur-veda*, there is definite acceptance of the Lord's supremacy in the following words:

jagad-yoner anicchasya
cid-ānandaika-rūpiṇaḥ
puṁso 'sti prakṛtir nityā
praticchāyeva bhāsvataḥ

acetanāpi caitanya-
yogena paramātmanaḥ
akarod viśvam akhilam
anityam nāṭakākṛtim

There is one Supreme Person who is the progenitor of this cosmic manifestation and whose energy acts as *prakṛti*, or the material nature, dazzling like a reflection. By such illusory action of *prakṛti*, even dead matter is caused to move by the cooperation of living energy of the Lord, and the material world appears like a dramatic performance to the ignorant eyes. The ignorant person, therefore, may even be a scientist or physiologist in the drama of *prakṛti*, while the sane person knows *prakṛti* as the illusory energy of the Lord. By such a conclusion, as confirmed by the *Bhagavad-gītā*, it is clear that the living entities are also a display of the Lord's superior energy (*parā prakṛti*), just as the material world is a display of the Lord's inferior energy (*aparā prakṛti*). The superior energy of the Lord cannot be as good as the Lord, although there is very little difference between the energy and the possessor of the energy, or the fire and the heat. Fire is possessed of heat, but heat is not fire. This simple thing is not understood by the man with a poor fund of knowledge who falsely claims that the fire and heat are the same. This energy of the fire (namely heat) is explained here as a reflection, and not directly fire. Therefore the living energy represented by the living entities is the reflection of the Lord, and never the Lord Himself. Being the reflection of the Lord, the existence of the living entity is dependent on the Supreme Lord, who is the original light. This material energy may be compared to darkness, as actually it is darkness, and the activities of the living entities in the darkness are reflections of the original light. The Lord should be understood by the context of this verse. Nondependence of both the energies of the Lord is explained as *māyā*, or illusion. No one can make a solution of the darkness of ignorance simply by the reflection of light. Similarly, no one can come out of material existence simply by the reflected light of the common man; one has to receive the light from the original light itself. The reflection of sunlight in the darkness is unable to drive out the darkness, but the sunlight outside the reflection can drive out the darkness completely. In darkness no one can see the things in a room. Therefore a person in the dark is afraid of snakes and scorpions, although there may not be such things. But in the light the things in the room can be clearly seen, and the fear of snakes and scorpions is at once removed. Therefore one has to take shelter of the light of the Lord, as in the *Bhagavad-gītā* or the *Śrīmad-Bhāgavatam*, and not the reflective personalities who have no touch with the Lord. No one should hear *Bhagavad-gītā* or *Śrīmad-Bhāgavatam* from a person who does not believe in the existence of the Lord. Such a person is already doomed, and any association with such a doomed person makes the associater also doomed.

According to the *Padma Purāṇa*, within the material compass there are innumerable material universes, and all of them are full of darkness. Any living being, beginning from the Brahmās (there are innumerable Brahmās in innumerable universes) to the insignificant ant, are all born in darkness, and they require factual light from the Lord to see Him directly, just as the sun can be seen only by the direct light of the sun. No lamp or manmade torchlight, however powerful it may be, can help one see the sun. The sun reveals itself. Therefore the action of different energies of the Lord, or the Personality of Godhead Himself, can be realized by the light manifested by the causeless mercy of the Lord. The impersonalists say that God cannot be seen. God can be seen by the light of God and not by man-made speculations. Here this light is specifically mentioned as *vidyāt*, which is an order by the Lord to Brahmā. This direct order of the Lord is a manifestation of His internal energy, and this particular energy is the means of seeing the Lord face to face. Not only Brahmā but anyone who may be graced by the Lord to see such merciful direct internal energy can also realize the Personality of Godhead without any mental speculation.

TEXT 35

यथा महान्ति भूतानि भूतेषूच्चावचेष्वनु ।
प्रविष्टान्यप्रविष्टानि तथा तेषु न तेष्वहम् ॥३५॥

yathā mahānti bhūtāni
bhūteṣūccāvaceṣv anu

praviṣṭāny apraviṣṭāni
tathā teṣu na teṣv aham

yathā—just as; *mahānti*—the universal; *bhūtāni*—elements; *bhūteṣu ucca-avaceṣu*—in the minute and gigantic; *anu*—after; *praviṣṭāni*—entered; *apraviṣṭāni*—not entered; *tathā*—so; *teṣu*—in them; *na*—not; *teṣu*—in them; *aham*—Myself.

TRANSLATION

O Brahmā, please know that the universal elements enter into the cosmos and at the same time do not enter into the cosmos; similarly, I Myself also exist within everything created, and at the same time I am outside of everything.

PURPORT

The great elements of material creation, namely earth, water, fire, air and ether, all enter into the body of all manifested entities—the seas, mountains, aquatics, plants, reptiles, birds, beasts, human beings, demigods and everyone materially manifested—and at the same time such elements are differently situated. In the developed stage of consciousness, the human being can study both physiological and physical science, but the basic principles of such sciences are nothing but the material elements and nothing more. The body of the human being and the body of the mountain, as also the bodies of the demigods, including Brahmā, are all of the same ingredients—earth, water, etc.—and at the same time the elements are beyond the body. The elements were created first, and therefore they entered into the bodily construction later, but in both circumstances they entered the cosmos and also did not enter. Similarly, the Supreme Lord, by His different energies, namely the internal and external, is within everything in the manifested cosmos, and at the same time He is outside of everything, situated in the kingdom of God (Vaikuṇṭhaloka) as described before. This is very nicely stated in the *Brahma-saṁhitā* (5.37) as follows:

ānanda-cinmaya-rasa-pratibhāvitābhis
tābhir ya eva nija-rupatayā kalābhiḥ

goloka eva nivasaty akhilātma-bhūto
govindam ādi-puruṣaṁ tam ahaṁ bhajāmi

"I worship the Personality of Godhead, Govinda, who, by expansion of His internal potency of transcendental existence, knowledge and bliss, enjoys in His own and expanded forms. Simultaneously He enters into every atom of the creation."

This expansion of His plenary parts is also more definitely explained in the same *Brahma-saṁhitā* (5.35) as follows:

eko 'py asau racayituṁ jagad-aṇḍa-koṭiṁ
yac-chaktir asti jagad-aṇḍa-cayā yad-antaḥ
aṇḍāntara-stha-paramāṇu-cayāntara-sthaṁ
govindam ādi-puruṣaṁ tam ahaṁ bhajāmi

"I worship the Personality of Godhead, Govinda, who, by one of His plenary portions, enters into the existence of every universe and every particle of the atoms and thus unlimitedly manifests His infinite energy all over the material creation."

The impersonalists can imagine or even perceive that the Supreme Brahman is thus all-pervading, and therefore they conclude that there is no possibility of His personal form. Herein lies the mystery of His transcendental knowledge. This mystery is transcendental love of Godhead, and one who is surcharged with such transcendental love of Godhead can without difficulty see the Personality of Godhead in every atom and every movable or immovable object. And at the same time he can see the Personality of Godhead in His own abode, Goloka, enjoying eternal pastimes with His eternal associates, who are also expansions of His transcendental existence. This vision is the real mystery of spiritual knowledge, as stated by the Lord in the beginning (*sarahasyaṁ tad-aṅgaṁ ca*). This mystery is the most confidential part of the knowledge of the Supreme, and it is impossible for the mental speculators to discover by dint of intellectual gymnastics. The mystery can be revealed through the process recommended by Brahmājī in his *Brahma-saṁhitā* (5.38) as follows:

premāñjana-cchurita-bhakti-vilocanena
santaḥ sadaiva hṛdayeṣu vilokayanti

yaṁ śyāmasundaram acintya-guṇa-svarūpaṁ
govindam ādi-puruṣaṁ tam ahaṁ bhajāmi.

"I worship the original Personality of Godhead, Govinda, whom the pure devotees, their eyes smeared with the ointment of love of Godhead, always observe within their hearts. This Govinda, the original Personality of Godhead, is Śyāmasundara with all transcendental qualities."

Therefore, although He is present in every atom, the Supreme Personality of Godhead may not be visible to the dry speculators; still the mystery is unfolded before the eyes of the pure devotees because their eyes are anointed with love of Godhead. And this love of Godhead can be attained only by the practice of transcendental loving service of the Lord, and nothing else. The vision of the devotees is not ordinary; it is purified by the process of devotional service. In other words, as the universal elements are both within and without, similarly the Lord's name, form, quality, pastimes, entourage, etc., as they are described in the revealed scriptures or as performed in the Vaikuṇṭhalokas, far, far beyond the material cosmic manifestation, are factually being televised in the heart of the devotee. The man with a poor fund of knowledge cannot understand, although by material science one can see things far away by means of television. Factually, the spiritually developed person is able to have the television of the kingdom of God always reflected within his heart. That is the mystery of knowledge of the Personality of Godhead.

The Lord can award anyone and everyone liberation (*mukti*) from the bondage of material existence, yet He rarely awards the privilege of love of Godhead, as confirmed by Nārada (*muktiṁ dadhāti karhicit sma na bhakti-yogam*). This transcendental devotional service of the Lord is so wonderful that the occupation keeps the deserving devotee always rapt in psychological activities, without deviation from the absolute touch. Thus love of Godhead, developed in the heart of the devotee, is a great mystery. Brahmājī previously told Nārada that the desires of Brahmājī are never unfulfilled because he is always absorbed in the transcendental loving service of the Lord; nor has he any desire in his heart save and except the transcendental service of the Lord. That is the beauty and mystery of the process of *bhakti-yoga*. As the Lord's desire is infallible because He is *acyuta*, similarly the desires of the devotees in the transcendental service of the Lord are also *acyuta*, infallible. This is very difficult, however, for the layman to understand without knowledge of the mystery of devotional service, as it is very difficult to know the potency of touchstone. As touchstone is rarely found, a pure devotee of the Lord is also rarely to be seen, even amongst millions of liberated souls (*koṭiṣv api mahāmune*). Out of all kinds of perfections attained by the process of knowledge, *yoga* perfection in devotional service is the highest of all and the most mysterious also, even more mysterious than the eight kinds of mystic perfection attained by the process of yogic performances. In the *Bhagavad-gītā* (18.64) the Lord therefore advised Arjuna about this *bhakti-yoga:*

sarva-guhyatamaṁ bhūyaḥ
śṛṇu me paramaṁ vacaḥ

"Just hear from Me again about the most confidential part of the instructions in *Bhagavad-gītā.*" The same was confirmed by Brahmājī to Nārada in the following words:

idaṁ bhāgavataṁ nāma
yan me bhagavatoditam
saṅgraho 'yaṁ vibhūtīnāṁ
tvam etad vipulīkuru

Brahmājī said to Nārada, "Whatever I have spoken to you about the *Bhāgavatam* was explained to me by the Supreme Personality of Godhead, and I am advising you to expand these topics nicely so that people may easily understand the mysterious *bhakti-yoga* by transcendental loving service to the Lord." It is to be noted here that the mystery of *bhakti-yoga* was disclosed to Brahmājī by the Lord Himself. Brahmājī explained the same mystery to Nārada, Nārada explained it to Vyāsa, Vyāsa explained it to Śukadeva Gosvāmī, and that same knowledge is coming down in the unalloyed chain of disciplic succession. If one is fortunate enough to have received the knowledge in the transcendental disciplic succession, surely he will have the chance to understand the mystery of the Lord and that of the *Śrīmad-Bhāgavatam*, the sound incarnation of the Lord.

TEXT 36

एतावदेव जिज्ञास्यं तत्त्वजिज्ञासुनात्मनः ।
अन्वयव्यतिरेकाभ्यां यत् स्यात् सर्वत्र सर्वदा ॥३६॥

etāvad eva jijñāsyaṁ
tattva-jijñāsunātmanaḥ
anvaya-vyatirekābhyāṁ
yat syāt sarvatra sarvadā

etāvat—up to this; *eva*—certainly; *jijñāsyam*—is to be inquired; *tattva*—the Absolute Truth; *jijñāsunā*—by the student; *ātmanaḥ*—of the Self; *anvaya*—directly; *vyatirekābhyām*—indirectly; *yat*—whatever; *syāt*—it may be; *sarvatra*—in all space and time; *sarvadā*—in all circumstances.

TRANSLATION

A person who is searching after the Supreme Absolute Truth, the Personality of Godhead, most certainly search for it up to this, in all circumstances, in all space and time, and both directly and indirectly.

PURPORT

To unfold the mystery of *bhakti-yoga,* as it is explained in the previous verse, is the ultimate stage of all inquiries or the highest objective for the inquisitive. Everyone is searching after self-realization in different ways—by *karma-yoga,* by *jñāna-yoga,* by *dhyāna-yoga,* by *rāja-yoga,* by *bhakti-yoga,* etc. To engage in self-realization is the responsibility of every living entity developed in consciousness. One who is developed in consciousness certainly makes inquiries into the mystery of the self, of the cosmic situation and of the problems of life, in all spheres and fields—social, political, economic, cultural, religious, moral, etc.—and in their different branches. But here the goal of all such inquiries is explained.

The *Vedānta-sūtra* philosophy begins with this inquiry about life, and the *Bhāgavatam* answers such inquiries up to this point, or the mystery of all inquiries. Lord Brahmā wanted to be perfectly educated by the Personality of Godhead, and here is the answer by the Lord, finished in four nutshell verses, from *aham eva* to this verse, *etāvad eva.* This is the end of all self-realization processes. Men do not know that the ultimate goal of life is Viṣṇu, or the Supreme Personality of Godhead, due to being bewildered by the glaring reflection in the darkness, and as such everyone is entering into the darkest region of material existence, driven by the uncontrolled senses. The whole material existence has sprung up because of sense gratification, desires based principally on the sex desire, and the result is that in spite of all advancement of knowledge, the final goal of all the activities of the living entities is sense gratification. But here is the real goal of life, and everyone should know it by inquiries put before a bona fide spiritual master expert in the science of *bhakti-yoga*, or from a living personality of *Bhāgavatam* life. Everyone is engaged in various kinds of scriptural inquiries, but the *Śrīmad-Bhāgavatam* gives answers to all of the various students of self-realization: this ultimate objective of life is not to be searched out without great labor or perseverance. One who is imbued with such sincere inquiries must ask the bona fide spiritual master in the disciplic succession from Brahmājī, and that is the direction given here. Because the mystery was disclosed before Brahmājī by the Supreme Personality of Godhead, the mystery of all such inquiries regarding self-realization must be put before such a spiritual master, who is directly the representative of the Lord, acknowledged in that disciplic succession. Such a bona fide spiritual master is able to clear up the whole thing by evidence from the revealed scriptures, both direct and indirect. Although everyone is free to consult the revealed scriptures in this connection, one still requires the guidance of a bona fide spiritual master, and that is the direction in this verse. The bona fide spiritual master is the most confidential representative of the Lord, and one must receive direction from the spiritual master in the same spirit that Brahmājī received it from the Personality of Godhead, Lord Kṛṣṇa. The bona fide spiritual master in that bona fide chain of disciplic succession never claims to be the Lord Himself, although such a spiritual master is greater than the Lord in the sense that he can deliver the Lord by his personally realized experience. The Lord is not to be found simply by education or by a good fertile brain, but surely He can be found by the sincere student through the transparent medium of the bona fide spiritual master.

The revealed scriptures give directions directly to this end, but because the bewildered living entities are blinded by the glaring reflection in the darkness, they are unable to find the truth of the revealed scriptures. For example, in the *Bhagavad-gītā* the whole direction is targeted toward the Personality of Godhead Lord Śrī Kṛṣṇa, but for want of a bona fide spiritual master in the line of Brahmājī or the direct hearer, Arjuna, there are different distortions of the revealed knowledge by many unauthorized persons who just want to satisfy their own whims. Undoubtedly the *Bhagavad-gītā* is accepted as one of the most brilliant stars in the horizon of the spiritual sky, yet the interpretations of this great book of knowledge have so grossly been distorted that every student of the *Bhagavad-gītā* is still in the same darkness of glaring material reflections. Such students are hardly enlightened by the *Bhagavad-gītā*. In the *Gītā* practically the same instruction is imparted as in the four prime verses of the *Bhāgavatam*, but due to wrong and fashionable interpretations by unauthorized persons, one cannot reach the ultimate conclusion. In the *Bhagavad-gītā* (18.61) it is clearly said:

īśvaraḥ sarva-bhūtānāṁ
hṛd-deśe 'rjuna tiṣṭhati
bhrāmayan sarva-bhūtāni
yantrārūḍhāni māyayā

The Lord is situated in the hearts of all living beings (as Paramātmā), and He is controlling all of them in the material world under the agency of His external energy. Therefore it is clearly mentioned that the Lord is the supreme controller and that the living entities are controlled by the Lord. In the same *Bhagavad-gītā* (18.65) the Lord directs as follows:

man-manā bhava mad-bhakto
mad-yājī māṁ namaskuru
mām evaiṣyasi satyaṁ te
pratijāne priyo 'si me

It is clear from this verse of the *Bhagavad-gītā* that the direction of the Lord is that one should be God-minded, a devotee of the Lord, a worshiper of the Lord, and must offer all obeisances unto Lord Kṛṣṇa. By so doing, the devotee will undoubtedly go back to Godhead, back to home.

Indirectly it is said that the whole Vedic social construction of human society is so made that everyone acts as a part and parcel of the complete body of the Lord. The intelligent class of men, or the *brāhmaṇas,* are situated on the face of the Lord; the administrative class of men, the *kṣatriyas,* are situated on the arms of the Lord; the productive class of men, the *vaiśyas,* are situated on the belt of the Lord; and the laborer class of men, the *śūdras,* are situated on the legs of the Lord. Therefore the complete social construction is the body of the Lord, and all the parts of the body, namely the *brāhmaṇas,* the *kṣatriyas,* the *vaiśyas* and the *śūdras,* are meant to serve the Lord's whole body conjointly; otherwise the parts become unfit to be coordinated with the supreme consciousness of oneness. Universal consciousness is factually achieved by coordinated service of all concerned to the Supreme Personality of Godhead, and that alone can insure total perfection. Therefore even the great scientists, the great philosophers, the great mental speculators, the great politicians, the great industrialists, the great social reformers, etc., cannot give any relief to the restless society of the material world because they do not know the secret of success as mentioned in this verse of the *Bhāgavatam,* namely that one must know the mystery of *bhakti-yoga.* In the *Bhagavad-gītā* (7.15) also it is said:

na māṁ duṣkṛtino mūḍhāḥ
prapadyante narādhamāḥ
māyayā 'pahṛta-jñānā
āsuraṁ bhāvam āśritāḥ

Because the so-called great leaders of human society are ignorant of this great knowledge of *bhakti-yoga* and are always engaged in ignoble acts of sense gratification, bewildered by the external energy of the Lord, they are stubborn rebels against the supremacy of the Supreme Personality of Godhead, and they never agree to surrender unto Him because they are fools, miscreants and the lowest type of human beings. Such faithless nonbelievers may be highly educated in the material sense of the term, but factually they are the greatest fools of the world because by the influence of the external, material nature all their so-called acquisition of knowledge has been made null and void. Therefore all advancement of knowledge in the present context of things is being misused by cats and dogs fighting with one another for sense gratification, and all acquisition of knowledge in science, philosophy, fine arts, nationalism, economic development, religion and great activities are being spoiled by being used as dresses for dead men. There is no utility in the dresses used for covering a coffin of a dead body save getting false applause from the ignorant public. The *Śrīmad-Bhāgavatam* therefore says again and again that without attainment of the status of *bhakti-yoga*, all the activities of human society are to be considered absolute failures only. It is said:

parābhavas tāvad abodha-jāto
yāvan na jijñāsata ātma-tattvam
yāvat kriyās tāvad idaṁ mano vai
karmātmakaṁ yena śarīra-bandhaḥ
(*Bhāg.* 5.5.5)

As long as one is blind to inquiring after self-realization, all material activities, however great they may be, are all different kinds of defeat because the aim of human life is not fulfilled by such unwanted and profitless activities. The function of the human body is to attain freedom from material bondage, but as long as one is fully absorbed in material activities, his mind will be overwhelmed in the whirlpool of matter, and thus he will continue to be encaged in material bodies life after life.

evaṁ manaḥ karma-vaśaṁ prayuṅkte
avidyayātmany upadhīyamāne
prītir na yāvan mayi vāsudeve
na mucyate deha-yogena tāvat
(*Bhāg.* 5.5.6)

It is one's mind that generates different kinds of bodies for suffering different kinds of material pangs. Therefore as long as the mind is absorbed in fruitive activities, the mind is understood to be absorbed in nescience, and thus one is sure to be subjected to material bondage in different bodies again and again until one develops a transcendental love for Godhead, Vāsudeva, the Supreme Person. To become absorbed in the transcendental name, quality, form and activities of the Supreme Person,

Vāsudeva, means to change the temper of the mind from matter to absolute knowledge, which leads one to the path of absolute realization and thus frees one from the bondage of material contact and encagements in different material bodies.

Śrīla Jīva Gosvāmī Prabhupāda therefore comments on the words *sarvatra sarvadā* in the sense that the principles of *bhakti-yoga*, or devotional service to the Lord, are apt in all circumstances; i.e., *bhakti-yoga* is recommended in all the revealed scriptures, it is performed by all authorities, it is important in all places, it is useful in all causes and effects, etc. As far as all the revealed scriptures are concerned, he quotes from the *Skanda Purāṇa* on the topics of Brahmā and Nārada as follows:

saṁsāre 'smin mahā-ghore
janma-mṛtyu-samākule
pūjanaṁ vāsudevasya
tārakaṁ vādibhiḥ smṛtam

In the material world, which is full of darkness and dangers, combined with birth and death and full of different anxieties, the only way to get out of the great entanglement is to accept loving transcendental devotional service to Lord Vāsudeva. This is accepted by all classes of philosophers.

Śrīla Jīva Gosvāmī also quotes another common passage, which is found in three *Purāṇas*, namely the *Padma Purāṇa*, *Skanda Purāṇa* and *Liṅga Purāṇa*. It runs as follows:

āloḍya sarva-śāstrāni
vicārya ca punaḥ punaḥ
idam ekaṁ suniṣpannaṁ
dhyeyo nārāyaṇaḥ sadā

"By scrutinizingly reviewing all the revealed scriptures and judging them again and again, it is now concluded that Lord Nārāyaṇa is the Supreme Absolute Truth, and thus He alone should be worshiped."

The same truth is also indirectly described in the *Garuḍa Purāṇa* as follows:

pāraṁ gato 'pi vedānāṁ
sarva-śāstrārtha-vedy api
yo na sarveśvare bhaktas
taṁ vidyāt puruṣādhamam

"Even though one may have gone to the other side of all the *Vedas*, and even though one is well versed in all the revealed scriptures, if one is not a devotee of the Supreme Lord, he must be considered the lowest of mankind." Similarly, it is also stated in *Śrīmad-Bhāgavatam* (5.18.12) indirectly as follows:

yasyāsti bhaktir bhagavaty akiñcanā
sarvair guṇais tatra samāsate surāḥ
harāv abhaktasya kuto mahad-guṇā
mano-rathenāsati dhāvato bahiḥ

One who has unflinching devotion unto the Supreme Personality of Godhead must have all the good qualities of the demigods, and contrarily one who is not a devotee of the Lord must be hovering in the darkness of mental speculation and thus must be engaged in material impermanence. *Śrīmad-Bhāgavatam* (11.11.18) says:

śabda-brahmaṇi niṣṇāto
na niṣṇāyāt pare yadi
śramas tasya śrama-phalo
hy adhenum iva rakṣataḥ

"One may be well versed in all the transcendental literature of the *Vedas*, but if he fails to be acquainted with the Supreme, then it must be concluded that all of his education is like the burden of a beast or like one's keeping a cow without milking capacity."

Similarly, the liberty of discharging loving transcendental service to the Lord is invested in everyone, even the women, the *śūdras*, the forest tribes, or any other living beings born in sinful conditions.

te vai vidanty atitaranti ca deva-māyāṁ
strī-śūdra-hūṇa-śabarā api pāpa-jīvāḥ

yady adbhuta-krama-parāyaṇa-śīlaśikṣās
tiryag-janā api kimu śruta-dhāraṇā ye
(*Bhāg.* 2.7.46)

The lowest of human beings can be elevated to the highest stage of devotional life if they are trained by the bona fide spiritual master well versed in the transcendental loving service of the Lord. If the lowest can be so elevated, then what to speak of the highest, who are well versed in the Vedic knowledge? The conclusion is that devotional service to the Lord is open for all, regardless of who they are. That is the confirmation of its application for all kinds of performers of the service.

Therefore the devotional service of the Lord with perfect knowledge through the training of a bona fide spiritual master is advised for everyone, even if one happens not to be a human being. This is confirmed in the *Garuḍa Purāṇa* as follows:

kīṭa-pakṣi-mṛgāṇāṁ ca
harau sannyasta-cetasām
ūrdhvām eva gatiṁ manye
kiṁ punar jñāninām nṛṇām

"Even the worms, birds and beasts are assured of elevation to the highest perfectional life if they are completely surrendered to the transcendental loving service of the Lord, so what to speak of the philosophers amongst the human beings?"

Therefore there is no need to seek properly qualified candidates for discharging devotional service to the Lord. Let them be either well behaved or ill trained, let them be either learned or fools, let them be either grossly attached or in the renounced order of life, let them be liberated souls or desirous of salvation, let them be inexpert in the discharge of devotional service or expert in the same, all of them can be elevated to the supreme position by discharging devotional service under the proper guidance. This is also confirmed in the *Bhagavad-gītā* (9.30,32) as follows:

api cet sudurācāro
bhajate mām ananya-bhāk

sādhur eva sa mantavyaḥ
samyag vyavasito hi saḥ

māṁ hi pārtha vyapāśritya
ye 'pi syuḥ pāpa-yonayaḥ
striyo vaiśyās tathā śūdrās
te 'pi yānti parāṁ gatim

Even if a person is fully addicted to all sorts of sinful acts, if he happens to be engaged in the loving transcendental service of the Lord under proper guidance, he is to be considered the most perfect holy man without a doubt. And thus any person, whatsoever and whosoever he or she may be—even the fallen woman, the less intelligent laborer, the dull mercantile man, or even a man lower than all these—can attain the highest perfection of life by going back home, back to Godhead, provided he or she takes shelter of the lotus feet of the Lord in all earnestness. This sincere earnestness is the only qualification that can lead one to the highest perfectional stage of life, and unless and until such real earnestness is aroused, there is a difference between cleanliness or uncleanliness, learning or nonlearning, in the material estimation. Fire is always fire, and thus if someone touches the fire, knowingly or unknowingly, the fire will act in its own way without discrimination. The principle is: *harir harati pāpāni duṣṭa-cittair api smṛtaḥ.* The all-powerful Lord can purify the devotee of all sinful reactions, just as the sun can sterilize all sorts of infections by its powerful rays. "Attraction for material enjoyment cannot act upon a pure devotee of the Lord." There are hundreds and thousands of aphorisms in the revealed scriptures. *Ātmārāmāś ca munayaḥ:* "Even the self-realized souls are also attracted by the transcendental loving service of the Lord." *Kecit kevalayā bhaktyā vāsudeva-parāyaṇāḥ:* "Simply by hearing and chanting, one becomes a great devotee of Lord Vāsudeva." *Na calati bhagavat-padāravindāl lavanimiṣārdham api sa vaiṣṇavāgryaḥ:* "A person who does not move from the lotus feet of the Lord even for a moment or a second is to be considered the greatest of all Vaiṣṇavas." *Bhagavat-pārṣadatāṁ prāpte mat-sevayā pratītaṁ te:* "The pure devotees are convinced of attaining the association of the Personality of Godhead, and thus they are always engaged in the transcendental loving service of the Lord." Therefore in all continents, in all planets, in all universes, devotional service to the Lord, or *bhakti-yoga*, is current, and that is the statement of the *Śrīmad-Bhāgavatam* and allied scriptures. Everywhere means in every part of the creation of the Lord. The Lord can be served by all the senses, or even simply by the mind. The South Indian *brāhmaṇa* who served the Lord simply on the strength of his mind also factually realized the Lord. Success is guaranteed for a devotee who fully engages any one of his senses in the mode of devotional service. The Lord can be served by any ingredient, even the most common commodity—a flower, a leaf, a fruit or a little water, which are available in any part of the universe and without cost—and thus the Lord is served universally by the universal entities. He can be served simply by hearing, He can be served simply by chanting or reading about His activities, He can be served simply by adoring Him and accepting Him.

In the *Bhagavad-gītā* it is stated that one can serve the Lord by offering the result of one's own work; it does not matter what one does. Generally men may say that whatever they are doing is inspired by God, but that is not all. One should actually work on behalf of God as a servant of God. The Lord says in the *Bhagavad-gītā* (9.27):

yat karoṣi yad aśnāsi
yaj juhoṣi dadāsi yat
yat tapasyasi kaunteya
tat kuruṣva mad-arpaṇam

Do whatever you like or whatever may be easier for you to do, eat whatever you may eat, sacrifice whatever you can sacrifice, give whatever you may give in charity, and do whatever you may undertake in penance, but everything must be done for Him only. If you do business or if you accept some employment, do so on behalf of the Lord. Whatever you may eat, you may offer the same to the Lord and be assured that He will return the food after eating it Himself. He is the complete whole, and therefore whatever He may eat as offered by the devotee is accepted because of the devotee's love, but again it is returned as *prasāda* for the devotee so that he can be happy by eating. In other words, be a servant of

God and live peacefully in that consciousness, ultimately returning home, back to Godhead.

It is said in the *Skanda Purāṇa:*

yasya smṛtyā ca nāmoktyā
tapo-yajña-kriyādiṣu
nūnaṁ sampūrṇatām eti
sadyo vande tam acyutam

"I offer my obeisances unto Him, the infallible, because simply by either remembering Him or vibrating His holy name one can attain the perfection of all penances, sacrifices or fruitive activities, and this process can be universally followed." It is enjoined (*Bhāg.* 2.3.10):

akāmaḥ sarva-kāmo vā
mokṣa-kāma udāra-dhīḥ
tīvreṇa bhakti-yogena
yajeta puruṣaṁ param

Though a person be full of desires or have no desires, he may follow this path of infallible *bhakti-yoga* for complete perfection." One need not be anxious to propitiate each and every demigod and goddess because the root of all of them is the Personality of Godhead. As by pouring water on the root of the tree one serves and enlivens all the branches and leaves, so by rendering service unto the Supreme Lord one automatically serves every god and goddess without extraneous effort. The Lord is all-pervading, and therefore service unto Him is also all-pervading. This fact is corroborated in the *Skanda Purāṇa* as follows:

arcite deva-deveśe
śaṅkha-cakra-gadā-dhare
arcitāḥ sarva-devāḥ syur
yataḥ sarva-gato hariḥ

When the Supreme Lord, the Personality of Godhead, who carries in His hands a conchshell, wheel, club and lotus flower, is worshiped, certainly all other demigods are worshiped automatically because Hari, the Personality of Godhead, is all-pervading. Therefore, in all cases, namely nominative, objective, causative, dative, ablative, possessive and supportive, everyone is benefited by such transcendental loving service to the Lord. The man who worships the Lord, the Lord Himself who is worshiped, the cause for which the Lord is worshiped, the source of supply, the place where such worship is done, etc.—everything is benefited by such an action.

Even during the annihilation of the material world, the process of *bhakti-yoga* can be applied. *Kālena naṣṭā pralaye vāṇīyam:* the Lord is worshiped in devastation because He protects the *Vedas* from being annihilated. He is worshiped in every millennium or *yuga.* As it is said in *Śrīmad-Bhāgavatam* (12.3.52):

kṛte yad dhyāyato viṣṇuṁ
tretāyāṁ yajato makhaiḥ
dvāpare paricaryāyāṁ
kalau tad dhari-kīrtanāt

In the *Viṣṇu Purāṇa* it is written:

sa hānis tan mahac chidraṁ
sa mohaḥ sa ca vibhramaḥ
yan-muhūrtaṁ kṣaṇaṁ vāpi
vāsudevaṁ na cintayet

"If even for a moment remembrance of Vāsudeva, the Supreme Personality of Godhead, is missed, that is the greatest loss, that is the greatest illusion, and that is the greatest anomaly." The Lord can be worshiped in all stages of life. For instance, even in the wombs of their mothers Mahārāja Prahlāda and Mahārāja Parīkṣit worshiped the Lord; even in his very childhood, at the age of only five years, Dhruva Mahārāja worshiped the Lord; even in full youth, Mahārāja Ambarīṣa worshiped the Lord; and even at the last stage of his frustration and old age Mahārāja Dhṛtarāṣṭra worshiped the Lord. Ajāmila worshiped the Lord even at the point of death, and Citraketu worshiped the Lord even in heaven and in hell. In the *Narasiṁha Purāṇa* it is said that as the hellish inhabitants began to chant the holy name of the Lord they began to be elevated from hell towards heaven. Durvāsā Muni has also supported this view: *mucyeta yan-nāmny udite nārako 'pi.* "Simply by chanting the holy name of the Lord the inhabitants of hell became released from their hellish persecution." So the conclusion of *Śrīmad-Bhāgavatam*, as given by Śukadeva Gosvāmī to Mahārāja Parīkṣit, is:

etan nirvidyamānānām
icchatām akuto-bhayam
yoginām nṛpa nirṇītam
harer nāmānukīrtanam

"O King, it is finally decided that everyone, namely those in the renounced order of life, the mystics, and the enjoyers of fruitive work, should chant the holy name of the Lord fearlessly to achieve the desired success in their pursuits." (*Bhāg.* 2.1.11)

Similarly, as indicated indirectly in various places in revealed scriptures:

1. Even though one is well versed in all the *Vedas* and scriptures, if one is not a devotee of the Supreme Lord, the Personality of Godhead, he is considered to be the lowest of mankind.
2. In the *Garuḍa Purāṇa*, *Bṛhan-nāradīya Purāṇa* and *Padma Purāṇa*, the same is repeated: What is the use of Vedic knowledge and penances for one who is devoid of devotional service to the Lord?
3. What is the comparison of thousands of *prajāpatis* to one devotee of the Lord?
4. Śukadeva Gosvāmī said (*Bhāg.* 2.4.17) that neither the ascetic, nor one who is greatly munificent, nor one who is famous, nor the great philosopher, nor the great occultist, nor anyone else can achieve the desired result without being engaged in the service of the Lord.
5. Even if a place is more glorious than heaven, if there is no glorification of the Lord of Vaikuṇṭha or His pure devotee, it should at once be quitted.
6. The pure devotee refuses to accept all the five different types of liberation in order to be engaged in the service of the Lord.

The final conclusion, therefore, is that the glories of the Lord must be always and everywhere proclaimed. One should hear about His glories, one should chant about His glories, and one should always remember His glories because that is the highest perfectional stage of life. As far as fruitive work is concerned, it is limited to an enjoyable body; as far as *yoga* is concerned, it is limited to the acquirement of mystic power; as far as empiric philosophy is concerned, it is limited to the attainment of transcendental knowledge; and as far as transcendental knowledge is concerned, it is limited to attainment of salvation. Even if they are adopted, there is every chance of discrepancies in discharging the particular type of functions. But adoption of the transcendental devotional service of the Lord has no limit, nor is there fear of falling down. The process automatically reaches the final stage by the grace of the Lord. In the preliminary stage of devotional service there is an apparent requisite for knowledge, but in the higher stage there is no necessity of such knowledge. The best and guaranteed path of progress is therefore engagement in *bhakti-yoga*, pure devotional service.

The cream of *Śrīmad-Bhāgavatam* in the foregoing four *ślokas* is sometimes squeezed out by the impersonalist for different interpretations in their favor, but it should be carefully noted that the four *ślokas* were first described by the Personality of Godhead Himself, and thus the impersonalist has no scope to enter into them because he has no conception of the Personality of Godhead. Therefore, the impersonalist may squeeze out any interpretations from them, but such interpretations will never be accepted by those who are taught in the disciplic succession from Brahmā, as will be cleared up in the following verses. Besides that, the *śruti* confirms that the Supreme Truth Absolute Personality of Godhead never reveals Himself to anyone who is falsely proud of his academic knowledge. The *śruti-mantra* clearly says (*Kaṭha Up.* 1.2.23):

nāyam ātmā pravacanena labhyo
na medhayā na bahudhā śrutena
yam evaiṣa vṛṇute tena labhyas
tasyaiṣa ātmā vivṛṇute tanuṁ svām

The whole matter is explained by the Lord Himself, and one who has no approach to the Lord in His personal feature can rarely understand the purport of *Śrīmad-Bhāgavatam* without being taught by the *bhāgavatas* in the disciplic succession.

TEXT 37

एतन्मतं समातिष्ठ परमेण समाधिना ।
भवान् कल्पविकल्पेषु न विमुह्यति कर्हिचित् ॥३७॥

etan mataṁ samātiṣṭha
parameṇa samādhinā
bhavān kalpa-vikalpeṣu
na vimuhyati karhicit

etat—this; *matam*—the conclusion; *samātiṣṭha*—remain fixed; *parameṇa*—by the supreme; *samādhinā*—concentration of the mind; *bhavān*—yourself; *kalpa*—intermediate devastation; *vikalpeṣu*—in the final devastation; *na vimuhyati*—will never bewilder; *karhicit*—anything like complacence.

TRANSLATION

O Brahmā, just follow this conclusion by fixed concentration of mind, and no pride will disturb you, neither in the partial nor in the final devastation.

PURPORT

As in the *Bhagavad-gītā*, Tenth Chapter, the Personality of Godhead, Lord Kṛṣṇa, has summarized the whole text in four verses, namely, *ahaṁ sarvasya prabhavaḥ*, etc., so the complete *Śrīmad-Bhāgavatam* has also been summarized in four verses, as *aham evāsam evāgre*, etc. Thus the secret purpose of the most important Bhāgavatite conclusion has been explained by the original speaker of the *Śrīmad-Bhāgavatam*, who was also the original speaker of the *Bhagavad-gītā*, the Personality of Godhead, Lord Śrī Kṛṣṇa. There are many grammarians and nondevotee material wranglers who have tried to present false interpretations of these four verses of the *Śrīmad-Bhāgavatam* but the Lord Himself advised Brahmājī not to be deviated from the fixed conclusion the Lord had taught him. The Lord was the teacher of the nucleus of *Śrīmad-Bhāgavatam* in four verses, and Brahmā was the receiver of the knowledge. Misinterpretation of the word *aham* by the word jugglery of the impersonalist should not disturb the mind of the strict followers of the *Śrīmad-Bhāgavatam. Śrīmad-Bhāgavatam* is the text of the Personality of Godhead and His unalloyed devotees, who are also known as the *bhāgavatas*, and any outsider should have no access to this confidential literature of devotional service. But unfortunately the impersonalist, who has no relation to the Supreme Personality of Godhead, sometimes tries to interpret *Śrīmad-Bhāgavatam* by his poor fund of knowledge in grammar and dry speculation. Therefore, the Lord warns Brahmā (and, through Brahmā, all future devotees of the Lord in the disciplic succession of Brahmā) that one should never be misled by the conclusion of the so-called grammarians or by other men with a poor fund of knowledge, but must always fix the mind properly, via the *paramparā* system. No one should try to give a new interpretation by dint of mundane knowledge. And the first step, therefore, in pursuance of the system of knowledge received by Brahmā, is to approach a bona fide *guru* who is the representative of the Lord following the *paramparā* system. No one should try to squeeze out his own meaning by imperfect mundane knowledge. The *guru*, or the bona fide spiritual master, is competent to teach the disciple in the right path with reference to the context of all authentic Vedic literature. He does not attempt to juggle words to bewilder the student. The bona fide spiritual master, by his personal activities, teaches the disciple the principles of devotional service. Without personal service, one would go on speculating like the impersonalists and dry speculators life after life and would be unable to reach the final conclusion. By following the instructions of the bona fide spiritual master in conjunction with the principles of revealed scriptures, the student will rise to the plane of complete knowledge, which will be exhibited by development of detachment from the world of sense gratification. The mundane wranglers are surprised that one can detach himself from the world of sense gratification, and thus any attempt to be fixed in God realization appears to them to be mysticism. This detachment from the sensory world is called the *brahma-bhūta* stage of realization, the preliminary stage of transcendental devotional life (*parā bhaktiḥ*). The *brahma-bhūta* stage of life is also known as the *ātmārāma* stage, in which one is fully self-satisfied and does not hanker for the world of sense enjoyment. This stage of full satisfaction is the proper situation for understanding the transcendental knowledge of the Personality of Godhead. The *Śrīmad-Bhāgavatam* (1.2.20) affirms this:

evaṁ prasanna-manaso
bhagavad-bhakti-yogataḥ
bhagavat-tattva-vijñānaṁ
mukta-saṅgasya jāyate

Thus in the completely satisfied stage of life, exhibited by full detachment from the world of sense enjoyment as a result of performing devotional service, one can understand the science of God in the liberated stage.

In this stage of full satisfaction and detachment from the sensory world, one can know the mystery of the science of God with all its confidential intricacies, and not by grammar or academic speculation. Because Brahmā qualified himself for such reception, the Lord was pleased to disclose the purpose of *Śrīmad-Bhāgavatam.* This direct instruction by the Lord to any devotee who is detached from the world of sense gratification is possible, as stated in the *Bhagavad-gītā* (10.10):

teṣāṁ satata-yuktānāṁ
bhajatāṁ prīti-pūrvakam
dadāmi buddhi-yogaṁ taṁ
yena mām upayānti te

Unto the devotees who are constantly engaged in the Lord's transcendental loving service (*prīti-pūrvakam*), the Lord, out of His causeless mercy upon the devotee, gives direct instructions so that the devotee may make accurate progress on the path returning home, back to Godhead. One should not, therefore, try to understand these four verses of *Śrīmad-Bhāgavatam* by mental speculation. Rather, by direct perception of the Supreme Personality of Godhead, one is able to know all about His abode, Vaikuṇṭha, as was seen and experienced by Brahmājī. Such Vaikuṇṭha realization is possible by any devotee of the Lord situated in the transcendental position as a result of devotional service.

In the *Gopāla-tāpanī Upaniṣad* (*śruti*) it is said, *gopa-veśo me puruṣaḥ purastād āvirbabhuva:* the Lord appeared before Brahmā as a cowboy, that is, as the original Personality of Godhead, Lord Śrī Kṛṣṇa, Govinda, who is later described by Brahmājī in his *Brahma-saṁhitā* (5.29):

cintāmaṇi-prakara-sadmasu kalpavṛkṣa-
lakṣāvṛteṣu surabhīr abhipālayantam
lakṣmī-sahasra-śata-sambhrama-sevyamānaṁ
govindam ādi-puruṣaṁ tam ahaṁ bhajāmi

Brahmājī desires to worship the original Personality of Godhead, Lord Śrī Kṛṣṇa, who resides in the topmost Vaikuṇṭha planet, known as Goloka Vṛndāvana, where He is in the habit of keeping *surabhi* cows as a cowboy and where He is served by hundreds and thousands of goddesses of fortune (the *gopīs*) with love and respect.

Therefore Lord Śrī Kṛṣṇa is the original form of the Supreme Lord (*kṛṣṇas tu bhagavān svayam*). This is also clear from this instruction. The Supreme Personality of Godhead is Lord Kṛṣṇa, and not directly Nārāyaṇa or the *puruṣa-avatāras*, which are subsequent manifestations. Therefore *Śrīmad-Bhāgavatam* means consciousness of the Supreme Personality of Godhead Lord Śrī Kṛṣṇa, and *Śrīmad-Bhāgavatam* is the sound representation of the Lord as much as the *Bhagavad-gītā* is. Thus the conclusion is that *Śrīmad-Bhāgavatam* is the science of the Lord in which the Lord and His abode are perfectly realized.

TEXT 38

श्रीशुक उवाच
सम्प्रदिश्यैवमजनो जनानां परमेष्ठिनम् ।
पश्यतस्तस्य तद् रूपमात्मनो न्यरुणद्धरिः ॥३८॥

śrī-śuka uvāca
sampradiśyaivam ajano
janānāṁ parameṣṭhinam
paśyatas tasya tad rūpam
ātmano nyaruṇad dhariḥ

śrī-śukaḥ uvāca—Śrī Śukadeva Gosvāmī said; *sampradiśya*—fully instructing Brahmājī; *evam*—thus; *ajanaḥ*—the Supreme Lord; *janānām*—of the living entities; *parameṣṭhinam*—unto the supreme leader, Brahmā; *paśyataḥ*—while he was seeing; *tasya*—His; *tat rūpam*—that transcendental form; *ātmanaḥ*—of the Absolute; *nyaruṇat*—disappeared; *hariḥ*—the Lord, the Personality of Godhead.

TRANSLATION

Śukadeva Gosvāmī said to Mahārāja Parīkṣit: The Supreme Personality of Godhead, Hari, after being seen in His transcendental form, instructing Brahmājī, the leader of the living entities, disappeared.

PURPORT

In this verse it is clearly mentioned that the Lord is *ajanaḥ*, or the Supreme Person, and that He was showing His transcendental form (*ātmano rūpam*) to Brahmājī while instructing him in the summarization of *Śrīmad-Bhāgavatam* in four verses. He is *ajanaḥ*, or the Supreme Person, amongst *janānām*, or all persons. All living entities are individual persons, and amongst all such persons Lord Hari is supreme, as confirmed in the *śruti-mantra, nityo nityānāṁ cetanaś cetanānām.* So there is no place for impersonal features in the transcendental world as there are impersonal features in the material world. Whenever there is *cetana*, or knowledge, the personal feature comes in. In the spiritual world everything is full of knowledge, and therefore everything in the transcendental world, the land, the water, the tree, the mountain, the river, the man, the animal, the bird—everything—is of the same quality, namely *cetana*, and therefore everything there is individual and personal. *Śrīmad-Bhāgavatam* gives us this information as the supreme Vedic literature, and it was personally instructed by the Supreme Personality of Godhead to Brahmājī so that the leader of the living entities might broadcast the message to all in the universe in order to teach the supreme knowledge of *bhakti-yoga.* Brahmājī in his turn instructed Nārada, his beloved son, the same message of *Śrīmad-Bhāgavatam,* and Nārada, in his turn, taught the same to Vyāsadeva, who again taught it to Śukadeva Gosvāmī. Through Śukadeva Gosvāmī's grace and by the mercy of Mahārāja Parīkṣit we are all given *Śrīmad-Bhāgavatam* perpetually to learn the science of the Absolute Personality of Godhead, Lord Kṛṣṇa.

TEXT 39

अन्तर्हितेन्द्रियार्थाय हरये विहिताञ्जलिः ।
सर्वभूतमयो विश्वं ससर्जेदं स पूर्ववत् ॥३९॥

antarhitendriyārthāya
haraye vihitāñjaliḥ
sarva-bhūtamayo viśvaṁ
sasarjedaṁ sa pūrvavat

antarhita—on the disappearance; *indriya-arthāya*—unto the Personality of Godhead, the objective of all senses; *haraye*—unto the Lord; *vihita-añjaliḥ*—in folded hands; *sarva-bhūta*—all living entities; *mayaḥ*—full of; *viśvam*—the universe; *sasarja*—created; *idam*—this; *saḥ*—he (Brahmājī); *pūrva-vat*—exactly like before.

TRANSLATION

On the disappearance of the Supreme Personality of Godhead, Hari, who is the object of transcendental enjoyment for the senses of devotees, Brahmā, with folded hands, began to re-create the universe, full with living entities, as it was previously.

PURPORT

The Supreme Personality of Godhead, Hari, is the object for fulfilling the senses of all living entities. Illusioned by the glaring reflection of the external energy, the living entities worship the senses instead of engaging them properly in fulfilling the desires of the Supreme.

In the *Hari-bhakti-sudhodaya* (13.2) there is the following verse:

akṣṇoḥ phalaṁ tvādṛśa-darśanaṁ hi
tanoḥ phalaṁ tvādṛśa-gātra-saṅgaḥ
jihvā-phalaṁ tvādṛśa-kīrtanaṁ hi
sudurlabhā bhāgavatā hi loke

"O devotee of the Lord, the purpose of the visual sense is fulfilled simply by seeing you, and to touch your body is the fulfillment of bodily touch.

The tongue is meant for glorifying your qualities because in this world a pure devotee of the Lord is very difficult to find."

Originally the senses of the living entity were awarded for this purpose, namely to engage them in the transcendental loving service of the Lord or that of His devotees, but the conditioned souls, illusioned by the material energy, became captivated by sense enjoyment. Therefore the whole process of God consciousness is meant to rectify the conditional activities of the senses and to re-engage them in the direct service of the Lord. Lord Brahmā thus engaged his senses in the Lord by re-creating the conditioned living entities to act in the re-created universe. This material universe is thus created and annihilated by the will of the Lord. It is created to give the conditioned soul a chance to act to return home, back to Godhead, and servants like Brahmājī, Nāradajī, Vyāsajī and their company become busy with the same purpose of the Lord: to reclaim the conditioned souls from the field of sense gratification and return them to the normal stage of engaging the senses in service of the Lord. Instead of doing so, i.e. converting the actions of the senses, the impersonalists began to make the conditioned souls sense-less, and the Lord also sense-less. That is improper treatment for the conditioned souls. The diseased condition of the senses may be treated by curing the defect, but not uprooting the senses altogether. When there is some disease in the eyes, the eyes may be cured to see properly. Plucking out the eyes is no treatment. Similarly, the whole material disease is based on the process of sense gratification, and liberation from the diseased condition is re-engagement of the senses to see the beauty of the Lord, hear His glories, and act on His account. Thus Brahmājī created the universal activities again.

TEXT 40

प्रजापतिर्धर्मपतिरेकदा नियमान् यमान् ।
भद्रं प्रजानामन्विच्छन्नातिष्ठत् स्वार्थकाम्यया ।।३९।।

prajāpatir dharma-patir
ekadā niyamān yamān
bhadraṁ prajānām anvicchann
ātiṣṭhat svārtha-kāmyayā

prajā-patiḥ—the forefather of all living entities; *dharma-patiḥ*—the father of religious life; *ekadā*—once upon a time; *niyamān*—rules and regulations; *yamān*—principles of control; *bhadram*—welfare; *prajānām*—of the living beings; *anvicchan*—desiring; *ātiṣṭhat*—situated; *sva-artha*—own interest; *kāmyayā*—so desiring.

TRANSLATION

Thus once upon a time the forefather of living entities and the father of religiousness, Lord Brahmā, situated himself in acts of regulative principles, desiring self-interest for the welfare of all living entities.

PURPORT

One cannot be situated in an exalted position without having undertaken a regulative life of rules and regulations. An unrestricted life of sense gratification is animal life, and Lord Brahmā, in order to teach all concerned within the jurisdiction of his generations, taught the same principles of sense control for executing higher duties. He desired the welfare of all as servants of God, and anyone desiring the welfare of the members of his family and generations must conduct a moral, religious life. The highest life of moral principles is to become a devotee of the Lord because a pure devotee of the Lord has all the good qualities of the Lord. On the other hand, one who is not a devotee of the Lord, however qualified he may be in the mundane sense of the term, cannot be qualified with any good quality worthy of the name. The pure devotees of the Lord, like Brahmā and persons in the chain of disciplic succession, do not do anything to instruct their subordinates without acting accordingly themselves.

TEXT 41

तं नारदः प्रियतमो रिक्थादानामनुव्रतः ।
शुश्रूषमाणः शीलेन प्रश्रयेण दमेन च ॥४०॥

taṁ nāradaḥ priyatamo
rikthādānām anuvrataḥ
śuśrūṣamāṇaḥ śīlena
praśrayeṇa damena ca

tam—unto him; *nāradaḥ*—the great sage Nārada; *priyatamaḥ*—very dear; *riktha-ādānām*—of the inheritor sons; *anuvrataḥ*—very obedient; *śuśrūṣamāṇaḥ*—always ready to serve; *śīlena*—by good behavior; *praśrayeṇa*—by meekness; *damena*—by sense control; *ca*—also.

TRANSLATION

Nārada, the most dear of the inheritor sons of Brahmā, always ready to serve his father, strictly follows the instructions of his father by his mannerly behavior, meekness and sense control.

TEXT 42

मायां विविदिषन् विष्णोर्मायेशस्य महामुनिः ।
महाभागवतो राजन् पितरं पर्यतोषयत् ॥४१॥

māyāṁ vividiṣan viṣṇor
māyeśasya mahā-muniḥ
mahā-bhāgavato rājan
pitaraṁ paryatoṣayat

māyām—energies; *vividiṣan*—desiring to know; *viṣṇoḥ*—of the Personality of Godhead; *māyā-īśasya*—of the master of all energies; *mahā-muniḥ*—the great sage; *mahā-bhāgavataḥ*—the first-class devotee of the Lord; *rājan*—O King; *pitaram*—unto his father; *paryatoṣayat*—very much pleased.

TRANSLATION

Nārada very much pleased his father and desired to know all about the energies of Viṣṇu, the master of all energies, for Nārada was the greatest of all sages and greatest of all devotees, O King.

PURPORT

Lord Brahmā, being the creator of all living beings in the universe, is originally the father of several well-known sons, like Dakṣa, the *catuḥ-sanas*, and Nārada. In three departments of human knowledge disseminated by the *Vedas*, namely fruitive work (*karma-kāṇḍa*), transcendental knowledge (*jñāna-kāṇḍa*), and devotional service (*upāsanā-kāṇḍa*),

Devarṣi Nārada inherited from his father Brahmā devotional service, whereas Dakṣa inherited from his father fruitive work, and Sanaka, Sanātana, etc., inherited from their father information about *jñāna-kāṇḍa*, or transcendental knowledge. But out of them all, Nārada is described here as the most beloved son of Brahmā because of good behavior, obedience, meekness and readiness to render service unto the father. And Nārada is famous as the greatest of all sages because of his being the greatest of all devotees. Nārada is the spiritual master of many famous devotees of the Lord. He is the spiritual master of Prahlāda, Dhruva and Vyāsa, down to the forest animal hunter Kirāta. His only business is to turn everyone to the transcendental loving service of the Lord. Therefore all these features of Nārada make him the dearmost son of his father, and all this is due to Nārada's being a first-class devotee of the Lord. The devotees are always anxious to know more and more about the Supreme Lord, the master of all energies. As confirmed in the *Bhagavad-gītā* (10.9):

mac-cittā mad-gata-prāṇā
bodhayantaḥ parasparam
kathayantaś ca māṁ nityaṁ
tuṣyanti ca ramanti ca

The Supreme Lord is unlimited, and His energies are also unlimited. No one can know them completely. Brahmājī, being the greatest living entity within this universe and being directly instructed by the Lord, must know more than anyone within this universe, although such knowledge may not be complete. Thus it is the duty of everyone to ask about the unlimited Lord from the spiritual master in the disciplic succession of Brahmā, which descends from Nārada to Vyāsa, from Vyāsa to Śukadeva and so on.

TEXT 43

तुष्टं निशाम्य पितरं लोकानां प्रपितामहम् ।
देवर्षिः परिपप्रच्छ भवान् यन्मानुपृच्छति ॥४३॥

tuṣṭaṁ niśāmya pitaraṁ
lokānāṁ prapitāmaham

devarṣiḥ paripapraccha
bhavān yan mānupṛcchati

tuṣṭam—satisfied; *niśāmya*—after seeing; *pitaram*—the father; *lokānām*—of the whole universe; *prapitāmaham*—the great-grandfather; *devarṣiḥ*—the great sage Nārada; *paripapraccha*—inquired; *bhavān*—yourself; *yat*—as it is; *mā*—from me; *anupṛcchati*—inquiring.

TRANSLATION

The great sage Nārada also inquired in detail from his father, Brahmā, the great-grandfather of all the universe, after seeing him well satisfied.

PURPORT

The process of understanding spiritual or transcendental knowledge from the realized person is not exactly like asking an ordinary question from the schoolmaster. The schoolmasters in the modern days are paid agents for giving some information, but the spiritual master is not a paid agent. Nor can he impart instruction without being authorized. In the *Bhagavad-gītā* (4.34), the process of understanding transcendental knowledge is directed as follows:

tad viddhi praṇipātena
paripraśnena sevayā
upadekṣyanti te jñānaṁ
jñāninas tattva-darśinaḥ

Arjuna was advised to receive transcendental knowledge from the realized person by surrender, questions and service. Receiving transcendental knowledge is not like exchanging dollars; such knowledge has to be received by service to the spiritual master. As Brahmājī received the knowledge directly from the Lord by satisfying Him fully, similarly one has to receive the transcendental knowledge from the spiritual master by satisfying him. The spiritual master's satisfaction is the means of assimilating transcendental knowledge. One cannot understand transcendental knowledge simply by becoming a grammarian. The *Vedas* declare (*Śvetāśvatara Upaniṣad* 6.23):

yasya deve parā bhaktir
yathā deve tathā gurau
tasyaite kathitā hy arthāḥ
prakāśante mahātmanaḥ

"Only unto one who has unflinching devotion to the Lord and to the spiritual master does transcendental knowledge become automatically revealed." Such relationship between the disciple and the spiritual master is eternal. One who is now the disciple is the next spiritual master. And one cannot be a bona fide and authorized spiritual master unless one has been strictly obedient to his spiritual master. Brahmājī, as a disciple of the Supreme Lord, received the real knowledge and imparted it to his dear disciple Nārada, and similarly Nārada, as spiritual master, handed over this knowledge to Vyāsa and so on. Therefore the so-called formal spiritual master and disciple are not facsimiles of Brahmā and Nārada or Nārada and Vyāsa. The relationship between Brahmā and Nārada is reality, while the so-called formality is the relation between the cheater and cheated. It is clearly mentioned herewith that Nārada is not only well behaved, meek and obedient, but also self-controlled. One who is not self-controlled, specifically in sex life, can become neither a disciple nor a spiritual master. One must have disciplinary training in controlling speaking, anger, the tongue, the mind, the belly and the genitals. One who has controlled the particular senses mentioned above is called a *gosvāmī.* Without becoming a *gosvāmī* one can become neither a disciple nor a spiritual master. The so-called spiritual master without sense control is certainly the cheater, and the disciple of such a so-called spiritual master is the cheated.

One should not think of Brahmājī as a dead great-grandfather, as we have experience on this planet. He is the oldest great-grandfather, and he is still living, and Nārada is also living. The age of the inhabitants of the Brahmaloka planet is mentioned in the *Bhagavad-gītā.* The inhabitants of this small planet earth can hardly calculate even the duration of one day of Brahmā.

TEXT 44

तस्मा इदं भागवतं पुराणं दशलक्षणम् ।
प्रोक्तं भगवता प्राह प्रीतः पुत्राय भूतकृत् ॥४४॥

tasmā idaṁ bhāgavataṁ
purāṇaṃ daśa-lakṣaṇam
proktaṁ bhagavatā prāha
prītaḥ putrāya bhūta-kṛt

tasmai—thereupon; *idam*—this; *bhāgavatam*—the glories of the Lord or the science of the Lord; *purāṇam*—Vedic supplement; *daśa-lakṣaṇam*—ten characteristics; *proktam*—described; *bhagavatā*—by the Personality of Godhead; *prāha*—said; *prītaḥ*—in satisfaction; *putrāya*—unto the son; *bhūta-kṛt*—the creator of the universe.

TRANSLATION

Thereupon the supplementary Vedic literature, Śrīmad-Bhāgavatam, which was described by the Personality of Godhead and which contains ten characteristics, was told with satisfaction by the father [Brahmā] to his son Nārada.

PURPORT

Although the *Śrīmad-Bhāgavatam* was spoken in four verses, it had ten characteristics, which will be explained in the next chapter. In the four verses it is first said that the Lord existed before the creation, and thus the beginning of the *Śrīmad-Bhāgavatam* includes the *Vedānta* aphorism *janmādy asya. Janmādy asya* is the beginning, yet the four verses in which it is said that the Lord is the root of everything that be, beginning from the creation up to the supreme abode of the Lord, naturally explain the ten characteristics. One should not misunderstand by wrong interpretations that the Lord spoke only four verses and that therefore all the rest of the 17,994 verses are useless. The ten characteristics, as will be explained in the next chapter, require so many verses just to explain them properly. Brahmājī had also advised Nārada previously that he should expand the idea he had heard from Brahmājī. Śrī Caitanya Mahāprabhu instructed this to Śrīla Rūpa Gosvāmī in a nutshell, but the disciple Rūpa Gosvāmī expanded this very elaborately, and the same subject was further expanded by Jīva Gosvāmī and even further by Śrī Viśvanātha Cakravartī Ṭhākura. We are just trying to follow in the footsteps of all these authorities. So *Śrīmad-Bhāgavatam* is not like ordinary fiction or mundane literature. It is unlimited in strength, and however one may expand it according to one's own ability, *Bhāgavatam* still cannot be finished by such expansion. *Śrīmad-Bhāgavatam*, being the sound representation of the Lord, is simultaneously explained in four verses and in four billion verses all the same, inasmuch as the Lord is smaller than the atom and bigger than the unlimited sky. Such is the potency of *Śrīmad-Bhāgavatam*.

TEXT 45

नारदः प्राह मुनये सरस्वत्यास्तटे नृप ।
ध्यायते ब्रह्म परमं व्यासायामिततेजसे ॥४५॥

nāradaḥ prāha munaye
sarasvatyās taṭe nṛpa
dhyāyate brahma paramaṁ
vyāsāyāmita-tejase

nāradaḥ—the great sage Nārada; *prāha*—instructed; *munaye*—unto the great sage; *sarasvatyāḥ*—of the River Sarasvatī; *taṭe*—on the bank; *nṛpa*—O King; *dhyāyate*—unto the meditative; *brahma*—Absolute Truth; *paramam*—the Supreme; *vyāsāya*—unto Śrīla Vyāsadeva; *amita*—unlimited; *tejase*—unto the powerful.

TRANSLATION

In succession, O King, the great sage Nārada instructed Śrīmad-Bhāgavatam unto the unlimitedly powerful Vyāsadeva, who meditated in devotional service upon the Supreme Personality of Godhead, the Absolute Truth, on the bank of the River Sarasvatī.

PURPORT

In the Fifth Chapter of the First Canto of *Śrīmad-Bhāgavatam*, Nārada instructed the great sage Vyāsadeva as follows:

atho mahā-bhāga bhavān amogha-dṛk
śuci-śravāḥ satya-rato dhṛta-vrataḥ

urukramasyākhila-bandha-muktaye
samādhinānusmara tad viceṣṭitam

"O greatly fortunate, pious philosopher, your name and fame are universal, and you are fixed in the Absolute Truth with spotless character and infallible vision. I ask you to meditate upon the activities of the Personality of Godhead, whose activities are unparalleled."

So in the disciplic succession of the Brahma-sampradāya, the practice of *yoga* meditation is not neglected. But because the devotees are *bhakti-yogīs*, they do not undertake the trouble to meditate upon the impersonal Brahman; as indicated here, they meditate on *brahma paramam*, or the Supreme Brahman. Brahman realization begins from the impersonal effulgence, but by further progress of such meditation, manifestation of the Supreme Soul, Paramātmā realization, takes place. And progressing further, realization of the Supreme Personality of Godhead is fixed. Śrī Nārada Muni, as the spiritual master of Vyāsadeva, knew very well the position of Vyāsadeva, and thus he certified the qualities of Śrīla Vyāsadeva as fixed in the Absolute Truth with great vow, etc. Nārada advised meditation upon the transcendental activities of the Lord. Impersonal Brahman has no activities, but the Personality of Godhead has many activities, and all such activities are transcendental, without any tinge of material quality. If the activities of the Supreme Brahman were material activities, then Nārada would not have advised Vyāsadeva to meditate upon them. And the *paraṁ brahma* is Lord Śrī Kṛṣṇa, as confirmed in the *Bhagavad-gītā*. In the Tenth Chapter of the *Bhagavad-gītā*, when Arjuna realized the factual position of Lord Kṛṣṇa, he addressed Lord Kṛṣṇa in the following words:

paraṁ brahma paraṁ dhāma
pavitraṁ paramaṁ bhavān
puruṣaṁ śāśvataṁ divyam
ādi-devam ajaṁ vibhum

āhus tvām ṛṣayaḥ sarve
devarṣir nāradas tathā
asito devalo vyāsaḥ
svayaṁ caiva bravīṣi me

Arjuna summarized the purpose of the *Bhagavad-gītā* by his realization of Lord Śrī Kṛṣṇa and thus said, "My dear Personality of Godhead, You are the Supreme Absolute Truth, the Original Person in the eternal form of bliss and knowledge, and this is confirmed by Nārada, Asita, Devala and Vyāsadeva, and, above all, Your personal self has also confirmed it." (Bg. 10.12–13)

When Vyāsadeva fixed his mind in meditation, he did it in *bhakti-yoga* trance and actually saw the Supreme Person with *māyā*, the illusory energy, in contraposition. As we have discussed before, the Lord's *māyā*, or illusion, is also a representation because *māyā* has no existence without the Lord. Darkness is not independent of light. Without light, no one can experience the contraposition of darkness. However, this *māyā*, or illusion, cannot overcome the Supreme Personality of Godhead, but stands apart from Him (*apāśrayam*).

Therefore, perfection of meditation is realization of the Personality of Godhead along with His transcendental activities. Meditation on the impersonal Brahman is a troublesome business for the meditator, as confirmed in the *Bhagavad-gītā* (12.5): *kleśo 'dhikataras teṣām avyaktāsakta-cetasām.*

TEXT 46

यदुताहं त्वया पृष्टो वैराजात् पुरुषादिदम् ।
यथासीत्तदुपाख्यास्ते प्रश्नानन्यांश्च कृत्स्नशः ॥४६॥

yad utāhaṁ tvayā pṛṣṭo
vairājāt puruṣād idam
yathāsīt tad upākhyāste
praśnān anyāṁś ca kṛtsnaśaḥ

yat—what; *uta*—is, however; *aham*—I; *tvayā*—by you; *pṛṣṭaḥ*—I am asked; *vairājāt*—from the universal form; *puruṣāt*—from the Personality of Godhead; *idam*—this world; *yathā*—as it; *āsīt*—was; *tat*—that; *upākhyāste*—I shall explain; *praśnān*—all thc questions; *anyān*—others; *ca*—as well as; *kṛtsnaśaḥ*—in great detail.

TRANSLATION

O King, your questions as to how the universe became manifested from the gigantic form of the Personality of Godhead,

as well as other questions, I shall answer in detail by explanation of the four verses already mentioned.

PURPORT

As stated in the beginning of the *Śrīmad-Bhāgavatam*, this great transcendental literature is the ripened fruit of the tree of Vedic knowledge, and therefore all questions that can be humanly possible regarding the universal affairs, beginning from its creation, are all answered in the *Śrīmad-Bhāgavatam*. The answers depend only on the qualification of the person who explains them. The ten divisions of *Śrīmad-Bhāgavatam*, as explained by the great speaker Śrīla Śukadeva Gosvāmī, are the limitation of all questions, and intelligent persons will derive all intellectual benefits from them by proper utilization.

Thus end the Bhaktivedanta purports of the Second Canto, Ninth Chapter, of the Śrīmad-Bhāgavatam, *entitled "Answers by Citing the Lord's Version."*

CHAPTER TEN

Bhāgavatam Is the Answer to All Questions

TEXT 1

श्रीशुक उवाच
अत्र सर्गो विसर्गश्च स्थानं पोषणमूतयः ।
मन्वन्तरेशानुकथा निरोधो मुक्तिराश्रयः ॥ १ ॥

śrī-śuka uvāca
atra sargo visargaś ca
sthānaṁ poṣaṇam ūtayaḥ
manvantareśānukathā
nirodho muktir āśrayaḥ

śrī-śukaḥ uvāca—Śrī Śukadeva Gosvāmī said; *atra*—in this *Śrīmad-Bhāgavatam; sargaḥ*—statement of the creation of the universe; *visargaḥ*—statement of subcreation; *ca*—also; *sthānam*—the planetary systems; *poṣaṇam*—protection; *ūtayaḥ*—the creative impetus; *manvantara*—changes of Manus; *īśa-anukathāḥ*—the science of God; *nirodhaḥ*—going back home, back to Godhead; *muktiḥ*—liberation; *āśrayaḥ*—the *summum bonum.*

TRANSLATION

Śrī Śukadeva Gosvāmī said: In the Śrīmad-Bhāgavatam there are ten divisions of statements regarding the following: the creation of the universe, subcreation, planetary systems, protection by the Lord, the creative impetus, the change of Manus, the science of God, returning home, back to Godhead, liberation, and the summum bonum.

TEXT 2

दशमस्य विशुद्ध्यर्थं नवानामिह लक्षणम् ।
वर्णयन्ति महात्मानः श्रुतेनार्थेन चाञ्जसा ॥ २ ॥

daśamasya viśuddhy-arthaṁ
navānām iha lakṣaṇam
varṇayanti mahātmānaḥ
śrutenārthena cāñjasā

daśamasya—of the *summum bonum; viśuddhi*—isolation; *artham*—purpose; *navānām*—of the other nine; *iha*—in this *Śrīmad-Bhāgavatam; lakṣaṇam*—symptoms; *varṇayanti*—they describe; *mahā-ātmānaḥ*—the great sages; *śrutena*—by Vedic evidences; *arthena*—by direct explanation; *ca*—and; *añjasā*—summarily.

TRANSLATION

To isolate the transcendence of the summum bonum, the symptoms of the rest are described sometimes by Vedic inference, sometimes by direct explanation, and sometimes by summary explanations given by the great sages.

TEXT 3

भूतमात्रेन्द्रियधियां जन्म सर्ग उदाहृतः ।
ब्रह्मणो गुणवैषम्याद्विसर्गः पौरुषः स्मृतः ॥ ३ ॥

bhūta-mātrendriya-dhiyāṁ
janma sarga udāhṛtaḥ
brahmaṇo guṇa-vaiṣamyād
visargaḥ pauruṣaḥ smṛtaḥ

bhūta—the five gross elements (the sky, etc.); *mātrā*—objects perceived by the senses; *indriya*—the senses; *dhiyām*—of the mind; *janma*—creation; *sargaḥ*—manifestation; *udāhṛtaḥ*—is called the creation; *brahmaṇaḥ*—of Brahmā, the first *puruṣa; guṇa-vaiṣamyāt*—by interaction of the three modes of nature; *visargaḥ*—re-creation; *pauruṣaḥ*—resultant activities; *smṛtaḥ*—it is so known.

TRANSLATION

The elementary creation of sixteen items of matter—namely the five elements [fire, water, land, air and sky], sound, form, taste, smell, touch, and the eyes, ears, nose, tongue, skin and mind—is known as sarga, whereas subsequent resultant interaction of the modes of material nature is called visarga.

PURPORT

In order to explain the ten divisional symptoms of the *Śrīmad-Bhāgavatam*, there are seven continuous verses. The first of these under reference pertains to the sixteen elementary manifestations of earth, water, etc., with material ego composed of material intelligence and mind. The subsequent creation is a result of the reactions of the above-mentioned sixteen energies of the first *puruṣa*, the Mahā-Viṣṇu incarnation of Govinda, as later explained by Brahmā in his treatise *Brahma-saṁhitā* (5.47) as follows:

yaḥ kāraṇārṇava-jale bhajati sma yoga-
nidrām ananta-jagadaṇḍa-saroma-kūpaḥ
ādhāra-śaktim avalambya parāṁ sva-mūrtiṁ
govindam ādi-puruṣaṁ tam ahaṁ bhajāmi

The first *puruṣa* incarnation of Govinda, Lord Kṛṣṇa, known as the Mahā-Viṣṇu, goes into a *yoga-nidrā* mystic sleep, and the innumerable universes are situated in potency in each and every hair hole of His transcendental body.

As mentioned in the previous verse, *śrutena* (or with reference to the Vedic conclusions), the creation is made possible from the Supreme Personality of Godhead directly by manifestation of His particular energies. Without such a Vedic reference, the creation appears to be a product of material nature. This conclusion comes from a poor fund of knowledge. From Vedic reference it is concluded that the origin of all energies (namely internal, external and marginal) is the Supreme Personality of Godhead. And as explained hereinbefore, the illusory conclusion is that creation is made by the inert material nature. The Vedic conclusion is transcendental light, whereas the non-Vedic conclusion is material darkness. The internal potency of the Supreme Lord is identical with the

Supreme Lord, and the external potency is enlivened in contact with the internal potency. The parts and parcels of the internal potency which react in contact with the external potency are called the marginal potency, or the living entities.

Thus the original creation is directly from the Supreme Personality of Godhead, or Parambrahman, and the secondary creation, as a reactionary result of the original ingredients, is made by Brahmā. Thus the activities of the whole universe are started.

TEXT 4

स्थितिर्वैकुण्ठविजयः पोषणं तदनुग्रहः ।
मन्वन्तराणि सद्धर्म ऊतयः कर्मवासनाः ॥ ४ ॥

sthitir vaikuṇṭha-vijayaḥ
poṣaṇaṁ tad-anugrahaḥ
manvantarāṇi sad-dharma
ūtayaḥ karma-vāsanāḥ

sthitiḥ—the right situation; *vaikuṇṭha-vijayaḥ*—the victory of the Lord of Vaikuṇṭha; *poṣaṇam*—maintenance; *tat-anugrahaḥ*—His causeless mercy; *manvantarāṇi*—the reign of the Manus; *sat-dharmaḥ*—perfect occupational duty; *ūtayaḥ*—impetus to work; *karma-vāsanāḥ*—desire for fruitive work.

TRANSLATION

The right situation for the living entities is to obey the laws of the Lord and thus be in perfect peace of mind under the protection of the Supreme Personality of Godhead. The Manus and their laws are meant to give right direction in life. The impetus for activity is the desire for fruitive work.

PURPORT

This material world is created, maintained for some time, and again annihilated by the will of the Lord. The ingredients for creation and the subordinate creator, Brahmā, are first created by Lord Viṣṇu in His first and second incarnations. The first *puruṣa* incarnation is Mahā-Viṣṇu, and the second *puruṣa* incarnation is the Garbhodakaśāyī Viṣṇu, from whom Brahmā is created. The third *puruṣa-avatāra* is the Kṣīrodakaśāyī Viṣṇu, who lives as the Supersoul of everything in the universe and maintains the creation generated by Brahmā. Śiva is one of the many sons of Brahmā, and he annihilates the creation. Therefore the original creator of the universe is Viṣṇu, and He is also the maintainer of the created beings by His causeless mercy. As such, it is the duty of all conditioned souls to acknowledge the victory of the Lord and thus become pure devotees and live peacefully in this world, where miseries and dangers are always in existence. The conditioned souls, who take this material creation as the place for satisfaction of the senses and thus are illusioned by the external energy of Viṣṇu, remain again to be subjected to the laws of material nature, creation and destruction.

In the *Bhagavad-gītā* it is said that beginning from the topmost planet of this universe down to the lowest planet, Pātālaloka, all are destructible, and the conditioned souls may travel in space either by good or bad work or by modern spacecraft, but they are sure to die everywhere, although the duration of life in different planets is different. The only means to attain eternal life is to go back home, back to Godhead, where there is no more rebirth as in the material planets. The conditioned souls, being unaware of this very simple fact because of forgetting their relationship with the Lord of Vaikuṇṭha, try to plan out a permanent life in this material world. Being illusioned by the external energy, they thus become engaged in various types of economic and religious development, forgetting that they are meant for going back home, back to Godhead. This forgetfulness is so strong due to the influence of *māyā* that the conditioned souls do not at all want to go back to Godhead. By sense enjoyment they become victims of birth and death repeatedly and thus spoil human lives which are chances for going back to Viṣṇu. The directive scriptures made by the Manus in different ages and millenniums are called *sad-dharma*, good guidance for the human beings, who should take advantage of all the revealed scriptures for their own interest, to make life's successful termination. The creation is not false, but it is a temporary manifestation just to give a chance for the conditioned souls to go back to Godhead. The desire to go back to Godhead and functions performed in that direction form the right path of work. When such a regulative path is accepted, the Lord gives all protection to His devotees by His causeless mercy, while the nondevotees risk their own activities to bind themselves in a chain of fruitive reactions. The word *sad-dharma* is significant in this connection. *Sad-dharma*, or duty performed for going back to Godhead and thus becoming His unalloyed devotee, is the only pious activity; all others may pretend to be pious, but actually they are not. It is for this reason only that the Lord advises in the *Bhagavad-gītā* that one give up all so-called religious activities and completely engage in the devotional service of the Lord to become free from all anxieties due to the dangerous life of material existence. To work situated in *sad-dharma* is the right direction of life. One's aim of life should be to go back home, back to Godhead, and not be subjected to repeated births and deaths in the material world by getting good or bad bodies for temporary existence. Herein lies the intelligence of human life, and one should desire the activities of life in that way.

TEXT 5

अवतारानुचरितं हरेश्चास्यानुवर्तिनाम् ।
पुंसामीशकथाः प्रोक्ता नानाख्यानोपबृंहिताः ॥ ५ ॥

avatārānucaritaṁ
hareś cāsyānuvartinām
puṁsām īśa-kathāḥ proktā
nānākhyānopabṛṁhitāḥ

avatāra—incarnation of Godhead; *anucaritam*—activities; *hareḥ*—of the Personality of Godhead; *ca*—also; *asya*—of His; *anuvartinām*—followers; *puṁsām*—of the persons; *īśa-kathāḥ*—the science of God; *proktāḥ*—is said; *nānā*—various; *ākhyāna*—narrations; *upabṛṁhitāḥ*—described.

TRANSLATION

The science of God describes the incarnations of the Personality of Godhead and His different activities together with the activities of His great devotees.

PURPORT

During the course of the existence of the cosmic manifestation, the chronology of history is created, recording the activities of the living entities. People in general have a tendency to learn the history and narrations of different men and times, but due to a lack of knowledge in the science of Godhead, they are not apt to study the history of the incarnations of the Personality of Godhead. It should always be remembered that the material creation is created for the salvation of the conditioned souls. The merciful Lord, out of His causeless mercy, descends to various planets in the material world and acts for the salvation of the conditioned souls. That makes the history and narrations worth reading. *Śrīmad-Bhāgavatam* offers such transcendental topics of the Lord in relationship with great devotees. Therefore the topics of the devotees and the Lord are to be given respectful aural reception.

TEXT 6

निरोधोऽस्यानुशयनमात्मनः सह शक्तिभिः ।
मुक्तिर्हित्वान्यथारूपं स्वरूपेण व्यवस्थितिः ॥ ६ ॥

nirodho 'syānuśayanam
ātmanaḥ saha śaktibhiḥ
muktir hitvānyathā rūpaṁ
sva-rūpeṇa vyavasthitiḥ

nirodhaḥ—the winding up of the cosmic manifestation; *asya*—of His; *anuśayanam*—the lying down of the *puruṣa* incarnation Mahā-Viṣṇu in mystic slumber; *ātmanaḥ*—of the living entities; *saha*—along with; *śaktibhiḥ*—with the energies; *muktiḥ*—liberation; *hitvā*—giving up; *anyathā*—otherwise; *rūpam*—form; *sva-rūpeṇa*—in constitutional form; *vyavasthitiḥ*—permanent situation.

TRANSLATION

The merging of the living entity, along with his conditional living tendency, with the mystic lying down of the Mahā-Viṣṇu is called the winding up of the cosmic manifestation. Liberation is

the permanent situation of the form of the living entity after he gives up the changeable gross and subtle material bodies.

PURPORT

As we have discussed several times, there are two types of living entities. Most of them are ever liberated, or *nitya-muktas,* while some of them are ever conditioned. The ever-conditioned souls are apt to develop a mentality of lording over the material nature, and therefore the material cosmic creation is manifested to give the ever-conditioned souls two kinds of facilities. One facility is that the conditioned soul can act according to his tendency to lord it over the cosmic manifestation, and the other facility gives the conditioned soul a chance to come back to Godhead. So after the winding up of the cosmic manifestation, most of the conditioned souls merge into the existence of the Mahā-Viṣṇu Personality of Godhead, lying in His mystic slumber, to be created again in the next creation. But some of the conditioned souls, who follow the transcendental sound in the form of Vedic literatures and are thus able to go back to Godhead, attain spiritual and original bodies after quitting the conditional gross and subtle material bodies. The material conditional bodies develop out of the living entities' forgetfulness of their relationship with Godhead, and during the course of the cosmic manifestation, the conditioned souls are given a chance to revive their original status of life with the help of revealed scriptures, so mercifully compiled by the Lord in His different incarnations. Reading or hearing of such transcendental literatures helps one become liberated even in the conditional state of material existence. All the Vedic literatures aim at devotional service to the Personality of Godhead, and as soon as one is fixed upon this point, he at once becomes liberated from conditional life. The material gross and subtle forms are simply due to the conditioned soul's ignorance and as soon as he is fixed in the devotional service of the Lord, he becomes eligible to be freed from the conditioned state. This devotional service is transcendental attraction for the Supreme on account of His being the source of all pleasing humors. Everyone is after some pleasure of humor for enjoyment, but does not know the supreme source of all attraction (*raso vai saḥ rasaṁ hy evāyaṁ labdhvānandī bhavati*). The Vedic hymns inform everyone about the supreme source of all pleasure;

the unlimited fountainhead of all pleasure is the Personality of Godhead, and one who is fortunate enough to get this information through transcendental literatures like *Śrīmad-Bhāgavatam* becomes permanently liberated to occupy his proper place in the kingdom of God.

TEXT 7

आभासश्च निरोधश्च यतोऽस्त्यध्यवसीयते ।
स आश्रयः परं ब्रह्म परमात्मेति शब्द्यते ॥ ७ ॥

ābhāsaś ca nirodhaś ca
yato 'sty adhyavasīyate
sa āśrayaḥ paraṁ brahma
paramātmeti śabdyate

ābhāsaḥ—the cosmic manifestation; *ca*—and; *nirodhaḥ*—and its winding up; *ca*—also; *yataḥ*—from the source; *asti*—is; *adhyavasīyate*—become manifested; *saḥ*—He; *āśrayaḥ*—reservoir; *param*—the Supreme; *brahma*—Being; *paramātmā*—the Supersoul; *iti*—thus; *śabdyate*—called.

TRANSLATION

The supreme one who is celebrated as the Supreme Being or the Supreme Soul is the supreme source of the cosmic manifestation as well as its reservoir and winding up. Thus He is the Supreme Fountainhead, the Absolute Truth.

PURPORT

Synonyms for the supreme source of all energies, as explained in the very beginning of the *Śrīmad-Bhāgavatam*, are *janmādy asya yataḥ, vadanti tat tattva-vidas tattvaṁ yaj jñānam advayam/ brahmeti paramātmeti bhagavān iti śabdyate*, called Parambrahma, Paramātmā or Bhagavān. The word *iti* used here in this verse completes the synonyms and thus indicates Bhagavān. This will be further explained in the later verses, but this Bhagavān ultimately means Lord Kṛṣṇa because the *Śrīmad-Bhāgavatam* has already accepted the Supreme Personality of

Godhead as Kṛṣṇa. *Kṛṣṇas tu bhagavān svayam.* The original source of all energies, or the *summum bonum,* is the Absolute Truth, which is called Parambrahma, etc., and Bhagavān is the last word of the Absolute Truth. But even with the synonyms for Bhagavān, such as Nārāyaṇa, Viṣṇu and Puruṣa, the last word is Kṛṣṇa, as confirmed in the *Bhagavad-gītā: ahaṁ sarvasya prabhavo mattaḥ sarvaṁ pravartate,* etc. Besides that, the *Śrīmad-Bhāgavatam* is the representation of Lord Kṛṣṇa as a sound incarnation of the Lord.

kṛṣṇe sva-dhāmopagate
dharma-jñānādibhiḥ saha
kalau naṣṭa-dṛśām eṣaḥ
purāṇārko 'dhunoditaḥ
(*Bhāg.* 1.3.43)

Thus by general conclusion Lord Kṛṣṇa is the ultimate source of all energies, and the word Kṛṣṇa means that. And to explain Kṛṣṇa or the science of Kṛṣṇa, the *Śrīmad-Bhāgavatam* has been prepared. In the First Canto of *Śrīmad-Bhāgavatam* this truth is indicated in the questions and answers by Sūta Gosvāmī and great sages like Śaunaka, and in the First and Second Chapters of the canto this is explained. In the Third Chapter this subject is more explicit, and in the Fourth Chapter even more explicit. In the Second Canto the Absolute Truth as the Personality of Godhead is further emphasized, and the indication is the Supreme Lord Kṛṣṇa. The summary of *Śrīmad-Bhāgavatam* in four verses, as we have already discussed, is succinct. This Supreme Personality of Godhead in the ultimate issue is confirmed by Brahmā in his *Brahma-saṁhitā* as *īśvaraḥ paramaḥ kṛṣṇaḥ sac-cid-ānanda-vigrahaḥ.* So it is concluded in the Third Canto of the *Śrīmad-Bhāgavatam.* The complete subject matter is elaborately explained in the Tenth and Eleventh Cantos of the *Śrīmad-Bhāgavatam.* In the matter of the changes of the Manus or *manvantaras,* such as the Svāyambhuva-*manvantara* and Cākṣuṣa-*manvantara,* as they are discussed in the Third, Fourth, Fifth, Sixth and Seventh Cantos of *Śrīmad-Bhāgavatam,* Lord Kṛṣṇa is indicated. In the Eighth Canto the Vaivasvata-*manvantara* explains the same subject indirectly, and in the Ninth Canto the same purport is there. In the Twelfth Canto the same is further explained, specifically regarding the different incarnations of the Lord. Thus it is concluded by studying the complete *Śrīmad-Bhāgavatam* that Lord Śrī Kṛṣṇa is the ultimate *summum bonum*, or the ultimate source of all energy. And according to the grades of worshipers, the indications of the nomenclature may be differently explained as Nārāyaṇa, Brahmā, Paramātmā, etc.

TEXT 8

योऽध्यात्मिकोऽयं पुरुषः सोऽसावेवाधिदैविकः ।
यस्तत्रोभयविच्छेदः पुरुषो ह्याधिभौतिकः ॥ ८ ॥

yo 'dhyātmiko 'yaṁ puruṣaḥ
so 'sāv evādhidaivikaḥ
yas tatrobhaya-vicchedaḥ
puruṣo hy ādhibhautikaḥ

yaḥ—one who; *adhyātmikaḥ*—is possessed of the sense organs; *ayam*—this; *puruṣaḥ*—personality; *saḥ*—he; *asau*—that; *eva*—also; *adhidaivikaḥ*—controlling deity; *yaḥ*—that which; *tatra*—there; *ubhaya*—of both; *vicchedaḥ*—separation; *puruṣaḥ*—person; *hi*—for; *ādhibhautikaḥ*—the visible body or the embodied living entity.

TRANSLATION

The individual person possessing different instruments of senses is called the adhyātmic person, and the individual controlling deity of the senses is called adhidaivic. The embodiment seen on the eyeballs is called the adhibhautic person.

PURPORT

The supreme controlling *summum bonum* is the Personality of Godhead in His plenary portion of Paramātmā, or the Supersoul manifestation. In the *Bhagavad-gītā* (10.42) it is said:

athavā bahunaitena
kiṁ jñātena tavārjuna
viṣṭabhyāham idaṁ kṛtsnam
ekāṁśena sthito jagat

All the controlling deities like Viṣṇu, Brahmā and Śiva are different manifestations of the Paramātmā feature of the Supreme Personality of Godhead Śrī Kṛṣṇa, who exhibits himself in such manners by entering into each and every universe generated from Him. But still apparently there are divisions of the controller and controlled. For example, in the food-controlling department the controller of food is a person made of the same ingredients as the person who is controlled. Similarly, each and every individual in the material world is controlled by the higher demigods. For example, we have our senses, but the senses are controlled by superior controlling deities. We cannot see without light, and the supreme controller of light is the sun. The sun-god is in the sun planet, and we, the individual human beings or any other being on this earth, are all controlled by the sun-god as far as our eyes are concerned. Similarly, all the senses we have are controlled by the superior demigods, who are also as much living entities as we are, but one is empowered while the other is controlled. The controlled living entity is called the adhyātmic person, and the controller is called the adhidaivic person. All these positions in the material world are due to different fruitive activities. Any individual living being can become the sun-god or even Brahmā or any other god in the upper planetary system by a higher grade of pious work, and similarly one becomes controlled by the higher demigods by lower grades of fruitive activities. So every individual living entity is subject to the supreme control of the Paramātmā, who puts everyone in different positions of the controller and the controlled.

That which distinguishes the controller and controlled, i.e. the material body, is called the adhibhautic *puruṣa.* The body is sometimes called *puruṣa,* as confirmed in the *Vedas* in the following hymn: *sa vā eṣa puruṣo 'nna-rasamayaḥ.* This body is called the *anna-rasa* embodiment. This body depends on food. The living entity which is embodied does not eat anything, however, because the owner is spirit in essence. The material body requires replacement of matter for the wearing and tearing of the mechanical body. Therefore the distinction between the individual living entity and controlling planetary deities is in the *anna-rasamaya* body. The sun may have a gigantic body, and the man may have a smaller body, but all these visible bodies are made of matter; nonetheless, the sun-god and the individual person, who are related as the controller and the controlled, are the same spiritual parts and parcels of the Supreme Being, and it is the Supreme Being who places different parts and parcels in different positions. And thus the conclusion is that the Supreme Person is the shelter of all.

TEXT 9

एकमेकतराभावे यदा नोपलभामहे ।
त्रितयं तत्र यो वेद स आत्मा स्वाश्रयाश्रयः ॥ ९ ॥

ekam ekatarābhāve
yadā nopalabhāmahe
tritayaṁ tatra yo veda
sa ātmā svāśrayāśrayaḥ

ekam—one; *ekatara*—another; *abhāve*—in the absence of; *yadā*—because; *na*—does not; *upalabhāmahe*—perceptible; *tritayam*—in three stages; *tatra*—there; *yaḥ*—the one; *veda*—who knows; *saḥ*—he; *ātmā*—the Supersoul; *sva*—own; *āśraya*—shelter; *āśrayaḥ*—of the shelter.

TRANSLATION

All three of the above-mentioned stages of different living entities are interdependent. In the absence of one, another is not understood. But the Supreme Being who sees every one of them as the shelter of the shelter is independent of all, and therefore He is the supreme shelter.

PURPORT

There are innumerable living entities, one dependent on the other in the relationship of the controlled and the controller. But without the medium of perception, no one can know or understand who is the controlled and who is the controller. For example, the sun controls the power of our vision, we can see the sun because the sun has its body, and the sunlight is useful only because we have eyes. Without our having eyes, the sunlight is useless, and without sunlight the eyes are useless. Thus they are interdependent, and none of them is independent. Therefore the natural question arises concerning who made them interdependent. The one who has made such a relationship of interdependence must be ultimately completely independent. As stated in the beginning of the *Śrīmad-Bhāgavatam,* the ultimate source of all interdependent objectives is the complete independent subject. This ultimate source of all interdependence is the Supreme Truth or Paramātmā, the Supersoul, who is not dependent on anything else. He is *svāśrayāśrayaḥ.* He is only dependent on His self, and thus He is the supreme shelter of everything. Although Paramātmā and Brahman are subordinate to Bhagavān, because Bhagavān is Puruṣottama or the Superperson, He is the source of the Supersoul also. In the *Bhagavad-gītā* (15.18) Lord Kṛṣṇa says that He is the Puruṣottama and the source of everything, and thus it is concluded that Śrī Kṛṣṇa is the ultimate source and shelter of all entities, including the Supersoul and Supreme Brahman. Even accepting that there is no difference between the Supersoul and the individual soul, the individual soul is dependent on the Supersoul for being liberated from the illusion of material energy. The individual is under the clutches of illusory energy, and therefore although qualitatively one with the Supersoul, he is under the illusion of identifying himself with matter. And to get out of this illusory conception of factual life, the individual soul has to depend on the Supersoul to be recognized as one with Him. In that sense also the Supersoul is the supreme shelter. And there is no doubt about it.

The individual living entity, the *jīva,* is always dependent on the Supersoul, Paramātmā, because the individual soul forgets his spiritual identity whereas the Supersoul, Paramātmā, does not forget His transcendental position. In the *Bhagavad-gītā* these separate positions of the *jīva-ātmā* and the Paramātmā are specifically mentioned. In the Fourth Chapter, Arjuna, the *jīva* soul, is represented as forgetful of his many, many previous births, but the Lord, the Supersoul, is not forgetful. The Lord even remembers when He taught the *Bhagavad-gītā* to the sun-god some billions of years before. The Lord can remember such millions and billions of years, as stated in the *Bhagavad-gītā* (7.26) as follows:

vedāhaṁ samatītāni
vartamānāni cārjuna
bhaviṣyāṇi ca bhūtāni
māṁ tu veda na kaścana

The Lord in His eternal blissful body of knowledge is fully aware of all that happened in the past, that which is going on at the present and also what will happen in the future. But in spite of His being the shelter of both the Paramātmā and Brahman, persons with a poor fund of knowledge are unable to understand Him as He is.

The propaganda of the identity of cosmic consciousness with the consciousness of the individual living entities is completely misleading because even such a person or individual soul as Arjuna could not remember his past deeds, although he is always with the Lord. And what can the tiny ordinary man, falsely claiming to be one with the cosmic consciousness, know about his past, present and future?

TEXT 10

पुरुषोऽण्डं विनिर्भिद्य यदासौ स विनिर्गतः ।
आत्मनोऽयनमन्विच्छन्नपोऽस्राक्षीच्छुचिः शुचीः ॥१०॥

puruṣo 'ṇḍaṁ vinirbhidya
yadāsau sa vinirgataḥ
ātmano 'yanam anvicchann
apo 'srākṣīc chuciḥ śucīḥ

puruṣaḥ—the Supreme Person, Paramātmā; *aṇḍam*—the universes; *vinirbhidya*—making them each separately situated; *yadā*—when; *asau*—the same; *saḥ*—He (the Lord); *vinirgataḥ*—came out; *ātmanaḥ*—of Himself; *ayanam*—lying in place; *anvicchan*—desiring; *apaḥ*—water; *asrākṣīt*—created; *śuciḥ*—the most pure; *śucīḥ*—transcendental.

TRANSLATION

After separating the different universes, the gigantic universal form of the Lord [Mahā-Viṣṇu], which came out of the causal ocean, the place of appearance for the first puruṣa-avātara, entered into each of the separate universes, desiring to lie on the created transcendental water [Garbhodaka].

PURPORT

After analysis of the living entities and the Supreme Lord, Paramātmā, the independent source of all other living beings, Śrīla

Śukadeva Gosvāmī is now presenting the prime necessity for devotional service to the Lord, which is the only occupational business of all living entities. The Supreme Lord Śrī Kṛṣṇa and all His plenary portions and extensions of plenary portions are nondifferent from one another, and thus the supreme independence is in each and every one of them. In order to prove this, Śukadeva Gosvāmī (as promised to King Parīkṣit) describes herein the independence of the *puruṣa-avatāra* Personality of Godhead, even in the sphere of the material creation. Such activities of the Lord are also transcendental, and therefore they are also *līlā*, or pastimes, of the absolute Lord. Such pastimes of the Lord are very conducive to the hearers for self-realization in the field of devotional service. Some may argue, why not then relish the transcendental *līlā* of the Lord as exhibited in the land of Mathurā and Vṛndāvana, which are sweeter than anything in the world? Śrīla Viśvanātha Cakravartī Ṭhākura replies that the pastimes of the Lord in Vṛndāvana are meant to be relished by advanced devotees of the Lord. Neophyte devotees will misunderstand such supreme transcendental activities of the Lord, and therefore the Lord's pastimes in the material sphere related to creation, maintenance and destruction are verily relishable by the *prākṛta*, or mundane devotees of the Lord. As the *yoga* system mainly based on bodily exercises is meant for the person who is too much attached to the bodily conception of existence, similarly the Lord's pastimes related to the creation and destruction of the material world are for those who are too materially attached. For such mundane creatures the functions of the body and the functions of the cosmic world through physical laws in relationship with the Lord are also therefore included in understanding of the lawmaker, the Supreme Personality of Godhead. The scientists explain the material functions by so many technological terms of material law, but such blind scientists forget the lawmaker. The *Śrīmad-Bhāgavatam* points out the lawmaker. One should not be amazed by the mechanical arrangement of the complicated engine or dynamo, but one should praise the engineer who creates such a wonderful working machine. That is the difference between the devotee and the nondevotee. Devotees are always full with praising the Lord, who directs the physical laws. In the *Bhagavad-gītā* (9.10) the direction of the Lord upon the material nature is described as follows:

mayādhyakṣeṇa prakṛtiḥ
sūyate sacarācaram
hetunānena kaunteya
jagad viparivartate

"The material nature full of physical laws is one of My different energies; therefore it is neither independent nor blind. Because I am transcendentally all-powerful, simply by My glancing over material nature, the physical laws of nature work so wonderfully. The actions and reactions of the physical laws work on that account, and thus the material world is created, maintained and annihilated again and again."

Men with a poor fund of knowledge, however, become astonished by studying the physical laws both within the construction of the individual body and within the cosmic manifestation, and foolishly they decry the existence of God, taking it for granted that the physical laws are independent, without any metaphysical control. The *Bhagavad-gītā* (9.11) replies to this foolishness in the following words:

avajānanti māṁ mūḍhā
mānuṣīṁ tanum āśritam
paraṁ bhāvam ajānanto
mama bhūta-maheśvaram

"The foolish men [*mūḍhāḥ*] do not know the Personality of Godhead in His eternal form of bliss and knowledge." The foolish man thinks of the transcendental body of the Lord as something like his own, and therefore he cannot think of the unlimited controlling power of the Lord, who is not visible in the acting of the physical laws. The Lord is, however, visible to the naked eyes of people in general when He descends Himself by His own personal potency. Lord Kṛṣṇa incarnated Himself as He is and played very wonderful parts as the Lord Himself, and the *Bhagavad-gītā* concerns such wonderful actions and knowledge. Yet foolish men will not accept Lord Kṛṣṇa as the Supreme Lord. Generally they consider the infinitesimal and infinite features of the Lord because they themselves are unable to become either the infinitesimal or the infinite, but one should know that the infinite and infinitesimal sizes of the Lord are not His highest glories. The most wonderful manifestation of the Lord's power is exhibited when the infinite Lord becomes visible to our eyes as one of us. Yet His activities are different from those of the finite beings. Lifting a mountain at the age of seven years and marrying sixteen thousand wives in the prime of His youth are some of the examples of His infinite energy, but the *mūḍhas*, after seeing them or hearing about them, decry them as legendary and take the Lord as one of them. They cannot understand that the Lord Śrī Kṛṣṇa, although in the form of a human being by His own potency, is still the Supreme Lord with full potency as the supreme controller.

When, however, the *mūḍhas* give submissive and aural reception to the messages of the Lord as in the *Śrīmad Bhagavad-gītā* or in the *Śrīmad-Bhāgavatam* through the channel of disciplic succession, such *mūḍhas* also become devotees of the Lord by the grace of His pure devotees. And for this reason only, either in the *Bhagavad-gītā* or in the *Śrīmad-Bhāgavatam*, the pastimes of the Lord in the material world are delineated for the benefit of those men with a poor fund of knowledge.

TEXT 11

तास्ववात्सीत् स्वसृष्टासु सहस्रंपरिवत्सरान् ।
तेन नारायणो नाम यदापः पुरुषोद्भवाः ॥११॥

tāsv avātsīt sva-sṛṣṭāsu
sahasraṁ parivatsarān
tena nārāyaṇo nāma
yad āpaḥ puruṣodbhavāḥ

tāsu—in that; *avātsīt*—resided; *sva*—own; *sṛṣṭāsu*—in the matter of creation; *sahasram*—one thousand; *parivatsarān*—years of His measurement; *tena*—for that reason; *nārāyaṇaḥ*—the Personality of Godhead named Nārāyaṇa; *nāma*—name; *yat*—because; *āpaḥ*—water; *puruṣa-udbhavāḥ*—emanated from the Supreme Person.

TRANSLATION

That Supreme Person is not impersonal and therefore is distinctively a nara, or person. Therefore the transcendental water

created from the Supreme Nara is known as nāra. And because He lies down on that water, He is known as Nārāyaṇa.

TEXT 12

द्रव्यं कर्म च कालश्च स्वभावो जीव एव च ।
यदनुग्रहतः सन्ति न सन्ति यदुपेक्षया ॥१२॥

dravyaṁ karma ca kālaś ca
svabhāvo jīva eva ca
yad-anugrahataḥ santi
na santi yad-upekṣayā

dravyam—physical elements; *karma*—action; *ca*—and; *kālaḥ*—time; *ca*—also; *sva-bhāvaḥ jīvaḥ*—the living entities; *eva*—certainly; *ca*—also; *yat*—whose; *anugrahataḥ*—by the mercy of; *santi*—exist; *na*—does not; *santi*—exist; *yat-upekṣayā*—by negligence.

TRANSLATION

One should definitely know that all material ingredients, activities, time and modes, and the living entities who are meant to enjoy them all, exist by His mercy only, and as soon as He does not care for them, everything becomes nonexistent.

PURPORT

The living entities are the enjoyers of the material ingredients, time, modes, etc., because they want to lord it over the material nature. The Lord is the supreme enjoyer, and the living entities are meant to assist the Lord in His enjoyment and thus participate in the transcendental enjoyment of everyone. The enjoyer and the enjoyed both participate in enjoyment, but, deluded by the illusory energy, the living entities want to become the enjoyer like the Lord, although they are not meant for such enjoyment. The *jīvas,* the living entities, are mentioned in the *Bhagavad-gītā* as the Lord's superior nature, or *parā prakṛti,* and so also it is mentioned in the *Viṣṇu Purāṇa.* Therefore the living entities are never the *puruṣas,* or the factual enjoyers. As such, the spirit of enjoyment by the living entity in the material world is false. In the spiritual world the living entities are pure in nature, and therefore they are associates in the enjoyment of the Supreme Lord. In the material world the spirit of enjoyment of the living entities by dint of their own actions (*karma*) gradually fades by the laws of nature, and thus the illusory energy dictates in the ears of the conditioned souls that they should become one with the Lord. This is the last snare of the illusory energy. When the last illusion is also cleared off by the mercy of the Lord, the living entity again becomes reinstated in his original position and thus becomes actually liberated. For this attainment of liberation from the material clutches, the Lord creates the material world, maintains it for some time (one thousand years of His measurement, as stated in the previous verse), and then again annihilates it by His will. The living entities are therefore completely dependent on the mercy of the Lord, and all their so-called enjoyments by scientific improvement are crushed into dust when the Lord desires.

TEXT 13

एको नानात्वमन्विच्छन् योगतल्पात् समुत्थितः ।
वीर्यं हिरण्मयं देवो मायया व्यसृजत् त्रिधा ॥१३॥

eko nānātvam anvicchan
yoga-talpāt samutthitaḥ
vīryaṁ hiraṇmayaṁ devo
māyayā vyasṛjat tridhā

ekaḥ—He, one alone; *nānātvam*—varieties; *anvicchan*—so desiring; *yoga-talpāt*—from the bedstead of mystic slumber; *samutthitaḥ*—thus generated; *vīryam*—the semina; *hiraṇmayam*—golden hue; *devaḥ*—the demigod; *māyayā*—by the external energy; *vyasṛjat*—perfectly created; *tridhā*—in three features.

TRANSLATION

The Lord, while lying on His bed of mystic slumber, generated the seminal symbol, golden in hue, through external energy out of His desire to manifest varieties of living entities from Himself alone.

PURPORT

In the *Bhagavad-gītā* (9.7–8) the creation and annihilation of the material world are stated as follows:

sarva-bhūtāni kaunteya
prakṛtiṁ yānti māmikām
kalpa-kṣaye punas tāni
kalpādau visṛjāmy aham

prakṛtiṁ svām avaṣṭabhya
visṛjāmi punaḥ punaḥ
bhūta-grāmam imaṁ kṛtsnam
avaśaṁ prakṛter vaśāt

"At the end of each millennium the creative forces, namely the material nature and the living entities who struggle in the material nature, all merge together into the transcendental body of the Lord, and again when the Lord desires to manifest them, all of them are again displayed by the Lord.

"Therefore the material nature is working under the control of the Lord. All of them, under the agency of material nature and under the control of the Lord, are thus repeatedly created and annihilated by the will of the Lord."

As such, before the creation or manifestation of the material cosmic world, the Lord exists as total energy (*mahā-samaṣṭi*), and thus desiring Himself to be diffused to many, He expands Himself further into multitotal energy (*samaṣṭi*). From the multitotal energy He further expands Himself into individuals in three dimensions, namely adhyātmic, adhidaivic and adhibhautic, as explained before (*vyaṣṭi*). As such, the whole creation and the creative energies are nondifferent and different simultaneously. Because everything is an emanation from Him (the Mahā-Viṣṇu or Mahā-samaṣṭi), nothing of the cosmic energies is different from Him; but all such expanded energies have specific functions and display as designed by the Lord, and therefore they are simultaneously different from the Lord. The living entities are also similar energy (marginal potency) of the Lord, and thus they are simultaneously one with and different from Him.

At the stage of nonmanifestation, the living energies remain potent in the Lord, and when they are let loose in the cosmic manifestation they are exhibited differently in terms of different desires under the modes of nature. Such differential manifestations of the living energies are conditional states of the living entities. The liberated living entities, however, in the *sanātana* (eternal) manifestation, are unconditionally surrendered souls, and therefore they are not subject to the conditions of creation and annihilation. So this creation takes place by the glance of the Lord from His bedstead of mystic slumber. And thus all the universes and the lord of the universe, Brahmā, are again and again manifested and annihilated.

TEXT 14

अधिदैवमथाध्यात्ममधिभूतमिति प्रभुः ।
अथैकं पौरुषं वीर्यं त्रिधाभिद्यत तच्छृणु ॥१४॥

adhidaivam athādhyātmam
adhibhūtam iti prabhuḥ
athaikaṁ pauruṣaṁ vīryaṁ
tridhābhidyata tac chṛṇu

adhidaivam—the controlling entities; *atha*—now; *adhyātmam*—the controlled entities; *adhibhūtam*—the material bodies; *iti*—thus; *prabhuḥ*—the Lord; *atha*—in this way; *ekam*—one only; *pauruṣam*—of His Lordship; *vīryam*—potency; *tridhā*—in three; *abhidyata*—divided; *tat*—that; *śṛṇu*—just hear from me.

TRANSLATION

Just hear from me how the potency of His Lordship divides one into three, called the controlling entities, the controlled entities and the material bodies, in the manner mentioned above.

TEXT 15

अन्तःशरीर आकाशात् पुरुषस्य विचेष्टतः ।
ओजः सहो बलं जज्ञे ततः प्राणो महानसुः ॥१५॥

antaḥ śarīra ākāśāt
puruṣasya viceṣṭataḥ
ojaḥ saho balaṁ jajñe
tataḥ prāṇo mahān asuḥ

antaḥ śarīre—within the body; *ākāśāt*—from the sky; *puruṣasya*—of Mahā-Viṣṇu; *viceṣṭataḥ*—while so trying, or willing; *ojaḥ*—the energy of the senses; *sahaḥ*—mental force; *balam*—bodily strength; *jajñe*—generated; *tataḥ*—thereafter; *prāṇaḥ*—the living force; *mahān asuḥ*—the fountainhead of everyone's life.

TRANSLATION

From the sky situated within the transcendental body of the manifesting Mahā-Viṣṇu, sense energy, mental force and bodily strength are all generated, as well as the sum total of the fountainhead of the total living force.

TEXT 16

अनुप्राणन्ति यं प्राणाः प्राणन्तं सर्वजन्तुषु ।
अपानन्तमपानन्ति नरदेवमिवानुगाः ॥१६॥

anuprāṇanti yaṁ prāṇāḥ
prāṇantaṁ sarva-jantuṣu
apānantam apānanti
nara-devam ivānugāḥ

anuprāṇanti—follow the living symptoms; *yam*—whom; *prāṇāḥ*—senses; *prāṇantam*—endeavoring; *sarva-jantuṣu*—in all living entities; *apānantam*—stop endeavoring; *apānanti*—all others stop; *nara-devam*—a king; *iva*—like; *anugāḥ*—the followers.

TRANSLATION

As the followers of a king follow their lord, similarly when the total energy is in motion, all other living entities move, and when the total energy stops endeavoring, all other living entities stop sensual activities.

PURPORT

The individual living entities are completely dependent on the total energy of the supreme *puruṣa.* No one has independent existence, just as no electric lamp has independent effulgence. Each and every electrical instrument depends fully on the total powerhouse, the total powerhouse depends on the reservoir of water for generating electricity, water depends on the clouds, the clouds depend on the sun, the sun depends on creation, and the creation depends on the movement of the Supreme Personality of Godhead. Thus the Supreme Personality of Godhead is the cause of all causes.

TEXT 17

प्राणेनाक्षिपता क्षुत् तृडन्तरा जायते विभोः ।
पिपासतो जक्षतश्च प्राङ्मुखं निरभिद्यत ॥१७॥

prāṇenākṣipatā kṣut tṛḍ
antarā jāyate vibhoḥ
pipāsato jakṣataś ca
prāṅ mukhaṁ nirabhidyata

prāṇena—by the living force; *ākṣipatā*—being agitated; *kṣut*—hunger; *tṛṭ*—thirst; *antarā*—from within; *jāyate*—generates; *vibhoḥ*—of the Supreme; *pipāsataḥ*—being desirous to quench the thirst; *jakṣataḥ*—being desirous to eat; *ca*—and; *prāk*—at first; *mukham*—the mouth; *nirabhidyata*—was opened.

TRANSLATION

The living force, being agitated by the virāṭ-puruṣa, generated hunger and thirst, and when He desired to drink and eat, the mouth opened.

PURPORT

The process by which all living beings in the womb of the mother develop their sense organs and sense perceptions appears to follow the same principles in the case of the *virāṭ-puruṣa,* the sum total of all living entities. Therefore the supreme cause of all generation is not impersonal or without desire. The desires for all kinds of sense perception and sense organs exist in the Supreme, and thus they take place in the individual persons. This desire is the nature of the supreme living being, the Absolute Truth. Because He has the sum total of all mouths, the individual living entities have mouths. Similarly with all other senses and sense organs. Here the mouth is the symbolic representation of all sense organs, for the same principles apply to the others also.

TEXT 18

मुखतस्तालु निर्भिन्नं जिह्वा तत्रोपजायते ।
ततो नानारसो जज्ञे जिह्वया योऽधिगम्यते ॥१८॥

mukhatas tālu nirbhinnaṁ
jihvā tatropajāyate
tato nānā-raso jajñe
jihvayā yo 'dhigamyate

mukhataḥ—from the mouth; *tālu*—the palate; *nirbhinnam*—being generated; *jihvā*—the tongue; *tatra*—thereupon; *upajāyate*—becomes manifested; *tataḥ*—thereupon; *nānā-rasaḥ*—various tastes; *jajñe*—became manifested; *jihvayā*—by the tongue; *yaḥ*—which; *adhigamyate*—become relished.

TRANSLATION

From the mouth the palate became manifested, and thereupon the tongue was also generated. After this all the different tastes came into existence so that the tongue can relish them.

PURPORT

This gradual process of evolution suggests the explanation of the controlling deities (*adhidaiva*) because Varuṇa is the controlling deity for all relishable juices. Therefore the mouth becomes the resting place for the tongue, which tastes all the different juices, of which the controlling deity is Varuṇa. This suggests, therefore, that Varuṇa was also generated along with the development of the tongue. The tongue and the palate, being instrumental, are *adhibhūtam*, or forms of matter, but the functioning deity, who is a living entity, is *adhidaiva*, whereas the person undergoing the function is *adhyātma*. Thus the three categories are also explained as to their birth after the opening of the mouth of the *virāṭ-puruṣa*. The four principles mentioned in this verse serve to explain the three main principles, namely the *adhyātma*, *adhidaiva* and *adhibhutam*, as explained before.

TEXT 19

विवक्षोर्मुखतो भूम्नो वह्निर्वाग् व्याहृतं तयोः ।
जले चैतस्य सुचिरं निरोधः समजायत ॥१९॥

vivakṣor mukhato bhūmno
vahnir vāg vyāhṛtaṁ tayoḥ
jale caitasya suciraṁ
nirodhaḥ samajāyata

vivakṣoḥ—when there was a need to speak; *mukhataḥ*—from the mouth; *bhūmnaḥ*—of the Supreme; *vahniḥ*—fire or the controlling deity of fire; *vāk*—vibration; *vyāhṛtam*—speeches; *tayoḥ*—by both; *jale*—in the water; *ca*—however; *etasya*—of all these; *suciram*—a very, very long time; *nirodhaḥ*—suspension; *samajāyata*—did continue.

TRANSLATION

When the Supreme desired to speak, speeches were vibrated from the mouth. Then the controlling deity Fire was generated from the mouth. But when He was lying in the water, all these functions remained suspended.

PURPORT

The peculiarity of the gradual development of the different senses is simultaneously supported by their controlling deities. It is to be understood, therefore, that the activities of the sense organs are controlled by the will of the Supreme. The senses are, so to speak, offering a license for the conditioned souls, who are to use them properly under the control of the controlling deity deputed by the Supreme Lord. One who violates such controlling regulations has to be punished by degradation to a lower status of life. Consider, for example, the tongue and its controlling deity, Varuṇa. The tongue is meant for eating, and men, animals and birds each have their different tastes because of different licenses. The taste of human beings and that of the swine are not on the same level. The controlling deity, however, awards or certifies a particular type of body when the particular living entity develops a taste in terms of different modes of nature. If the human being develops taste without discrimination, as does the swine, then the controlling deity is certainly certified for the next term to award him the body of a swine. The swine accepts any kind of foodstuff, including stools, and a human being who has developed such indiscriminate taste must be prepared for a degraded life in the next life. Such a life is also God's grace because the conditioned soul desired a body like that for perfectly tasting a particular type of foodstuff. If a man gets the body of a swine it must be considered the grace of the Lord because the Lord awards the facility. After death the next body is offered by superior control, not blindly. A human being, therefore, must be on his guard as to what sort of body he is going to have in the next life. An irresponsible life of indiscrimination is risky, and that is the declaration of all scriptures.

TEXT 20

नासिके निरभिद्येतां दोधूयति नभस्वति ।
तत्र वायुर्गन्धवहो घ्राणो नसि जिघृक्षतः ॥२०॥

nāsike nirabhidyetāṁ
dodhūyati nabhasvati
tatra vāyur gandha-vaho
ghrāṇo nasi jighṛkṣataḥ

nāsike—in the nostrils; *nirabhidyetām*—being developed; *dodhūyati*—rapidly blowing; *nabhasvati*—air respiration; *tatra*—thereupon; *vāyuḥ*—air; *gandha-vahaḥ*—smelling odor; *ghrāṇaḥ*—sense of smell; *nasi*—in the nose; *jighṛkṣataḥ*—desiring to smell odors.

TRANSLATION

Thereafter, when the supreme puruṣa desired to smell odors, the nostrils and respiration were generated, the nasal instrument and odors came into existence, and the controlling deity of air, carrying smell, also became manifested.

PURPORT

The nasal instrument, odor, and the controlling deity air, smelling, etc., all became manifested simultaneously when the Lord desired to smell. The Vedic *mantras* confirm this statement in the *Upaniṣads'* statement that everything is first desired by the Supreme before the subordinate living entity can act upon it. The living entity can see only when the Lord sees, the living entity can smell when the Lord smells, and so on. The idea is that the living entity cannot do anything independently. He can simply think of doing something independently, but he cannot act independently. This independence in thinking is there by the grace of the Lord, but the thinking can be given shape by the grace of the Lord, and therefore the common saying is that man proposes and God disposes. The whole explanation is on the subject of the absolute dependence of the living entities and absolute independence of the Supreme Lord. Less intelligent persons claiming to be on an equal level with God must first prove themselves to be absolute and independent, and then they must substantiate their claim to being one with God.

TEXT 21

यदात्मनि निरालोकमात्मानं च दिदृक्षतः ।
निर्भिन्ने ह्यक्षिणी तस्य ज्योतिश्चक्षुर्गुणग्रहः ॥२१॥

yadātmani nirālokam
ātmānaṁ ca didṛkṣataḥ
nirbhinne hy akṣiṇī tasya
jyotiś cakṣur guṇa-grahaḥ

yadā—while; *ātmani*—unto Himself; *nirālokam*—without any light; *ātmānam*—His own transcendental body; *ca*—also other bodily forms; *didṛkṣataḥ*—desired to look upon; *nirbhinne*—due to being sprouted;

hi—for; *akṣiṇī*—of the eyes; *tasya*—of Him; *jyotiḥ*—the sun; *cakṣuḥ*—the eyes; *guṇa-grahaḥ*—the power of seeing.

TRANSLATION

Thus when everything existed in darkness, the Lord desired to see Himself and all that was created. Then the eyes, the illuminating god Sun, the power of vision and the object of sight all became manifested.

PURPORT

The universe is by nature dense darkness, and therefore the total creation is called *tamas*, or darkness. The night is the real feature of the universe, for then one cannot see anything, including oneself. The Lord, out of His causeless mercy, first desired to see Himself and all the creation as well, and thus the sun became manifested, the power of vision for all living entities became possible, and the objects of vision were also manifested. This means that the whole phenomenal world became visible after the creation of the sun.

TEXT 22

बोध्यमानस्य ऋषिभिरात्मनस्तज्जिघृक्षतः ।
कर्णौ च निरभिद्येतां दिशः श्रोत्रं गुणग्रहः ॥२२॥

bodhyamānasya ṛṣibhir
ātmanas taj jighṛkṣataḥ
karṇau ca nirabhidyetāṁ
diśaḥ śrotraṁ guṇa-grahaḥ

bodhyamānasya—desiring to understand; *ṛṣibhiḥ*—by the authorities; *ātmanaḥ*—of the Supreme Being; *tat*—that; *jighṛkṣataḥ*—when He desired to take up; *karṇau*—the ears; *ca*—also; *nirabhidyetām*—became manifested; *diśaḥ*—the direction or the god of air; *śrotram*—the power of hearing; *guṇa-grahaḥ*—and the objects of hearing.

TRANSLATION

By development of the desire of the great sages to know, the ears, the power of hearing, the controlling deity of hearing, and

the objects of hearing became manifested. The great sages desired to hear about the Self.

PURPORT

As stated in the *Bhagavad-gītā*, by advancement of knowledge one should try to know about the Supreme Lord, the *summum bonum* of everything. Knowledge does not mean knowledge only of the laws of nature or physical knowledge, which are working by the direction of the Lord. The scientists are eager to hear about the physical laws working in material nature. They are eager to hear through the medium of radio and television about things taking place far away from them on other planets, but they should know that the power of hearing and the instruments for hearing were given to them by the Lord for hearing about the Self, or about the Lord. Unfortunately the power of hearing is misused in hearing the vibrations of mundane affairs. The great sages were interested in hearing about the Lord through Vedic knowledge and nothing more. That is the beginning of aural reception of knowledge.

TEXT 23

वस्तुनो मृदुकाठिन्यलघुगुर्वोष्णशीतताम् ।
जिघृक्षतस्त्वङ् निर्भिन्ना तस्यां रोममहीरुहाः ।
तत्र चान्तर्बहिर्वातस्त्वचा लब्धगुणो वृतः ॥२३॥

vastuno mṛdu-kāṭhinya-
laghu-gurv-oṣṇa-śītatām
jighṛkṣatas tvaṅ nirbhinnā
tasyāṁ roma-mahī-ruhāḥ
tatra cāntar bahir vātas
tvacā labdha-guṇo vṛtaḥ

vastunaḥ—of all matter; *mṛdu*—softness; *kāṭhinya*—hardness; *laghu*—lightness; *guru*—heaviness; *oṣṇa*—warmness; *śītatām*—coldness; *jighṛkṣataḥ*—desiring to perceive; *tvak*—the touch sensation; *nirbhinnā*—distributed; *tasyām*—in the skin; *roma*—hairs on the body; *mahī-ruhāḥ*—as well as the trees, the controlling deities; *tatra*—there;

ca—also; *antaḥ*—within; *bahiḥ*—outside; *vātaḥ tvacā*—the sense of touch or the skin; *labdha*—having been perceived; *guṇaḥ*—objects of sense perception; *vṛtaḥ*—generated.

TRANSLATION

When there was a desire to perceive the physical characteristics of matter, such as softness, hardness, warmth, cold, lightness and heaviness, the background of sensation, the skin, the skin pores, the hairs on the body and their controlling deities (the trees) were generated. Within and outside the skin is a covering of air through which sense perception became prominent.

PURPORT

The physical characteristics of matter, such as softness, are subjects of sense perception, and thus physical knowledge is the subject matter of the touch sensation. One can measure the temperature of matter by touching with the hand, and one can measure the weight of an object by lifting it with the hand and thus estimate its heaviness or lightness. The skin, the skin pores and the hairs on the body are all interdependent with the touch sensation. The air blowing within and outside the skin is also an object of sense perception. This sense perception is also a source of knowledge, and therefore it is suggested here that physical or physiological knowledge is subordinate to the knowledge of the Self, as above mentioned. Knowledge of Self can expand to the knowledge of phenomena, but physical knowledge cannot lead to knowledge of the Self.

There is, however, an intimate relation between the hairs on the body and the vegetation on the body of the earth. The vegetables are nourishment for the skin both as food and medicine, as stated in the Third Canto: *tvacam asya vinirbhinnāṁ viviśur dhiṣṇyam oṣadhīḥ.*

TEXT 24

हस्तौ रुरुहतुस्तस्य नानाकर्मचिकीर्षया ।
तयोस्तु बलवानिन्द्र आदानमुभयाश्रयम् ॥२४॥

hastau ruruhatus tasya
nānā-karma-cikīrṣayā

tayos tu balavān indra
ādānam ubhayāśrayam

hastau—the hands; *ruruhatuḥ*—manifested; *tasya*—His; *nānā*—various; *karma*—work; *cikīrṣayā*—being so desirous; *tayoḥ*—of them; *tu*—however; *balavān*—to give strength; *indraḥ*—the demigod in heaven; *ādānam*—activities of the hand; *ubhaya-āśrayam*—dependent on both the demigod and the hand.

TRANSLATION

Thereafter when the Supreme Person desired to perform varieties of work, the two hands and their controlling strength, and Indra, the demigod in heaven, became manifested, as also the acts dependent on both the hands and the demigod.

PURPORT

In every item we can note with profit that the sense organs of the living entity are never independent at any stage. The Lord is known as the Lord of the senses (Hṛṣīkeśa). Thus the sense organs of the living entities are manifested by the will of the Lord, and each organ is controlled by a certain type of demigod. No one, therefore, can claim any proprietorship of the senses. The living entity is controlled by the senses, the senses are controlled by the demigods, and the demigods are the servants of the Supreme Lord. That is the arrangement in the system of creation. The whole thing is controlled ultimately by the Supreme Lord, and there is no independence either of the material nature or of the living entity. The illusioned living entity who claims to be the lord of his senses is under the clutches of the external energy of the Lord. As long as a living entity continues to be puffed up by his tiny existence, he is to be understood to be under the stringent control of the external energy of the Lord, and there is no question of liberation from the clutches of illusion (*māyā*), however much one may declare himself a liberated soul.

TEXT 25

गतिं जिगीषतः पादौ रुरुहातेऽभिकामिकाम् ।
पद्भ्यां यज्ञः स्वयं हव्यं कर्मभिः क्रियते नृभिः ॥२५॥

gatiṁ jigīṣataḥ pādau
ruruhāte 'bhikāmikām
padbhyāṁ yajñaḥ svayaṁ havyaṁ
karmabhiḥ kriyate nṛbhiḥ

gatim—movement; *jigīṣitaḥ*—so desiring; *pādau*—the legs; *ruruhāte*—being manifested; *abhikāmikām*—purposeful; *padbhyām*—from the legs; *yajñaḥ*—Lord Viṣṇu; *svayam*—personally Himself; *havyam*—the duties; *karmabhiḥ*—by one's occupational duty; *kriyate*—caused to be done; *nṛbhiḥ*—by different human beings.

TRANSLATION

Thereupon, because of His desiring to control movement, His legs became manifested, and from the legs the controlling deity named Viṣṇu was generated. By His personal supervision of this act, all varieties of human being are busily engaged in dutiful occupational sacrifice.

PURPORT

Every human being is engaged in his particular occupational duty, and such activities are visible as men go hither and thither. This is very prominently visible in big cities of the world: people are going all over the cities with great concern, from one place to another. This movement is not limited only to the cities, but is also visible outside the cities from one place to another, or from one city to another, by different means of vehicles. Men are moving by cars and rails on the roads, by subways within the earth and by planes in the sky for the purpose of business success. But in all these movements the real purpose is to earn wealth for comfortable life. For this comfortable life the scientist is engaged, the artist is engaged, the engineer is engaged, the technician is engaged, all in different branches of human activity. But they do not know how to make the activities purposeful to fulfill the mission of human life. Because they do not know this secret, all their activities are targeted towards the goal of sense gratification without control, and therefore by all this business they are unknowingly entering into the deep regions of darkness.

Because they have been captivated by the external energy of the Supreme Lord, they have completely forgotten the Supreme Lord Viṣṇu, and thus they have taken it for granted that this life, as presently manifested under the conditions of material nature, is all in all for enjoying the highest amount of sense gratification. But such a wrong conception of life cannot give anyone the desired peace of mind, and thus in spite of all advancement in knowledge by use of the resources of nature, no one is happy in this material civilization. The secret is that at every step they should try to execute sacrifices toward the path of world peace. The *Bhagavad-gītā* (18.45–46) also advises the same secret in the following verses.

sve sve karmaṇy abhirataḥ
saṁsiddhiṁ labhate naraḥ
sva-karma-nirataḥ siddhiṁ
yathā vindati tac chṛṇu

yataḥ pravṛttir bhūtānāṁ
yena sarvam idaṁ tatam
sva-karmaṇā tam abhyarcya
siddhiṁ vindati mānavaḥ

The Lord said to Arjuna: "Just hear from Me how one can attain the highest perfection in life simply by discharging his specified occupational duty. Man can attain the highest perfection of life by worshiping the Supreme Lord and by performing sacrifice for the sake of the Supreme Lord Viṣṇu, who is all-pervading and by whose control every living being acquires his desired facilities, according to his personal propensity."

There is no harm in having different propensities in life because every human being is proportionately independent to chalk out the plan of his life by different occupations, but one should make it a point in his life to know perfectly well that he is not independent absolutely. One is certainly under the control of the Supreme Lord and under different agencies. Knowing this, one should make it a point that by his work and the result of his labor he serves the Supreme Lord as prescribed by the authorities expert in the transcendental loving service of the Supreme Lord Viṣṇu. For performing such occupational duties of life the leg is the most important instrument of the body because without the help of the legs one cannot move from one place to another, and therefore the Lord has special control over the legs of all human beings, which are meant for performing *yajñas.*

TEXT 26

निरभिद्यत शिश्नो वै प्रजानन्दामृतार्थिनः ।
उपस्थ आसीत् कामानां प्रियं तदुभयाश्रयम् ॥२६॥

nirabhidyata śiśno vai
prajānandāmṛtārthinaḥ
upastha āsīt kāmānāṁ
priyaṁ tad-ubhayāśrayam

nirabhidyata—came out; *śiśnaḥ*—the genitals; *vai*—certainly; *prajā-ānanda*—sex pleasure; *amṛta-arthinaḥ*—aspiring to taste the nectar; *upasthaḥ*—the male or female organ; *āsīt*—came into existence; *kāmānām*—of the lustful; *priyam*—very dear; *tat*—that; *ubhaya-āśrayam*—shelter for both.

TRANSLATION

Thereupon, for sexual pleasure, begetting offspring and tasting heavenly nectar, the Lord developed the genitals, and thus there is the genital organ and its controlling deity, the Prajāpati. The object of sexual pleasure and the controlling deity are under the control of the genitals of the Lord.

PURPORT

The heavenly pleasure for the conditioned soul is sexual pleasure, and this pleasure is tasted by the genitals. The woman is the object of sexual pleasure, and both the sense perception of sexual pleasure and the woman are controlled by the Prajāpati, who is under the control of the Lord's genitals. The impersonalist must know from this verse that the Lord is not impersonal, for He has His genitals, on which all the pleasurable objects of sex depend. No one would have taken the trouble to maintain children if there were no taste of heavenly nectar by means of sexual intercourse. This material world is created to give the conditioned souls a chance for rejuvenation for going back home, back to

Godhead, and therefore generation of the living being is necessary for upkeep of the purpose of creation. Sexual pleasure is an impetus for such action, and as such one can even serve the Lord in the act of such sexual pleasure. The service is counted when the children born of such sexual pleasure are properly trained in God consciousness. The whole idea of material creation is to revive the dormant God consciousness of the living entity. In forms of life other than the human form, sexual pleasure is prominent without any motive of service for the mission of the Lord. But in the human form of life the conditioned soul can render service to the Lord by creating progeny suitable for the attainment of salvation. One can beget hundreds of children and enjoy the celestial pleasure of sexual intercourse, provided he is able to train the children in God consciousness. Otherwise begetting children is on the level of the swine. Rather, the swine is more expert than the human being because the swine can beget a dozen piglets at a time, whereas the human being can give birth to only one at a time. So one should always remember that the genitals, sexual pleasure, the woman and the offspring are all related in the service of the Lord, and one who forgets this relationship in the service of the Supreme Lord becomes subjected to the threefold miseries of material existence by the laws of nature. Perception of sexual pleasure is there even in the body of the dog, but there is no sense of God consciousness. The human form of life is distinct from that of the dog by the perception of God consciousness.

TEXT 27

उत्सिसृक्षोर्धातुमलं निरभिद्यत वै गुदम् ।
ततः पायुस्ततो मित्र उत्सर्ग उभयाश्रयः ॥२७॥

utsisṛkṣor dhātu-malaṁ
nirabhidyata vai gudam
tataḥ pāyus tato mitra
utsarga ubhayāśrayaḥ

utsisṛkṣoḥ—desiring to evacuate; *dhātu-malam*—refuse of eatables; *nirabhidyata*—became open; *vai*—certainly; *gudam*—the evacuating hole; *tataḥ*—thereafter; *pāyuḥ*—the evacuating sense organ; *tataḥ*—

thereafter; *mitraḥ*—the controlling demigod; *utsargaḥ*—the substance evacuated; *ubhaya*—both; *āśrayaḥ*—shelter.

TRANSLATION

Thereafter, when He desired to evacuate the refuse of eatables, the evacuating hole, anus, and the sensory organ thereof developed along with the controlling deity Mitra. The sensory organ and the evacuating substance are both under the shelter of the controlling deity.

PURPORT

Even in the matter of evacuating stool, the refuse is controlled, so how can the living entity claim to be independent?

TEXT 28

आसिसृप्सोः पुरः पुर्या नाभिद्वारमपानतः ।
तत्रापानस्ततो मृत्युः पृथक्त्वमुभयाश्रयम् ॥२८॥

āsisṛpsoḥ puraḥ puryā
nābhi-dvāram apānataḥ
tatrāpānas tato mṛtyuḥ
pṛthaktvam ubhayāśrayam

āsisṛpsoḥ—desiring to go everywhere; *puraḥ*—in different bodies; *puryāḥ*—from one body; *nābhi-dvāram*—the navel or abdominal hole; *apānataḥ*—was manifested; *tatra*—thereupon; *apānaḥ*—stopping of the vital force; *tataḥ*—thereafter; *mṛtyuḥ*—death; *pṛthaktvam*—separately; *ubhaya*—both; *āśrayam*—shelter.

TRANSLATION

Thereafter, when He desired to move from one body to another, the navel and the air of departure and death were combinedly created. The navel is the shelter for both, namely death and the separating force.

PURPORT

The *prāṇa-vāyu* continues the life, and the *apāna-vāyu* stops the living force. Both the vibrations are generated from the abdominal hole, the navel. This navel is the joint from one body to the other. Lord Brahmā was born of the abdominal hole of Garbhodakaśāyī Viṣṇu as a separate body, and the same principle is followed even in the birth of any ordinary body. The body of the child develops from the body of the mother, and when the child is separated from the body of the mother, it is separated by cutting the navel joint. And that is the way the Supreme Lord manifested Himself as separated many. The living entities are therefore separated parts, and thus they have no independence.

TEXT 29

आदित्सोरन्नपानानामासन् कुक्ष्यन्त्रनाडयः ।
नद्यः समुद्राश्च तयोस्तुष्टिः पुष्टिस्तदाश्रये ॥२९॥

āditsor anna-pānānām
āsan kukṣy-antra-nāḍayaḥ
nadyaḥ samudrāś ca tayos
tuṣṭiḥ puṣṭis tad-āśraye

āditsoḥ—desiring to have; *anna-pānānām*—of food and drink; *āsan*—there became; *kukṣi*—the abdomen; *antra*—the intestines; *nāḍayaḥ*—and the arteries; *nadyaḥ*—the rivers; *samudrāḥ*—seas; *ca*—also; *tayoḥ*—of them; *tuṣṭiḥ*—sustenance; *puṣṭiḥ*—metabolism; *tat*—of them; *āśraye*—the source.

TRANSLATION

When there was a desire to have food and drink, the abdomen and the intestines and also the arteries became manifested. The rivers and seas are the source of their sustenance and metabolism.

PURPORT

The controlling deities of the intestines are the rivers, and those of the arteries, the seas. Fulfillment of the belly with food and drink is the cause of sustenance, and the metabolism of the food and drink replaces the waste of the bodily energies. Therefore, the body's health is dependent on healthy actions of the intestines and the arteries. The rivers and the seas, being the controlling deities of the two, keep the intestines and the arteries in healthy order.

TEXT 30

निदिध्यासोरात्ममायां हृदयं निरभिद्यत ।
ततो मनश्चन्द्र इति सङ्कल्पः काम एव च ॥३०॥

nididhyāsor ātma-māyāṁ
hṛdayaṁ nirabhidyata
tato manaś candra iti
saṅkalpaḥ kāma eva ca

nididhyāsoḥ—being desirous to know; *ātma-māyām*—own energy; *hṛdayam*—the location of the mind; *nirabhidyata*—was manifested; *tataḥ*—thereafter; *manaḥ*—the mind; *candraḥ*—the controlling deity of the mind, the moon; *iti*—thus; *saṅkalpaḥ*—determination; *kāmaḥ*—desire; *eva*—as much as; *ca*—also.

TRANSLATION

When there was a desire to think about the activities of His own energy, then the heart (the seat of the mind), the mind, the moon, determination and all desire became manifested.

PURPORT

The heart of every living entity is the seat of the Supersoul, Paramātmā, a plenary expansion of the Supreme Personality of Godhead. Without His presence the living entity cannot get into the working energy according to his past deeds. The living entities who are conditioned in the material world are manifested in the creation in terms of respective inclinations inherent in them, and the requisite material body is offered to each and every one of them by the material energy under the direction of the Supersoul. This is explained in the *Bhagavad-gītā* (9.10). When, therefore, the Supersoul is situated in the heart of the conditioned soul, the requisite mind is manifested in the conditioned soul, and he becomes conscious of his occupation as one is conscious of his duty after waking up from slumber. Therefore the material mind of the living entity develops when the Supersoul sits on his heart, after which the mind, the controlling deity (moon), and then the activities of the mind (namely thinking, feeling and willing) all take place. The activities of the mind cannot begin without the manifestation of the heart, and the heart becomes manifested when the Lord wants to see the activities of the material creation.

TEXT 31

त्वक्चर्ममांसरुधिरमेदोमज्जास्थिधातवः ।
भूम्यप्तेजोमयाः सप्त प्राणो व्योमाम्बुवायुभिः ॥३१॥

tvak-carma-māṁsa-rudhira-
medo-majjāsthi-dhātavaḥ
bhūmy-ap-tejomayāḥ sapta
prāṇo vyomāmbu-vāyubhiḥ

tvak—the thin layer on the skin; *carma*—skin; *māṁsa*—flesh; *rudhira*—blood; *medaḥ*—fat; *majjā*—marrow; *asthi*—bone; *dhātavaḥ*—elements; *bhūmi*—earth; *ap*—water; *tejaḥ*—fire; *mayāḥ*—predominating; *sapta*—seven; *prāṇaḥ*—breathing air; *vyoma*—sky; *ambu*—water; *vāyubhiḥ*—by the air.

TRANSLATION

The seven elements of the body, namely the thin layer on the skin, the skin itself, the flesh, blood, fat, marrow and bone, are all made of earth, water and fire, whereas the life breath is produced by the sky, water and air.

PURPORT

The construction of the whole material world is prominently made by three elements, namely earth, water and fire. But the living force is produced by sky, air and water. So water is the common element in both the gross and subtle forms of all material creation, and it should be noted herewith that due to necessity, water, being most prominent in the material creation, is the principal element of all the five. This material body is thus an embodiment of the five elements, and the gross manifestation is perceived because of three, namely earth, water, and fire. Sensations of touch are perceived due to the thin layer on the skin, and bone is as good as hard stone. The breathing air of life is produced of sky, air and water, and therefore open air, regular bath and ample space in which to live are favorable for healthy vitality. Fresh produce from the earth like grains and vegetables, as well as fresh water and heat, is good for the upkeep of the gross body.

TEXT 32

गुणात्मकानीन्द्रियाणि भूतादिप्रभवा गुणाः ।
मनः सर्वविकारात्मा बुद्धिर्विज्ञानरूपिणी ॥३२॥

guṇātmakānīndriyāṇi
bhūtādi-prabhavā guṇāḥ
manaḥ sarva-vikārātmā
buddhir vijñāna-rūpiṇī

guṇa-ātmakāni—attached to the qualities; *indriyāṇi*—the senses; *bhūta-ādi*—material ego; *prabhavāḥ*—influenced by; *guṇāḥ*—the modes of material nature; *manaḥ*—the mind; *sarva*—all; *vikāra*—affection (happiness and distress); *ātmā*—form; *buddhiḥ*—intelligence; *vijñāna*—deliberation; *rūpiṇī*—featuring.

TRANSLATION

The sense organs are attached to the modes of material nature, and the modes of material nature are products of the false ego. The mind is subjected to all kinds of material experiences (happiness and distress), and the intelligence is the feature of the mind's deliberation.

PURPORT

Illusioned by the material nature, the living entity identifies with false ego. More clearly, when the living entity is entrapped by the material body, he at once identifies with the bodily relationships, forgetting his own identity as spirit soul. This false ego associates with different modes of material nature, and thus the senses become attached to the modes of material nature. Mind is the instrument for feeling different material experiences, but intelligence is deliberative and can change everything for the better. The intelligent person, therefore, can attain salvation from the illusion of material existence by proper use of intelligence. An intelligent person can detect the awkward position of material existence and thus begin to inquire as to what he is, why he is subjected to different kinds of miseries, and how to get rid of all miseries, and thus, by good association, an advanced intelligent person can turn towards the better life of self-realization. It is advised, therefore, that an intelligent person associate with the great sages and saints who are on the path of salvation. By such association, one can receive instructions which are able to slacken the conditioned soul's attachment for matter, and thus the intelligent man gradually gets rid of the illusion of matter and false ego and is promoted to the real life of eternity, knowledge and bliss.

TEXT 33

एतद्भगवतो रूपं स्थूलं ते व्याहृतं मया ।
मह्यादिभिश्चावरणैरष्टभिर्बहिरावृतम् ॥३३॥

etad bhagavato rūpaṁ
sthūlaṁ te vyāhṛtaṁ mayā
mahy-ādibhiś cāvaraṇair
aṣṭabhir bahir āvṛtam

etat—all these; *bhagavataḥ*—of the Personality of Godhead; *rūpam*—form; *sthūlam*—gross; *te*—unto you; *vyāhṛtam*—explained; *mayā*—by me; *mahī*—the planets; *ādibhiḥ*—and so on; *ca*—unlimitedly; *avaraṇaiḥ*—by coverings; *aṣṭabhiḥ*—by eight; *bahiḥ*—external; *āvṛtam*—covered.

TRANSLATION

Thus by all this, the external feature of the Personality of Godhead is covered by gross forms such as those of planets, which were explained to you by me.

PURPORT

As explained in the *Bhagavad-gītā* (7.4), the separated material energy of the Personality of Godhead is covered by eight kinds of material coverings: earth, water, fire, air, sky, mind, intelligence and false ego. All these are emanations from the Personality of Godhead as His external energy. These coverings are just like the covering of clouds for the sun. The cloud is a creation of the sun, yet it actually covers the eyes so that one cannot see the sun. The sun cannot be covered by the clouds. The cloud can at utmost extend a few hundreds of miles in the sky, but the sun is far greater than millions of miles. So a hundred-mile covering is not competent to cover millions of miles. Therefore, one of the various energies of the Supreme Personality of Godhead cannot, of course, cover the Lord. But these coverings are created by Him to cover the eyes of the conditioned souls who want to lord it over the material nature. Actually the conditioned souls are covered by the illusory creative cloud of matter, and the Lord reserves the right of not being exposed to their eyes. Because they have no eyes of transcendental vision and because they cannot see the Personality of Godhead, they therefore deny the existence of the Lord and the transcendental form of the Lord. The covering of the gigantic material feature is accepted by such men with a poor fund of knowledge, and how this is so is explained in the following verse.

TEXT 34

अतः परं सूक्ष्मतममव्यक्तं निर्विशेषणम् ।
अनादिमध्यनिधनं नित्यं वाङ्मनसः परम् ॥३४॥

ataḥ paraṁ sūkṣmatamam
avyaktaṁ nirviśeṣaṇam
anādi-madhya-nidhanaṁ
nityaṁ vāṅ-manasaḥ param

ataḥ—therefore; *param*—transcendental; *sūkṣmatamam*—finer than the finest; *avyaktam*—unmanifested; *nirviśeṣaṇam*—without material features; *anādi*—without beginning; *madhya*—without an intermediate stage; *nidhanam*—without end; *nityam*—eternal; *vāk*—words; *manasaḥ*—of the mind; *param*—transcendental.

TRANSLATION

Therefore beyond this [gross manifestation] is a transcendental manifestation finer than the finest form. It has no beginning, no intermediate stage and no end; therefore it is beyond the limits of expression or mental speculation and is distinct from the material conception.

PURPORT

The gross external body of the Supreme is manifested at certain intervals, and thus the external feature or form of the Supreme Personality of Godhead is not the eternal form of the Lord, which has no beginning, no intermediate stage and no end. Anything which has a beginning, interim and end is called material. The material world is begun from the Lord, and thus the form of the Lord, before the beginning of the material world, is certainly transcendental to the finest, or the finer material conception. The ether in the material world is considered to be the finest. Finer than the ether is mind, intelligence, and false ego. But all eight of the outward coverings are explained as outer coverings of the Absolute Truth. The Absolute Truth is therefore beyond the expression and speculation of the material conception. He is certainly transcendental to all material conceptions. This is called *nirviśeṣaṇam.* One should not, however, misunderstand *nirviśeṣaṇam* as being without any transcendental qualifications. *Viśeṣaṇam* means qualities. Therefore *nir* added to it means that he has no material qualities or variegatedness. This nullifying expression is described in four transcendental qualifications, namely unmanifested, transcendental, eternal, and beyond the conception of mind or word. Beyond the limits of words means negation of the material conception. Unless one is transcendentally situated, it is not possible to know the transcendental form of the Lord.

TEXT 35

अमुनी भगवद्रूपे मया ते ह्यनुवर्णिते ।
उभे अपि न गृह्णन्ति मायासृष्टे विपश्चितः ॥३५॥

amunī bhagavad-rūpe
mayā te hy anuvarṇite

ubhe api na gṛhṇanti
māyā-sṛṣṭe vipaścitaḥ

amunī—all these; *bhagavat*—unto the Supreme Personality of Godhead; *rūpe*—in the forms; *mayā*—by me; *te*—unto you; *hi*—certainly; *anuvarṇite*—described respectively; *ubhe*—both; *api*—also; *na*—never; *gṛhṇanti*—accepts; *māyā*—external; *sṛṣṭe*—being so manifested; *vipaḥ-citaḥ*—the learned one who knows.

TRANSLATION

Neither of the above forms of the Lord, as just described unto you from the material angle of vision, is accepted by the pure devotees of the Lord who know Him well.

PURPORT

The impersonalists think of the Absolute Personality of Godhead in two different ways, as above mentioned. On the one hand they worship the Lord in His *viśva-rūpa*, or all-pervading universal form, and on the other they think of the Lord's unmanifested, indescribable, subtle form. The theories of pantheism and monism are respectively applicable to these two conceptions of the Supreme as gross and subtle, but both of them are rejected by the learned pure devotees of the Lord because they are aware of the factual position. This is very clearly mentioned in the Eleventh Chapter of the *Bhagavad-gītā*, which records Arjuna's experience of the *viśva-rūpa* of the Supreme Lord Śrī Kṛṣṇa.

adṛṣṭa-pūrvaṁ hṛṣito 'smi dṛṣṭvā
bhayena ca pravyathitaṁ mano me
tad eva me darśaya deva rūpaṁ
prasīda deveśa jagan-nivāsa
(Bg. 11.45)

Arjuna, as a pure devotee of the Lord, never previously saw the contemplated universal form of the Lord (*viśva-rūpa*), but when he did see it, his curiosities were satisfied. But he was not happy to see such a form of the Lord because of his attachment as a pure devotee. He was afraid to see the gigantic form of the Lord. He therefore prayed to the Lord to assume His four-handed Nārāyaṇa or Kṛṣṇa form, which alone could please Arjuna. Undoubtedly the Lord has the supreme potency to exhibit Himself in multifarious forms, but the pure devotees of the Lord are interested in His forms as eternally exhibited in the abode of the Lord, known as the *tripād-vibhūti* or kingdom of God. The Lord in the *tripād-vibhūti* abode exhibits Himself in two forms, either with four hands or with two hands. The *viśva-rūpa* exhibited in the material manifestation has unlimited hands and unlimited dimensions with everything unlimited. The pure devotees of the Lord worship Him in His Vaikuṇṭha forms as Nārāyaṇa or Kṛṣṇa. Sometimes the same Vaikuṇṭha forms of the Lord are in the material world also by His grace as Śrī Rāma, Śrī Kṛṣṇa, Śrī Narasiṁhadeva, etc., and thus the pure devotees also worship them. Usually the features shown in the material world have no existence in the Vaikuṇṭha planets, and thus they are not accepted by the pure devotees. What the pure devotees worship from the very beginning are eternal forms of the Lord existing in the Vaikuṇṭha planets. The nondevotee impersonalists imagine the material forms of the Lord, and ultimately they merge in the impersonal *brahmajyoti* of the Lord, whereas the pure devotees of the Lord are worshipers of the Lord both in the beginning and also in the perfect stage of salvation, eternally. The worship of the pure devotee never stops, whereas the worship of the impersonalist stops after his attainment of salvation, when he merges in the impersonal form of the Lord known as the *brahmajyoti*. Therefore the pure devotees of the Lord are described here as *vipaścita*, or the learned who are in the knowledge of the Lord perfectly.

TEXT 36

स वाच्यवाचकतया भगवान् ब्रह्मरूपधृक् ।
नामरूपक्रिया धत्ते सकर्माकर्मकः परः ॥३६॥

sa vācya-vācakatayā
bhagavān brahma-rūpa-dhṛk
nāma-rūpa-kriyā dhatte
sakarmākarmakaḥ paraḥ

saḥ—He; *vācya*—by His forms and activities; *vācakatayā*—by His transcendental qualities and entourage, *bhagavān* the Personality of

Godhead; *brahma*—absolute; *rūpa-dhṛk*—by accepting visible forms; *nāma*—name; *rūpa*—form; *kriyā*—pastimes; *dhatte*—accepts; *sa-karma*—engaged in work; *akarmakaḥ*—without being affected; *paraḥ*—transcendence.

TRANSLATION

He, the Personality of Godhead, manifests Himself in a transcendental form, being the subject of His transcendental name, quality, pastimes, entourage and transcendental variegatedness. Although He is unaffected by all such activities, He appears to be so engaged.

PURPORT

Whenever there is a need of material creation, the transcendental Personality of Godhead accepts forms in the material world for creation, maintenance and destruction. One should be intelligent enough to know His activities in truth and not be biased to conclude that He descends to the material world by accepting a form created by material nature. Any form accepted from the material nature has its affection for everything done in the material world. A conditioned soul who accepts a material form for undergoing a certain term of material activities is subjected to the laws of matter. But here in this verse it is clearly stated that although the forms and activities of the Lord appear to be the same as those of a conditioned soul, they are supernatural and impossible for the conditioned soul. He, the Supreme Personality of Godhead, is always unaffected by such activities. In the *Bhagavad-gītā* (4.14) the Lord says:

na māṁ karmāṇi limpanti
na me karma-phale spṛhā
iti māṁ yo 'bhijānāti
karmabhir na sa badhyate

The Lord is never affected by the activities which He apparently performs by His different incarnations and personalities, nor does He have any desire to achieve success by fruitive activities. The Lord is full by His different potencies of wealth, strength, fame, beauty, knowledge and renunciation, and thus He has no reason for physical exertion like the conditioned soul. Therefore an intelligent person who can distinguish between the transcendental activities of the Lord and the activities of the conditioned souls is also not bound by the reactions of activities. The Lord as Viṣṇu, Brahmā and Śiva conducts the three modes of material nature. From Viṣṇu is born Brahmā, and from Brahmā is born Śiva. Sometimes Brahmā is a separated part of Viṣṇu, and sometimes Brahmā is Viṣṇu Himself. Thus Brahmā creates the different species of life all over the universe, which means that the Lord creates the whole manifestation either by Himself or through the agency of His authorized deputies.

TEXTS 37–40

प्रजापतीन्मनून् देवानृषीन् पितृगणान् पृथक् ।
सिद्धचारणगन्धर्वान् विद्याध्रासुरगुह्यकान् ॥३७॥
किन्नराप्सरसो नागान् सर्पान् किम्पुरुषान्नरान् ।
मातृ रक्षःपिशाचांश्च प्रेतभूतविनायकान् ॥३८॥
कूष्माण्डोन्माद वेतालान् यातुधानान् ग्रहानपि ।
खगान्मृगान् पशून् वृक्षान् गिरीन्नृप सरीसृपान् ॥३९॥
द्विविधाश्चतुर्विधा येऽन्ये जलस्थलनभौकसः ।
कुशलाकुशला मिश्राः कर्मणां गतयस्त्विमाः ॥४०॥

prajā-patīn manūn devān
ṛṣīn pitṛ-gaṇān pṛthak
siddha-cāraṇa-gandharvān
vidyādhrāsura-guhyakān

kinnarāpsaraso nāgān
sarpān kimpuruṣān narān
mātṝ rakṣaḥ-piśācāṁś ca
preta-bhūta-vināyakān

kūṣmāṇḍonmāda-vetālān
yātudhānān grahān api
khagān mṛgān paśūn vṛkṣān
girīn nṛpa sarīsṛpān

dvi-vidhāś catur-vidhā ye 'nye
jala-sthala-nabhaukasaḥ
kuśalākuśalā miśrāḥ
karmaṇāṁ gatayas tv imāḥ

prajā-patīn—Brahmā and his sons like Dakṣa and others; *manūn*—the periodical heads like Vaivasvata Manu; *devān*—like Indra, Candra and Varuṇa; *ṛṣīn*—like Bhṛgu and Vasiṣṭha; *pitṛ-gaṇān*—the inhabitants of the Pitā planets; *pṛthak*—separately; *siddha*—the inhabitants of the Siddha planet; *cāraṇa*—the inhabitants of the Cāraṇa planet; *gandharvān*—the inhabitants of the Gandharva planets; *vidyādhra*—the inhabitants of the Vidyādhara planet; *asura*—the atheists; *guhyakān*—the inhabitants of the Yakṣa planet; *kinnara*—the inhabitants of the Kinnara planet; *apsarasaḥ*—the beautiful angels of the Apsarā planet; *nāgān*—the serpentine inhabitants of Nāgaloka; *sarpān*—the inhabitants of Sarpaloka (snakes); *kimpuruṣān*—the monkey-shaped inhabitants of the Kimpuruṣa planet; *narān*—the inhabitants of earth; *mātṝ*—the inhabitants of Mātṛloka; *rakṣaḥ*—the inhabitants of the demoniac planet; *piśācān*—the inhabitants of Piśācaloka; *ca*—also; *preta*—the inhabitants of Pretaloka; *bhūta*—the evil spirits; *vināyakān*—the goblins; *kūsmāṇḍa*—will-o'-the-wisp; *unmāda*—lunatics; *vetālān*—the jinn; *yātudhānān*—a particular type of evil spirit; *grahān*—the good and evil stars; *api*—also; *khagān*—the birds; *mṛgān*—the forest animals; *paśūn*—the household animals; *vṛkṣān*—the ghosts; *girīn*—the mountains; *nṛpa*—O King; *sarīsṛpān*—reptiles; *dvi-vidhāḥ*—the moving and the standing living entities; *catuḥ-vidhāḥ*—living entities born from embryos, eggs, perspiration and seeds; *ye*—others; *anye*—all; *jala*—water; *sthala*—land; *nabha-okasaḥ*—birds; *kuśala*—in happiness; *akuśalāḥ*—in distress; *miśrāḥ*—in mixed happiness and distress; *karmaṇām*—according to one's own past deeds; *gatayaḥ*—as result of; *tu*—but; *imāḥ*—all of them.

TRANSLATION

O King, know from me that all living entities are created by the Supreme Lord according to their past deeds. This includes Brahmā and his sons like Dakṣa, the periodical heads like Vaivasvata Manu, the demigods like Indra, Candra and Varuṇa, the great sages like

Bhṛgu, Vyāsa and Vasiṣṭha, the inhabitants of Pitṛloka and Siddhaloka, the Cāraṇas, Gandharvas, Vidyādharas, Asuras, Yakṣas, Kinnaras and angels, the serpentines, the monkey-shaped Kimpuruṣas, the human beings, the inhabitants of Mātṛloka, the demons, Piśācas, ghosts, spirits, lunatics and evil spirits, the good and evil stars, the goblins, the animals in the forest, the birds, the household animals, the reptiles, the mountains, the moving and standing living entities, the living entities born from embryos, from eggs, from perspiration and from seeds, and all others, whether they be in the water, land or sky, in happiness, in distress or in mixed happiness and distress. All of them, according to their past deeds, are created by the Supreme Lord.

PURPORT

The varieties of living entities are mentioned in this list, and, with no exception from the topmost planet down to the lowest planet of the universe, all of them in different species of life are created by the Almighty Father, Viṣṇu. Therefore no one is independent of the Supreme Personality of Godhead. In the *Bhagavad-gītā* (14.4) the Lord therefore claims all living entities as His offspring in the following verse:

sarva-yoniṣu kaunteya
mūrtayaḥ sambhavanti yāḥ
tāsāṁ brahma mahad yonir
ahaṁ bīja-pradaḥ pitā

The material nature is compared to the mother. Although every living being is seen to come out of the mother's body, it is still a fact that the mother is not the ultimate cause of such a birth. The father is the ultimate cause of birth. Without the father's seed, no mother can give birth to a child. Therefore the living beings in different varieties of forms and positions within the innumerable universes are all born of the seeds of the Almighty Father, the Personality of Godhead, and only to the man with a poor fund of knowledge they appear to be born of the material nature. Being under the material energy of the Supreme Lord, all living entities beginning from Brahmā down to the insignificant ant are manifested in different bodies according to their past deeds.

The material nature is one of the energies of the Lord (Bg. 7.4). The material nature is inferior in comparison to the living entities, the superior nature. The superior nature and inferior nature of the Lord combine to manifest all universal affairs.

Some of the living entities are relatively happy in better conditions of life, whereas others are in distressed conditions of life. But factually, none of them are actually happy in material conditional life. No one can be happy in prison life, although one may be a first-class prisoner and another a third-class prisoner. The intelligent person should not try to be promoted from third-class prison life to first-class prison life, but should try to be released from the prison altogether. One may be promoted to first-class prisoner, but the same first-class prisoner is again degraded to a third-class prisoner in the next term. One should try to be free from prison life and go back home, back to Godhead. That is the real goal for all types of living entities.

TEXT 41

सत्त्वं रजस्तम इति तिस्रः सुरनृनारकाः ।
तत्राप्येकैकशो राजन् भिद्यन्ते गतयस्त्रिधा ।
यदैकैकतरोऽन्याभ्यां स्वभाव उपहन्यते ॥४१॥

sattvaṁ rajas tama iti
tisraḥ sura-nṛ-nārakāḥ
tatrāpy ekaikaśo rājan
bhidyante gatayas tridhā
yadaikaikataro 'nyābhyāṁ
sva-bhāva upahanyate

sattvam—the mode of goodness; *rajaḥ*—the mode of passion; *tamaḥ*—the mode of darkness; *iti*—thus; *tisraḥ*—the three; *sura*—demigod; *nṛ*—human being; *nārakāḥ*—one who is suffering hellish conditions; *tatra api*—even there; *ekaikaśaḥ*—another; *rājan*—O King; *bhidyante*—divide into; *gatayaḥ*—movements; *tridhā*—three; *yadā*—

at that time; *ekaikataraḥ*—one in relation with another; *anyābhyām*—from the other; *sva-bhāvaḥ*—habit; *upahanyate*—develops.

TRANSLATION

According to the different modes of material nature—the mode of goodness, the mode of passion and the mode of darkness—there are different living creatures, who are known as demigods, human beings and hellish living entities. O King, even a particular mode of nature, being mixed with the other two, is divided into three, and thus each kind of living creature is influenced by the other modes and acquires its habits also.

PURPORT

The living entities individually are being conducted by a particular mode of nature, but at the same time there is every chance of their being influenced by the other two. Generally, all conditioned souls in the material encagement are influenced by the mode of passion because every one of them is trying to lord it over the material nature to fulfill his individual desire. But in spite of the individual mode of passion, there is always the chance of being influenced by the other modes of nature by association. If one is in good association he can develop the mode of goodness, and if in bad association he may develop the mode of darkness or ignorance. Nothing is stereotyped. One can change his habit by good or bad association, and one has to become intelligent enough to discriminate between good and bad. The best association is the service of the devotees of the Lord, and by that association one can become the highest qualified man by the grace of the Lord's pure devotees. As we have already seen in the life of Śrīla Nārada Muni, he became the topmost devotee of the Lord simply by the association of pure devotees of the Lord. By birth he was the son of a maidservant and had no knowledge of his father and no academic education, even of the lowest status. But simply by associating with the devotees and by eating the remnants of their foodstuff, he gradually developed the transcendental qualities of the devotees. By such association, his taste for chanting and hearing the transcendental glories of the Lord became prominent, and because the glories of the Lord are nondifferent from the Lord, he got direct association with the Lord by means of sound representation. Similarly, there is the life of Ajāmila

(Sixth Canto), who was the son of a *brāhmaṇa* and was educated and trained properly in the discharge of the duties of a *brāhmaṇa,* but who in spite of all this, because he contacted the bad association of a prostitute, was put into the path of the lowest quality of *caṇḍāla,* or the last position for a human being. Therefore the *Bhāgavatam* always recommends the association of the *mahat,* or the great soul, for opening the gate of salvation. To associate with persons engaged in lording it over the material world means to enter into the darkest region of hell. One should try to raise himself by the association of the great soul. That is the way of the perfection of life.

TEXT 42

स एवेदं जगद्धाता भगवान् धर्मरूपधृक् ।
पुष्णाति स्थापयन् विश्वं तिर्यङ्नरसुरादिभिः ॥४२॥

sa evedaṁ jagad-dhātā
bhagavān dharma-rūpa-dhṛk
puṣṇāti sthāpayan viśvaṁ
tiryaṅ-nara-surādibhiḥ

saḥ—He; *eva*—certainly; *idam*—this; *jagat-dhātā*—the maintainer of the entire universe; *bhagavān*—the Personality of Godhead; *dharma-rūpa-dhṛk*—assuming the form of religious principles; *puṣṇāti*—maintains; *sthāpayan*—after establishing; *viśvam*—the universes; *tiryak*—living entities lower than the human beings; *nara*—the human beings; *sura-ādibhiḥ*—by the demigodly incarnations.

TRANSLATION

He, the Personality of Godhead, as the maintainer of all in the universe, appears in different incarnations after establishing the creation, and thus He reclaims all kinds of conditioned souls amongst the humans, the nonhumans and the demigods.

PURPORT

The Supreme Personality of Godhead Viṣṇu incarnates Himself in different societies of living entities to reclaim them from the clutches of illusion, and such activities of the Lord are not limited only to human society. He incarnates Himself even as a fish, hog, tree and many other forms, but less intelligent persons who have no knowledge of Him deride Him even if He is in human society as a human being. The Lord therefore says in the *Bhagavad-gītā* (9.11):

avajānanti māṁ mūḍhā
mānuṣīṁ tanum āśritam
paraṁ bhāvam ajānanto
mama bhūta-maheśvaram

As we have already discussed in the previous verses, it is concluded that the Lord is never a product of the material creation. His transcendental position is always unchanged. He is the eternal form of knowledge and bliss, and He executes His almighty will by His different energies. As such, He is never the subject of reactions for any of His acts. He is transcendental to all such conceptions of actions and reactions. Even if He is visible in the material world, the exhibition is only of His internal energy, for He is above the good and bad conceptions of this material world. In the material world the fish or the hog may be considered lower than the man, but when the Lord appears as a fish or hog, He is neither of them in the material conception. It is His causeless mercy that He appears in every society or species of life, but He is never to be considered one of them. Conceptions of the material world such as good and bad, lower and upper, important and insignificant, are estimations of the material energy, and the Supreme Lord is transcendental to all such conceptions. The words *paraṁ bhāvam*, or transcendental nature, can never be compared to the material conception. We should not forget that the potencies of the Almighty Lord are always the same and do not decrease because the Lord assumes the form of a lower animal. There is no difference between Lord Śrī Rāma, Lord Śrī Kṛṣṇa and His incarnations as a fish and hog. He is all-pervading and simultaneously localized at any and every place. But the foolish person with a poor fund of knowledge, for want of that *paraṁ bhāvam* of the Lord, cannot understand how the Supreme Lord can take the form of a man or a fish. One compares everything to one's own standard of knowledge, as the frog in the well considers the sea to be like the well. The frog in the well cannot even think of the sea, and when such a frog is informed of the greatness of the sea, it takes the conception of the sea as being a little greater than the well. As such, one who is foolish about the transcendental science of the Lord will find it difficult to understand how Lord Viṣṇu can equally manifest Himself in every society of living entities.

TEXT 43

ततः कालाग्निरुद्रात्मा यत्सृष्टमिदमात्मनः ।
संनियच्छति तत् काले घनानीकमिवानिलः॥४३॥

tataḥ kālāgni-rudrātmā
yat sṛṣṭam idam ātmanaḥ
sanniyacchati tat kāle
ghanānīkam ivānilaḥ

tataḥ—thereafter, at the end; *kāla*—destruction; *agni*—fire; *rudra-ātmā*—in the form of Rudra; *yat*—whatever; *sṛṣṭam*—created; *idam*—all these; *ātmanaḥ*—of His own; *sam*—completely; *niyacchati*—annihilates; *tat kāle*—at the end of the millennium; *ghana-anīkam*—bunches of clouds; *iva*—like that of; *anilaḥ*—air.

TRANSLATION

Thereafter, at the end of the millennium, the Lord Himself in the form of Rudra, the destroyer, will annihilate the complete creation as the wind displaces the clouds.

PURPORT

This creation is very appropriately compared to clouds. Clouds are created or situated in the sky, and when they are displaced they remain in the same sky without manifestation. Similarly, the whole creation is made by the Supreme Personality of God in His form of Brahmā, it is maintained by Him in the form of Viṣṇu, and it is destroyed by Him in the form of Rudra, or Śiva, all in due course. This creation, maintenance and destruction are nicely explained in the *Bhagavad-gītā* (8.19–20) as follows:

bhūta-grāmaḥ sa evāyaṁ
bhūtvā bhūtvā pralīyate

rātry-āgame 'vaśaḥ pārtha
prabhavaty ahar-āgame

paras tasmāt tu bhāvo 'nyo
'vyakto 'vyaktāt sanātanaḥ
yaḥ sa sarveṣu bhūteṣu
naśyatsu na vinaśyati

The nature of the material world is that it is first created very nicely, then it develops very nicely and stays for a great number of years (even beyond the calculation of the greatest mathematician), but after that it is again destroyed during the night of Brahmā, without any resistance, and at the end of the night of Brahmā it is again manifested as a creation to follow the same principles of maintenance and destruction. The foolish conditioned soul who has taken this temporary world as a permanent settlement has to learn intelligently why such creation and destruction take place. The fruitive actors in the material world are very enthusiastic in the creation of big enterprises, big houses, big empires, big industries and so many big, big things out of the energy and ingredients supplied by the material agent of the Supreme Lord. With such resources, and at the cost of valuable energy, the conditioned soul creates, satisfies his whims, but unwillingly has to depart from all his creations and enter into another phase of life to create again and again. To give hope to such foolish conditioned souls who waste their energy in this temporary material world, the Lord gives information that there is another nature, which is eternally existent without being occasionally created or destroyed, and that the conditioned soul can understand what he should do and how his valuable energy may be utilized. Instead of wasting his energy in matter, which is sure to be destroyed in due course by the supreme will, the conditioned soul should utilize his energy in the devotional service of the Lord so that he can be transferred to the other, eternal nature, where there is no birth, no death, no creation, no destruction, but permanent life instead, full of knowledge and unlimited bliss. The temporary creation is thus exhibited and destroyed just to give information to the conditioned soul who is attached to temporary things. It is also meant to give him a chance for self-realization, and not for sense gratification, which is the prime aim of all fruitive actors.

TEXT 44

इत्थंभावेन कथितो भगवान् भगवत्तमः ।
नेत्थंभावेन हि परं द्रष्टुमर्हन्ति सूरयः ॥४४॥

ittham-bhāvena kathito
bhagavān bhagavattamaḥ
nettham-bhāvena hi paraṁ
draṣṭum arhanti sūrayaḥ

ittham—in these features; *bhāvena*—the matter of creation and destruction; *kathitaḥ*—described; *bhagavān*—the Personality of Godhead; *bhagavat-tamaḥ*—by the great transcendentalists; *na*—not; *ittham*—in this; *bhāvena*—features; *hi*—only; *param*—most glorious; *draṣṭum*—to see; *arhanti*—deserve; *sūrayaḥ*—great devotees.

TRANSLATION

The great transcendentalists thus describe the activities of the Supreme Personality of Godhead, but the pure devotees deserve to see more glorious things in transcendence, beyond these features.

PURPORT

The Lord is not only the creator and destroyer of the material manifestations of His different energies. He is more than a simple creator and destroyer, for there is His feature of *ānanda*, or His pleasure feature. This pleasure feature of the Lord is understood by the pure devotees only, and not by others. The impersonalist is satisfied simply by understanding the all-pervasive influence of the Lord. This is called Brahman realization. Greater than the impersonalist is the mystic who sees the Lord situated in his heart as Paramātmā, the partial representation of the Lord. But there are pure devotees who take part in the direct pleasure (*ānanda*) potency of the Lord by factual reciprocation of loving service. The Lord in His abode called the Vaikuṇṭha planets, which are eternal manifestations, always remains with His associates and enjoys transcendental loving services by His pure devotees in different transcendental humors. The pure devotees of the Lord thus undergo a practice of that devotional service to the Lord during the manifestation of the creation and take full advantage of the manifestation by qualifying themselves to enter into the kingdom of God. The *Bhagavad-gītā* (18.55) confirms this:

bhaktyā mām abhijānāti
yāvān yaś cāsmi tattvataḥ
tato māṁ tattvato jñātvā
viśate tad anantaram

By development of pure devotional service one can factually know the Lord as He is and thus be trained in the bona fide service of the Lord and be allowed to enter into the direct association of the Lord in so many capacities. The highest glorious association with the Lord is made possible in the planet of Goloka Vṛndāvana, where Lord Kṛṣṇa enjoys Himself with the *gopīs* and His favorite animals, the *surabhi* cows. A description of this transcendental land of Kṛṣṇa is given in the *Brahma-saṁhitā*, which is considered by Lord Śrī Caitanya to be the most authentic literature in this connection.

TEXT 45

नास्य कर्मणि जन्मादौ परस्यानुविधीयते ।
कर्तृत्वप्रतिषेधार्थं माययारोपितं हि तत् ।।४५।।

nāsya karmaṇi janmādau
parasyānuvidhīyate
kartṛtva-pratiṣedhārthaṁ
māyayāropitaṁ hi tat

na—never; *asya*—of the creation; *karmaṇi*—in the matter of; *janma-ādau*—creation and destruction; *parasya*—of the Supreme; *anuvidhīyate*—it is so described; *kartṛtva*—engineering; *pratiṣedha-artham*—counteract; *māyayā*—by the external energy; *āropitam*—is manifested; *hi*—for; *tat*—the creator.

TRANSLATION

There is no direct engineering by the Lord for the creation and destruction of the material world. What is described in the Vedas

about His direct interference is simply to counteract the idea that material nature is the creator.

PURPORT

The Vedic direction for the creation, maintenance and destruction of the material world is this: *yato vā imāni bhūtāni jāyante. yena jātāni jīvanti. yat prayanty abhisaṁviśanti,* i.e., everything is created by Brahman, after creation everything is maintained by Brahman, and after annihilation everything is conserved in Brahman. Gross materialists without any knowledge of Brahman, Paramātmā or Bhagavān conclude material nature to be the ultimate cause of the material manifestation, and the modern scientist also shares this view that the material nature is the ultimate cause of all the manifestations of the material world. This view is refuted by all Vedic literature. The Vedānta philosophy mentions that Brahman is the fountainhead of all creation, maintenance and destruction, and *Śrīmad-Bhāgavatam,* the natural commentation on the *Vedānta* philosophy, says, *janmādy asya yato 'nvayād itarataś cārtheṣv adhijñaḥ svarāṭ,* etc.

Inert matter is undoubtedly energy with potential to interact, but it has no initiative of its own. *Śrīmad-Bhāgavatam* therefore comments on the aphorism *janmādy asya* by saying *abhijñaḥ* and *svarāṭ,* i.e., the Supreme Brahman is not inert matter, but He is supreme consciousness and is independent. Therefore inert matter cannot be the ultimate cause of the creation, maintenance and destruction of the material world. Superficially material nature appears to be the cause of creation, maintenance and destruction, but material nature is set into motion for creation by the supreme conscious being, the Personality of Godhead. He is the background of all creation, maintenance and destruction, and this is confirmed in the *Bhagavad-gītā* (9.10):

mayādhyakṣeṇa prakṛtiḥ
sūyate sa-carācaram
hetunānena kaunteya
jagad viparivartate

The material nature is one of the energies of the Lord, and she can work under the direction of the Lord (*adhyakṣeṇa*). When the Lord throws His transcendental glance over the material nature, then only can the material nature act, as a father contacts the mother, who is then able to conceive a child. Although it appears to the layman that the mother gives birth to the child, the experienced man knows that the father gives birth to the child. The material nature therefore produces the moving and standing manifestations of the material world after being contacted by the supreme father, and not independently. Considering material nature to be the cause of creation, maintenance, etc., is called "the logic of nipples on the neck of a goat." The *Caitanya-caritāmṛta* by Śrīla Kṛṣṇadāsa Kavirāja Gosvāmī describes this logic of *ajā-gala-stana-nyāya* as follows (as explained by His Divine Grace Śrī Śrīmad Bhaktisiddhānta Sarasvatī Gosvāmī Mahārāja): "The material nature, as the material cause, is known as *pradhāna*, and as efficient cause is known as *māyā*. But since it is inert matter, it is not the remote cause of creation." Kavirāja Gosvāmī states as follows:

ataeva kṛṣṇa mūla-jagat-kāraṇa
prakṛti——kāraṇa yaiche ajā-gala-stana
(Cc. *Ādi* 5.61)

Because Kāraṇārṇavaśāyī Viṣṇu is a plenary expansion of Kṛṣṇa, it is He who electrifies the matter to put it in motion. The example of electrification is quite appropriate. A piece of iron is certainly not fire, but when the iron is made red-hot, certainly it has the quality of fire through its burning capacity. Matter is compared to the piece of iron, and it is electrified or made red-hot by the glance or manipulation of the supreme consciousness of Viṣṇu. Only by such electrification is the energy of matter displayed in various actions and reactions. Therefore the inert matter is neither efficient nor the material cause of the cosmic manifestation. Śrī Kapiladeva has said:

yatholmukād visphuliṅgād
dhūmād vāpi sva-sambhavāt
apy ātmatvenābhimatād
yathāgniḥ pṛthag ulmukāt
(*Bhāg.* 3.28.40)

The original fire, its flame, its sparks and its smoke are all one, for fire is still fire yet is different from the flame, flame is different from sparks, and sparks are different from the smoke. In every one of them, namely in the flames, in the sparks and in the smoke, the integrity of fire is present, yet all of them are differently situated with different positions. The cosmic manifestation is compared to the smoke because when smoke passes over the sky so many forms appear, resembling many known and unknown manifestations. The sparks are compared to living entities, and the flames are compared to material nature (*pradhāna*). One must know that each and every one of them is effective simply because of being empowered by the quality of the original fire. Therefore all of them, namely the material nature, the cosmic manifestation and the living entities, are but different energies of the Lord (fire). Therefore those who accept the material nature as the cosmic manifestation's original cause (*prakṛti*, the cause of creation according to Sāṅkhya philosophy) are not correct in their conclusion. The material nature has no separate existence without the Lord. Therefore, setting aside the Supreme Lord as the cause of all causes is the logic of *ajā-gala-stana-nyāya*, or trying to milk the nipples on the neck of a goat. The nipples on the neck of a goat may seem like sources of milk, but to try to get milk from such nipples will be foolish.

TEXT 46

अयं तु ब्रह्मणः कल्पः सविकल्प उदाहृतः ।
विधिः साधारणो यत्र सर्गाः प्राकृतवैकृताः ॥४६॥

ayaṁ tu brahmaṇaḥ kalpaḥ
savikalpa udāhṛtaḥ
vidhiḥ sādhārano yatra
sargāḥ prākṛta-vaikṛtāḥ

ayam—this process of creation and annihilation; *tu*—but; *brahmaṇaḥ*—of Brahmā; *kalpaḥ*—his one day; *sa-vikalpaḥ*—along with the duration of the universes; *udāhṛtaḥ*—exemplified; *vidhiḥ*—regulative principles; *sādhāraṇaḥ*—in summary; *yatra*—wherein; *sargāḥ*—creation; *prākṛta*—in the matter of material nature; *vaikṛtāḥ*—disbursement.

TRANSLATION

This process of creation and annihilation described in summary herein is the regulative principle during the duration of Brahmā's one day. It is also the regulative principle in the creation of mahat, in which the material nature is dispersed.

PURPORT

There are three different types of creation, called *mahā-kalpa*, *vikalpa* and *kalpa*. In the *mahā-kalpa* the Lord assumes the first *puruṣa* incarnation as Kāraṇodakaśāyī Viṣṇu with all the potencies of the *mahat-tattva* and the sixteen principles of creative matter and instruments. The creative instruments are eleven, the ingredients are five, and all of them are products of *mahat*, or materialistic ego. These creations by the Lord in His feature of Kāraṇodakaśāyī Viṣṇu are called *mahā-kalpa*. The creation of Brahmā and dispersion of the material ingredients are called *vikalpa*, and the creation by Brahmā in each day of his life is called *kalpa*. Therefore each day of Brahmā is called a *kalpa*, and there are thirty *kalpas* in terms of Brahmā's days. This is also confirmed in the *Bhagavad-gītā* (8.17) as follows:

sahasra-yuga-paryantam
ahar yad brahmaṇo viduḥ
rātiṁ yuga-sahasrāntāṁ
te 'ho-rātra-vido janāḥ

In the upper planetary system the duration of one complete day and night is equal to one complete year of this earth. This is accepted even by the modern scientist and attested by the astronauts. Similarly, in the region of still higher planetary systems the duration of day and night is still greater than in the heavenly planets. The four *yugas* are calculated in terms of the heavenly calendars and accordingly are twelve thousand years in terms of the heavenly planets. This is called a *divya-yuga*, and one thousand *divya-yugas* make one day of Brahmā. The creation during the day of Brahmā is called *kalpa*, and the creation of Brahmā is called *vikalpa*. When *vikalpas* are made possible by the breathing of Mahā-Viṣṇu, this is called a *mahā-kalpa*. There are regular and systematic cycles of these *mahā-kalpas, vikalpas* and *kalpas.* In answer to Mahārāja Parīkṣit's question about them, Śukadeva Gosvāmī answered in the *Prabhāsa-khaṇḍa* of the *Skanda Purāṇa.* They are as follows:

prathamaḥ śveta-kalpaś ca
dvitīyo nīla-lohitaḥ
vāmadevas tṛtīyas tu
tato gāthāntaro 'paraḥ

rauravaḥ pañcamaḥ proktaḥ
ṣaṣṭhaḥ prāṇa iti smṛtaḥ
saptamo 'tha bṛhat-kalpaḥ
kandarpo 'ṣṭama ucyate

sadyotha navamaḥ kalpa
īśāno daśamaḥ smṛtaḥ
dhyāna ekādaśaḥ proktas
tathā sārasvato 'paraḥ

trayodaśa udānas tu
garuḍo 'tha caturdaśaḥ
kaurmaḥ pañcadaśo jñeyaḥ
paurṇamāsī prajāpateḥ

ṣoḍaśo nārasiṁhas tu
samādhis tu tato 'paraḥ
āgneyo viṣṇujaḥ sauraḥ
soma-kalpas tato 'paraḥ

dvāviṁśo bhāvanaḥ proktaḥ
supumān iti cāparaḥ
vaikuṇṭhaś cārṣṭiṣas tadvad
valī-kalpas tato 'paraḥ

saptaviṁśo 'tha vairājo
gaurī-kalpas tathāparaḥ

māheśvaras tathā proktas
tripuro yatra ghātitaḥ
pitṛ-kalpas tathā cānte
yaḥ kuhūr brahmaṇaḥ smṛtā

Therefore the thirty *kalpas* of Brahmā are: (1) Śveta-kalpa, (2) Nīlalohita, (3) Vāmadeva, (4) Gāthāntara, (5) Raurava, (6) Prāṇa, (7) Bṛhat-kalpa, (8) Kandarpa, (9) Sadyotha, (10) Īśāna, (11) Dhyāna, (12) Sārasvata, (13) Udāna, (14) Garuḍa, (15) Kaurma, (16) Nārasiṁha, (17) Samādhi, (18) Āgneya, (19) Viṣṇuja, (20) Saura, (21) Soma-kalpa, (22) Bhāvana, (23) Supuma, (24) Vaikuṇṭha, (25) Arciṣa, (26) Valī-kalpa, (27) Vairāja, (28) Gaurī-kalpa, (29) Māheśvara, (30) Paitṛ-kalpa.

These are Brahmā's days only, and he has to live months and years up to one hundred, so we can just imagine how many creations there are in *kalpas* only. Then again there are *vikalpas*, which are generated by the breathing of Mahā-Viṣṇu, as stated in the *Brahma-saṁhitā* (*yasyaika-niśvasita-kālam athāvalambya jīvanti loma-vilajā jagad-aṇḍa-nāthāḥ*). The Brahmās live only during the breathing period of Mahā-Viṣṇu. So the exhaling and inhaling of Viṣṇu are *mahā-kalpas*, and all these are due to the Supreme Personality of Godhead, for no one else is the master of all creations.

TEXT 47

परिमाणं च कालस्य कल्पलक्षणविग्रहम् ।
यथा पुरस्ताद्व्याख्यास्ये पाद्मं कल्पमथो शृणु ॥४७॥

parimāṇaṁ ca kālasya
kalpa-lakṣaṇa-vigraham
yathā purastād vyākhyāsye
pādmaṁ kalpam atho śṛṇu

parimāṇam—measurement; *ca*—also; *kālasya*—of time; *kalpa*—a day of Brahmā; *lakṣaṇa*—symptoms; *vigraham*—form; *yathā*—as much as; *purastāt*—hereafter; *vyākhyāsye*—shall be explained; *pādmam*—by the name Pādma; *kalpam*—the duration of a day; *atho*—thus; *śṛṇu*—just hear.

TRANSLATION

O King, I shall in due course explain the measurement of time in its gross and subtle features with the specific symptoms of each, but for the present let me explain unto you the Pādma-kalpa.

PURPORT

The present duration of a *kalpa* of Brahmā is called the Varāha-kalpa or Śvetavarāha-kalpa because the incarnation of the Lord as Varāha took place during the creation of Brahmā, who was born on the lotus coming out of the abdomen of Viṣṇu. Therefore this Varāha-kalpa is also called Pādma-kalpa, and this is testified by *ācāryas* like Jīva Gosvāmī as well as Viśvanātha Cakravartī Ṭhākura in pursuance of the first commentator, Svāmī Śrīdhara. So there is no contradiction between the Varāha and the Pādma-kalpa of Brahmā.

TEXT 48

शौनक उवाच

यदाह नो भवान् सूत क्षत्ता भागवतोत्तमः ।
चचार तीर्थानि भुवस्त्यक्त्वा बन्धून् सुदुस्त्यजान् ॥४८॥

śaunaka uvāca
yad āha no bhavān sūta
kṣattā bhāgavatottamaḥ
cacāra tīrthāni bhuvas
tyaktvā bandhūn sudustyajān

śaunakaḥ uvāca—Śrī Śaunaka Muni said; *yat*—as; *āha*—you said; *naḥ*—unto us; *bhavān*—your good self; *sūta*—O Sūta; *kṣattā*—Vidura; *bhāgavata-uttamaḥ*—one of the topmost devotees of the Lord; *cacāra*—practiced; *tīrthāni*—places of pilgrimage; *bhuvaḥ*—on the earth; *tyaktvā*—leaving aside; *bandhūn*—all relatives; *su-dustyajān*—very difficult to give up.

TRANSLATION

Śaunaka Ṛṣi, after hearing all about the creation, inquired from Sūta Gosvāmī about Vidura, for Sūta Gosvāmī had previously

informed him how Vidura left home, leaving aside all his relatives, who were very difficult to leave.

PURPORT

The *ṛṣis* headed by Śaunaka were more anxious to know about Vidura, who met Maitreya Ṛṣi while traveling to the pilgrimage sites of the world.

TEXTS 49–50

क्षत्तुः कौशारवेस्तस्य संवादोऽध्यात्मसंश्रितः ।
यद्वा स भगवांस्तस्मै पृष्टस्तत्त्वमुवाच ह ॥४९॥
ब्रूहि नस्तदिदं सौम्य विदुरस्य विचेष्टितम् ।
बन्धुत्यागनिमित्तं च यथैवागतवान् पुनः ॥५०॥

kṣattuḥ kauśāraves tasya
saṁvādo 'dhyātma-saṁśritaḥ
yad vā sa bhagavāṁs tasmai
pṛṣṭas tattvam uvāca ha

brūhi nas tad idaṁ saumya
vidurasya viceṣṭitam
bandhu-tyāga-nimittaṁ ca
yathaivāgatavān punaḥ

kṣattuḥ—of Vidura; *kauśāraveḥ*—as that of Maitreya; *tasya*—their; *saṁvādaḥ*—news; *adhyātma*—in the matter of transcendental knowledge; *saṁśritaḥ*—full of; *yat*—which; *vā*—anything else; *saḥ*—he; *bhagavān*—His Grace; *tasmai*—unto him; *pṛṣṭaḥ*—inquired; *tattvam*—the truth; *uvāca*—answered; *ha*—in the past; *brūhi*—please tell; *naḥ*—unto us; *tat*—those matters; *idam*—here; *saumya*—O gentle one; *vidurasya*—of Vidura; *viceṣṭitam*—activities; *bandhu-tyāga*—renouncing the friends; *nimittam*—the cause of; *ca*—also; *yathā*—as; *eva*—also; *āgatavān*—came back; *punaḥ*—again (at home).

TRANSLATION

Śaunaka Ṛṣi said: Let us know, please, what topics were discussed between Vidura and Maitreya, who talked on transcendental

subjects, and what was inquired by Vidura and replied by Maitreya. Also please let us know the reason for Vidura's giving up the connection of his family members, and why he again came home. Please also let us know the activities of Vidura while he was in the places of pilgrimage.

PURPORT

Śrī Sūta Gosvāmī was narrating the topics of the creation and destruction of the material world, but it appears that the *ṛṣis* headed by Śaunaka were more inclined to hear of transcendental subjects, which are on a higher level than the physical. There are two classes of men, namely those too addicted to the gross body and the material world, and others, on the higher level, who are interested more in transcendental knowledge. *Śrīmad-Bhāgavatam* gives facility to everyone, both to the materialist and to the transcendentalist. By hearing *Śrīmad-Bhāgavatam* in the matter of the Lord's glorious activities both in the material world and in the transcendental world, men can derive equal benefit. The materialists are more interested in the physical laws and how they are acting, and they see wonders in those physical glamors. Sometimes, due to physical glamors, they forget the glories of the Lord. They should know definitely that physical activities and their wonders are all initiated by the Lord. The rose in the garden gradually takes its shape and color to become beautiful and sweet not by a blind physical law, although it appears like that. Behind that physical law is the direction of the complete consciousness of the Supreme Lord, otherwise things cannot take shape so systematically. The artist draws a picture of a rose very nicely with all attention and artistic sense, and yet it does not become as perfect as the real rose. If that is the real fact, how can we say that the real rose has taken its shape without intelligence behind the beauty? This sort of conclusion is due to a poor fund of knowledge. One must know from the above description of creation and annihilation that the supreme consciousness, being omnipresent, can take care of everything with perfect attention. That is the fact of the omnipresence of the Supreme Lord. Persons, still more foolish than the gross materialists, however, claim to be transcendentalists and claim to have such supreme all-pervading consciousness, but offer no proof. Such foolish persons cannot know what is going on behind the next wall, yet they are falsely proud of possessing the cosmic, all-pervading consciousness of the Supreme Person. For them also, hearing of *Śrīmad-Bhāgavatam* is a great help. It will open their eyes to see that simply by claiming supreme consciousness one does not become supremely conscious. One has to prove in the physical world that he has such supreme consciousness. The *ṛṣis* of Naimiṣāraṇya, however, were above the gross materialists and the false transcendentalists, and thus they were always anxious to know the real truth in transcendental matters, as discussed by authorities.

TEXT 51

सूत उवाच
राज्ञा परीक्षिता पृष्टो यदवोचन्महामुनिः ।
तद्वोऽभिधास्ये श‍ृणुत राज्ञः प्रश्नानुसारतः ॥५१॥

sūta uvāca
rājñā parīkṣitā pṛṣṭo
yad avocan mahā-muniḥ
tad vo 'bhidhāsye śṛṇuta
rājñaḥ praśnānusārataḥ

sūtaḥ uvāca—Śrī Sūta Gosvāmī replied; *rājñā*—by the King; *parīkṣitā*—by Parīkṣit; *pṛṣṭaḥ*—as asked; *yat*—what; *avocat*—spoke; *mahā-muniḥ*—the great sage; *tat*—that very thing; *vaḥ*—unto you; *abhidhāsye*—I shall explain; *śṛṇuta*—please hear; *rājñaḥ*—by the King; *praśna*—question; *anusārataḥ*—in accordance with.

TRANSLATION

Śrī Sūta Gosvāmī explained: I shall now explain to you the very subjects explained by the great sage in answer to King Parīkṣit's inquiries. Please hear them attentively.

PURPORT

Any question that is put forward may be answered by quoting the authority, and that satisfies the saner section. That is the system even in the law court. The best lawyer gives evidence from the past judgment of the court without taking much trouble to establish his case. This is called the *paramparā* system, and learned authorities follow it without manufacturing rubbish interpretations.

īśvaraḥ paramaḥ kṛṣṇaḥ
sac-cid-ānanda-vigrahaḥ
anādir ādir govindaḥ
sarva-kāraṇa-kāraṇam
(*Brahma-saṁhitā* 5.1)

Let us all obey the Supreme Lord, whose hand is in everything, without exception.

Thus end the Bhaktivedanta purports of the Second Canto, Tenth Chapter, of the Śrīmad-Bhāgavatam, *entitled "Bhāgavatam Is the Answer to All Questions."*

END OF THE SECOND CANTO

Appendixes

About the Author

His Divine Grace A.C. Bhaktivedanta Swami Prabhupāda appeared in this world in 1896 in Calcutta, India. He first met his spiritual master, Śrīla Bhaktisiddhānta Sarasvatī Gosvāmī, in Calcutta in 1922. Bhaktisiddhānta Sarasvatī, a prominent religious scholar and the founder of sixty-four Gauḍīya Maṭhas (Vedic institutes), liked this educated young man and convinced him to dedicate his life to teaching Vedic knowledge. Śrīla Prabhupāda became his student, and eleven years later (1933) at Allahabad he became his formally initiated disciple.

At their first meeting, in 1922, Śrīla Bhaktisiddhānta Sarasvatī Ṭhākura requested Śrīla Prabhupāda to broadcast Vedic knowledge through the English language. In the years that followed, Śrīla Prabhupāda wrote a commentary on the *Bhagavad-gītā*, assisted the Gauḍīya Maṭha in its work and, in 1944, started *Back to Godhead*, an English fortnightly magazine. Maintaining the publication was a struggle. Singlehandedly, Śrīla Prabhupāda edited it, typed the manuscripts, checked the galley proofs, and even distributed the individual copies. Once begun, the magazine never stopped; it is now being continued by his disciples in the West and is published in over thirty languages.

Recognizing Śrīla Prabhupāda's philosophical learning and devotion, the Gauḍīya Vaiṣṇava Society honored him in 1947 with the title "Bhaktivedanta." In 1950, at the age of fifty-four, Śrīla Prabhupāda retired from married life, adopting the *vānaprastha* (retired) order to devote more time to his studies and writing. Śrīla Prabhupāda traveled to the holy city of Vṛndāvana, where he lived in very humble circumstances in the historic medieval temple of Rādhā-Dāmodara. There he engaged for several years in deep study and writing. He accepted the renounced order of life (*sannyāsa*) in 1959. At Rādhā-Dāmodara, Śrīla Prabhupāda began work on his life's masterpiece: a multivolume annotated translation of the eighteen-thousand-verse *Śrīmad-Bhāgavatam* (*Bhāgavata Purāṇa*). He also wrote *Easy Journey to Other Planets*.

After publishing three volumes of the *Bhāgavatam*, Śrīla Prabhupāda came to the United States, in September 1965, to fulfill the mission of his spiritual master. Subsequently, His Divine Grace wrote more than sixty volumes of authoritative annotated translations and summary studies of the philosophical and religious classics of India.

When he first arrived by freighter in New York City, Śrīla Prabhupāda was practically penniless. Only after almost a year of great difficulty did he establish the International Society for Krishna Consciousness, in July of 1966. Before his passing away on November 14, 1977, he guided the Society and saw it grow to a worldwide confederation of more than one hundred *āśramas*, schools, temples, institutes and farm communities.

In 1968, Śrīla Prabhupāda created New Vrindaban, an experimental Vedic community in the hills of West Virginia. Inspired by the success of New Vrindaban, now a thriving farm community of more than two thousand acres, his students have since founded several similar communities in the United States and abroad.

In 1972, His Divine Grace introduced the Vedic system of primary and secondary education in the West by founding the Gurukula school in Dallas, Texas. Since then, under his supervision, his disciples have established children's schools throughout the United States and the rest of the world, with the principal educational center now located in Vṛndāvana, India.

Śrīla Prabhupāda also inspired the construction of several large international cultural centers in India. The center at Śrīdhāma Māyāpur in West Bengal is the site for a planned spiritual city, an ambitious project for which construction will extend over many years to come. In Vṛndāvana, India, are the magnificent Kṛṣṇa-Balarāma Temple and International Guesthouse, and Śrīla Prabhupāda Memorial and Museum. There is also a major cultural and educational center in Bombay. Other centers are planned in a dozen important locations on the Indian subcontinent.

Śrīla Prabhupāda's most significant contribution, however, is his books. Highly respected by the academic community for their authority, depth and clarity, they are used as standard textbooks in numerous college courses. His writings have been translated into over fifty languages. The Bhaktivedanta Book Trust, established in 1972 to publish the works of His Divine Grace, has thus become the world's largest publisher of books in the field of Indian religion and philosophy.

In just twelve years, in spite of his advanced age, Śrīla Prabhupāda circled the globe fourteen times on lecture tours that took him to six continents. In spite of such a vigorous schedule, Śrīla Prabhupāda continued to write prolifically. His writings constitute a veritable library of Vedic philosophy, religion, literature and culture.

References

The purports of *Śrīmad-Bhāgavatam* are all confirmed by standard Vedic authorities. The following authentic scriptures are cited in this volume. For specific page references, consult the general index.

Āyur-veda

Bhagavad-gītā

Bhagavat-sandarbha

Bhakti-rasāmṛta-sindhu

Brahma-saṁhitā

Brahma-vaivarta Purāṇa

Bṛhad-āraṇyaka Upaniṣad

Bṛhan-nāradīya Purāṇa

Caitanya-caritāmṛta

Garga Upaniṣad

Garuḍa Purāṇa

Gopāla-tāpanī Upaniṣad

Hari-bhakti-sudhodaya

Īśopaniṣad

Kaṭha Upaniṣad

Krama-sandarbha

Liṅga Purāṇa

Mahābhārata

Manu-saṁhitā

Muṇḍaka Upaniṣad

Nārada-pañcarātra

Narasiṁha Purāṇa

Padma Purāṇa

Rāmāyaṇa

Sāṅkhya-kaumudī

Śikṣāṣṭaka

Skanda Purāṇa

Śrīmad-Bhāgavatam

Śvetāśvatara Upaniṣad

Vāmana Purāṇa

Vedānta-sūtra

Viṣṇu Purāṇa

GLOSSARY

A

Ācārya—an ideal teacher, who teaches by his personal example; a spiritual master.

Acintya-bhedābheda-tattva—Lord Caitanya's doctrine of the "inconceivable oneness and difference" of God and His energies.

Ahiṁsā—nonviolence.

Ārati—a ceremony for greeting the Lord with chanting and offerings of food, lamps, fans, flowers and incense.

Arcana—the devotional process of Deity worship.

Āśrama—one of four spiritual orders of life. *See also: Brahmacarya; Gṛhastha; Vānaprastha; Sannyāsa*

Aṣṭa-siddhis—the eight mystic perfections acquired by *yoga* practice.

Asura—an atheistic demon; a gross materialist.

Avatāra—a descent, or incarnation, of the Supreme Lord.

Avyakta—unmanifest.

B

Bhagavad-gītā—the discourse between the Supreme Lord, Kṛṣṇa, and His devotee Arjuna expounding devotional service as both the principal means and the ultimate end of spiritual perfection.

Bhakta—a devotee of the Supreme Lord.

Bhakti-yoga—linking with the Supreme Lord by devotional service.

Brahmacarya—celibate student life; the first order of Vedic spiritual life.

Brahman—the Absolute Truth; especially the impersonal aspect of the Absolute.

Brāhmaṇa—a member of the intellectual, priestly class; the first Vedic social order.

Brahmavādīs—impersonalists among the transcendentalists.

C

Cetana—a conscious living entity.

D

Deva-dāsīs—female singers and dancers employed as servants of the Deity.

Dharma—religion; duty, especially everyone's eternal service nature.

E

Ekādaśī—a special day for increased remembrance of Kṛṣṇa, which comes on the eleventh day after both the full and new moon. Abstinence from grains and beans is prescribed.

G

Goloka Vṛndāvana (Kṛṣṇaloka)—the highest spiritual planet, Lord Kṛṣṇa's personal abode.

Gopīs—Kṛṣṇa's cowherd girl friends, who are His most surrendered and confidential devotees.

Gṛhastha—regulated householder life; the second order of Vedic spiritual life.

Guru—a spiritual master.

H

Hare Kṛṣṇa mantra—*See: Mahā-mantra*

J

Jīva-tattva—the living entities, atomic parts of the Supreme Lord.

K

Kali-yuga (Age of Kali)—the present age, characterized by quarrel. Last in the cycle of four ages, it began five thousand years ago.

Karatālas—hand cymbals used in *kīrtana.*

Karma—material, fruitive activity and its reactions.

Karma-kāṇḍa—the portions of the *Vedas* describing rituals to be performed for material benefit.

Karma-yoga—action in devotional service; also, fruitive actions performed in accordance with Vedic injunctions.

Karmī—one engaged in *karma* (fruitive activity); a materialist.

Kīrtana—the devotional process of chanting the names and glories of the Supreme Lord.

Kṛṣṇaloka—*See:* Goloka Vṛndāvana

Kṣatriya—a warrior or administrator; the second Vedic social order.

M

Mahā-mantra—the great chant for deliverance:
Hare Kṛṣṇa, Hare Kṛṣṇa, Kṛṣṇa Kṛṣṇa, Hare Hare
Hare Rāma, Hare Rāma, Rāma Rāma, Hare Hare.

Mantra—a transcendental sound or Vedic hymn, which can deliver the mind from illusion.

Mathurā—Lord Kṛṣṇa's abode, surrounding Vṛndāvana, where He took birth and to which He later returned after performing His childhood Vṛndāvana pastimes.

Māyā—the inferior, illusory energy of the Supreme Lord, which rules over this material creation; forgetfulness of one's relationship with Kṛṣṇa.

Māyāvādīs—impersonalist philosophers who conceive of the Absolute as ultimately formless and the living entity as equal to God.

Mṛdaṅga—a clay drum used for congregational chanting.

N

Nārāyaṇa-para—one who has dedicated his life to the Supreme Lord—Nārāyaṇa, or Kṛṣṇa.

P

Paramparā—a disciplic succession of bona fide spiritual masters.

Prajāpatis—the demigods in charge of populating the universe.

Prasādam—the Lord's mercy; food or other items spiritualized by being first offered to the Supreme Lord.

Puruṣa-avatāras—the three primary Viṣṇu expansions of the Supreme Lord who are involved in universal creation.

R

Ṛṣi—a sage.

S

Sac-cid-ānanda—the natural condition of spiritual life: eternal existence, full consciousness and unlimited happiness.

Sac-cid-ānanda-vigraha—the Lord's transcendental form, which is eternal and full of knowledge and bliss.

Saṅkīrtana—congregational or public glorification of the Supreme Lord, Kṛṣṇa, especially through chanting of the Lord's holy names.

Sannyāsa—renounced life; the fourth order of Vedic spiritual life.

Sarva-jña—one who knows everything—past, present and future.

Śāstra—revealed scripture, such as the Vedic literature.

Sāttvika—in the mode of goodness.

Śravaṇaṁ kīrtanaṁ viṣṇoḥ—the devotional process of hearing and chanting about Lord Viṣṇu, or Kṛṣṇa.

Śūdra—a laborer; the fourth of the Vedic social orders.

Svāmī—a controller of the mind and senses; the title of one in the renounced, or *sannyāsa*, order.

T

Tapasya—austerity; accepting some voluntary inconvenience for a higher purpose.

Tilaka—auspicious clay markings placed by devotees on the forehead and other parts of the body.

V

Vaikuṇṭha—the spiritual world, where there is no anxiety.

Vaiṣṇava—a devotee of the Supreme Lord—Viṣṇu, or Kṛṣṇa.

Vaiśyas—farmers and merchants; the third Vedic social order.

Vānaprastha—one who has retired from family life; the third order of Vedic spiritual life.

Varṇa—one of the four Vedic social-occupational divisions of society, distinguished by quality of work and situation with regard to the modes of nature (*guṇas*). *See also: Brāhmaṇa; Kṣatriya; Vaiśya; Śūdra*

Varṇāśrama-dharma—the Vedic social system of four social and four spiritual orders. *See also: Varṇa; Āśrama*

Veda-vāda-rata—one who gives his own explanation of the *Vedas;* a *smārta.*

Vedas—the original revealed scriptures, first spoken by Lord Kṛṣṇa.

Vibhūti—the opulence and power of the Supreme Lord.

Virāṭ-rūpa—the conception likening the physical form of the universe to the Lord's bodily form.

Viṣṇu—the Supreme Lord; Lord Kṛṣṇa's expansions in Vaikuṇṭha and for the creation and maintenance of the material universes.

Viṣṇu-tattva—the status or category of Godhead. The term applies to primary expansions of the Supreme Lord.

Vṛndāvana—Kṛṣṇa's eternal abode, where He fully manifests His quality of sweetness; the village on this earth in which He appeared five thousand years ago.

Vyāsadeva—the incarnation of Lord Kṛṣṇa who gave the *Vedas, Purāṇas, Vedānta-sūtra* and *Mahābhārata* to mankind.

Y

Yajña—a Vedic sacrifice; also, the Supreme Lord, the goal and enjoyer of all sacrifices.

Yogī—a transcendentalist striving for union with the Supreme.

Yugas—ages in the life of a universe, occurring in a repeated cycle of four.

Sanskrit Pronunciation Guide

Throughout the centuries, the Sanskrit language has been written in a variety of alphabets. The mode of writing most widely used throughout India, however, is called *devanāgarī*, which means, literally, the writing used in "the cities of the demigods." The *devanāgarī* alphabet consists of forty-eight characters: thirteen vowels and thirty-five consonants. Ancient Sanskrit grammarians arranged this alphabet according to practical linguistic principles, and this order has been accepted by all Western scholars. The system of transliteration used in this book conforms to a system that scholars in the last fifty years have accepted to indicate the pronunciation of each Sanskrit sound.

Vowels

अ a आ ā इ i ई ī उ u ऊ ū ऋ ṛ

ॠ ṝ ऌ ḷ ए e ऐ ai ओ o औ au

Consonants

Gutturals:	क ka	ख kha	ग ga	घ gha	ङ ṅa
Palatals:	च ca	छ cha	ज ja	झ jha	ञ ña
Cerebrals:	ट ṭa	ठ ṭha	ड ḍa	ढ ḍha	ण ṇa
Dentals:	त ta	थ tha	द da	ध dha	न na
Labials:	प pa	फ pha	ब ba	भ bha	म ma
Semivowels:	य ya	र ra	ल la	व va	
Sibilants:	श śa	ष ṣa	स sa		
Aspirate:	ह ha	Anusvāra: ं ṁ	Visarga: ः ḥ		

Numerals

० -0 १-1 २-2 ३-3 ४-4 ५-5 ६-6 ७-7 ८-8 ९-9

The vowels are written as follows after a consonant:

ा ā ि i ी ī ु u ू ū ृ ṛ ॄ ṝ े e ै ai ो o ौ au

For example: क ka का kā कि ki की kī कु ku कू kū

कृ kṛ कॄ kṝ के ke कै kai को ko कौ kau

Generally two or more consonants in conjunction are written together in a special form, as for example: क्ष kṣa त्र tra

The vowel "**a**" is implied after a consonant with no vowel symbol.

The symbol virāma (्) indicates that there is no final vowel: क्

The vowels are pronounced as follows:

a — as in **but**
ā — as in **far** but held twice as long as **a**
ai — as in **aisle**
au — as in **how**
e — as in **they**
i — as in **pin**
ī — as in **pique** but held twice as long as **i**
ḷ — as in **lree**
o — as in **go**
ṛ — as in **rim**
ṝ — as in **reed** but held twice as long as **ṛ**
u — as in **push**
ū — as in **rule** but held twice as long as **u**

The consonants are pronounced as follows:

Gutturals
(pronounced from the throat)
k — as in **kite**
kh — as in **Eckhart**
g — as in **give**
gh — as in **dig-hard**
ṅ — as in **sing**

Labials
(pronounced with the lips)
p — as in **pine**
ph — as in **up-hill** (not **f**)
b — as in **bird**
bh — as in **rub-hard**
m — as in **mother**

Cerebrals
(pronounced with tip of tongue against roof of mouth)

ṭ — as in tub
ṭh — as in light-heart
ḍ — as in dove
ḍh — as in red-hot
ṇ — as in sing

Dentals
(pronounced as cerebrals but with tongue against teeth)

t — as in tub
th — as in light-heart
d — as in dove
dh — as in red-hot
n — as in nut

Aspirate

h — as in home

Anusvāra

ṁ — a resonant nasal sound like in the French word *bon*

Palatals
(pronounced with middle of tongue against palate)

c — as in chair
ch — as in staunch-heart
j — as in joy
jh — as in hedgehog
ñ — as in canyon

Semivowels

y — as in yes
r — as in run
l — as in light
v — as in vine, except when preceded in the same syllable by a consonant, then like in swan

Sibilants

ś — as in the German word s*prechen*
ṣ — as in shine
s — as in sun

Visarga

ḥ — a final **h**-sound: **aḥ** is pronounced like **aha**; **iḥ** like **ihi**

There is no strong accentuation of syllables in Sanskrit, or pausing between words in a line, only a flowing of short and long (twice as long as the short) syllables. A long syllable is one whose vowel is long (**ā, ai, au, e, ī, o, ṝ, ū**) or whose short vowel is followed by more than one consonant (including **ḥ** and **ṁ**). Aspirated consonants (consonants followed by an **h**) count as single consonants.

Index of Sanskrit Verses

This index constitutes a complete listing of the first and third lines of each of the Sanskrit poetry verses of this volume of *Śrīmad-Bhāgavatam*, arranged in English alphabetical order. The first column gives the Sanskrit transliteration; the second, the chapter-verse reference. Apostrophes are alphabetized as *a*'s.

A

B

C

D

T

U

Index of Verses Quoted

This index lists the verses quoted in the purports and footnotes of this volume of *Śrīmad-Bhāgavatam*. Numerals in boldface type refer to the first or third lines of verses quoted in full; numerals in roman type refer to partially quoted verses.

General Index

Numerals in boldface type indicate references to translations of the verses of *Śrīmad-Bhāgavatam.*

A

B

C

L

M

O

S

U

W

Y